"What a brilliant collection of cutting edge chapters that skillfully describe the critical challenges for those working on reproductive justice, evidence-based policy making, and the persistent inequities that face women in particular—whether because of gender, class or race. Faculty in schools of public health and women, gender and sexuality studies programs will find this the best such collection to date. More comprehensive than anything of its kind I have ever seen."

—**Judy Norsigian,** Executive Director, Our Bodies Ourselves

"In *Reproduction and Society,* editors Carole Joffe and Jennifer Reich have compiled an impressive 'best of' collection of readings on the social and political significance of reproduction. Contributors from diverse disciplinary and professional backgrounds have applied themselves to contraception, pregnancy, policy and more; the result is a volume that is as compelling as it is informative."

—**Jeanne Flavin,** Sociology, Fordham University, Board President, National Advocates for Pregnant Women, and author of *Our Bodies, Our Crimes: the Policing of Women's Reproduction in America*

"Feminist sociologists Carole Joffe and Jennifer Reich have created a timely and valuable resource that illuminates the personal and political implications of key reproductive experiences. As editors, they have drawn from outstanding scholarship in a range of disciplines to examine contraception, abortion, assisted reproduction, pregnancy and childbirth through diverse, interrelated sociological lenses: feminist analyses of governance and institutional control; intersectionality, reproductive justice and social movements. If we are ever to achieve reproductive justice in the U.S., we need this book for its informed and thoughtful consideration of the complexity of issues facing women and men whose reproductive options are shaped by culture, ideology and politics. This book is a must-read for the generation most affected by U.S. reproductive policies—future parents—and is destined to become a classic in the sociology of reproduction."

—**Christine H. Morton,** author of *Birth Ambassadors: Doulas and the Re-Emergence of Woman-Supported Birth in America,* founder of ReproNetwork.org, and research sociologist at Stanford University

Reproduction and Society: Interdisciplinary Readings

A collection of essays, framed with original introductions, *Reproduction and Society: Interdisciplinary Readings* helps students to think critically about reproduction as a social phenomenon. Divided into six rich and varied sections, this book offers students and instructors a broad overview of the social meanings of reproduction and offers opportunities to explore significant questions of how resources are allocated, individuals are regulated, and how very much is at stake as people and communities aim to determine their own family size and reproductive experiences. This is an ideal core text for courses on reproduction, family, gender and sexualities.

Carole Joffe is a Professor in the Advancing New Standards in Reproductive Health (ANS-IRH) program at the Bixby Center for Global Reproductive Health at the University of California, San Francisco. She is also professor emerita of sociology at the University of California, Davis. In 2013, Professor Joffe received the Lifetime Achievement Award from the Society of Family Planning. She is the author of several books and numerous articles on various aspects of reproductive health and reproductive politics.

Jennifer Reich is Associate Professor of Sociology at the University of Colorado, Denver. She is the author of *Fixing Families: Parents, Power, and the Child Welfare System* (Routledge, 2005), which won the American Sociological Association section on Race, Gender, and Class Distinguished Contribution to Scholarship Book Award in 2007 and was a finalist for the prestigious C. Wright Mills Award from the Society for the Study of Social Problems in 2006. She has written more than 20 articles and book chapters on gender, reproductive politics, family policy, and welfare.

PERSPECTIVES ON GENDER

Edited by Myra Marx Ferree, University of Wisconsin, Madison.

Reproduction and Society: Interdisciplinary Readings

Edited by
Carole Joffe and Jennifer Reich

Routledge
Taylor & Francis Group

NEW YORK AND LONDON

First published 2015
by Routledge
711 Third Avenue, New York, NY 10017

and by Routledge
2 Park Square, Milton Park, Abingdon, Oxon, OX14 4RN

Routledge is an imprint of the Taylor & Francis Group, an informa business

Library of Congress Cataloging-in-Publication Data
Reproduction and society : interdisciplinary readings / edited by Carole Joffe and Jennifer Reich.
    pages cm.—(Perspectives on gender)
  Includes bibliographical references and index.
  1. Family size—Social aspects.   2. Human reproduction—Social aspects.   3. Reproductive rights—Social aspects.   4. Birth control—Social aspects.   I. Joffe, Carole E.   II. Reich, Jennifer A.
  HQ760.R47 2015
  304.6'3—dc23
  2014011791

ISBN: 978-0-415-73102-7 (hbk)
ISBN: 978-0-415-73103-4 (pbk)
ISBN: 978-1-315-75422-2 (ebk)

Typeset in Sabon and Helvetica Neue
by Apex CoVantage, LLC

Dedicated to those health care professionals and advocates who strive, often against great odds, to make possible high quality, respectful, and compassionate reproductive health care to women and men in the United States and globally.

CONTENTS

Section III: Reproductive Technologies 99

Introduction

Section IV: Pregnancy and Birth 137

Introduction

This chapter by psychologists Ramaswami Mahalingam and Madeline Wachman examines structural and cultural factors that shape attitudes toward female infants and how these views lead to complex consequences that include extreme neglect of girls in the form of sex-selective abortion and female infanticide.

This excerpt from an address given by then-First Lady Hillary Rodham Clinton to the United Nations Conference on Women highlights the circumstances of women globally and the challenges to their health and well-being.

SERIES FOREWORD

Reproduction and Society, by Carole Joffe and Jennifer Reich

This interdisciplinary reader adds a new and much needed perspective to the long-running series of "Perspectives on Gender" books that it has been my privilege to edit. The intent of the series has always been to add high-quality scholarship to illuminate the workings of gender in society, especially in ways that recognize the intersectional impacts of class and race on and with gender. Moreover, the scope of the series is geographically broad, drawing attention to changes over time and variation between countries in how gender relations are organized. The books in this series have therefore also always been various in their specific focus, even though unified by a relational view of gender as a matter of power that is exercised in diverse, interactive forms.

The series as a whole has deliberately engaged diversity as a necessary perspective on gender. This has been expressed in its range of topics from micro to macro analyses of gender transformations, the mix of quantitative and qualitative methods employed, and the strong emphasis on making sure that gender was seen as intersectional with race and class. The centrality of social change to the titles in this series has implied an emphasis on contested power relations, social movements, and historical transformations in work, family and politics. These two themes of diversity and change have been admirably combined now in this single volume.

It has been my pleasure and privilege to help authors in the series frame the concerns in their manuscripts to make visible our collective commitment to intersectionality and social change while also staying true to their individual voices. If we succeeded, readers will be able to recognize the collective energy in the series as well as the distinctive contributions of each individual book. Both Carole Joffe and Jennifer Reich are well-recognized experts in the field of reproduction—before, during and after conception, pregnancy, childbirth and in relation to the challenges of raising children in the shadow of the state.

I find myself particularly enthusiastic about this book because it so nicely weaves these themes into a political understanding of reproduction as both a physically significant and yet fully social constructed experience that is placed at the center of women's lives. There is simply no other book that tackles so comprehensively the problematic of reproduction. But this book is no mere gap-filler. It is a contribution in itself to theorizing the scope and meaning of reproduction as a societal relationship, one by no means less important than production, consumption, nationalism, or trade. Most importantly, the perspective Joffe and Reich offer differs from more narrowly life-course or psychological accounts of women's involvement in reproduction. They place all aspects of reproduction into a frame that is social and political rather than individual or developmental, and they use intersectionality as a lens to make the parameters of reproductive injustice clear. These they identify as gendered, but not only as about gender as a binary societal relationship.

Rather than making "difference" from men the definition of either women or gender, Joffe and Reich look to the social organization of embodied people in hierarchical relations in which the work of societal reproduction figures centrally. Thus while this book is interdisciplinary to the core, it is also fundamentally an account of the particular decisions, policies, practices and political struggles that shape the relations in which reproduction is situated in this particular historical moment. Moreover, thinking about reproduction as a social as well as biological act has been fruitful for understanding the ways that women and men are related to the state—via motherhood or military service—and why the state cares differently about the reproductive work being done depending on the race, class and sexualities of those doing it. Refraining from political polemics, the book nonetheless embraces an understanding of reproduction as a political act in the sense of making a new generation of the body politic.

If, when, and how women do or do not become pregnant, bear and raise children, and raise their own voices to claim authority over the process has already been the subject of a vast array of feminist scholarship as well as philosophical and practical political debates. Indeed, the thorniest issue for a book like this is to take a clear position on what matters most and why, and here the collection succeeds brilliantly. The particular contribution of this volume is to choose skillfully among the most insightful work and integrate the diversity of the perspectives offered there into a coherent account of the gendering of reproduction. The selections are then placed in their historical, political and scholarly context by section introductions that capture and condense the contributions of so many other outstanding scholars that a single volume necessarily omits.

The range of work is impressive not only for the attention it pays to including the diversity of women's experiences with the ways reproduction is organized but also for its exceptional understanding of reproductive matters at all levels from the individual to the interactional to the institutional and ideological. There is clear commitment to a feminist perspective: the importance of all women's lives; women's agency in the face of structural obstacles; recognition of various degrees of risk, choice, and control encountered in relations of reproduction that differ by gender in relation to race, nationality, and class. Rather than a political program with obligatory answers, the feminist perspective of this book offers a series of tough questions about what real reproductive justice would look like.

In sum, while this book is admirably suited for classroom use, it is also an integrative contribution to gender scholarship, framing the issues of reproduction broadly but distinctively as being matters of inclusive and intersectional justice. Acknowledging controversies, even among feminists, but also putting the variety of perspectives into a well-thought-out framework, the authors add a comprehensive take on matters of reproduction to the other concerns about gender and justice that this series has stressed.

Myra Marx Ferree
Series Editor

PREFACE

Surrogacy, egg and sperm donation, controversies of birth control access, the right to choose one's childbirth experience, or stories of reproductive technologies gone awry are now common discussions in news, politics, and even popular culture. Questions of the social and political—as opposed to biological—dimensions of human reproduction surround us. Scholarly studies in this arena have exploded over the last forty years or so, a development that was set in motion with the re-emergence of a woman's movement in the United States and elsewhere, and the *Roe v. Wade* decision legalizing abortion in 1973. Since then, a variety of forces, ranging from advances in reproductive technology, to the growing inequality in U.S. society (and how this affects people's reproductive possibilities) have only increased this attention to reproduction. Courses in a variety of disciplines focusing on this topic have become increasingly common in universities.

This sustained attention among scholars has led to many excellent book-length examinations of particular aspects of reproduction (such as pregnancy loss, abortion, contraception, or surrogacy). Such treatments, however, do not lend themselves to adequately educating the student who needs a broader overview of the social meanings of reproduction that covers a range of sites and forms of reproductive control within its cultural and political contexts. This book fills this gap. We designed this volume to support these discussions, help students to think critically about reproduction as a social phenomenon, and provide a resource for those teaching about these issues. *Reproduction and Society* contains original essays that frame each section. These short introductions by the editors offer descriptive information about the scale and scope of the topic, highlight particularly important themes, and introduce the readings. These introductory essays are followed by a selection of four to seven reprints from the best work in this field. We draw on the work of senior scholars, who have produced classics in the study of reproduction, as well as those written by younger scholars who are pushing the field forward. The authors represented in this volume are mainly drawn from the social sciences, but we also include the writings of health care professionals, lawyers, environmental scientists, psychologists, advocates and journalists—voices that reflect the rich diversity of this field. We have assembled a text with plainly written, engaging sections that will have wide appeal to undergraduate and graduate students and others who are new to the study of reproduction.

In the main introduction, co-authored by the editors, we present an overview of the field of reproduction. We also make clear to readers our understanding of a *feminist perspective* on reproduction that considers gender to be indelibly linked to reproduction, and explain how such a perspective informs this book. We introduce readers to the historic institutional and individual biases that created anxieties about demographic changes in the U.S. and world-wide and which have led to legal and social regulation of reproduction. We discuss the fairly recently articulated goal of *reproductive justice* (as opposed to the more individualized focus on *reproductive rights*) by advocates and scholars as a vehicle for securing and defending individuals' rights to plan and execute their reproductive lives. We explain that this book's main focus is the United States, although in each section there is some attention to global issues, as well as to the increasingly diverse population of the U.S. We then follow this intro-duction with six substantive sections on various aspects of reproduction: contraception and sterilization; abortion; reproductive technologies; pregnancy and birth; groups targeted for specific reproductive policies (e.g., immigrants, incarcerated women, disabled women); and return with a concluding section on reproductive justice.

Two key ideas about reproduction run through the entire book. The first, as the title implies, is the intense interest that virtually all societies have in human reproduction, osten-sibly one of the most private of all acts. We suggest that the concepts of both *regulation* and *stratification* are crucial to understanding how reproduction is transformed from a private act into a public issue. Approaching the topic in this way offers us a framework to explain to readers how societies encourage reproduction among some women, but seek to prevent it among others, as illustrated, for example, by sterilization campaigns, both past and present. We demonstrate the factors—race, class, ethnicity, disability, incarceration, income status—that make women (and sometimes men) most likely to be targeted for regulation by those in power. Indeed, we suggest that reproduction serves as a prime concrete illustration of the intersectionality that has been so widely theorized by feminist scholars.

Our view of reproductive policies as always containing both *liberatory and coercive pos-sibilities* is also a major theme of this volume. Or, as we sometimes have phrased it, the "too much too little" dilemma of reproduction. For example, we argue, on the one hand, that reproductive health services are essential for women to be able to participate equally in soci-ety, and at the present moment, in both the U.S. and globally, there is "too little" access for many women to these services. Yet, at the same time, we offer examples of "too much" ser-vice being offered to certain groups in a coercive manner, e.g. the disproportionate location of family planning clinics in minority neighborhoods when the U.S. government first became involved in this service in the 1970s, the forced abortions that have long characterized policy in China, the notorious vasectomy campaign aimed at poor villagers in India in the 1970s, or sterilization abuse in the U.S.

Reproduction and Society is suitable as a main text in courses focusing on reproduction, irrespective of what departments or programs offer them. The book can also serve as a use-ful supplement to courses on the family, gender, health care, social problems, and sexuality. Reproduction as a field of study offers opportunities to explore significant questions of how resources are allocated, individuals are regulated, and how very much is at stake as people and communities aim to determine their own family size and reproductive experiences.

ACKNOWLEDGMENTS

Our greatest debt is to our friend and colleague Tracy Weitz, who originally urged us to compile this volume, and who has greatly enriched us over the years with her profound understanding of reproductive issues. We also are very grateful to Jeanne Flavin, who gave us excellent feedback as this work was taking shape and to Myra Marx Ferree who also gave highly useful advice. At Routledge, we thank Samantha Barbaro, Margaret Moore, Karyn Morrison, Emily How, Jennifer Ferguson, and Sarah Olney. We also thank the Packard Foundation for its support of this work.

We would also like to thank our reviewers:

Karl Wielgus	Anoka-Ramsey Community College
Cindy Stearns	Sonoma State University
Kristen Karlberg	SUNY Purchase
Catherine Harnois	Wake Forest University

Carole Joffe additionally thanks her colleagues in the ANSIRH (Advancing New Standards in Reproductive Health) program at the University of California, San Francisco for their encouragement of this project and for their many lively conversations about the topics raised in this book. She finally thanks Elise Belusa and Chelsea Simms for their excellent research assistance.

Jennifer Reich is grateful for the community of scholars of reproduction whose ideas and passion inform this work, and especially to Zakiya Luna and Emily Mann. Peter Adler and Jonathan Wynn provided pragmatic advice and encouragement. She is grateful to Dave, Harrison, Lilia, and Jonas Scudamore for their support and patience.

INTRODUCTION

Reproduction and the Public Interest in Private Acts

Carole Joffe and Jennifer Reich

In the United States, opponents of comprehensive reproductive rights promote so-called "Personhood" measures which would give fertilized eggs the same legal status as live human beings. Since the passage of the Affordable Care Act (ACA or "Obamacare"), the massive healthcare reform bill in 2010, opponents have filed numerous lawsuits challenging the requirement that contraception services be provided. In the not too distant past of the 1960s, poor women, disproportionately African American and Latina, were sterilized without their knowledge or informed consent—a practice that has not entirely disappeared. More routine use of assisted reproduction, including sperm and ovum donation, surrogacy, or in vitro fertilization, has, on the one hand, made the dream of pregnancy and parenting possible for thousands of people to whom it was previously unavailable. Yet, on the other hand, the field of assisted reproduction has raised new questions about which practices are ethical and who can access these technologies—including discriminatory practice or lack of affordability. More commonly, the contemporary birth scene in the United States is marked both by a renewed interest on the part of many women in natural childbirth, including midwifery and home births, *and* a birth rate by Caesarean section that is far higher than that of any other industrialized country.

Conflictual reproductive politics are not unique to the United States. Elsewhere in the world, groups in various European countries express concern about a "demographic winter"—where birth rates have fallen below replacement levels among the native-born population and correspondingly riser higher ones among immigrants—and these anxieties have fueled anti-immigrant demagoguery (Joyce 2008). Beyond their other functions of humiliation and dominance, the mass rapes and forced impregnation that so often accompany wars, in places as diverse as Bosnia, Bangladesh, and the Congo, serve also, in the words of United Nations officials, as "ethnic cleansing," that is, insuring that their enemies' populations will include the children of the victors (United Nations 1994). In China, longstanding policies of a one-child limit, which involves forced abortions (Greenhalgh 2005), have only recently been partially relaxed (Denyer and Wan 2013), while in El Salvador and Nicaragua, the absolute ban on abortion for any reason has led to the deaths, injuries, and imprisonment of numerous women (Muth 2013).

These examples, and many possible others, help us see that reproduction—broadly defined as the processes by which new humans are potentially brought forth into the world—is not simply a biological process, but one laden with symbolic, political, philosophical, and ideological meanings. The examples also make clear that reproduction, ostensibly one of the most private and personal of all human activities, is, in fact, deeply a matter of public concern. The readings in this book demonstrate that numerous aspects of reproduction are both highly contested, and subject to considerable regulation. The enormous interest that various groups—nation states, religious groups, political parties, various ethnic groups—have in reproductive matters points to the challenges women face in determining their own procreative futures. While we argue that such involvement by external parties is always a feature of the reproductive landscape, in all societies and all time periods, in recent years the conflicts over reproductive policies have notably intensified in the United States. Indeed, this book was prepared in the midst of what some have deemed a "war on women" in the United States because of the harsh restrictions politicians have imposed not only on abortion but also on related reproductive services.

In this book, mainly focusing on the United States, we explore the issue we have identified above: why do private acts of reproduction arouse such controversy and how is reproductive behavior regulated? In pursuing this question, we continue in a more recent tradition of analyzing reproduction that is somewhat different from the way that many social scientists have previously investigated this topic. Before the mid-1970s, sociologists interested in reproduction mainly collaborated with medical and health care professionals and scholars. The focus was on the role of social conditions and how factors such as health status and income affected conception, pregnancy, labor, and delivery. These issues are still of interest and are reflected in the readings in this volume. However, two interrelated events of the 1970s—the re-emergence of a women's movement in the United States, known as "second wave feminism," and the U.S. Supreme Court decision, *Roe v. Wade* in 1973, which legalized abortion—led both to a renewed interest in reproductive matters and to a new approach to the subject among many scholars who came of age in that era and beyond.

The "personal is political" was one of the defining insights of second wave feminism in the 1970s and distinguished it from the first wave of the movement, which had mainly shied away from issues of sexuality and reproduction. Accordingly, scholars in a range of disciplines influenced by this most recent version of feminism began to investigate, typically with a critical eye, such topics as the historically varied movements for "reproductive freedom," the character of reproductive health services, the cultural meanings of infertility and childlessness and of course the enormous social conflict set off by the *Roe* decision (Ehrenreich and English 2005; Ginsberg 1989; Ginsberg and Rapp 1995; Gordon 2002; Morgan and Michaels 1999; Petchesky 1990). Furthermore, the immediate, strong backlash to *Roe* alerted scholars to the fact that reproductive issues were no less central to the ascendant New Right (now known as the Religious Right) of that era than they were to feminism itself (Petchesky 1990). An explosion of scholarship, initially stimulated by these two events, and which continues to expand to this day, grew to encompass both theoretical and empirical explorations of the many aspects of reproduction.

In this volume, our approach is fundamentally sociological—that is, we are interested in such questions as the societal conflicts that reproductive issues so often generate, the nature of the institutional settings in which reproductive services take place, who has access to these services, and so on. But we are in strong agreement with those who argue that the richness of the field of reproduction can best be grasped through interdisciplinary work. Accordingly, in this volume, we draw on a wide range of disciplines for the best scholarship in this arena, including anthropology, history, law, and medicine.

KEY THEMES IN THE STUDY OF REPRODUCTION

Although the sections in this book are divided mainly along the lines of the different areas of reproductive services, e.g. contraception, abortion, pregnancy, and so on, certain key themes reappear in all these areas that are core to the study of reproduction. We offer here a brief discussion of each, which we hope will help the reader make theoretical sense of the discussions included in this volume, but also can help in the examination of other aspects of gender, inequality, social movements, and reproductive politics.

Feminist Perspectives on Reproduction

Much of the current, and in our view strongest, scholarship in the field of reproduction, as already suggested, is written from a feminist perspective. What does this mean? Most fundamentally, this approach views control of their fertility as essential for women to gain full citizenship, and to be able to participate in "public" as well as in private life. Accordingly, some of the most interesting writing in this field has explored the tensions between women's own desires regarding reproduction and the demands of the nation state. These tensions are seen, for example, in the calls to "reproduce the nation" faced by women in societies as varied as contemporary Turkey (Altiok 2013), and numerous countries of the former Eastern European Soviet bloc after the fall of communism (Gal and Kligman 2000).

Such official governmental dictates, often accompanied by religious and cultural ones, can result from the aftereffects of war, and the perceived need to repopulate; in some instances, the demands stem from anxiety about the changing position of women and the desires of some to reverse these gains and get women out of the paid workforce and "back home." A number of observers of the ongoing reproductive struggles in the United States, particularly the abortion conflict, have viewed these battles as primarily a backlash against the social changes first set in motion by the woman's movement of the 1970s (Gordon 2002; Luker 1984; Di Mauro and Joffe 2009). At the same time, leaders in countries concerned with a rising population or a perceived inability to meet the needs of all of its citizens will call for reduced childbirth. China, with its many years of strictly enforced one-child policies has long been the best known example of this, but modern Iran, though an extremely conservative Islamic state, nonetheless very actively promoted smaller families through widely available birth control because of similar concerns about a too rapidly growing population, which led to "the largest and fastest drop in fertility ever recorded" (Weiss 2012).

The attempt to regulate women's reproduction, however, goes far beyond the official statements of government bodies. A useful and comprehensive approach to the very broad question of both what is demanded of women with respect to reproduction and how such demands are enforced, comes from the feminist anthropologists Lynn Morgan and Elizabeth Roberts (2013) who have recently articulated the concept of "reproductive governance." They define this as "the mechanisms through which different historical configurations of actors—such as state, religious, and international financial institutions, NGOs, and social movements—use legislative controls, economic inducements, moral injunctions, direct coercion, and ethical incitements to produce, monitor, and control reproductive behaviors and population practices."

This reproductive governance formulation leads us to note the impositions of very stark policies, such as the absolute ban on abortion and contraception, for example, during the reign of the Communist dictator Nicolae Ceaucescu (Kligman 1998) in Romania from 1965 to 1989 (a policy that led to many children being abandoned or orphaned because of their mothers' unsafe abortions), or the fines historically imposed on Chinese women who violated the one-child policy. But this formulation also encompasses "softer" approaches, such as the "carrot" of generous maternity (and in some cases, paternity) benefits as an inducement to increased reproduction, as for example in various European countries concerned about low birth rates. Still another dimension of reproductive governance is the public health campaigns that seek to stigmatize certain behaviors and promote others; prime examples of this in the U.S. context are the periodic drives against teenage pregnancy, often involving posters on subways and buses, or the signs in bars cautioning pregnant women of the link between alcohol use and birth defects.

Coercion, as suggested above, is frequently an element in the regulation of reproduction. Although we most often think of this phenomenon in terms of the withholding of services, particularly abortion and contraception, and thus forcing childbirth, coercion can also take the form of aggressively promoting, or even imposing, unwanted services on women and, less often, men. An example of the latter is the notorious vasectomy campaign that took place in rural India in the 1970s that set quotas for local officials to achieve millions of sterilizations each year—a campaign so thoroughly discredited for its insensitivity that it was one factor in bringing down the Indian government of that time (Bhagat 2004). Therefore, a major focus of feminists who study reproduction, particularly in a global context, has been a critique of "population controllers"—those groups who have advocated for a massive infusion of contraception as a means to address world overpopulation (Dixon-Mueller 1993). Though feminists, obviously, have in other contexts been highly supportive of contraception, they have taken issue with population controllers on such matters as the testing of contraceptive methods on women in the developing world, and the coercive manner with which contraceptive services have often been delivered. These tensions came to a head at two United Nations Conferences in Cairo and Beijing in the mid-1990s, as will be discussed in the final section of this book.

Feminist health activists and scholars, moreover, have been severely critical of pharmaceutical companies whose products, such as the first generation of oral contraception (the "pill") and the earliest IUDs (intrauterine devices) proved to be unsafe (Seaman 1994; Seaman and Eldridge 2012). Indeed, the significantly increased safety of the birth control pills and IUDs (now referred to as "IUCs" or "intrauterine contraception") currently in use can be in great measure attributed to the feminist health activism of the 1970s. For example, the concerns that activists such as Seaman raised about the high estrogen levels in the first commercially available pills led to Senate hearings, and as a result of these hearings, a health warning was added to the pill, the first informational insert for any prescription drug (Watkins 2001).

These various examples show us that feminist analysts view reproduction as a complex terrain, always containing both liberatory and coercive possibilities. Though currently in the United States and elsewhere in the world, arguably the main problem with respect to women's reproductive self-determination is a matter of "too little"—as both contraception and abortion are restricted, assisted reproduction is out of reach for poorer women, and women in the developing world do not have enough safe pregnancy and maternity care—the problem in other places and other historical times is one of "too much," as women are subjected to reproductive services against their will.

Finally with respect to feminism, in spite of the enormous outpouring of writing on reproduction, there is not a uniform feminist "position" on various aspects of this huge field. For example, assisted reproduction is a particular area where they have been sharp divisions among feminists: some have applauded the emergence of these new technologies, while others have been severely critical, claiming they exploit poorer women because of the financial incentives to sell their eggs or rent their wombs for surrogacy. Even the issue of abortion, though it receives near universal support by feminists, is not supported by all who claim that identity, as is illustrated by the group called Feminists for Life. Moreover, as is discussed in the final section of this book, even among the feminist supporters of abortion, there is some division as to how much the defense of abortion should occur within a single issue movement, as opposed to a broader movement for reproductive justice, which addresses issues beyond abortion.

Race, Class and Reproduction

Issues of race and class are central to virtually every area of reproduction discussed in this volume. Indeed, this field offers numerous concrete examples of the "intersectionality" of gender, race and class that has been so widely theorized by feminist scholars (Crenshaw 1991; Collins and Andersen 2007). To return to the point mentioned above, that of the numerous instances of governments urging that women reproduce more, we can now add that it is not simply "women" who are the targets of these exhortations; rather, some women's reproduction is desired more than others, and conversely, reproduction by others is discouraged, if not forcibly prevented. The anthropologists Faye Ginsburg and Rayna Rapp (1995) have referred to this phenomenon as *stratified reproduction*. A historical example of this comes from the United States, in the early 20th century, a time when a belief in eugenics (the idea that the human race could be improved through selective breeding) was far more accepted by the general public than it is today. In 1905, the then-president Theodore Roosevelt famously condemned the "race suicide" that he claimed was underway in the United States because the birth rates of native born women from a Northern European background were lower than those of recent immigrants from Ireland, Italy and Eastern Europe (Gordon 2002). In contemporary times, the Roma, also known as gypsies, have been subjected to coerced sterilizations in various European countries (Albert 2011), just as poor, mainly women of color were in the United States in the 1960s.

At certain historical points, there have been sterilization campaigns of the "unfit," in ways that often include race and class dimensions, but go beyond them. For example, the state of Virginia in the 1920s had a policy of compulsory sterilization of the "feebleminded," a policy that was upheld in the 1927 U.S. Supreme Court case, *Buck v. Bell*. Another example is the Nazis' orders to German doctors to sterilize patients suffering from mental illness, physical illness, and conditions such as alcoholism (Caplan 1992), in addition to the better-known campaigns against Jews, homosexuals and gypsies.

An often overlooked but still salient issue in the contemporary United States, relevant to this issue of stratified reproduction, concerns women receiving TANF (Temporary Assistance to Needy Families) or, as it is more commonly referred to, "welfare." As is discussed further in Section V, as part of a major overhaul of welfare in 1996 (at which time, TANF replaced an older program, Aid to Families with Dependent Children), states were permitted to impose "family caps" on recipients. This policy allowed states to exclude a child born after a woman was initially declared eligible for support from receiving additional funding. Interestingly, the welfare reform measure, and especially the family cap provision, brought a rare moment of unity between the reproductive rights movement and the anti-abortion movement: the former arguing that this policy interfered with reproductive freedom, and the latter decrying that such a policy would inevitably lead to higher abortion rates among welfare recipients (Joffe 1995). What all these disparate examples have in common, quite obviously, is a desire by those in power to mold the population of a given country along particular lines, whether racial, ethnic, or economic (and often, of course, these categories overlap). In this light, the situation in the contemporary United States presents a particularly interesting contradiction:

the family cap provision reveals, like the earlier sterilization campaigns, that there is hostility to births among the poorest women (disproportionately women of color)—yet at the same time, there is now also a powerful political opposition to birth control and abortion services.

Social class and race status has implications for reproduction in other ways as well. In the United States, women of a lower socioeconomic status are more likely to have infertility issues and they are more likely to give birth to low weight babies, and newborns with other health problems. These disparities are a function of several factors, including lessened access to regular primary care and prenatal care. Additionally, poorer women are more likely to live in areas with environmental hazards that impact both fertility and birth outcomes. With respect to infertility problems, assisted reproduction is usually not covered by health insurance plans, and despite the popular image of a career-driven 40-year-old with a ticking biological clock as the prime candidate for infertility treatment, it is in fact lower income women who most need such services but typically can't afford them.

When we look at these issues from a racial standpoint, we find that African American women have the highest rate of infertility in the United States (11.5%), followed by Hispanic women at 7.4% and white women at 7% (McCarthy-Keith et al. 2010). Black women's higher exposure to lead during pregnancy, because their geographical location, has been linked to the higher rate of miscarriage among this group (Mukherjee et al. 2013) and may also account for higher rates of premature birth, low birth weight and developmental delays.

Until the advent of the ACA, even those patients with health insurance did not always have prenatal or maternity care benefits. The poorest individuals in the United States are eligible for Medicaid, a health care program that does cover prenatal and maternity care, but millions of women, typically the "working poor," are caught in the unfortunate situation of earning too much to qualify for Medicaid but not enough to be able to afford their own health insurance. Because of some states' refusal to expand Medicaid eligibility, an option permitted by the 2012 Supreme Court decision on the ACA (Kaiser Family Foundation 2013), many of these women will not have health care, including prenatal and maternity care, even with the full roll-out of the ACA. Undocumented immigrant women are the most vulnerable, with respect to reproductive and other health care. They have been excluded from the ACA and often their first contact with the health care system during a pregnancy is when they show up at hospital emergency rooms to give birth. With respect to abortion, no federal funds are permitted to be used in the United States for abortion (except in cases of rape, incest, and threats to the life of the pregnant woman) and 33 states forbid the use of state Medicaid dollars for this purpose. The lack of public funding for abortion disproportionately affects poor women (more than often, women of color) who are most likely to need an abortion and least able to pay for one. All forms of FDA-approved contraception are covered in the ACA, but, as earlier noted, numerous states and businesses have filed lawsuits challenging this, and at the time of this writing the issue is unresolved. In June 2014, as this book was in press, the Supreme Court ruled in the *Hobby Lobby* case that corporations with religious objections did not have to provide contraceptive coverage.

Globally, the lack of adequate maternity care and safe abortion services for the poor are acknowledged public health crises. The World Health Organization estimates that about 358,000 women (the overwhelming majority of whom are in developing countries) die each year from pregnancy-related causes, and millions more suffer complications, including chronic disease and sterility, from unsafe birth and abortions (World Health Organization 2010). While in the developed world, as some selections in this book point out, there have been significant critiques of the excessive medicalization of normal pregnancies, in the developing world much of the death and injury is due to a lack of trained health care personnel, and insufficient access to quality clinic facilities.

The Institutional Settings Where Reproductive Services Take Place

In this volume, we view an examination of the reproductive services that women (and to a lesser extent men) receive and the settings in which they take place as crucial components of the study of reproduction. Focusing on the point of service delivery leads us to consider such questions as, what is the actual content of "reproductive services?" For example, do such services only involve clinical interventions, such as a physical exam and a prescription for a medication, such as birth control pills, or do these services involve a counseling component as well? If so, does such counseling have a particular ideological slant? For example, in a number of states, largely in the south and Midwest, public funding for family planning services is diverted to so-called "crisis pregnancy centers," which offer pregnancy tests, but also give misleading or inaccurate information about both contraception and abortion (Bryant and Levi 2012). Who, we must also ask, has access to reproductive services? Who provides such services? How much choice should individuals have in finding the kind of care they want?

Historically speaking, key reproductive events in a woman's life such as contraceptive efforts, births, and abortions took place apart from institutional settings and without professional assistance. As an obvious example, women gave birth in their own homes and were assisted by family members or neighbors. Over time, especially in the industrialized world, these events began to take place in hospitals and clinics—and with the rise of assisted reproduction, even conception itself now takes place in specialized facilities, as when sperm and egg are combined in a petri dish in an in vitro fertilization (IVF) clinic. To be sure, access to these various service settings varies enormously: women in developing countries, as already suggested, do not have adequate access to facilities offering either safe birth or safe abortions, and only a tiny portion of women in those countries can afford assisted reproductive services. In what perhaps may be seen as a historical irony, some clinicians in the United States now struggle for the legal right to assist at a home birth.

Even in the United States, access to various reproductive services is very unevenly distributed, along both economic and geographic lines. Abortion, for example, is not available in nearly 90% of U.S. counties and, as of this writing, several states have only one remaining facility. Family planning services, which include cancer screenings, and testing for sexually transmitted infections as well as contraceptive services, have been the subject of intense political attacks, and a number of states have successfully prevented Planned Parenthood facilities—the largest deliverer of such services in the United States—from receiving public funding. Women living in predominately rural areas have problems finding an obstetrician/gynecologist to care for them during their pregnancies as nearly half of all U.S. counties are without such a specialist (ACOG 2012). (However, these women typically do have access to primary care providers, nurse practitioners and various kinds of midwives, which many argue are just as adequate for serving women with normal pregnancies as are specialists.)

As elsewhere in the health care system, the occupational groups that have developed over time to offer reproductive services show interesting divisions along "turf" lines. For example, in the U.S. context, there are longstanding battles between midwives and physicians over the right of the former to legally offer maternity care, and to assert their vision of the ideal "low tech" birthing experience against the increasingly high tech one promoted by many obstetricians. And even within the world of midwifery there exists competition between different classes of midwives—those trained and certified through university-based programs and those who have developed their skills through an "apprentice" route.

Given the high degree of politicization that is a feature of much of the reproductive landscape in the contemporary United States, it is not surprising that there are deep ideological schisms among providers of reproductive services. With respect to abortion, there are organized groups within the major relevant professional associations, such as the American College of Obstetricians and Gynecologists (ACOG), of anti-abortion doctors as well as pro-choice ones. Independent groups such as the Christian Medical and Dental Society not only oppose abortion but also contraception for unmarried persons and many of the procedures associated with assisted reproduction (Christian Medical and Dental Society 2013). A particularly interesting, and consequential development in the ongoing ideological battle over reproductive health services is the recent rise of the "health care refusal" movement: initially started by pharmacists who refused to fill prescriptions for emergency contraception (EC), who believed (incorrectly, according to medical experts) that EC could cause an abortion of an existing pregnancy, the refusal movement has spread to a wide variety of health care workers, including doctors, nurses, ambulance dispatchers, receptionists, schedulers, and so on. Essentially, these health care workers argue that they should not be forced to participate in any aspect of health care service delivery which violates their conscience (National Women's Law Center 2013). Courts in different states have come to different conclusions as to whether such refusals are legally permissible and some states have passed statutes protecting practitioners who refuse to provide services because of conscious objection. While most such refusals involve abortion or contraception, healthcare workers in the field of assisted reproduction have refused to provide services to certain categories of patients, such as single women and homosexuals. The recent rapid spread of mergers between Catholic hospitals and secular ones, actions undertaken as cost saving measures, has had significant consequences for the availability of reproductive health care in the United States The newly merged entities are obliged to operate under the Catholic Health Care Directives, which means there can be no provision of contraception, sterilization, assisted reproduction, or abortion on hospital grounds, even to victims of rape or to women facing serious health risks from pregnancy (Freedman and Stulberg 2013).

The world of reproductive services has also seen the continual creation of new occupational roles. Genetic counseling, for example, is an occupation that developed as prenatal diagnosis became more widely available (Rapp 1999). Similarly, the role of the abortion counselor arose in the first freestanding abortion clinics in NY and Washington, DC, places which legalized abortion several years before the *Roe* decision, as new patient needs were identified (Joffe 2013). Doulas are a more recent example of new occupations developing in the reproductive health world: they are non-medical persons, nearly always women, who serve as labor coaches and offer emotional assistance before, during, and after the birth as well. Use of doulas has increased in popularity in the United States recently, and some doulas also offer their services for abortions. Even lay persons have been drawn into paid service in the assisted reproduction world, as men sell their sperm for insemination, and women sell their eggs, and serve as economically compensated surrogate or gestational mothers (Almeling 2011), as is discussed in Section III.

As we consider the institutional settings, availability of services, and kinds of providers available, we should also pose the admittedly far more subjective but equally important question: how are women treated in various reproductive settings? Common sense tells us that those with more resources are far more likely to be able to choose service settings in which patients are treated respectfully and able to make decisions about the type of services offered. The issue of how women are treated has received much attention from feminist health advocates and will be addressed in the next section. Here, we will merely point out one of the extremes of dis-respectful, indeed unacceptable, treatment of women in a reproductive context: the practice of having incarcerated women give birth in shackles, as is discussed at greater length in one of the readings in Section V. In this example, we can begin to identify the ways that providers, institutional contexts, resources, and systems of inequality structure women's experiences and allow them to be treated in ways that can only be viewed as inhumane.

Reproduction and Social Movements

The field of reproduction has long been the scene of an immense amount of social move-ment activity. The leading example of this in the U.S. context, of course, is the highly visible abortion conflict. The extent to which the abortion issue dominates American politics, more than forty years after the *Roe* decision, is striking, and, to many outside the United States, puzzling. Both the supporters and opponents of abortion are well organized into movements that operate at the national, state and local levels. The abortion conflict manifests in elections ranging from presidential contests to those for school board seats, in cultural struggles over what is permissible in television shows, in educational contexts where discussions of abor-tion, whether in medical schools or high schools, is contested, and virtually everywhere else in American society.

What accounts for this staying power of abortion as one of the most divisive aspects of American politics? Obviously, for many on both sides of the debate, abortion arouses deep passions on religious and moral grounds. But we argue that to understand a conflict of this magnitude, one must go beyond those issues and examine abortion in far broader terms. As Linda Gordon (2002, 320), a leading historian of reproduction, has put it:

> No one issue dramatizes the basic cultural/political fissures in the United States . . . more than abor-tion does . . . The abortion debate is not only about abortion; it is also about deep differences in social values that spill over into a variety of other issues related to sex and reproduction.

Similarly, our approach in this book is to see the ongoing battles over abortion care, and related reproductive health services, as stemming from a clash between two world-views over the proper place of women in society and the legitimacy of non-procreative sexuality.

Contraception is perhaps the most dramatic contemporary example of the "spill over" to which Gordon refers. For a long time, contraception was seen as "common ground" in the abortion battle—something both supporters and opponents of abortion could agree on as a path to decrease the need for abortion. However, this common understanding is disap-pearing, as we have seen in the continuing furor over contraception coverage in the ACA. Some opponents of abortion first criticized contraception as "supportive of the abortion mentality," arguing that those who use contraception to prevent birth would likely choose an abortion if the contraception failed. More recently, the dominant argument of contracep-tion opponents has been to reframe contraception itself as an "abortifacient," a rhetorical strategy that started with EC and then spread to regular oral contraception, and is applied to intrauterine devices ("IUDS") as well (Di Mauro and Joffe 2009). Although medically inaccurate, this strategy has worked to make contraception more politically controversial in recent years than it has been than at any time in the last 50 years.

Similarly, the field of assisted reproduction has been deeply affected by the abortion con-flict. During IVF embryos are created by mixing sperm and egg in a lab, and after cell division and an examination of the quality of those cells, one or two embryos will be inserted into a woman's uterus in hopes it implants and grows. In fact, more embryos are often created than are actually used. As a result, there exist divisions about what to do with these extra embryos, which are commonly frozen for additional attempts if needed, are discarded, or donated for research. Abortion opponents object to the destruction of these embryos, claiming they are "unborn persons" and see the use of such embryos for research purposes as equally reprehensible. Abortion opponents also object to the use of pre-implantation diagnosis of embryos used in IVF because of the likely destruction of those embryos found to be carrying anomalies.

To be sure, not all current reproductive battles that have attracted activism should be categorized as standoffs between liberals *versus* conservatives or feminists *versus* traditionalists. Given the centrality of reproductive issues to contemporary feminism, health activists from that movement have been involved in just about all of these battles, but the opponents have differed. For example, as earlier mentioned, the history of the introduction of new contraceptive methods in the United States has seen repeated instances in which feminists have mobilized against pharmaceutical companies. Activism in the realm of pregnancy and birth is particularly interesting because it has often involved participation by those on both sides of the abortion divide, but who in this instance are united in their demands for less routine use of technology (such as fetal monitors) in labor and for the legitimacy of midwife-assisted birth and home births, to name just a few points of communality. In this case, the targets of the activists are the obstetrical establishment and insurance companies. And while these strange bedfellows approach questions differently, they sometimes find common goals, even if those goals are underscored by different ideological beliefs about reproduction.

The interface of reproductive health and the environment is one of the newer sites of activism in the reproductive world. At this point, this activism is primarily led by scientists whose research calls attention to the rising rates of infertility and birth defects that can be attributed to environmental degradation. The main targets of activists are chemical companies and governments—both national and local—who, activists claim, are not doing enough to address these problems. In this instance, reproductive health advocates have allied with other activists who oppose environmental degradation. This issue is explored in greater detail in Section IV.

Reproductive movements based in the United States have for many years engaged global reproductive issues as well. Abortion, contraception, and HIV education and services are the subjects of most of this engagement, as advocates from different sides in the "culture wars" seek to influence politics and help develop services in the Global South, as the developing world is often referred to. For example, Human Life International, an anti-abortion group, has a presence in over sixty countries; the organization works assiduously to prevent any moves toward liberalization of abortion laws and also promotes policies that discourage condom distribution. On the other side, the group Catholics for Choice has long worked in Latin America to promote safe abortion and contraceptive services. Perhaps the most historic engagement of U.S. reproductive rights activists with global allies took place at two U.N. Conferences in Cairo and Beijing in the mid-1990s. There, despite massive pushback from the Vatican and a handful of conservative governments, activists achieved historic breakthroughs in getting delegates to agree to a range of reproductive services that must be made available to women in member U.N. nations, though abortion, not surprisingly, was a major point of conflict. Since those meetings, there has been mixed success in implementing the results of Cairo and Beijing, as we discuss in Section VI, and both the successes and failures of those conferences still resonate today.

Finally, though most social movement activity in the U.S. reproductive world, as suggested above, deals with advocating for or against various governmental policies or corporate practices, yet another consequential target for movement activists is reproductive health care settings themselves. Perhaps the most dramatic example of this has been the transformation, over the last 40 years or so, of how birth takes place in the United States Although they are so commonplace now that it is difficult to imagine they were ever controversial, many birth practices are the outcomes of political activism. Among these, hospitals now permit partners and other close associates in labor and delivery rooms; a range of options exist, for those experiencing normal pregnancies, as to the level of pain control measures received during labor; and freestanding birthing centers and home births attended by midwives are options available to some women—even as feminist health activists continue to decry the high rate of Caesarean sections in the United States.

In the following sections, we present short introductions that offer an overview of the topic that follows. We have then provided selected readings in several key areas of reproduction to explore these issues in greater detail. These include: contraception, abortion, assisted reproduction, pregnancy and labor, reproductive policies targeted at special groups of women, and the emergence of national and global movements for reproductive justice.

SECTION I
Contraception and Sterilization

Contraception and sterilization, the subjects of this section, are particularly fascinating phenomena to consider, as they embody the "too much/too little" paradox discussed in the introduction. On the one hand, each represents services that women and men throughout history have very much desired so they can control their own fertility and determine their own family size. On the other hand, both contraception and (especially) sterilization have in different contexts been used by those in power to control women's fertility—sometimes without their consent or knowledge.

As an overview, birth control generally refers to intentional methods to prevent pregnancy. As readers doubtless know, women ovulate once a month and release an ovum (or egg), creating a window during which time sperm can potentially fertilize that ovum. Once fertilized, that ovum will migrate to the uterus and implant in the uterine lining where it can begin to grow into a fetus, and then a baby. Birth control is a broad category that encompasses different types of technologies. First, barrier methods, such as condoms, diaphragms, cervical caps and sponges, are those that use a device to block sperm from coming in contact with an egg. This category also includes spermicides that can kill sperm before fertilization can occur. Second, hormonal methods are those that aim to stop ovulation, or fertilization, such as oral contraceptives, emergency contraception (sometimes referred to as the "morning after pill"), injectable contraceptives (like Depo Provera) that are given in a shot about once every twelve weeks, or implantable contraceptives, like Implanon, which can be inserted into a woman's body and remain effective for several years. A new generation of intrauterine devices, sometime referred to as LARC (long lasting reversible contraception) has replaced earlier IUDs (intrauterine devices) and is widely considered to be much safer than the first generation, which were very controversial because of numerous injuries they caused, and in the case of one form, the Dalkon Shield, even some deaths (Kolata 1987). Third, sterilization methods are those that aim to permanently end reproductive capabilities, either by cutting the vas deferens in a man's body so sperm cannot exit, or by blocking a woman's fallopian tubes so ovulation cannot occur. "Natural family planning" is a birth control method that teaches women how to recognize they are ovulating and to abstain from sex at that time.

Women's own desire to control their fertility is a historical constant, as the first pages from the selection of historian Linda Gordon's *Moral Property of Women* show. Indeed, one of the very first known medical textbooks, published in China in approximately 2700 BC, contained information on contraception (and abortion, Riddle 1992). Some societies have passed laws to limit, regulate, or criminalize use of birth control. Whether legal or illegal, it remains true that contraception has always been—and continues to be—controversial in some quarters, including the contemporary United States.

Some of the controversy over birth control is rooted in religion. Although the Catholic Church's prohibition on contraception (with the exception of natural family planning methods,) is well known, other religions have also opposed or insisted on limiting its use, including, for example, the Orthodox branch of Judaism and some denominations of Christianity. The reasons for religious or governmental clampdowns on contraception are varied and not mutually exclusive. Sometimes this is because of disapproval of sexual activity that is separate from the possibility of procreation and especially when this occurs outside of marriage; in other instances it is because of a drive to re-populate a society after war or other natural disasters; and in some cases, the reason is a desire to reinforce traditional gender roles, in which women's primary role is to bear children and maintain the home. The particular reasons for promoting or rejecting birth control typically represent cultural, political and economic currents in a society and vary across time and place. To illustrate this, we offer here a very brief history of the changing status of birth control in the U.S., but we encourage readers to explore this interesting issue in other places and eras.

In the United States, until the 19th century, contraception was practiced quite widely. The invention of vulcanized rubber in the mid-1800s allowed for better access to methods like condoms and syringes, but many people relied on a variety of folk methods, many of which were ineffectual or dangerous (and as Gordon points out in Chapter 1, there is ample evidence of abortion and infanticide occurring in that period). During this time, there were few attempts at regulation. Starting in the late 1800s and into the first quarter of the 20th century, birth control became a highly contested political issue for the first time. The two chief antagonists in this conflict were Anthony Comstock (1844–1915) and Margaret Sanger (1879–1966). Comstock was a deeply religious and socially conservative man who founded an organization, the New York Society for the Suppression of Vice, and led a decades-long crusade against what he termed "obscene, lewd, or lascivious" material. He began his campaign because of his objections to the pornography that he saw openly displayed in New York city shops; yet, what is noteworthy for our purposes is that among the types of material he classified as "obscene" were information about birth control and abortion, as well as educational material on health and even anatomy textbooks. Building his political connections, Comstock eventually became a U.S. Postal Inspector and with his supporters succeeded in persuading Congress to pass the Comstock Act of 1873, which made illegal "an obscene book, pamphlet, paper, writing, advertisement, circular, print, picture, drawing or other representation . . . or other article of an immoral nature, or any drug or medicine, or any article whatever, for the prevention of conception, or for causing unlawful abortion, or shall advertise the same for sale" (Tone 2001). About twenty states also passed similar laws, known together as the Comstock Laws, which would last for more than seventy years.

Comstock's greatest adversary was Margaret Sanger (Chesler 1993). Sanger was a public health nurse whose work among immigrant women in the tenements of the Lower East Side of New York exposed her to the deaths and injuries among this population caused by uncontrolled pregnancy, childbearing, and unsafe abortions. She learned about the most effective forms of contraception that were available at this time in Europe, including a very early version of the diaphragm, and began to write and lecture about women's right to decide when and if to have children. She and her sister opened the first birth control clinic in the U.S. in the Brownsville section of Brooklyn in 1916. Her clinic was immediately shut down by police and Sanger and her sister were arrested and jailed. In the following decades, Sanger repeatedly clashed with Comstock and local authorities who enforced the Comstock Act as she continued to advocate for birth control. In 1921, Sanger founded the American Birth

Control League, which eventually became the Planned Parenthood Federation of America. A lifelong crusader for women's reproductive self-determination, one of her later achievements was securing the funding for the research that eventually led to the development of oral contraception, known ubiquitously as "the pill."

Though Margaret Sanger is acknowledged as the single most influential individual in the struggle to bring birth control to women, both in the U.S. and elsewhere, she remains to this day a controversial figure. Failing to receive support for her work from other quarters, she accepted financial aid from some of the leading eugenicists of her time. Eugenicists in England and the U.S. aimed to promote reproduction among people they viewed as desirable, namely white, Protestant, wealthy—those like themselves—and to limit or control the reproduction of those they viewed as genetically unfit. As the historian Rickie Solinger (2013, 8) explains in writing about this period, "The field of eugenics generally defined the 'unfit' as nonwhites, mixed-race persons, immigrants, and poor and working class whites, as well as people with handicaps and criminal records." Because of this connection and statements she made (some of which have been taken out of context), Sanger's legacy has been sullied as she has been accused of being both a eugenicist and a racist. There is no question Sanger had organizational ties to the eugenicist movement. Yet, she also received support and accolades from many African American ministers, social workers and leading intellectuals of that time, including W. E. B. Dubois, and Martin Luther King, Jr., which belies these claims. The historian Ellen Chesler (1993), Sanger's premier biographer, challenges these allegations of racism, noting that while

> most birth control facilities conformed to the segregation mores of the day, she opened an integrated clinic in Harlem in the early 1930s. Later, she facilitated birth control and maternal health programs for rural black women in the South, when local white health officials there denied them access to any New Deal-funded services

Nevertheless, groups opposed to legal abortion, access to birth control, or Planned Parenthood clinics more generally, have kept this charge of racism alive, and have used it to try to build sympathy to their position among communities of color in the U.S.

As the 20th century progressed, the legal—and cultural—status of birth control gradually began to change. Several court decisions allowed physicians to prescribe contraception for the prevention of disease or on health grounds, (e.g. prescribing it for women whose health would clearly suffer if pregnant). During World War II the U.S. Army issued thousands of condoms to soldiers as a means of preventing sexually transmitted infections, increasing the cultural acceptance for birth control. In 1965, the U.S. Supreme Court in the landmark decision of *Griswold v Connecticut*, acknowledged a "right to privacy" in the Constitution of the United States and overturned a Connecticut law barring the use of contraceptives by married persons, seen as one of the last state Comstock laws. Several years later, in the 1972 decision, *Eisenstadt v Baird*, the Court established the right of unmarried persons to use contraception. By then, with women entering college and the workforce in unprecedented numbers, and premarital sex becoming more common, the demand for reliable birth control use was dramatically increasing (May 2010).

The birth control pill, which started to become available to American women in the mid-1960s, became inextricably linked to these changes in the lives of American women. By the end of the decade, the federal government became involved in the distribution of family planning services—contraception along with cancer screenings—to low income women and teenagers, through the passage of Title X of the Public Health Service Act in 1970. Given the intense political polarization that now exists over contraception in American politics, it is interesting to note that one of the chief sponsors of Title X was George H. W. Bush, the future Republican president and then a congressman from Texas, and the bill was signed into law by Richard Nixon, a Republican president.

The government's funding of birth control through Title X quickly became controversial. Though the program was intended to serve people on the basis of their incomes, critics noted that clinics were disproportionately located in African American communities (Littlewood 1977). Black militants of that era, associated with groups such as the Black Panthers, alleged that the program aimed to further "black genocide"; there were demonstrations against Title X facilities and in the city of Cleveland a clinic was set on fire (May 2010).

This controversy in the African American community over publicly provided birth control brought to the fore gender issues as well as racial ones. As the selection in this section from a classic piece by the late black feminist writer Toni Cade Bambera suggests, African American women in that era understood the complexities of birth control access. She acknowledges that Black women may have had reason to mistrust the motivations of those targeting their communities with birth control—but makes clear her belief that women in her community nevertheless wanted birth control in order to promote their own objectives of raising healthy children.

Since its establishment in 1970, there have been numerous unsuccessful efforts by conservative politicians to abolish Title X, although its supporters decry its inadequate levels of funding. It remains the only federal program devoted solely to family planning, though other programs, e.g. Medicaid in some states, devote some of their resources to this purpose. No Title X funds are allowed to be used for abortions, but the fact that Planned Parenthood affiliates receives about 25% of Title X contracts—and some Planned Parenthood clinics also provide abortions—is yet another reason that many conservatives are opposed to this program.

Contraception, some fifty years after the *Griswold* decision made it legal, is a strongly held value of Americans, and its use is virtually universal: The Centers for Disease Control (2010) has reported that "over 99%" of American women have ever used contraception for pregnancy prevention in the context of sexual intercourse. (This excludes the many women who use oral contraception for medical reasons, such as severe acne, endometriosis, or other health conditions.) But the high rate of usage does not mean that contraception is used consistently or correctly. Nearly half of all pregnancies occurring in the U.S. are unplanned—the highest rate among developed countries—and lower income women have a far incidence of such pregnancies than higher income ones (Guttmacher Institute 2013a). Several reasons account for this high rate, including the fact that the most effective methods are the more expensive ones, and thus far, not all women needing assistance with paying for contraception are able to get this help. As already mentioned, the outcome of legal challenges to the contraceptive coverage provision in the ACA will be very consequential in addressing this problem.

For those women with the resources to use contraception regularly, the economic rewards have been considerable. The economic journalist Annie Lowrey's brief piece in this section, "The Economic Impact of the Pill," summarizes some of the key research on this topic. Researchers have argued that use of the pill—currently the most popular form of contraception among American women—has played a large role in facilitating the entrance of women into traditionally male professions and increased women's wages.

But in spite of the value placed on contraception by Americans, its widespread (if erratic) usage, and its well-documented economic benefits, contraception today has reemerged as a hot-button issue in U.S. politics. Once seen by both those who support and oppose abortion as common ground, because of the potential to reduce the need for abortions, contraception has gradually been reframed by influential social conservatives as a *form* of abortion and thus in some circles, the former has become nearly as demonized as the latter (Di Mauro and Joffe 2009).

Sterilization, the second most widely used birth control method in the U.S., has a history even more marked by controversy, with the strongest critics in this case being feminist health activists. Starting in the early the 20th century, a period in which, as we have noted, eugenic beliefs were widely held, sterilization of those deemed "unfit," often without their consent, was a widespread practice in many states. There were legal efforts to challenge state-ordered sterilization. In a famous U.S. Supreme Court case 1927, *Buck v Bell*, the Court upheld this practice of involuntary sterilization. Accepting the state of Virginia's claim that Carrie Buck and her mother were "feeble-minded" and "promiscuous," and that it was in the state's interest to sterilize them, Justice Oliver Wendell Holmes, wrote in the 8–1 majority opinion the now notorious statement, "Three generations of imbeciles are enough." The Virginia sterilization law remained in place until it was repealed in 1974 (Schoen 2005).

Sterilization abuse again came to public attention in the 1960s when it became known that thousands of poor women, many of whom were on public assistance, and disproportionately women of color, were being subjected to coercive sterilization. These procedures took place for the most part in Southern states (Schoen 2005), but also in California, where doctors mainly targeted Mexican immigrants, as the sociologist Elena Gutiérrez discusses in the selection in this chapter from her book, *Fertile Matters*. The outcry against these practices mainly came from feminist health activists of that period; one of the leading reproductive rights groups of the 1960s was CARASA (Committee on Abortion Rights and against Sterilization Abuse, Petchesky 1984). The furor raised when the news of coerced sterilization became widely known led to strict new regulations on when sterilization could occur, including waiting periods between when women signed consent and could undergo the surgery. Intended to protect women, these new regulations became cumbersome and many women have found them onerous—again an example of the "too much/too little" paradox that so often accompanies reproductive policies.

Human rights groups continue to identify forced sterilization around the world, such as the recent cases that have come to light involving the Roma (also known as "gypsies") in several European countries, as mentioned in the introduction to this book. However, in the United States, sterilization abuse was thought to be a thing of the past, with some still living victims in North Carolina, for example, finally receiving apologies and financial compensation (Lombardo and Hardin 2013). But, to widespread shock, in 2013 investigators revealed that at least 250 female inmates in California prisons were sterilized without the required approval between the late 1990s and 2010 (Johnson 2013b). This reemergence of sterilization abuse more than fifty years after the aforementioned scandals in the South and California, and the resulting backlash that created new regulations, is a disturbing reminder of how powerful are the cultural inclinations to curtail the reproduction of the most vulnerable women in society and those who are deemed, by those in power, as unfit to reproduce—in this case, incarcerated women.

CONTRACEPTION, HEALTH AND THE FUTURE

Our argument throughout the introduction to this section is that birth control is both a tool for individual self-determination and a potential weapon to be used by those with power to limit the reproduction of others. Part of the challenge for scholars and activists alike has been

Table 1.1 Contraceptive Reliability

Method	Perfect use	Actual use
Proportion of women who will become pregnant in the first year of use		
Vasectomy	0.10	0.15
Tubal ligation	0.5	0.5
IUD	0.6	0.8
IUD w/ hormone release (Mirena)	0.2	0.2
Injectable (Depo Provera)	0.2	6
Cervical ring (Nuva ring)	0.3	9
Patch	0.3	9
Oral contraceptive	0.3	9
Diaphragm	6	12
Male condom	2	18
Female condom	5	21
Spermacides	18	28
Natural family planning	4	24
Withdrawal	4	22
No method	85	85

Source: Guttmacher Institute

to define the line when policies facilitate women and men's abilities to access birth control they want, and when such policies become coercive.

Birth control also highlights changing cultural norms. First, it allows individual to be sexually active with a much lower risk of pregnancy, as Table 1.1 shows. For some, this represents a threat to traditional definitions of family and sexuality. Second, the ability to control one's own fertility has facilitated women's abilities to complete education, obtain graduate degrees, and enter the workforce in greater numbers. This represents a potential transformation in workplaces and family life that some find to be a threat. Third, birth control also allows women to escape many of the health risks associated with pregnancy. it is worth noting here that the Institutes of Medicine, the body of medical experts charged by Congress to review medical evidence and make recommendations improve the nation's health, issued a report in 2011 defining contraception as a key part of women's health and thus, something that should be included as part of comprehensive preventative care (Institute of Medicine 2011). While this finding was controversial for many of the reasons noted above, it also represents a core understanding that birth control is an important tool in promoting a healthy population and individual health and wellbeing. This underscores the need to ensure access to birth control, particularly to those who could least afford it, even as those efforts must protect against the possibility of coercion that we have seen historically.

CHAPTER 1

The Folklore of Birth Control

Linda Gordon

There is a prevalent myth, in our technological society, that birth control technology came to us with modern medicine. This is far from the truth, as modern medicine did almost nothing prior to the 1950s to improve on birth control devices that were literally more than a millennium old. It is important to look at this heritage of traditional birth control if we are to understand the birth control movement, for that movement took its strength from women's understanding of the suppression of actual possibilities.

Birth control was not invented by scientists or doctors. It is a part of folk culture, and women's folklore in particular, in nearly all societies. Even though women rarely had a formal or absolute right to decide unilaterally when to bear children and when not to, women's birth control practice was usually respectable. At other times it was practiced illegally, its technology passed on by an underground of midwives and wisewomen.

An extensive folklore of birth control was handed down from generation to generation in most traditional societies. Some of these practices have remained so unchanged that, for example, vaginal sponges sold in the 1990s were virtually identical to those used several thousand years before Christ. The variety of attempts to prevent conception, and the creativity behind them, tells us something about how much people wanted control over reproduction. New inventions, after all, do not fall from the sky. They are

developed by practice—through trial and error—in response to people's needs. A cataloging of the extent, variety, and ingenuity of these practices is eloquent testimony to the intensity of women's concern.

Differences in birth control methods have social significance, in part because some techniques are more amenable to being used independently and even secretly by women, some give full control to men, while others are more likely to be used cooperatively. A list of birth control methods might look like this: infanticide; abortion; sterilization; withdrawal by the male (*coitus interruptus*); suppositories designed to form an impenetrable coating over the cervix; diaphragms, caps, or other devices, which are inserted into the vagina over the cervix and withdrawn after intercourse; intrauterine devices; internal medicines—potions or pills; douching and other forms of action after intercourse designed to kill or drive out the sperm; condoms; and varieties of the rhythm methods, based on calculating the woman's fertile period and abstaining from intercourse during it.[1] All these techniques were practiced in the ancient world and in modern preindustrial societies. Indeed, until modern hormonal chemicals there were no essentially new birth control devices, only improvements of the old.

People have been designing homemade contraceptive formulas and performing homemade abortions for years. These folk techniques cannot compete with today's methods for effectiveness and safety, but when they were developed they were extraordinary achievements. On a societal level, even a small percentage of effectiveness produces an impact on the birth rate. Today women want 100 percent certainty that their pregnancies will be voluntary, a reasonable and practicable desire. But the development of that desire was itself produced by its historic possibility. Lacking that kind of effective contraception, women in preindustrial societies did not form such high expectations.

For our purposes, however, birth control attempts in preindustrial societies are significant whether or not they worked. They are evidence not only of the desire to control reproduction but also of the conviction that it is proper to do so and of the aspiration to do so. Today we need to combine the sophistication of modern chemistry and medicine with the attitude of these women and men of long ago, who believed that birth control was their responsibility and took responsibility for experimenting and judging what was best for themselves.

What we know today of the traditional use of these techniques represents only a fraction of what once existed. We have only sparse observations, and what information we have often comes from foreign travelers, merchants, even colonizers/invaders of other cultures who are hardly sensitive to their social organization, let alone the private culture of women. Anthropologists produce more reliable information, but they too are often handicapped by their cultural insensitivity and, when male, by their sex. Some of our information comes from the written records of ancient societies; but these records, too, were often based on the impressions of historians whose limitations were not dissimilar from those of modern anthropologists. What follows is only a sample drawn from inadequate information—a double handicap. But the sample serves a specific end: to demystify the technology of birth control.

In preindustrial societies one solution to periodic overpopulation or overburdened mothers was infanticide, the killing of newborn babies. The anthropologist Ralph Linton argued that infanticide met the needs of primitive groups more efficiently than contraception.[2] Contraception, at the level of technology available in most preindustrial societies, resulted in hit-or-miss population limitation. Infanticide provided not only precise population control but also control of the size and spacing of individual families.

Although women had the most to gain from reproduction control, infanticide was nevertheless frequently a direct expression of male supremacy. Not only have male babies been more valued, but female children were sometimes so valueless, despised, and even burdensome that a portion of them were systematically killed.

In these societies, infanticide was most distinctly not murder (assuming that "murder" refers to illegitimate, illegal killing). Infanticide was legal and respectable, fully distinguished in law and in custom from criminal homicide, even from justifiable homicide. Just as the Right to Life movement argues that a fetus is as much a living being as an infant, so in infanticide-practicing society it seemed that a newborn baby was no more a living being than a fetus. Certainly societies that have permitted infanticide have not defined newborn infants as human.

Nor was it just the "primitives" whose moral codes permitted infanticide. Both approval and condemnation are found in preliterate as well as highly advanced societies. Aristotle and Plato recommended infanticide for eugenic reasons.[3] The Romans legislated against infanticide, perhaps because, in conformity with their imperialist policies, they sought to expand their population, whereas the Greeks preferred to curb or stabilize theirs.[4] Nevertheless, infanticide persisted throughout the Roman period as a widespread and rarely prosecuted crime. Tacitus, the Roman historian, found it odd and foolish that the Jews did not practice infanti- cide.[5] For the Christians, the emphasis on the eternal life of the soul in heaven or hell rede- fined the moral issue. The sin of infanticide became not just a matter of human life but of the potential damnation of an immortal soul if it passed out of the body before baptism. It followed from this that killing a newborn child was a worse sin than killing a baptized adult.[6] But even Christianity was for a long time unable to secure full conformity to its commandments in this area, and throughout the Middle Ages, in Christian Europe, infan- ticide by exposure was not unusual.[7]

Are we, today, at a higher stage of moral development than these classical worthies or medieval sinners? Perhaps, but the fact that we have developed better methods of birth control makes it a bit too easy for us to claim superiority. Moreover, ignorance and shame still give rise to occasional infanticide in the United States.

Abortion has always been far more prev- alent than infanticide. One anti-abortion argument is that abortion violates some age- old and God-given "natural law," but the historical evidence dissolves that illusion.

Birth control before conception, if it can be done, is less painful and safer than birth control after conception. But contraception, as we call it today, was not easy to arrange in the premodern world. Effective contra- ception required at least a rudimentary understanding of the process of conception. Moreover, it usually required forethought, and an antagonistic male could sabotage a woman's attempts to contracept. Developing contraceptive techniques that work required a scientific trial-and-error process of study that was difficult in earlier times, given the lack of privacy and the superstition that frequently surrounded sexual intercourse. Considering these obstacles, the contracep- tive knowledge accumulated in the ancient world is impressive.

Some of that ancient technology was lost over the centuries, often due to religious

and moral suppression of birth control. The better methods, which required more prepa- ration, were probably the first to disappear. But the suppression was never complete. When the first birth control clinics opened in Europe and America in the early twen- tieth century, their records showed that the majority of women coming to the clinics for the first time had used contraception previously.[8]

In traditional reproduction control attempts, little or no distinction was made between abortion and contraception; reproduction seemed a process with no sharply differen- tiated stages prior to birth. So many of the same potions described above as aborti- facients were also used at an earlier stage. Magical as well as medical, potions were often concocted of symbolically sterile ingre- dients, as teas made from fruitless plants.[9] Despite almost universal failure to prevent conception through taking internal medicine, the same recipes used in ancient societies and in medieval Europe continued in use in the modern world.

The single most common contraceptive method in history, throughout the world, is *coitus interruptus,* or withdrawal—the male withdrawing his penis before ejacula- tion so that his semen is deposited outside the vagina. Unlike potions, this can be an effective method. Withdrawal was tra- ditionally used in Africa, in Australasia, throughout Islamic society, and in Europe. Judaism and Roman Catholicism both condemned the practice, but in medieval Europe its practice was common enough to be frequently attacked in the canonical writings as a "vice against nature," one of the several species of lust. A related con- traceptive practice is *coitus obstructus,* recommended in several ancient Sanskrit texts: "If one, at the time of sexual enjoy- ment, presses firmly with the finger on the fore part of the testicle, turns his mind to other things, and holds his breath while doing so . . ."[10]

These practices are dependent on considerable male will and skill. Women's analogous methods were physical exertions—such as jumping and running—designed to expel semen from the body after intercourse or to prevent it from reaching the uterus. Sneezing was recommended by the physicians of ancient Greece, by rabbis, and, as late as 1868, in an anonymous birth control pamphlet. These were not particularly effective techniques, and the more canny ancient doctors advised combining them with additional precautions. A common myth was that a woman's passivity during intercourse would make her less likely to conceive. The converse myth—that for intercourse to be fruitful the woman must be active—reveals an understandable association between passion and fertility. By the Middle Ages, Christian influence had succeeded in reversing this folk belief: too much female passion ought to be avoided, for it would make intercourse sterile.

Douching, which could have been effective, was apparently not widespread. Spermicidal substances, such as citrus fruit juice, were identified but used in less effective ways. The ancient Greek physician Aëtios knew the spermicidal properties of vinegar, but instead of recommending it to women as a douche, he suggested applying it to the penis. In the nineteenth century attempts to kill sperm by bathing the penis in some spermicidal lotion remained common, judging by the recipes for such lotions in home-remedy books. For example, "Take bichloride of mercury, 25 parts; milk of almonds, 400 parts; alcohol, 100 parts; rose-water, 1000 parts. Immerse the glands in a little of the mixture, as before, and be particular to open the orifice of the urethra so as to admit the contact of the fluid. This may be used as often as convenient, until the orifice of the urethra feels tender on voiding the urine. Infallible, if used in proper time."[11] Douching would have been less painful, and some nineteenth-century household management books recommended it and offered recipes for the liquid.[12]

The most effective traditional contraceptive techniques were various sorts of pessaries, which aimed to block the cervix. Pessaries were particularly effective when combined with spermicides. Numerous ancient formulas for pessaries have been recently discovered, tested, and found effective, such as ancient Egyptian recipes using crocodile dung or a mixture of honey and natron (natural sodium carbonate) or a natural gum. Although none of the substances is strongly spermicidal, all are of a consistency that, at body temperature, would form an impenetrable covering over the cervix. Islamic medical writings offer thirteen different prescriptions for pessaries. Both Islamic and Sanskrit sources suggest rock salt, a good spermicide. An Indian work of the first century B.C. suggests rock salt dipped in oil, which is even better, since the oil would retard the motility of sperm and clog the cervix. Oil inside the vagina is one of the most continuous practices in folk contraception. Aristotle suggested oil of cedar or olive oil. Women of the U.S. Midwest in the twentieth century have used lard. Marie Stopes, an English birth control champion of the early twentieth century, reported high effectiveness rates with the use of oil and nothing else.[13]

Another form of pessary was a solid object used to occlude the cervix. This type of contraceptive was also widespread in preindustrial societies, such as Africa, where women used plugs of chopped grass or cloth. On Easter Island women used algae or seaweed. Japanese prostitutes used balls of bamboo tissue paper, Islamic and Greek women used wool, and Slovak women used linen rags. Geography ruled, and women used what they could get. The most effective natural cervical cap—the sponge—was first used by people who lived by the sea and was the most effective contraceptive in use until the development of the rubber diaphragm. If properly used, a sponge will not only block the cervix but will also absorb semen and can be saturated with a spermicidal fluid. Sponges were promoted by birth control clinics as late as 1930, and a study done in New York at that time found a 50 percent success rate among women using sponges even without medical advice.[14]

As to condoms, many tropical peoples used coverings for the penis for a variety of purposes, such as protection against tropical disease or insect bites, as marks of rank, as amulets, or merely as decoration. A linen sheath was promoted as a specifically anti-venereal disease precaution by the Italian anatomist Fallopius (discoverer of the "Fallopian tubes"), an early authority on syphilis, in 1564. In the eighteenth century these devices were being made of animal membrane, thus waterproof and effective as a contraceptive. By this time, sheaths for the penis were widespread, often given to men by prostitutes, and they had acquired a wealth of charming nicknames and euphemisms: the English riding coat, assurance caps, the French letter, bladder policies, instruments of safety, condoms, cundums, and, of course, prophylactics. Through the mid-nineteenth century, books of home remedies gave instructions for making condoms, as for example:

> Take the caecum of the sheep; soak it first in water, turn it on both sides, then repeat the operation in a weak ley of soda, which must be changed every four or five hours, for five or six successive times; then remove the mucous membrane with the nail; sulphur, wash in clean water, and then in soap and water; rinse, inflate and dry. Next cut it to the required length, and attach a piece of ribbon to the open end. Used to prevent infection or pregnancy. The different qualities consist in extra pains being taken in the above process, and in polishing, scenting, &c.[15]

A few groups used internal condoms for women: in one location women inserted into their vaginas seed pods about five inches long with one end cut off.

Occasionally ancient peoples tried to practice a rhythm method. To do so successfully they would have needed either an exact knowledge of the physiology of contraception or a sophisticated observation of a large number of cases—neither of which was likely. (A precise and commonly accepted identification of the fertile period of the human female was not made until 1924.) So these practices were often faulty: for example, East African Nandi women and the great Greek gynecologist Soranus agreed that avoiding intercourse for a few days after menstruation would prevent conception. A somewhat more effective—and very widespread—practice was prolonging the suckling of infants, which reduces fertility to some degree.

Midwives in Java performed external manipulations that caused the uterus to tip, or become retroflexed, thus preventing conception. This procedure was usually done after either abortion or childbirth. An anthropologist visiting Java in 1897 found 50 percent of the women with retroflexed uteruses, but the midwives told him that they could restore the uterus to its normal position by massage whenever a woman wanted a child.

The most ambitious forms of contraception practiced in the preindustrial world were surgical sterilizations, which were unusually invasive. Some groups of Australians performed surgery in which the cervix was cut and forced to heal in an open position.[16] Others did ovariectomies (removal of the ovaries). Of less clear intent was subincision of males, in which the urethra was surgically opened at the base of the penis so that both urine and semen emerged at a point just on top of the testicles. Subincision did not entirely prevent conception, and there is no clear evidence that it was performed with any population control intent, but it did make conception less likely with each act of intercourse.

The wide array of birth control techniques used in preindustrial societies discloses something vital to understanding the modern birth control movement: that the burden of involuntary childbearing was not the result of *lack* of technology but of the *suppression* of technology. This means that childbearing cannot be considered the cause, or at least not the simple, exclusive cause, of women's subject status, because efforts—sometimes successful—to transcend the biological, and thereby to reshape some of the operations of gender, were present in the earliest known human societies.

The first political battle about contraception concerned the safety of the Pill, and it aligned the new feminists of the late 1960s against the birth control establishment, the pharmaceutical companies, and even the federal government. The feminist challenge helped to create lasting improvements in drug safety and consumers' right to information.[17]

Soon after the Pill became available in the continental United States, women who took it began to complain in large numbers of the same side effects that had been reported in Puerto Rico, where it was first tested: bloating, weight gain, nausea, vomiting, stomach pain, headaches, and rashes. As in the Puerto Rico trials, physicians, population controllers, and researchers trivialized or even discounted these complaints. Many women quit using the Pill, but many others started, so there was no economic incentive for Searle, the lone U.S. manufacturer, to question its product, and the population control establishment had no political incentive to do so.

In 1961 came the first reports of Pill-related deaths from pulmonary embolisms (blood clots traveling to the lungs). Then four more deaths were reported in the *British Medical Journal*. Norway banned the Pill. Searle, Gregory Pincus (who had conducted the Puerto Rico trials), and the Population Council responded, first by denying the connection between health dangers and the Pill and then by saying that if there was a connection it was a 1-in-500,000 event. The Food and Drug Administration accepted these responses. By the end of 1962 there had been 272 reported cases of blood clots, thrombophlebitis, or strokes among Pill users, a ratio at least 135 times greater than that which Searle had allowed. Still, it was not until 1969 that the FDA conducted a study and found that women using the Pill were more than four times as likely to develop blood clots as nonusers.

These suspicions and denials occurred just as the women's movement was inspiring challenges rather than deference to professionals (overwhelmingly male) who claimed to be authorities on women. One of the first manifestos in that challenge was Barbara Seaman's book *The Doctors' Case against the Pill*, published in 1969. This journalist did such masterful research and so carefully scrutinized the scientific research that her case—confirming the severe risks of high-dose oral contraceptives—could not be impeached (although it is revealing of the still developing confidence of the new feminism that in her title she felt she had to draw on traditional expertise, the "doctors' case," to legitimate her findings). Seaman soon had a large social movement behind her, raising questions and demanding public answers.

The fight was in part a consumer rights struggle, and Seaman has been called the women's Ralph Nader. The public outcry led Wisconsin Democratic senator Gaylord Nelson, chairman of the Subcommittee on Monopoly of the Select Committee on Small Business, to hold hearings in 1970 on the dangers of the Pill and whether consumers were getting adequate information about those dangers. The hearings provided one of the first stages on which the new women's movement could command attention. Frustrated by Nelson's refusal to let even a single woman testify as a consumer of contraception, the Washington, D.C.-based Women's Liberation seized the floor and the attention of the media, disrupting the proceedings and demanding to be heard. One poll found that an astonishing 87 percent of American women between the ages of twenty-one and forty-five followed the hearings. They heard politicians such as Bob Dole, then a Republican senator from Kansas, joke that reporting the dangers of the Pill would make women so terrified they would need tranquilizers as well as birth control. "'We must not frighten millions of women into disregarding the considered judgments of their physicians about the use of oral contraceptives,'" he declaimed.[18] Still, the FDA stalled; and it did not agreed to require informative patient inserts in prescription drug packaging until 1978.

Debate about the Pill may have overemphasized the danger of death and illness but it underemphasized the discomforts. The "harmless" side effects such as nausea, rashes, weight gain, and bloating, belittled by physicians and researchers,[19] were more influential than long-term health risks in reducing oral contraceptive use. For example, the Pill "dropout" began in 1967, before there was much publicity about its dangers. Most women who had stopped using oral contraceptives by 1982 had done so on their own initiative—only one-third had been advised by a doctor to discontinue use.[20] Women were "saved" from the Pill's dangers not primarily by health professionals but mainly by their own feelings and the efforts of feminist organizations.

The next major contraceptive battle concerned intrauterine devices. Debate about the Pill ended by making it safer. Debate about IUDs began similarly but ended quite differently. IUDs were extremely promising when introduced in the early 1960s, but now only 1 percent of contracepting American women use them. This disappointment was not due to feminist and consumer pressure but to the faulty structure of contraceptive testing and marketing in the United States.

IUDs have been used since antiquity. But as with many modern contraceptives, the demand that made large-scale manufacture profitable developed only later, about the same time that the Pill came on the market. At first the FDA did not claim authority to regulate IUDs. By the early 1970s several hundred gynecologists had "carved and twisted various metals, plastics, and fibers" for use as IUDs, and at least three million U.S. women and seven million women abroad received inadequately tested devices.[21] The women's health movement, which had learned from its experience with the Pill, began to see miserable and dangerous reactions in many users, notably pain and bleeding, pelvic inflammatory disease, septic abortions, uterine perforations, anemia, embedding, and even fragmentation of the devices.[22] But the pharmaceutical companies that made and sold IUDs did no testing to learn whether these problems were inherent in the principle behind IUDs or the result of a particular shape or composition.

The development of the oral contraceptive created a giant leap in birth control technology but did little to alter the fundamentally political bases of birth control issues. In the 1970s, the debate about contraception differed from that about abortion by remaining, for the most part, immune from the conservative critique of sexual permissiveness and the subversion of the family Contraception was still publicly defined as a marital aid, and political disputes focused on safety. Planned Parenthood's quiet conversion to providing contraceptive services to the unmarried occurred without major national opposition because opponents were so focused on abortion. This began to change in the 1980s, however, when epidemics of teenage pregnancy and HIV/AIDS stimulated more aggressive proposals for making contraceptives easily accessible. . .

STERILIZATION AND ITS ABUSES

Disappointment in high-tech contraception also promoted a turn to sterilization, which has been the most common form of birth control for U.S. women over the age of twenty-five since the late 1970s.[23] The women's health movement has not been a particularly strong proponent of sterilization, preferring temporary methods that allow women to change their minds about reproduction. Furthermore, widespread patterns of coercive sterilization provoked a strong movement against sterilization abuse.

Forcible sterilization is not new. The first eugenic sterilization programs, adopted by thirty states during the 1920s, forcibly sterilized some 64,000 "feebleminded" or "genetically defective" people. Disproportionately used in southern states, sterilization was imposed on many blacks, American Indians, and poor whites whose alleged "feeblemindedness," if any symptoms of it actually existed, was more likely the result of poor health and little or no education. Yet even in these overtly, nakedly eugenical programs, some of the sterilized women were willing, even eager clients. As one study shows, among women deprived of access to other forms of birth control, often so poor that their existing children were malnourished, ill clothed, and uneducated, approximately 6 percent of those sterilized had requested the surgery. During the 1960s that figure rose to 20 percent.[24]

Even in the textbook case of sterilization abuse that occurred in Puerto Rico, it is not always easy to distinguish voluntary from forced sterilization. Starting in the 1920s, sterilization was heavily promoted in Puerto Rico as a primary form of birth control. By 1949, 18 percent of childbirths were followed by sterilization. Between the 1930s and the 1970s, one-third of Puerto Rican women of childbearing age had been sterilized.[25] Many women welcomed the opportunity to acquire a reliable form of birth control, but their choices were limited—by the availability of cheap or free sterilization in contrast to expensive contraception; by a creative rewriting of Catholic doctrine that treated contraception as a vice but blinked at sterilization; by the fact that sterilization required no cooperation from husbands and could even be hidden from men. One study showed that 22 percent of unmarried Puerto Rican women knew about *la operación* but only 1 percent had heard of the diaphragm and only 12 percent knew anything about condoms.[26] In Puerto Rico sterilization became legitimated more than contraception because it was medicalized—surgery performed in a hospital while under anesthesia. Conversely, contraception became associated with prostitutes and thus doubly immoral. But aren't all birth control choices constrained? Perhaps for the majority of the world's people, constraint is a matter of degree.

Many politicized Puerto Ricans denounced the sterilization campaign as a tool of colonialism. They saw it as a eugenics as well as a population control policy, a judgment difficult to contest. Prior to attaining commonwealth status and the right to elect its own governor, Puerto Rico was led by a governor appointed by the U.S. government. In 1932 he declared that Puerto Rico's population problem was a matter not only of high quantity but also of low quality.[27] No one could argue that the purpose of U.S. public and private investment in population control in Puerto Rico was to increase Puerto Rican women's reproductive autonomy.

Women of higher class, race, and national status faced paternalism of another kind. While impoverished Puerto Rican women were being pressured into sterilization, many prosperous white women in the United States were denied sterilization as a birth control option. Most doctors stuck to the indications for sterilization recommended by the American College of Obstetricians and Gynecologists (ACOG), which relied on a formula (the woman's age multiplied by the number of children she had) to determine whether a woman was a candidate for sterilization. If the result was 120 or more, she was approved, but only if two doctors plus a psychiatrist also recommended the surgery. Responding to pressure from women, ACOG liberalized its guidelines in 1969–70 and sterilizations increased substantially. Left unchallenged were the medical establishment's assumption of authority to decide when women could be sterilized and the refusal of most medical insurance providers to pay for elective sterilization. The liberalization also reflected the general cultural shifts of the post–World War II period toward a more positive view of small families and marital sexual activity, combined with the impact of population control arguments.[28] A 1982 study showed that 30 percent of former users of the Pill had turned to sterilization as their birth control alternative.[29]

Was the increase in surgical sterilization a net gain for reproductive and sexual freedom? Not necessarily, because even when the surgery was voluntary the context often constrained women's choices. Many women enjoyed being free from the hassle of using contraceptives, but they preferred contraception over sterilization because it left open the option of further childbearing.

The ambiguity of the meanings of sterilization can be seen in class, race, and sex differences. Overall, 11 percent of American men in the mid-1990s had chosen surgical sterilization compared to 28 percent of women. Among couples, approximately 5 percent relied on vasectomy for contraception, while 15 percent relied on female sterilization.[30] Female sterilization is a poor person's birth control, most commonly relied on by women with less than a high school education or a household income below 150 percent of the federal poverty level. Vasectomy, by contrast, is more common among middle- and higher-income men and twenty-nine times more common among whites than blacks. Among whites, the more education a woman has received, the less likely she is to be sterilized for contraceptive purposes; with men, the correlation with education is reversed.[31] Overall, female sterilizations are medically more complex, and class differences influence how invasive the sterilization surgery will be: poor women are more likely to have hysterectomies than

tubal ligations.[32] Public funds can be used to cover most of the cost of sterilizations for the poor, while there is little public funding for abortion or contraception. These differentials raise troubling questions. Vasectomies are safer, simpler, and generally easier to reverse than tubal ligations, and certainly safer and simpler than hysterectomies, so why aren't they the dominant method? Does the preponderance of poor and less well educated women suggest that sterilization might not be their method of choice if they had full access to the information, training, medical care, and money that contraception and abortion require?

The civil rights and women's movements entered the debate in the early 1970s to challenge sterilization abuse. The campaign was jump-started by the Young Lords Party, a Puerto Rican civil rights group in New York City that questioned the high rate of sterilization not only on the island of Puerto Rico but also among Puerto Ricans in New York, where the sterilization rate was seven times that among Anglo-Americans and twice the rate among African Americans.[33] Led by an unusually strong feminist group within the organization, the Young Lords exposed the blatant coercion behind the sterilization of Puerto Rican women. Coercive sterilization appears to have been growing in the 1960s, part of the conservative backlash against welfare and civil rights, and it was overwhelmingly a eugenic practice, considering that the victims were primarily poor, black, Hispanic, and especially Native American. What differentiated this practice from that in earlier decades was a greater attempt to hide the coercion, so that it required more ambitious investigation to develop the proof that soon began to emerge.

It is not surprising that the new feminism, which revived the distinction between individual reproductive rights and population control, actively opposed coercive sterilization. But women's liberation supporters, a predominantly white and prosperous group in the early 1970s, had to be taught about sterilization abuse by people of color.[34] Insensitivity to what constituted coercion was related to the individual rights, or choice, perspective of the women's movement, and it was the socialist feminist branch of the movement that initiated and led the campaign against sterilization abuse.

In 1973, civil rights activists helped bring a number of lawsuits against physicians charged with performing coerced sterilizations. These were almost all abuses of poor, nonwhite, or mentally retarded women; virtually no abuses against white or middleclass women were documented.[35] In 1974, responding to this pressure, the Department of Health, Education, and Welfare issued guidelines for all sterilization procedures paid for with federal funds that would ensure informed consent and prohibit the sterilization of women younger than twentyone. Then public interest groups—the American Civil Liberties Union, the Public Citizen—and federal agencies—the Centers for Disease Control, the General Accounting Office—studied hospital compliance with the new standards. Their findings were cause for alarm: one report indicated that 76 percent of hospitals were disregarding the guidelines, while a second report placed the figure at 94 percent; another study found that 700 sterilizations had been illegally performed on underage patients.[36] The GAO report on Indian Health Service hospitals found not one of them to be in compliance.[37] Women were commonly approached during childbirth for their consent to be sterilized: "I used to make my pitch while sewing up the episiotomy when the anesthesia started wearing off," said a medical resident to a *Los Angeles Times* reporter. Others were threatened shortly before delivery with losing their welfare payments, their Medicaid payments, or withdrawal of obstetrician's services unless they consented to sterilization.[38]

In the early 1970s sterilization abuse was mainly understood in civil rights, civil liberties, anti-imperialist, and class-conscious terms. Gender analysis was underdeveloped and many condemnations of sterilization entirely ignored women's desire for reproduction control. Indeed, the opponents of sterilization abuse sometimes fell into the same conflation of all forms of reproduction control that had characterized both population control and anti–birth control groups in earlier decades. For example, the radical health research group Health/PAC criticized all federal funding of birth control services and took the book *Our Bodies, Ourselves* to task for offering a positive view of sterilization as a reproduction control option.[39] This unqualified condemnation of sterilization was in part provoked by the fact that the influential Association for Voluntary Sterilization opposed the federal guidelines, as did Planned Parenthood, on the grounds that they were paternalistic, deprived women of choice, and interfered with the doctorpatient relationship. With this kind of political polarization, it is not surprising that the gendered meanings of sterilization were rendered invisible. Surveys did not point out that vasectomies were never imposed on men or that nearly all Medicaid sterilizations were being performed on women.[40] By contrast, some feminist groups, representing a more privileged group of women, had difficulty in understanding the problem. For example, at its 1978 national convention the National Organization for Women (NOW), by a narrow majority to be sure, voted to condemn the thirty-day waiting period.[41]

The left wing of the women's liberation movement began to organize against sterilization abuse and was particularly active in New York City, where it was able to build a coalition that included the National Black Feminist Organization, Health/PAC, the Puerto Rican Socialist party, the Lower East Side Neighborhood Health Center, and the local branch of NOW. Pressure from this coalition won tougher guidelines from the city's Health and Hospital Corporation in

1977. In 1978, the Department of Health, Education, and Welfare issued yet more regulations, extending the required waiting period for federally funded sterilizations from three to thirty days, requiring translators where necessary, and banning the signing of consent forms during labor, childbirth, or abortion. But noncompliance rates remained high: surveys of hospitals done again in 1979 found that 70 percent were not even in compliance with the 1974 guidelines.[42]

Out of this struggle came a more complex analysis of sterilization abuse and a new type of feminist reproductive rights group that extended its concerns to all forms of interference with reproductive autonomy. These groups insisted that the right to have children safely and to be able to keep them in good health was as much a reproductive right as the freedom not to bear children. They also pointed out that there could be no truly free choice as long as either right was interfered with. The leading such group was New York's Committee for Abortion Rights and Against Sterilization Abuse (CARASA), which led the fight against coercive sterilization to substantial victories. The National Women's Health Network organized an even larger coalition in New York in 1979, uniting CARASA with the Committee to End Sterilization Abuse, the Mexican-American Women's National Association, the Center for Constitutional Rights, and the Chicana Nurses Association, among others, to monitor the compliance of New York City hospitals with the new city laws,[43] thus appropriating an aspect of state power.

The New York City coalition in turn became part of a national coalition, the Reproductive Rights National Network, known as R2N2, which was established in 1981 and came to include eighty member groups. This network further developed and communicated feminist thinking about reproductive rights, and its national newsletter was very influential. R2N2 was committed to a multi-issue approach, hoping

to change the movement's primary identification as white, heterosexual, and middle class. It united not only abortion rights and prevention of sterilization abuse but also demands for better maternity and infant care for those who chose to give birth.

The campaign against sterilization abuse represented in some ways the high point of the reproductive rights work of the women's health movement. At the peak of feminist power, it succeeded in eliminating some of the worst abuses and raising the consciousness of medical workers about patients' rights to informed consent.

NOTES

1. In addition to these deliberate birth control methods, all societies have social regulations that affect the birth rate. Late marriages, of course, produce a lower birth rate because there are more years between generations. Prestigious groups that require celibacy—such as monastics—are common in many societies. Preindustrial societies frequently have taboos on sexual intercourse for long periods after childbirth and sometimes even during lactation. There is no proof, however, that such customs are intended to have a population control function; and indeed they are usually described as having other purposes by the people who practice them. For the sake of clarity, therefore, I have omitted them from consideration in this survey, and I consider only methods with conscious birth control purpose.
2. Norman E. Himes, *Medical History of Contraception* (1936; rpt., New York: Gamut Press, 1963); and Linton letter to Himes, quoted in ibid., 52.
3. Thomas R. Malthus, *An Essay on Population* (London: J. M. Dent, 1960–61), 1:141–42; William Graham Sumner, *Folkways* (1906; rpt., New York: New American Library, 1940), 272; Himes, *Medical History of Contraception*, 79.
4. W. E. H. Lecky, *A History of European Morals from Augustus to Charlemagne* (1869; rpt., New York: Appleton, 1877), 2:27.
5. Malthus, *Essay on Population* 1:chaps. 13–14; John J. Noonan Jr., *Contraception: A History of Its Treatment by Catholic Theologians and Canonists* (Cambridge, Mass.: Harvard University Press, 1965), 85–86.
6. Lecky, *History of European Morals*, 2:23; Glanville Williams, *The Sanctity of Life and the Criminal Law* (New York: Knopf, 1957), 16.
7. David Bakan, *The Slaughter of the Innocents* (Boston: Beacon, 1972), 35–36; Edward Westermarck, *The Origin and Development of the Moral Ideas* (London: Macmillan and Co., 1906), 1:411–13.

8. See, for example, Marie E. Kopp, *Birth Control in Practice: Analysis of Ten Thousand Case Histories of the Birth Control Clinical Research Bureau* (New York: McBride, 1934), 133; Lella Secor Florence, *Birth Control on Trial* (London: Allen and Unwin, 1930), 91; Raymond Pearl, "Contraception and Fertility in 4,945 Married Women: A Second Report on a Study in Family Limitation," *Human Biology* 6 (1934): 355–401.

9. For example, Nicholas Culpeper, *Complete Herbal* (n.d.; rpt., London: W. Foulsham, n.d.), 39–41.

10. Quoted in Himes, *Medical History of Contraception*, 118.

11. *The United States Practical Receipt Book; or, Complete Book of Reference* (Philadelphia: Lindsay and Blakiston, 1844), 29.

12. Ibid.

13. Marie C. Stopes, "Positive and Negative Control of Conception in Its Various Technical Aspects," *Journal of State Medicine* (London) 39 (1931): 354–60.

14. Kopp, *Birth Control in Practice*, 133.

15. *U.S. Practical Receipt Book*, 87.

16. Aptekar, *Anjea*, 122–26.

17. My synopsis of the political battles over oral contraceptives is indebted to Andrea Tone, *Devices and Desires: A History of Contraceptives in America* (New York: Hill and Wang, 2001); Paul Vaughan, *The Pill on Trial* (New York: Coward-McCann, 1970); and Elizabeth Siegel Watkins, *On the Pill: A Social History of Oral Contraceptives, 1950–1970* (Baltimore: Johns Hopkins University Press, 1998).

18. Quoted in Tone, *Devices and Desires*, 249–50.

19. Judith Bruce, "User's Perspectives on Contraceptive Technology and Delivery Systems: Highlighting Some Feminist Issues," *Technology in Society: An International Journal* 9:3–4 (1987): 359–83. Bruce quotes Bernard Berelson, president of the Population Council in the 1960s: "'When uninformed women encountered minor difficulties they tended to discontinue. . . . dissatisfied women have spread adverse gossip and encouraged others to discontinue'" (359–60).

20. William F. Pratt and Christine A. Bachrach, "What Do Women Use When They Stop Using the Pill?," *Family Planning Perspectives* 19:6 (Nov.–Dec. 1987): 257–65; Rosalind Pollack Petchesky, *Abortion and Woman's Choice: The State, Sexuality, and Reproductive Freedom* (New York: Longman, 1984), 188. By contrast, Jacqueline Darroch Forrest and Stanley K. Henshaw, in "What U.S. Women Think and Do about Contraception," *Family Planning Perspectives* 15:4 (July–Aug. 1983): 157–66, attribute the decline of oral contraceptive use to the impact of "adverse propaganda." The situation was substantially different in the Third World, where high-dosage pills were urged and sometimes dumped upon women often lacking any other contraceptive alternatives.

21. Ruzek, *Women's Health Movement*, 43. Note that the FDA apparently could have claimed authority to screen IUDs, on the basis of Supreme Court decisions, but did not do so.

22. My synopsis of the conflicts about IUDs is indebted to Morton Mintz, *At Any Cost: Corporate Greed, Women, and the Dalkon Shield* (New York: Pantheon Books, 1985); Richard B. Sobol, *Bending the Law: The Story of the Dalkon Shield Bankruptcy* (Chicago: University of Chicago Press, 1991); and Nicole J. Grant, *The Selling of Contraception: The Dalkon Shield Case, Sexuality, and Women's Autonomy* (Columbus: Ohio State University Press, 1992). Like oral contraceptives, IUDs were tested on poor minority women, largely Chicanas. An excellent early summary of IUD problems is in Katherine Roberts, "The Intrauterine Device as a Health Risk," *Women and Health,* July–Aug. 1977, pp. 21–30.

23. Forrest and Fordyce, "U.S. Women's Contraceptive Attitudes and Practice"; Rosalind Pollack Petchesky, "'Reproductive Choice' in the Contemporary United States: A Social Analysis of Female Sterilization," in *And the Poor Get Children: Radical Perspectives on Population Dynamics*, ed. Karen Michaelson (New York: Monthly Review Press, 1981), 51; Forrest and Henshaw, "What U.S. Women Think and Do." Thanks to Susan Jew at the Alan Guttmacher Institute for information used in this discussion.

24. The figures are from a North Carolina study by Johanna Schoen, summarized in "Between Choice and Coercion: Women and the Politics of Sterilization in North Carolina, 1929–1975," *Journal of Women's History* 13:1 (Spring 2001): 132–56.

25. Annette B. Ramírez de Arellano and Conrad Seipp, *Colonialism, Catholicism, and Contraception: A History of Birth Control in Puerto Rico* (Chapel Hill: University of North Carolina Press, 1983).

26. Cited in Jennifer A. Nelson, "'Abortions under Community Control': Feminism, Nationalism, and the Politics of Reproduction among New York City's Young Lords," *Journal of Women's History* 13:1 (Spring 2001): 167.

27. Ibid., 168.

28. Some critics have suggested as a further incentive that gynecologists and obstetricians were short of work, and especially surgical work, as a result of the falling birth rate and that residents needed more surgical practice. See Robert E. McGarrah, "Voluntary Female Sterilization: Abuses, Risks, and Guidelines," *Hastings Center Report*, June 1974, p. 6, quoted in Barbara Caress, "Sterilization," *Health/PAC Bulletin* 62 (Jan.–Feb. 1975): 4.

29. Pratt and Bachrach, "What Do Women Use?," 263.

30. This information was found online at http://www.nichd.nih.gov/publications/pubs/vasect.htm.

31. Online at http://www.agi-usa.org/pubs/teen_preg_sr_0699.html.

32. Petchesky, "'Reproductive Choice' in the Contemporary United States."

33. Nelson, "'Abortions under Community Control,'" 169.

34. Helen Rodriguez-Trias, "The Women's Health Movement: Women Take Power," in *Reforming Medicine: Lessons of the Lost Quarter Century,* ed. Victor and Ruth Sidel (New York: Pantheon, 1984), 107–26.

35. The double standard here—forcing sterilization on poor women, barring prosperous women from sterilization—is reminiscent of that regarding employment—requiring it of poor mothers, condemning it in prosperous mothers.

36. Robert E. McGarrah, staff attorney for the Public Citizen, to Caspar Weinberger, Secretary of HEW, Jan. 20, 1975; Ted Bogue and Daniel W Sigelman, Sterilization Report no. 3, *Public Citizen,* July 17, 1979; ACLU, Hospital Survey of Sterilization Policies, 1975, all in BWHBC Archives, folder "Sterilization Abuse."

37. "Sterilization Abuse," *Network News* (NWHN), Sept. 1979, BWHBC Archives.

38. Quoted in Caress, "Sterilization," 5; Claudia Dreifus, "Sterilizing the Poor," in *Seizing Our Bodies: The Politics of Women's Health,* ed. Claudia Dreifus (New York: Random House, 1977), 105–20.

39. Caress, "Sterilization," 11.

40. Petchesky, *Abortion and Woman's Choice,* 180.

41. Rebecca Staton and Meredith Tax for CARASA to Eleanor Smeal of NOW, Aug. 10, 1978; *CARASA News,* Nov. 2, 1978, pp. 3–5, both in BWHBC Archives.

42. Bogue and Sigelman, Sterilization Report no. 3; *Family Planning Perspectives* 11:6 (Nov.–Dec. 1979): 366–67.

43. NWHN, "Sterilization Abuse."

CHAPTER 2

The Pill—Genocide or Liberation?

Toni Cade Bambera

To offer contemporary readers some context for this selection, the essay from which it is drawn was written in the late 1960s by Toni Cade, a leading African American author and activist of that era. The timing of the essay is noteworthy for the ferment that was occurring in African American communities across the country, with the development of militant political groups such as the Black Panthers and riots in major American cities protesting the oppressive conditions in which many African Americans lived. That period saw the first federal legislation to make birth control available to the poor—but clinics were disproportionately located in Black communities, leading to accusations of "black genocide" on the part of some (mainly male) community leaders.

. . . I've been made aware of the national call to the Sisters to abandon birth control, to not cooperate with an enemy all too determined to solve his problem with the bomb, the gun, the pill; to instruct the welfare mammas to resist the sterilization plan that has become ruthless policy for a great many state agencies; to picket family-planning centers and abortion-referral groups, and to raise revolutionaries. And it seems to me that once again the woman has demonstrated the utmost in patience and reasonableness when she counters, "What plans do you have for the care of me and the child? Am I to persist in the role of Amazon workhorse and house slave? How do we break the cycle of child-abandonment-ADC-child?"

It is a noble thing, the rearing of warriors for the revolution. I can find no fault with the idea. I do, however, find fault with the notion that dumping the pill is the way to do it. You don't prepare yourself for the raising of super-people by making yourself vulnerable—chance fertilization, chance support, chance tomorrow—nor by being celibate until you stumble across the right stock to breed with. You prepare yourself by being healthy and confident, by having options that give you confidence, by getting yourself together, by being together enough to attract a together cat whose notions of fatherhood rise above the Disney caliber of man-in-the-world-and-woman-in-the-home, by being committed to the new consciousness, by being intellectually and spiritually and financially self-sufficient to do the thing right. You prepare yourself by being in control of yourself. The pill gives the woman, as well as the man, some control. Simple as that. . . .

On the other hand, I would never agree that the pill really liberates women. It only helps. It may liberate her sexually (assuming that we don't mean mutually exploitive when we yell "sexual equality"), but what good is that if in other respects her social role remains the same? And it is especially doubtful that the pill can liberate her in these other areas—note how easily the sexual freedom has been absorbed into the commodity framework, used to push miniskirts, peeka-boo blouses, and so forth so we can go on being enslaved to consumerism. But the pill gives her choice, gives her control over at least some of the major events in her life. And it gives her time to fight for liberation in those other areas. But surely there would be no need to shout into her ear about dumping the pill if the Brother was taking care of business on a personal plane and analyzing the whole issue of liberation on a political plane. Men are invariably trying to create a woman who will answer their needs, assuage their fears, boost their morale, confirm their romantic fantasies, lull them into the comforting notion that they are ten steps ahead simply because she is ten paces behind. And this invariably makes her not very true to herself. Women who've thought about this whole question have my support. The Brothers who merely rant and rave set my teeth on edge.

CHAPTER 3

The Fertility of Women of Mexican Origin

A Social Constructionist Approach

Elena Gutiérrez

"I think what we are trying to show is that throughout the entire period that the doctors were not using medical reasons to perform these sterilizations, but were using social reasons. That is very pertinent to this case."[1]

Attorney Antonia Hernández spoke these words as she implored federal district court judge Jesse Curtis to hear the testimony of her next witness. Along with co-counsel Charles Nabarette, Hernández represented ten women of Mexican origin filing a class-action civil suit against physicians at the University of Southern California-Los Angeles County Medical Center (LACMC). The plaintiffs in the case of *Madrigal v. Quilligan,* which was tried in 1978, accused the doctors of coercively sterilizing each of them between June 1971 and March 1974. Many alleged that hospital personnel forced them into signing consent forms while under the duress of labor pains, or that they were never approached and informed about the procedure at all. All of the women had various levels of English comprehension, and most testified that they did not understand that tubal ligation would irreversibly terminate their childbearing. The plaintiffs filed suit against state and federal officials, and the administrators and doctors at LACMC for violation of their constitutionally guaranteed right to procreate.[2] In addition to financial compensation, the plaintiffs requested that the U.S. Department of Health, Education and Welfare require federally funded hospitals to provide thorough sterilization counseling and consent forms in Spanish.[3] On this, the sixth day of the trial, tension in the courtroom was high.

The contested witness was Karen Benker, a medical student at the University of Southern California Medical School, and an employee of the Women's Hospital of LACMC during the period when the alleged forced sterilizations of countless Mexican-origin women occurred. As the only witness who had observed the alleged coercive practices of the doctors firsthand and was willing to testify in court, Benker's observations confirmed Hernández's argument that the sterilization of her clients at this hospital was "socially motivated."[4]

What Dr. Benker would share with the court could prove that the coercive sterilization of these ten plaintiffs was not incidental, accidental, or medically necessary, but was part of a concerted attempt by the doctors at the Women's Hospital of LACMC to reduce the birth rate of Mexican-origin women. Based on this testimony, Hernández would maintain that many of the physicians deceptively pushed women into sterilization in accordance with an attitude widespread in the hospital community that the high childbearing rates of Mexican-origin women contributed to many social problems and could be effectively remedied through sterilization.

"THEY BREED LIKE RABBITS"

The Forced Sterilization of Mexican-Origin Women

Antonia Hernández had just begun her first job as a staff attorney at the Los Angeles County Center for Law and Justice when Bernard Rosenfeld, a resident at LACMC, approached her with data proving that women were being coercively sterilized there.[1] Rosenfeld provided her with information on more than 180 cases of primarily Spanish-surname women who were sterilized during childbirth. All were approached by hospital staff who recommended the procedure during the late stages of their labor, after they had already been administered large doses of Demerol or Valium. Many of the women required emergency cesarean sections, and following their deliveries there was no signed consent form for tubal ligation or any other record of their agreement to the procedure in their files.

Rosenfeld had gone through the medical records of hundreds upon hundreds of Spanish-surname patients; reviewing their indications for cesarean section, he recognized a clear pattern of coercion. The notes on one twenty-three-year-old patient with one child read: "Failure to deliver baby with forceps. Caesarean section needed. Consents signed in markedly distressed handwriting, in English. No medical indication for sterilization." A month and a half later, upon a visit to the Family Planning Clinic to request birth control, this patient was fitted with an intra-uterine device (IUD), which she wore for at least a year before she learned that she had been sterilized.[2] With so many similar cases documented, Rosenfeld believed that the data proved what he had seen with his own eyes during his medical residency: the targeted and coercive sterilization of African American and Mexican women.

Hernández followed up on Rosenfeld's information, locating and talking with many of the women whom he suspected had been coercively sterilized. In an interview with the author, she recalled:

> I remember driving around city terrace. It took a long time. All I can tell you is that this case consumed my life. . . . I must have interviewed a hundred women. I remember driving all over East L.A. with a map looking for addresses of these women. And then I had the difficult job of saying to many of the women, "Do you know you were sterilized?" It was a very painful process. And some of them knew, but they all had the misconception that their tubes were tied but could be untied.

Hernández was often faced with the responsibility of encouraging each woman to take legal action. However, many women who wanted to participate in the lawsuit could not because their statute of limitations had expired; others were worried that if they testified against the hospital, they or members of their family would be deported. In the end, two separate cases were filed against LACMC.

Andrade et al. v. Los Angeles County-usc Medical Center was filed by Richard Cruz, a lawyer most noted for his founding of Católicos Por La Raza, a Catholic Chicano activist organization. Cruz also worked with assistance from the offices of Belli, Ashe, and Choulos, who provided co-counsel and split the costs of the case.[3] Cruz's clients were forcibly sterilized between 1972 and 1973, and because their complaints fell within the statue of limitations, each asked for $2 million in compensation for what they had endured as a result of their sterilization.[4] Their suit charged nurses and doctors at LACMC with battery and claimed that "the government in combination with the University of Southern California and health professionals and administrators accomplished a massive 'push' of unlawful sterilization operations between 1968 and 1974 at defendant hospital."[5] Cruz also argued that there was "no way around the word genocide" when considering the

abuses that occurred, and he condemned the medical practitioners on moral grounds.[6] It is unclear why *Andrade* never went to court. Before examining the details of what occurred at LACMC, it is important to understand the context that made sterilization a common practice.

THE ADVENT OF SURGICAL STERILIZATION

Academics and others typically define sterilization abuse as "the misinformed, coerced, or unknowing termination of the reproductive capacity of women and men."[7] The long and well-researched history of sterilization abuse in the United States has demonstrated that practitioners of coercive sterilization have targeted their subjects according to race, class, and gender.[8] As historian Adelaida Del Castillo has noted, sterilization abuse of Mexican-origin peoples for eugenic reasons had occurred previously. Before sterilization was widely available, individual judges would make parole and other conditions of probation dependent upon sterilization. In 1966, for example, Nancy Hernández was sentenced to jail when she refused to agree to be sterilized for a misdemeanor conviction.[9]

During the 1970s, several circumstances directly precipitated sterilization abuse nationwide. For one thing, medical regulations governing sterilization options for most women had become less restrictive. Earlier sterilization was guided by an age-parity formula, whereby a doctor would only sterilize a woman if her age multiplied by the number of her children exceeded 120. In 1970 the American College of Obstetrics and Gynecology withdrew this standard, offering millions of women access to the procedure.[10] The liberalization of medical guidelines for sterilization was coupled with increased availability of funding. Governmental grants to the poor increased substantially after 1965, most notably through passage of the Family Planning Services and Population

Research Act in 1970. While in 1965 only $5 million of federal money was available for family planning services for the poor, in 1979 the government distributed $260 million for this purpose.[11]

Government financing for sterilization procedures in particular was substantial. Prior to 1969 the government had prohibited federally supported family planning services from subsidizing sterilization and abortion services. Funds for sterilization became accessible officially in 1971, with Medicaid covering 90 percent of the cost. Most federal funds were offered through the Office of Economic Opportunity (OEO), which was established to fight the "war on poverty."[12] The combination of technical advances in tubal ligation surgery, increased availability of federal funding, and relaxed requirements for the procedures led to sterilization becoming the most popular form of birth control in the United States.[13]

California long held the highest rates of sterilization in the nation, and these developments increased those rates even more.[14] Sterilizations at the Women's Hospital of LACMC exemplified the extraordinary surge in the numbers of women undergoing such procedures. During the two-year period between July 1968 and July 1970, elective hysterectomy increased by 742 percent, elective tubal ligation by 470 percent, and tubal ligation after delivery by 151 percent.[15]

AN "EPIDEMIC" OF STERILIZATION ABUSE REVEALED

Despite the dramatic increase in rates of sterilization through the 1970s, no medical community boards or governmental officials monitored these procedures. No safeguards to prevent widespread abuses were in effect during the first three years that publicly funded sterilization procedures were available, although OEO-funded family planning clinics were asked to refrain from performing the operation until a set of federal guidelines could be administered. Although guidelines were printed in 1972, the U.S. government did not distribute them to clinics until 1974.[16] Within this unregulated environment, many coerced sterilizations occurred without much notice until the case of the Relf sisters captured public attention.

In June 1973, Mary Alice and Katie Relf, two African American sisters in their early teens, were sterilized in a Montgomery, Alabama hospital even though neither of the girls, nor their parents, gave permission for, or even knew about, the operations. The hospital paid for these operations using OEO funds. Although Mrs. Relf signed an "X" on a consent form she could not read, neither she nor her daughters were advised of the specific nature of the "shots" the nurse advised were necessary. Realizing later that their daughters had been unwittingly sterilized, the parents reported the incident to the Southern Poverty Law Center. National objection to the treatment of the Relf sisters forced the federal Department of Health, Education, and Welfare to suspend the availability of federal funds for the sterilization of minors and the "mentally incompetent" until the government enacted regulations. However, coercive sterilization of adults continued unchecked.[17]

One major study in this era, conducted and coauthored by Drs. Bernard Rosenfeld and Sidney Wolfe, and later published by the Ralph Nader Health Research Group in 1973, exposed several reputable teaching institutions for coercively targeting poor women of color for sterilization. The report verified that doctors at some of the nation's most prestigious hospitals pressured women into consenting to sterilization.[18]

Based on medical journal articles, observation, and interviews with medical students and doctors trained in hospitals across the nation, the report revealed an "epidemic of sterilization . . . in . . . almost every major American teaching hospital in the past two years."[19] In most cases, women were not adequately informed of the range of birth control options available to them nor the permanence of the sterilization operation. Moreover, many were unaware that they had been sterilized. In almost every major medical teaching hospital in the country, the number of elective tubal ligations had at least doubled between the years of 1971 and 1973.[20] On finding that most of the victimized women were low-income minorities, the authors of the report charged that doctors and other hospital personnel acted out of racist attitudes regarding "overpopulation" and "ideal family size."[21] Studies also showed that of the many cases of coercive sterilization reported, none documented abuses against white women.[22] In fact, doctors often tried to talk white middle-class women out of sterilization surgery.[23]

While doctors and others targeted African American women in the South, Native American women suffered from rampant sterilization abuse at Indian Health Service (IHS) clinics. Dr. Connie Uri, who interviewed many native women sterilized while under duress or without complete information, became their advocate. The national attention that she brought to these abuses resulted in a study requested by Senator James Abourzek and conducted by the General Accounting Office (GAO). The report revealed that many women had felt coerced into sterilization by the IHS and under threat of losing their welfare benefits if they did not agree to the operation. In the four IHS areas examined in the GAO study, 3,406 sterilizations were performed between 1973 and 1976, an estimated one-quarter of all Native Americans sterilized during those three years.[24] Many of these women were under the age of twenty-one, a violation of the moratorium called by the Department of Health, Education, and Welfare in 1974.

Elsewhere I have argued that although sterilization abuse of women of color was widespread across the nation at this time, institutions in different regions of the country coerced women in numerous ways, using a variety of justifications.[25] The sterilization abuse of women of Mexican origin followed a pattern similar to that of other women of color, but several factors distinguish what occurred at LACMC from other cases. For example, abuses that have received widespread national attention, such as *Relf v. Weinberger* and *Walker v. Pierce,* occurred in the South and targeted African American women receiving public assistance. The case of *Madrigal v. Quilligan,* on the other hand, took place in Los Angeles and involved mostly poor Mexican immigrant women with limited English-speaking ability—none of whom were receiving public assistance. These differences raise unique issues of citizenship, regional racial politics, language, and culture. How these factors shaped the sterilization abuse of Mexican-origin women is best exemplified in the case of *Madrigal v. Quilligan.*

FORCED STERILIZATION AT LOS ANGELES COUNTY MEDICAL CENTER

Prior to the promulgation of the 1974 guidelines, there had been no "official" policy regulating the practice of sterilization at the Women's Hospital at LACMC.[26] Although the Department of Health, Education, and Welfare's regulations were implemented nationwide in May 1974, they remained unenforced at LACMC in December of that year.[27] During the late 1960s, the hospital received substantial federal funds for the development and improvement of the Obstetrics-Gynecology Department, much of which was funneled toward rebuilding the Women's Hospital facility within which these services were housed. During this period several new doctors with prestigious credentials joined the Women's Hospital staff under the newly appointed direction of Dr. Edward James Quilligan.[28] The new staff, well-funded and practicing in upgraded facilities, began at once to promote birth control to their female patients.[29] In addition, several of the doctors were involved in contraceptive studies conducted on LACMC patients and published in esteemed medical journals.[30]

"Birth control" in this case included rampant sterilization abuse at LACMC, yet this was only one aspect of the systematic effort by the hospital staff to reduce the birthrate of their mostly minority clientele. Several other programs reflected the department's attempt to cut the birthrate of the Mexican and African American populations, who made up the majority of the hospital's patients. Bilingual family planning counselors actively visited each new mother prior to her discharge from the ward to ensure her commitment to practice some form of birth control; no woman was released until this was promised. Counselors aggressively recommended IUDS, a long-term method of birth control that women themselves cannot regulate.[31]

Dr. Karen Benker recounted that "the drive to insert IUDS was so great that the women actually did not receive a postpartum checkup or have any of their questions about their baby or their health answered. They were merely placed on the table one after another and an IUD was popped into place."[32] In her affidavit Benker stated that these facts demonstrate "the great emphasis that the department did put on 'cutting the birth rate of the Mexican and Negro population.'"

Doctors implemented the most effective form of birth control during delivery when they terminated the childbearing capabilities of women of Mexican origin by tubal ligation. As was common in teaching hospitals across the nation, LACMC students were encouraged to conduct several surgical procedures to refine their skills. According to Dr. Bernard Rosenfeld, coauthor of the Health Research Group Report and a resident in the Obstetrics-Gynecology Department at LACMC during this period, staff doctors would often congratulate residents on the number of postpartum tubal ligations accomplished within a week's time.[33] Similarly, residents

reportedly encouraged interns to press women into agreeing to a sterilization procedure. In one instance, after a patient had refused a resident's solicitations for sterilization, the resident's supervisor remarked, "Talk her into it. You can always talk her into it." In June 1973 a resident told new interns, "I want you to ask every one of the girls if they want their tubes tied, regardless of how old they are. Remember everyone you get to get her tubes tied means two tubes [i.e., two procedures] for some resident or intern."[34] Rosenfeld estimated that 10 to 20 percent of the physicians at LACMC "actively pushed sterilization on women who either did not understand what was happening to them or who had not been given all the facts regarding their options."[35]

Physicians most often approached women for sterilization while they were in the last stages of labor, during their wait in the Active Labor Room, where they stayed until actual delivery. Here women in the most painful stages of labor were attached to fetal monitors and placed in beds side by side. Dr. Karen Benker recalled the scene as one of "crowding, screams of pain, bright lights, lack of sleep by patients and staff, and an 'assembly-line' approach so that many women were literally terrified of what was happening at the time they signed the consents. Of course, this was especially true of non-English-speaking mothers who were left with no explanation of what was happening."[36] Dr. Benker's acknowledgment that non-English-speaking women were "of course" more likely to experience medical mistreatment speaks to the critical importance of language in the sterilization abuse cases that occurred at LACMC. Most residents and doctors were not bilingual; most knew only a few obstetrical-related words. There was "virtually no one available" to interpret for Spanish-speaking women. Often women were sterilized on the basis of one question, "¿Más niños?" (More babies?)[37] While some nurses or translators tried to communicate with Spanish-speaking women, as illustrated below, the doctors apparently took advantage of the women's inability to understand English and manipulated them into consenting to sterilization.[38]

Residents and nurses often approached women to sign consent forms immediately before childbirth. Medical personnel gave women in labor a shot of Valium or Demerol in preparation for the delivery, and they shoved consent forms into the hands of laboring women while they were too groggy to understand or notice that they were signing forms granting permission for their own sterilization.[39] Dr. Benker described seeing this type of coercion "on almost a daily basis": "The doctor would hold a syringe in front of the mother who was in labor pain and ask her if she wanted a pain killer; while the woman was in the throes of a contraction the doctor would say, 'Do you want the pain killer? Then sign the papers. Do you want the pain to stop? Do you want to have to go through this again? Sign the papers.'"[40]

Moreover, hospital staff did not fully explain the irreversible nature of the sterilization procedure. Many women agreed to the surgery believing that their tubes were being tied temporarily and that they could be untied later and their fertility restored. A physician first asked María Figueroa if she wanted tubal ligation as she was being prepared for surgery. She specifically recalled that the doctor told her the procedure entailed the "tying of a woman's tubes" and she could later have them untied. She initially rejected the procedure, but tired from her labor and of the doctor's urgings, Mrs. Figueroa agreed to sterilization if she delivered a boy. As it turned out, she was sterilized even though she delivered a baby girl.[41]

In many instances LACMC patients were not just subjected to a single incident of coercion but were harassed continually by nurses and doctors. Helena Orozco, a plaintiff in the *Madrigal* trial, had repeatedly declined sterilization throughout her prenatal care at the hospital. She had discussed sterilization with her husband prior to labor, and Mrs. Orozco told the nurses, "We decided not to."[42] However, after numerous solicitations from the doctor and nurses, and while crying from intense pain during labor, Mrs. Orozco signed the consent for sterilization because, in her words, "I just wanted them to leave me alone, sign the papers and get it over with. . . . I was in pain on the table when they were asking me all those questions, and they were poking around my stomach, and pushing with their fingers up there. I just wanted to be left alone."[43] Mrs. Orozco also agreed to the operation because "I thought he [the doctor] meant tying tubes only. Then they could be untied later. . . . If they would have put the word 'sterilization' there, I would not have signed the papers."[44] Because she believed the procedure to be reversible, Mrs. Orozco planned to have her tubes untied in three years and did not find out until a year and a half later that she could never again have children.

Hospital personnel also strategically limited communication between laboring women and their husbands. For example, when a patient adamantly resisted sterilization, the doctor would warn the husband that his wife's health was in danger, hoping that the husband would then pressure his wife to submit to the procedure.[45] Such manipulative gender dynamics were apparent in the case of Dolores Madrigal, who refused sterilization from the outset of her stay at LACMC. After Mrs. Madrigal had refused the recommendations of several nurses that she take care of herself and agree to a tubal ligation, doctors talked with Mr. Madrigal in another room, telling him that his wife would die if she had another child.[46] Ten minutes later, a nurse returned to Mrs. Madrigal and informed her, laughing, that her husband had agreed to the sterilization procedure, and again presented her with a consent form to sign.[47]

Women requiring cesarean section delivery were at greatest risk of coercive sterilization.

According to Dr. Benker, once it became clear that a cesarean was going to be necessary, the resident was "extremely aggressive" in pushing for sterilization. Many doctors lied to patients, telling them that state law only allowed three cesarean sections and that sterilization was therefore required after childbirth. Maria Hurtado recalled that her doctor "brought someone from outside and explained to her to ask me why I wanted so many children since the State of California only permitted three Cesareans."[48] While unconscious following the delivery of her child, Mrs. Hurtado was given a tubal ligation without her consent. It was not until requesting birth control during her six-week postpartum visit that she recalled a receptionist at the hospital telling her, "Lady, forever you will not be able to have any more children."[49]

Doctors sometimes told patients that they might even die during future childbirths if they were not sterilized after their cesarean.[50] Upon the cesarean delivery of her third child, Consuelo Hermosillo was advised by her doctor that sterilization would be necessary, because a fourth pregnancy would most likely be life-threatening.[51] While medicated, Ms. Hermosillo signed the consent forms, without full comprehension of their content. Likewise, Estela Benavides feared her doctor's warnings that another child delivered by cesarean could be life-threatening, and she consented to a tubal ligation while hemorrhaging during her labor. She made this hard decision, she stated, out of her commitment to continue to care for her existing children.[52]

THE PHYSICIANS' PERSPECTIVE

The physicians' attitudes toward the LACMC clientele, and their perceptions of their own role in providing a panacea for overpopulation, were intricately linked. As authors of the Health Research Group study asserted, "Sometimes the doctors involved held very strong beliefs about population control, others admittedly held strong views about class prejudice—others simply believed all persons on welfare should have their tubes tied."[53] Dr. Rosenfeld recalled once talking to a colleague about coercing patients into sterilization when the other physician said, "Well, if we're going to pay for them, we should control them."[54]

These attitudes were prevalent at LACMC and across the nation during this time. While under general anesthesia in preparation for a cesarean delivery, Jovita Rivera was approached by a doctor who told her that she should have her "tubes tied" because her children were a burden on the government. Ironically, Ms. Rivera was not receiving public assistance, nor were any of the plaintiffs in the Madrigal case. However, because physicians and other hospital personnel perceived these women as welfare recipients, they were considered prime candidates for tubal ligation.[55]

The doctors would also make use of patients' racial/ethnic identity and immigrant status to coerce them into sterilization. Many physicians "would express very prejudiced remarks about patients who did not speak English—Mexican American patients" and referred to them as "beans."[56] After four hours in the delivery room in advanced labor, Georgina Hernández was approached by her doctor, who first commented that Mexicans are very poor and cannot provide for a large family, and then suggested that she be sterilized. Although Mrs. Hernández resisted her doctor's urgings and did not recall signing a consent form, she was surgically sterilized during the delivery of her fourth child.[57] Other women were threatened with deportation if they were not sterilized. In a San Diego hospital, "one resident would be so furious if a woman declined (sterilization) that he would say, 'We know you're here illegally and if you don't consent to have a tubal, we'll call the feds [immigration officials] and get you deported.'"[58]

Patients were even roughly handled by some physicians. One doctor slapped a patient and told her to shut up as she cried out in labor pains. Some medical workers expressed moralistic references to the woman's sexual activity. For example, a doctor might observe that if a woman had not had sex, she would not be in pain right now. According to Dr. Benker, these biased attitudes and behaviors were common practice on the obstetrical floor.

The individual experiences of the women involved in the Madrigal trial suggest a range of manipulations of power and privilege that coalesced at LACMC to rob women of Mexican origin of their reproductive liberty. Not only do these incidents demonstrate the ways patriarchal, class-based, and racial ideas were used by hospital personnel to coerce Mexican-origin women into sterilization, they also show how ideological notions impact medical practice. The salient aspects of these ideas are further illuminated by the legal proceedings surrounding the case.

NOTES

Part One

1. Trial transcript, 828, *Madrigal v. Quilligan* (C.D. Cal., 7 June 1978) (No. CV-75-2057-EC). Trial transcript and other case pleadings are available in the Carlos Vélez-Ibañez Sterilization Archives, Chicano Studies Library, University of California, Los Angeles (hereafter referred to as Vélez Archives).
2. The first line of the complaint reads, "This is a suit against State officials and others acting under color of state law to redress the violation of the plaintiffs' constitutional right to procreate and their constitutional right to due process of law." Plaintiffs' First Amended Complaint, *Madrigal v. Quilligan* (C.D. Cal., 25 November 1975) (No. CV-75-2057-EC), p. 1, Vélez Archives.
3. Plaintiffs' Proposed Findings of Fact and Conclusions of Law, *Madrigal v. Quilligan* (C.D. Cal., 22 June 1978) (No. CV-75-2057-EC), Vélez Archives.
4. Antonia Hernández, Charles Nabarette, and Karen Benker each reported to me that several other staff members corroborated Dr. Benker's story. Although willing to speak "off the record," they feared retribution and the permanent loss of a job in medicine if they were involved in the case. Hernández, Nabarette, and Benker interviews.

Part Two

1. Rosenfeld had first gone to the Southern Poverty Law Center, which funded some of the initial case costs and legal advice. See Elizabeth Shalen, Esq., to Kent Russel, Esq., 11 May 1974; and Morris Dees to Mr. Melvin Belli, 17 December 1972, Box 15, Folder 4, Ricardo Cruz/Católicos por La Raza Papers (hereafter referred to as Cruz Papers).
2. Bernard Rosenfeld, Notes on Medical File, File 72, Notes, personal papers of Bernard Rosenfeld, in author's collection (hereafter referred to as Rosenfeld Papers).
3. Kent A. Russel to Ricardo Cruz, 18 June 1974, Box 15, Folder 4, Cruz Papers.
4. Mike Goodman, "Women Ask $6 Million From County in Sterilization Claim," *Los Angeles Times*, 21 November 1974, Rosenfeld Papers.
5. "First Amended Complaint for Damages," *Virginia Andrade et al. v. Los Angeles County, University of Southern California Medical Center, et al.*, 6 November 1975, No. C126404, p. 4, Rosenfeld Papers.
6. See, for example, Richard Cruz Testimony at California State Hearings on Proposed Sterilization Regulations, Los Angeles, 113–122, RG 5, Box 54, Folder 9, MALDEF Papers.
7. Clarke, "Subtle Sterilization Abuse."
8. Although heavily concentrated on the early part of the century, the most comprehensive account of sterilization abuse during the twentieth century is Reilly, *The Surgical Solution*. For late-twentieth-century sterilization abuse historiography, see Donovan, "Sterilizing the Poor and Incompetent"; Littlewood, *The Politics of Population Control*; Shapiro, *Population Control Politics*; and Davis, *Women Under Attack*. This was not the first occurrence of massive sterilization abuses in the United States. During the late nineteenth and early twentieth centuries, sterilization of the "unfit" was advocated for achieving racial purity and race progress. For discussions of sterilization during this period, see Haller, *Eugenics*; and Chase, *The Legacy of Malthus*. Puerto Rican women also suffered a disproportionate amount of sterilization abuse; see Ramírez de Arellano and Seipp, *Colonialism, Catholicism, and Contraception*; and López, "Agency and Constraint."
9. "Cruel and Unusual?" *Newsweek* 67 (13 June 1966): 46; "Criminal Justice: Jail or Sterilization?" *Time Magazine* 87 (3 June 1966): 46.
10. Shapiro, *Population Control Politics*.
11. Ibid.
12. A 1967 study conducted by the Office of Economic Opportunity (OEO) determined birth control to be the most "cost-effective" method of poverty prevention. In 1968, the OEO sponsored a county-by-county study designed to ascertain how many indigent women were provided with family planning services; a total of 5.3 million were found to be "in-need," with only 85 percent of those receiving services. See "Birth Control Effectiveness," *Science*,

12 May 1967; U.S. Office of Economic Opportunity, *Need for Subsidized Family Planning Services*; and Hern, "Family Planning and the Poor." Advocacy for birth control as an effective way to treat poverty grew during the 1960s. See Shepard, "Birth Control for the Poor"; and "Welfare Birth Control," 157.

13. Gordon, *Women's Body, Women's Right*; Petchesky, *Abortion and Women's Choice*; National Center for Health Statistics, *Trends in Contraceptive Practice*.
14. Reilly, *The Surgical Solution*.
15. Health Research Group, *A Health Research Group Study*.
16. Historians of sterilization abuse have noted the "spurious political considerations" that deterred the implementation of federal sterilization regulations. Most suggest that because 1972 was an election year, the White House purposefully suppressed the regulations, fearing that it would hinder Nixon's re-election. See Littlewood, *The Politics of Population Control*; Shapiro, *Population Control Politics*.
17. The case of *Relf v. Weinberger* (later merged with a similar suit by the National Welfare Rights Organization) aimed to force the federal government to establish stringent guidelines to regulate doctor behavior and protect patients from possible abuse. The case was crucial in establishing the requirement of informed consent and federal regulations regarding sterilization that were implemented in April 1974. See *Relf et al. v. Weinberger et al.*, Civil Action No. 73–1557, U.S. Dist. Ct., Washington, D.C., 15 March 1974.
18. Robert Kistler, "Women 'Pushed' Into Sterilization, Doctor Charges: Thousands Victimized at Some Inner-City Teaching Hospitals, Report Claims," *Los Angeles Times*, 2 December 1974, pp. 1, 3, 26–28; and Les Payne, "U.S. Sterilization Abuses Disclosed," *Los Angeles Times*, 5 January 1975.
19. Pointing to class differentials in medical care, "Such abuses . . . historically have found fertile climates in the nation's giant, core-city teaching complexes such as the USC-Los Angeles County Medical Center, where medicine is high volume, often impersonal— and practiced on patients who are generally poor, frightened and uneducated." See Health Research Group, *A Health Research Group Study*; and Kistler, "Women 'Pushed' Into Sterilization," 1.
20. Health Research Group, *A Health Research Group Study*.
21. Hernández, "Chicanas and the Issue of Involuntary Sterilization."
22. Gordon, *Women's Body, Women's Right*.
23. Roberts, *Killing the Black Body*.
24. Dillingham, "Indian Women and IHS Sterilization Practices"; "Sterilization of Native Americans"; and "Sterilization Update."
   A full copy of the Abourzek Report, released in November 1976, can be found in RG 5, Box 910, Folder 5, MALDEF Papers.
   The in-depth research of Dr. Connie Uri, which investigated beyond those four Indian Health Service areas, indicate that even more Native women were sterilized. For narrative accounts of sterilization abuse of Native American women, see Joan Burnes, "Shocking Sterilization Statistics Surface," *Indian Country Today*, 24 August 1994, p. 8; "Sterilization of Native Women to IHS Charged," *Akwesasne Notes* (Early Winter 1974): 6–7; Larson, "And Then There Were None," 61; and Lou, "The Sterilization of American Indian Women," 43, 51, 57, 100. See also Richard M. Harley, "Indian Women Plan to Sue U.S. in Sterilization Cases," *Christian Science Monitor*, 27 May 1977, p. 6, for an account of legal action taken on behalf of Native women who were coercively sterilized.
25. Gutiérrez, "Policing 'Pregnant Pilgrims.'"
26. Not until 22 February 1974 was it specified that "patients will not be approached for the first time concerning sterilization when they are in active labor" in a memo dispersed to all staff by Dr. Quilligan. Deposition of Roger Freeman, 12, *Madrigal v. Quilligan* (No. CV-75-2057-EC) (29 June 1977), (Vélez Papers). I am indebted to Carlos Vélez-Ibañez, who graciously shared personal collected materials (Vélez Papers) from the *Madrigal* case that are not available in the Vélez Archives.
27. Robert Kistler, "Many U.S. Rules on Sterilization Abuses Ignored Here," *Los Angeles Times*, 3 December 1974, sec. 1, pp. 3, 24–26. Dr. Quilligan told a *Los Angeles Times* reporter that he did "not recall" the guidelines distributed on 18 April 1974.
28. The information in this section is based on Karen Benker's "Statement on Sterilization Abuse," n.d., Vélez Archives (hereafter referred to as Benker Statement).
29. Although definitive statistics are unavailable, it was reported by the head of Obstetrics/Gynecology, Dr. Quilligan, that the "predominate race" that frequented LACMC was Mexican American (trial transcript, 740).
30. Selected publications from doctors eventually named as defendants in the *Madrigal* trial include Brenner et al., "Ectopic Pregnancy Following Tubal Sterilization Surgery," *Obstetrics and Gynecology* 49(3) (March 1977): 323–324; Bernstein et al., "Clinical Experience with the Cu-7 Intrauterine Device," *Contraception* 6(2) (August 1972): 99–107; E.J. Quilligan, "Contraception After Pregnancy," *Journal of Reproductive Medicine* 21 (5, Suppl.) (November 1978): 250–251; Tyler et al., "Long-term Studies of Oral Contraceptives and IUDs at the Family Planning Centers of Greater Los Angeles," *Journal of Reproductive Medicine* 8(4) (April 1972): 162–164; Tyler et al., "Present Status on Injectable Contraceptives: Results of Seven-Years Study," *Fertility and Sterility* 21(6) (June 1970): 469–481; and Zuspan et al., "Discussion (On Current Concepts of Contraception)," *Journal of Reproductive Medicine* 21 (5, Suppl.) (November 1978): 257–271.
   As "experts" in the field, several doctors also provided public testimony regarding contraceptive usage. See "Statement before the Subcommittee on

Intergovernmental Relations, House Committee on Government Operations," 12 June 1973; Mishell et al., "The Need for Development of New Methods of Contraception," Statement, 2 May 1978; in *U.S. House of Representatives Select Committee on Population and Development: Research in Population and Development: Needs and Capacities,* vol. 3, Hearings, 2–4 May, 1978 (Washington, D.C.: U.S. Government Printing Office, 1978), 374–380; Mishell et al., Population Control Statement on IUDS, Submitted to the U.S. Congress, House, Committee on Governmental Operations, Subcommittee on Intergovernmental Relations, 12 June 1973.

31. See Gordon, *Women's Body, Women's Right,* 423–424, for a succinct discussion of the problematic uses of the IUD.

32. Benker Statement, p. 2.

33. Rosenfeld documented his personal observations while a resident at LACMC, and his accounts were used by the attorneys for the Southern Poverty Law Center in the Relf case against HEW over the adoption of sterilization guidelines. Rosenfeld was also scheduled to serve as a witness in the *Madrigal* case but did not testify out of fear of retribution. See *Madrigal v. Quilligan,* trial transcript, 1445,1449. His contract was not renewed at the Women's Hospital because of his involvement in unveiling sterilization abuses there.

34. Health Research Group, *A Health Research Group Study,* 7–8.

35. Narda Zacchino and Kris Lindgren, "Plaintiffs Lose Suit Over 10 Sterilizations," *Los Angeles Times,* 1 July 1978, sec. B1.

36. Benker Statement, p. 5.

37. Ibid.; see also "Deposition of Dr. Karen Benker," 6 September 1977, 32, Vélez Papers.

38. Juan Nieto, an intern at LACMC, reported that he had experienced similar treatment—"particularly of Mexican-Americans"—at a hospital in Colorado where he completed his medical training. Suggesting a pattern of abuse of Mexican-origin women throughout the Southwest, Nieto was sure that Spanish-speaking patients "had no idea the procedure urged on them was permanent" (Bernard Rosenfeld, interview notations, Rosenfeld Papers).

39. Ibid.

40. Benker Statement, p. 3.

41. Georgina Torres-Rizk, "Sterilization Abuses Against Chicanas in Los Angeles," 2 December 1976, pp. 1–2, RG 9, Box 95, Folder 4, MALDEF Papers.

42. Trial transcript, 18. Mrs. Orozco testified that doctors almost cheered when she finally signed the consent (19).

43. Trial transcript, 370. All of the following quotes from the women involved in the *Madrigal* case were taken directly from the court transcript. During the trial the women all testified in Spanish, with their words translated by a court translator, then transcribed by the court reporter.

44. Trial transcript, 383.

45. Benker Statement, 4.

46. Trial transcript, 453.

47. Ibid., 454. Preferring the husband's decision regarding sterilization over the woman's is also evidenced in Dr. Quilligan's admission in the situation of another patient; although Mrs. Melvina Hernández was sterilized without her knowledge, he said, "We wouldn't have done it without the husband's permission" (Goodman, "Women Ask $6 Million," *Los Angeles Times,* 21 November 1974, sec. 1, pp. 1, 25). However, the doctors would also lie to the husbands, telling them that their wives would die unless they were sterilized, or that they were signing forms to consent for a cesarean-section delivery only. Gabriel Acosta, fearing for his wife's life, believed that he was only signing a consent to an emergency cesarean section. See Diane Ainsworth, "Mother No More," *Reader,* 26 January 1979, pp. 1, 4–9.

48. Trial transcript, 406.

49. Ibid., 416.

50. Benker Statement, p. 3.

51. "He told me, in these words: 'Lady, the limit for cesarean are three by law. So, you have to decide whether you want to risk the next one, because I think the next one you can die because you are rated here in the history as a patient of high risk'" (trial transcript, 665).

52. The words of Mrs. Benavides clearly reflect that she was fearing for her life: "They told me the reason was that if I got pregnant again the baby would probably be in the same position, and something else could happen serious. . . . I thought maybe I could die. . . . I thought if I had another child something could happen to me." Moreover, she testified that her only concern was for the daughters she already had: "The only thing I thought about was the girls. That is why I asked the question, that if I accepted that operation, I want it to be all right for my girls" (trial transcript, 126–129).

53. Kistler, "Women 'Pushed' Into Sterilization," 1.

54. Ibid.

55. The actual versus the perceived welfare status of the plaintiffs proves problematic in the case. In fact, the defendants opposed the plaintiffs' case as a class action because they are supposed to represent "a class of persons receiving medical and/or other aid from federal or state governmentally funded sources." Because this is not "uniformly true" of all the plaintiffs (many did receive aid after their sterilization), the case was never considered a class action suit. See "Affidavit of Nancy L. Menzies," 13 July 1977, RG 5, Box 946, Folder 10, MALDEF Papers.

56. Deposition of Dr. Karen Benker, 6 September 1977, Vélez Papers.

57. Torres-Rizk, "Abuses Against Chicanas," 2; and "Interview of Georgina Hernández," 9 May 1978, 10, Vélez Papers.

58. Kistler, "Women 'Pushed' Into Sterilization," 2.

CHAPTER 4

The Economic Impact of the Pill

Annie Lowrey

The recent controversy over contraception and health insurance has focused on who should pay for the pill. But there is a wealth of economic evidence about the value of the pill – to taxpayers, as my colleague Motoko Rich writes, as well as to women in general.

Indeed, as the economist Betsey Stevenson has noted, a number of studies have shown that by allowing women to delay marriage and childbearing, the pill has also helped them invest in their skills and education, join the work force in greater numbers, move into higher-status and better-paying professions and make more money over all.

One of the most influential and frequently cited studies of the impact the pill has had on women's lives comes from Claudia Goldin and Lawrence F. Katz. The two Harvard economists argue that the pill gave women "far greater certainty regarding the pregnancy consequences of sex." That "lowered the costs of engaging in long-term career investments," freeing women to finish high school or go to college, for instance, rather than settling down.

The pill also helped make the marriage market "thicker," they write. By decoupling sex from marriage, young people were able to put off getting married and spend more time shopping around for a prospective partner.

Those changes have had enormous impacts on the economy, studies show: increasing the number of women in the labor force, raising the number of hours that women work and giving women access to traditionally male and highly lucrative professions in fields like law and medicine.

A study by Martha J. Bailey, Brad Hershbein and Amalia R. Miller helps assign a dollar value to those tectonic shifts. For instance, they show that young women who won access to the pill in the 1960s ended up earning an 8 percent premium on their hourly wages by age 50.

Such trends have helped narrow the earnings gap between men and women. Indeed, the paper suggests that the pill accounted for 30 percent – 30 percent! – of the convergence of men's and women's earnings from 1990 to 2000.

Interestingly, the study also found that the pill had the greatest economic benefits for women with average IQ scores. "Almost all of the wage gains accrued to women in the middle of the IQ distribution," the paper said. For this group, it said, women with early access to the pill "enjoyed greater hourly wages throughout their twenties and the premium grew to a statistically significant 20 percent at ages 30 to 49." Why? The pill helped "middle ability" women in "planning for and opting into paid work," the researchers theorized.

SECTION II
Abortion

Abortion, the subject of this section, sparks the most controversy of all reproductive issues, and the "abortion wars," as this book shows, impact other reproductive health services in a variety of ways. Abortion is defined as the intentional termination of a pregnancy after a fertilized egg or pre-embryo has implanted in the uterine wall, usually several days to more than a week after conception. There are several different techniques for performing abortion, which we discuss later. The editors of this book both support safe and legal access to abortion, but recognize that abortion raises complex ethical and religious issues for many, including, no doubt, many readers of this volume. But abortion is not only the most divisive issue in American domestic politics, and a core issue of modern conservatism. It also must be understood as a medical procedure that over a million women in the United States and forty-four million women worldwide seek each year. Moreover, it is important to understand that abortion care constitutes some health professionals' *work*—work that involves elements of risk and stigma (in the United States) found nowhere else in medicine. It is this approach to the abortion issue—as a health care service—that shapes most of the selected readings in this section.

The extent to which societies are divided about abortion varies according to time and place. For example, the enormous polarization around the issue that now exists in the United States should not blind us to the fact that in most contemporary western European countries, and even in the United States prior to the mid-19th century, abortion is/was not particularly controversial. The one historical constant about abortion is that whether legal or not, controversial or not, women have always sought abortion, in every society for which written records exist. As the anthropologist George Devereux concluded (1954, 98), after an exhaustive review of materials from 350 ancient and preindustrial societies, "there is every indication that abortion is an absolutely universal phenomenon, and that it is impossible even to construct an imaginary social system in which no woman would ever feel at least compelled to abort." In fact, we know that the ability to control one's own fertility—that is, the number of off-spring one has—is a fundamental desire, across geography, history, legal context, and cultures.

Today, approximately 40% of the world's women live in places where abortion is illegal, mainly on the African continent (South Africa being the major exception) and most of Latin America. But the abortion rate (abortions per thousand women, aged 15–44) is higher in Latin America and Africa than it is in the United States and Europe, reflecting both inadequate contraceptive availability in the developing world, as well as an ample market of illegal provision. As reported by the Guttmacher Institute (2013b), the leading research organization tracking reproductive events both in the United States and globally, nearly half of all abortions occurring worldwide are unsafe—that is, these procedures are not performed by a competent provider and/or in a facility with minimal medical standards—and nearly all of these unsafe procedures take place in the developing world. The World Health Organization (2014) has estimated that some 47,000 women die each year from unsafe abortion, again, nearly all occurring in the developing world, or Global South, while others put that figure even higher.

In the developed world, or Global North, in contrast, legal abortion is a very safe procedure, and medical researchers have concluded that in the United States, abortion is fourteen times safer than childbirth, with respect to the likelihood of a woman dying (Raymond and Grimes 2012). But despite its safety, abortion has had a very turbulent history in the United States and continues to do so. As the selection in this section from *Doctors of Conscience: The Struggle to Provide Abortion before and after Roe v Wade* by sociologist Carole Joffe shows, abortion prior to the 1850s was quite widespread and largely unregulated. It was physicians, in the newly founded American Medical Association (1847), who led the efforts to criminalize abortion. By the 1870s all states had made abortions illegal, leading to a century of criminalization, until the *Roe v Wade* decision in 1973. During this period illegal abortion was widely practiced by a variety of practitioners—some well-trained, some not; some ethical, some not. Many women, desperate to control their own reproduction, took matters into their own hands, often with tragic results. The selection from *Doctors of Conscience* also describes the range of providers to which women were exposed, and the public health consequences that occur when abortion is illegal. The selection additionally conveys the dismay that many young physicians of the pre-*Roe* era felt about the deaths and injuries they observed when they knew the procedure could be safely done under proper conditions. In conjunction with the feminist health movement of the 1960s, many of these "doctors of conscience" began to call for the legalization of abortion, and by 1970 the AMA reversed its historic position on abortion. In 1973, the U.S. Supreme Court ruled in the decision *Roe v Wade* that abortion was a decision left to physicians and their patients and could not be restricted up to the point of viability of the fetus (usually understood as 24 weeks of gestation, or the end of the second trimester of pregnancy), with states free to regulate abortion after that point in pregnancy. Nearly all states prohibit abortions after 24 weeks, unless there is a threat to the pregnant woman's life, or she is facing a severe health condition. This decision had far-reaching effects in increasing women's access to services and eliminating many of the risks associated with illegal abortion.

Since the *Roe v Wade* decision, more than a million abortions have taken place in the United States each year (though no exact figures are available, some researchers have estimated that a similar number of illegal procedures took place in the years leading up to *Roe*). About half of all pregnancies taking place in the United States are unintended, and of these about four in ten end in abortion. In 2010, the last year for which data are available as this book goes to press, about 1.21 million abortions were performed in the United States. At current rates, researchers estimate that 3 in 10 American women will have an abortion by the age 45. Women in their 20s account for more than half of all abortions, while 18% of those getting abortions are teenagers. About 61% of current abortion patients already have one or more children. Women obtaining abortions also come from all religious backgrounds: 38% of women obtaining abortions identify as Protestant, and 28% as Catholic. 42% of women obtaining abortions have incomes below 100% of the federal poverty level (about $11,000 for a single woman with no children) (Guttmacher Institute 2013a).

Nearly 90% of abortions take place in the first twelve weeks of pregnancy, and nearly all of these take place in freestanding clinics. Only about 1% of abortions take place after 20 weeks of gestation; of those procedures that take place after 20 weeks, some are due to genetic anomalies of the fetus discovered late in pregnancy; some are because the pregnancy presents a serious health risk to the pregnant woman; others are due to women having difficulties in raising the funds for an abortion (pushing her later and later in pregnancy, and thus raising the cost even more); and some women, often younger teens, simply do not realize they are pregnant until fairly late in the pregnancy.

Women seek abortions for a variety of personal reasons, but there are definitely patterns in their motivation. According to Guttmacher researchers, American women explain their decision in ways that "underscore their understanding of the responsibilities of parenthood and family life." Three-fourths of women cite concern for or responsibility to other individuals; three-fourths say they cannot afford a child; three-fourths say that having a baby would interfere with work, school or the ability to care for other children; and half say they do not want to be a single parent or are having problems with their husband or partner (Finer et al. 2005).

There are several methods of abortion currently in use in the United States. Most abortions in the first trimester (12 weeks) take place by a procedure known as *aspiration*: these are performed either by use of a vacuum aspiration machine, or for abortions early in the first trimester, by use of a hand-held device, called a "manual vacuum aspirator." (The MVA is also widely in use in the developing world, where electricity can be erratic.) Another method of abortion which has more recently come into use is known as *medication abortion*: this regimen, which is typically used in the United States up through nine weeks of pregnancy, involves women taking two drugs, mifepristone (formerly known as "RU-486" or the "abortion pill"), which causes fetal demise, and misoprostol, a widely used ulcer drug, which also has the effect of causing uterine contractions. Approximately 20% of abortions taking place in the U.S use this mifepristone–misoprostol combination, with follow-up care from a physician. Misoprostol, which is sold under the trade name Cytotec, is available on over the counter status in some developing countries, and women in those countries who have trouble accessing legal abortion have long used misoprostol to commence bleeding. If their abortion is not complete, they then present at a hospital, claiming to be in the process of miscarrying. As abortion access has become more difficult in many states in the United States, misoprostol use has increased, particularly along the U.S./Mexican border (Tan 2012).

Starting around 13 or 14 weeks of gestation, many doctors use a method called "*dilation and extraction*" (D and E), which often takes place over two days. On the first day, clinicians insert *lamineria* (a seaweed preparation), which softens the woman's cervix, and a physician then completes the procedure by removing the contents of the uterus the next day. *Intact D and E* is a variant of the standard D and E method, in which the fetus' body is removed intact, after its skull has been collapsed; this method has in the past been occasionally used by doctors in those cases where they felt it to be the safest method available to best protect the health of the pregnant woman. However, abortion opponents sensationalized this procedure, referring to it as "partial birth abortion," a term that does not exist in the medical literature, but conveys, out of context, highly upsetting imagery. Capitalizing on this inflammatory image, conservatives in the U.S. Congress, in an unprecedented interference with doctors' ability to exercise medical judgment, secured the votes to ban this single medical procedure (except when necessary to save a woman's life). This law was then upheld by the Supreme Court in 2007. The Court's decision in that case *Gonzalez v Carhart* was particularly disappointing to women's health advocates not only because of the willingness to overrule medical judgment, but also because, for the first time, the Court found an abortion law constitutional that did not allow an exception to preserve women's health (Greenhouse 2007). The decision further dismayed many observers because of the majority's endorsement of the alleged negative mental health effects of abortion, an idea widely disputed by mental health professionals (APA 2014).

In the rare cases of post-24 week abortions, doctors typically use the *induction* method, in which women are given an injection which causes fetal demise, and then are given medications which cause uterine contractions and the expulsion of the fetus. These later abortions, typically of wanted pregnancies gone horribly wrong, can be extremely upsetting for women and their families, and counseling is a particularly important part of such procedures.

Access to all forms of abortion has become increasingly difficult since the 1973 decision. Nearly 90% of U.S. counties are without an abortion provider, and given the U.S. population distribution, this means about one out of three American women lives in a county without a provider. This poses particular difficulties for women who live in rural areas, especially those without access to transportation. Since *Roe*, state legislatures have imposed hundreds of restrictions on abortion. As of 2013, twenty-six states require women seeking abortions to wait between 24–72 hours between meeting with a provider and completing the procedure, an additional barrier to women without transportation or childcare. Seventeen states require women to be told information in counseling that is medically untrue, including that abortion causes breast cancer, infertility or suicidal thoughts, or that fetuses feel pain (Gold and Nash 2007). The majority of states require that teenagers seeking abortion have their parents' consent and/or that their parents be notified of their plans to terminate their pregnancies. This is particularly challenging for some teens who feel they cannot safely inform their parents of their need for an abortion. All states that require parental notification or consent also provide a process for these teens known as "judicial bypass," in which a judge can grant permission instead. This process is explored in the excerpt from the sociologist Helena Silverstein's 2009 book, *Girls on the Stand: How Courts Fail Pregnant Minors*.

The longstanding practice of state legislatures passing abortion restrictions intensified after the 2010 elections, in which Republicans took control of many state legislatures and governorships and conservative politicians passed an unprecedented number of such restrictions. Some of these, known as "TRAP laws" (Targeted Regulation of Abortion Providers) require clinics to spend hundreds of thousands of dollars in physical upgrades, in order to conform to the physical requirements of an ambulatory surgical center. Although ostensibly about patient safety, these regulations only apply to clinics that provide abortions and not to any other comparable healthcare setting where one would assume patient safety would be equally important. Critics of these laws argue that the requirements of these laws, which specify things like the size of janitor closets and the width of hallways, have nothing to do with abortion patient safety, and everything to do with the goal of shutting clinics down (Center for Reproductive Rights 2013). Indeed, some clinics have been forced to close because they were unable to afford the upgrades demanded by such laws. As of this writing, a number of states are down to one clinic.

Cost represents another barrier to access to legal abortion. Though the cost of an abortion varies from region to region, the average cost of a first trimester procedure in 2014, was about $450, with costs rising considerably for procedures later in pregnancy. Due to the passage in 1976 by Congress of a law known as the Hyde Amendment, no federal funds are allowed to be used for abortions, except under the very limited circumstances of rape, incest, and threats to the life of the pregnant woman. (Some 15 states do allow state Medicaid funds to be used for abortions for poor women on this program.) Given that so many of current abortion recipients have incomes below the official poverty line, even the cost of a first trimester procedure is often very difficult to come by.

Of the numerous controversies that always swirl around abortion, the racial and ethnic composition of abortion recipients has provoked the most recent attention. African American women and Latinas are disproportionately overrepresented in the pool of recipients. African American women, for example, are four times as likely as white women to have an abortion, and, as mentioned earlier, nearly half of all abortion patients have incomes below the poverty line. There are several reasons why women of color and women in severe poverty (which are often overlapping categories) are more likely to seek out abortion services. The most significant one reflects the disparities in access to basic health care that exist in American society. Access to a regular health care provider, comprehensive sex education, and subsidized contraception (especially for the more effective kinds, which are more expensive) have historically been denied to many of the most vulnerable women in our society. The Affordable Care Act, and especially its stated objective of providing all FDA-approved contraceptives without a co-payment in the context of preventative care, may help address these groups' high rate of unintended pregnancy, though, as mentioned, this coverage may be overturned by the Supreme Court. Even if this aspect of the ACA is allowed to stand, however, as the sociologist Tracy Weitz points out in the selection in this section from her article, "Rethinking the Mantra that Abortion Should be 'Safe, Legal and Rare,'" the realities of contraceptive failure rates demonstrate the fallacy of claiming that abortion can ever be truly "rare."

The high rates of abortion within communities of color have spurred some groups to renew the cries of "black genocide" that first appeared in the 1970s, with the spread of federally funded birth control, as discussed in the last section. In a notorious campaign oriented at the African American community, an anti-abortion foundation, in conjunction with some anti-abortion groups within that community, sponsored a series of billboards placed in Black neighborhoods across the country, claiming, for example, that "the most endangered place for a black child is in his mother's womb," and comparing abortion to slavery. This campaign proved to be very divisive and groups headed by women of color succeeded in a number of cities in having these billboards taken down. In a selection from an editorial he wrote with Carole Joffe, "Race, reproductive politics and reproductive health in the contemporary United States," Dr. Willie Parker, an African American obstetrician/gynecologist, reflects on why he repudiates the billboard campaigns and feels committed to providing abortions to women in his community. We return to this topic again in Section VI.

The abortion provider workforce—doctors, nurses, counselors, managers and others who work at abortion providing facilities—have faced challenges found nowhere else in U.S. medicine. Although the vast majority of the anti-abortion movement uses peaceful means, such as picketing, to express their opposition, there has always been a small, extremely violent wing of the movement. Since shortly after the *Roe* decision, providers have been subjected to thousands of incidents of vandalism and fire-bombings at their workplaces, and stalking and death threats at their homes and places of worship. Extremists have hounded the children of providers at their schools. Eight members of this community have been assassinated (four doctors, two clinic receptionists, a clinic security guard, and a volunteer escort) between 1993 and 2009. Since the passage of the FACE Act (Freedom of Access to Clinic Entrances) in 1992, which made it a federal crime to inhibit access to clinics, the large scale clinic "invasions" that were common in the 1980s have subsided, but nearly all abortion providing facilities experience some forms of harassment that often impacts patients as well as providers. For example, along with peaceful protesters, many clinics must contend with abortion opponents who engage in aggressive "sidewalk counseling," typically screaming through bullhorns at patients entering clinics, terrifying them in the process.

Providers also face a different kind of challenge from medical colleagues. Though most of the medical profession supports legal abortion, many are averse to the stigma and controversy that abortion provision so frequently brings. Therefore, relatively few hospitals have established abortion services, and many group practices in obstetrics and gynecology and primary care medicine (the two specialties which produce the most abortion providers) expressly forbid their members to become involved in abortion care. In the selection from her book, *Willing and Unable: Doctors' Constraints in Abortion Care*, sociologist Lori Freedman describes the difficulties doctors trained in abortion procedure have in finding suitable places to practice. The marginality of abortion in medical circles has led to the creation of a number of advocacy and educational groups among medical students and clinicians who support abortion rights, with Medical Students for Choice, the National Abortion Federation and the Abortion Care Network being among the most prominent.

So where does the abortion issue stand in American society, more than forty years after legalization? The views of the American people as a whole are best described as polarized, and in some ways contradictory. Polls consistently show a small majority of Americans supporting abortion in the first trimester of pregnancy, with support dropping off for abortions later in pregnancy. Yet, interestingly, later abortions—those done after 20 weeks of gestation—represent, as mentioned, only about 1% of all abortions performed in the United States. These procedures are often done for reasons of fetal anomalies, which often can only be discovered late in pregnancy—and these anomalies are among the reasons for an abortion that gain the highest approval from Americans.

Polls, of course, can only tell us so much about people's feelings on such a complex subject as abortion. Many Americans have more nuanced views. Individuals may object to abortions generally, but support friends or family when faced with an unintended pregnancy. As we have discussed, desires to control one's own family size are highly personal and symbolically meaningful. One place we can see this is in the complex reactions of men whose partners have abortions, which are discussed in the selection by sociologist Jennifer Reich from her article "Not ready to fill his father's shoes: A masculinist discourse of abortion."

In contemplating the future of abortion in American society, it is hard at this point to be optimistic that there will be less conflict, or that all women who want to access it will be able to. Even if *Roe* is not overturned—and that will depend on the outcome of presidential elections and the makeup of the Supreme Court, which continues to hear challenges to abortion regulation—the numerous state-imposed restrictions will likely lead to more clinics closing. The barriers to access—cost, lack of a provider, and the many regulations—will continue to affect women in rural communities and poor women more than wealthier women and those in urban areas. Although some, on both sides of the abortion divide, hope to see adoption as a "common ground" solution to this conflict, research suggests this is unlikely: very few American women are willing to make babies available for adoption—about 1%, according to a government study (U.S. Department of Health and Human Services 2005). Whatever the future course of reproductive politics in the United States, one thing is certain: in this country, as elsewhere, abortion will always be one necessary element in the spectrum of women's reproductive health services.

CHAPTER 5

A selection from *Doctors of Conscience*

The Struggle to Provide Abortion Before and After Roe v. Wade

Carole Joffe

The relationship of organized medicine and abortion in the United States has always been marked by strain and ambivalence. What emerges from an overview of this relationship, from the nineteenth century through the *Roe* era, is a portrait of a profession increasingly splintered. While dominant medical organizations have at times taken strong stands against legal abortion, and at other times been conspicuous for their silence, other segments of the profession – notably progressive factions within obstetrics and gynecology and public health – have found their colleagues' antiabortion stands to be untenable and have worked assiduously for acceptance of abortion within medical circles. The point of this [selection] is to convey the cross pressures about the abortion issue that individual physicians in practice and training . . . felt in the years leading up to *Roe*.

Until the middle of the nineteenth century, abortion was only minimally regulated in the United States. The prevailing standard was that abortions that occurred before "quickening" (which generally occurs between the fourth and sixth months of pregnancy) were not regulated at all, and there was minimal attempt to police abortions that occurred afterward. Abortion apparently was commonly practiced, and abortion services were freely advertised in newspapers, offered by practitioners of widely varying degrees of medical training and credentials. Much of the abortion activity of the period consisted

of women's attempts to give themselves abortions using various herbs and drugs, which they either purchased from an apothecary or ordered through the mail. The drive to criminalize abortion, which started in mid-century and peaked by the early 1880s, when all the states had enacted antiabortion statutes, stemmed from a variety of motivations, including societal anxiety about the declining birth rates of Anglo-Saxon women in comparison to those of newly arriving immigrants. The Roman Catholic Church and many Protestant clergy, which up to this point had been silent on the abortion question, also participated in the campaign.

But as recent scholarship has demonstrated, the most important force in the campaign to criminalize abortion were the physicians.[1] The American Medical Association (AMA), founded in 1847, made the abortion struggle one of its highest priorities. The argument of these physicians, in brief, was that abortion was both an immoral act and a medically dangerous one, given the incompetence of many of the practitioners then. The abortion campaign of the nineteenth century thus is most usefully understood as a key component of a larger battle then under way: the attempt of "regular" or "elite" physicians (that is, those who were university-trained) to attain professional dominance over the wide range of "irregular" medical practitioners-healers, homeopaths, and the like-who had flourished throughout the first part of the nineteenth century. Abortion was a particularly fruitful territory over which to stake claims of professional monopoly, both because so much of the irregulars' activity was apparently abortion-based and because much abortion work was being done by laypeople with no claims whatsoever to medical credentials.[2]

The objective of regular physicians was not simply to abolish all abortions, however. Rather, the AMA argument, which ultimately prevailed, was that physicians should control the terms under which "approved" abortions were performed-that is, "legal" abortions were now to be confined to those performed in a hospital, for "medically indicated" reasons.

As with virtually all social conflicts over reproductive matters,[3] the nineteenth century AMA campaign against abortion contained an explicit dimension of gender politics. The arguments used then by many of the antiabortion physicians prefigure in many instances the rhetoric of the antiabortion movement of the present time: abortion represents a threat to male authority and the "traditional role" of women; abortion is a symbol of uncontrolled female sexuality, and an "unnatural" act. Above all, the aborting woman is selfish and self-indulgent. As the authors of the AMA's Committee on Criminal Abortion wrote in 1871 about this woman:

> She becomes unmindful of the course marked out for her by Providence, she overlooks the duties imposed on her by the marriage contract. She yields to the pleasures – but shrinks from the pains and responsibilities of maternity; and, destitute of all delicacy and refinement, resigns herself, body and soul, into the hands of unscrupulous and wicked men. Let not the husband of such a wife flatter himself that he possesses her affection. Nor can she in turn ever merit even the respect of a virtuous husband. She sinks into old age like a withered tree, stripped of its foliage; with the stain of blood upon her soul, she dies without the hand of affection to smooth her pillow.[4]

One well-known result of the "century of criminalization" that resulted from the efforts of the AMA was a flourishing market in illegal abortion. In addition to the abortions women attempted to give themselves, illegal abortions were done by nurses and midwives, lay abortionists, and physicians. A study published by Frederick Taussig in 1936 estimated a half-million illegal abortions were taking place in the United States annually; the Kinsey Report in 1953 suggested that nine out of ten premarital pregnancies among its respondents were aborted, while over 20 percent of the married women in the sample reported having had an abortion while married.[5] Estimates of illegal abortion in the 1950s and in the years immediately leading up to *Roe* range as high as 1.2 million per year.

This highly erratic system of illegal abortion inevitably carried with it a high degree of medical risk and of patient exploitation. Anywhere from one thousand to five thousand women per year are estimated to have died from illegal abortions in the pre-*Roe* era and many thousands more were injured.[6] Moreover, the accounts of women who obtained illegal abortions in that era often describe intolerable situations:

> "More than the incredible filth of the place, and my fear on seeing it; more than the fear that I would surely become infected; more than the fact that the man was an alcoholic, and was drinking throughout the procedure – a whiskey glass in one hand, and a sharp instrument in the other; more than the indescribable pain, the most intense pain I have ever been subjected to; more than the humiliation of being told, 'You can take your pants down now, but you shoulda' – ha! ha! – kept them on before'; more than the degradation of being asked to perform a deviant sex act after he had aborted me . . . more than the hemorrhaging and the peritonitis and the hospitalization that followed; more even than the gut-twisting fear of being 'found out' and locked away for perhaps 20 years; more than all these things, those pitchy stairs

and that dank, dark hallway and the door at the end of it stay with me and chill my blood still."[7]

"Preparations for doing this were very complicated and anxiety-filled. I had to stand on a street corner in Washington, D.C., holding a copy of *Time* magazine. A woman was supposed to approach me and ask if I had a problem. . . . The next stage happened a week later. I was picked up by a car . . . by someone who took me to a place where there was a long black limousine waiting. . . . We left Washington, and the car stopped, and the driver said, 'And now, for fun, we're going to put these little goggles over your eyes'. . . . And then we arrived at a farmhouse. . . . There were guards standing around with guns. . . . I just remember being terrified."[8]

Reginald Berry, an African-American, was a resident in a large general hospital on the East Coast in the late 1960s. Though his hospital, which served a largely minority low-income population, had no shortage of tragedies associated with illegal abortion, for Berry, the most shattering incident of all was the death of one of his fellow residents from an abortion. The woman, whose abortion may have been self-administered, did not admit herself to the hospital until it was too late to save her. Berry and others in his group of residents were grief-stricken, not only because of the loss of a treasured colleague, but because of their conviction that they could have prevented her death had she only turned to them for an abortion. "She was a smart girl, one of the most brilliant girls I have ever known in my life. . . . She could have had any one of us to do it for her. . . . I would have done it."

But whether or not they experienced unwanted pregnancies in their own lives, all of the physicians interviewed for this study in the course of their medical training came face to face with the consequences of illegal abortion. For most, the first encounter with illegal abortion came during residency, in the hospital emergency room. Some encountered patients who claimed to be miscarrying – also known medically as "spontaneously aborting" – and the residents' role would be to complete the procedure with a D. & C. As the residents soon came to realize, however, many of these "miscarriages" in fact were abortions that had been initiated outside the hospital. In a minority of cases, moreover, patients would not have an abortion in process – spontaneous or otherwise-and would attempt to simulate such a condition to obtain a D. & C.[9] Alice Wilkins, while a resident in a county hospital in southern California in the 1940s, experienced such a case. "A patient was brought in to the hospital, just streaming with blood. So I went in to complete the procedure, and I became very suspicious when I saw no blood in the vagina at all. It later turned out that her boyfriend worked in a slaughterhouse and had brought home a lot of animal blood to make it appear she was hemorrhaging." Especially when they occurred at the beginning of the young physicians' residencies, such incidents introduced the often naive doctors to the desperate lengths to which women with unwanted pregnancies were willing to go.

But most patients who appeared at the hospital were in the process of genuine miscarriage, and residents became aware of the wide-often, to them, astonishing-range of methods then in use to induce abortion. Peters McPherson had been a resident at a large public hospital in New Orleans in the 1940s. "We had a woman who somehow or other managed to get a catheter [a hollow tube] into her cervix and poured turpentine down there and literally cooked the lining of her uterus. . . . It was like she got gasoline in there and lit it. We had to take her uterus out." Another common practice for women attempting abortions themselves was to use potassium permanganate tablets. These tablets, widely available over the counter, were placed by pregnant women directly in their vaginas to induce bleeding, and thus to convince medical authorities that they were miscarrying. But as Stan Oliver, who cared for a number of women who had used this method, recalled, "These tablets just eroded the vagina and the women hemorrhaged like hell; [the tablets] lacerated their cervixes." Other doctors reported seeing women in emergency rooms who had used not only the proverbial coat hanger, but also Lysol, broken Coke bottles, catheters, and a variety of other objects.[10] Horace Freeman, who had been a resident in Harlem in the mid–1940s, said, with a sigh, "I have taken everything out of the human vagina that one could imagine ever fitting in there."

Whether their attempted abortions were self-induced or performed by others, many of the abortion patients in emergency rooms were in serious, often life-threatening medical condition because of these attempts. Ken Gordon had been the chief obstetrical resident in the mid–1950s at a public hospital in a large East Coast city. One of Gordon's most powerful memories is of a twenty-two-year-old woman who came to the hospital in septic shock.

What happens there, the infection is so overwhelming, the bacteria produce toxins that lead to a collapse of the cardiovascular system. These patients have no blood pressure, no pulse – in some cases, there is absolutely nothing you can do to reverse the situation. We gave the girl blood, cortisone, hydrocortisone – nothing was working, she was not responsive. We finally figured the only chance we had was to do a hysterectomy. We took her to the O.R., but Anesthesia said, "We won't give her anesthesia, without getting blood pressure or a pulse. We can't monitor where we are, and so we might kill her with the anesthesia." So I had to do something I don't recommend to anybody, which is a hysterectomy under local anesthesia. We got the uterus out – I still have a picture of it in my teaching files – it was basically a bag of pus. We found a coiled up catheter in there. When we were all done, I was walking along beside her in the corridor – they were taking her back to her bed. And one of the tragedies of this septic shock is that people remain lucid until the end, and she was holding my hand, and saying, "Doctor, help me, I'm dying." And I knew she was, and I knew there was not a blessed

other thing we could do for her, and before she got to her bed, around midnight, she died, and I have been haunted by that girl ever since.

For those recipients of illegal abortions who were aborted by the D. & C. method, perforation of the uterus was a particular hazard. Describing that procedure, Gordon said, "I always used to tell medical students it was like being blindfolded and trying to scrape wet cotton balls out of a wet paper bag, and getting all the balls without tearing the bag. . . . The uterus was so soft, it was very easy to poke something through the uterus." Numerous respondents gave horrified accounts – in some cases nearly fifty years after the fact – of the gruesome aftereffects of botched D. & C.'s. Taylor Buckley, who was chief resident on an obstetrical ward in a big city general hospital in the early 1940s, recalled one such case.

A doctor brought her in. He called me and said, "Will you admit her on your service? She's got a strangulated hernia." I said, "Well, why don't you send her to general surgery?" He said, "I think it's in your field." She came in and she had a loop of bowel hanging out of her vagina wrapped in newspaper and that was the "strangulated hernia." And what he [the abortionist] did was perforate the uterus. He pulled out the bowel with his aborting instruments and he thought it was fetal bowel. She had literally over thirty inches of bowel hanging out of her vagina. And the poor woman should have died from several causes – bowel obstruction, septicemia, and everything else. I operated and did a bowel resection, pulled this damn dirty bowel out of the uterus and vagina, and she lived. But many others died.

A number of respondents in recollecting the consequences of failed abortion attempts they had witnessed pointed out the special intensity that often characterized the relationship between resident and patient in these situations. As Irving Goodman put it, "We were the ones that always had to take care of these patients. . . . We got to be fairly close to the patient because, when you are in your residency, you were really involved with her on a very frequent basis because you had to see her, literally, every two hours. The medical problems were so intense and prolonged that you got to know your patient. And you began to realize the desperation behind which the action was taken."

A corollary to the enormous compassion that many of these young doctors came to feel toward their patients was their enormous rage at the illegal abortionists who had done such inept work. In the case of the massive perforation cited above, for example, the abortionist was known to Taylor Buckley. "He was a referring doctor to our clinic, a general practitioner in our neighborhood. I can still see the bastard's dirty fingernails." Buckley went on to declaim against the "shady, incompetent" abortionists who preyed on vulnerable women, arguing, as many other respondents in this study did, that many were physicians who were simply too inept to succeed at a mainstream medical practice. To be sure, the anger this group felt toward illegal abortionists is complex; . . . many of these physicians themselves, including Buckley, sought providers of illegal abortion to whom they could refer patients. The challenge, obviously, was to find providers who were both medically competent and ethical.

For many respondents, their increasing recognition of the immense pressures illegal abortions were putting on already burdened hospitals further illustrated the irrationality of abortion restrictions. Numerous subjects recalled the "septic tanks," as residents referred to the special wards in big city hospitals that were reserved for those suffering septicemia (infection of the bloodstream) from illegal abortions. Louise Thomas, a resident in a New York City hospital in the late 1960s, spoke of the "Monday morning abortion lineup": "What would happen is that the women would get their paychecks on Friday, Friday night they would go to

their abortionist and spend their money on the abortion. Saturday they would start being sick and they would drift in on Sunday or Sunday evening, either hemorrhaging or septic, and they would be lined up outside the operating room to be cleaned out Monday morning. There was a lineup of women on stretchers outside the operating room, so you knew if you were an intern or resident, when you came in on Monday morning, that was the first thing you were going to do."

The most evocative description of the immense demands placed on public hospitals by illegal abortion came from Renee Giardino, who also had been a resident during the same period in a county hospital in the New York area.

There were two gyn wards. They were supposed to have thirty-two beds each, but they had to have beds all up and down the hallways. They were always full [because of illegal abortions]. They must have had one hundred and forty beds in those wards. . . . The residents would get duties of twenty-four-hour periods, and in that period, you'd get ten to twelve admissions. They walked into the emergency room bleeding. The first thing the doctor down there did was send them for an X-ray to see what was in their belly – to see if there were knitting needles, hooks, catheters up their belly. . . . Then when they got to the ward, the first thing you did besides examine them was to do a culture for gas gangrene. It was a standard we had, whether they had a fever or not, to take this culture, because if they had gas gangrene, you really had to take drastic measures, like surgery, heavy duty antibiotics, and all that kind of stuff. Until the suction curettage came through, the routine was that you accumulated all the women until two o'clock in the morning when all the major surgery was done, and the last gunshot wound had been cleared out of the emergency room – then the first-year residents dragged the patients down to the operating room and started doing the D. & C.'s at two o'clock in the morning. That's when the operating room was quiet. . . . There would be two or three operating rooms going at the same time.

Between 2:00 and 6:00 A.M. you could get a certain number of D. & C.'s done and clean up the women who weren't septic, scrape their uteruses and get them back upstairs so they could be discharged in a day or two. If they were hemorrhaging profusely, we didn't make them wait until 2:00 A.M. Were they treated badly? I don't know. Everybody at County got treated badly just because we were all so overworked, under stress, and overwhelmed. I don't think they were treated any more badly.

For many of the physicians active in the pre-*Roe* period, the presence of the police in hospital wards was yet another contributing factor to their growing sympathy for abortion patients. The amount of police interrogation of illegal abortion recipients varied widely. Thus, depending on where they were, and when, a number of respondents were routinely forced to deal with police themselves, or to see their patients subjected to cross-examination. Miriam Harkin recalls with remorse her collusion with police in the Midwest in the 1940s. "Well, when I was an intern we'd see these women coming in with illegal abortions. And what bothers me now is that at that stage of my career we were all so indoctrinated how terrible abortion is. If someone came in with an illegal, we would grill her, 'Who did it? Who did it?' We were treating her like a criminal, instead of treating her like a patient. And I participated in that too, and then I thought, 'Am I crazy?! What's going on here?!'"

Some residents learned to circumvent the police whenever feasible because of the strain this imposed on their patients. In New York state in the 1950s and 1960s, for example, physicians in hospitals were required to report "all illegal abortions or suspected illegal ones" to the district attorney. Like many others interviewed, Rosalind Greene, then a resident in a New York hospital, found this requirement untenable. "Women would never admit to having an induced abortion. But that was the law; you were supposed to inform them of anyone you suspected

of having an induced abortion. When we saw how they hassled the women, we never called them unless we thought the woman was going to die. If we thought the woman was going to die we knew there would be an investigation afterwards, and therefore we felt we had to call."

For some residents, the experience of seeing a very sick woman refuse to give in to pressure to reveal the name of her abortionist was a transforming experience. Ed Lever, a resident at University Hospital in the Midwest in 1960, recalled such a case, in which he was essentially ordered by his superiors to find out the name of the abortionist in question so a police report could be made.

This was a young woman with an acute septic abortion, and she had been to a criminal abortionist in Chicago. . . . She was in the process of dying of sepsis and I asked her if she would tell me who did this, and she said no, and she died. And that was the thing that sort of solidified it for me [commitment to legal abortion]. . . . It was starting to impress me that women felt that strongly about an unwanted pregnancy, that they would go to that length, knowing the risks involved – these people must have been awfully frightened and they must have felt very strongly about what they wanted to do. . . . I had always been taught in medical school that physicians were always to be the advocates of the patient and all of a sudden I was no longer an advocate, I was an adversary. That got me terribly upset.

To be sure, some physicians were torn between compassion for abortion patients who were being grilled by policemen and their own rage at incompetent abortionists whose victims would routinely show up in the hospital emergency room. Taylor Buckley, for example, recounted a case in which he thought notifying the police to be highly appropriate. "One case, I recall, where an abortionist infected a girl badly and he pulled an arm off of a fetus that was about twenty weeks, I guess. And she finally came to us with the most horrible story. She had been locked up in his office for forty-eight hours while he was trying to abort her. And he was guzzling bottles of whiskey while taking care of her. And she was in sad shape when she came in. . . . And she very definitely located the guy, he was not far away from the hospital. The cops went and brought him in, and in her feeble state she said, 'That's the man.' All of us had to go to court on that one. But she died and the guy was set free."

Dealing with senior physicians, and particularly with the hospital therapeutic abortion committees, was often another formative experience for the residents. In these hospital situations – working with senior colleagues who were in a position to affect the younger physicians' careers – some of these future abortion providers experienced firsthand the cruelty and hypocrisy that could characterize the medical establishment's response to abortion. Ed Lever had a particularly shattering encounter with his department head.

A young woman in her twenties, the mother of one child, and a severe diabetic, was admitted to the hospital and I was asked to see her in consultation. . . . She was critically ill, dying in fact from the complications of diabetes. She also was pregnant. I went to the head of my department, Dr. Morgan [not his real name]. . . . I presented the case to him and I said that I thought in order to prolong her life we better terminate the pregnancy and he said, "We don't do that." I said, "What do you mean? We would be doing it to save her life, and there are such statutes on the book," and I went to the library and got the statute and showed it to him, and he said, "We don't do abortions," and she died. And this so upset me. She was going to die eventually but her life could have been prolonged.

Tania Meadows also recalled the callousness of the abortion committee in her West Coast hospital in the early 1960s. "Well, there was a woman who wanted an abortion who was very emotionally disturbed. She was married with one child who had some very severe congenital malformation that

was not considered hereditary. They were both on welfare, she and her husband. They were utterly down and out. They were desperate and she was applying for an abortion and was turned down. She was turned down because she was married, and it was felt – I can't remember the exact words the committee used – that a married woman should have her children, and since they had one, another one would 'complete their family.'" The unfairness that Meadows confronted in this abortion committee was profoundly upsetting to her, and, as she later realized, was instrumental in leading her to a "feminist" analysis of the abortion issue. "It was the first time I had really come up against discrimination of the kind that was incomprehensible to me. . . . The people on these committees were really at that time and at that place viewing women as reproductive machines."

The hospital abortion committees often operated on a quota basis, and the residents and young practitioners came to realize that their clinic patients were competing for precious slots with the private patients of their superiors. Virtually everyone interviewed for this study commented on the inherent unfairness of abortion provision before legalization. Thomas Darrow's observation about the small Southern hospital in which he was a resident in the 1960s was typical. "It all depended on who you were. As long as you were the banker's daughter, the doctor's daughter, the golf buddy's daughter, it was always taken care of." Morris Fischer recounts the experience, common to many of those interviewed, of being approached by an antiabortion colleague whose daughter needed an abortion. "I said to him, 'I'll do the abortion and now your daughter will be fresh as a daisy, clean as a pin, and you are relieved of a terrible tragedy that otherwise would have occurred in your family. How do you reconcile that with what you do in the Committee meetings, where you forbid abortions for other patients?' He answered, 'I have a different code for my family.'" Yet another hypocritical twist came with some residents' realization that some of the illegal abortions (presented as miscarriages) that they were called upon to complete had been induced by the attending physicians who were their supervisors—attendings who had, in many cases, shown little sympathy for the clinic patients admitted with incomplete abortions. Horace Freeman recalled that a certain portion of his abortion cases during his residency were "abortions that were started around the corner in the offices of my own attending. . . . It was just a service to the patient, plus a fee."[11]

Quite obviously, there are many factors that led this group of physicians to commit to some degree of abortion activity before abortion was legalized, and to remain committed after *Roe*. Some spoke quite movingly of early childhood memories of a beloved relative or family friend dying of an illegal abortion; others . . . spoke of their own traumatic searches for a safe abortion. Some attributed their abortion involvement to longstanding family traditions of participation in progressive social movements. Some had life changing experiences in the developing world. Some respondents—especially, though not exclusively, female—either explicitly or implicitly used the language of feminism to explain their initial pull toward abortion work.

But none of these factors alone . . . accounts for these physicians' eventual commitment to abortion work. The one experience all these physicians did share, however, was having faced the medical results of illegal abortion. Eugene Fox, describing his reaction to a patient's death early in his residency, captured the defining experience of all these "conscience" physicians: "I could not understand why she died. There were a lot of things I did not know at the time. One of the things I didn't know was the lengths to which some women would go to get an abortion."

NOTES

1. This following discussion of the history of abortion, and particularly the role of physicians in the antiabortion campaign of the nineteenth century, draws on Kristin Luker, *Abortion and the Politics of Motherhood* (Berkeley: University of California Press, 1984); James Mohr, *Abortion in America: The Origins and Evolution of National Policy, 1800–1900* (New York: Oxford University Press, 1978); Rosalind P. Petchesky, *Abortion and Women's Choice*, rev. ed. (Boston; Northeastern University Press, 1990); and Carroll Smith-Rosenberg, "The Abortion Movement and the AMA, 1850–1880," in her Disorderly Conduct: Visions of Gender in Victorian America (New York: Knopf, 1985), pp. 217–44.

2. As Smith-Rosenberg writes in "The Abortion Movement and the AMA," "Abortion-related ads provided a lucrative source of income for the new urban newspapers. By the 1840s, ads for abortafacients filled their pages . . . Physicians, midwives, and many others who specialized in gynecological ailments, whatever their formal training, set up special clinics, advertised their fee scales, solicited customers, printed cards, even sent business agents out into agrarian areas and smaller towns to solicit business . . . By mid-century, abortion had become a big business" (pp. 225–26).

3. Two of the strongest statements within contemporary feminist scholarship of this connection between reproductive conflicts and gender politics are Petchesky, *Abortion and Woman's Choice*, and Linda Gordon, *Woman's Body, Woman's Right* (Baltimore; Penguin, 1977). As Petchesky writes with respect to abortion conflict in our own time, *"abortion is the fulcrum of a much broader ideological struggle in which the very meanings of the family, the state, motherhood, and young women's sexuality are contested"* (p. xi, emphasis hers).

4. Quoted in Smith-Rosenberg, "The Abortion Movement and the AMA," pp. 256–57. For a contemporary antiabortion statement, which presents the abortion-seeking woman in a similar light, see Connaught Marshner, *The New Traditional Woman* (Washington, D.C.: Free Congress Research and Educational Foundation, 1982).

5. Mohr, *Abortion in America*, p. 6

6. As with estimates of the frequency of illegal abortion, estimates of death from illegal abortion have been highly contested, with the antiabortion movement, in particular, accusing the pro-choice movement of inflating the figures. Numerous commentators have pointed out how difficult it is to make such an estimate, given the likelihood that many abortion deaths were listed as something else, in order to mask the shame associated with illegal abortion. Writing in 1948. Christopher Tietze suggested a figure of approximately one thousand abortions per year, while a well-regarded study in 1962 offered the estimate of five thousand deaths per year. Christopher Tietze, "Abortion as a Cause of Death," *Journal of Public Health* 38 (1948): 1434–41; Zad

Leavy and Jerome M. Kummer, "Criminal Abortion: Human Hardship and Unyielding Laws," *Southern California Law Review* 35 (1962): 126.

7. National Abortion Rights Action League, *Facing a Future Without Choice: A Report on Reproductive Liberty in America* (Washington, D.C.: National Abortion Rights Action League, 1992), p. 16.

8. Ellen Messer and Kathryn May, *Back Rooms: Voices from the Illegal Abortion Era* (New York: St. Martin's Press), pp. 148–49.

9. Maginnis, P. and Phelan, L. 1969. *Abortion Handbook for Responsible Women*. San Francisco: Contact Books.

10. For a review of the most common techniques of illegal abortion – both self-induced and performed by others – see Richard Schwartz, *Septic Abortion* (Philadelphia: J.B. Lippincott, 1968); Gordon Horobin, ed. *Experience with Abortion* (New York: Cambridge University Press, 1973), and Potts et al., *Abortion*, pp. 253–76. For an account of the medical challenges that were involved in treating certain types of illegal abortions, see Michael Burnhill, "Treatment of Women Who Have Undergone Chemically Induced Abortions," *Journal of Reproductive Medicine* 30 (1985): 610–14.

11. Bernard Nathanson, Aborting America (Garden City, N.Y.: Doubleday, 1979), pp. 19–22.

CHAPTER 6

Practice Constraints and the Institutionalized Buck-Passing of Abortion Care

Lori Freedman

I had a lot [of residents] that were just 100 percent pro-choice who have never done an abortion in private practice . . . In a conservative state like [this one in the Midwest], if you get the reputation that your group performs abortions, all of a sudden the other groups have a marked increase in their patient load.

> Dr. Davis Chasey, retired founder and director of a residency abortion clinic

For decades, abortion rights activists and scholars have argued that abortion should be integrated into mainstream medical care and hence treated as a legitimate part of full-spectrum reproductive health services (Lindheim 1979; Rose 2007). In theory, getting abortion services out of the clinics and into doctors' offices would reduce stigma and make abortion care less marginalized and vulnerable to violent attack by antiabortionists. To many in the pro-choice movement, this seems a straightforward solution requiring only the politicization of physicians and

their commitment to continuing to provide abortions after residency. However, this strategy fails to take into account the substantial decline in physician autonomy since the dominance of managed care. Although numerous physicians have become politically active around abortion during medical school and residency,[1] the commitment appears to be too costly for most physicians to sustain. The *willing* physicians in this chapter explain how integrating abortion into mainstream medical services is quite difficult. Mainstream medicine passed the buck on abortion long ago, and many physicians find it both regrettable and easier that way.

ABORTION STIGMA, PROFESSIONAL CIVILITY, AND CONSERVATIVE COMMUNITY PRESSURE

In many parts of the country, both urban and rural, the legacy of the pre-*Roe* "abortionist" is alive and well. The stigma associated with this label is pervasive yet unusual as far as stigmas go in that this one is associated with an otherwise high-status individual: a physician. Regardless, the label is "deeply discrediting," in the words of Erving Goffman, from his seminal introduction of stigma to the field of sociology (Goffman 1963: 3). The word *abortionist* confers the imagery of a physician who does little else besides abortion and may be not skillful enough to do well in general or mainstream medicine. It also connotes bad intentions. In Carole Joffe's study of doctors who provided abortion before legalization, one physician remembered that "'abortionist' was such a dirty word, it was just one step above pervert, or child abuser . . . to be called an abortionist in the 1950s, you were the scum of the earth" (Joffe 1995: 76). Also, by the mere association with abortion, especially at that time, doctors were seen as condoning a "sexually immoral" lifestyle. Remarking on how perceptions of physicians providing illegal abortions (and those parading as physicians) affected future generations of abortion providers, Joffe writes, "Abortion practices in the pre-*Roe* period created a complex legacy for physicians active after *Roe,* given the enduring images of inept 'quacks' and 'butchers' and the associations with criminality and greed" (Joffe 1995: 52). After legalization, some of Joffe's abortion providers found that their status increased little and that the label abortionist stuck in certain medical environments, regardless of the legal legitimization. One physician objected, "I'm no more an abortionist than I am an obstetrician or a hysterectomist or any other procedure that I do" (Joffe 1995: 153).

In a review of the sociological literature on stigma since Goffman (1963), Bruce Link and Jo Phelan (2001) found four principles consistent among stigmas. These can be applied neatly to abortion providers. First, Link and Phelan argue that stigmas are widely used to distinguish and label difference—as in *abortionist* rather than *ob-gyn or physician.* Second, the label is associated with a negative

attribute, in this case, a morally deficient or technically incompetent physician. Third, the stigma allows the user to separate "us" from "them," much as the "quack" is singled out from legitimate physicians. Finally, status loss and discrimination result—exactly what was feared by several physicians in my study and widely experienced decades ago by Joffe's abortion-providing physicians.

Many physicians I spoke with, like Joffe's physician, regard the idea of being labeled for one of the many surgical procedures they perform as absurd. For those in small-town private practices, however, the prospect of being identified with abortion in this way is profoundly threatening. For example, Dr. Bill Spellman in the Midwest said: "I didn't plan on doing abortions in my private practice for a lot of reasons. It's too small of a community to really do *that* . . . it's tough if you do abortions electively in your own private practice because then you get labeled as an *abortionist,* which, a guy [here], he got labeled like that." Similarly, regarding his small southern town, Dr. Kevin Dougherty remarked, "There's a history in the city that I'm in. There was a practice that did offer abortions and were *run out of town.*"

The subjects at the center of this controversy, physicians, are normally high-status individuals; they have a long way to fall from grace. Additionally, the individuals in my study were often new parents, new homeowners, new members of a practice—all, of course, because I selected a group that had graduated only five to ten years before from their residency programs. Therefore, many saw themselves as relatively vulnerable—an unlikely characterization of physicians. These doctors had student loans and mortgages to repay; at the same time, they needed to prove themselves as worthy members of their private-practice groups.

Dr. John Brill wanted to continue providing abortions in his private practice, as he had done in his first job after residency, but after moving to a small, conservative town in the West to be closer to family, he no longer saw it as a possibility. "It's a small town and none of the ob-gyns perform abortions," he said. "There is one abortion clinic in town. And the provider who comes up from [the city two and a half hours away] to perform abortions is *vilified* within the community. To perform abortions in this community means being '*evil.*'"

For Dr. Brill, it was as if he had entered a new world. He recently had come from a western urban area where he was, among other things, an abortion provider. Yet his move placed him in a cultural and political context where he quickly decided he must hide that identity. With the aforementioned commuting provider planning to retire soon, Dr. Brill was contacted by the local abortion clinic in its search for a new physician director: "They called me up and said, 'Hey, we heard that you might be the person.' I was like, 'Well, you know, that's real nice but I don't think I can be the guy running the [abortion] clinic.' . . . I didn't turn them down. I said I'd be happy to have a dialogue, but I don't think I can be, you know, 'Doctor Abortion Provider,' the only one in this town." This was not a simple decision for Dr. Brill. Politically, he is very sympathetic to abortion rights; however, he is deeply concerned that any connection to abortion would undermine him professionally:

It's frustrating because it's a service that is desperately needed, and it would completely destroy my ability to practice medicine in town. And that's a difficult position to be in. Do I sacrifice myself for the greater good? But then I can't take care of my wife and kids? I don't like thinking about it too much. It sort of burns me when I have to think about it too much . . . It's a real sort of strong Christian community, so a lot of the family practice docs in town, they're strong Christians. And that's your referral base. And so to be labeled as the evil abortion doctor is a great way to make no friends amongst the ob-gyns and to have no family practice docs refer patients to you.

Dr. Brill identified professional failure, and the economic effect of that on his family, as a major risk to providing abortions. He worried that other physicians would not refer their patients to him and his practice would be, in a sense, boycotted by the community. For Dr. Brill and doctors similarly situated, the local stigma of abortion is both palpable and personal.

Some physicians had the unpleasant experience of being screened by patients with strong antiabortion views, further reiterating the sentiment that abortion practice is risky for their reputations in their communities and the financial success of the medical groups with which they practice. Five of the six doctors who shared these stories practice in the Midwest in cities of varying sizes. One such physician, Dr. Stacy Kern, had an uncomfortable encounter with a couple who were looking for a physician who, like themselves, would be opposed to abortion:

I had a patient who came in for obstetrical care with me as a new ob patient . . . And we had about a forty-minute new [prenatal] visit, which is a long time, because we had a lot of stuff to talk about. And at the very end of the discussion her husband said to me, "Well, we just feel so much more comfortable with you because we've had some experiences where practitioners think it's okay to, like, do abortions or something. And I just don't see how anybody could ever believe that—you know, to deliver babies and then to kill babies and to be okay with that" . . .

Well, first I thought, oh dear . . . And I just sort of looked [at them] and I said, "Well, you're talking to one of those people" . . . Oh my God, the room was just like—there's this deep inhalation . . . I said, "Listen, I'm sorry but, you know, if somebody needs a safe procedure, I feel that you have to offer them a safe procedure . . . I'll step out and you two can talk and I'll be back in a few minutes." And I stepped out and actually had a family practice resident shadowing me that day. When we got through, her eyes were [bulging wide]. And I said, "I don't think she'll be staying with me" . . . Well, about five minutes later I went back, and they're all packed up [and said,] "We'll be going elsewhere."

While disconcerting to Dr. Kern, the interaction ended peacefully. Dr. Bill Spellman was not so lucky, and in his case, the patient was initially deceptive, which eroded his confidence in counseling patients about pregnancy options for the future:

> I got burnt on it once so I'm always leery. A woman came in and started talking to me directly about how she wanted to get a termination. She brought it up, she wanted to talk about it, and so I said, "Well, there's this and this and this available out there." And she says, "Would there be any way that you could perform this? I really think that we have a link here and I really want you to do this." And I felt very bad for her because of the whole story behind it. And I said, "Well," I said, "I've done these before." And right then she stood up and she said, "I knew it. I knew it all along. You're a baby killer," and walked out of the room . . . She wrote this long letter to the people who ran the office that I worked for basically telling them just what an absolute scumbag I was and all these other things. So since that point— you know, burned once, I'm not going to do it again—when somebody comes in and wants to talk about [abortion], I talk to them a little bit, I have them leave, and I have them come back for another visit.

Dr. Spellman now gives patients with unwanted pregnancies reading materials about pregnancy options from ACOG, a presumably uncontroversial source of information, and talks to them at the second visit about whether they want a referral to an abortion clinic. He feels this has successfully weeded out one or two similar patients, but he credits the professional embarrassment and personal discomfort of this interaction with making him even more sensitive to the stigma and contention surrounding abortion in his community.

Physicians practicing in small and mid-sized towns worried significantly about the consequences of involvement with abortion. Most of these doctors practiced in groups where policies on abortion are made for the practice as a whole. Dr. Spellman thinks it would be challenging to persuade the partners of his midwestern group practice to provide abortions in their town even if they did want to:

> If you start doing elective terminations in your practice, then the community will just kind of view you as that one thing. The right-to-life people are really, really, really organized in this and they're very, very good about getting that word out within seconds about somebody. And, you know, it's—you hate to say it—you practice in the real world . . . I think if we were in LA or in Phoenix, Arizona, or something like that, I don't think the partners would give a crap. Because it's such a big place that, you know, who cares if two or three thousand or a hundred thousand people believe that you're an abortion clinic when there's still 2.4 million more people out there? Here we only have a couple hundred thousand people . . . They guard their reputation a lot in these communities. It's one of the things that really makes a practice.

Essentially, he argues that performing abortions means facing professional sanctions such as losing patients and losing business, that the antiabortion activists will bring so much attention to the matter that the entire ob-gyn practice will be viewed as "an abortion clinic." Whether practicing solo or in a group, doctors in relatively small or politically conservative communities felt a stigma that made abortion practice seem incompatible with general medical practice.

Most of the physicians in my study feared the social and professional consequences of performing abortions and maintained collegiality and civility by not performing them after residency. Those I spoke with who performed abortions regularly, and not exclusively for genetic or medical indications, lived in areas around the country that were less politically conservative and/

or worked in relatively protective university settings where multiple layers of bureaucracy as well as the way that the clinic is physically embedded within a larger medical facility made them less visible to the outside world. Indeed, almost all of the physicians I interviewed trained in such protective university environments. Graduation was a rude awakening for some.

THREATS, INTIMIDATION, AND VIOLENCE

Not all professional sanctions were feared, anticipated, and then avoided. Some physicians reported having direct confrontations with colleagues regarding abortion. An important characteristic of most stigmas is that their subjects must agree to the "rules"; that is, they must recognize that they are stigmatized, and if they do not, there will be consequences for such "deviance" (Goffman 1963).[2] Those with power over the stigmatized may impose the consequences in the form of direct discrimination (Link and Phelan 2001). Physicians encounter various types of intimidation and violence when they provide (or consider providing) abortions. These can be viewed as a type of such stigma enforcement. Several physicians I spoke with who wanted to continue performing abortions met with uncomfortable interactions out in the "real world." Indeed, these interactions were uncomfortable enough to keep them "in line" and to significantly shape their practice patterns.

Many physicians found out at job interviews how abortion would be viewed in the private practices they hoped to join. Some declined job offers because of abortion prohibitions, and some did not. Still others had little choice in the matter given the limited job opportunities in their area. For example, Dr. Kern was tied to the area because of her husband's work. She took a job in one of the two existing ob-gyn practices in her midsized city in the Midwest, and by the time I met her she had worked in both. Speaking of the second group practice, she said: "In this group, you interview with all of the different physicians that are partners. And the one partner who's very senior in the group and very pro-life, basically his only job is to sit with you and just tell you . . . 'If you join this group you will not be performing abortion procedures. And if that's a problem for you, then you will work elsewhere. Okay?'"

Dr. Kern's experience of being told by her superior that abortion would not be tolerated in his practice was not unique. Dr. Kevin Dougherty's first job was in a small town in the South. He was unsure of his personal intent to provide abortions, but the group let him know quickly that it was not an option. He was not surprised by this, however. He explained to me why he felt it was important to respect a medical group's desire to avoid abortion:

My feeling about it is that everybody is pinned down by their business climate—I mean, my business climate right now is absolutely antagonistic towards even the idea of *this* . . . In private practice, you certainly don't want—if you get a sense that *that* is not going to go over well, you don't push *that* . . . it's not just your own practice [that] is in jeopardy, but you're also putting your partners' practice in jeopardy by being associated with them . . . They knew that I had done *that* in the past. They made clear undertones about the fact that, "You know, we're not going to be doing *that*."—"Okay, got it!" And I don't feel strongly enough about it to, to say, "I'm going to do it and go out and"—You know, there's only so much up-starting that you can do, especially without having a lot of your own patients yet. So I have remained fairly quiescent about it.

Dr. Dougherty did not want to "make waves" so early in his career. In addition to maintaining professional civility with his private-practice partners, he worried, as Dr. Brill did, about having enough patients and losing business by being associated with abortion. Because medicine has remained largely privatized in the United States, physician practices are subject to market forces like all other businesses.

Dr. Spellman, like Dr. Kern, had limited job choices because he wanted to stay close to family. He took a job in a private practice in a midwestern urban area where he was told point-blank not to do abortions and was even threatened:

> The guy that I replaced out there . . . I don't know how old he was. He looked ancient to me when I first met him. And I took over his patient practice. So they'd already interviewed me and accepted me for the job and I already signed the contract. So I went out there and-I don't even know why I was riding around with this guy—but he took me to lunch and . . . we get back to his office and I was supposed to follow him in on a few patients for—I don't even know the real reasons. But he leaned across the desk and said, *"If I ever find out you did elective abortion any time in your professional life, you'll never practice medicine in* [this state] *again. Do you understand that?"* And I went, "Okay." And he goes, "As far as I know, you've never done an abortion, have you?" And I said, "Yeah, a lot for genetic reasons and lots of other things." He said, "From this point on out—I'll take that as you saying no—from this point on." And I'm thinking to myself, you're leaving this practice. You have nothing to do with it. You don't even own it. So it kind of rankled me a little bit that he came across that strong.

This was a very disturbing way for Dr. Spellman to start his career. However, as he suspected, the older physician had less power to manage his future practice than he threatened during that conversation:

> I thought, "Yep, that just confirms it. I just can't do abortion electively in clinic." But I said to my partners, "But there's a need for people that have (A) genetic problems, and (B) have, you know, [fetal] demises. And if you don't have somebody to do these [abortions], what are they going to do? [Are] you going to

do hysterectomies on these people?" . . . And they're like, "Well, we'll figure out a way." So one thing led to another, and boom, boom, boom, I got referrals, usually one or two a week, of [abortions] to do over that time of people with either [fetal] demises or with severe genetic anomalies or other anomalies.

Such a turn of the tides is not an uncommon abortion story. Many physicians want both distance from abortion and someone skilled to send their patients to; this is part of what Joffe considers to be the deep ambivalence around abortion in American medicine (Joffe 1995). While many physician organizations publicly take an antiabortion stance, individual physicians often empathize with the predicaments of their patients, especially when they involve fetal anomalies. Dr. Spellman's colleagues had to refer their patients to him because they had not been trained or had not maintained their surgical skills in second-trimester abortions and could not perform these procedures safely even if they had wanted to. His partners were grateful that they had a conveniently located physician to, in a certain sense, do their "dirty work," a term used sociologically by Everett Hughes to describe work that is perceived as unsavory and/or degrading, but necessary (Hughes and Coser 1994). That is, although Dr. Spellman's partners may have been unwilling or unable to participate in abortion training and care, on some level they understood certain abortions as necessary for their patients. The relatively tolerant practice culture was short-lived, however. Dr. Spellman continued:

> And then as time went on, another partner came to the group who was super conservative as far as his thoughts about most issues in the world. And he wanted me to sign a contract with the group that said I would not do terminations on certain genetic problems like [Down syndrome] and things like that, because they weren't fatal anomalies . . . he was just him being him trying to control things, which is what he did with

all aspects of the practice, not just that. I would never sign anything like that as long as I live.

Dr. Spellman resisted control by both his predecessor and his colleague, to an extent. But as he mentioned, he quickly gave up any expectation of doing elective abortions because of the strength of the stigma and the antiabortion sentiment in his region.

Midwesterners and small-town physicians were not the only ones to feel personally threatened by the stigma and controversy of abortion in their practices. Dr. Qui Qan Wong took a job in what she described as a highly Catholic northeastern suburb near her residency after graduation. She was surprised how her medical practices were policed by staff members at the hospital, which she described as a public and not religiously affiliated institution. She first learned that abortion would not be acceptable in her practice when she tried to schedule a second-trimester abortion for a fatal genetic indication. Dr. Wong explained that since she did not grow up assimilated into American culture, she was quite surprised to discover that abortion was such a polarizing issue:

You know, maybe it's my stupidity. I didn't realize there was that much, you know, anti-abortion feeling out there. I guess in residency, you just live [in the hospital], so you don't get as much outside. It wasn't until I started to be on my own, I started to feel this sort of real antiabortion environment that we have . . .

One [case] that really wasn't an abortion but it was for medical reasons . . . and I felt that it should be done, you know, because I had a relationship with the patient, [but I] was told, "No way"—and had the nurses come and say, "You are not doing that" . . . It was a fetal anomaly . . . that baby wasn't going to survive no matter what. And even that, they won't let me do it . . . I called . . . and [the surgery scheduler] said, "Wait a minute," and then they got somebody else on the phone with me and said, "You can't do it."

An abortion for a fetal anomaly, especially a fatal one, was not considered a "moral"

issue in Dr. Wong's residency program. As her words convey, it was considered medically necessary. But she soon learned that no abortion was considered necessary in her new hospital culture, and although she had preferred to take care of her patient herself, she ultimately referred the patient to her residency abortion service.

Dr. Wong was shocked to discover that even pharmacists were involved in her practices around abortion,[3] through a very threatening conflict over a drug that is associated with medication abortion but widely used for other conditions as well:

I have pharmacists who call me who refuse to give the medication Cytotec.[4] They said, "That's abortion medication, I'm not going to give it," even though the time that he called me about wasn't for abortion. It was for a [different gynecological] issue. He said, "I know that's abortion," and I was like, "Well, that's not what I'm using it for," and he said, "I'm not going to give it." And he started yelling at me on the phone and said, "I'm going to put your name on the Web!"

He was threatening me . . . He said, "Well, I refuse and I'm tearing up the prescription so she's not going to get it anywhere else." So the poor lady had to come back and get the prescription . . . I was just like, my God! But there are a few of them around [this northeastern urban area]—pharmacists—who, literally, will not fill Cytotec.

By threatening Dr. Wong with posting her name on the Web, the pharmacist threatened to publicly name her as an abortion provider to potentially violent antiabortion activists. This was not a threat she took lightly. An abortion provider had been shot at the local abortion clinic only a few years before.

Fear of violence was not nearly as prevalent in the physician interviews as I would have thought, but it was noticeably more salient for those who had practiced near protesters or near victims of violence. Dr. Tiffany Howell had significant exposure to protesters when she moonlighted for an abortion clinic in a western urban area. By the time of the interview, she had moved to a conservative midsized city in the Midwest.

> The antiabortion forces are definitely real and they're definitely out there and can make your life hard. In [the city were I worked before,] they picketed [the abortion clinic] every day, and the doctors that had been working there for years and years and years had people at their house all the time, picketing at their house—one of them had sent flyers to all his neighbors talking about how he was an abortionist and all this kind of—so they make it difficult for you . . .
>
> I didn't go [work at the clinic] as often [as the other doctors]—but [the protesters] eventually figured out who I was and they found out what my name was . . . they would yell your name out as you're walking into the clinic and stuff and take your picture. And it's intimidating. It's intimidating as a provider. And when you go to [work there], they ask you if you want to have a bulletproof vest to wear and you're like, "Oh, dear" . . . But it's true, people have been shot who are abortion providers. It has happened . . . I 'd like to do abortions, but I don't know if I'll ever do them here.

In recent decades, the label abortionist has done more than signify stigma and defamation that could result in professional failure. It has been used to identify targets of violence. And those who have not accepted the terms of the stigma (that they should not provide abortions, and if they do it should be hidden) have at times experienced violence in the form of clinic or physician attack. Stigma and violence as well as economic and professional failure are what physicians fear. These are the perceived and real risks of involvement with abortion care and the reasons why many individuals, group practices, and large institutions distance themselves from abortion practice.

NO-ABORTION POLICIES

Physicians in all areas of the country referred to *no-abortion policies* in their private-practice groups, HMOs, and hospitals,

although they rarely used those words. Unlike their approach to any other medical procedure, and for reasons unrelated to skill level or technological resources, many medical groups make a concerted effort to take a stand on whether they provide abortions or not. Sometimes the reasoning for this appeared individual and arbitrary, as in the cases above where a superior had antiabortion sentiments and was able to control the practice of employed physicians. But the widespread existence of these prohibitions betrays their structural nature as a response to the stigma and contention surrounding abortion and results in the institutionalized buck-passing of abortion care.

Only one physician I spoke with, Dr. Brill, is in private practice alone. Consistent with the major shifts in medicine toward managed care during the past few decades (Freidson 1970; Hafferty and Light 1995; Hartley 2002; Haug 1988; Madison and Konrad 1988), the rest of the physicians practice in large private-practice groups, HMOs, the military, or academic institutions. Physician autonomy over decisions about abortion practice is severely curtailed by this restructuring. Physicians found out both informally and formally about the abortion policies in their practice settings. Abortion "policies" were conveyed in a variety of ways beyond threats and intimidation. Such policies were observed in order to avoid conflict. The protocols determining how abortions get done and who does them differed widely, but the tendency to separate them from other aspects of ob-gyn care, and for coworkers to police those boundaries, was similar in cities around the country, both big and small.

NOTES

1. The organization Medical Students for Choice has proliferated and become active in many medical schools, and private sources of funding have enabled residency programs to improve abortion training and the teaching curriculum, which includes a politicizing component.

2. Goffman, who wrote briefly about several types of deviants who resisted their prescribed stigma, might have grouped abortion providers among "social deviants." He writes: "those who come together into a sub-community or milieu may be called *social deviants*, and their corporate life a deviant community . . . prostitutes, gypsies, carnival workers, hobos, winos, show people" (Goffman 1963: 143). Abortion providers have been their own conferences and national organizations to help protect physicians from harm and support their professional endeavors. Specialized organizations may be typical for particular subspecialties in medicine, but not for particular surgical procedures. This is a distinction of social, not medical, significance.

3. Pharmacists have been very vocal in a national "right of refusal," or "conscience clause," movement that lobbies for the right for a variety of practitioners to refuse to provide any treatment or medication to which they object, including contra-

ceptive pills, emergency contraception, and in this case, misoprostol.

4. Cytotec, known by the generic name misoprostol, is approved by the Food and Drug Administration for use with ulcers, but it is universally used off-label for obstetrical care, namely, to induce uterine contractions and soften the cervix during childbirth. It is also used to facilitate medication abortion, in which case it is typically paired with mifepristone (RU-486 or the "French abortion pill") or methotrexate, a common cancer drug that works similarly to mifepristone and is more readily accessible to physicians but that has more uncomfortable side effects. Antiabortion legislation has created prohibitive amounts of paperwork requirements for mifepristone (Joffe and Weitz 2003). Cytotec/misoprostol can, however, cause an abortion if used by itself in the right doses. It is commonly used for this purpose throughout the world, especially in many Latin American countries, where it is sold in pharmacies over the counter.

CHAPTER 7

Rethinking the Mantra that Abortion Should be "Safe, Legal, and Rare"

Tracy A. Weitz

Abortion is the most contested social issue of our time.[1] Recent events, including the assassination of Dr. George Tiller, an abortion provider in Kansas, and the fight over health care reform, demonstrate the intense polarization of the ongoing debate over abortion.[2] This article examines how the desire to find an end to the abortion wars led to the widespread adoption of the rhetorical mantra that abortion should be "safe, legal, and rare." By tracing the history and consequences of this paradoxical position, this paper provides insight into the intractability of the abortion conflict in the United States. The paper begins with a review of the transition from libratory to consolatory language regarding the role of abortion in society. I then argue that women's health and well-being are harmed when desires to

resolve the social conflict over abortion are prioritized over women's need for abortion. Additionally, the adoption of the mantra that abortion should be rare increases the stigma associated with abortion. I demonstrate how focusing on making abortion rare reduces access to care and sets up unrealistic goals related to the number of abortions that should occur in the United States.

Analysis of fertility patterns in the United States find that before ending her reproductive years, one in three women will have an abortion.[3] Perhaps the most powerful argument there is for the legality and morality of abortion is its commonness. An alternative approach to that of wanting abortion to be rare would recognize the importance of abortion access for women and the meaning of abortion for women's equality. This new approach does not shy away from the difficult conversations about abortion but rather accepts abortion as a highly contentious issue in modern society and one for which there is no simple solution.

FROM LIBRARY TO CONCILIATORY LANGUAGE REGARDING THE ROLE OF ABORTION IN SOCIETY

Within the feminist movement, the *Roe v. Wade* decision [410 U.S. 113, 1973] recognizing the constitutional right to abortion was greeted with libratory language about women's freedom and right to bodily autonomy. Not only was abortion necessary to save women's lives, the argument forwarded by physician advocates for legal abortion, it was central to women's place in society. Abortion was articulated as a way for women to shape the destiny and course of their lives and the right to abortion became synonymous with notions of modern feminism. "Abortion on demand" and "abortion without apology" were two slogans adopted by radical feminists to express an unqualified support for both the right to abortion and the use of abortion.[4]

The 1970s were also a time of growing strength of the anti-abortion movement. Single issue politics expanded through the formation of political action committees (PACs) with the sole purpose of electing candidates who were opposed to abortion rights. Efforts culminated in the 1980 election of Ronald Reagan as a "pro-life" president who would use the executive branch to forward an anti-abortion agenda.[5]

In the 1980s, the nature of the fight over abortion shifted dramatically from a struggle to change the legal status of abortion to a larger culture war over the social meaning of abortion. As articulated by abortion rights opponents, the goal was to change the hearts and minds of the American public and make abortion a non-normative practice that is

unworthy of societal approval. The strategies were multidimensional and included humanizing the fetus through the widespread distribution of fetal images and exposing the "truth" about abortion by disseminating graphic images of the abortion procedure.[6]

Abortion clinics and their patients became the direct target of large-scale anti-abortion demonstrations at which anti-abortion activists blockaded clinics in order to prevent women from obtaining abortions. The most famous of these were the Siege on Atlanta, GA during the 1988 Democratic National Convention and the Summer of Mercy in Wichita, KS in 1991. In Kansas, thousands of pro-life protesters converged on the city over a forty-two-day period and more than 2,500 protesters were arrested.[7] While many direct-action efforts were nonviolent, some activists began advocating for more violent tactics designed to shut down the clinics through bombings, arsons, buric acid attacks, and even the direct killing of physicians.[8] Pro-choice groups responded with active clinic defense strategies and national marches. Media coverage was extensive and focused on the direct conflict between the supporters and opponents of abortion in public spaces.[9] Consequently, abortion became understood by the American public as an angry hostile debate between two sides both aimed at winning at all costs.

The amped up volatility of the abortion debate in the United States led many in politics and public advocacy to desire a way to end the abortion war. It was at this point in the history of abortion in the United States that the phrase "safe, legal, and rare" entered into the common discourse about what American's should think about abortion. As the phrase suggests, the goal is to resolve the conflict over abortion by maintaining its legality but reducing its use.

The first national figure to adopt this approach was Bill Clinton during his 1992 presidential campaign. On his first day in office President Clinton, while reversing the anti-abortion policies of the Reagan-Bush I administrations, invoked this new paradoxical approach of affirming abortion rights within the context of wanting lower use of abortion: his vision was "an America where abortion is safe, legal and rare."[10] Since the phrase's introduction in the mid-1990s, most pro-choice politicians have used it in answering a question about their support for abortion rights.[11] The mainstream press also recognizes the wide acceptance of this position. In 2003, *USA Today* wrote about abortion: "[A] right most Americans want preserved: reproductive choice that makes abortions safe, legal and rare."[12]

Advocacy organizations also began to adapt to this new desire for a middle ground to end the conflict. For example, NARAL, first formed in 1967 as the National Association for the Repeal of Abortion Laws and with legalization changed its name to the National Abortion Rights Action League in 1973. In 1993 NARAL changed its name to the National Abortion and Reproductive Rights Action League and launched the "Real Choices" campaign "to highlight the goals of its expanded mission: to preserve access to abortion while working to enact policies to make abortion less necessary." In 2003 the organization would go even further changing its name to "NARAL Pro-Choice America." In this iteration NARAL became an expression rather than an acronym, removing the word abortion from its name entirely. In 2005 NARAL's work prioritized a "prevention first campaign" to reduce the need for abortion.

A CRITIQUE OF THE GOAL OF MAKING ABORTION "RARE"

What could be wrong about wanting abortion to be "rare?" At first glance the declaration seems imminently reasonable as it could be interpreted as the desire to make abortion rare in an individual woman's life. She would thus have the healthcare,

contraception, gender equity, social change, and economic resources she needs to control her fertility. It is probably true that most women do not proactively desire to have an abortion in their lives. However, acknowledging women's individual desires to avoid an unintended pregnancy is qualitatively different from a social goal of making abortion rare on the aggregate.

First and foremost the desire to make abortion "rare" creates an immediate normative judgment about abortion. While a major piece of art may be "rare" and thus even more valued, such is not the meaning in this case. Rather "rare" suggests that abortion is happening more than it should, and that there are some conditions for which abortions should and should not occur. It separates good abortions from bad abortions. It creates an understanding that women's individual decision making is somehow responsible for the violent disruptive social conflict over abortion in the United States. The general sentiment is that if women were just more responsible we as a nation would be less polarized over abortion. In an op-ed in the *New York Times* entitled "This Is the Way the Culture Wars End," liberal columnist William Saletan explained this location of blame: "This isn't a shortage of pills or condoms. It's a shortage of cultural and personal responsibility. It's a failure to teach, understand, admit or care that unprotected sex can lead to the creation—and the subsequent killing, through abortion—of a developing human being."[13]

Such individualization of responsibility is harmful to women. Abortion is currently one of the most stigmatized events in a woman's life and the widespread endorsement of "rare" both produces and reproduces this stigma.[14] A recent review of mental health and abortion found profound psychological implications of stigma. According to experimental studies stigmatization can create negative cognitions, emotions, and behavioral reactions that can adversely affect social, psychological, and biological functioning. Societal stigma is seen as particularly pernicious because it leads to internalized stigma in which women adopt the negative societal beliefs and stereotypes about themselves.[15]

The inherent delegitimization of abortion in the call for it to be "rare" was pointed out early on by a conservative anti-abortion blogger "[T]he phrase actually brings up an important question: if abortion is merely a medical procedure—a simple choice, then why should it be rare?"[16] Recently Pastor Rick Warren, who provided the invocation at President Obama's inauguration, reiterated the critique when challenging Obama's pro-choice position: "Now, I don't understand the, the idea of it should be rare and, and less. Well, either you believe it's life or you don't. It—why would you believe it should be rare? Because if, if it's not—if a baby, a fetus is not a life, then why restrict it?"[17]

As this sentiment suggests, support for making abortion rare, presupposes that abortion is wrong and somehow different than other health care. This ongoing marginalization of abortion as a different type of health care, one in which the goal is reduced use rather than expanded access and enhanced quality, has contributed to the significant decline in the number of locations where abortions are performed in the United States. In 2004, only 1,787 facilities continued to provide abortion care and 86 percent of counties were without a known abortion provider.[18] Increased access to care is not part of the "rare" message and efforts to expand services could be construed as working against the goal of making it less frequently used.

Similarly, the call for abortion to be rare negates mandates for routine training in abortion. In the United States today, less than half of all obstetrics and gynecology residency programs offer routine training in abortion care and only 11 of the 480 family practice programs acknowledge attention to abortion care within the curriculum.[19]

More insidious, the uniform acceptance that fewer abortions is good creates the inability to recognize the consequences of reduced access or to accept credit for efforts that actual increase the number of abortions. For example, in 2009, the Guttmacher Institute released a reanalysis of earlier data regarding the effect of Medicaid restrictions on women's use of abortion. Abortion opponents quickly utilized the data to demonstrate the success of their efforts at reducing abortion: "Overall, the results indicate that there is a very strong consensus among both the public-health researchers and economists that public funding restrictions lower abortion rates."[20] Instead of supporting the conclusion that the number of abortion in the United States should be higher than it is given barriers to care, the Guttmacher Institute released a statement qualifying their findings: "The availability of coverage, while important at the individual level, cannot be expected to increase the overall numbers of abortion more than nominally—if at all."[21] The author of this statement was a proponent of the "rare" mantra.[22]

The third critique is that the call for abortion to be "rare" legitimizes efforts to restrict its use. Prior to 1989, laws interfering with a woman's right to abortion were ruled unconstitutional. The shift in the composition of the Court under the Reagan and Bush I administrations led to the 1989 and 1992 *Webster* and *Casey* Supreme Court decisions establishing a threshold of "undue burden" for the constitutionality of state-based restrictions.[23] Under this new legal regime, states can demonstrate a preference against abortion through the implementation of waiting periods, parental involvement, mandatory information, and scripted provider speech requirements; since 1994, almost every state has done so. These laws vary in their construction and studying the effects of these laws is difficult but suggests that additional barriers to abortion disproportionately affect traditionally vulnerable populations.[24]

For example, the most severe waiting periods require two in-person visits to the clinic with a prescribed time between visits. In a world where many women lack paid sick leave and childcare, access to a provider in their community, and affordable transportation/lodging, a two-visit requirement may be insurmountable to some women.

Mandatory information laws often include significant amounts of misinformation.[25] For example, six states require that women be informed of the unsubstantiated link between abortion and breast cancer, eight states the unsupported ability of a fetus to feel pain at a certain point in gestation, and seven states the supposed long-term negative mental health consequences.[26] Each of these claims is contrary to recognized science.[27] The content of scripted provider speech continues to negatively evolve. For example, in South Dakota physicians must tell a women that the abortion will "terminate the life of a whole, separate, unique, living human being; that the pregnant woman has an existing relationship with that unborn human being, and that the relationship enjoys protection under the U.S. Constitution and under the laws of South Dakota; and that by having an abortion, her existing relationship and her existing constitutional rights with regards to that relationship will be terminated."[28] Notions that abortion should be "rare" contribute the environment in which these pejorative laws are seen as acceptable.

The fourth flaw in the call for abortion to be "rare" is that it sets up an expectation that abortion can be reduced to a specific number at which the country will come to an agreement about abortion being acceptable and uncontroversial. Central to the rare argument is a belief that the conflict surrounding abortion is related to frequency.

Unfortunately, numbers have little to do with ongoing opposition to abortion and the rarity of some abortions seem to be their reason for aversion. Take for example the situation of George Tiller, MD, the physician

recently killed in Wichita, KS. In addition to having a robust practice of first-trimester and early second-trimester procedures, Dr. Tiller also provided medically indicated abortions in the third trimester. While these abortions were "rare" in numerical sense, occurring only 2,400 times a year in the entire country, they were the abortions for which he was most reviled.[29] The rarity of these procedures did not provide any protection for Dr. Tiller. Instead the specialness of those abortions provided evidence that such abortions were abnormal.

Other examples support the argument that the frequency of abortion is unrelated to the size or strength of the conflict. For example, one of the largest fights over abortion in recent years was waged in South Dakota when in 2006 the state legislature banned abortion and the ban was narrowly reversed in two public referendum. Ironically, in 2005, the year prior to the ban, only 790 women obtained abortions in South Dakota, suggesting that frequency and controversy are not associated.[30] Likewise, in Texas a 2003 law mandating that abortions after sixteen weeks be performed only in facilities licensed as ambulatory surgical facilities led to a 87 percent decline in the number of later abortions performed in 2004 in that state.[31] The conflict over abortion in Texas, however, remains unchanged. Finally, the significant decline in the teen pregnancy and abortion rates in California between 1996 and 2000 did not result in a subsequent reduction in the fight over abortion among adolescents.[32] California still experienced resource-intensive ballot initiative fights over parental consent in 2004, 2005, and 2007.[33]

But just how far could the United States reduce the number of abortions and would that meet the threshold for "rare"? The answer to this question employs the standard set by the NIH Office of Rare Diseases Research which defines a rare disease as one having a prevalence of fewer than 200,000 affected individuals in the United States.[34] Currently there are 1.2 million abortions per year in the United States. Thus the number of abortions would need to decline by 83 percent to meet this threshold. Such a reduction is both unrealistic at a practical level and impossible with current conceptive options. All contraceptive methods have failures—both due to the method themselves and due to user errors. Currently 54 percent of all abortions happen to women using birth control.[35] For the purposes of this argument let us assume that all women used contraception perfectly over the course of their sexual lives when not trying to get pregnant and used the method with the very lowest failure rate, the intrauterine contraception or IUC. With 61 million women of reproductive age and a desire for an average of two children per woman, the number of unintended pregnancies would still be greater than 200,000 per year.[36]

The Netherlands provides an example of what might be more realistic and possible. With one of the lowest abortion rates in the world at 8.4 per 1,000 women, there are still over 34,000 abortions per year—not meeting the incidence rate for "rare" given the population of only 16 million.[37] While held up as a model for family planning and sexuality education, abortion happens routinely in the Netherlands.[38] And U.S.-based pro-life groups remain loudly opposed to abortion in Netherlands.[39] In August 2009, the World Congress of Families, an international coalition of pro-family groups, held their fifth international meeting in Amsterdam. U.S. pro-life groups were well represented and very active in opposing Dutch policies on abortion.

ACCEPTING THE DIFFICULTY OF THE ABORTION DEBATE IN THE U.S.

As this article suggests the rhetorical strategy to support making abortion "safe, legal, and rare" does not achieve the underlying goal of reducing the social conflict over abortion and has real consequences for women's health and well-being, including reducing access to care, increasing stigma, justifying restrictions, and establishing unattainable goals. Consequently, it is unrealistic to equate the debate over abortion to the number of abortions that occur and to assume that a reduction would be met by an equal reduction in the strength of the conflict. While serving as a short term diversion for those seeking to avoid immediate conflict, the strategy of wanting abortion to be "rare" does nothing to secure the ongoing right to abortion that is grounded in real access to excising that right. A more realistic approach to securing the right to have and use abortion requires work to articulate abortion as a social good and to significantly increase access to services. Advocates for abortion rights should be realistic that such changes represent fundamental shifts in the role and power of women in society and thus will not happen without social conflict and debate. The linguistic trick of affirming the right to abortion while simultaneously devaluing it is both harmful and ineffective as a strategy to securing rights. Instead I proposed a four part approach: 1) acceptance that abortion is a polarizing issue in the U.S.; 2) acknowledgement that abortion has and will always be part of the human condition; 3) validation of the rights of women to equal participation in society and control over their reproductive lives; and 4) engagement in the hard conversations about abortion regarding the moral status of life, the extent of the rights and autonomy of women, the limits of the state to intervening in personal decisions, and the role of religion in public life. Finally, I remind the reader that the desire to help an individual woman achieve her reproductive desires by avoiding an abortion is a laudable goal, not because it reduces the need for abortion, but because it is what that woman wants for her life.

NOTES

1. For more analysis of the current abortion controversy in the United States, see Alesha E. Doan, *Opposition & Intimidation: The Abortion Wars & Strategies of Political Harassment* (Ann Arbor:

University of Michigan Press, 2007); Krista Jacob, *Abortion under Attack: Women on the Challenges Facing Choice* (Emeryville, CA: Seal Press, 2006); Carole E. Joffe, *Dispatches from the Abortion Wars: The Costs of Fanaticism to Doctors, Patients, and the Rest of Us* (Boston, MA: Beacon Press, 2009); Scott Klusendorf, *The Case for Life: Equipping Christians to Engage the Culture* (Wheaton, IL: Crossway Books, 2009); Eyal Press, *Absolute Convictions: My Father, a City, and the Conflict That Divided America* (New York: Henry Holt and Co., 2006); and Melody Rose, *Safe, Legal, and Unavailable? Abortion Politics in the United States* (Washington DC: CQ Press, 2007).

2. For discussion of the assassination of Dr. Tiller, see David Barstow, "An Abortion Battle, Fought to the Death," *New York Times*, 26 July 2009, A1; Peter Slevin, "Slaying Raises Fears on Both Sides of Abortion Debate," *Washington Post*, 2 June 2009 A1. For abortion in the health reform debate, see David D. Kirpatrick, "Health Bill Revives Abortion Groups," *New York Times*, 24 November 2009; Sharon Lerner, "Round Two: The Coming Battle over Abortion Funding" *The Nation* [online], 23 November 2009, http://www.thenation.com/doc/20091207/lerner.

3. Stanley K. Henshaw and Kathryn Kost, "Trends in the Characteristics of Women Obtaining Abortions, 1974–2004," (New York City: Guttmacher Institute, 2008).

4. Betty Friedan, "Abortion: A Women's Civil Right (Chicago: First National Conference for Repeal of Abortion Laws, 1969)," in *It Changed My Life: Writings on the Women's Movement*, ed. Betty Friedan (Cambridge, MA: Harvard University Press, 1998); Janet Hadley, *Abortion: Between Freedom and Necessity* (Philadelphia, PA: Temple University Press, 1996); Rosalind P. Petchesky, *Abortion and Woman's Choice: The State, Sexuality, and Reproductive Freedom*, rev. ed. (Boston, MA: Northeastern University Press, 1990); Ruth Rosen, *The World Split Open: How the Modern Women's Movement Changed America* (New York: Viking, 2000); Ninia Baehr, *Abortion without Apology: A Radical History for the 1990s* (Boston, MA: South End Press, 1990).

5. Karen O'Connor, *No Neutral Ground? Abortion Politics in an Age of Absolutes* (Boulder, CO: Westview Press, 1996); Rose, *Safe, Legal, and Unavailable?*

6. James Davidson Hunter, *Culture Wars: The Struggle to Define America* (New York: Basic Books, 1991); Teresa R. Wagner, *Back to the Drawing Board: The Future of the Pro-Life Movement* (South Bend, IN: St. Augustine's Press, 2003); Marvin N. Olasky, *Abortion Rites: A Social History of Abortion in America* (Washington DC; Lanham, MD: Regnery Pub., Distributed by National Book Network, 1995); Rosalind P. Petchesky, "Fetal Images: The Power of Visual Culture in the Politics of Reproduction," *Feminist Studies* 13, no. 2 (1987): 263–92; Jon A. Shields, *The Democratic Virtues of the Christian Right* (Princeton, NJ: Princeton University Press, 2009).

7. Rescues during this time were organized by the group Operation Rescue. For more on the history of rescues, see Patricia Baird-Windle and Eleanor J. Bader, *Targets of Hatred: Anti-Abortion Terrorism* (New York: Palgrave for St. Martin's Press, 2001); Philip F. Lawler, *Operation Rescue: A Challenge to the Nation's Conscience* (Huntington, IN: Our Sunday Visitor, 1992); Jerry Reiter, *Live from the Gates of Hell: An Insider's Look at the Antiabortion Underground* (Amherst, NY: Prometheus Books, 2000); and Mark Allan Steiner, *The Rhetoric of Operation Rescue: Projecting the Christian Pro-Life Message* (New York: T & T Clark, 2006).

8. Carol Mason, *Killing for Life: The Apocalyptic Narrative of Pro-Life Politics* (Ithaca, NY: Cornell University Press, 2002); Joseph M Scheidler, *Closed: 99 Ways to Stop Abortion* (Westchester, IL: Crossway Books, 1985).

9. O'Connor, *No Neutral Ground?*

10. Robin Toner, "Settling In: Easing Abortion Policy; Clinton Orders Reversal of Abortion Restrictions Left by Reagan and Bush," *New York Times*, 23 January 1993, 1.

11. For example, Senator Barbara Boxer from San Francisco, CA and an outspoken supporter of abortion rights invoked the phrase in her remarks regarding the thirtieth anniversary celebration of *Roe v. Wade*, *30 Faces of Roe: Personal Perspectives on Roe V. Wade's 30th Anniversary*, Center for Reproductive Law and Policy, 2003, *www.reproductiverights.org/crt_roe_30faces.html*; and Hilary Clinton used the phrase in her speech to family planning advocates in 2005, *Remarks by Senator Hillary Rodham Clinton to the NYS Family Planning Providers*, 24 January 2005, http://clinton.senate.gov/~clinton/speeches/2005125A05.html.

12. "'Partial-Birth' Abortion Ban Sets Stage for Broader Fight," *USA Today*, 23 October 2003, 14A.

13. William Saletan, "This Is the Way the Culture Wars End," *New York Times*, 22 February 2009, 11.

14. For more discussion of abortion stigma, see Jennifer Baumgardner, *Abortion & Life* (New York: Akashic Books, 2008); Marlene Gerber Fried, "Abortion in the United States: Barriers to Access," *Health and Human Rights* 4, no. 2 (2000): 174–94; Anuradha Kumar, Leila Hessini, and Ellen M. H. Mitchell, "Conceptualising Abortion Stigma," *Culture, Health & Sexuality: An International Journal for Research, Intervention and Care* 11, no. 6 (2009): 1–15; Lisa L. Littman, Christina Zarcadoolas, and Adam R. Jacobs, "Introducing Abortion Patients to a Culture of Support: A Pilot Study," *Archives of Women's Mental Health* 12, no. 6 (2009): 419–31.

15. Brenda Major et al., "Abortion and Mental Health: Evaluating the Evidence," *American Psychologist* 64, no. 9 (2009): 863–90. For additional reviews of the mental health implications of abortion, see Gail Erlick Robinson et al., "Is There An 'Abortion Trauma Syndrome'? Critiquing the Evidence,"

Harvard Review of Psychiatry 17, no. 4 (2009): 268–90.

16. Casey's Critical Thinking, "Safe, Legal and Rare," 2003, http://www.hoshuha.com/articles/safe.html.

17. *Meet the Press' Transcript for Nov. 29, 2009*, http://www.msnbc.msn.com/id/34079938/ns/meet_the_press/page/3/.

18. Rachel K. Jones et al., "Abortion in the United States: Incidence and Access to Services, 2005," *Perspectives in Sexual and Reproductive Health* 40, no. 1 (2008): 6–16.

19. Katherine L Eastwood et al., "Abortion Training in United States Obstetrics and Gynecology Residency Programs," *Obstetrics and Gynecology* 108, no. 2 (2006): 303–8; Ruth Lesnewski, Linda Prine, and Marji Gold, "New Research Abortion Training as an Integral Part of Residency Training," *Family Medicine* 35, no. 6 (2003): 386–87.

20. Michael New, political science professor at the University of Alabama, as quoted in Steven Ertelt, "Study: Abortion Funding Cuts Reduce Abortions: Why Does Obama Want More?" LifeNews.com, 17 July 2009, http://www.lifenews.com/nat5238.html.

21. Susan Cohen, "Politics Distorts Facts on Impact of Abortion Coverage," RHRealityCheck.org, 5 December 2009, http://www.rhrealitycheck.org/blog/2009/08/04/politics-distorts-facts-impact-abortion-coverage.

22. Susan A. Cohen, "A Message to the President: Abortion Can Be Safe, Legal and Still Rare," *Guttmacher Report on Public Policy* 4, no. 1 (2001): 1–2, 14.

23. *Webster v. Reproductive Health Services* [492 U.S. 490, 1989] and *Planned Parenthood of Southeastern Pennsylvania v. Casey* [505 U.S. 833, 1992].

24. Amanda Dennis et al., *The Impact of Laws Requiring Parental Involvement for Abortion: A Literature Review* (New York: Guttmacher Institution, 2009); Stanley K. Henshaw et al., *Restrictions on Medicaid Funding for Abortions: A Literature Review* (New York: Guttmacher Institute, 2009); Theodore J. Joyce et al., *The Impact of State Mandatory Counseling and Waiting Period Laws on Abortion: A Literature Review* (New York: Guttmacher Institute, 2009).

25. Chinué Turner Richardson and Elizabeth Nash, "Misinformed Consent: The Medical Accuracy of State-Developed Abortion Counseling Materials," *Guttmacher Policy Review* 9, no. 4 (2006): 6–11.

26. Guttmacher Institute, *State Policies in Brief. Counseling and Waiting Periods for Abortion* (New York: Guttmacher Institute, 2009).

27. Tracy A. Weitz, "What Physicians Need to Know About the Legal Status of Abortion in the United States," *Clinical Obstetrics and Gynecology* 52, no. 2 (2009): 130–39.

28. S.D. Codified Laws § 34-23A-10.1

29. For statistics on medically indicated abortions in the third trimester, see Henshaw and Kost, "Trends in the Characteristics of Women Obtaining Abortions, 1974–2004," Table 4. As an example of this animosity, see one of hundreds of websites set up to expose Dr. Tiller's later abortion practices: "George Tiller: America's most notorious abortionist,".http://www.dr-tiller.com. This website takes a revealing look at "Tiller the Killer".

30. Guttmacher Institute, *State Facts About Abortion: South Dakota* (New York: Guttmacher Institute, 2008), http://www.guttmacher.org/pubs/sfaa/pdf/south_dakota.pdf.

31. Bonnie Scott Jones and Tracy A. Weitz, "Legal Barriers to Second-Trimester Abortion Provision and Public Health Consequences," *American Journal of Public Health* 99, no. 4 (2009): 623–30.

32. *Decline in Unintended Pregnancies in California: California State Senate and Assembly Districts* (San Francisco, CA: The UCSF Bixby Center for Reproductive Health Research and Policy, 2007); Guttmacher Institute, *U.S. Teenage Pregnancy Statistics National and State Trends and Trends by Race and Ethnicity* (New York: Guttmacher Institute, 2006).

33. Proposition 73 in 2005, Proposition 85 in 2006 and Proposition 4, 2008.

34. Rare Diseases and Related Terms, National Institutes of Health, Office of Rare Diseases Research, 2009, http://rarediseases.info.nih.gov/RareDiseaseList.aspx.

35. Rachel K. Jones, Jacqueline E Darroch, and Stanley K. Henshaw, "Contraceptive Use among U.S. Women Having Abortions in 2000–2001," *Perspectives on Sexual and Reproductive Health* 34, no. 6 (2002): 294–303.

36. The following calculation is provided by Diana Greene Foster, and is a gross estimate based on the most idealized situation in which only women who want to be pregnant do not use the most effective method of contraception and all unintended pregnancies while contracepting result in abortion. There are currently 62 million U.S. women in their childbearing years (15–44). Of these, 43 million women of reproductive age are sexually active and do not want to become pregnant, but could become pregnant if they fail to use a contraceptive method. As the typical U.S. woman wants only two children, to achieve this goal she must use contraceptives for roughly three decades: six months of trying to conceive, nine months of pregnancy and three months of postpartum infecundity results. If every woman used an IUC for every year she is trying to avoid pregnancy (with a 0.8 percent chance of failure per year): 43,000,000 *(27/30)*0.008 = 309,600 abortions per year. If the 10 million who are sterilized stay sterilized and the rest adopt IUCs: 33,000,000 *(27/30)*0.008 = 237,600 abortions per year. Data for this calculation is drawn from sources cited in the Guttmacher Institute's *Facts on Contraceptive Use* (New York: Guttmacher Institute, 2008), http://www.guttmacher.org/pubs/fb_contr_use.html#1.

37. The U.S. abortion rate is 21 per 1,000. For more discussion of abortion rates in other countries, see Gilda Sedgh et al., "Induced Abortion: Estimated Rates and Trends Worldwide," *The Lancet* 370, no. 9595 (2007): 1338–45.

38. Sue Alford and Debra Hauser, *Adolescent Sexual Health in Europe and the U.S.—Why the Difference?*, Advocates for Youth, September 2009, http://www.advocatesforyouth.org/storage/advfy/documents/fsest.pdf.

39. Joseph Meaney, "Laying the Netherlands to Sleep," insidecatholic.com, 14 October 2009, http://insidecatholic.com/Joomla/index.php?option=com_content&task=view&id=7043&Itemid=48.

CHAPTER 8

Race, Reproductive Politics and Reproductive Health Care in the Contemporary United States

Willie Parker and Carole Joffe

To paraphrase Leo Tolstoy, who famously wrote that all unhappy families are unhappy in their own way, we can say that all nations confront the thorny issue of demographics, but each in its own, typically controversial, way. Various European countries, for example, have anxieties about a "demographic winter," which is a below replacement birth rate of the native population, which has led to corresponding fears about rising birth rates among Muslim immigrants. China, driven by worries about overpopulation, has instituted coercive reproductive policies that many observers find unacceptably harsh. The United States, a country marked by extreme stratification on both racial and economic grounds, is a particularly interesting case to consider from a demographic lens because there has been a history both of targeting the birth rates of people of color *and* at the same time deep political divisions about the provision of reproductive health services—particularly abortion but increasingly, as the current election season reveals, contraception as well.

We, a sociologist and physician, respectively, write here of our dismay about the contemporary state of reproductive politics in the United States and particularly the cynical manipulation of racial themes by the opponents of abortion and birth control. However, we are acutely aware of the mixed legacy of the United States with respect to demographic issues. To name but a few examples, in 1905, President Theodore Roosevelt warned of "race suicide" because of his concern about falling birth rates among white Anglo-Saxon women and the higher rates among immigrants.[1] In the 1927 Supreme Court case, *Buck v Bell*, the Court upheld a statute instituting compulsory sterilization of the unfit, including the mentally retarded, "for the protection and health of the state."[2] In the 1960s, impoverished African-American and Latina women, along with some poor whites, were subjected to coerced sterilizations, often without these women fully understanding to what they had ostensibly agreed.[3] When the first federally funded family planning centers were established in the early 1970s, as a result of the passage of Title X, they were disproportionately located in African-American communities, although the language of the legislation did not mention race but rather the income status of the intended recipients.[4]

Co-existing with these events, however, has been a longstanding reproductive freedom movement in the United States, made up of clinicians and lay activists alike.

Starting in the early 20th century, doctors and nurses, along with lay allies, fought for the legalization of first, birth control, and, later, abortion, seeing the particular damage done to the most vulnerable women in the absence of such services. In the 1960s and 1970s, feminist health activists raised an outcry about the sterilization abuses mentioned above; indeed, among the most prominent of the reproductive rights organizations to emerge from the "second wave" feminism of that era was CARASA, the Committee for Abortion Rights and Against Sterilization Abuse, providing a template for the principle that abortion rights should ideally be considered in a broader context that includes the right to *have* children.[5] That generation of feminist activists also severely criticized the then-common practice of testing new contraceptive methods on Third World women. Today, there are numerous reproductive rights/reproductive justice groups hard at work in the United States, a number of them specifically concerned with the situation of women of color.

In short, this very brief recapitulation of reproductive struggles in the United States reveals the truism that the world of sexual and reproductive health services is a complex terrain, always containing both liberatory and coercive possibilities, and always with particular implications for people of color in a white-dominated society. But with respect to present-day conflicts, no figure's legacy has been more contested than that of Margaret Sanger, the founder of the organization that eventually became Planned Parenthood. Anti-abortion forces for years have accused Sanger of being a racist and a eugenicist. Currently, these groups have pounced upon the high rate of abortion within the African-American community—black women have abortions at nearly four times the rate of white women and have joined forces with some conservative groups within that community to mount a vigorous campaign against Planned Parenthood in particular

and abortion provision more generally. Starting in Atlanta, and spreading to other cities, these groups have sponsored controversial billboards — some proclaiming that "black children are an endangered species" and others comparing abortion to slavery.

As Ellen Chesler, Sanger's premier biographer, has argued, such accusations are a distortion of Sanger's record.[6] Although Sanger did receive some support from eugenicist organizations (at a time when eugenics was a far more mainstream movement than it is currently), her record cannot be construed as "racist." Among her supporters were numerous black ministers, leading African-American intellectuals such as W.E.B. Dubois, and prominent community leaders such as Mary McLeod Bethune, founder of the National Council for Negro Women. In 1966, when Dr. Martin Luther King accepted the first Margaret Sanger award from Planned Parenthood, he praised Sanger for "her courage and vision," comparing her struggle for birth control to the civil rights movement. One of the most effective critiques of the billboard campaign, and against the larger agenda of demonizing Planned Parenthood, has come from Sistersong, a coalition of reproductive justice groups of women of color. As Loretta Ross, the executive director of the group told the *New York Times*, "The reason we have so many Planned Parenthoods in the black community is because leaders in the black community in the '20s and '30s went to Margaret Sanger and asked for them. Controlling our fertility was part of our uplift out of poverty strategy, and it still works".[7]

This manipulation of the history of race and reproduction by those involved in the billboard campaigns and similar efforts obscures the contemporary facts of life faced by the most vulnerable black women. These women experience high rates of unintended pregnancy, low use of the most effective forms of contraception, deep poverty, inadequate educational opportunities, unacceptable levels of intimate partner violence and, very often, lack of support from their churches. It should come as no surprise that these same women would have the highest rates of abortion in this country. Given the conditions, these women need—among many other services—access to comprehensive health care that includes both family planning and abortion. Yet, abortion has long been excluded from most mainstream health care institutions and sources of public funding, and during the current political season, we have watched with dismay the severe attacks on contraceptive coverage as well. The isolation of abortion, in particular, from the rest of health care has contributed to its stigmatization and has helped the development of conspiracy theories, such as we see in the billboard campaign. We decry the inflammatory, false rhetoric of "black genocide" that has been used in this campaign by anti-abortion extremists, and we are hardly the first to point to the hypocrisy of those who oppose contraception and abortion, yet just as fervently oppose any spending for social services.

One of us (WP), speaking from my perspective as a member of the African American community and as a women's health provider, asserts that this attempt to manipulate my community is made possible by our unresolved issues regarding gender roles and sexuality in a modern context. The failure of our community to promote the agency of our mothers, sisters and partners, and to deal forthrightly with sexual matters, leaves us treating abortion and HIV-related issues as "open secrets." This evasion results in exorbitant rates for both. To truly confront these issues, our community desperately needs medically accurate sexuality education, improved health literacy and a constructive engagement of religious and spiritual leaders, given the central importance of religion in the African-American community. This type of empowerment effort towards shared reproductive health responsibility is the only effective rebuttal to the mischief occurring with race and reproduction in our

community. To paraphrase Dr. King, just as individual wealth is always a function of the commonwealth, thus it too holds true that compromising the reproductive health and rights of individual black women results in jeopardizing the collective well-being of black communities.

If to know is to become responsible, my awareness of black women's unmet reproductive health needs requires me to provide family planning and abortion care to those most in demand for them. Doing so represents a dual sense of responsibility that I feel as both a women's health provider and as a member of the African-American community. I join with those in my community who have articulated a vision of reproductive justice, defined as creating a society that enables all women and families to have the children they want, the resources needed to raise them, and the ability to prevent or end the pregnancies that they do not want. I call on my fellow health care providers, of all races, to trust women to make the good and tough decisions about when and whether to expand their families. A fundamental respect for fairness necessitates it, and a respect for human rights demands it.

In conclusion, as already noted, we write in a period of unprecedented political attack on women's health issues—not just abortion, but also contraception and a range of other reproductive health services. Even the seemingly long settled issue of the importance of programs to combat domestic violence is now being resisted by conservative forces.[8] This "war on women," as it has come to be known, has galvanized a countermovement of health activists, both women and men, who have effectively and creatively protested these developments in a variety of ways. We are greatly heartened by this mobilization, although its eventual impact on elections and restrictive measures is unclear at this time. We close by reminding our readers of what is perhaps obvious: the stakes in this "war" are inevitably the highest for the most vulnerable in our society—those poor women of color about whom we have written in this editorial.

NOTES

1. Roosevelt T. On American Motherhood. Available at http://www.nationalcenter.org/TRooseveltMotherhood.html (accessed February 6, 2012).
2. Buck v. Bell, 274 U.S. 200 (1927). Available at http://www.oyez.org/cases/1901-1939/1926/1926_292 (accessed February 6, 2012).
3. Schoen J. Choice and coercion: birth control, sterilization, and abortion in public health and welfare. Chapel Hill: University of N. Carolina Press; 2005.
4. Gordon L. The moral property of women: a history of birth control politics in America. Urbana, IL: University of Illinois Press; 2002. p. 289–91.
5. Petchesky R. Abortion and woman's choice: the state, sexuality and reproductive freedom. Boston: Northeastern University Press; 1990. p. 392.
6. Chesler E. Was Planned Parenthood's founder racist? Salon 2012 Nov 2. Available at http://www.salon.com/writer/ellen_chesler/ (accessed February 6, 2012).
7. Dewans S. Antiabortion ads split Atlanta. New York Times 2012 Feb 5. Available at http://www.nytimes.com/2010/02/06/us/06abortion.html?scp=1&sq=Shaila%20Dewan%20Margaret%20Sanger&st=cse (accessed February 6, 2012).
8. Joffe C. All common ground lost: the right's opposition to the Violence Against Women Act. Rhrealitycheck.org. Available at http://www.rhrealitycheck.org/article/2012/03/16/all-common-ground-lost-rightsopposition-to-violence-against-women-act (accessed March 20, 2012).

Chapter 9

Not Ready to Fill His Father's Shoes

A Masculinist Discourse of Abortion

Jennifer Reich

There are approximately 62 million women of reproductive age living in the United States. While approximately six million become pregnant each year, about half of those pregnancies are unintended (Alan Guttmacher Institute 2004). In turn, half of these unintended pregnancies are terminated by abortion (Alan Guttmacher Institute 1999). Although women from a wide range of socioeconomic, racial, religious, marital, and childbearing backgrounds seek abortions, abortion remains controversial. A portion of this controversy swirls around questions of what the appropriate role should be for men who co-conceive.

This article unpacks this issue by examining how men faced with unintended pregnancies that culminated in elective abortions articulate their desired outcomes and account for their decisions to terminate the pregnancies.

In doing so, I expose how men's narratives reveal the ways that reproductive decisions reflect their gendered social selves. Arendell (1992) argues in her own research on men's narratives of divorce that "how men define their situations and act in divorce points to their positions in a gender-structured society and to their understandings of the nature of social practices, relationships, and selves" (p. 152). From this, Arendell provides a rich examination of "a masculinist discourse of divorce" in which the men interviewed "shared a set of dispositions, practices, and explanations with which they managed their identities, situations, and emotional lives" (p. 153).

Lupton and Barclay (1997), in their study of discourses of fatherhood, argue that "the discourses available at a certain historical moment construct the ways we think or talk about, or respond to, phenomena. As such, they are both enabling and constraining human action and notions of reality. Discourses may be regarded as assemblages of knowledges that serve to produce notions of the human subject" (p. 5). From this orientation, Lupton and Barclay argue that the meanings of fatherhood are best understood by examining the discourses used to represent it. Following the example of these authors, this article explicates a masculinist discourse of abortion.

Using data collected during in-depth interviews with twenty men involved in thirty abortions (of fetuses they co-conceived), this article looks at how men accounted for their own desired outcomes of unplanned pregnancies, the meaning of potential fatherhood for them, and the decision to terminate those pregnancies. Specifically, I show how men's narratives reflected their understandings of procreation as a chance to reproduce themselves and to satisfy their romantic notions of fatherhood, requiring their satisfaction of the role of the good provider and contingent on their desire to participate in a traditional male-headed nuclear family. To be clear, this article does not aim to capture the realities of the abortion experience but rather the discourses of abortion that—constructed and reshaped over time—reflect men's cultural understandings of pregnancy, abortion, and masculinity. In examining these narratives and men's efforts to retrospectively frame the abortion experience in terms of their conceptions of masculine competence, we can see the cultural dominance of narrowly defined fatherhood and how such constructions reify meanings of hegemonic masculinity (Connell 1995) and of traditional notions of family formation.

MANAGING THE MASCULINE SELF

The concept of a masculine discourse presumes gender is socially constructed, with meanings that exist in and change between specific historical, social, and cultural contexts (Kimmel 1996). As Connell (1995) points out, individuals undertake "gender projects" to make sense of themselves as gendered beings (Armato and Marsiglio 2002). In doing so, individuals respond to and reinterpret cultural expectations of being gendered or of how to "do gender" (West and Zimmerman 1987). Nowhere can this be seen as clearly as in the realm of social expectations of men around reproduction. Men frequently encounter messages calling for social and sexual responsibility around contraception (Blaney 1997; Hollos and Larsen 2004; Kaiser Family Foundation 1997; Oudshoorn 2004) and even childbirth participation (Mardorossian 2003). Most commonly, men have been able to establish themselves as competent in the realm of the family, as they achieve the role of the good provider (Bernard 1981).

More recently, competent fatherhood—particularly for unmarried men—has been equated with providing significant social and financial resources to their children (Curran and Abrams 2000; Dowd 2000; Jump and Haas 1987; Lamb 2000; Whitehead and Popenoe 1999). In reverse, male irresponsibility has been defined as male absence from their children's lives, failure to pay child support (embodied in the label *deadbeat dads*), and to some extent, presumed refusal to marry women who have become pregnant by them. Further defining incompetent fatherhood, a recent body of literature has attempted to connect male absence to poor life outcomes for children (Blankenhorn 1996; Comanor and Phillips 1998; Popenoe 1996). Taken together, these cultural expectations require competent fathers to be present, financially supportive, ideally married to the mother of their children and thus heterosexual, and a decisive force in the family. At the heart of definitions of competent fatherhood are meanings of competent masculinity (Holland and Scourfield 2000; Oudshoorn 2004; Reich 2005). Even as the expectations and definitions of fathers may vary by race, class, ethnicity, sexual orientation, or age, the cultural meanings and expectations of fatherhood and masculinity remain entwined.

LITERATURE ON MEN AND ABORTION

Little is known about how men make sense of abortion in their lives, since the body of academic writings on men and abortion is notably thin. Some research investigates opinions of who should have the right to decide pregnancy outcome (Embree 1998; Rosenwasser, Wright, and Barber 1987). Other research reports men's attitudes about abortion (Marsiglio and Shehan 1993; Miller 1994; Osborn and Silkey 1980) or perceptions of men's roles in contraception, reproduction, or pregnancy in general (Brindis et al. 1998; Edwards 1994; Grady et al. 1996; Marsiglio, Hutchinson, and Cohan 2001; Wegner et al. 1998). However, far less research has been conducted in the area of men's own experiences with abortion. A small body of research attempts to identify what roles men play in abortion, including when they are informed about unintended pregnancy and abortion (Henshaw and Kost 1992), which characteristics among men and women predict abortion (Zavodny 2001), and how men affect decisions regarding pregnancy outcome (Evans 2001; Kero et al. 1999). Illustrating the salience of cultural views about male responsibility, research has shown that adolescent and adult males identify responsibility as central to definitions of masculinity and that abortion may be an expression of responsibility (Kero and Lalos 2000; Marcell, Raine, and Eyre 2003). However, even as men articulate the importance of responsibility and may internalize expectations to behave responsibly, it is not clear how that value is actualized in pregnancy prevention or abortion decisions.

Outside this broad and ill-defined view of responsibility, few studies explore how men feel about their unintended pregnancies and abortions or construct meaning around them. Those that do often draw on data collected in interviews or surveys of nonrandomly sampled men, largely from abortion clinic waiting rooms (Holmberg and Wahlberg 2000; Kero and Lalos 2004; Shostak 1987; Shostak, McLouth, and Seng 1990; Wade 1978) or a men's counseling group that met during the partners' abortion procedures (Gordon and Kilpatrick 1977). Because of sampling, these studies inevitably overrepresent the perspectives of those most engaged in their relationships and do not reflect the majority of abortions. One recent study found that only 22 to 25 percent of women came to or left the abortion procedure with the man by whom they became pregnant (Beenhakker et al. 2004). Thus, not enough is known of the men who did not accompany partners, including those informed of the pregnancy only after its termination. Furthermore, virtually no studies evaluate men's constructions of meaning of the abortion experience later in life[1] or evaluate how the experience informs their sense of self. This research begins to address this void.

METHOD

This research analyzes the narrative accounts of thirty abortion stories collected from twenty different men during in-depth, one-on-one interviews. Multiple abortion experiences of the same man are sometimes referenced independently of each other, since the men referenced them as separate experiences and in all but two cases, had conceived with different women. In presenting these separate events, I am able to demonstrate how the experiences are not only different between men but also between relationships involving the same man.[2]

Participants were recruited through advertisements in two California regional newspapers—one daily and one free weekly—that ran for approximately two weeks, through flyers placed around a large public university campus and the surrounding communities, and through snowball sampling techniques. In all, thirty men volunteered; eight were excluded after they disclosed that although they felt they had faced the prospect of dealing with an unplanned pregnancy, they eventually learned that the woman had not actually been pregnant, while two others did not attend interview appointments. As such, twenty interviews were completed.

Interviews were conducted in comfortable private or semiprivate locations suggested by participants. Interviews were guided by an interview schedule that asked men about their past and present romantic or sexual relationships; context and detail of any pregnancies in which they were involved; the details surrounding the abortion(s), including how the pregnancy occurred and how the decision to terminate the pregnancy was reached; how they felt, looking back, about the abortion, including what they wished had gone differently; and how they felt the abortion had affected their lives. Interviews lasted between forty minutes and three hours. All interviews were conducted by the author, a young white woman. A growing body of work provides reflexive analysis of qualitative data collection and suggests that gender informs the interactions between interviewer and participant, although it is unclear how it influences the information yielded (Arendell 1997; Behar and Gordon 1995; Krieger 1991; Schwalbe and Wolkomir 2001). Schwalbe and Wolkomir suggest that the interview is an opportunity to signify masculinity "inasmuch as men can portray themselves as in control, powerful, autonomous and rational" while also a threat, as the interviewer maintains control, asks questions, and "does not simply affirm a man's masculinity displays" (p. 91). These threats and opportunities are in effect a gendered interaction; as men are inevitably defining

masculinity in their interviews, they do so in ways differently than they might for a male interviewer or an older researcher. Given that many of the men confided that they had never told anyone their abortion stories before or would never tell their male friends, I suspect that the cross-gender dynamic facilitated greater disclosure. Having said that, it is important to acknowledge that discussions of abortion, contraception, and reproduction can be sensitive. I believe that by providing the participants with a comfortable location and assurance of confidentiality, they disclosed honestly. Nonetheless, it is important to acknowledge that the interview is in itself a social interaction that affects how information is communicated (Hutchinson, Marsiglio, and Cohan 2002; Schwalbe and Wolkomir 2001).

DESCRIPTION OF PARTICIPANTS

At the time of the interview, participants ranged in age from 20 to 67, with eight men between the ages of 20–24, four men between 26–30, seven men between 34–45, and one man of 67. All self-identified as heterosexual. Fifteen of the twenty men had never been married, two were married at the time of the interview, two were divorced, and one was both divorced and widowed. Only one participant—the 67-year-old man—had been married to the woman who had the abortion (they eventually divorced, and he went on to become twice widowed). Only one of the men interviewed (Tim, age 24) was still involved with the woman who had the abortion, while only one participant (Carlos, age 21) reported asking the woman who had the abortion if she objected to his participation in the interview (the two were no longer involved). Fifteen participants self-identified as white, three as Latino, and two as African American (including one who identified as biracial).

The men reflected a wide array of professions, including student (both graduate and undergraduate), homemaker, waiter, security guard, retail salesman, auto mechanic, security guard, drug treatment counselor, nightclub disk jockey, writer, self-employed, and retired. Thirteen of the twenty were raised with a religion; of those, eight reported that they are still religious, although four changed their religious affiliation sometime during their adult life (not reported as connected to any particular experience).[3] None self-identified as pro-life or antiabortion. Although several voiced general discomfort with abortion, none voiced a desire to see abortion outlawed or criminalized, and none reported involvement with any abortion-related organization. All the elective abortions were described as occurring in the first trimester and resulting from unintended pregnancies. Of the twenty men, six were involved with multiple abortions: one with five (Aaron, age 20), one with three (Gary, age 26), and four with two. Of those four, two of the men experienced two abortions with the same woman (Tim, age 24, and Patrick, age 35). The other two men were involved with two abortions with two different women (Jon, age 40, and Brendan, age 21). The men with three or more abortions reported that each was with a different woman. There was a wide range of time elapsed between abortions and interviews. The shortest time was approximately three months. The longest was more than thirty years.

The men described their desired pregnancy outcomes at the time as they remembered them, which was not necessarily indicative of how they made sense of the experience at the time. In three abortions, the men were not told about the pregnancy until after it was terminated. In five of the abortions, the men recalled wanting to see the pregnancy continue, even as some recalled having chosen to defer to the woman's decision. In ten abortions, the men described having made the decision, even as it required the woman to terminate the pregnancy when she was inclined to continue it. Sixteen abortions—the majority—involved men and women reaching mutual decisions or men describing a process of withholding their own preferences until the women were able to reach their own decisions and then deferring to those choices.[4]

LIMITATIONS OF SAMPLE

This study is not based on a random sample and thus is not generalizable. Because participation was voluntary, the men presumably applied some amount of significance to the abortions to motivate them to volunteer.[5] I do not wish to further a belief that most men whose partners have had abortions, with or without their knowledge, apply equal significance. However, studying the qualitative responses of these men offers unique insight into how men understand their role in an accidental pregnancy, the decision to terminate that pregnancy, and how such experiences intersect with dominant meanings of masculinity, particularly as constructed and narrated with temporal distance from the experience.

This study has the advantage of sampling men beyond the clinic waiting room and accessing men who are, in all but one case, no longer involved with the women who had been pregnant. At the same time, the men often had temporal distance from the experience and had shaped their sense of the pregnancy and accompanying relationship over time. This has the strength of providing narratives that are less emotionally laden than are those of men actively involved in the termination of the pregnancy. It is also limited by relying on men's more distant recollections that are more divorced emotionally from the experience. I did not interview couples and have no way of knowing how the men's accounts of events may differ or be similar to those of their partners. However, one of the aims of this study is to understand how men construct a narrative of the experience and to examine what discourses these narratives reflect. As such, their precise recollection of details or the ways their stories differ from those of their female partners are of less relevance.

CHOOSING OR NOT CHOOSING FATHERHOOD

In deciding what they wanted the outcome of the unplanned pregnancy to be, the men described a process of examining their own desire to become fathers or rather to take on the identity of father (and accompanying responsibilities). The men overwhelmingly discussed their own process of decision making in terms of their desire to satisfy the cultural expectations of competent fatherhood. In accounting for the decision to terminate an unplanned pregnancy, the men drew on several factors: their relative desire to reproduce themselves, their evaluation of self in relation to the image of idealized fatherhood, and whether they felt ready to take on the roles of the provider and head of household. The men also discussed the relative desirability or appropriateness of the pregnant woman in their imagined father-headed family. For the latter, the men evaluated the women who had become pregnant to assess whether they might be a good choice to mother their children or to serve as their counterpart in the family they envisioned heading.

REPRODUCING HIMSELF

The occurrence of unintended pregnancy has its own meanings for men. A few of the men voiced the ability to conceive—or as one man described it, "siring a child"—as a sign of virility (Throsby and Gill 2004). Similarly, Gary, a 26-year-old Latino hotel desk clerk responsible for three pregnancies that all ended in abortion, joked, "Maybe it's the Hispanic in me. I just want to have kids." He continued, "Unfortunately, I thought it was some sort of pride thing."

In reflecting on their preparedness to become fathers, many of the men articulated abstract projections of themselves in their imagined children. Some men described potential fatherhood as presenting a chance at immortality. For example, Patrick, a 35-year-old white self-employed builder of custom furniture, described "procreation" as when "a part of yourself goes on to live in the future." Other men described fatherhood as offering a reflection of themselves. Such was the case for Jim, a white homemaker in his late forties with four children by three mothers. Jim is estranged from his first two children (now adults) who have one mother, is close to his college-age daughter from a second woman, and now married for a third time, is actively involved in raising his eight-year-old son from that marriage. Jim, who disagreed with a woman he dated between his second and third marriages when she opted to terminate an unintended pregnancy, explained his objection and how his view of abortion has changed since having children:

> Particularly if you've had kids, and I have, I think of what a reflection of your own life kids can be. You know, you look at yourself, you see yourself in your own kids, and once you've been able to experience that, then to make a decision that you're not going to [be a] father has a lot of misgivings.

Although Jim references the experience of having children as imbuing the abortion experience with particular meaning, men who had children were not the only ones to describe fatherhood as a reflection of themselves. For example, Aaron, a 20-year-old childless black man who is a student and disk jockey and who had been involved in five abortions, explained that he could not help but think about "what it would be like to have a kid, a little Aaron running around."

Seeing oneself reproduced was an issue for the few men who articulated a desire to never have children. For example, Sam, a 39-year-old white graduate student, described his motivation to see his unintended pregnancy end in abortion and his desire to remain childless as in part stemming from his lack of desire to see a reflection of himself. He remarked, "I don't feel a need to have a little one of me running around and seeing myself in this child. I don't really want to see my faults, neuroses, and psychoses and bringing them up and putting them in my child, which I [would] do one way or another." Further demonstrating the understanding of fatherhood as a reproduction of self, the men interviewed overwhelmingly referred to the unborn fetus as a "he" or discussed what their sons would need. A few used gender-neutral terms. None envisioned the fetus as a "she."

ROMANTIC NOTIONS OF FATHERHOOD

A second way the men described the process of deciding about pregnancy outcome reflected a belief that children promised to lend a greater meaning to one's life or to bring out one's best qualities. Twenty-nine-year-old Eric, a white auto mechanic, described wondering after the abortion "what it would be like to have a child. I get along great with kids. Everywhere I go, kids like me, and I don't know why because I'm an introvert, but with kids you sit down next to them—" Similarly, Carlos, a 21-year-old Latino college student and café manager, noted, "I think I'll realize more why I was put here on earth when I become a parent, 'cause I love kids and I want to be a dad so bad, I think right now, more than anything, almost too much."

As these quotes illustrate, the men imagined children as potentially bringing out their best qualities or providing emotional fulfillment. Even though some of the men in this study imagined this emotional satisfaction, very few reported a process of evaluating their own emotional maturity or

whether they would have time to participate in the day-to-day responsibilities of parenting, including providing or arranging child care, preparing meals, or dressing and bathing their children. Fatherhood appeared to be considered in abstract, romanticized ways. As Liss-Levinson (1981) asserts, "The traditional male sex role places a high value on external control and evaluation of behavior. Parenting is simply not reinforced by these means . . . While the role of father is certainly part of the traditional male image, the notion of parenting, or the actual caring for the child, is not part of the image" (p. 23). This does not necessarily mean that the men did not consider such issues but that discussing these issues, which may reflect the "conduct of motherhood," was not part of the narrative they believed was most relevant (LaRossa 1995).

The men's assessment of their own readiness for fatherhood was closely related to their own romantic construction of fatherhood. As de Beauvoir (1952) wrote, "The life of the father has a mysterious prestige . . . It is through him that the family communicates with the rest of the world; he incarnates that immense, difficult and marvelous world of adventure; he personifies transcendence, he is God" (p. 27). The men in this study evaluated how they measured up to the mystique of fatherhood and whether they felt prepared to assume that identity. A key aspect of their constructions of fatherhood was a consideration of their abilities to be directly involved in activities with their imagined children. Most often, the men discussed their abilities to play sports, underscoring the centrality of sports and athletics to definitions of masculinity (McKay, Messner, and Sabo 2000; Messner 1987; Sabo 1998).

Men's readiness or reticence to become fathers who could participate in these activities shaped many respondents' desired pregnancy outcomes. Matt, a 21-year-old white college student and nightshift security guard, explained, "[My father] was never the type where he'd coach me or get athletically involved, but I want to do that because I think that's pretty much how I became the person I am, through sports." Similarly, Alex, a 24-year-old biracial doorman at a bar, explained "I got a boy [friend] whose dad's like only 48 now and he's 25 or 26 . . . and he goes skiing with him and shit and everything, you know. It's cool, like hanging with one of the fellas instead of being with someone's dad. And that would be cool."

Participants frequently described considering the reproductive histories of their own fathers in reaching their decisions. In these stories, the men both reflected on their own abilities to accomplish what they perceived their fathers did as men and also often voiced a desire to avoid their own fathers' mistakes, including having children early and in less than ideal relationships. For example, Alex recalled thinking as he left the abortion clinic about how his parents had gotten married because of an unplanned pregnancy. He explained, "That was the only drawback, when I thought about that. I guess I was the same age as my dad at the time. I thought, man, fuck that! I was a punk. Yeah, I think, I'm sure he could have had way more fun without me." Similarly, 24-year-old Tim, a white college student, described his decision to persuade his girlfriend to have an abortion, referencing his own parents' failed marriage: "I didn't want to make the same mistakes my parents had . . . so I talked to her and basically, I was one-sided. There was no way I was going to have this baby." In pointing to the ways their own fathers failed, the men also constructed their idealized notions of the kinds of fathers they plan to be.

The men also drew on images of fathers as authoritative and in control in weighing their own willingness to assume the identity. Again, several men drew on stories of their own fathers. For example, Patrick's narrative included detailed accounts of his father's efforts to force him into law school so that he "would fill his shoes, become part of the law

firm." However, in characterizing his father, Patrick, 35, described his father in terms of admiration and respect, explaining, "I have nothing but praise for him . . . he was a really great dad and I [could] count [on him] for emotional stability; what he has taught me has held me above water more than anything else." This description of his own father as both domineering and reliable is informative and taken together shapes Patrick's view of what he should become if he becomes a father. Later in the interview, as Patrick discussed his sadness about the two abortions with which he was involved (and had insisted on), he compared himself to the Old Testament's greatest patriarch, Abraham, and described his guilt about the abortions, explaining, "God says sacrifice your own son and he was gonna do it . . . and [my] pain was about taking my own child's life." In using such cultural imagery, both in his reverent descriptions of his own father—who had misunderstood his own son's interests—and then in his construction of the fetus as his child and himself as a fatherlike servant of God, Patrick reifies his image of fathers as omnipotent. Although Patrick's frame of reference was more dramatic than that of other men, several men drew on descriptions of their own fathers as wise, respected, or authoritative in their evaluation of their preparedness to become a father, an assessment made when facing an unintended pregnancy.

ROLE OF THE PROVIDER

The majority of the men interviewed provided self-evaluations of their relative abilities to financially support a child or family in describing their own deliberations leading up to the abortion. In doing so, the men drew heavily on cultural expectations of competent masculinity as requiring men to be good providers (Bernard 1981; Coltrane 1998; Gerson 1997). As Bernard writes, "Success in the good-provider role came to define masculinity itself. The good provider had to win, to succeed, to dominate" (p. 240). Wally's description of his wife's abortion illustrates this dynamic. In discussing his wife's choice to terminate a pregnancy despite his objections, Wally, a 67-year-old white man and retired drug treatment counselor, provided great detail about how much he was earning at the time and how able he would have been to support that addition to the family, noting that "while we certainly hadn't planned on a third child so soon, financially we could hack it."

Several of the childless men defined their desire for children as contingent on reaching some future point when they would be able to financially support them. Twenty-one-year-old Carlos explained,

I'm really looking forward to [fatherhood]. I want to be situated well enough so that I can give my kid all the tools he needs so he can have no limit to what he wants to do. I want to be financially stable, to provide, and have school behind me and hopefully be in the beginning stages of having my own restaurant or clothing store or something.

Similarly, 20-year-old Aaron described the lifestyle he envisions living in ten years as "sitting back, counting my money [and] married." As he described his desire to see his girlfriend continue the pregnancy (the third unplanned pregnancy with a third woman), he described his financial stability as justification for that desire: "We were gonna get a place. I mean, I was working. I was making good money at the time and we were gonna raise our kid."

For Patrick, the desire to be both married and to be the primary breadwinner was intertwined. He explained that his girlfriend Liz "got pregnant and I knew that I didn't want to marry her, so ultimately I had to make the decision. I told her, 'I think it's best that since I cannot support you right now . . . and I don't want to marry you right now' [that you terminate the pregnancy]." Despite

the fact that, according to Patrick, Liz had inherited a sizable amount of money and could have continued the pregnancy without needing financial support, Patrick nonetheless justified his unwillingness to marry her as due to his lack of income. In doing so, he reveals the salience of traditional meanings of competent masculinity as hinging on being a provider. Furthermore, this story shows how men like Patrick assume that reproduction should occur within marriage and that the perceived marriageability of the woman affects their understanding of pregnancy outcome. This issue is explored in greater detail in the following section.

DESIRING A MALE-HEADED FAMILY

A fourth way the men reflected on the meaning of the abortion experience and communicated their preference to see the pregnancy terminated was to describe their desire for a traditional nuclear family and to assess whether this pregnancy with this woman would facilitate that. Because almost all the men were unmarried at the time of the unplanned pregnancy, the possibility of continuing this pregnancy challenged this traditional vision of family. Illustrating this, Tim, 24, explained,

I've always wanted a paradigm family situation. I want to have one child, or children with one person. I want to be the breadwinner of the family. I want her to have motherly duties. I'm gonna have fatherly duties . . . I know it's paternalistic, it's macho. Whatever you want to call it, these are my feelings. And I want what I never had. I want a family.

Tim convinced his girlfriend to have two abortions after two unplanned pregnancies, in large part because of how those pregnancies interrupted his plans for the kind of family he wanted. At the time of the interview, more than two years after the first abortion, he was still dating her. Yet in narrating his strong preference to see both pregnancies terminated, Tim considered the kind of family he wants and whether his girlfriend would fit. Tim came to this position after his disappointment in having grown up with a single mother and having a father he only visited on weekends. It is likely he wants what he called "a paradigm family situation" both because he would like to provide that to his future child and because such a family arrangement can guarantee ongoing access and contact with his children. Like Tim, almost none of the men interviewed described a situation in which they could envision sharing a child without also being the head of household in a heterosexual nuclear family, even though they may be motivated differently.

The men's articulated desire for a paradigmatic male-headed family also drew on perceptions of the women who had been pregnant. For the few men who described deeply loving the women, the abortion process reflected greater ambivalence. For example, Aaron refers to finding out that "a part of me was inside her" as significant. With another woman, Aaron recalls thinking a lot about "what the two of us created." Both quotes—drawing on experiences with different women in different pregnancies—illustrate how he thought of the fetus as a symbol of intimacy. This was not widespread.

More common, about one-third of the participants in this study described the women who had had the abortions as "obsessive," "possessive," "unstable," or unsuitable to mother what was often described as "my child." For example, 24-year-old Alex reflected on his support for the abortion, explaining, "I didn't want the responsibility, and I'm not sure I wanted my kid with her. When you have a kid, you know what I mean, that's it. You have a child, you take care of it, you know; but I can't even take care of myself, and she infuriates me sometimes."

Similarly, Gary, 26, described in negative terms the second woman who became pregnant by him and terminated the pregnancy. In articulating both the discomfort of the procedure itself and his difficulties engaging her emotionally, he explained that she was "very negative and always whining about something's wrong with her all the time and it was definitely, she was high maintenance and so that really, um, took away some of my sympathy at the time."

A large subset described the importance of having children with the right person and could describe their image of such a person. For example, Tim, the only man in the study still involved with the woman who had the abortions (two), described his uncertainty about whether to commit to Debra, his girlfriend of five years. In explaining why he insisted on both abortions, he explained, "I want a little family structure . . . That's what everyone dreams about, and I want my dreams to come true. And I think if I had a child with Debra it might mess, it might mess that up, because I'm not sure she's the perfect person."

The notion that the woman who had become pregnant was not "the perfect person" ran through many of the stories. Patrick, 35, referring to his girlfriend of seven years, commented, "You know, [a college friend] warned me. He said, 'She's crazy. You should stay away from that girl. She's nuts.' [I said] 'I can handle it.' Sure, right. Well, it screwed up my life." In describing his decision to insist that she terminate the pregnancy and his own ambivalence about having done so, he contemplates, "Why did I want to, you know, take my own child? Why did I want to do that? Well, [because] in having a child with Liz, that would be forever . . . I would always be a father to that child to a woman that I really wanted no part of." Although the first abortion with her was after the first year of the relationship, he continued his relationship with Liz for another six years. Patrick, like many men in this study, recast the woman who became pregnant in terms of moral failure or personal shortcoming. There is little doubt that this recasting occurred after the termination of the relationship and perhaps served to justify such an ending. It also occurred equally among the men, irrespective of whether they reported having wanted the pregnancy to continue or not. Furthermore, this rhetoric supports a cultural view that women who engage in nonmarital sex, particularly when they become pregnant or infected with a sexually transmitted disease, are morally tainted and as such are no longer motherly (Nack 2002; Reich 2005; Umansky 1998).

The narrative of the women as failed or inadequate also serves to portray the men's desire to be seen as competent. This can perhaps be seen most clearly in the men's comments about hypothetical future partners. Illustrating this connection, 21-year-old Matt explained his choice to only have intercourse with women who could potentially be a significant partner: "I can't wait to have kids. It seems the older I get, the more moral I become . . . I don't pull the trigger unless the feeling is there." Thus, potential sexual partners are imagined as potential mothers, and in imagining their potential selves, the men draw heavily on the kinds of relationships and family forms they would like to achieve. Few men imagined a friendship with a woman in which they could share parenting without having a romantic relationship with the accompanying entitlements of head of household. The men who were best able to imagine such a relationship were most likely to have agreed mutually on abortion.

CONCLUSION

Unintended pregnancy and resulting abortion provide an important vantage point from which to examine how men conceptualize their masculine identities and what Marsiglio, Hutchinson, and Cohan (2001) term their "procreative selves." As men identify an embodied experience of reproduction post-conception (and in fact in many cases do not learn of the pregnancy until after it is terminated), understanding abortion experiences requires examining cultural discourses of reproduction and fatherhood and the related dimensions of masculinity.

In this study, the men's narratives of their abortion experiences reflect aspects of hegemonic masculinity. First, the men often conceptualized reproduction as a chance to reproduce themselves, to gain immortality, or to bring out their best qualities. Second, the men relied on romantic cultural images of fatherhood, including the prescribed role of playing sports or being an authoritative figure. The men reflected on their own fathers' lives and procreative histories to construct their images of the kinds of fathers they would like to be. Third, the men evaluated their relative ability to be a good provider in deciding whether they wanted to see the pregnancy continue. The men who felt they could provide were often frustrated that the pregnant woman chose to terminate the pregnancy. Other men imagined a future masculine self who was financially self-reliant and able to provide. Fourth, the men overwhelmingly communicated their desire to have a paradigmatic male-headed nuclear family. In establishing their desire for such a family form, they evaluated the woman who was pregnant and frequently suggested that she was not "the perfect one" or possessed traits that made her less than ideal to mother their children.

Taken together, these men's patterned narratives form a masculinist discourse of abortion. Revealed in such discourse is the way that men's reproductive decisions are heavily embedded in cultural definitions of heterosexual middle-class fatherhood. Of some surprise, there was little discernible difference between the men, irrespective of race, ethnicity, class, education level, or age. In part, this may be because of the limited size of the sample. Yet in part, it also likely reflects the dominant culture of fatherhood that defines competent masculinity in narrow terms. The men who in most cases planned to eventually become fathers hoped to be good ones. As the men's discourse reflected aspirational fatherhood, they used the same cultural terms of competent masculinity. There was little variation between men based on their desired pregnancy outcome, as they recounted it. This suggests that over time, the narratives the men deployed to account for the terminated pregnancy—even though they may have originally desired a different outcome—rely on the same available cultural scripts. Such scripts were deployed during the interview to construct a masculine self. Because this study does not utilize interviews with couples or dyads in the abortion and draws on men's recollections of the abortion experience, it is difficult to say whether these dynamics were as dominant in their decision-making experience at the time of the unintended pregnancy as the narratives would suggest. Nonetheless, the strong patterned narratives that represent this masculinist discourse explicate the significance and cultural accessibility of this discourse. Presumably, the men strived to provide their best presentation of self in their narratives. In doing so, they chose to use these tropes of competent masculinity. The use of this masculinist narrative does not preclude the very real possibility that there are more complex emotional processes occurring internally that were not fully revealed during the interview. In fact, the process of constructing a masculine self during an interview with a female researcher may limit a willingness to disclose the full range of emotions experienced. Irrespective of what emotions may or may not have been felt, what remains relevant is that as men travel through their social worlds and selectively disclose about their abortion experience, these are the narratives they put forth. Thus, these narratives represent the public understanding of men's experience of abortion.

Finally, there is great importance in understanding a masculine discourse of abortion. As policymakers, agencies, and public service campaigns aim to alter men's reproductive and familial behavior, it is important to recognize the extent to which men have internalized such cultural messages and the ways they do and do not affect behavior. Without stronger understanding of the ways that men's behaviors are shaped by their own perceptions of masculinity and goals for their future masculine and paternal selves, such programs and campaigns will be ineffective.

NOTES

1. Kero and Lalos (2004) examined abortion experiences up to twelve months after the experience.
2. Given that this study did not collect data from the women in the abortion dyad, the context of relationships and how these relational issues shaped the abortion experience are not adequately explored here. This is a ripe area for future research.
3. Three respondents were raised Jewish, of which two still practice. One is Mormon, one is Baptist, and one identifies as Protestant. Three were raised Presbyterian; one still practices, one is now Episcopalian, and one reports exercising Eastern philosophy. One was raised Episcopalian and Baptist and only loosely identifies with either. Three were raised Catholic, of which two loosely still practice.
4. For a more detailed discussion of how these men accounted for the decision-making process, see Reich and Brindis (forthcoming).
5. Similar observations were made by Terry Arendell (1997), who conducted interviews with divorced men.

CHAPTER 10

Facing the Fetus

Helena Silverstein

On a Saturday afternoon of the following spring, with a warm mist of rain falling, [Julian] McPhillips pulls his car off the busy Montgomery thoroughfare into the edge of a retail parking lot and lowers his driver-side window. "This is one of two we've done, over the years," he says, pointing to the billboard above. "The message changes from time to time, but the theme is the same."

In stark black-and-white, the sign features a drawing of a fetus inside the uterus, alongside the text, "Before I formed thee in the womb, I knew thee . . . (Jeremiah 1:5)." A telephone number for Sav-A-Life is listed below. (The other billboard reads, "Abortion Stops a Beating Heart: Please consider the Alternatives, Including Adoption." The same telephone number appears).

"The people at Sav-A-Life tell us they've had a very good response, that a number of women have come in because of the billboard and changed their minds and not had an abortion," he says.

—Carroll Dale Short,
The People's Lawyer[1]

When a minor appears before a judge to petition for a bypass of parental involvement, we expect the setting to be neutral, unadorned by a billboard such as the one described here. Yet some judges have gone one better, appointing attorneys to serve as guardians for the unborn. These judges have placed walking and talking pro-life advertisements in the center of bypass proceedings, claiming the legitimacy of the rule of law for what is nothing more than pro-life propaganda. This chapter tells the story of guardianship appointments in Alabama.[2]

"PROVIDENCE FOR THE UNBORN"

On July 6, 1998, a pregnant minor, three months shy of her eighteenth birthday, sought a waiver of parental consent from the juvenile court in Montgomery County.[3] The minor's petition was put before Judge W. Mark Anderson, one of three judges responsible for reviewing bypass requests in Montgomery. In accordance with internal courthouse procedures, the court intake officer assigned the minor legal counsel. Reaching beyond ordinary procedures, the judge appointed a guardian ad litem to represent the fetus. Such guardians are officers of the court and are normally appointed to represent parties incapacitated by age or other disability.

Judge Anderson had presided over bypass hearings prior to this case. In fact, Anderson had previously made clear both his opposition to abortion and his willingness to grant waiver requests. In an earlier bypass case, he wrote a lengthy judicial order that expressed his "fixed opinion that abortion is wrong"[4] and his belief that the minor's decision to terminate her pregnancy would compound one mistake with another more terrible one—namely, the death of her unborn child. Still, Anderson waived parental consent upon finding that the minor was sufficiently mature and informed to have the abortion and upon concluding that, given the maturity finding, the law allows the judge no alternative but to grant the bypass. The order noted that the minor would turn eighteen in a month and could wait until then to have the abortion without a judicial bypass. But quoting from Shakespeare and referring to Macbeth's plan to assassinate his own father, Anderson reportedly wrote, "like Macbeth, 'If it were done when 'tis done, then 'twere well It were done quickly.'"[5]

Anderson selected attorney Julian McPhillips, an avid supporter of Sav-A-Life, to serve as guardian for the fetus in the July 1998 case.[6] "Though many people in [Montgomery] were surprised when Judge Anderson appointed an advocate for the anonymous teenager's baby," explains Carroll Dale Short, author of McPhillips's biography, "nobody who knew McPhillips was surprised at the judge's choice of attorney. He's possibly the area's most high-visibility figure in the pro-life arena, with a successful record of defending anti-abortion protesters who are arrested outside city clinics."[7]

When the minor's court-appointed counsel, Beverly Howard, received notice that a guardian would represent "Baby Ashley" at the hearing, she filed a motion to strike the appointment. Anderson denied the motion, basing his authority for the appointment on Rule 17(c) of the Alabama Rules of Civil Procedure. Rule 17(c) states that "when the interest of an infant unborn or unconceived is before the court, the court may appoint a guardian ad litem for such interest."[8] Anderson justified his use of Rule 17(c) by noting the importance of giving the "unborn child" an "opportunity to have a voice, even a vicarious one, in the decision making."[9] He did not appeal to the Alabama Parental Consent Statute, for neither it nor any other involvement statute that is currently in effect includes provisions concerning the appointment of fetal representation.[10]

Howard also filed a motion asking the judge to recuse himself from the case, given his previously declared opposition to abortion. Anderson rejected this motion as well, explaining that his personal views would not interfere with his ability to follow the law. In support of this contention, Anderson pointed to the fact that his attitudes about abortion did not prevent him from approving previous bypass petitions.

Bypass hearings in Alabama and elsewhere ordinarily take less than thirty minutes. In these hearings, it is typical for the lawyer and the judge to question the minor in an effort to elicit testimony that speaks to the two-pronged bypass test. A minor usually answers questions that address her level of education, grades, future plans, career interests, and employment history. Her attorney commonly inquires about the medical aspects and risks of the procedure. A minor can also expect questions about whether she has considered alternatives to abortion, what plans she has made to handle any physical or emotional consequences, why she would choose abortion over other alternatives, and why she would make such a choice without involving her parents.

During this bypass hearing, Howard posed questions along these lines, yielding testimony concerning the minor's level of maturity and her familiarity with abortion and its alternatives. Answering Howard's inquiries, the minor testified that she was a high school honors student with a college scholarship in hand. She managed her own money, investigated the financial assistance available should she have a child, and received counseling from Sav-A-Life about the alternatives to abortion.[11] She explained the risks of abortion and expressed her view that proceeding with childbirth would interfere with her ability to pursue college. The petitioner also expressed fears about her father discovering her pregnancy, saying that he "had been known to point a gun at boys who looked at her provocatively."[12]

In his position as guardian, McPhillips called two witnesses on behalf of the fetus, over the repeated objections of the minor's counsel. These witnesses included a physician who testified about the physical development of the fetus and the executive director of a Sav-A-Life center who testified about alternatives to abortion and her experiences with postabortive women.

Anderson allowed the guardian considerable latitude not only in calling witnesses but also in questioning the petitioner. During an extensive cross-examination, McPhillips put many questions to the minor about the life and death of the fetus. For example, McPhillips asked the young woman whether she was aware that the "baby" already had a heartbeat. "And you are not concerned after you have had the abortion that some day you may wake up and say my gosh, what have I done to my own baby?"[13] Though the minor acknowledged that she might experience regret, McPhillips persisted: "You are not worried about being haunted by this? Here you have the chance to save the life of your own baby. . . . And still you want to go ahead and snuff out the life of your own baby?"[14]

McPhillips invoked religion in pursuing this line of inquiry. Over protests from Howard, he asked the minor whether she was familiar with Bible scripture in which God says to the prophet Jeremiah: "Before I formed thee in the womb, I knew thee." McPhillips also asked the minor if she had prayed about her decision. After acknowledging that she had and indicating her belief that abortion is a sin, McPhillips asked if she was willing to "pay the price for this sin?"[15] "You say that you are aware that God instructed you not to kill your own baby, but you want to do it anyway? And are you saying here today that notwithstanding everything that you want to interfere with God's plan for your baby?"[16]

Among her many objections, Howard protested the use of the term "kill," to which McPhillips insisted, "Your honor, it's killing. I didn't say 'murder,' although it's murder."[17] This provoked another objection from Howard, who argued that bypass hearings do not extend the right to kill but rather determine whether a minor is in a position to make a decision about abortion without parental consent. In an effort to make the questioning "more palatable," Anderson suggested that the parties refer to the procedure as "cooperating in the termination of the life of the unborn child."[18] McPhillips, though, was undeterred:

> If you sugarcoat it too much, she doesn't understand what she's doing. Killing is what she would be doing. She may choose not to. But if in the event you choose to have an abortion, I'd like to ask her if she realizes that there's a life

there. Does she understand that a beating heart is going to be put to an end?[19]

After a four-hour hearing that generated some 150 pages of transcript, Anderson granted the bypass. Taking the opportunity to voice his own views about abortion and the life of the unborn, the judge offered the minor these reflections:

> I know this has not been an easy afternoon. . . . We're dealing with a decision that is going to stop a beating heart. . . . But what we have done here today is not for the purpose of giving you a hard time. . . . I feel that we are dealing with a human life and the end of the human life. . . . Whatever that decision is and whatever you do, I hope God will be with you.[20]

Anderson also expressed his views in his written order granting the bypass. He praised the guardian's performance, stating that McPhillips had done

> a yeoman's job of protecting the interests of his ward, to the extent that this unfortunate law allows. What we call life is but a brief passage in eternity. There must be a special providence for the unborn who not only are deprived of the opportunity to live but of having a saving faith in spite of the sin whose commission is the natural inheritance of man.[21]

Despite these comments, Anderson indicated that he felt "confined to issue the waiver of parental consent" pursuant to state law:[22]

> From the record made through almost four hours of testimony and arguments of the most acrimonious nature, it is clear to the court that a waiver is not in best interest of this young woman. It certainly is not in the best interest of the unborn child. Those findings are abundantly clear from the efforts and evidence of Mr. McPhillips. But unfortunately those two findings are not determinative of the issue raised by this proceeding. This court is bound to uphold to the law, however distasteful that may be and regardless of whether the law is

consistent with this court's fixed opinions. This is the law. Required consent shall be waived if . . . the minor is mature and well informed enough to make the abortion decision on her own. . . . The court hereby grants the minor's petition for waiver of consent.[23]

SILENCE IS GOLDEN

The provisions enumerated in the Alabama parental consent statute afford minors the right to appeal a judge's denial of a bypass petition.[24] No other party is explicitly given the right to appeal. This fact notwithstanding, McPhillips sought and received a stay of Anderson's order, and appealed the decision to the Court of Civil Appeals.

By challenging Anderson's order, McPhillips provided the Alabama appellate courts an opportunity to rule on the permissibility of guardianship appointments. Both the Court of Civil Appeals and the Alabama Supreme Court, to which the case eventually fell, passed up this opportunity.

Rather than ruling on the broad question of whether guardian appointments are legally appropriate in the context of bypass hearings, the Court of Civil Appeals confined itself to the narrow question of whether a guardian, once appointed, has the right to appeal the grant of a bypass petition. In a one-page per curiam opinion dismissing the appeal, the appellate court explains that the right to an appeal in such cases is "purely statutory."[25] Furthermore,

> [t]he legislature did not provide a right to appeal from the granting of a petition for a waiver of parental consent. The statute specifically states that an appeal may lie for any "minor" to whom the court "denies" the petition. This specific wording does not leave room for judicial interpretation. In this case no minor was denied a waiver. Therefore, there is no right to appeal.[26]

Faced with this dismissal, McPhillips appealed to the Supreme Court of Alabama. In a ruling issued on August 3, 1998, the high court affirmed Anderson's decision to grant the bypass of consent.[27] All the justices concurred in the finding that the minor proved herself to be sufficiently mature and well informed to proceed with the abortion absent parental involvement. Nevertheless, the ruling was sharply divided over the issue of whether a guardian can appeal the grant of a bypass petition. The court's per curiam ruling, joined by four justices and concurred with by a fifth,[28] states:

> The Legislature, as the Court of Civil Appeals correctly noted, did not provide a right to appeal from an order granting a petition for a waiver of parental consent. We can conclude only that the Legislature understood its subordinance to the Supremacy Clause of the United States Constitution and that it recognized that, pursuant to the United States Supreme Court's decision in *Roe v. Wade* (1973), it could not constitutionally confer upon a nonviable fetus the right to appeal, through a guardian ad litem, an order granting a minor's request to have an abortion.[29]

The opinion rejects the right of the fetus to appeal through a guardian but neither rejects nor confirms the trial court's authority to appoint the guardian ad litem in the first place. Instead, the ruling, like the decision of the Court of Civil Appeals, is silent on this point.[30]

Diverging from this opinion, four justices expressly addressed the legitimacy of guardianship appointments and argued in favor of the guardian's right to appeal. The opinion of these justices supports Anderson's application of Rule 17(c) and cites precedent requiring the appointment of a guardian to represent the interests of an unborn child during certain types of divorce proceedings:[31]

> If a guardian ad litem is required for an unborn child when its legitimacy is at stake, then, a fortiori, it would appear that the appointment of a guardian ad litem, although not specifically provided for in the Parental Consent Statute,

would at least be authorized, if not required, in a case such as this one, involving a minor who is seeking a waiver of parental consent to have an abortion.[32]

Having established their position on the legitimacy of guardianship appointments, the dissenters also argue that "[i]t is well settled that a guardian ad litem appointed to protect the interests of the unborn has a right to appeal."[33] Furthermore,

> it seems clear that the Legislature intended, in adopting the Parental Consent Statute, to preserve the life of the unborn, and it deliberately was doing what it could within the constraints of the Federal Constitution, as interpreted by the Supreme Court of the United States, to accomplish that purpose. . . . The general rule of law is that guardians ad litem are desirable in many proceedings to ensure that the proceedings will have the adversariness necessary for the full presentation of the issues, and in the proceedings now here for review such an appointment would be consistent with the purpose and intent of the Legislature in adopting the Parental Consent Statute. . . . [W]e conclude that the Legislature, when it provided the minor a right to appeal, did not intend to prohibit a guardian ad litem appointed to represent the interest of an unborn child from appealing from an adverse order. Stated differently, we do not believe that the Legislature, by failing specifically to provide in the Parental Consent Statute for a guardian ad litem's right to appeal, intended, by omission, to defeat such a right of appeal.[34]

With four justices indicating that a trial court may appoint a guardian ad litem to represent the fetus in bypass hearings, and with another five justices remaining silent on this point, Alabama trial courts retain the discretion to designate an agent to speak on behalf of the unborn. Indeed, as McPhillips explained,

> the [Alabama] Supreme Court decision was a victory at least on this point. . . . Four judges were saying I should be a guardian for the

unborn, but the others didn't even comment on the issue of whether I should have the right to be a guardian ad litem. I talked to the judge, Judge Anderson, and he deserved an award for being a profile in courage, and we took that as a green light for there being a right to have a guardian, and so he continued to appoint guardians for the unborn.[35]

ONGOING USE OF FETAL REPRESENTATIVES

In an effort to explicitly sanction that which the Alabama Supreme Court did not, the Alabama legislature in 1999 considered a bill requiring that an attorney be appointed to represent the state in bypass cases and granting to the trial court the option of designating a guardian to represent the unborn.[36] Drafted by the president of the Alabama Pro-Life Coalition, the bill died in committee but not before being endorsed by then Alabama Attorney General William Pryor.[37] According to one news report, Pryor, one of President George W. Bush's controversial appointments to the federal bench,[38] was reported as saying that an "attorney representing the government should be involved to protect the state's interest in preserving life."[39] In addition, "Pryor said he envisioned attorneys with networks like Alabama Lawyers for Life, of which he used to be a member, agreeing to represent the state for free and 'potentially' taking an adversarial [position] against abortions."[40]

Notwithstanding this legislative failure and given the green light provided by the Alabama Supreme Court, Judge Anderson has made it a routine practice to appoint guardians at bypass hearings. Judge John Cappel, also of Montgomery County, has adopted this practice.[41] As a result, since the 1998 case in which McPhillips served as guardian, at least three different attorneys have represented the unborn in at least seventeen bypass hearings.[42]

Those who have represented the unborn since McPhillips admit that their common objective is to protect the fetus' interest in being born. As one guardian explained, "In a nutshell, my role is to protect the interest of the unborn child, and I believe my role, through the questions, is to see if I can change the child's mind and convince her to carry the child to term."[43] Another explained that "the law is clear: if this girl is mature enough, then they have a right to make that choice. My job is to see if she meets those conditions."[44] But this job, the guardian said, is secondary: "I'm there representing the unborn, my goal primarily is to save that unborn fetus' life. . . . The unborn fetus has no voice other than my voice, and if we don't make sure that the voice is heard, at least to the limit of the law, then that unborn fetus doesn't have a chance."[45]

To give the fetus a chance, guardians try to demonstrate to the minor that there is a living human being growing inside her body, that she may suffer physically and emotionally as a result of aborting the fetus, that some women who have abortions develop psychological problems and may even become suicidal, that there are many families willing to adopt, and that money is available to assist with both prenatal care and the raising of children. They do so through extensive cross-examination.[46]

One guardian explained that the questions presented during cross-examination overlap to some extent with those posed to the minor by her counsel. Among these questions are "Where do they intend to spend the night? What are the risks?"[47] In addition, this guardian also asks: "Have you talked with anybody who had an abortion before? Do you know that people who suffer abortions tend to be more suicidal? . . . [H]ave you watched any videos?"[48]

Similarly, as another guardian explained, "I'll go through preliminary questions, her school activities, what her career plans are, do they have a job, do they have a bank account, what kind of level of maturity they have in general."[49] This guardian continues

through a list of some seventy questions to inquire

[i]f they've seen pictures of the baby, of the fetus; if they've talked to a medical doctor. And then a whole series of questions about how the procedure is performed, what the risks are, what the complications might be, what they will do in the event they confront complications. I discuss psychological and emotional consequences, post-abortion syndrome in men and in mothers as well. Ask if they've talked to any adults, a minister, counselor at school, clinic; if they've seen videos or printed materials about the procedure. And then I ask them about alternatives: raising it themselves, adoption, Catholic Social Services. There are a number of agencies that will take the child. I usually ask if they've been to any pro-life agencies. Do they believe this is in their best interest? I ask if she thinks abortion is wrong. Then a couple of scenarios: if there was a couple in their church, well educated and they couldn't have a child and they really wanted one, would she consider giving the child to them for adoption? I try to get them to think if there are alternatives. . . . Usually we'll ask do they go to church, what church, what's the view of the church regarding abortion, have they thought about whether there are churchgoers who would want to adopt, do they attend regularly.[50]

Owing to the fact that guardians are obligated to advance the interest of the fetus, the questions put to the minor are in many instances designed to compel her to consider the nature of human life, personhood, and killing. A minor will typically be asked whether she believes abortion is wrong and whether choosing abortion runs counter to her religious views. If the minor answers either of these questions affirmatively, she will be expected to resolve the discord between her beliefs and her decision to terminate her pregnancy. Indeed, one guardian went so far as to ask a minor who already had a child whether she could imagine killing that child. When the minor said no, the guardian pressed her to explain how she could justify aborting the fetus she was carrying if she could not conceive of killing her born child.

Guardians sometimes use fear to persuade the minor to forgo her intended course of action. Consider the following report of a guardian's questions, taken from a dissenting opinion in an appeal of a bypass denial:

> The minor testified that she and her boyfriend plan to marry when they are older and that they have discussed having three children. The lawyer the trial judge appointed to represent the fetus asked if the minor, knowing that "one of the risks that you are going to face is the possibility that you will be sterile after this procedure," was "willing to place your future three children at risk." The lawyer then asked, if she died as a result of the abortion, "Would that not take away not only your three children but your boyfriend's future wife and his three children?" The lawyer also asked if the minor had ever heard of post-abortion syndrome in men. He asked if she was aware that men are "very often affected psychologically by their child being taken in abortion" and if she was willing to "place [her boyfriend] at the same risk" she was taking. The lawyer also said to the minor: "If you did have a complication and you had to go to the hospital, your church congregation is going to find out what's happened. How is that going to effect [sic] your going to church every Sunday?"[51]

While guardians use cross-examination as the primary method for advocating birth over abortion, some guardians have called witnesses to present evidence on behalf of the fetus.[52] Like McPhillips, two other guardians brought in the director of a Sav-A-Life center to testify about the psychological effects of abortion. These guardians also put on the record the testimony of a woman who had previously undergone an abortion. These "experts" were called "to try and put out information," one guardian explained.[53] "That lady who had had the abortion said once if she said it twenty times, 'if I had known then what I know now, I would never

have done what I did.' So information is the tool."[54] With that testimony presented, the guardian asked the minor "whether she knew what she was getting into."[55]

Additional opportunities for appellate review have emerged with the continued use of guardians, but these have yielded little beyond the 1998 decision.[56] In 1999, the Court of Civil Appeals considered a case in which a minor's appeal of a bypass denial was accompanied by a guardian's motion to file a brief in support of the judge's order. Overturning the judge's denial of the bypass request, the Court also rejected the guardian's motion. In a footnote and without explanation or support, the Court of Civil Appeals wrote that "[a] majority of the [Alabama Supreme] court did not address whether the trial court had the authority to appoint a guardian for the fetus. Likewise, in this case, we do not address the propriety of appointing the guardian, and we have denied the guardian's motion to file a brief in support of the trial court's order."[57]

In 2001, a minor appealed a judicial order denying her bypass request and directly raised the question of whether the trial court had violated her constitutional rights by designating an agent for the fetus.[58] The Alabama Supreme Court ruled that the trial judge had erred in denying the bypass and offered the following characterization of the guardian's participation:

> [T]his was not a nonadversarial proceeding. [The minor] was cross-examined by a lawyer appointed to represent the fetus, and she adhered to her testimony and to her position that an abortion was the most appropriate course of action for her, despite being given full exposure, through an extended cross-examination, to opposing viewpoints that strongly emphasized the negative effect of the abortion procedure and that advocated the benefits of having a child.[59]

While explicitly acknowledging that the presence of a guardian generated an adversarial hearing, the court sidestepped the opportunity to address the propriety of designating agents for the fetus. "[I]n light of our holding," the court explained, "we pretermit any discussion of [the minor's] argument concerning the trial court's appointment of a lawyer to represent the fetus."[60]

One Alabama Supreme Court justice has registered criticism of guardian appointments. In a harshly worded dissent challenging both the denial of a bypass request and the appointment of fetal representation, Justice Douglas Inge Johnstone characterized such appointments as gratuitous and claimed the petitioner was "a victim of prejudice against abortion."[61] Quoting from the hearing transcript, the dissent criticized the trial judge's statement to the minor that appointing "a lawyer to represent your unborn child" allows "someone to represent the silent voice in this case."[62] Johnstone argued that "[g]ratuitously appointing a guardian ad litem for the 'silent voice' casts the inquiry as a contest between a baby struggling to save its own life and the mother fighting to kill the baby."[63]

NOTES

1. Carroll Dale Short, *The People's Lawyer: The Colorful Life and Times of Julian L. McPhillips, Jr.* (Montgomery, Ala.: NewSouth Books, 2000), 306.
2. The information I present about guardianship appointments derives from several sources, including the interviews drawn upon in Chapter 6. In this chapter I cite interviews only when they are the source of a direct quotation. I do not identify the names of those interviewed, except where the participants have consented to my inclusion of their names.
3. *See Ex parte* Anonymous, 720 So. 2d 497 (Ala. 1998) at 499. The ruling does not specify that the minor sought the waiver in Montgomery County.
4. Amy Bach, "No Choice for Teens," *Nation*, October 11, 1999, 7.
5. Interview, April 23, 2001.
6. Short, *The People's Lawyer*, 320, 306.
7. *Id.* at 307.
8. Quoted in *Ex parte* Anonymous, 720 So. 2d at 499 n.2.
9. Quoted in Bach, "No Choice for Teens," 7.
10. As noted in Chapter 2, some parental involvement laws incorporate provisions allowing for or mandating the appointment of a guardian ad litem to protect the interests of the minor. *See, e.g., KRS* § 311.732 (3)(c) (2004). While the Alabama parental consent statute does not mention such appointments, the Alabama Supreme Court has held "that the attorney to be appointed under the parental consent act is to be a guardian ad litem [for the minor], and that future appointments should be so designated and shall entail the responsibilities attendant to such appointments." *Ex parte* Anonymous, 531 So. 2d 901 (Ala. 1988) at 905.
11. *See* Bach, "No Choice for Teens," 7.
12. *Id.*
13. *Id.*
14. *Id.*
15. Interview, April 23, 2001.
16. Quoted in Bach, "No Choice for Teens," 7.
17. Interview, April 23, 2001.
18. *Id.*
19. *Id.*
20. *Id.*
21. *Id.*
22. *Ex parte* Anonymous, 720 So. 2d at 504.
23. Interview, April 23, 2001.
24. *Ala. Code* § 26–21–4(h) (2004).
25. *In re* Anonymous, 720 So. 2d 497 (Ala. Civ. App. 1998) at 497.
26. *Id.*
27. *Ex parte* Anonymous, 720 So. 2d 497 (Ala. 1998).
28. Justices Reneau Almon, Janie Shores, J. Gorman Houston, and Mark Kennedy joined the per curiam opinion. Justice Ralph Cook concurred, without opinion.
29. *Ex parte* Anonymous, 720 So. 2d at 499–500 (citations omitted).
30. The court's opinion addresses a separate issue raised by McPhillips—namely, whether the judicial waiver provision deprives parents of due process of law. The court notes the legislature's intention "to foster 'the family structure,' to preserve the family 'as a viable social unit,' and to protect 'the rights of parents to rear children who are members of their household.'" *Id.* at 500 (quoting *Ala. Code* § 26–21–1(a) (1975)). Nevertheless, the court concludes, and with little elaboration, that the statute does not unconstitutionally deny the due process rights of custodial parents. *Id.*
31. *See Ex parte* Martin, 565 So. 2d 1 (Ala. 1989).
32. *Ex parte* Anonymous, 720 So. 2d at 502 (Hooper, C. J., Maddox, J., See, J., and Lyons, J., concurring specially in part and dissenting in part).
33. *Id.*
34. *Id.* at 502–3.
35. Interview, April 23, 2001.
36. *See* S.B. 389, 1999 Ala. Reg. Sess. (1999). Sections 26–21–4 (i)-(j) of the proposed legislation would have provided for the following:

    (i) . . . [T]he Attorney General or his or her representative shall participate as an advocate for the state to examine the petitioner and any witnesses, and to present evidence for the purpose of providing the court with a sufficient record upon which to make an informed decision and to do substantial justice.

(j) In the court's discretion, it may appoint a guardian ad litem for the interests of the unborn child of the petitioner who shall also have the same rights and obligations of participation in the proceeding as given to the Attorney General.

37. *See* Jay Reeves, "Bill Would Involve State Attorneys in Juvenile Abortion Cases," Associated Press State and Local Wire, February 23, 1999. That the bill died in committee was reported to me by the Legislative Reference Service of the State of Alabama.

38. Senate Democrats filibustered Pryor's nomination to the Eleventh Circuit Court of Appeals, prompting President Bush to install Pryor as a recess appointment. *See* Neil A. Lewis, "Bypassing Senate for Second Time, Bush Seats Judge," *New York Times*, February 21, 2004. Pryor eventually earned Senate approval after a compromise that avoided a vote to eliminate filibusters of judicial nominees. Carl Hulse, "Bipartisan Group in Senate Averts Judge Showdown," *New York Times*, May 24, 2005.

39. Quoted in Reeves, "Bill Would Involve State Attorneys in Juvenile Abortion Cases."

40. *Id.*

41. Although there may be instances of such appointments that I have yet to discover, reports suggest that most judges who handle bypass petitions in Alabama typically do not assign a guardian to give a voice to the fetus. Outside of Alabama, there have been some reported cases of guardian appointments at bypass hearings in Florida, Indiana, and Louisiana. *See* Chapter 9 in this volume.

42. McPhillips was not called on in these cases to act as guardian ad litem. One attorney was appointed to handle two of these cases, a second attorney handled one case, and a third attorney has routinely served in this capacity. There was an additional instance in which a guardian was appointed to represent the fetus, but the minor, in the end, did not pursue the waiver option and the hearing was cancelled. There have likely been other instances in which guardians have served as fetal representatives. The seventeen I count since the McPhillips hearings are ones I have been able to document either by way of interviews or through appellate court rulings.

43. Interview, May 23, 2001.

44. Interview, April 26, 2001.

45. *Id.*

46. For example, the Alabama Supreme Court relayed the questioning of a minor by one guardian:

The lawyer appointed for the fetus, described in the record as a guardian ad litem, subjected [the minor] to a probing cross-examination concerning her knowledge of the negative consequences of undergoing an abortion and the possible consequences, including depression, sterility, and death. The appointed lawyer's cross-examination also explored at some length [the minor's] knowledge of the alternatives to abortion, including having her family help raise the baby or placing the baby for adoption. *Ex parte* Anonymous, 810 So. 2d 786 (Ala. 2001) at 789.

47. Interview, May 16, 2001.

48. *Id.*

49. Interview, May 23, 2001.

50. *Id.*

51. *In re* Anonymous, 810 So. 2d 784 (Ala. Civ. App. 2001) at 785 (Yates, J., dissenting).

52. Among the witnesses called were the executive director of Sav-A-Life, the director of COPE Crisis Pregnancy Center, and a woman who testified about her post-abortive experiences. *See In re* Anonymous, 733 So. 2d 429 (Ala. Civ. App. 1999).

53. Interview, April 26, 2001.

54. *Id.*

55. *Id.*

56. The U.S. Supreme Court has not faced the opportunity to address the constitutionality of these appointments. But the Florida Supreme Court did, finding in one case that "the appointment of a guardian ad litem for the fetus was clearly improper." *In re* T. W., 551 So. 2d 1186 (1989) at 1190.

57. *In re* Anonymous, 733 So. 2d 429 (Ala. Civ. App. 1999) at 431 n.1. The denial of the guardian's motion prompted a separate, one-paragraph concurrence written by Presiding Judge William Robertson and joined by Judge William Thompson. Agreeing that the trial court erred in failing to grant the bypass request, Robertson expressed his disagreement with the majority's decision to deny the guardian's motion to file a brief. Citing the Alabama Supreme Court's ruling on guardianship appointments, Robertson argued:

[I]t appears that Rule 17(c), Ala. R. Civ. P., would permit the appointment of a guardian ad litem to represent the interests of the fetus. It follows that when the trial court has made such an appointment, the guardian should be entitled to appear before an appellate court that is considering whether the trial court properly denied a waiver of parental consent to the minor . . . and should be allowed to submit a brief in support of the trial court's judgment, as the guardian sought to do here. *Id.* at 433 (Robertson, J., concurring in the result).

58. *Ex parte* Anonymous, 810 So. 2d 786 (Ala. 2001).

59. *Id.* at 791.

60. *Id.* at 795.

61. *Ex parte* Anonymous, 889 So. 2d 525 (Ala. 2003) at 527 (Johnstone, J. dissenting).

62. *Id.*

63. *Id.*

SECTION III
Reproductive Technologies

In 1978 Louise Brown was born to her parents, John and Lesley Brown, at a community hospital in England. After nine years of trying to conceive and discovering that Lesley had blocked fallopian tubes, Louise's birth seemed a miracle to her parents. In fact, her birth was seen as miraculous across the globe. Louise Brown was the first baby ever born from a process of in vitro fertilization (IVF) where the ovum from her mother was fertilized by sperm from her father and then implanted days later into her mother's body. Often referred to as the world's first "test tube baby," Louise Brown's conception and birth raised new questions. Would the baby be healthy? How would technology affect women's roles? Who should control this technology? What ethical issues did this technology raise? As Louise Brown noted on her thirty-fifth birthday in 2013, "When I was born they all said it shouldn't be done and that it was messing with God and nature but it worked and obviously it was meant to be" (BBC News 2013). Today, more than 5.5 million babies have been born by IVF, while even newer technological advances continue to expand the ways families are built. In the U.S. the Centers for Disease Control and Prevention estimate that 1% of all babies born are the result of assisted reproductive technologies (CDC 2013a). While these births to families that might otherwise not have children have been greatly welcomed, the use of technologies raises new legal and social questions.

Every pregnancy requires sperm and egg to provide genetic material that provide cells that divide to form a zygote. When that zygote implants inside the uterus, it grows into an embryo, then a fetus, and eventually, a baby. Most of the time, that genetic material—the sperm and the egg—come together from sexual intercourse between a man and a woman who will become parents to that baby. They might choose to raise that baby or place it for adoption, but they are defined at birth as parents.

Reproductive technologies create new possibilities for how pregnancies happen and who is defined as a parent. Laws defining who is a parent were written in most states when there were few deviations from traditional procreation. For example, the woman who gave birth to a baby was always the legal mother. As genetics and gestation have become decoupled, that assumption has become now more complicated. This section examines these questions in greater detail.

ASSISTED REPRODUCTIVE TECHNOLOGIES

First, we provide a brief overview of the technologies that are commonly used in assisted reproduction and the processes used. These are relatively straight-forward. However, the implications for how they matter in meanings of family and gender are more complex, which the following readings illustrate.

Artificial insemination (AI) is a technology where sperm is taken from a man's body and placed in a woman's body to fertilize an ovum. In its least clinical forms, women can self-inseminate using a syringe or turkey baster and sperm from a donor. In its more advanced form, sperm might be placed inside the uterus to increase chances of successful fertilization. The sperm might come from a man who wants to be a father or from a donor who is willing to offer sperm so someone else can have a child, but who does not intend to parent that child. Sperm donors are sometimes known—as in the case of friends who want to support a woman who wants a baby—or can be anonymous—like in the case of sperm banks, as the selection in this section from the sociologist Rene Almeling's book, *Sex Cells*.

In vitro fertilization (IVF) describes a procedure in which sperm fertilize an ovum outside of a woman's body, in a clinical setting. Then, after the pre-embryo has successfully begun cell division, that pre-embryo is implanted in a woman's uterus so it can grow to a full-term fetus. The ovum may or may not come from the woman who wants to be a mother. The woman in whose body the embryo is implanted might be the woman who wants to be a mother (defined below), but it can also be a woman who is willing to be a surrogate for someone else who wants to be a parent. IVF has a variety of uses. For example, a woman might opt for IVF if she is having hard time becoming pregnant but wants to be a mother. In this case, she might use her own ovum, which would be taken from her body to be fertilized (by her partner's sperm or from a donor) and then implanted. A woman might also choose to use someone else's ovum. There are many reasons for this. A woman might carry a genetic disease and doesn't want to pass it down to her offspring. She might have a hard time becoming pregnant. She might be older and have a better chance of becoming pregnant with a donated ovum. In lesbian families, a woman might want to carry a pregnancy but use her partner's ovum so they can both have a biological tie to their child. A woman also may have an embryo implanted so she can gestate a baby for someone else. This arrangement is known as surrogacy.

Surrogacy has an old history. Many biblical stories cite surrogate motherhood relationships where a man could impregnate another woman who would relinquish the child to him and his wife, and surrogacy arrangements were allowed in ancient cultures when a woman was unable to conceive. In traditional surrogacy, the woman who becomes pregnant also contributes her ovum. As technology has become more reliable and readily available, women can serve as gestational surrogates where they use someone else's ovum, possibly from a donor or from the socially intended mother and then after IVF carry the pregnancy to term. Some women serve as surrogates for family members or friends. There are examples of women carrying a pregnancy for her adult daughter and her husband, giving birth to her own grandchildren, or serving as a surrogate for a sister or friend. In commercial surrogacy, women are paid to gestate a baby for an individual or couple who want a baby.

SOCIAL IMPLICATIONS OF ASSISTED REPRODUCTIVE TECHNOLOGIES

Technologies are relatively unchanging in application, but can lead to various permutations of family. For example, a woman can use her ovum and her husband's sperm and hire a surrogate to carry the pregnancy. A lesbian couple might use one woman's ovum, donor sperm, and the partner's uterus to carry the pregnancy. A gay couple might use one man's sperm, the ovum from the other man's sister, and a surrogate to have a baby. There are even examples of couples using donor ovum, donor sperm, and a surrogate to have a baby. Each of these permutations uses technology to yield different social outcomes. They also complicate how we understand who counts as a parent and how we feel about the relationships between each party. The sociologist Josh Gamson's selection in this section demonstrates these complexities.

Most surrogacy arrangements—about 95%—go smoothly (Saul 2009). Yet, occasionally, disputes arise. In 1986, one such case was important for establishing legal precedent on how traditional surrogacy contracts could be treated. In this case, Mary Beth Whitehead agreed to serve as a surrogacy for Bill and Elizabeth Stern. Elizabeth "Betsy" Stern was not infertile, but had multiple sclerosis and was fearful a pregnancy might exacerbate her condition. Mary Beth Whitehead was a white woman with two children of her own who agreed to be impregnated with Bill Stern's sperm and to relinquish the baby to the Sterns after birth. However, when the baby was born, Whitehead announced she had changed her mind and no longer wished to give the baby to the Sterns. In making sense of this unusual contract, the courts ruled that Whitehead's actions were very similar to those of a birth mother who promises a baby for adoption and then changed her mind. They also made clear they did not recognize the surrogacy contract as legal. Thus, the legal decision dictated that she could not be forced to give the baby to the Sterns. The case was sent to family court where a judge evaluated what was in the child's best interests. The Sterns were then granted custody, with Whitehead receiving visitations (*New York Times* 1988).

A second case helped to clarify the legal meanings of surrogacy. In 1993 Marc Calvert, a white man, and his wife, Crispina Calvert, a Filipina, hired Anna Johnson to be a surrogate for them. Using their own genetic material, the embryo was implanted in Johnson's body. Anna Johnson, an African American single mother of one three-year-old daughter, worked as a nurse and occasionally received public assistance and thought surrogacy would help support her family. However, six months into her pregnancy, Johnson announced that she felt a connection to the fetus and no longer wished to give the baby up. Although Johnson's claim sounded like Whitehead's, the court saw one significant difference: genetics. Whitehead, who was able to establish some parental rights, was genetically related to the baby, whereas Johnson was not. In this case, Johnson was not granted any rights to the baby. As courts have interpreted surrogacy disputes, they consider genetics, but they are also willing to consider what the original intent of the contract was, and what the court views to be in the best interest of the child. In a similar case (*Baker v Kehoe*), a woman, Amy Kehoe, used donor ovum and donor sperm, to have twins by a surrogate. After the babies were born, the surrogate, Laschell Baker, sued for custody of the babies after discovering that Ms. Kehoe had been treated for psychosis eight years prior. Arguing that she would be a better mother and that there was a risk Ms. Kehoe could relapse, Ms. Baker persevered in the Michigan courts, where surrogacy contracts are unenforceable, and gained custody of the twins (Saul 2009).

Given the complexity surrogacy contracts raise, many states opt to simply outlaw them or do not address them in law at all. As of 2011, Washington, DC was the only region to make surrogacy a crime punishable by jail and Illinois is the only state to carefully define how a contract should be followed and enforced. Other states take different approaches. Some states prohibit enforcement of surrogacy contracts, though they occur anyway. Seven states allow surrogacy contracts but specify conditions in which they are legal, including the marital status of the contracting parents, infertility diagnosis, or the surrogate has a prior child. Seven states permit surrogacy but provide limited details for enforcement. Seven more states lack statutes about surrogacy but have court orders acknowledging it. The remaining 22 states have no official position in statute nor case law, which many attorneys interpret as allowed because it is not prohibited (Hinson & McBrien 2011). Faced with uneven interpretation and enforcement, and sizeable cost, many couples look for other options for surrogacy, and India has emerged as a new marketplace for surrogacy. Recent estimates are that the surrogacy industry in India is a $2.5 billion market, with an estimated 25,000 foreign couples visiting India for surrogacy services (Bhowmick 2013). Reproductive tourism, that is, traveling to utilize reproductive technologies not available in one's own country or because they are more affordable in other places, is growing.

Surrogacy contracts—in the U.S. and abroad—almost always occur between two parties with unequal resources and power; the socially intended parents almost always have more economic resources than the women with whom they are contracting to be a surrogate. Commercial surrogates are also highly incentivized by the financial benefits of being a surrogate, raising issues of whether they freely choose these roles or are vulnerable to coercion. This inequality between the two parties makes for additional challenges in thinking through the social implications of these relationships. Sociologist Sharmila Rudrappa's article in this section examines these issues, and shows how surrogates in India both face potential exploitation, but are also able to derive wealth and self-determination for their families from their work as surrogates.

THE PROMISE AND PERILS OF ARTS

Reproductive technologies are expensive and not entirely successful. According to the Centers for Disease Control, success from IVF for a woman who is younger than 35 years in age is 40%. As women age, the likelihood of success diminishes: a woman 38–40 has a 22% success rate, while women over 40 have a success rate of about 12%, dropping to 5% after 43 years of age. Success rates also vary from clinic to clinic, depending on technique and experience, and depend on the reasons for infertility (CDC 2013b). As mentioned, treatments are expensive and only sometimes covered by health insurance. A 2006 survey found that only 20% of employers covered infertility treatment as part of health insurance (Andrews 2011). This raises other questions about whether limits should be placed on women who want to use these technologies. Given the social importance applied to having genetic children, how realistically do women understand these costs, as well as the risks? Sociologist Laura Mamo's selection in this section, from her book *Queering Reproduction*, explores many of these issues, including what kinds of families should also have access to these technologies. Mamo's selection raises the new possibilities and challenges for same sex couples that have come with developments in assisted reproduction.

Assisted reproductive treatments are expensive and risky. Women can experience serious health complications from the hormones used to stimulate ovulation for ovum donation and IVF, the long-term effects of which are not well studied. The increased risk of multiple births is also a significant problem. During IVF, doctors commonly transfer more than one pre-embryo in hopes that one will successfully implant. Yet, it is not uncommon for more than one to implant, increasing rates of twins or triplets, which carry risks of prematurity, long-term health outcomes, and high healthcare costs. While shows like the former reality show, *John and Kate Plus Eight*, celebrated the use of IVF and life with multiples, the costs can be hefty. This industry is largely unregulated, with doctors expected to follow agreed upon professional standards. While they are required to report their success rates to the CDC, which are made public to potential consumers, they also are expected to electively exercise appropriate caution. Indeed, the notorious case of Nadya Suleman—dubbed by the media as "Octomom"—and her doctor, Dr. Michael Kamrava, is arguably the best known instance of an IVF case in which no such caution was shown. The doctor complied with Suleman's request that he implant eight embryos in her (all of which resulted in live births) although she was already the mother of six children, also born by IVF. The resulting public uproar contributed to a medical review which resulted in the suspension of Kamrava's license (Muhajer 2011).

Reproductive technologies, once unusual or scary, have become more common—so much so that they are increasingly making their way into popular culture. Relatively unknown at the time Louise Brown was born, they are commonly referenced in movies, where women go out and get pregnant on their own, sperm is lost or switched, surrogates are hired and behave in ways that contradict the aims of the contracting mother (often to great hilarity), women donate eggs for money, or a sperm donor learns of his many off-spring. The "new normalcy" of reproductive technologies allows audiences to understand what they are, but their representations in popular culture also reveal the way in which these technologies potentially disrupt traditional definitions of family. Like other areas of reproduction that we discuss in this book, assisted reproduction contains both liberatory and coercive possibilities. Individuals and couples are able to have children and create new families that otherwise would not be possible—yet at the same time, poorer women are at risk of exploitation by richer men and women to sell their eggs and rent their wombs, and middle income individuals and couples are similarly at risk of being exploited by unethical clinics and amassing huge expenses that they cannot afford in the quest to have a biological child.

CHAPTER 11

Selling Genes, Selling Gender

Rene Almeling

Contemporary egg agencies and sperm banks operate within the context of a thriving medical marketplace. In many cases, the programs are founded or staffed by physicians, nurses, and psychologists. They cultivate networks with referring physicians, belong to professional medical associations, set goals for expanding their businesses, charge a variety of fees for different services, and develop official protocols for dealing with donors and recipients. Even when the donation program staff members are not actually clinicians, they are part of the broader medical market for sex cells and, as such, are able to draw on the cultural power of medical authority in shaping the structure and meaning of egg and sperm donation.[1]

To stay in business, donation programs must recruit "sellable" donors who provide "high-quality" gametes to recipients who "shop around." In the words of OvaCorp's psychologist, "Medically, the invention of IVF really broke it down to [fallopian] tubes, eggs, uterus, sperm. To this day, that's how we solve the problem. Do you need sperm or eggs, or do you need both? Or do you need a uterus? What do you got, what do you need, and what can you give up psychologically? Then sort of broker what you need." But even as egg agencies and sperm banks engage in similar practices—advertising to recruit donors, screening applicants, monitoring the production of bodily goods, and setting fees—a detailed comparison of their organizational processes reveals that what makes an egg donor sellable is not what makes a sperm donor sellable and that the definition of "high quality" is not the same for women and men.

This chapter details the daily business practices of two egg agencies, OvaCorp and Creative Beginnings, and two sperm banks, CryoCorp and Western Sperm Bank. Economic rhetoric permeates all four programs, but staff members are very aware of being in a unique business. They discuss "people-management" strategies and point out that they are not "manufacturing toothpaste" or "selling pens." They also consistently refer to the women and men who produce eggs and sperm as "donors" who "help" recipients, and they refer to the donor-recipient exchange as a "win-win situation." But as will become clear, cultural beliefs about sex and gender shape this confluence of economic logic and altruistic rhetoric so that in egg agencies donation means giving a gift while in sperm banks it means performing a job.

RECRUITING "SELLABLE" DONORS

To find donors, egg agencies and sperm banks advertise in a variety of forums (college newspapers, free weekly magazines, radio, and websites), hold donor information sessions, and encourage previous donors to refer siblings, friends, and roommates. Cryo-Corp and Western Sperm Bank are located within blocks of prestigious four-year universities, and their advertising is directed at cash-strapped college students. The marketing director of CryoCorp, which requires that donors be enrolled in or have a degree from a four-year university, explained that the location was a deliberate choice because "the owners of the sperm bank thought that that was a good job match, and it really works out well for the students. They're young and therefore healthy. They don't have to make a huge time commitment. They can visit the sperm bank anytime." Nevertheless, the staff members at sperm banks lament difficulties in recruiting men and offer hefty "finder's fees" to current donors who refer successful applicants.

In contrast, OvaCorp and Creative Beginnings receive several hundred applications from women each month. Creative Beginnings' founder explained the impetus behind her marketing strategy. "We appeal to the idea that there's an emotional reward, that they're going to feel good about what they've done, that it's a win-win situation, that they're going to help someone with something that person needs, and they're going to get something they need in return." Both agencies report that "young moms are the best donors. They pay the best attention and show up for appointments" because they understand the importance of a child to recipient clients.

When a potential donor calls or e-mails a program for the first time, the staff initiates an extensive screening process by asking about family health history (including physical, mental, and genetic disease) and social characteristics. Some screening standards are based on biomedical guidelines for genetic material most likely to result in pregnancy. For example, ASRM (American Society of Reproductive Medicine) issues guidelines for age and height/weight ratios, which are followed closely by egg agencies

to select donors who will respond well to fertility medications. But some of the guidelines reflect recipient requests for socially desirable characteristics, such as the height minimums set by sperm banks at around 5 feet 8 inches.

Even some of the nominally biomedical factors are better understood as social characteristics, as evident in this donor manager's discussion of Western Sperm Bank's standards.

> We have to not take people that are very overweight because of a sellable issue. It becomes a marketing thing; some of the people we don't accept. Also height becomes a marketing thing. When I'm interviewing somebody to be a donor, of course personality is really important. Are they gonna be responsible? But immediately I'm also clicking in my mind: Are they blond? Are they blue-eyed? Are they tall? Are they Jewish? So [I'm] not just looking at the [sperm] counts and the [health] history but also can we sell this donor? And anyone that's [willing to release identifying information to offspring at age eighteen], obviously we will ignore a lot; even if they're not quite as tall as we'd like, we'll take them. Or maybe if they're a little chunky, we'll still take them, because we know that [their willingness to release identifying information] will supersede the other stuff.

Likewise, in explaining the screening process for women applying to be donors, Creative Beginnings' office manager said, "this is a business, and we're trying to provide a service." Later that day, her assistant noted that recipients "basically go shopping and they want this and they want that."

OvaCorp's donor manager also emphasized social characteristics, including education level and attractiveness, in describing what makes an egg donor "sellable."

> You will find that a donor's selling tool is her brains and her beauty. That's a donor's selling point, as opposed to she's a wonderful person. That's nice. But bottom line, everyone wants

someone that's either very attractive, someone very healthy, and someone very bright. That's her selling point/tool. That's why I also work with women who don't have children, because I get a higher level of academia with a lot of our single donors because they're not distracted by kids.

Research on how recipients select donors suggests that staff members are responding to their clients' interest in attractive and intelligent donors whose phenotypes are similar to their own.[2] Egg agencies and sperm banks use education as a signifier of genetic-based intelligence, but as the donor manager quoted above suggests, women without children have more time to pursue additional schooling.[3]

During this early phase of recruitment, egg agency staff members are also assessing an applicant's level of responsibility, which is often glossed as "personality" or "helpfulness," as in this interview with the assistant director of Creative Beginnings.

Assistant Director: Personality is a big thing. We always want this to be a positive experience, if it is going to bring them to a different point in their life instead of just doing it to do it. A lot of them don't care about the money; they just want to help somebody, and that's all the more reason to continue with them.

Rene: So if donors don't ever meet the recipient, though, why would their personality matter technically?

Assistant Director: Well, we don't really look at the personality for them to meet the recipient. If they have a good personality, then we can trust them. They really want to go forward with this. They're more likely to continue with the process by getting their profile finished in a timely manner, getting their pictures into us and all the release forms that they need. Then it just shows responsibility.

At the same time, according to Creative Beginnings' founder, the staff is responding to recipients who "want to know that the person donating is a good person. They

want to know that person wasn't doing it for the money, that person's family history is good, that person was reasonably smart, that they weren't fly-by-nights, drug abusers, or prostitutes." Intersecting with gendered expectations about egg donors having, or at least expressing, altruistic motivations are class-based concerns around defining "appropriate" donors.

Sperm banks, in stark contrast, *expect* men to be financially motivated, and the staff speaks directly about responsibility rather than couching it in terms of altruistic motivations. Western Sperm Bank's donor manager explained,

Aside from personality, the other thing that makes me fall in love with a donor is someone that's responsible. It is so rare to get someone that's truly responsible, that comes in when he's supposed to come in or at least has the courtesy to call us and say, "I can't make it this week, but I'll come in next week twice." Then of course the second thing that makes him ideal is that he has consistently very high [sperm] counts, so I rarely have to toss anything on him [i.e., reject his sperm sample]. And then, I guess the third thing would be someone that has a great personality, that's just adorable, caring, and sweet. There are donors, that their personalities, I think, ugh. They have great [sperm] counts, they come in when they're supposed to, but I just don't like them. That's a personal thing, and I think, huh, I don't want more of those babies out in the world.

Although egg agencies and sperm banks are interested in responsible women and men who fulfill their obligations, donors are also expected to embody notions of American femininity or masculinity. Staff members expect egg donors to conform to one of two gendered stereotypes: highly educated and physically attractive or caring and motherly with children of their own. Sperm donors, on the other hand, are generally expected to be tall and college educated with consistently high sperm counts.

In terms of other characteristics, egg agencies and sperm banks work to recruit donors from a variety of racial, ethnic, and religious backgrounds to satisfy a diverse recipient population. In fact, race/ethnicity is genetically reified to the degree that it serves as the basis for program filing systems. In Creative Beginnings' office, there is a cabinet for "active donor" files. The top two drawers are labeled "Caucasian," and the bottom drawer is labeled "Black, Asian, Hispanic." During a tour of CryoCorp, the founder lifted sperm samples out of the storage tank filled with liquid nitrogen and explained that the vials are capped with white tops for Caucasian donors, black tops for African American donors, yellow tops for Asian donors, and red tops for donors with "mixed ancestry." All four programs complain about the difficulty of recruiting African American, Hispanic, and Asian donors, and Jewish donors are in demand for Jewish clients. In one case, even though a director thought a particular egg donor applicant was too interested in the financial compensation, she was accepted into the program because she was Catholic, reflecting the director's interest in diversifying the donor catalog.

The final phase of recruitment involves reproductive endocrinologists, psychologists, and geneticists or genetic counselors, who serve as professional stamps of approval in producing sex cells for sale.[4] Applicants are examined by a physician and tested for blood type, Rh factor, drugs, and sexually transmitted infections. Both egg agencies require a psychological evaluation and the Minnesota Multiphasic Personality Inventory, but neither sperm bank requires that donors be psychologically screened. All four programs require that donors prepare a detailed family health history for three generations (and thus do not generally accept adoptees). In some programs, this history is evaluated by genetic counselors or geneticists, who might request specific genetic tests. In at least one case, though, test results revealing the mutation that causes cystic fibrosis were not enough to disqualify an "extraordinary" egg donor. The founder of Creative Beginnings explained,

> All the time there are calls coming in about problems or questions. Like today, there is a donor who's mixed. She's got Black and Caucasian, and her cystic fibrosis screening turned out that she's a carrier.[5] She's a really pretty girl, and the recipient really wants her badly because she's fair skinned, she's very pretty, and the recipient knows that this donor is extraordinary. But then [the recipient is] torn because her husband's saying, "Well, do we want to introduce something into our gene pool?" They could go ahead and use her, but the husband just has to be tested to see if he's a carrier.

As part of describing why she is the "right person" to open a commercial egg agency, the founder of Creative Beginnings criticized other programs for just this scenario, which underscores the difficulty of refusing paying clients who become attached to a particular donor.

Staff members at each of the four programs view donor screening as a staged process that requires more of a monetary investment at every step. According to one of OvaCorp's psychologists, the psychological screening in egg donation is often performed before the medical tests because it is cheaper. Similarly, in sperm donation, banks confirm that a donor passes one set of tests before advancing him because, according to a Western Sperm Bank donor screener, "at each step of the game, we're spending more money on them." CryoCorp's marketing director takes this rationale a step further: "Once someone goes through our screening process, it's in our best interest to continue him in the program, because we've invested a huge amount of money, thousands and thousands of dollars. So the more vials we can collect before he drops out of the program, the better, especially if that donor's a popular donor."

In this first stage in the process of gamete donation, there are structural similarities in that both egg agencies and sperm banks expend funds on recruitment and employ a range of medical and social standards to garner "sellable" donors. But comparing how staff evaluates donors and their genetic material reveals how gendered stereotypes shape the definition of "high-quality" eggs and sperm. Both women and men are screened for infectious and genetic diseases, which suggests parallel concerns raised by the exchange of bodily tissue. However, "girls who just want to lay their eggs for some quick cash" are rejected, while men are expected to be interested in making money.

These gendered expectations correspond to traditional norms of women as selfless caregivers and men as emotionally distant breadwinners, a link between individual reproductive cells and cultural norms of motherhood and fatherhood that is made especially clear in the psychological evaluations, which are required of egg donors but not sperm donors. In addition to being evaluated for psychological stability, women are asked how they feel about "having their genetics out there." Sperm banks do not require that men consider this question with a mental health professional, which suggests that women are perceived as more closely connected to their eggs than men are to their sperm.

The majority of women and men who apply to donation programs are not accepted. Both sperm banks reject more than 90% of applicants, most because they do not have the exceptionally high sperm counts that are required because freezing sperm in liquid nitrogen significantly reduces the number that are motile. Both egg agencies estimate that they reject over 80% of women who apply.[6] In short, donor recruitment is time intensive, rigorous, and costly. As staff members sift through hundreds of applications, the framing of egg donation as an altruistic win-win situation and sperm donation as an easy job shapes subsequent staff/donor interactions, from constructing individualized donor profiles to the actual sale of sex cells.

CONSTRUCTING DONOR PROFILES

Once applicants pass the initial screening with program staff, they are invited to fill out a "donor profile." These are lengthy documents with questions about the donor's physical characteristics, family health history, and educational attainment; in some programs, standardized test scores, GPA, and IQ scores are requested. There are also open-ended questions about hobbies, likes and dislikes, and motivations for donating. Once approved by staff, egg donor profiles, along with current pictures, are posted on an agency's password-protected website under the woman's first name. The donor then waits to be selected by a recipient before undergoing medical, psychological, and genetic screening.

In contrast, sperm banks do not post profiles until donors pass the medical screening and produce enough samples to be listed for sale on the bank's publicly accessible website. Western Sperm Bank's donor manager explained,

> From the moment the donor is signed on, it's really nine months before we even see any profit from them. They have six months worth of quarantine [for HIV], and then another three months before we can really release enough inventory so that people aren't upset at us. If we release five vials and twenty women call, only two women are going to be happy. The others are going to be really upset that that's all we got on him this month.

Sperm banks are much more concerned about donor anonymity, so men's profiles are assigned an identification number and do not include current photographs.[7] Both banks do offer a "photo-matching service," in which recipients pay staff to select donors with specified phenotypes.

Profiles serve as the primary marketing tool for both the program and the donor. For donation programs, posted profiles represent the full range of donors available and thus are used to recruit recipient clients. The founder of Creative Beginnings explained that she would prefer not to have profiles on the website because she thinks they are impersonal but that she needs them to be "competitive" with other programs.[8] For donors, the profiles are the primary basis a recipient will use to select them. Typically, recipients also consult with staff about which donors to choose; occasionally, egg recipients will ask to meet a donor, but under no circumstances are sperm recipients allowed to meet donors. If a donor's profile is not appealing, recipients are not likely to express interest in purchasing that donor's sex cells.

This explains why programs spend a great deal of energy encouraging applicants to complete the profiles and, in the case of egg donation, to send in attractive pictures. During an informational meeting for women interested in becoming egg donors, Creative Beginnings' staff members offered explicit advice about how they should appeal to recipients.

Assistant Director: The profile really gives recipients a chance to get to know you on another level. Even though it's anonymous, it feels like it's personal. It feels like they're making a connection with you. They want to feel like it's less clinical than just looking it up on the website, and they want to see which girl best suits their needs. It's about who looks like they could fit into my family and who has the characteristics that I would like in my offspring? You can never be too conceited or too proud of your accomplishments because they really like to feel like, wow, this is a really special and unique person. And they want to feel like they're helping you just like you're helping them. They know that money is a good motivator, but they also want to feel like you're here for some altruistic purposes. So I always say to let your personality show, but also you can kind of look at the question and

think, if I were in their position, how would I want somebody to answer that question? I don't want you to be somebody that you're not, but think of being sensitive to their needs and feelings when you're answering them. That's the big portion of it. The pictures are another portion. We always ask for one good head-and-shoulder shot. It's whatever is your best representation, flattering, and lets you come out.

Donor Assistant: You don't want something where your boobs are hanging out of your top [*laughter*]. These people are not looking for sexy people.

Assistant Director: We get girls who send in pictures from their homecoming dance, but everybody takes those pictures where they're half-wasted, and they've got their drink in one hand arid their cigarette in another. Recipients don't need to see it. It's like your parents: ignorance is bliss.

Egg donors are encouraged by agency staff to construct properly feminine profiles for the recipients, who are continually referenced as an oblique "they" who will be reading the donors' answers and making judgments about their motivations. Although it is important for the "girls" to let their "personalities" shine through, the recipients do not necessarily need to know about their flaws, such as wearing revealing clothing, drinking, or smoking.[9]

If a donor's profile is deemed unacceptable by staff or if she sends in unattractive pictures, an agency will "delete" her from the database. Creative Beginnings' office manager explained, "We have to provide what our client wants, and that's a specific type of donor. Even though [the recipients] may not be the most beautiful people on the face of the earth, they want the best. So that's what we have to provide to them." In contrast, sperm recipients are not allowed to see photographs of donors, and thus men's physical appearance is not held to similarly high standards.

NOTES

1. On the ways in which medicine is influenced by market forces, see Conrad and Leiter (2004), Light (2004), and McKinley and Stoekle (1988). On the cultural power of medical authority, see Parsons (1951), Freidson (1970), and Starr (1982).
2. Becker (2000) and Becker, Butler, and Nachtigall (2005). These studies are limited to heterosexual couples and do not include systematic comparisons of how recipients select egg donors versus sperm donors.
3. Rindfuss, Morgan, and Offutt (1996).
4. There is less screening of recipients. Creative Beginnings asks for recipients' health histories and doctors' names to confirm that they actually do "need" egg donation. OvaCorp and both sperm banks require certification that recipients are working with a doctor.
5. Being a "carrier" means that an individual has one copy of a defective gene that causes a disease but that person will not develop the disease. To develop the disease, a person must have two copies of the defective gene, one copy inherited from each biological parent. If both parents are carriers, there is a 25% chance the child will have cystic fibrosis and a 50% chance the child will be a carrier.
6. A study of attrition at Oregon Health Sciences University (OHSU) reports a similar rate (Gorrill et al. 2001). Researchers tracked all inquiries from potential egg donors for ten months in 1999.

Of these, 315 women responded to the program's advertisements; 124 returned profiles; 82 were invited to an orientation session (the others were rejected based on age, weight, smoking, and/or family health history); 64 attended the orientation; and 56 began screening. Of those screened, 13 were rejected for medical or psychological reasons; 5 completed the screening but were lost despite follow- up efforts; and 38, or 12% of the women who initially inquired, entered the donor pool. OHSU estimated the cost of bringing one donor into the pool at $1,869.
7. Throughout its long history, donor insemination has been marked by extensive secrecy (see Chapter 1). CryoCorp and Western Sperm Bank do not share adult photos of sperm donors with recipients, but there are a few banks that do, including Gametes Inc.
8. The founder of another major egg agency on the West Coast had a similar response to online profiles. "The biggest change came with the Internet, because that made donors immediately available. It became a catalog for choosing people. It had the bonus that a lady from Australia can get online and see donors immediately [but] the detracting element of depersonalizing it and making the donors seem like a commodity or an object, rather than a person. So that was really hard."
9. It is not uncommon for egg agency staffers to refer to the donors as "girls."

CHAPTER 12

India's Reproductive Assembly Line

Sharmila Rudrappa

"If you asked me two years ago whether I'd have a baby and give it away for money, I wouldn't just laugh at you, I would be so insulted I might hit you in the face," said Indirani, a 30-year old garment worker and gestational surrogate mother. "Yet here I am today. I carried those twin babies for nine months and gave them up." Living in the southern Indian city of Bangalore, married at 18, and with two young children of her own, she had delivered twins a month earlier for a Tamil couple in the United States.

I met Indirani when she was still pregnant and living in a dormitory run by Creative Options Trust for Women, Bangalore's only surrogacy agency at the time. COTW works with infertility specialists who rely on the Trust to recruit, house, care for, and monitor surrogate mothers for their clients. Straight and gay couples arrive from all over India and throughout the world to avail themselves of Bangalore's expertise in building biological families. Indirani and other mothers introduced me to 70 other surrogates they had gotten to know through their line of work. Some of them, including Indirani herself, double as recruiting agents, bringing new laborers into Bangalore's reproductive assembly line.

India is emerging as a key site for transnational surrogacy, with industry profits projected to reach $6 billion in the next few years, according to the Indian Council for Medical Research. In 2007, the *Oprah* show featured Dr. Nayna Patel in the central Indian town of Anand, Gujarat, who was harnessing the bodies of rural Gujarati women to produce babies for American couples. Subsequent newspaper articles and TV shows, as well as blogs by users of surrogacy, popularized the nation as a surrogacy destination for couples from the United States, England, Israel, Australia and to a lesser extent Italy, Germany, and Japan.

The cities of Anand, Mumbai, Delhi, Hyderabad, and Bangalore have become central hubs for surrogacy due to the availability of good medical services, inexpensive pharmaceuticals, and, most importantly, cheap and compliant labor. The cost of surrogacy in India is about $35,000–40,000 per baby, compared to the United States, where it can run as high as $80,000, which makes it particularly appealing to prospective parents. It is working class women who make India's reproductive industry viable. In Bangalore, the garment production assembly line is the main conduit to the reproduction assembly line, as women move from garment factories, to selling their eggs, to surrogacy.

Indirani's life typifies that of other women in Bangalore's garment factories. Paid low wages, she works intermittently in one of the city's many garment factories. She quit when she became pregnant, and joined the line again when her two children attended school, taking time away when she was sick, or to care for sick family members. Bangalore's reproduction industry affords women like her the possibility of extracting greater value from their bodies once they have been deemed unproductive workers in garment factories. Because of its life affirming character, Indirani and others see surrogacy, however exploitative, as a more meaningful and creative option than factory work.

RENT-A-WOMB: SURROGATE MOTHERS IN GUJARAT, INDIA

The popular understanding is that women who have large debt burdens and are destitute opt to become surrogate mothers. But while they are in debt, the 70 mothers I met were not among the poorest in Bangalore. Many were part of dual or multiple income households, and tended to be garment workers who earn more than the average working woman in the city.

Former surrogate mothers, who also work as recruiting agents, have extensive networks among women in prime reproductive age in their own extended families, and among neighbors and friends who work as maids, cooks, street sweepers, or construction workers. Because cuts in food, education, and medical subsidies due to state divestment, along with volatile markets and global financial crises, lead to unsteady factory work and low wages, their greatest recruiting success is among garment workers.

Like garment workers in sweatshops across the world, women in Bangalore are underpaid and overworked. In order to meet short production cycles set by global market demands, they work at an inhumanely fast pace, with few or no breaks. They frequently suffer from headaches, chest pain, ear and eye pain, urinary tract infections, and other health problems. Sexual harassment and abuse are rampant on the production line. The supervisors, almost all men, castigate women in sexually derogatory terms when they do not meet production quotas, and often grope the women as they instruct them on how to work better. "Sometimes," says Indirani, "I wouldn't take a lunch break when pieces piled up. I didn't want to be shamed in front of everyone. I would go to any length to avoid calling the supervisor's attention to me."

Indirani earned $100 to $110 monthly, depending upon her attendance, punctuality, and overtime hours. Frequently, she and her co-workers were unable to meet the inordinately high production targets and were required by supervisors to stay past regular working hours to meet their quotas. "Playing" catch-up, however, did not necessarily result in overtime pay. Indirani's husband became suspicious if her paycheck did not reflect her overtime hours. He wondered whether she was really at the factory, or whether she was cavorting with another man. Indirani, like many of the women I interviewed, reported that she felt debased at work and at home.

Prior research on Bangalore's female garment workers suggests that they work an average of 16 hours a day in the factory and at home doing laundry, cooking, taking care of children, and commuting to work. Working in the factory all day, and then returning home to complete household tasks was absolutely exhausting. Indirani's friend Suhasini, who was also a surrogate mother, avoided garment work altogether. Her mother, sister, and other women family members had worked the line, and she knew it was not what she wanted for her life. "But I need money," she told me. "For us," she says, "surrogacy is a boon." She describes Mr. Shetty who started COTW, as "a god to us." When I met her again in December 2011, Suhasini was receiving hormonal injections so that she could be a surrogate mother for a second time.

For much of her working life Indirani has been intermittently employed in one of Bangalore's many garment factories. She quit when pregnant, and joined the line again when her two children attended school. She also stopped factory work when she was sick, or had to care for sick family members. From the perspective of the garment factories, when Indirani is healthy she is a valuable worker for the firm. But during her pregnancies and illnesses, or when she has

to attend to her family's needs, she loses her value as a worker, and the company replaces her. She is, as anthropologist Melissa Wright calls it, a "disposable worker." Upon recovering her health, or managing family chores efficiently, Indirani cycles back into the garment factory again, this time miraculously having regained her value for the production process. Over her working life, Indirani has shifted from being valuable, to becoming an undesirable worker who must seek other forms of employment to help support her family.

MAKING BABIES

Indirani and her auto-rickshaw worker husband have struggled for much of their married life to make ends meet, and to support their small children. Indirani's husband did not earn much money. He rented his vehicle from an acquaintance, and the daily rental and gasoline costs cut significantly into the household income. So Indirani and he decided to borrow money from her cousin to purchase an auto-rickshaw of their own. Their troubles worsened when they were unable to pay back the loan, and the cousin would often arrive at their door, demanding his money and screaming expletives at them. He would come to the factory on payday and take Indirani's entire paycheck. She said, "I'd work hard, facing all sorts of abuse. And at the end of it I wouldn't even see any money. I felt so bad I contemplated suicide." When a friend at work suggested that she sell her eggs to an agency called COTW for approximately $500, Indirani jumped at what she perceived as a wonderful opportunity. After "donating" her eggs, Indirani decided to try surrogacy; she became pregnant with twins on her first attempt.

When I asked Indirani whether the hormonal injections to prepare her for ova extraction, and subsequently for embryo implantation, were painful or scary, she avoided answering directly. "*Aiyo akka,*" she said. "When you're poor you can't afford the luxury of thinking about discomfort." When I told her about the potential long-term effects of hyperovulation, she shrugged. Her first priority was getting out of poverty; any negative health threats posed by ova extraction or surrogacy were secondary.

Indirani did not find surrogacy to be debasing work. She earned more money as a reproduction worker than she did as a garment worker, and found the process much more enjoyable. She was exhausted physically and emotionally working as a tailor in the factory and then cleaning, cooking, and taking care of her family. Upon getting pregnant, however, Indirani lived in the COTW dormitory. At first she missed her family, often wondering what her children were doing. Was her mother-in-law taking care of them? "I was in a different place surrounded by strangers," she recalled. But soon she began to like the dormitory. She didn't have to wake up by 5 am to prepare meals for the family, pack lunches for everyone, drop the children off at the bus stop so they could get to school, and then hop onto the bus herself to get to the garment factory. Instead, she slept in, and was served breakfast. She had no household obligations and no one made demands on her time and emotions. Surrogacy afforded her the luxury of being served by others. She did not remember a time in her life when she felt so liberated from all responsibilities.

SURVEILLANCE AND SISTERHOOD

As she got to know the other women in the COTW dormitory, Indirani began to feel as though she was on vacation. For Indirani and many of the surrogate mothers I interviewed, it was easier to talk with the friends they made in COTW than with childhood friends and relatives; they felt they had more common with one another. Through the surrogacy process, many women told me, they lost a baby but gained sisters for life.

Indirani's husband brought the children over to visit on some weekday evenings, and her daughter stayed overnight with her on weekends. Her older sister Prabha, also a garment worker who was similarly strapped for cash, joined her at COTW two months after Indirani arrived, becoming a gestational surrogate for a straight, white couple. Like most surrogates, she had no idea where they were from, or where her contract baby would live.

Noting the closed circuit cameras that monitored the mothers' every move in the dormitory, I asked how they felt about them. Indirani said they didn't bother her; in fact, most of the mothers did not register the cameras' presence. While this initially surprised me, I soon realized that they were accustomed to surveillance in their everyday lives. Living under the gaze of relatives and inquisitive neighbors, and housed in one-two room homes where it was common for six to eight households to share a bathroom, notions of privacy were quite foreign. Surveillance at the dormitory was benign in comparison to the surveillance and punishment meted out for supposed infractions on the garment shop floor, where long conversations with teammates, taking a few minutes of rest, or going on breaks were all curtailed. In comparison, surveillance at COTW, designed to check on whether the women were having sex with their men folk who visited the facilities, seemed relatively banal.

The surrogate mothers delivered their babies through caesarian surgeries between the 36th and 37th week of gestation in order to conform to the scheduling needs of potential parents. Indirani was initially fearful of going under the knife, but she saw many mothers survive caesarians and was no longer anxious. In the end, she found the caesarian method of delivering the twins she had carried easier than the vaginal births of her own two children.

The $4000 Indirani earned was far less than the $7000 the surrogacy agency charged for the children. While she was legally entitled to a larger amount because she carried twins, Indirani made no more money than those mothers pregnant with singletons. Her take-home pay actually ended up being less than $4000 after she paid the recruiting agent $200 and bought small, obligatory gifts for the COTW staff who cared for her during her pregnancy. Indirani had the option of staying on in the dormitory for up to two months after delivering her twins, but like all the mothers I interviewed, she chose not to do so because COTW charged for post-natal care, and for food and board. She could not afford to lose her hard-earned money on what she perceived as a luxury, so she returned home within days of delivery to all the household work that waited. Within a week of returning home, her remaining earnings went directly to her cousin, the moneylender. Still, knowing her debts were paid off gave her peace of mind.

Indirani claimed she does not feel any attachment to the twins she carried. "They were under contract. I couldn't bring myself to feel anything for them," she told me. "They were never mine to begin with, and I entered into this knowing they were someone else's babies." It is hard enough for her to take care of her own two children, she said. "Why do you think I'm going through all this now? What would I do with two more? They are burdens I cannot afford." On the other hand, some mothers professed deep attachments to the babies they had given up. Roopa, a divorced mother who gave birth to a baby girl three years ago, always celebrated her contract baby's birthday. "June 21st *akka*," she said, "I cook a special meal. My daughter doesn't know why we have a feast, but it's my way of remembering my second child. I still cry for that little girl I gave away. I think about her often. I could never do this again."

LIFE OUT OF WASTE

Regardless of how they felt about the babies they had given up, the women almost all said they derived far more meaning from surrogacy than they did working under the stern labor regimes of the garment factory. In our conversations, time and again, women described the many ways they are deemed worthless in the garment factory. Their labor powers exhausted, their sexual discipline suspect, their personal character under question, they are converted to waste on the shop floor—until they are eventually discarded. On the other hand, Bangalore's reproduction industry, they said, gave them the opportunity to be highly productive and creative workers once more.

Indirani contrasted the labor processes in producing garments and producing a baby: the latter was a better option, she said. "Garments? You wear your shirt a few months and you throw it away. But I make you a baby? You keep that for life. I have made something so much bigger than anything I could ever make in the factory." Indirani observed that while the people who wore the garments she'd worked on would most probably never think about her, she was etched forever in the minds of the intended parents who took the twins she bore.

Indirani and the other mothers I met did not necessarily see selling eggs or surrogacy as benign processes. Nor did they misread their exploitation. However, given their employment options and their relative dispossession, they believed that Bangalore's reproduction industry afforded them greater control over their emotional, financial, and sexual lives. In comparison to garment work, surrogacy was easy.

Surrogacy was also more meaningful for the women than other forms of paid employment. Because babies are life-affirming in ways garments are obviously not, surrogacy allowed women to assert their moral worth. In garment work their sexual morality was constantly in question at the factory and at home. At the dormitory, in contrast, they were in a women-only space, abstaining from sex, and leading pure, virtuous lives.

Through surrogacy, Indirani said, she had built a nuclear family unit and fulfilled one infertile woman's desire to be a mother. In the process, she had attempted to secure the future of her own family and her own happiness. As a garment worker Indirani felt she was being slowly destroyed, but as a surrogate mother she said she was creating a new world. She was ready to go through surrogacy once again to earn money for her children's private schooling. The last time we met in December 2011, Indirani asked me, "If anyone you know wants a surrogate mother, will you think of me? I want to do this again."

CHAPTER 13

Debates over Lesbian Reproduction within Lesbian/Gay and Feminist Communities

Laura Mamo

As the lesbian and women's health movements expanded access to information about insemination and lesbian motherhood became more common, debates erupted within feminist and lesbian and gay communities.

IS LESBIAN REPRODUCTION LIBERATORY?

Feminism in the 1970s was informed by two divergent theoretical ideas about motherhood. One considered motherhood—like any other connection to men—to be in the service of patriarchal oppression and the continued subordination of women to men. The other viewed motherhood as a distinctive woman's experience, as well as a source and reflection of women's unique power. As lesbian parenthood became more common, these positions fueled controversies, with some lesbians viewing motherhood and parenting as conventions of heterosexuality, and others seeing them as unique expressions of alternative, chosen family forms able to transform dominant conventions of gender and sexuality.

DOES LESBIAN REPRODUCTION DEMONSTRATE NORMALCY OR MARK TRANSGRESSIVENESS?

Some of the questions that fueled debate three decades ago continue to spark controversy, including one that concerns assimilation and resistance. Divisions in queer politics, for example, were fraught over whether or not to embrace all alternative cultural practices in an effort to ally the marginalized to resist dominant gender, sexual, and other norms. Others, however, focused their political struggles on state recognition and, thus, inclusion in civil-rights entitlements, a position that asserted that gays and lesbians were just like everyone else and should therefore be recognized as part of mainstream social and cultural life.

Does having children, and thereby demonstrating normalcy, pave the road toward equal civil rights for lesbians? Can the act of parenting and forming a family destabilize dominant constructions of gender, sexuality, and the family? In wider culture(s), pronatalism historically ebbs and flows; for lesbians, being or becoming a mother is never an obvious or easy social identity to achieve. Although resisting the dominant script of women-as-natural-mothers has long been a part of lesbian activism, the prescription to reproduce that upholds "traditional values" is not only alive and well, but in many ways it is staging a comeback. The controversy continues over whether and to what degree lesbian parenting is a consequence of normalization and the pronatalism of dominant culture and to what degree it marks a continued transgressiveness from feminisms and queer cultures.

WHAT ARE THE MEANINGS AND CONSEQUENCES OF LESBIANS' USE OF REPRODUCTIVE TECHNOLOGIES?

Lesbian and gay identity politics of the 1980s and 1990s and queer politics and theories contributed to analyses of the meaning and potential consequences of reproductive technologies for social life. Would they lead to acceptance and integration of lesbian and gay lives into the mainstream? If so, would this remove discrimination and open an avenue for social justice? Or would lesbian use of reproductive technologies further marginalize more alternative queer lives and thus lead to further discrimination and social injustice?

Questions about the social impact of reproductive technologies are not limited to discussions of queer reproduction; scholars have repeatedly debated whether reproductive technologies are progressive, having the potential to sever the link between sexuality and reproduction for women, or regressive, representing power and a patriarchal strategy to keep women tied to motherhood. In *The Dialectic of Sex* (1970), for example, Shulamith Firestone famously advocated the use of technology to free women from "the tyranny of reproduction." Patriarchy, the root of women's oppression, was about the control of women's bodies, fertility, and sexuality by men. Access to effective

contraceptive and birth technologies could liberate women from that oppression: biology need not be destiny. This stance relied on a social-constructionist argument of the gendered social order and the construction of gender itself. Although a form of technological determinism, Firestone asserted, a "technological fix" (i.e., an artificial womb) would free women from the tyranny of their own biology. Not all feminists shared this viewpoint.

Throughout the 1980s, many voiced concerns about assisted-reproduction technologies as reinforcing the "cult of motherhood," pointing to the historical continuities of the ideology of motherhood. Others argued, from a radical or cultural feminist position, that such technologies were means by which men could appropriate reproductive capacities, the ultimate source of female power, from women. A powerful example was Gena Corea's (1985) image of the "mother machine," a future in which women become professional breeders—a prescient thought given the professional surrogates who work today (see also Corea 1984, 1987). By the 1980s, heterosexual donor insemination was widely accepted as a treatment for infertility, despite objections from feminists who argued that the medicalization and professionalization of fertility and childbirth were forms of male-dominated social control of women's bodies (Corea 1985; Rothman 1986).

Lesbian feminism receded in the 1980s, along with the feminist sex wars, the validation of lesbian sex as a distinctive source of pleasure as well as danger, and the recognition of butch-femme as an erotic system that fostered and shaped women's desire (see Snitow 1980; Vance 1982). But the theoretical debates regarding the consequences of assisted reproduction continued to unfold. By the 1990s, feminist theorizing by Jana Sawicki (1991) and others who examined assisted-reproduction technologies dismissed one-dimensional thinking, arguing that it failed to take into account the ways in which a practice or institution could empower some women and disempower others. Furthermore, such accounts captured neither the interplay between domination and resistance nor the ways they could coexist in the same set of practices and/or institutions.

FROM TURKEY BASTER TO BIOTECHNOLOGICAL ACCOMPLISHMENT

Esther—the lesbian who self-inseminated without success, stopped trying, then resumed her efforts four years later—responded to a request for volunteers that I had placed in the newsletter of a nonprofit sperm bank that serves lesbians. After a phone conversation in which she agreed to participate in the research, she invited me to her home to conduct the interview.

At the time of our interview, Esther was thirty-five years old. She had begun trying to get pregnant in her late twenties. She described herself as a white, Jewish, lefty liberal at the height of her career, having recently been promoted to executive director of a nonprofit organization. Her annual income, $35,000 per year, qualified her to purchase a condominium in a housing complex with assistance from a middle-income-housing grant program in San Francisco.

In 1997, when Esther resumed her efforts to get pregnant after a four-year hiatus, she encountered a changed set of assumptions and protocols. This time around, purchasing semen from a sperm bank involved her in a full fertility work-up. After receiving the work-up, Esther purchased a box of six ovulation-predictor kits from her provider at a cost of $19.99 and went home to wait for her next cycle to begin. Nine days after the first day of her next period, Esther began using the ovulation sticks every morning to predict when she would ovulate. The day the line turned from white to blue indicated that her ovulation was imminent (and would occur in twenty-four to forty-four hours),

and she knew her "best chance" of conceiving was approaching. Esther phoned the infertility clinic and scheduled an IUI (intrauterine insemination) for the next day.

As an HMO member, Esther was not concerned about the monthly cost of office visits for each procedure; she would be required to provide only a $5 copayment. The cost of purchasing sperm from a sperm bank—approximately $150 per insemination—would not be covered by her HMO because she did not have an official diagnosis of infertility based on the *International Classification of Diseases* or the guidelines of her HMO, but instead simply lacked a source of sperm.

When after six cycles she was still not pregnant, Esther scheduled an appointment with the infertility specialist to determine why. They discussed possible next steps, including additional technologies and pharmaceutical drugs she might try. Esther decided to continue inseminating without the use of hormone therapy for three additional cycles of IUI. If these were not successful, they would add clomiphene citrate (Clomid), an oral medication used to stimulate egg development, to her insemination routine. On the seventh cycle, before initiating the use of Clomid, Esther conceived, but she miscarried a few weeks later. The miscarriage was emotionally devastating, but after taking a few months off, Esther started again, immediately using Clomid. She also added human chorionic gonadotrophin, another ovulation stimulant and a hormone used to produce ovarian progesterone during the first trimester to protect against miscarriage. She continued to use IUI technology for the inseminations.

In our interview, Esther described these cycles as "very scientific. . . . I was doing the Clomid and they had me come in for a sonogram to get a visual on the eggs. They were doing more lab tests to see how I was reacting to the hormones and they also did some extra blood tests to rule out things that may cause miscarriages, lupus and some other stuff." Esther continued, "In the beginning, it was very important to me that I did it at home and that I lit candles on my altar. And now I could care less. It's the end; the means is not the issue anymore. Now, I am very clear with myself. There are decision changes as you get on the path. Everyone says, 'I'll never go further than this,' and then everyone ends up going further."

In addition to these biomedical interventions, Esther described other strategies she employed to enhance her fertility. "Oh, I also changed my diet a bit, less sugar, alcohol, and caffeine. I took those prenatal supplements and I started doing yoga to increase my strength and energy flow. I don't know if it will help, but I may as well try." At the end of the interview, Esther paused and said, "It's really interesting because a couple months ago they changed the name of the clinic from the infertility clinic to the fertility clinic. It's like they want to destigmatize these procedures and capture a wider market." At the time of our interview, Esther had completed the second month of trying to conceive with the help of fertility drugs, and was not yet pregnant. Although she had been pursuing pregnancy as a single woman, she described her hopes that her new relationship might develop into a coparenting partnership. As we talked, her partner was preparing dinner in the next room. Esther's story shares qualities with those told by the other thirty-five women I interviewed: an expectation that getting pregnant can and will be an easy, low-tech process organized mostly outside of medical worlds; a tendency to draw on both women's health resources and biomedical re-sources; and a nonlinear trajectory—her pregnancy plans were disrupted by life events, shaped by emotional ups and downs, and required a lot of work.

What comes across most dramatically in Esther's story is her shift from self-empowerment to patient status. What was once espoused by women's health movements as

a simple procedure that any women could "control" is today often a biotechnical process requiring increased reliance on medical expertise and services. This process carries health risks, legal risks, and an assumption of technoscientific progress as measured by the continuous introduction of new technologies that promise to be more advanced and efficient.

This broader trend in medicine has shaped lesbian reproduction as well as heterosexual reproduction. Although social movements have redefined homosexuality in nonmedical terms, the medicalization of bodies and bodily processes has been uneven and complicated. At times, and under certain conditions, medicalization is an encroachment into people's social lives. At other times, it is a welcome resource for ameliorating and making sense of social lives. There are no simple analyses or one-way arrows. The lingering feminist health ideals of the 1970s and 1980s often coexist with biomedical expertise and services. Even as many social movements have resisted medicalization, individuals have turned to medical discourses and services as a matter of everyday pragmatism to meet their goals.

The Ultimate Guide to Pregnancy for Lesbians (Pepper 1999), a key self-help resource for lesbians seeking parenthood, exemplifies this unevenness. Written by a new lesbian mom, the book offers a firsthand account of "the conception roller coaster" and provides a step-by-step guide for conception, beginning with one's first ovulation kit and moving toward increasing technological sophistication. Although it in part reflects feminist health ideals, this account is ultimately a hybrid. The author first states, "The best expert is you . . . follow your OWN intuition. Because only you and your partner (if you have one) can sense how your body is responding and what feels right to you. Intuition is a powerful tool in this process. Go with it!" In describing how to get pregnant, she advises, "Make the first time special, then move on." The special first time refers to the at-home, do-it-yourself procedure; moving on refers to IUI, which usually takes place in a medical office. The latter, Pepper argues, "is more effective because it lets the sperm, which are often 'spun' to shake out the dead or less effective swimmers, bypass the long journey through the cervical mucus and the vagina, placing it closer to the egg" (ibid., 66).

In another self-help account (R. 2000) a lesbian couple and their known donor quickly learn that insemination will not be the demedicalized, legally sanctioned procedure they had hoped for. First, in order to receive legal protection, they have to enter the medical field. Second, in order to reduce expenses, the recipient has to be given a diagnosis of infertility before she receives a physical exam. And third, they have to find an Ob-Gyn who will counter standard practices by performing an insemination with "live," not frozen and tested sperm. Similar hybrid stories have appeared on feminist Web sites, in gay and lesbian magazines, and in other newspapers and media. Each and all of these images and events contribute substantially to the cultural climate in which lesbian reproduction takes place today.

CONTEMPORARY LESBIAN REPRODUCTION

By 2000, assisted reproduction in the form of vaginal insemination (often self-insemination in the context of women's health movements) and IUI techniques had fully entered the mainstream. Both are now widely viewed as legitimate, relatively low-cost procedures for achieving pregnancy when few biophysical constraints are present. Alongside low-tech, assisted-reproduction technologies exists a large-scale biomedical infertility delivery service system: Fertility Inc. (This term denotes the corporate contours of this highly profitable medical sector and all the services and products it encompasses.)

As this system has evolved, assisted-reproduction practices have become more likely to draw on Fertility Inc.'s highly commercialized and commodified set of biomedical fertility and infertility services. While self-insemination and alternative health information remain accessible, conception and its information resources are most often accomplished by accessing Fertility Inc. and thereby purchasing a variety of biomedical services, information, and technologies.

Throughout the 1990s, biomedicine co-opted many of the ideals of women's health activism. Women's health centers, for example, are now big business for biomedicine. In creating such centers, biomedicine has not only profited but also effectively displaced the many centers that grew out of the feminist health movement, replacing them with clinics devoid of the original feminist spirit of patient empowerment (e.g., Worcester and Whatley 1988).

ADVANCES AND RESISTANCES

In the final year of the twentieth century, a baby was born to two mothers. Fertilization took place in a petri dish, with eggs harvested from one woman and sperm from an anonymous donor. Once an embryo formed, it was placed into the uterus of the woman's partner, who carried the baby to term (Crummy 2000). Neither woman received a medical diagnosis of infertility, yet their reproductive bodies became the objects of biomedicine.

Today, artificial insemination is a routine medical treatment and an accepted form of assisted reproduction. But questions remain. Has the medicalization of assisted reproduction and its associated discourses effectively established the legitimacy of these services *as well as* an increased need for them (Hartouni 1997, 74)? If so, for whom? The legitimacy of artificial insemination and other infertility treatments continues to rely on an implicit (and often explicit) heterosexual frame.

Insurance policies reflect this fact. In the United States insurance policies generally cover the costs of assisted reproduction for married couples only. In Oklahoma, for example, doctors are not allowed to provide IVF services to single women; this effectively excludes lesbians who by law are unmarried. Doctors are, however, permitted to provide IUI services to single women. Therefore, while social movements have opened up the possibility for lesbians to have children, institutional structures continue to position these same women outside the category of legitimate users. But this picture is complicated: corporate medicine certainly wants these consumers for reasons of profit and some lesbian health organizations have transformed themselves into sperm banks and alternative-insemination service providers.

LOOKING AHEAD

Despite the demedicalization of homosexuality in 1974, ideas of same-sex sexuality as nonprocreative and therefore unnatural continue to shape institutional practices concerning appropriate and actual users of assisted reproduction. Of course, what and who counts as an "appropriate" user of such services has fluctuated across the decades. What remained consistent is *the* configuration of the heterosexual, married couple as normative users of assisted-reproduction technologies. Assisted reproduction has, therefore, secured heterosexual privilege (as well as race and class hierarchies). Contemporary practices of lesbians' achieving pregnancy have resulted from a confluence of these discursive worlds.

In October 2005 the Indiana legislature tried to pass a law that required "intended parents" using assisted reproduction to be married to each other, thereby denying parenthood to single, lesbian, and gay male persons and creating a category of "unlawful reproduction." Such legislation reflected *the* political tenor of the times. The 2004

presidential elections marked a return to "family values": eleven states passed amendments to define marriage as being between a man and a woman. Current policy actions around marriage, domestic-partner benefits, and adoption situate lesbian mothers and queer families on unstable ground. These policies not only threaten the legitimacy of same-sex relationships and the bonds between parents and children but also the ways in which people are recognizable as belonging to families, citizenry, and social life. It is easy to regard marriage-definition laws as strategies for both protecting and shoring up the heterosexual nuclear family. Assisted-reproduction technologies and ad hoc family formations "trouble the normal" and construct new ways of knowing about kinship, of becoming related, and of destabilizing the nature-culture divide.

WHY DO SUCH POLICIES SEEK TO LIMIT LESBIANS' REPRODUCTION?

As the sociologist Amy Agigian (2004) eloquently argues, lesbians' use of artificial insemination provokes many fears, including homophobia, fear of losing fathers' rights, fear of combining stranger and kin, and fear of mixing racial types. During the twentieth century, a high value was placed on maintaining the opposite-sex, two-parent family as the dominant family unit (both symbolically and in actuality) and on sustaining the sanctity of marriage and importance of paternity as key aspects of family ideology.

These attempts to maintain the gendered social order, with its reliance on heterosexuality and the nuclear family form, are not surprising given the potential of reproductive technologies to delink sexuality, procreation, parenthood, and blood ties from their seemingly natural web (Haraway 1997). Whether or not such technologies fulfill this potential and under what circumstances requires in-depth analysis. As I will argue, lesbian reproduction does not represent liberation from gender norms and the sexual and reproductive order, nor does it merely reinforce that order. Further, reproduction has always been and will continue to be stratified as groups are differentially supported and constrained in exercising their reproductive rights (Collins 1999).

ENFORCING BIOPOWER

The history of assisted reproduction is a history of the enforcement of biopower. That is, when a race, class, and gender lens is applied, it becomes clear that across the centuries, stratified reproduction has been enacted through efforts to support, impede, and otherwise control the reproduction of certain groups.

Articulations of biopower may be found both in scientific research and in its application in clinical "treatments." Such articulations affect not only research and healthcare practices but also the dissemination of knowledges and differential access to technologies. Over time, they give life new interpretations and forms, making life itself problematic. In short, assisted reproduction challenges previously held notions of "nature" and "life itself." The professional organization of infertility services and its associated discourses have constructed conceptive technologies as legitimate means to achieve pregnancy for married heterosexual couples unable to fulfill their "natural" desire to procreate (Hartouni 1997, 74). However, the use of such technologies by those not considered "appropriate" reproducers (according to dominant social ideas) is still viewed as problematic. Although this dominant discourse shapes practices of use of reproductive technologies, it does not have the power to stop their use by lesbian women.

CHAPTER 14

The Belly Mommy and the Fetus Sitter
The Reproductive Marketplace and Family Intimacies[1]

Joshua Gamson

A NEW WORLD OF RELATIONAL LIFE

Few experiences are more intensely personal and intimate than making a life. When the intended parents, while bringing an extra penis to the mix, lack two of the biological components required for reproduction, the intimacies involved become more complex. When out of necessity the process is approached with intense, self-conscious intention, involving the help of egg donors and surrogates, when it goes against the grain of medical and legal institutions and social conventions, the process yields unusual and intricate relationships. So it was for me. Our first daughter resulted from the egg of a close friend, fertilized by the sperm of either me or my husband Richard—we know which one, but don't disclose that publicly—carried by my college girlfriend, supported by her then husband, and birthed by her near the home of my parents, who helped sponsor the whole expensive endeavor and greeted newborn Reba Sadie, along with several other members of our families of origin, in the maternity ward of Martha's Vineyard

Hospital. Our second, Madeleine Blanche, resulted from the egg of a friend, fertilized by the sperm of either me or Richard, carried by a woman from Kentucky who was a complete stranger before we met her through a surrogacy agency, and birthed by her near her own home in Bowling Green, with the surrogate's mother in the delivery room and Reba, my parents, and my mother-in-law in the waiting room.

As I will recount, much in these two creation processes was different. One brought together people who already had thick friendship ties to one another, while the second was built largely on a relationship brokered by commercial agents. They also had quite a bit in common. Each involved exchanges of money, facilitated in part by social class, and negotiations with unfriendly or uncomprehending institutional forces. And each engaged a relatively new sort of approach to the deeply intimate process of reproduction, in which key parts of the process were "outsourced" to others. They offer an interesting opportunity to consider the novel forms of intimacy opened up by contemporary reproductive medicine, especially for those for whom the choice to parent remains institutionally and socially controversial, and to consider more broadly the dynamics of intimacy within market-based reproduction.

Indeed, many people, scholars included, see egg donation and surrogacy as quintessential examples of the encroachment of a market mentality into aspects of intimate life that had previously been insulated from commercial forces. For instance, in her recent book, *The Outsourced Self: Intimate Life in Market Times*, Arlie Russell Hochschild (2012) details what she calls the "outsourcing" of intimacy, a "strange new emotional capitalism" (13) in which the market has become present "in our bedrooms, at our breakfast tables, in our love lives, entangled in our deepest joys and sorrows" (222). Chief among her examples is surrogacy, in which "a person can now legally purchase an egg

from one continent, sperm from another, and implant it in a 'womb for rent' in yet another" (73). She describes a couple who, turning to a surrogacy clinic in India, "saw their relationship with the surrogate as a mutually beneficial transaction," and "imagined themselves as outsourcers paying a stranger to provide a professionally supervised service," establishing with the gestational carrier "the sort of relationship one might establish with an obstetrician or dentist" (83). She describes an Indian surrogate who, "instructed to remain emotionally detached from her clients, her babies, and even from her womb," while doing "an extraordinarily personal thing," entered transactions that were "cursory, businesslike, and spanned differences in language, culture, ethnicity, nation, and, most of all, social class" (93).

Reading that, I wondered: Was that us? Was my family's creation part of the transformation of one of the most intimate human experiences into a commercial transaction, turning conception and childbirth into services, alienating ourselves and the women involved from our bodies and our babies, replacing the personal and the attached with the impersonal and detached? There is certainly something to that; everywhere we turned in our family creation process we encountered market-based activity and rhetoric. Our own class advantages, and to a degree also gender ones, made the whole thing possible in the first place. And like many of the people Hochschild interviewed, all of us involved seemed to struggle with, resist, and accommodate ourselves to market logic: trying to "protect the personal from the purchased," to find the line past which intimate life became "too commercial," to hold onto the "spirit of the gift," to seize back intimate moments from the marketplace (Hochschild 2012, 13, 95, 225). To Hochschild, such actions are mechanisms for coping with "the basic imbalance between market, state, and civic life" that shows up in the commercial outsourcing of personal lives (225).

Hochschild's concerns, many of which I share, take their place within a larger body of thinking about the relationship between markets and intimate social life. As Viviana Zelizer has described them, perspectives on this relationship take several forms. Some see the marketplace and intimate relationships as "hostile worlds," with contact between them leading inevitably to "moral contamination and degradation" (Zelizer 2000, 818). Others suggest that "intimate transfers—be they of sex, babies, or blood—operate according to principles identical with transfers of stock shares and used cars" (Zelizer 2000, 825) and should be understood as simply another transactional type. Still others argue that commercialized intimacy is "nothing but the result of coercive, and more specifically patriarchal, power structures" (Zelizer 2000, 826), serving the interests of the more powerful partners in a gendered hierarchy. Zelizer suggests another, more nuanced approach, which she calls "differentiated ties": intimacy and marketplace are neither hostile, equivalent, nor reducible to coercion, but instead embedded together in social relations, as "people incessantly match different forms of payment to their various intimate relations" (Zelizer 2000, 826).

Pieces of each of these perspectives shows up in my family-making stories, but none of them alone quite seems to get it right. As I here tell the stories of conceiving and creating my own family, I want to consider what is and isn't captured in these concerns about market-linked reproduction, and to unravel some of the complexities of outsourced personal life. One is quickly evident just from the fact that I was *able* to build a family as I did. Although I was constantly aware of and wary of the role of the market elements of the process, I was also aware that without those transactions I would remain excluded from biological reproduction. For some of us, facing medical, biological, and/or social obstacles, the commercialized aspects of reproduction have been important

facilitators of family creation and relationships that were otherwise proscribed. In fact, it is not just capitalist entrepreneurs (for instance, those behind the many for-profit fertility clinics and surrogacy agencies) who have used market transactions to open up parenthood options, but also entrepreneurial activists (like the women who established sperm banks in the 1980s) (Mundy 2007). The expansion of who can become parents, when, and how—including, it turned out, by "outsourcing" parts of the process—has resulted not just from commercialization forces, and not just from advances in reproductive medicine, but also from social movements. Without feminism, it is hard to imagine women pursuing parenthood solo (Hertz 2006); without lesbian and gay organizing, the legal and social obstacles to same-sex parenting would have been insurmountable (Lewin 2009). In this context, the marketplace seemed to me neither a moral contaminator nor a coercive force but one mechanism for achieving both a personal and collective goal: the freedom to make the relationships that we want to make, not just the ones that are defined as legitimate by, say, heteronormative social forces and traditional family structures (Stacey 2011).

At an everyday level, my stories suggest, the relationship between marketplace and intimacies is not exclusively one in which the market colonizes personal life and we accommodate ourselves to it or push back against it. In many ways, in the creation of our family, the market indeed pushed against intimacies, replacing connection with commerce; in other ways, it produced intimacies, even as other institutions, such as law and medicine, were hostile or ill-equipped for this kind of family making. In some ways, financial transactions highlighted class differences and undercut the closeness of peers; in other ways, they generated balance and offset differences. Sometimes operating outside of the marketplace was a welcome relief from the ways it pushed people apart; at other times, the detachments it provided were themselves a welcome relief. Sometimes we were suspicious of and resisted the logic of the marketplace; at other times, we sought out and embraced it.

MAKING REBA SADIE

From the very beginning, considerations of the commercialized aspects of family creation were primary in my and Richard's decision-making. For a variety of reasons, some form of biological ties between us and any future baby was very important to Richard, and less so to me. I had no objections to biological reproduction itself, and felt no particular obligation to pursue adoption instead. Instead, my worries echoed the scholarly troubling of commodified intimate life relations. The idea of shopping for eggs, as though procreation was equivalent to a trip to the grocery store, rubbed me the wrong way; the idea of basically renting a woman's womb seemed even creepier, given the degree to which many men have proceeded as if entitled to access women's bodies through purchase, violence, or both. What I wanted, and Richard, too, I think, was something that felt more connected, organic, consensual, and intimate.

Then, just after New Years in 2004, I had a dream. In it, my college girlfriend, her freckled cheeks ruddy, her red hair matted with sweat, was having a baby. After my coffee, I gave Tamar a call. We hadn't spoken in about a year, but I told her about the dream and asked her if she and her husband were maybe on the way to a baby.

"Nah," she said. She and her husband Andy had decided against kids. Tamar mentioned only one regret. "I kind of wanted to experience pregnancy and childbirth. I was born into this body, you know, and I feel like I'm missing the chance to experience one of the most amazing things you can do in this kind of body."

"So you're saying you'd like to be pregnant and give birth to a child, but not raise it," I summarized.

"Exactly," she said.

"Have I got a deal for you," I said.

"I'll mull it over," she said. I figured she was kidding.

To my surprise, Tamar called back a few weeks later to discuss the possibility of carrying our baby. She came to our ongoing conversations with lists of discussion topics. Interestingly, among the things she requested was payment, not so much because she needed the money but so that she could treat the experience at least partially as a job, and perhaps because it seemed to balance things, by transforming a pure gift into an exchange of sorts. She also wanted to know how we would feel about her breastfeeding, at least for the first week or two. I'd been reading a lot of surrogacy websites, most of which saw a carrier's emotional attachment to the child she was carrying as the first step towards her decision to screw over the intended parents and keep the kid.

"I'm not worried about getting attached to this baby," Tamar said. "I want to feel attached to this baby. I hope you want that, too." It was exactly what I wanted: attachment and detachment combined. Given the health benefits of breast milk, Tamar also proposed to pump her breasts for the first six weeks and FedEx the milk to California.

"You drive a hard bargain," I told her. I knew she was in.

Not long after, looking for materials to paste into a birthday book for Tamar's upcoming birthday, I found several articles sent to me by her late mother, a psychologist, including an invited address she'd given to the American Psychological Association on Judaism and feminism. In it, she quotes a paper Tamar, then nineteen, had written about the separation of male and female in the creation story, and their reconciliation through the improbable pregnancies of Sarah (pregnant at ninety with Isaac) and Rebecca (barren for twenty years, only to give birth to twins Jacob and Esau). The logic of the interpretation wasn't easy to follow, but Tamar, her mother reported, "caused pregnancy to represent in symbol that which it is in biological fact, a unification of independent beings who require each other for the creation of new life." Tucked nearby was a letter Nancy had written to me after my break-up with Tamar. "When I think about what 'might have been' between Tamar and you," she had, "it is more often in terms of the large collection of baby items we have squirreled away in our minds for the first grandchild, for which you and Tamar looked like the most likely and most welcome candidates." I made a copy of the letter, and pasted the original onto a page for Tamar's birthday book.

Richard and I set about pursuing both commercial and non-commercial avenues to the egg that might become our baby. I perused egg donors on fertility clinic sites, unhappily, and we began talking to family and friends, one of whom ultimately agreed to donate eggs. All the elements were in place: intimates, together, expanding a family by creating a baby.

In April, Team Baby descended on Northern Virginia, near Tamar and Andy and a reputable fertility institute. The fertility institute was located in a small, bland office park in Fairfax. Checking in at the front desk, we could fit our roles into none of their forms. Mom-kid combos beamed from the shiny covers of parenting magazines. The few waiting women and the receptionist watched us with curiosity and caution, as if our laughter might be mocking them. In the waiting room, we were incongruous, a bunch of fertile people loosed in the land of infertility.

While the donor's eggs were being harvested, I browsed the agency's brochures, one of which advertised the availability, for an additional fee, of eggs from women who "hold or are pursuing advanced degrees in medicine or another academic specialty," known at the institute as "doctoral donors."

"Daddy," I said, in my best spoiled voice, "I want a doctoral donor." No one was amused.

After dinner that night, Andy put Sister Sledge's "We Are Family" on the CD player. We pushed back the table and danced a little. *We are family. I got all my sisters with me. We are family. Get up everybody and sing.*

The doctor—who, by coincidence, Richard knew from medical school, where they were among the few African American students—made no mention of our unusual circumstances, and had no trouble recognizing that Richard and I were the intended parents, and that the egg donor and Tamar were not "staff" but members of a tight little team. When she called the next day, the news wasn't good. Only two eggs had fertilized, and neither of the embryos looked promising. The odds of a pregnancy, she said, were slim to none, which Richard told me was doctor talk for "it's not going to happen." I flew home to go back to work.

Tamar, who for months had been physically and mentally preparing for her role, wanted to follow it all the way through. Otherwise, she said, it would be like she'd trained for a relay race and never been handed the baton. Besides, we figured, we'd already paid for the procedure. That Monday morning, Tamar lay on the table, legs raised, with Andy and Richard on each side. The room was a bit cramped, and on one side was a small sliding window much like you'd find at a Burger King drive-thru. The window slid open, and a voice called out, in a manner that reminded Richard of a short-order cook, "Embryos for Gamson." They all held hands and watched on the ultrasound screen as a tiny dot gently traveled, like a slow-motion spitball, to its destination.

Tamar was told to lay low for the day. Andy went to work, and she and Richard got French fries and watched DVDs.

Two Thursdays later, Tamar called to tell us she was pregnant.

Tamar approached pregnancy with the conscientiousness and grit that I recognized from our college years. She studied fetal development, she researched, she charted.

She kept her receipts and tracked her expenses on Excel. She dealt with curiosity-seekers with finesse and smiling bite, disarming them with the isn't-it-wonderful news that she was carrying a baby for dear friends, two guys who could not have one on their own. I imagined she left little space for disapproval. She told me she saw her mission as personal and political.

Still, we had to sue her. We had already decided against having the birth in Virginia, where laws were hostile to surrogacy, let alone same-sex parenting. Our plan was to head up to Massachusetts, hang out at my parents' house on Martha's Vineyard, and have the baby in the one state where Richard and I were legally married. Without legal intervention, the baby's presumptive legal parents would be Tamar and Andy, in which case we'd have to adopt our own kid, or at best Tamar and the one of us who donated sperm would, in which case we'd still have a mess on our hands. Tamar and Andy wanted no legal responsibility for a baby and we wanted all of it, so we decided to get a court order so that, as our complaint to the Probate and Family Court of Dukes County, Commonwealth of Massachusetts, put it, "the child's birth record may be established in accordance with those true and accurate facts regarding the child's parentage." I couldn't help but admire the big balls of a system that so casually insisted our collaboration be recorded as a dispute, and charged us money to do so. What a perfect perversion: generosity reflected back to us as animosity. At least, I thought, we got the pleasure of being difficult to digest.

In mid-December of 2005, we road-tripped it together in Tamar's Subaru from Virginia to Massachusetts, she in the back seat with her ridiculous belly and a body pillow, Richard and I in the front. How strange to be here with them, I thought, these two who had walked in from different lifetimes, now laughing it up and arguing about who could be in the delivery room.

Andy arrived a couple of days later, and we all hunkered down like roosting birds in my parent's small guesthouse to await the baby. The fireplace was lit each morning as the coffee was brewing, and burned itself out after that evening's movie. We read fiction punctuated by meals. We stared spacily out at the bare trees. We entered a sort of group marriage, annoying one another with dishwasher-loading styles and inappropriate whistling; occasionally one dyad would peel off for a walk, an argument, or both. On Christmas Day, Richard cooked an elaborate meal that included mac-and-cheese, collard greens, and sweet potato pie; it was also the first night of Chanukah, so we lit several menorahs near the Christmas lights. We became bored, impatient, and a little chubby. We tried every trick we'd heard, or thought we'd heard, to get the fully cooked baby to emerge, but she stayed put, paddling about contentedly in her dark sea of amniotic fluid. Finally, after weeks of waiting, the calm, patient nurse-midwife at the Martha's Vineyard Hospital scheduled an induction.

My mother kept a sort of journal record of our stay, with brief, factual summaries of each day's events, entitled, "It Takes Two Fathers, a Surrogate, Her Husband, Three Grandparents, a Dog, Three Cousins, Two Aunts, an Uncle, Four Houses and an Island to Birth a Baby: Notes From a Modern Confinement." It includes entries like this one, from December 19th: "At the guesthouse, Josh washes loads of beautiful hand-me-downs that are probably already clean. J and R deal with the legal procedures that will allow them to be recognized as the legal parents of the baby."

In the hospital, our reputation had clearly preceded us—the Vineyard is a small town in the winter, and we were the talk of it—and the warm nurses knew exactly who was who and what was what. We all did our best to entertain and distract Tamar. We put some country music on the CD player, and Andy and Richard danced a goofy jig.

I massaged Tamar's back and Andy quietly sung, a capella, a Kate Wolf song in which a lilac and an apple converse about "life in another time." When it seemed that no amount of drugs, songs, stories, baths, and jigs would get this baby moving—the contractions were regular and painful, but didn't increase in intensity, and Tamar's uterus was barely dilated—we ordered a pizza, wheeled Tamar out to the waiting area, and agreed to try again the next day.

The next afternoon, the nurse-midwife broke Tamar's water. A few hours later, Tamar agreed to an epidural, both for pain reduction and to increase the odds of a vaginal delivery. Several hours later, now into the early hours of day three of her labor, Tamar looked wearily at Cathy. "Do you think it's safe to say we've tried everything?" she asked. "Do you think I've done everything I can to get this baby out?" The nurse-midwife nodded, and picked up the phone to call the doctor.

Richard and Andy and I, in scrubs, masks, and cap, stood inside the delivery room. Richard's little sister watched from a windowed room just above us. His mother and mine, who had slept overnight on matching couches in the maternity visiting area, were waiting outside the door; my father was on his way. From where I stood, Tamar reminded me of a woman in a magic show being sawed in half, divided as she was by a waist-level screen. The top half was placid, her eyes blinking slowly, her head turned a bit to look at her husband. It seemed to have no connection to the bottom half, where three men poked away frantically with gloved hands dripping blood, pulling out of it the nine pound creature we named Reba Sadie, after my grandmother and Richard's great-grandmother. Andy cut the umbilical cord.

One of the nurses asked who was to get her first. Richard and I, teary-eyed and exhausted, looked at each other and then pointed to Tamar. Tamar, cheeks ruddy, hair matted, crying, gazed dopily at the swaddled infant, and then the nurse brought her back over to me and Richard. Richard held her up towards the fluorescent-lit ceiling, Kunta Kinte style, crying and chuckling. We took her out to the hallway to meet her grandparents. My mother turned to Richard's. "Look at those lips," she whispered.

The day before we were all to leave, my parents made us dinner and left us to eat it while they babysat. Over fettuccine that night, we talked on video to future versions of Reba. The combination of sleep deprivation, hormones, wine, and intimacy proved irresistible, and pretty much anything anyone said made someone else cry. When Tamar reported on our success with feedings ("every two to three hours, we're keeping meticulous records, and one of your daddies is always there"), I filmed the tears coming to Richard's eyes.

"What do you want Reba to know about who you are and who you are to her?" I asked, recording. Just the question made me cry a little.

"I'm not sure who I am to her yet," Tamar answered, drying her tears without interrupting the drama of the moment. "She'll have to figure that out as she grows up. But who she is to me: She's this wonderful little person I helped bring into the world, and I'm really glad she's here. Her dads needed a little help birthing her, since neither one of them has a uterus, and I do, so she got put inside of me when she was two cells big, and she grew inside of me for nine months." She covered her mouth, crying hard now, but readying a punch line nonetheless. "I tried to take really good care of her, and I think I did a pretty good job, cause she came out really, really big."

"Why are you crying?" I asked.

"I'm crying because there's a lot of hormones right now," Tamar said, blowing her nose. "And I'm also crying because I'm going to miss her. I was very glad to help her grow and bring her into this world. It's really hard to let her go now that she's no longer inside me. I want to be part of her life. I will be part of her life." Looking back, it sounds like something you'd hear on *Oprah*, but at the time it was just like listening to the inside of a heart.

Andy cleared his throat, and pushed his long hair back behind his ears. He sang for Reba the song he'd made up earlier in the week. The tune was from the spiritual "Children, Go Where I Send Thee." Andy had inserted lyrics that were equal parts love and cheese. *Children, go where I send thee. How shall I send thee?* Andy sang. *I'm gonna send you one by one. One for the little bitty Reba, wrapped in swaddling clothing, lying in her daddies' arms, born born born on the Vineyard.* Everyone but Andy got a shout out in his song—Richard and me (two), the grandparents (three), Richard's siblings (four), my sister's family (five), the hospital stay itself (six), even the "luck of the embryos" (seven), the nurses (eight), and the Apgar score (nine). He ended not with the apostles, but with Tamar: *Ten for the belly mommy.*

The next morning, the four of us took a walk on the beach with my mother, her dog Rosie, and a bundled-up Reba, to say our goodbyes. We didn't talk much. When Tamar and Andy drove off, my mom held the baby while Richard and I chased after their car, waving and crying, like the movie wives of soldiers chasing the train carrying away their husbands.

We flew home to California when Reba was nine days old. In my carry-on bag was her birth record, handed to us the day before by Sandy, a rosy-cheeked hospital records clerk with braces on her teeth. When we'd first arrived at her department, Sandy had not known what to make of the group of us, but over the weeks she had made many phone calls regarding the issue of how the Commonwealth might allow her to provide a birth record that didn't say "mother" and "father." She had gradually become a

confederate. The birth certificate she produced listed Parent A and Parent B.

MAKING MADELEINE BLANCHE

A few years later, when Richard and I decided, over dinner at a casino buffet, that we wanted to conceive another child, we turned very quickly towards market-based surrogacy. Much as she had appreciated the experience, Tamar was not interested in another round; the odds of another friend offering to carry a baby for us seemed slim. Much as we had both appreciated the earlier process, the thought of going through an agency, who would set us up with paid strangers to help us out, gave both of us a surprising sense of relief. I had no regrets at all about the way we had made Reba, but it was filled with exhausting complexities: the weird combination of guilt and gratitude towards the egg donor, the gestational surrogate, and her husband; the intense period of group marriage and then the abrupt, painful separation; the ambiguous boundaries of familial relationships; the practical hassles of organizing such an elaborate production, including the medical and legal maneuverings. The thought of doing that again, while parenting a preschooler, just when we were beginning to get some sleep, seemed too exhausting for words. Hiring an agency to help, and working with an egg donor and gestational surrogate to whom we had no past relationship, now seemed not unsettling, cold, and overly mercantile, but sensible, clear, and clean.

Still, when I looked into surrogacy agencies that had specialties in same-sex family building, I found myself again uncomfortable: with the glossy brochures and high fees, and perhaps with the forced recognition that our way of becoming parents was really only available to us because we had the earning capacity, borrowing power, and family financial support to afford it. When I looked at the profiles of egg donors on various web sites, I could not feel a connection to any of them. "They're all smiley and young and blue-eyed," I complained to Richard. "Most of them say something like, 'I'm a people person.'" Where were the black women with attitude and the neurotic Jews, or the Jewish women with attitude and the neurotic African Americans?

Thankfully, we knew some of those. So we asked a close friend—a woman with a very sweet, deep attachment to Reba—if she'd consider donating eggs for our next child. She said she'd give it some thought.

We chose an agency, Circle Surrogacy, partly because they were based in Massachusetts—we had vague, naïve notions that they'd be more likely to be connected to surrogates in that state, where we had already established legal parentage once—and partly because their self-presentation was of a small, gay-run agency that viewed surrogates as people rather than as means-to-an-end vessels, and aimed to build rather than limit the relationships between surrogates and clients. That is, they tapped into and comforted the very anxieties about commercialized reproduction that I brought to the table. The first e-mail to us, in early 2008, announced that the president of the agency is "one half of a gay couple and the proud dad to two boys through traditional surrogacy," before mentioning that the agency fees had just increased but if we signed on by the end of the month we'd be under the previous fee structure. We met with the agency president and one of his colleagues a few weeks later in a San Francisco hotel, where they were attending a conference. Some similar agencies, they told us, do not like the surrogates and the clients to have too much contact, and monitor any contact they do have, for fear that they will become too bonded. They took a different approach, they said, encouraging as much contact as possible, under the belief that making a baby together can and should be an intimate bonding experience.

That sounded just right. Plus, we knew this could all take a long time and were ready to get started. We forked over the large agency fee, sent in the 21-page contract, and signed on. Paperwork and e-mails flooded our way. There was the Timing of Payments notice, the lengthy Explanation of the Matching Process, the Parenting Questionnaire, and the separate Father's Questionnaire. We had to send them our wills, choose a plan for purchasing insurance for a surrogate, and look for a psychologist to evaluate us. The social worker wanted to talk to us, and then her successor, and then hers. The case manager, and then her successor, offered to answer any questions we might have. We had many.

In March, as I was resignedly narrowing the pool of people-person egg donors, we got a call from the friend we'd asked to consider egg donation. She'd decided, after serious and careful deliberation, that she couldn't do it; among other things, she was concerned that in order to keep her non-familial relationship to a future child clear, she'd need to distance herself from us and our family. She said we might get a call from a mutual friend, Rachel, from whom she'd sought counsel while thinking it all through. Sure enough, that very evening, Rachel, who was finishing a Ph.D. in Environmental Economics and had a son a few months younger than Reba. She offered us her eggs.

"Are you fucking kidding me?" I said. "A doctoral donor! Do you know how much your eggs are worth on the open market?" Rachel laughed.

Later, Richard asked her if she would feel weird knowing that her son had a genetic sibling, and she had a genetic child, living nearby.

"That's not how I think about it at all," she said, in the direct, self-possessed, and no-nonsense manner I'd often admired. "An egg is made up of some cells. I am offering you some of my cells. That's it. Of course, I'd want to know and love any child that comes of this. But that's not my child." Richard and

I could not believe our luck—or rather, the kindness of our friends. After the conversation, we cried a little. The next day, I began making arrangements with Rachel for her to see a fertility doctor.

A few weeks later, I received an e-mail from a Circle social worker named Katherine. "We have found a potential carrier that we think will be a great match for you two! Gail is a thirty five year old single mother of three children, living in Kentucky. She is very excited about helping a couple to create a family as wonderful as hers. She has a very strong support network in Kentucky and feels ready to embark on this journey with the support of her mother, siblings, and close friends." She attached Gail's profile and a few photos. Gail, pale with shoulder-length light brown hair, smiled alone, and then with a baby, and then with a baby and an eight-year-old boy. She was a single mother of three kids, her profile said. She liked "reading, playing games, spending time with family, going to movies and concerts, doing crafts, swimming, many outside sports, and of course shopping." She was of German descent, a high school graduate and a widow. Her father was an alcoholic and her sisters were molested. "I have a really easy pregnancy and I love being a mom but for some people they aren't able to get pregnant so easily," she wrote. "I think if someone wants to be a parent then why shouldn't I help them when it's so easy for me. My family is complete and it wouldn't be my baby. I'd just be carrying it for someone else. It would be my job to protect it until it's born and then they can protect it." She listed her base fee as $20,000. She'd found the agency through a Google search.

Notwithstanding Katherine's enthusiastic exclamation points, there was nothing in particular that made Gail a "great match" for us beyond the fact that she had completed a form and we had completed a form. She was in a state whose laws were unsympathetic to surrogacy and hostile to same-sex relationship recognition. As it turned out, no one at the agency knew much of anything about Gail beyond what she provided in her profile, and they had no intentions of ever meeting her. Still, however careless the matching process, there she was: a woman in Kentucky who would consider carrying our child.

We talked to Gail on the phone the next week. She was nervous and giggling. We mostly made small talk about kids and movies. Towards the end, I asked her what she thought it would be like to carry a child that she wasn't going to raise.

"It's kind of like a babysitting job," she said, giggling. "I figure I'd be babysitting your baby for nine months." Though I figured it might be more emotionally complicated, I liked that: She would be our fetus sitter.

We flew Gail out to meet us in person. She had never flown before. Within a few hours, she had lost much of her nervousness. She was funny and fun loving, with a sense of adventure. I thought maybe that was part of the appeal for her, besides the money and the "why shouldn't I help?" motivation: a taste for something new, different, bigger and weirder than her everyday life in Bowling Green. We introduced her to Rachel, and they seemed to appreciate each other. By the end of the trip, we'd all agreed to try to have a baby together.

The agency, despite their sales pitch, did little to facilitate a relationship between us and Gail, aside from taking over financial transactions. We fought with them over nearly everything, even as their staff members dropped out and new ones popped up in their places. The agency wanted Gail's emotional support to come from a long-distance phone relationship, at a fee of $3,000, with a social worker who was authorized by signed waiver to report to the agency if "there is any threat to the health of the surrogate, if there is any threat to the health of the child, or if the surrogate is thinking of changing her mind." We insisted that she have access to face-to-face support by a mental health professional in her own locale, whose sole loyalty would be to her. The psychiatrist the agency required us to see assured us that was the standard of care according to the American Society for Reproductive Medicine.

"We believe our success in having the highest success rate in surrogacy and having every surrogate relinquish the child is in large part due to [the outside social worker's] extraordinary ability to provide support over the phone and to build a relationship of trust and understanding with the surrogates," the agency's president wrote to us in an e-mail. He offered the example of a surrogate who "developed intra partum depression taking a whole box of Tylenol, trying to kill herself when she was six months pregnant." The social worker had "jumped to the rescue":

> She got in touch with a psychiatrist, who prescribed the one type of antidepressant that was not dangerous for the baby and we jointly (and nicely) threatened the surrogate with a locked institution if she didn't take her medication every day and show up for every consultation with the psychiatrist we set up. She did both, and delivered a healthy child three months later.

He told another cautionary tale of a surrogate who changed her mind about "releasing" the baby inside of her, revealed this in a "chat room for unhappy surrogates," some of whom were part of the social worker's "remarkable cadre of loyal surrogates." They reported her disclosure to the social worker, who reported it to the agency, and through an "incredible intervention, the surrogate agreed to release the child." He suggested that while a local therapist might be "by the book," it would "compromise the surrogacy," and could cost much more. "I fear greatly," he said, "that we will lose control." I was not comforted. To him, this was a goal-oriented business transaction; to me, an intimate process. To the agency, she was a service provider, and not one who could opt out once she opted in; to me, she was a person who, much as I hoped would carry our baby, should remain in control of her own body and destiny. The notion that threats, cadres of chat-room tattlers, and incredible interventions would build trust and understanding seemed unlikely; the notion that all that mattered was the "rescue," "control," the "relinquishing" of a healthy baby, and a high agency "success rate," seemed to undermine claims that Gail herself was a priority. We would have to work on trust and intimacy on our own.

Over time, without giving it much thought, we built a friendship with Gail. It made sense to do the egg donation and fertilization in California—and it took two egg donation cycles and four in-vitro attempts to get pregnant—and on each subsequent trip we all relaxed around one another. We were all regulars at the local fertility clinic, where Gail, Richard, our doctor, and a nurse, who seemed as invested in our baby as we were, would cram into a tiny laboratory room and wait for the tall, skinny embryologist to present the needle that might contain our future child. For the second pregnancy attempt, we invited Gail to bring her kids, and we took them and Reba on a road trip to Monterey. We were there when Gail's children touched the ocean for the first time; we took them out to dinner, and showed them the Golden Gate Bridge. It was a strange kind of relationship: inherently familial, but also most likely short-term; starting and to some degree set to end with a market transaction, but also somehow much more; at once superficial and deep. I was curious about its constraints, but never able to really get past them. She was a single, working mother with limited income, being paid by two men, a doctor and a professor, to conceive and carry a child. Though I had no evidence of it, I wondered if her easygoing persona was in part a means of covering discomfort and even resentment, and of protecting a valuable financial opportunity. For our part, we were loose but also careful, aware of the costs of alienating Gail.

Finally, in early 2008, Gail was pregnant. Unlike Tamar, her approach to pregnancy was unworried and undetailed: She had done it before, and it didn't seem to require much extra attention beyond going to check-ups. She would work in her job as a clerk at a campground/amusement park until the day before giving birth, as she had with her own children. Richard and I had told our-selves not to micromanage the pregnancy, which was just as well, given how hard it was to reach Gail, who sent us short, "the baby is doing fine" updates every few weeks by phone and e-mail. On the rare occasions that someone from the agency spoke to Gail, we'd get a sunny, exclamation-point ridden, information-thin e-mail from a caseworker in Boston. Aside from one trip to Kentucky for the twenty-week ultrasound, our involve-ment with the pregnancy was disconcertingly minimal. It really was like having a babysit-ter for our fetus.

The surrogacy agency had recommended that we pursue second-parent adoption—in which a non-biological parent adopts after the baby's birth—but neither of us liked the idea of adopting our own child. We hired a lawyer to get from a California court a pre-birth order designating us as the parents, as we had done in Massachusetts. Just before the baby was born, after many forms and fees, we were legally deemed her parents by the Alameda County Family Court.

Richard and Reba flew in mid-September to Bowling Green, Kentucky to await the birth, and I joined them after a week. We had invited Gail to come to Massachusetts or to California for the birth, but between her work and her kids, that turned out to be too much adventure, even for Gail. I wasn't excited. I figured that Kentucky would be full of homophobia, guns and fatty foods, and maybe not so safe for a black man, a Jew and their black-Jewish daughter. Richard had gone with Gail to meet the obstetrician, who,

when faced with the requirements of our sur-rogacy plan, turned hostile and scheduled her labor to be induced on what later turned out to be a day he would be on a golfing trip. After the meeting, Richard, who is not prone to tears, cried on Gail's shoulder.

Not long after my arrival, while Richard and I were in a matinee of "Zombieland," our lawyer called to report that the local family court had refused to domesticate the Califor-nia court order, leaving things in legal limbo. She said she would threaten to sue Kentucky for violating the Full Faith and Credit clause of the Constitution and instructed us to get out of there as soon as the baby was born. I felt vaguely unsafe and out of sorts. People seemed to stare at us. One night I dreamed that the baby was born healthy, and then stolen.

But when Madeleine Blanche came along a few days later (full head of black hair, long eyelashes, tongue sticking out) that sense of danger had receded. Gail's mother had been with her throughout labor, and held her hand in the delivery room when it got rough. Richard and I had stood behind Gail, watch-ing the obstetrician, a kind, efficient, direct woman, work with Gail, as a forceful nurse ordered Gail to push. My parents and Rich-ard's mother were in the waiting room with Reba. When it was over, we said goodbye to Gail, who went to sleep while we went off to the maternity ward to be regularly awakened by a hungry baby. I wondered if Gail would feel lonely, but couldn't ask.

Our presence seemed to send the staff of women at the Bowling Green medical cen-ter into Southern hospitality overdrive: they dispensed diapers, advice and coffeecake. We chatted about 4-year-olds, work and the costs of preschool. Nurse Christie brought a button for Reba that said, "I'm a big sister!" Unfamiliar heads popped in and out. Not homophobia but a kind of homophilic curi-osity was swirling around us, turning us into objects of gossip but also of generosity. Anx-ieties about discrimination were one thing, but my assumptions about homophobia now seemed glib and snobbish.

The problem was getting out of there. One sympathetic young clerk had been instructed by hospital lawyers not to put our names down on the birth forms as parents, but Gail had declined to sign anything that gave her legal or financial responsibility for our baby. The clerk tried the form with just a father's name, but the computer spit it back, saying it required a mother. So she sent the forms, along with a copy of the California court order, to the Kentucky Office of Vital Statistics with neither Father nor Mother listed. Her small act of administrative disobedience was, to me, quite touching. The hospital released us and our legally parentless baby.

On our way out, we went to visit Gail, who had mostly been sleeping since the birth. She was dressed and out of bed. Surrounded by her family, she looked refreshed and ready to get back to her post-fetus-sitting life. She'd called to get help from Richard, since the hospital staff was asking her to wait to be released until "our lawyers get back to us." Gail knew Richard would know how to address this.

"You're not refusing to release this patient, are you?" he asked a blank looking administrator. "You can't legally keep her here, you know. Get her a wheelchair, please." Minutes later, a wheelchair arrived.

We chatted with Gail, her mother, and her teenaged daughter about Madeleine, and exchanged a few small gifts. Even as Gail held Maddy for a minute, we kept it light, but beneath it, I could feel a strong, thin thread connecting all of us for the rest of our lives, maybe more. I might have made that up.

At the airport, the airline agent refused to allow us to fly with the baby without a note from her pediatrician. "She's three days old and we live in California," Richard said. "I'm her doctor." I watched him dig around for his medical license and then scribble something on a piece of paper. When we boarded the plane, with only a release document from the hospital to identify Madeleine, going home with our children felt like some sort of escape attempt.

Months later, we still had no birth certificate. Smelling discrimination again, I indulged in self-righteous daydreams of lawsuits, but my suspicions proved unreliable. For Kentucky officials the problem turned out to be much more mundane than sexual taboo: they didn't want California telling them what to put on their forms. In the end, they issued a birth certificate saying that Gail was the mother, then sealed it and issued an amended one listing Richard and me as the parents.

Finally one day the birth certificate arrived. Somehow, with all the lawyering and money that preceded it, I was surprised that it was just a piece of paper. Then I noticed something: the California judge had directed Kentucky to list one of us as Mother and the other as Father, but Kentucky officials refused. Instead they labeled us Parent and Parent. Kentucky had out-liberaled California.

We picked up Reba from preschool. She was uninterested in the news, but happy for the celebratory dinner, through which the baby slept, eyelashes fluttering.

OUTSOURCING, MARKETPLACES AND INTIMACIES

Looking back at these experiences of family creation through the lens of market-mediated intimacies, and of the outsourcing of private life, there is certainly plenty of evidence that the marketplace is hostile to both short- and long-term intimacy. In our more overtly market-engaged experience— which resulted in Madeleine—we developed connection, trust, and attachments *in spite of* the actions of the commercial agency that made and managed the link between Gail and us. To the degree that we forged intimacy, it was limited and transitory. We came together for a specific purpose, and when that goal was reached, when Gail's "babysitting" job was done, we parted. Even in the case of conceiving Reba, which was much less market-based (though much was still outsourced), the path we took was very much informed by the desire to bypass the commercial surrogacy system, on the grounds that it was likely to be less deeply intimate, as indeed it turned out to be.

It also appears, quite predictably, that the stronger the market involvement, the weaker the intimate ties. For instance, our family's relationship to Gail is, and is likely to remain, a relatively weak, inconsistent one involving very little emotional disclosure. We send her holiday cards every year and photos of Maddy and Reba every few months. She sends occasional news about her kids: last I heard, the older one was deciding to stay in Bowling Green for college so she could be near her boyfriend, the middle one was asking to learn to play piano, and the littlest one was obsessed with horses. Our relationship to Tamar, and also to Andy—they are no longer together—was dramatically strengthened and deepened through Reba's creation. They had been friends, but they became family. Although the relationship with Andy has faded, we see him periodically and he remains in our loose kinship network. Our relationship with Tamar is more intensively and selfconsciously present. We see her a couple of times a year, and talk a few more. Although we have been cautious about using "mother" in association with Tamar, which we all agree is both inaccurate and confusing, we sometimes refers to Tamar as Reba's "belly mommy," which reminds Reba that she came into the world like everyone else. More routinely, she is known as Aunt Tamar. For the past two years, Aunt Tamar has taken Reba, without us, to her family reunion in Michigan; that family is already a mix of biological, half-biological, and by-marriage kin, and Reba joins the mix as a sort of special guest star.

These experiences are much more complex and nuanced than the critical concerns about the commodification and outsourcing of personal life might suggest. They serve as reminders, first, that the outsourcing of such private, personal experiences is not in itself destructive. Even with payment, these family creation processes produced unusual new relationships, or new depths to existing ones. We did not just arrange for others to provide the service of reproduction. We also brought people *in* to our family, expanding rather than simply delegating to others its intimacies. We became connected, literally combining elements of ourselves. Market transactions and agents did not determine the sorts of relationships that we developed, any more than, say, a matchmaker determines the type relationship between potential romantic partners. We made our own intimate idiocultures, temporary but with lasting effects, facilitated in part by commercial brokers or by financial transactions we chose. Indeed, at times, much as Zelizer (2000) describes, we used, or simply allowed, the market to "mark the character and range of the social relationship" we were enacting (Zelizer 2000, 842): most importantly, payment marked the boundary between a parental and non-parental relationship to the baby, a boundary all of us involved wanted and needed.

Between the adults, the relationships these experienced produced range from minimal intimacy to maximal. I've already weathered dramatic conflict and changes with Tamar since Reba's birth, and the connection has survived; I am not sure I'll see Gail again, or that either of us would feel that as a loss. Yet even we are permanently bound by the creatures we produced. That is its own kind of intimacy—a spiritual one, in a sense, if not always a practical one.

A couple of years ago, when she was four, Reba had asked me if Tamar, was at my wedding to Richard. She already knew the answer was yes—she regularly asked to hear "the wedding story" before bed and had seen the photos—but she seemed to want confirmation before she continued.

"So I've known her forever," Reba said.

"Yes," I replied. "Since you were an embryo. Maybe even before that. Hard to know."

"Before that," she said with certainty. "Because I was at your and Daddy's wedding. When I was a spirit. I was sitting on Tamar's lap."

NOTE

1 Note: A small portion of the material in this chapter is adapted from my piece, "My New Kentucky Baby," which appeared in the *New York Times Magazine* (May 22, 2011).

SECTION IV
Pregnancy and Birth

Pregnancy and birth issues dramatically highlight the main themes of this volume: the tensions between "too much" medical care given to some women and "too little" given to others; the coercive practices to which the most vulnerable women are subject; the importance of social movement activity in reshaping both cultural understandings of reproductive issues and the concrete way in which services are delivered; and most of all, this realm makes evident, once again, the huge disparities in positive pregnancy outcomes that exist along racial, economic, and geographical lines.

To first address the disparity between the situation of women in the developing world, or Global South, and that of women in the developed world, or Global North, this stark statement from the World Health Organization (WHO) speaks volumes: "The maternal mortality rate in developing countries is 240 per 100,000 births versus 16 per 100, 000 in developed countries" (WHO 2012). Put another way, worldwide, about 800 women die from pregnancy- or childbirth-related complications every day. In 2010, about 287,000 women died during and following pregnancy and childbirth and millions more continue to suffer complications, including chronic disease and sterility from unsafe childbirth and abortion.

The overwhelming majority of these deaths and injuries occur in the developing world and almost all, in the view of experts, could be prevented with adequate health care services. For example, all pregnant women need to have access to trained caregivers who can diagnose preeclampsia, a potentially life threatening complication of pregnancy, or who know how to stop the severe bleeding that can follow childbirth. Yet, according to WHO (2012), only 46% of women in low-income countries (especially in sub-Saharan Africa and South Asia) have access to skilled care during pregnancy and childbirth. Yet another reason accounting for the high level of maternal mortality in the Global South is the frequency of adolescent girls becoming pregnant; the risk of death from pregnancy and childbirth is highest for girls under the age of 15. However, in spite of these very dispiriting figures, progress is being made: WHO (2012) reports that between 1990 and 2010, maternal mortality worldwide dropped by almost 50%.

In the United States, the number of reported pregnancy-related deaths is relatively low: about 650 each year (CDC 2013e). Nevertheless, the United States in 2010 ranked 50th in the world for maternal mortality, with a worse record than almost all European countries as well as several countries in the Middle East and Asia (Coeytaux et al. 2011). Moreover, the United States' record has worsened in in recent years, going from 7.2 deaths per 100,000 live births in 1987 to a high of 17.8 deaths per 100,000 live births in 2009. Although the precise causes of the increase are unknown, the U.S. Centers for Disease Control and Prevention believe that there may be more women with chronic illnesses becoming pregnant (CDC 2013d). Yet clearly another cause, according to the public health researcher Francine Coeytaux and her colleagues, in their selection in this section, is the gap in access to health care, including prenatal care, that is most true for African American women. Rates of maternal mortality are not equally distributed, with African American women experiencing the highest rates with 35.6 deaths per 100,000 live births, in comparison to a rate of 11.7 deaths per 100,000 for white women and 17.6 deaths per 100,000 for women of other racial backgrounds (CDC 2013d). As Coeytaux et al. argue, "women who receive no prenatal care are three to four times more likely to die of pregnancy-related complications than women who do" (2011, 190), and they frame the maternal mortality situation in the United States as a "human rights failure." Hopefully, the Affordable Care Act, which did not go fully into effect until after their selection was written, will improve this situation by bringing many previously uninsured women into the health care system.

As discussed elsewhere in this volume, attitudes toward pregnancy and birth in the United States by those in power have always revealed preferences for reproduction among some women more than among others, and a willingness to exert coercive policies, as shown for example in the country's history of sterilization. But nowhere was the absolute authority of others over the reproduction of vulnerable women more evident than that of slave masters' power over slave women, as discussed in the selection in this section by law professor Dorothy Roberts. Contemporary examples of extreme control of women's pregnancy decisions include policies regarding incarcerated women, drug using women, and disabled women, and these are discussed in the following section.

For other American women, however, the history of pregnancy and birth issues, as they have unfolded in the United States over the last 150 years or so, is more complicated—and more promising—than simply one of the powerful controlling the decisions of the vulnerable. Rather, this history has been marked by two interrelated struggles over how pregnancy and birth issues should be handled: the first occurring among groups of health care providers, especially doctors and midwives; and the second between doctors and lay activists. The story of these struggles begins in the 19th century, where births typically occurred in women's homes, and were attended by midwives or simply family members and friends. But similar to the campaign to wrest control of abortion from midwives and lay people that was discussed in Section II, physicians of that era, as part of a professionalizing drive to differentiate themselves from the various categories of health care providers then common in American society, sought exclusive "ownership" of pregnancy management and birth. They were ultimately successful in moving the site of most births into hospitals, and assuring that prenatal care remained firmly under the control of physicians, as numerous scholars have documented (Wertz and Wertz 1989; Leavitt 1986; Ehrenreich and English 2005). If midwives were to remain legally involved in maternity care, this required them to work under the supervision of physicians, a situation that remains law to this day in many places in the United States, one which professional midwives continue to contest. (Interestingly, in the European context, the well-known campaign of violence against "witches" in the 15th and 16th centuries, as Ehrenreich and English have argued in their classic pamphlet, *Witches, Midwives and Nurses* (2010), was largely directed at midwives who assisted women with both childbirth and abortion).

Maternity care became increasingly medicalized in the 20th century. For example, throughout the 1940s and 1950s it was not uncommon for women in the United States to deliver babies while virtually unconscious—so-called "twilight sleep"—after receiving strong sedatives and a promise of painless birth. Obstetricians began to increasingly use fetal monitors on all pregnant women even when there was no indication of fetal distress. Similarly, pregnant women were increasingly subject to the use of pitocin, a medication that stimulates contraction of the uterus and can speed up labor. In many hospitals in mid-century and beyond, women were discouraged from breast feeding—a practice that was made more difficult by hospitals' habit of making available commercial formula to new mothers.

A variety of factors—the growing awareness among American women of "natural childbirth" methods that had been developed earlier in Europe, such as the Lamaze method, the formation of the LA Leche League in 1956 which advocated breast feeding, and most crucially, the rise of the feminist health movement of the late 1960s—led to a backlash against the physician-controlled, highly medicalized version of birth that had become the norm. Birth activists, with allies within medicine, were able to create a revolution of sorts with respect to the options available in maternity care in the United States. Some hospitals became more receptive to those women wanting some version of a natural birth, with either no drugs or far fewer than had been previously used; women's partners and other family members were able to be in the birthing suite, offering support to laboring women; progressive doctors and midwives established freestanding "birthing centers" which offered women such options as delivering in tubs of water, and which were less likely to make use of such technology as fetal monitors. In places where legally permitted, and where supportive doctors could be found to offer backup in case of emergency, some women were able to choose the option of home births attended by midwives. Many of these options are most available to women who can afford them, as they are rarely covered by insurance. The full range of birthing options now available in many places to American women—*albeit* ones who can purchase them—are discussed in the selection in this section from *Our Bodies, Ourselves*, the proverbial "bible" of the feminist health movement, which was first published in 1969, and continues publication to this day.

Yet alongside this remarkable record of success in demedicalizing the birth experience for some women, for others, birth practices have become even *more* medicalized. Nowhere is this seen more vividly—and disturbingly—than in the high rate of Caesarean section (or C-sections, a procedure by which the newborn is surgically removed through incisions in the mother's abdomen and uterus, rather than birth occurring though a vaginal delivery). The United States is one of the top three countries for C-sections in the world. In the United States, there are about 2,651,428 vaginal deliveries each year and about 1,293,267 Cesarean deliveries. This means that Cesarean deliveries account for about 32.8% of all deliveries in the United States (CDC 2013e). Globally, a C-section rate of between 10–15% is considered necessary and appropriate (Gibbons et al. 2010).

The reasons for the high rate of C-sections are complex. To some degree, there is a cultural belief that injury is avoidable through action, so that physicians who do more might be seen as better than those who do less. In the selection in this section from a recent book by the sociologist Theresa Morris, she suggests that this cultural belief and, especially, accompanying concerns about liability and malpractice, leads to high rates of unnecessary C-sections. Alongside these issues, she suggests also that economic pressures discourage physicians from attending long labors, which cost them time in their clinic with other patients, which results in more active management of labor through medications designed to speed labor along. This "speed-up," in turn, results in higher C-section rates.

There is no question that advanced technology and the specialized training available in contemporary obstetrics in the United States has saved the lives of numerous women and fetuses that in former times would have died. The frustration facing many birth activists, including many physicians as well as midwives, is why these advanced medical techniques are imposed on women whose pregnancies do not warrant such intervention. As the sociologist Barbara Katz Rothman wryly commented on the recent developments in American birthing practices, a situation which has seen both the return of midwives, the natural childbirth movement, the rise of freestanding birth centers *and* the high degree of C-sections and other interventions, "When it comes to motherhood, we live in a world that makes no sense" (2007, 3).

Dilemmas associated with technology also present themselves in the area of prenatal diagnosis. Ever-evolving technology has made it possible to become aware of a broad array of serious health outcomes and genetic permutations that develop in fetuses in pregnancy. Yet, who should decide about available testing, who should pay for it, how should information be communicated, and what those findings may mean raise new and important questions about individuals' and couples' decision-making when pregnant. The excerpt in this section from the anthropologist Rayna Rapp's classic book on prenatal testing and diagnoses demonstrates these issues and also points to interesting variations as to how people from different social classes and racial and ethnic groups approach prenatal diagnosis.

Some portion of wanted pregnancies end, either through miscarriage or stillbirth (or in abortion, on the basis of information gained from prenatal diagnosis). As parents face these heart-breaking outcomes, they do so as individuals with their own philosophical, social, religious, moral, and personal views. Nowhere can this be seen more clearly than in the anthropologist Linda Layne's research on experiences of pregnancy loss, part of which we have excerpted in this section.

Finally, environmental scientists with a particular interest in reproductive health are establishing a new front in social movement activity around pregnancy. The work of these scientists has demonstrated that women's exposure to environmental toxins presents new risks to their reproductive health and pregnancy outcomes: chemical exposures before and during pregnancy can lead to miscarriage and stillbirth, impaired fetal growth, low birth weight, preterm birth, learning disabilities, and infertility. This field of research also has implications for male infertility. Many of those involved in this research are also advocates for governmental action, for example to increase testing and regulation of certain chemicals, and to inform both health care professionals and the general public about the threats to reproductive health contained in certain chemicals. Already, there has been widespread publicity about the dangers of the chemical *bisphenol A*, known as "BPA," which has been widely used in various plastic products. As a result of the recent scrutiny given to BPA, the U.S. Food and Drug Administration (FDA) and agencies in various other countries have banned BPA's use in baby bottles, which previously had been very common (Tavernise 2012). This relatively new area of the interface of reproductive health issues and the environment is addressed in the selection in this section by Jackie Schwartz and Tracey Woodruff, two leading scientists in this field.

CHAPTER 15

Reproduction in Bondage

Dorothy Roberts

When Rose Williams was sixteen years old, her master sent her to live in a cabin with a male slave named Rufus. It did not matter that Rose disliked Rufus "cause he a bully." At first Rose thought that her role was just to perform household chores for Rufus and a few other slaves. But she learned the true nature of her assignment when Rufus crawled into her bunk one night: "I says, 'What you means, you fool nigger?' He say for me to hush de mouth. 'Dis my bunk, too,' he say." When Rose fended off Rufus's sexual advances with a poker, she was reported to Master Hawkins. Hawkins made it clear that she had no choice in the matter:

> De nex' day de massa call me and tell me, "Woman, I's pay big money for you, and I's done dat for de cause I wants yous to raise me chillens. I's put you to live with Rufus for dat purpose. Now, if you doesn't want whippin' at de stake, yous do what I wants."

Rose reluctantly acceded to her master's demands:

> I thinks 'bout massa buyin' me offen de block and savin' me from bein' sep'rated from my folks and 'bout bein' whipped at de stake. Dere it am. What am I's to do? So I'cides to do as de massa wish and so I yields.[1]

The story of control of Black reproduction begins with the experiences of slave women like Rose Williams. Black procreation helped to sustain slavery, giving slave masters an economic incentive to govern Black women's reproductive lives. Slave women's childbearing replenished the enslaved labor force: Black women bore children who belonged to the slaveowner from the moment of their conception. This feature of slavery made control of reproduction a central aspect of whites' subjugation of African people in America. It marked Black women from the beginning as objects whose decisions about reproduction should be subject to social regulation rather than to their own will.

For slave women, procreation had little to do with liberty. To the contrary, Black women's childbearing in bondage was largely a product of oppression rather than an expression of self-definition and personhood. As Henry Louis Gates, Jr., writes about the autobiography of a slave named Harriet Jacobs, it "charts in vivid detail precisely how the shape of her life and the choices she makes are defined by her reduction to a sexual object, an object to be raped, bred, or abused."[2] Even when whites did not interfere in reproduction so directly, this aspect of slave women's lives was dictated by their masters' economic stake in their labor. The brutal domination of slave women's procreation laid the foundation for centuries of reproductive regulation that continues today.

All of these violations were sanctioned by law. Racism created for white slaveowners the possibility of unrestrained reproductive control. The social order established by powerful white men was founded on two inseparable ingredients: the dehumanization of Africans on the basis of race, and the control of women's sexuality and reproduction. The American legal system is rooted in this monstrous combination of racial and gender domination. One of America's first laws concerned the status of children born to slave mothers and fathered by white men: a 1662 Virginia statute made these children slaves.[3]

Slave masters' control of Black women's reproduction illustrates better than any other example I know the importance of reproductive liberty to women's equality. Every indignity that comes from the denial of reproductive autonomy can be found in slave women's lives—the harms of treating women's wombs as procreative vessels, of policies that pit a mother's welfare against that of her unborn child, and of government attempts to manipulate women's child-bearing decisions through threats and bribes. Studying the control of slave women's reproduction, then, not only discloses the origins of Black people's subjugation in America; it also bears witness to the horrible potential threatened by official denial of reproductive liberty.

REPRODUCING THE LABOR FORCE

The Vitality of Slavery

The essence of Black women's experience during slavery was the brutal denial of autonomy over reproduction. Female slaves were commercially valuable to their masters not only for their labor, but also for their ability to produce more slaves. The law made slave women's children the property of the slaveowner. White masters therefore could increase their wealth by controlling their slaves' reproductive capacity. With owners expecting natural multiplication to generate as much as 5 to 6 percent of their profit, they had a strong incentive to maximize their

slaves' fertility. An anonymous planter's calculations made the point:

> I own a woman who cost me $400, when a girl, in 1827. Admit she made me nothing—only worth her victuals and clothing. She now has three children, worth over $3000 . . . I would not this night touch $700 for her. Her oldest boy is worth $1250 cash, and I can get it.[4]

Another report confirmed that "[a] breeding woman is worth from one-sixth to one-fourth more than one that does not breed."[5] Slave births and deaths were not recorded in the family Bible but in the slaveholder's business ledger.

The ban on importing slaves after 1808 and the steady inflation in their price made enslaved women's childbearing even more valuable. Female slaves provided their masters with a ready future supply of chattel. Black procreation not only benefitted each slave's particular owner; it also more globally sustained the entire system of slavery. Unlike most slave societies in the New World, which relied on the massive importation of Africans, the slave population in the United States maintained itself through reproduction.[6] As Massachusetts senator Charles Sumner deplored, "Too well I know the vitality of slavery with its infinite capacity of propagation."[7] Here lies one of slavery's most odious features: it forced its victims to perpetuate the very institution that subjugated them by bearing children who were born the property of their masters.

To be sure, female slaves were primarily laborers and their capacity to reproduce did not diminish their masters' interest in their work. As we will see below, when a female slave's role as worker conflicted with that of childbearer, concern for high productivity often outweighed concern for high fertility. Slaveholders were willing to overwork pregnant slaves at the expense of the health of both mother and child. But even if, as some historians contend, "slave childbearing and rearing were not among slaveowners' top priorities,"[8] there is convincing evidence that whites placed a premium on slave fertility and took steps to increase it. Indeed, it seems incredible that whites, who dominated every aspect of their slaves' existence, would neglect the attribute that produced their most vital resource—their workforce. Nor can we ignore the sentiments of slaveholders like Thomas Jefferson, who instructed his plantation manager in 1820, "I consider a woman who brings a child every two years as more profitable than the best man on the farm."[9] Slaveowners who overworked their pregnant slaves operated under general ignorance about prenatal health combined with stereotypes about Black women's natural propensity for childbirth. They were not fully aware of the extent of the damage their labor practices inflicted on their long-term human investment.

A more realistic assessment is that because female slaves served as both producers and reproducers, their masters tried to maximize both capacities as much as possible, with labor considerations often taking precedence. Even then, the grueling demands of field work constrained slave women's experience of pregnancy and child-rearing. Every aspect of slave women's reproductive lives was dictated by the economic interests of their white slave masters.

The Carrot and the Stick

Slaveholders devised a number of tactics to induce their female slaves to bear children. Although these methods were neither uniformly practiced nor uniformly successful, most slave masters used some techniques to enhance slave fertility. They rewarded pregnancy with relief from work in the field and additions of clothing and food, punished slave women who did not bear children, manipulated slave marital choices, and forced slaves to breed. The owner of one Georgia plantation, for example, gave slave families an extra weekly ration for the birth of a child; a Virginia planter rewarded new mothers with a small pig. Some women seemed especially to appreciate presents that recognized their femininity, such as a calico dress or hair ribbons. On P. C. Weston's estate, the *Plantation Manual* prescribed that "women with six children alive at any one time are allowed all Saturday to themselves."[10] Slave women were sometimes guaranteed freedom if they bore an especially large number of children. Rhoda Hunt's mother was promised manumission when she had her twelfth child, but died a month before the baby's due date.[11]

Even without these concrete rewards, slave women felt pressure to reproduce. Because a fertile woman was more valuable to her master, she was less likely to be sold to another owner. So women could reduce the chances of being separated from their loved ones if they had children early and frequently. In addition, women could expect some relief from their arduous work load in the final months of pregnancy. (Records show, however, that expectant mothers received little or no work relief before the fifth month.)[12] Although data are scanty, it appears that slave women had their first child at an earlier age than white women of the time. A Virginia slaveholder reported in the early 1860s that "the period of maternity is hastened, the average youth of negro mothers being nearly three years earlier than that of the free race."[13] The first generation of slaves born in America also had more children than their African mothers, who avoided pregnancy for two or more years while nursing their infants. It was natural increase, and not importation of slaves, that explained the enormous growth in the slave population to 1.75 million by 1825.

Women who did not produce children, on the other hand, were often sold off—or worse. Slaveholders, angered at the loss on their investment, inflicted cruel physical and psychological retribution on their barren female slaves. A report presented to the

General Anti-Slavery Convention held in London in 1840 revealed:

> Where fruitfulness is the greatest of virtues, barrenness will be regarded as worse than a misfortune, as a crime and the subjects of it will be exposed to every form of privation and affliction. Thus deficiency wholly beyond the slave's power becomes the occasion of inconceivable suffering.[14]

One witness testified that a North Carolina planter ordered a group of women into a barn, declaring he intended to flog them all to death. When the women asked what crime they had committed, the master replied, "Damn you I will let you know what you have done; you don't breed, I have not had a young one from one of you for several months." Slaveholders treated infertile slaves like damaged goods, often attempting to pawn them off on unsuspecting buyers. Southern courts established rules for dealing with sellers' misrepresentations about the fertility of slave women similar to rules governing the sale of other sorts of commodities.

Slave-Breeding

Another aspect of reproductive control made the common inducement of slave childbearing even more despicable. Some slaveowners also practiced *slave-breeding* by compelling slaves they considered "prime stock" to mate in the hopes of producing children especially suited for labor or sale. While slave masters' interest in enhancing slave fertility is well established, slave-breeding has been the subject of greater controversy. That debate, however, has revolved around the extent and purpose of the practice, not whether or not slaveholders engaged in it at all.

In their 1974 bombshell *Time on the Cross: The Economics of American Negro Slavery,* historians Robert Fogel and Stanley

Engerman contested the key assumptions about the management of slaves, the material conditions of slaves' lives, and the efficiency of slave agriculture. Among the myths they debunked was "the thesis that *systematic* breeding of slaves for sale in the market accounted for a major share of the net income or profit of slaveholders, especially in the Old South."[15] Their disagreement with prevailing accounts of forced mating centered on the claim that whites widely employed livestock breeding techniques to raise slaves for market. Fogel and Engerman argued that such a practice was unsupported by plantation records and would have interfered with slave masters' overriding objective of maintaining a stable workforce. Unlike animals, slaves would rebel against massive breeding, the authors argued, thus wiping out any potential gain achieved by pushing their fertility rate to its biological peak. Rather, planters usually encouraged fertility through the positive economic incentives described above.

But Fogel and Engerman did not dispute evidence that slaveowners at least occasionally engaged in breeding to enhance the productivity of their own plantations and more rarely to increase their slaves' marketability. In her extensive review of slave narratives, for example, Thelma Jennings discovered that about 5 percent of the women and 10 percent of the men referred to slave-breeding.[16]

It is from slaves' stories, such as Rose Williams's experience with Rufus, that we learn of the indignities of forced mating. Frederick Douglass recorded in his autobiography how Edward Covey purchased a twenty-year-old slave named Caroline as a "breeder." Covey mated Caroline with a hired man and was pleased when a pair of twins resulted. Douglass observed that the slaveowner was no more criticized for buying a slave for breeding than "for buying a cow and raising stock from her, and the same rules were observed, with a view to increasing the number and quality of the one as of the other."[17] Katie

Darling, an ex-slave from Texas, described the practice in these words: "massa pick out a p'otly man and a p'otly gal and just put 'em together. What he want am the stock."[18]

Slaveholders had a financial stake in male slaves' marital choices, as well, since the children of the union belonged to the *wife's* owner. Although marrying "abroad" was common, some masters forbade their male slaves to court a woman from another plantation. Nor could a slave marry a free Black man or woman. The obstacles to finding a mate of one's choosing led one slave to complain that Black men "had a hell of a time gittin' a wife durin' slavery. If you didn't see one on de place to suit you and chances was you didn't suit them, why what could you do?"[19] Slave marriages were not recognized by law; these were partnerships consecrated by slaves' own ceremonies and customs.

Slaveholders' interference with bonded men's intimate lives was often more blunt. Some masters rented men of exceptional physical stature to serve as studs. Using terms such as "stockmen," "travelin' niggers," and "breedin' niggers," slave men remembered being "weighed and tested," then used like animals to sire chattel for their masters.[20] Of course, this also meant forcing slave women to submit to being impregnated by these hired men. Jeptha Choice recalled fulfilling the role of stud: "The master was might careful about raisin' healthy nigger families and used us strong, healthy young bucks to stand the healthy nigger gals. When I was young they took care not to strain me and I was as handsome as a speckled pup and was in demand for breedin'." Elige Davison similarly reported that his master mated him with about fifteen different women; he believed that he had fathered more than one hundred children.[21] Although this was quite rare, some slaveholders also practiced a cruel form of negative breeding. An ex-slave reported that "runty niggers" were castrated "so dat dey can't have no little runty chilluns."[22]

VICTIMS OF "THE GROSSEST PASSION"

"Slavery is terrible for men," wrote Harriet Jacobs, "but it is far more terrible for women." Slave women's narratives often decried the added torment that women experienced under bondage on account of their sex. Female slaves were commonly victims of sexual exploitation at the hands of their masters and overseers. The classification of 10 percent of the slave population in 1860 as "mulatto" gives some indication of the extent of this abuse.[23] Most of these mixed-race children were the product of forced sex between slave women and white men. Of course, the incidence of sexual assault that did not end in pregnancy was far greater than these numbers reveal.

Black women's sexual vulnerability continued to be a primary concern of Black activists after Emancipation. A pamphlet entitled *The Black Woman of the South: Her Neglects and Her Needs*, published in 1881 by the prominent Black Episcopalian minister Alexander Crummel, emphasized the violation of female virtue:

> In her girlhood all the delicate tenderness of her sex has been rudely outraged. . . . No chance was given her for delicate reserve or tender modesty. From her childhood she was the doomed victim of the grossest passion. All the virtues of her sex were utterly ignored. If the instinct of chastity asserted itself, then she had to fight like a tiger for the ownership . . . of her own person. . . . When she reached maturity, all the tender instincts of her womanhood were ruthlessly violated.[24]

The law reinforced the sexual exploitation of slave women in two ways: it deemed any child who resulted from the rape to be a slave and it failed to recognize the rape of a slave woman as a crime.

Legislation giving the children of Black women and white men the status of slaves left female slaves vulnerable to sexual violation as a means of financial gain. Children born to slave women were slaves, regardless of the father's race or status. This meant, in short, that whenever a white man impregnated one of his slaves, the child produced by his assault was his property.

The fact that white men could profit from raping their female slaves does not mean that their motive was economic. The rape of slave women by their masters was primarily a weapon of terror that reinforced whites' domination over their human property.[25] Rape was an act of physical violence designed to stifle Black women's will to resist and to remind them of their servile status. In fact, as historian Claire Robertson points out, sexual harassment was more likely to have the immediate effect of interfering with the victim's productivity both physically and emotionally.[26] Its intended long-term effect, however, was the maintenance of a submissive workforce. Whites' sexual exploitation of their slaves, therefore, should not be viewed simply as either a method of slave-breeding or the fulfillment of slaveholders' sexual urges.

The racial injustice tied to rape is usually associated with Black men. We are more familiar with myths about Black men's propensity to rape white women, which served as the pretext for thousands of brutal lynchings in the South. In the words of Ida B. Wells, who crusaded against lynching during the nineteenth century, "white men used their ownership of the body of white female[s] as a terrain on which to lynch the black male."[27] But white men also exploited Black women sexually as a means of subjugating the entire Black community. After Emancipation, the Ku Klux Klan's terror included the rape of Black women, as well as the more commonly cited lynching of Black men. White sexual violence attacked not only freed Black men's masculinity by challenging their ability to protect Black women; it also invaded freed Black women's dominion over their own bodies.[28]

I nevertheless think that sexual exploitation belongs in a discussion of reproductive control. Because rape can lead to pregnancy, it interferes with a woman's freedom to decide whether or not to have a child. In addition, forced sex and forced procreation are both degrading invasions of a woman's bodily integrity; both pursue the same ultimate end—the devaluation of their female victim. Although sexual assault and slave-breeding are distinguishable, both were part and parcel of whites' general campaign to control slave women's bodies. A contemporary example of this point is the rape of Muslim women by Serbian soldiers as part of the Serbians' "ethnic cleansing" campaign. Here, too, rape was a form of mass terrorism inflicted on a group of subjugated women. But there are reports that soldiers boasted to their victims, "You will have a Serbian child."[29]

The law also fostered the sexual exploitation of slave women by allowing white men to commit these assaults with impunity. Slaves were at the disposal of their masters. Owners had the right to treat their property however they wished, so long as the abuse did not kill the chattel. Conversely, slave women had no recognizable interest in preserving their own bodily integrity. After all, female slaves legally could be stripped, beaten, mutilated, bred, and compelled to toil alongside men. Forcing a slave to have sex against her will simply followed the pattern. This lack of protection was reinforced by the prevailing belief among whites that Black women could not be raped because they were naturally lascivious.

Louisiana's rape law explicitly excluded Black women from its protection.[30] Although the language of the Virginia rape law applied to all women victims, there is not a single reported eighteenth-century case in which a white man was prosecuted for raping a female slave.[31] Even if the criminal code did recognize the rape of a slave, the law would have prevented the victim from testifying in court about the assault. An evidentiary rule in most slave-holding states disqualified Blacks from testifying against a white person.[32] In short, for most of American history the crime of rape of a Black woman did not exist.

Nor could Black women be raped by Black men. When a slave named George was charged with having sex with a child under the age of ten, his lawyer argued that the criminal code did not apply because the victim was also a slave. The Mississippi court dismissed the indictment, adopting the lawyer's contention that "[t]he crime of rape does not exist in this State between African slaves."[33] The laws that regulated sexual intercourse among whites were not relevant to slaves: "Their intercourse is promiscuous" and "is left to be regulated by their owners," the court wrote. A similar crime committed against a white woman was a capital offense.

SHATTERING THE BONDS OF MOTHERHOOD

The domination of slave women's reproduction continued after their children were born. Black women in bondage were systematically denied the rights of motherhood. Slavery so disrupted their relationship with their children that it may be more accurate to say that as far as slaveowners were concerned, they "were not mothers at all."[34]

Prenatal Property

Slave mothers had no legal claim to their children. Slave masters owned not only Black women but also their offspring, and their ownership of these children was automatic and immediate. In fact, the law granted to whites a devisable, *in futuro* interest in the potential children of their slaves. Wills frequently devised slave women's children before the children were born—or even conceived. In 1830, for example, a South Carolina slaveowner named Mary Kincaid

bequeathed a slave woman named Sillar to her grandchild and Sillar's two children to other grandchildren. Mary's will provided that if Sillar should bear a third child, it was to go to yet another grandchild.[35] Sillar's future baby became the property of a white master before the child took its first breath!

An 1823 case, *Banks' Administrator v. Marksberry*, confirmed a master's property interest in the reproductive capacity of his female slaves.[36] The case involved the following clause in a deed executed by Samuel Marksberry, Sr.: "to Samuel Marksberry, my younger son, I do likewise give my negro wench, Pen; and her increase from this time, I do give to my daughter, Rachel Marksberry." The plaintiff challenged the gift of Pen's "increase" on the ground that the testator had nothing to give at the time he wrote the will. The court, however, sided with Rachel Marksberry:

> He who is the absolute owner of a thing, owns all its faculties for profits or increase, and he may, no doubt, grant the profits or increase, as well as the thing itself. Thus, it is every day's practice, to grant the future rents or profits of real estate; and it is held, that a man may grant the wool of a flock of sheep, for years. The interest which the donor's daughter, Rachel, took in the increase of Pen, must indeed, from its nature, have been contingent at the time of the gift; but as the children of Pen were thereafter born, they would, by the operation of the deed, vest in the donee, and her title thus become complete.[37]

The court viewed the slave Pen just like any other piece of property that produces offspring, crops, or other goods. Marksberry owned not only the piece of property itself but also the goods that she bore, as well as her potential to bear future goods. In this way, the law ensured that the relationship between the master and slave existed prior to the bond between mother and child. Owning a slave woman's future children was another way of cementing whites' control of reproduction.

The Auction Block

Perhaps the most tragic deprivation was the physical separation of enslaved women from their children. It has been estimated that nearly half a million Africans were transported to the North American mainland between 1700 and 1861. Many of these Africans purchased or kidnapped from their homelands lost track of their family members forever.

For slaves in America, the auction block became the agonizing site of slave mothers' separation from their children. Because it was in slaveowners' economic interest to maintain stable, productive families, they did not frequently tear young children from their homes. But the law permitted such disruptions when it became expedient. A nineteenth-century South Carolina court ruled, for example, that children could be sold away from their mothers no matter how young because "the young of the slaves . . . stand on the same footing as other animals."[38] A planter might decide to sell a mother or her children to pay off a debt or to get rid of an unruly slave. Slaves were devised in wills, wagered at horse races, and awarded in lawsuits. Bonded families were disbanded when the heirs of an estate decided not to continue the patriarch's business.

A mother's relationship with her children might also be shattered when young children were hired or apprenticed out to labor for others, sometimes for as long as ten years. Mothers often learned the heartbreaking news only when a new master appeared to take their children away. They might even be denied the chance to kiss their babies goodbye. As novelist Toni Morrison so vividly imagined the experience, most of slave women's loved ones "got rented out, loaned out, bought up, brought back, stored up, mortgaged, won, stolen or seized. . . . Nobody stopped playing checkers just because the pieces included [their] children."[39]

Most whites owned slaves to work for them, not to sell on the market. Some slaveowners, however, were in the business of purchasing or breeding human chattel for profit. A matter of dispute, the bulk of historical evidence indicates that the interstate slave trade often broke up slave families.[40] Professional slave traders fed, washed, and oiled the slaves they acquired, and marched the merchandise, chained together, to market. On the way, a crying baby might be snatched from his mother and sold on the spot to the first slave gang that approached.

The auction was often a government-sponsored event, taking place on the courthouse steps. In fact, government agents conducted half of the antebellum sales of slaves at sheriffs', probate, and equity court sales.[41] The South Carolina courts, for example, "acted as the state's greatest slave auctioneering firm."[42] The slaves were paraded before potential buyers, who inspected their teeth and pulled back their eyelids as if they were purchasing a horse. The auctioneer sold each slave to the highest bidder. At auction, families might be mercilessly torn apart, with parents and children sold to different buyers. Josiah Henson remembered the moving scene when, as a young child, his family was splintered on the auction block:

> My brothers and sisters were bid off first, and one by one, while my mother, paralyzed with grief, held me by the hand. Her turn came and she was bought by Isaac Riley of Montgomery County. Then I was offered. . . . My mother, half distracted with the thought of parting forever from all her children, pushed through the crowd while the bidding for me was going on, to the spot where Riley was standing. She fell at his feet, and clung to his knees, entreating him in tones that a mother could only command, to buy her baby as well as herself, and spare to her one, at least, of her little ones. . . . This man disengag[ed] himself from her with . . . violent

blows and kicks. . . . I must have been between five and six years old.[43]

The Working Mother

More insidious than the physical separation of mother and child was the slave masters' control over child-rearing. If an enslaved woman was fortunate enough to keep her children with her, she was deprived of the opportunity to nurture them. Becoming a mother did not change her primary task, which was physical labor for her master. Since most slave mothers worked all day, their children were watched by other slaves who were too weak, too old, or too young to join them in the fields.[44] A Florida plantation owner, for example, entrusted forty-two children to the care of an elderly man and woman, assisted by older youngsters. Caregivers were often too inexperienced or overwhelmed to give proper attention to the children in their charge.

Mothers were often forced to leave their nursing babies at home for hours while they worked in the field. Charlotte Brooks remembered how her baby suffered from her long absences: "When I did go I could hear my poor child crying long before I got to it. And la, me! my poor child would be so hungry when I'd get to it!"[45] All of Charlotte's children, like many slave children, died at an early age "for want of attention." The infant mortality rate among slaves in 1850 was twice that of whites, with fewer than two out of three Black children surviving to age ten.[46] Death from malnutrition and disease was more likely to snatch a mother's children than sale to a new owner.

Mothers who were not allowed time out from work to return to their cabins had to bring their infants with them to the field. Slave women ingeniously combined mothering and hard labor. One North Carolina slave woman, for example, strapped her infant to her back and "[w]hen it get hungry she just slip it around in front and feed it

and go right on picking or hoeing."[47] On one plantation, the women dug a long trough in the ground to create a makeshift cradle, where they put their babies every morning while they toiled. A former slave named Ida Hutchinson recalled the tragic fate of those babies as their mothers picked cotton in the distance:

> When [the mothers] were at the other end of the row, all at once a cloud no bigger than a small spot came up and it grew fast, and it thundered and lightened as if the world were coming to an end, and the rain just came down in great sheets. And when it got so they could go to the other end of the field, that trough was filled with water and every baby in it was floating round in the water, drowned. [The master] never got nary a lick of labor and nary a red penny for any of them babies.[48]

Ida understood that the deaths of the babies meant a financial loss to the slave master— the infants' gruesome demise denied him both their future labor and the money he might have gotten from selling them to another owner. No one recorded the horror their mothers must have felt upon discovering their precious babies floating lifeless in their makeshift cradle.

SLAVE WOMEN'S CONFLICTING ROLES

The dual status of slave women as both producer and reproducer created tensions that perplexed their masters and injured their children. A slaveholder was caught in an impossible dilemma—how to maximize his immediate profits by extracting as much work as possible from his female slaves while at the same time protecting his long-term investment in the birth of a healthy child.[49] The two goals were simply incompatible. Pregnancy and infant care diminished time in the field or plantation house. Overwork hindered the chances of delivering a strong future workforce.

Bearing children who were their masters' property only compounded the contradictions that scarred slave women's reproductive lives. It separated mothers from their children immediately upon conception. This division between mother and child did not exist for white women of that era. The notion that a white mother and child were separable entities with contradictory interests was unthinkable, as was the idea of a white woman's work interfering with her maternal duties. Both violated the prevailing ideology of female domesticity that posited mothers as the natural caretakers for their children.

The First Maternal-Fetal Conflict

The conflict between mother and child was most dramatically expressed in the method of whipping pregnant slaves that was used throughout the South. Slaveholders forced women to lie face down in a depression in the ground while they were whipped. A former slave named Lizzie Williams recounted the beating of pregnant slave women on a Mississippi cotton plantation: "I[']s seen nigger women dat was fixin' to be confined do somethin' de white folks didn't like. Dey [the white folks] would dig a hole in de ground just big 'nuff fo' her stomach, make her lie face down an whip her on de back to keep from hurtin' de child."[50]

This description of the way in which pregnant slaves were beaten vividly illustrates the slaveowners' dual interest in Black women as both workers and childbearers. This was a procedure that enabled the master to protect the fetus while abusing the mother. It was the slaveholder's attempt to resolve the tough dilemma inherent in female bondage. As far as I can tell, the relationship between Black women and their unborn children created by slavery is the first example of maternal-fetal conflict in American history.

Feminists use the term "maternal-fetal conflict" to describe the way in which law,

social policies, and medical practice sometimes treat a pregnant woman's interests in opposition to those of the fetus she is carrying. The miracles of modern medicine, for example, that empower doctors to treat the fetus apart from the pregnant woman make it possible to imagine a contradiction between the two. If the mother opposes the physician's suggestions for the care of the fetus, courts often treat the standoff as an adversarial relationship between the pregnant woman and her unborn child. Pitting the mother's interests against those of the fetus, in turn, gives the government a reason to restrict the autonomy of pregnant women.

Some feminist scholars have refuted the maternal-fetal conflict by pointing to its relatively recent origin. Ann Kaplan has explored, for example, how current representations of motherhood in popular materials, such as magazines, newspapers, television, and films, allow the public to imagine a separation between mother and fetus. She gives examples of the recent focus on the fetus as an independent subject—sensational pictures in *Life* magazine of fetal development during gestation or a *New York Times* enlarged image of the fetus floating in space, attached to an umbilical cord extending out of frame and disconnected from the mother's body, which is not seen.[51] Rayna Rapp adds that these fetal images were not even possible fifty years ago: "Until well after World War II, there were no medical technologies for the description of fetuses independent of the woman in whose body a given pregnancy was growing. Now, sciences like 'perinatology' focus on the fetus itself, bypassing the consciousness of the mother, permitting [the] image of the fetus as a separate entity."[52] Others have attributed the current attention to the fetus as a separate subject to a backlash against the successes of the women's movement during the 1960s and 1970s.

But the beating of pregnant slaves reveals that slave masters created just such a conflict between Black women and their unborn children to support their own economic interests. The Black mother's act of bearing a child profited the system that subjugated her. Even without the benefit of perinatology and advanced medical technologies, slaveowners perceived the Black fetus as a separate entity that would produce future profits or that could be parceled out to another owner before its birth. The whipping of pregnant slaves is the most powerful image of maternal-fetal conflict I have ever come across in all my research on reproductive rights. It is the most striking metaphor I know for the evils of policies that seek to protect the fetus while disregarding the humanity of the mother. It is also a vivid symbol of the convergent oppressions inflicted on slave women: they were subjugated at once as Blacks and as females.

The Cycles of Work and Childbirth

The tension between slave women's productive and reproductive roles also appeared in the fascinating interplay between annual cycles of crop production and the birth of children. It seems that slaves' procreative activities were subtly orchestrated by the nature of the work they performed. By studying the reproductive careers of nearly a thousand slave women, Cheryll Ann Cody discovered that many bore their children in strong seasonal patterns that tracked plantation work and planting calendars.[53] Slave births on the plantations she surveyed were concentrated in the late summer and early fall. On the Ravenal cotton plantations in South Carolina, for example, one-third of the slave children were born during the months of August, September, and October.

Consider the reproductive history of Cate, one of the Ravenal family's slaves. Cate was nineteen when she had her first child, Phillip, in September 1848. Her second child, who died in infancy, was born in August two years later, followed the next August by a third child. Between 1853 and 1859, Cate gave birth to six more children like

clockwork—each born between September and January.

Why did slave women tend to give birth during this period? The timing of births, of course, relates back to the timing of conception. A large proportion of these women became pregnant during the months of November, December, and January when labor requirements were reduced owing to completion of the harvest and to harsh weather, giving slaves more time and energy to devote to their families. As an added factor, the more nutritious diet available after the fall harvest probably increased slave women's fecundity.

It turns out that the seasonality of conceptions and births had a devastating impact on the survival of slave infants. Late summer and early fall, when many slave women were in their last term of pregnancy, was also the time of the highest labor demand and the greatest sickness.[54] Slaves on cotton and rice plantations spent these months intensely harvesting the crop. There was also a heightened risk of contracting diseases such as typhus and malaria, particularly for slaves who worked in swampy rice fields—diseases that could damage the fetus. Although Cody focuses on the effects of hard work and disease on gestation, the season also took its toll on new mothers and their infants. A woman who gave birth during harvest time, when planters had the greatest need for workers, could expect to be called to the fields soon after the delivery. According to the records of an Alabama plantation, a slave named Fanny had a baby in early August 1844, and was back picking cotton by August 29.[55] Needless to say, Fanny's fragile baby could hardly have received the type of neonatal care required for healthy development.

Records reveal that season of birth made little difference on plantations with exceedingly high mortality rates: on the Ball rice plantation, for example, nearly half of all infants died before their first birthday, no matter when they were born. But on the

Gaillard cotton plantation, "children born during the summer, when their mother's labor was in highest demand, suffered nearly twice the level of infant mortality as those born after the harvest."[56] Data collected by economist Richard Steckel from three large South Carolina and Alabama cotton plantations confirm this finding: Steckel discovered that the average probability of infant death from February to April (the plowing and planting season) and from September to November (harvest) was 40.6 percent—nearly four times greater than neonatal losses in other months.[57] In the conflict between slave women's service as producers and as reproducers, children ended up the losers.

NOTES

1. Herbert G. Gutman, *The Black Family in Slavery and Freedom, 1750–1925* (New York: Pantheon, 1976), pp. 84–85.
2. Henry Louis Gates, Jr., "To be Raped, Bred, or Abused," *New York Timed Book Review,* Nov. 22, 1987, p. 12, reviewing Harriet Jacobs, *Incidents in the Life of a Slave Girl* (1987).
3. A. Leon Higginbotham, Jr., *In the Matter of Color: Race and the American Legal Process; The Colonial Period* (New York: Oxford University-Press, 1978), pp. 42–45, 252.
4. Gutman, *Black Family in Slavery and Freedom,* pp. 77–78.
5. W. E. B. Du Bois, *Black Reconstruction in America, 1860–1880,* ed. August Meier (New York: Atheneum, 1985 [1935]), p. 44.
6. Wilma King, *Stolen Childhood: Slave Youth in Nineteenth-Century America* (Bloomington: Indiana University Press, 1995), p. xvii.
7. Bernard Schwartz, ed., *Statutory History of the United States,* vol. 1, *Civil Rights* (New York: Chelsea House, 1970), p. 83.
8. Claire Robertson, "Africa into the Americas? Slavery and Women, the Family, and the Gender Division of Labor," in David Barry Gasper and Darlene Clark Hine, eds., *More Than Chattel: Black Women and Slavery in the Americas* (Bloomington: Indiana University Press, 1996), pp. 3, 27.
9. Thomas Jefferson to John W. Eppes, June 30, 1820, in Edwin Morris Betts, ed., *Thomas Jefferson's Farm Book: With Commentary and Relevant Extracts from Other Writings* (Princeton: Princeton University Press, 1953), p. 46.
10. Gutman, *Black Family in Slavery and Freedom,* p. 77.
11. George P. Rawick, ed., *The Amerian Slave: A Composite Autobiography,* supp. series 1, vol. 8 (Westport, Conn.: Greenwood, 1977), p. 1075.
12. Richard H. Steckel, "Women, Work, and Health Under Plantation Slavery in the United States," in Gaspar and Hine, *More Than Chattel,* pp. 43, 55.
13. Gutman, *Black Family in Slavery and Freedom,* p. 50.
14. bell hooks, *Ain't I a Woman? Black Women and Feminism* (Boston: South End Press, 1981), pp. 40–41.
15. Robert William Fogel and Stanley L. Engerman, *Time on the Cross: The Economics of American Negro Slavery* (Boston: Little, Brown, 1974), p. 78.
16. Thelma Jennings, "Us Colored Women Had to Go Through a Plenty," *Journal of Women's History* 1 (Winter 1990), pp. 45, 49–74.
17. Frederick Douglass, *Life and Times of Frederick Douglass* (New York: Crowell, 1966), pp. 118–19.
18. Quoted in George P. Rawick, *From Sundown to Sunup: The Making of the Black Community* (Westport, Conn.: Greenwood, 1972), p. 88.
19. Jacqueline Jones, *Labor of Love, Labor of Sorrow: Black Women, Work, and the Family from Slavery to the Present* (New York: Vintage, 1986), p. 34.
20. Catherine Clinton, "Caught in the Web of the Big House: Women and Slavery," in Walter Raser, R. Frank Saunders, and John L. Wakelyn, eds., *The Web of Southern Social Relations: Women, Family, and Education* (Athens: University of Georgia Press, 1985), pp. 19, 23.
21. Quoted in Rawick, *From Sundown to Sunup,* p. 88.
22. Clinton, "Caught in the Web of the Big House," p. 24.
23. Jones, *Labor of Love, Labor of Sorrow,* p. 37. Robert Fogel and Stanley Engerman estimate that "the share of Negro children fathered by whites on slave plantations probably averaged between 1 and 2 percent." *Time on the Cross,* p. 133.
24. Quoted in Beverly Guy-Sheftall, *Daughters of Sorrow: Attitudes Toward Black Women, 1880–1920* (Brooklyn, NY.: Carlson, 1990), p. 60.
25. Angela Y. Davis, *Women, Race, and Class* (New York: Vintage, 1983), pp. 23–24.
26. Robertson, "Africa into the Americas?" p. 25.
27. Quoted in Angela P. Harris, "Race and Essentialism in Feminist Legal Theory," *Stanford Law Review* 42 (1990), pp. 581, 600.
28. See Jacquelyn Dowd Hall, "'The Mind That Burns in Each Body': Women, Rape, and Racial Violence," in Ann Snitow et al., eds., *Powers of Desire: The Politics of Sexuality* (New York: Monthly Review Press, 1983), pp. 328, 332–33.
29. Caroline D. Krass, "Bringing the Perpetrators of Rape in the Balkans to Justice: Time for an International Criminal Court," *Denver Journal of International Law and Policy* 22 (Spring 1994), pp. 317, 320.
30. Judith Kelleher Schafer, "The Long Arm of the Law: Slave Criminals and the Supreme Court in Antebellum Louisiana," *Tulane Law Review* 60 (1986), pp. 2147, 1265.
31. A. Leon Higginbotham Jr. and Anne F. Jacobs, "The 'Law Only as an Enemy': The Legitimization of Racial Powerlessness Through the Colonial and Antebellum Criminal Laws of Virginia," *North Carolina Law Review* 70 (1992), pp. 969, 1055–56.

32. See A. Leon Higginbotham, *In the Matter of Color: Race and the American Legal Process* (New York: Oxford University Press, 1978), p. 146.

33. *George v. State*, 37 Miss. 316 (1859).

34. Davis, *Women, Race, and Class*, p. 7.

35. Kenneth M. Stampp, *The Peculiar Institution: Slavery in the Ante-Bellum South* (New York: Vintage, 1956), p. 205. On the law governing bequests of slaves not yet born, see Thomas D. Morris, *Southern Slavery and the Law, 1619–1860* (Chapel Hill: University of North Carolina Press, 1996), pp. 89–93.

36. *Banks' Administrator v. Marksberry*, 3 Littell's Rep. 275 (1823).

37. Ibid., p. 280.

38. Quoted in Davis, *Women, Race, and Class*, p. 7.

39. Toni Morrison, *Beloved* (New York: Plume, 1987), p. 23.

40. Stampp, *The Peculiar Institution*, p. 239; Herbert Gutman and Richard Sutch, "The Slave Family: Protected Agent of Capitalist Masters or Victim of the Slave Trade?" in Paul A. David et al., *Reckoning with Slavery* (New York: Oxford University Press, 1976), p. 94; Michael Tadman, *Speculators and Slaves: Masters, Traders, and Slaves in the Old South* (Madison: University of Wisconsin Press, 1989).

41. Thomas D. Russell, "South Carolina's Largest Slave Auctioneering Firm," *Chicago-Kent Law Review* 68 (1993), p. 1241.

42. Ibid.

43. Josiah Henson, *Father Henson's Story of His Own Life* (New York: Corinth Books, 1962), pp. 12–13, quoted in Julius Lester, *To Be a Slave* (New York: Laurel Leaf Library, 1976), pp. 48–49.

44. Wilma King, "'Suffer with Them till Death': Slave Women and Their Children in Nineteenth-Century America," in Gaspar and Hine, *More Than Chattel*, pp. 147, 152.

45. Octavio Albert, *The House of Bondage; or, Charlotte Brooks and Other Stories* (1890), pp. 3–4.

46. Jones, *Labor of Love, Labor of Sorrow*, p. 35.

47. Ibid., p. 14.

48. Quoted in Lester, *To Be a Slave*, p. 38.

49. Jones, *Labor of Love, Labor of Sorrow*, p. 19.

50. Michael P. Johnson, "Smothered Slave Infants: Were Slave Mothers at Fault?" *Journal of Southern History* 47 (1981), pp. 493, 513.

51. E Ann Kaplan, "Sex, Work, and Motherhood: The Impossible Triangle," *Journal of Sex Research* 27 (1990), pp. 409, 417.

52. Rayna Rapp, "Constructing Amniocentesis: Maternal and Medical Discourses," in Faye Ginsburg and Anna Loewenhaupt Tsing, eds., *Uncertain Terms: Negotiating Gender in American Culture* (Boston: Beacon Press, 1990), p. 33.

53. Cheryll Ann Cody, "Cycles of Work and of Childbearing: Seasonality in Women's Lives on Low-Country Plantations," in Gasper and Hine, *More Than Chattel*, p. 61. Ann Patton Malone discovered a similar seasonality in her study of 989 slave births from 15 Louisiana plantations recorded from 1822 through 1861. Ann Patton Malone, *Sweet Chariot: Slave Family and Household Structure in Nineteenth-Century Louisiana* (Chapel Hill: University of North Carolina Press, 1992), pp. 232–33.

54. Cody, "Cycles of Work and of Childbearing," p. 69.

55. King, "Suffer with Them till Death," p. 152.

56. Cody, "Cycles of Work and of Childbearing," p. 72.

57. Richard H. Steckel, "A Dreadful Childhood: The Excess Mortality of American Slaves," *Social Science History* 10 (1986), p. 427.

CHAPTER 16

Maternal Mortality in the United States

A Human Rights Failure

Francine Coeytaux, Debra Bingham, and Nan Strauss

With 99% of maternal deaths occurring in developing countries, it is too often assumed that maternal mortality is not a problem in wealthier countries. Yet, statistics released in September of 2010 by the United Nations place the United States 50th in the world for maternal mortality—with maternal mortality ratios higher than almost all European countries, as well as several countries in Asia and the Middle East.[1,2]

Even more troubling, the United Nations data show that between 1990 and 2008, while the vast majority of countries reduced their maternal mortality ratios for a global decrease of 34%, maternal mortality nearly doubled in the United States.[1] For a country that spends more than any other country on health care and more on childbirth-related care than any other area of hospitalization— US$86 billion a year—this is a shockingly poor return on investment.[3,4]

Given that at least half of maternal deaths in the United States are preventable,[5] this is not just a matter of public health, but a human rights failure.[6] The Universal Declaration of Human Rights states that "every human being has the right to a standard of living adequate for the health and well-being of himself and his family, including medical care and necessary social services".[7] This means that the United States health care system must provide health care services that are available, accessible, acceptable and of good quality.[8] In addition, the health care system must be free from discrimination, must be accountable and must ensure the active participation of women in decision-making. Yet, instead, too many women in the United States face shortages of providers and facilities and inadequate staffing; financial, bureaucratic, transport and language barriers; care that is not culturally appropriate or respectful; a lack of opportunity for informed decision-making and the lack of a system to ensure that all women receive high-quality, evidence-based care. The comparatively high rates of maternal deaths in the United States is an indicator of the failure to ensure that women have guaranteed life-long access to equitable, quality health care, including reproductive health services. Indeed, in countries such as Canada and the United Kingdom where maternal deaths are reviewed and universal access to health care is guaranteed, fewer women die of preventable causes during childbirth than in the United States.

1. OVERVIEW

The rise of maternal deaths in the United States is historic and worrisome. In 1987, maternal death ratios hit the all-time low of 6.6 deaths per 100,000 live births.[9] These ratios were essentially maintained for more than a decade. Around 2000, the ratio began to increase and has since nearly doubled, hovering between 12 and 15 deaths per 100,000 live births between 2003 and 2007.[10] The overarching statistics only scratch the surface: "near misses" (maternal complications so severe the woman nearly died) have also increased by 27% between 1998 and 2005, now affecting approximately 34,000 women a year;[11] and appalling disparities in maternal health outcomes exist between racial and ethnic groups, and among women living in different parts of the United States.

The leading complications causing maternal deaths in the United States overlap with the main global causes; hemorrhage, pregnancy-related hypertensive disorders and infection are among the top causes of death in both the United States and the developing world. Other leading causes of maternal death in the United States are thrombotic pulmonary embolism, cardiomyopathy, cardiovascular conditions, and other medical conditions, whereas in developing countries, other leading causes of death are obstructed labor and unsafe abortions.[12,13]

For the last 50 years, black women who give birth in the United States have been approximately four times as likely to die as white women.[14] The greater risk of death for black women does not simply reflect a greater risk of an underlying complication occurring; in a national study of five medical conditions that are common causes of maternal death and injury (preeclampsia, eclampsia, obstetric hemorrhage, abruption and placenta previa), black women did not have a significantly higher prevalence than white women of any of these conditions.[14] However, the black women in the study were two to three times more likely to die than the white women who had the same complication.[14] Likewise, a study comparing maternal outcomes for Mexican-born women and White non-Latina women in

California found that while Mexican-born women were less likely to suffer complications overall, they did face a greater risk of particular obstetric complications such as postpartum hemorrhage, major puerperal infections and third-and fourth-degree lacerations, suggesting that the intrapartum care they received may have been of poorer quality.[15]

Clearly, contrary to common assumptions, the racial and ethnic disparities in outcomes are not always due to women of color having a higher prevalence of diseases. But as these studies illustrate, women of color often are less likely to receive beneficial treatments that could have prevented their death or injury. As the studies above also demonstrate, disparities in outcomes occur when there is a mismatch between the need for efficacious treatments and access to quality services. Eliminating disparities faced primarily by women of color and poor women must be a priority. Improving the health of women alone will not eliminate disparities; we also need system-level improvements to ensure that all women receive high-quality, equitable maternity care.

2. REASONS FOR THE INCREASE IN MATERNAL MORTALITY

Some of the increase in reported deaths can be attributed to better case identification resulting from the shift from International Statistical Classification of Diseases and Related Health Problems (commonly known as ICD) death certificate codes version 9 to version 10 definitions and an increasing number of states adopting a pregnancy check box on death certificates.[16] While it is unclear how much of the increase is due to reporting, these changes alone do not adequately explain the near doubling of maternal deaths. Indeed, the rise in maternal mortality rates has caused sufficient alarm that The Joint Commission issued a Sentinel Alert on the topic.[17]

The explanations beyond better case ascertainment can be grouped into two categories: (a) the overall health and wellbeing of each woman and (b) the quality of the care a woman receives. It is well known that healthy women have better outcomes. However, overall good health is not sufficient to avoid complications or to eliminate preventable deaths. Women have limited options in what type of health care coverage is available to them, who care for them and whether their clinicians provide them with high-quality care. In addition, clinicians may struggle to provide high-quality care in a hospital system where financial constraints have led to less money for training, fewer nurses and doctors and higher rates of leader turnover. System-level improvements ensuring a uniformly high quality of care are also needed, and these improvements are beyond the control of the individual woman or an individual provider.

We have sufficient data to know that women in the United States face a range of barriers preventing them from obtaining the services they need for a safe and healthy pregnancy and childbirth.

3. BARRIERS AND PROBLEMS PUTTING MATERNAL HEALTH AT RISK

Complications of pregnancy often begin even before a woman becomes pregnant, when many women are uninsured and lack affordable access to primary care including contraceptive services and information. In the United States, nearly half of all pregnancies are unintended,[18] and women with unintended pregnancies are more likely to develop complications and face worse outcomes for themselves and their babies.[19] Of the 17.5 million women in the United States estimated to be in need of publicly funded family planning services and supplies, Medicaid and government-funded clinics (Title X clinics) cover just over half of this need, leaving more than 8 million women without affordable family planning information and services.[20] Policy and legislative measures also limit access to contraception for some.

For many women, the cost of health care puts comprehensive health care beyond reach. Low-income women are more likely to be uninsured prior to becoming pregnant, and consequently are more likely to enter pregnancy with unmanaged chronic health conditions that increase their pregnancy risks. For women who become eligible for publicly financed care upon becoming pregnant, complicated bureaucratic hurdles and a lack of providers willing to accept patients paying with Medicaid increase the likelihood that these women will face significant delays in obtaining early prenatal care.

Women who receive no prenatal care are three to four times more likely to die of pregnancy-related complications than women who do.[21] Those with high-risk pregnancies are 5.3 times more likely to die if they do not receive prenatal care.[22] Healthy People 2010—national health objectives developed in 1998 by US federal health agencies—set a goal of 90% of women receiving "adequate prenatal care" (defined as 13 prenatal visits beginning in the first trimester).[23] However, data suggest that, for 25% of women, their care falls short of this goal.[23] This figure rises to 32% for African American women and 41% for American Indian and Alaska Native women.[23]

Many women receive inadequate or poor-quality intrapartum care. Hospitals and clinics, particularly those serving low-income communities, are often overcrowded and understaffed.[24] Understaffing can create pressure to care for a high volume of patients, making it difficult or impossible to provide good-quality care.[25,26] The current economic downturn and the increased use of medical interventions during childbirth are is likely to exacerbate the problem of understaffing while increasing the pressure on facilities in medically underserved areas, as more people become uninsured.

Providing quality postpartum care in the United States would both help reduce maternal deaths and improve the overall health of women. Most health plans in the United States only cover a single visit to a health care provider around 6 weeks after birth unless the woman has a recognized complication. By contrast, in many countries in Europe, multiple home visits following birth are standard for all women. Increasing the standards in the United States would prevent complications—such as infection, deep vein thrombosis and postpartum hemorrhage—that can develop after women have returned home.

4.   OVERUSE OF MEDICAL INTERVENTIONS

In contrast to many countries where women lack access to life-saving medical interventions, women and infants are often exposed to more procedures than are medically necessary or beneficial. This overuse of medical procedures increases injuries as well as costs. Indeed, we are unaware of any study indicating that the 56% increase in the rate of surgical births from 1996 to 2008[27] has improved outcomes. However, there are data to show that the overuse of medical procedures has increased both infant[28] and maternal morbidity.[11,29]

Because all medical interventions carry risks, their use in situations when they are not demonstrated to offer benefits exposes women to risks that are unwarranted. For example, overuse of induction of labor and of cesarean sections, and lack of access to vaginal births after cesarean sections, all can lead to higher incidences of postpartum infection and higher rates of hysterectomies.[30,31]

Countries such as the United Kingdom and the Netherlands, where women have routine access to woman-centered care and where there is better match between medical need and the number of medical interventions performed, have fewer deaths and lower health care costs. Hospital systems in the United States such as Intermountain Health Care[32] and the Health Care Corporation of America[29] have also demonstrated that a reduction in the overuse of medical interventions hits the sweet spot where both costs are reduced and outcomes can be improved.

5. LACK OF DATA AND ACCOUNTABILITY

The lack of comprehensive data collection is masking the full extent of maternal mortality and morbidity in the United States and is hampering efforts to analyze and address the problems. Reporting of pregnancy-related deaths as a distinct category is mandatory in only six states, and despite efforts in some other states to use additional methods to track maternal deaths (such as death certificate pregnancy check boxes and data-linking birth certificates with death certificates of women of childbearing age), systematic undercounting of pregnancy-related deaths persists.[16]

Many states, and some other countries, most notably the United Kingdom, have established maternal mortality review processes that have successfully identified system problems, developed and disseminated recommendations and set priorities in order to improve maternal care and prevent unnecessary maternal deaths.[33-35] But 29 states have no such processes.[6] The establishment of a comprehensive nationwide system to collect and analyze data on maternal deaths, complications and performance measures is also needed to increase accountability, develop targeted solutions and reduce maternal deaths. In the United Kingdom, this type of systematic approach has worked. For example, the mortality review process in the United Kingdom led to recommendations for deep vein thrombosis prophylaxis for women who have surgical births, and implementation of these recommendations led to fewer deaths from this cause.

6. CALL TO ACTION

For more than 20 years, the authorities have failed to improve the outcomes and disparities in maternal health care. Recent health care reform focused on improving access to care and reducing the growth in health care spending. However, improving health care coverage alone would leave largely unaddressed the issues of discrimination, systemic failures, optimizing quality of care and accountability. It is essential that the debate goes beyond providing health care coverage and ensures access to quality health care for all in a way that is equitable and free from discrimination.

We must also initiate, support and advance positive legislative and policy developments at all levels of government that demonstrate potential to reduce maternal mortality. Recently, three new pieces of federal legislation were introduced by Representatives Lucille Roybal-Allard, Lois Capps, Eliot Engel and Sue Myrick to measure and improve the quality of maternal care; support research into and promotion of best maternity practices; identify and reduce shortages of maternity care providers; increase coordination and prioritization of maternal care within Health and Human Services, improve quality of maternal care by establishing quality measures, and help to create a stronger, more diverse maternity care workforce. Additional related bills are expected to be introduced in the coming months. Clear priorities include eliminating racial disparities, improving systems to ensure that care is of uniformly high quality for all women and expanding comprehensive performance measurement, data collection and analysis to provide the basis for developing and implementing concrete strategies to reduce maternal deaths.

We in the United States must lengthen our stride and lead by example if we are going to be a credible part of the international community advocating for the United Nations

Millennium Development Goal #5—the reduction of maternal mortality by three fourths by the year 2015. The United States is facing a public health crisis that requires us to scrutinize the situation from every angle possible, as quickly as possible, and implement the needed interventions to eliminate preventable maternal deaths and injuries. The first step we need to take is to honor the lives of the women who have died by investing the necessary resources to identify why they died and learn from their deaths in order to prevent other women from dying. There are no acceptable excuses when we consider the fact that we lag behind most developed countries and when numerous developing countries, such as Vietnam and Albania, with much fewer resources than the United States, are making strides towards meeting their goals of reducing preventable maternal deaths, while the United States is backsliding.[36]

It is a human tragedy when a woman dies giving birth; her death forever changes her community and family for all future generations. It is both a tragedy and a human rights failure when a woman dies needlessly of preventable causes in a country that lacks the political will to have prevented her death.

NOTES

1. WHO. Trends in maternal mortality: 1990 to 2008 estimates developed by WHO, UNICEF, UNFPA and The World Bank, World Health Organization 2010, Annex 1. 2010. http://whqlibdoc.who.int/publications/2010/9789241500265_eng.pdf. Last accessed: January 3, 2011.
2. Coeytaux F, Bingham D, Langer A. Reducing maternal mortality: a global imperative. Contraception 2011;83:95–8.
3. Organisation for Economic Co-operation and Development. OECD health data 2010—frequently requested data 2010. http://www.oecd.org/document/16/0,3343,en_2649_33929_2085200_1_1_1_1,00.html. Last accessed: January 3, 2011.
4. Andrews R. The National Hospital Bill: the most expensive conditions by payer, 2006, in Healthcare cost and utilization project, statistical brief. Health Cost Utilization Proj Stat Brief 2008:7. http://www.hcup-us.ahrq.gov/reports/statbriefs/sb59.pdf. Last accessed January 3, 2011.
5. Bacak S, Berg CJ, Desmarais J, Hutchins E, Locke E, editors. State maternal mortality review: accomplishments of nine states. Atlanta: Centers for Disease Control and Prevention; 2006. http://www.cdph.ca.gov/data/statistics/Documents/MO-CDC-ReportAccomplishments 9States.pdf.
6. Amnesty International. Deadly delivery: the maternal health care crisis in the USA. New York: Amnesty International USA; 2010. http://www.amnestyusa.org/dignity/pdf/DeadlyDelivery.pdf. Last accessed January 3, 2011.
7. United Nations. Universal Declaration of Human Rights, G.A. res. 217A (III), in United Nations Doc. A/810. 1948.
8. United Nations. Committee on Economic, Social and Cultural Rights, The right to the highest attainable standard of health. General comment no. 14 E/C.12/200/4. 2000: Geneva.
9. Health Resources and Services Administration. Maternal mortality. Child Health USA 2008–2009. http://mchb.hrsa.gov/chusa08/hstat/hsi/pages/204mm.html. Last accessed: January 3, 2011.
10. Xu J, Kochanek KD, Murphy SL, Tejada-Vera B. Final data for 2007, in National Vital Statistics Reports. Hyattsville (MD): National Center for Health Statistics; 2010.
11. Kuklina E, Meikle S, Jamieson D, et al. Severe obstetric morbidity in the US, 1998–2005. Obstet Gynecol 2009;113:293–9.
12. Berg CJ, Callaghan WM, Syverson C, Henderson Z. Pregnancy-related mortality in the United States, 1998 to 2005. Obstet Gynecol 2010;116:1302–9.
13. World Health Organization. Make every mother and child count. Geneva: WHO; 2005.
14. Tucker MJ, Berg CJ, Callaghan WM, Hsia J. The black–white disparity in pregnancy-related mortality from 5 conditions: differences in prevalence and case-fatality rates. Am J Pub Health 2007;97:247–51.
15. Guendelman S, Thornton D, Gould J, Hosang N. Social disparities in maternal morbidity during labor and delivery between Mexican-born and US-born white Californians, 1996–1998. Am J Pub Health 2005;95:2218–24.
16. Hoyert DL. Maternal mortality and related concepts. N.C.F.H. Statistics, Editor. 2007:1–13.
17. The Joint Commission. Preventing maternal death. January 26, 2010. Issue 44. http://www.jointcommission.org/sentinel_event_alert_issue_44_preventing_maternal_death/. Last accessed: January 3, 2011.
18. Finer L, Henshaw S. Disparities in rates of unintended pregnancy in the United States, 2994 and 2001. Perspect Sex Reprod Health 2008;38: 90–6.
19. D'Angelo D, et al. Preconception and interconception health status of women who recently gave birth to live-born infant–pregnancy risk assessment monitoring system (PRAMS), United States, 26 reporting areas, 2004. MMWR surveillance summaries, December 14, 2007:4 and 17. http://www.cdc.gov/mmwr/preview/mmwrhtml/ss5610a1.htm. Last accessed: January 3, 2011.
20. Guttmacher Institute. Contraceptive needs and services, 2006. http://www.guttmacher.org/pubs/win/allstates2006.pdf. Last accessed: January 3, 2011.

21. Chang J, et al. Pregnancy-related mortality surveillance–United States, 1991–1999, MMWR surveillance summaries. 2003. February 21: 1–8. http://www.cdc.gov/mmwr/preview/mmwrhtml/ss5202a1.htm#tab3. Last accessed: January 3, 2011.

22. Rosenberg D, Geller SE, Studee L, Cox SM. Disparities in mortality among high risk pregnant women in Illinois: a population based study. Ann Epidemiol 2006;16:26–32.

23. Healthy People 2010: Midcourse review. US Department of Health and Human Services. 2000.

24. Regenstein M, Huang J. Stresses to the safety net: the public hospital perspective, Kaiser Commission on Medicaid and the Uninsured, report no.7329, June 2005. http://www.kff.org/medicaid/7329.cfm. Last accessed: January 3, 2011.

25. Institute of Medicine. Keeping patients safe: transforming the work environment of nurses, in Institute of Medicine Committee on the Work Environment for Nurses and Patient Safety Board on Health Care Services. Washington, DC: National Academies Press; 2004. p. 229 and 386.

26. Association of Women's Health, Obstetric and Neonatal Nurses. Guidelines for Professional Registered Nurse Staffing for Perinatal Units. Washington, DC; 2010. http://www.awhonn.org/awhonn/store/productDetail.do;jsessionid=D54A4918DF5BC334CD4681C94ECD3108?productCode=SG-910. Last accessed: January 5, 2011.

27. Martin JA, Hamilton BE, Sutton PD, Ventura SJ, Mathews Osterman MJK. Births: Final data for 2008. National vital statistics reports; vol 59 no 1. Hyattsville (MD): National Center for Health Statistics. 2010. http://www.cdc.gov/nchs/data/nvsr/nvsr59/nvsr59_01.pdf. Last accessed: January 3, 2011.

28. Tita ATN, Landon MB, Spong CY, et al. Timing of elective cesarean delivery at term and neonatal outcomes. NEJM 2009;360:111–20.

29. Clark SL, Belfort MA, Byrum SL, Meyers JA, Perlin JB. Improved outcomes, fewer cesarean deliveries, and reduced litigation: results of a new paradigm inpatient safety. Am J Obstet Gynecol 2008;199:e1-105.e7.

30. Knight M, UKOSS. Peripartum hysterectomy in the UK: management and outcomes of the associated haemorrhage. BJOG 2007;114: 1380–7.

31. Leth RA, Møller JK, Thomsen RW, Uldbjerg N, Nørgaard M. Risk of selected postpartum infections after cesarean section compared with vaginal birth: a five-year cohort study of 32,468 women. Acta Obstet Gynecol Scand 2009;88:976–83.

32. Oshiro BT. Decreasing elective deliveries before 39 weeks of gestation in an integrated health care system. Obstet Gynecol 2009; 113:804–11.

33. Berg CJ, et al. Preventability of pregnancy-related deaths—results of a state-wide review. Obstet Gynecol 2005;106:1228–34.

34. Benbow A, Maresh M. Reducing maternal mortality: reaudit of recommendations in reports of confidential inquiries into maternal deaths. Brit Med J 1998;317:1431–2.

35. Confidential enquiries, Savings mothers' lives: reviewing maternal deaths to make motherhood safer—2003-2005. The seventh report of the confidential enquiries into maternal deaths in the United Kingdom, G. Lewis, Editor. London. 2007. p. 1–260.

36. Hill K, et al. Estimates of maternal mortality worldwide between 1990 and 2005: an assessment of available data. Lancet 2007;370:1311–9.

CHAPTER 17

Choosing Your Health Care Provider and Birth Setting

Boston Women's Health Collective

SOME QUESTIONS TO ASK MIDWIVES AND PHYSICIANS

- Are you covered by my insurance? Will I pay for any portion of my care?
- What is your training and how long have you been practicing?
- For how many births have you been the primary attendant in the past few years?
- What is your philosophy of childbirth, and who practices with you? Do the other providers in your group practice share your views, and how do you handle disagreements over care and treatment?
- How can I reach you? How can I have my questions answered between visits?
- Would you or someone you work with stay with me throughout labor? If not, do you allow or encourage the presence of doulas, labor assistants, and family and friends? What do you see as their role?

- Do you support moving around during labor, changing positions, and eating and drinking?
- What are your policies on continuous fetal monitoring, cutting the umbilical cord, and episiotomy?
  Under what circumstances would you transfer my care to an OB or MFM? (This is a question for midwives and family physicians.)
- Under what circumstances do you recommend inducing labor? About what proportion of your patients have labor induced?

ADDITIONAL QUESTIONS FOR MIDWIVES AND PHYSICIANS IN HOSPITALS

- What are your policies regarding monitoring the baby's heart rate in labor, using breaking the mother's bag of waters, using epidurals, and performing episiotomies?
- What are your reasons to do a cesarean? How often do you find it necessary? How do you try to avoid the need for a cesarean?

ADDITIONAL QUESTIONS FOR HOME-BIRTH MIDWIVES

- What are your medical backup and emergency care arrangements?
- What problems are you able to deal with at home and which ones require transfer to a hospital?
- What is your role if I transfer to a hospital?
- Do you have statistics from your practice? May I see them?
- What is your plan if another client is in labor when I am?
- Where will I go for any lab work?
- What is your experience with methods for inducing labor?
- What equipment and medications do you bring to the birth?
- What methods do you suggest for alleviating pain?

- Are you currently certified in neonatal resuscitation?
- Can you provide references?

SOME QUESTIONS TO ASK WHEN SELECTING A HOSPITAL

If you are considering giving birth in a particular hospital, look at its website and/or go on a tour to find answers to these questions:

- What kind of anesthesiology and pediatric coverage does the hospital offer? Does it have a blood bank available?
- What is its registered-nurse-to-patient ratio? What is it in active labor?
- What percentage of births at the hospital are cesarean deliveries? What percentage of women who are admitted for VBAC deliver vaginally?
- What are the routine policies for laboring women? How does the hospital deal with requests for nonroutine practices?
- What percentage of women have an epidural for labor?
- Are showers, tubs, or whirlpool baths available for laboring women?
- Can I labor, give birth, and recover in the same room?
- Are there restrictions on the number of people allowed in the labor and delivery room at once? Under what circumstances would I be separated from my companions?
- What is the rooming-in policy for babies, and under what circumstances would my baby be separated from me?
- What are the routine newborn care policies? Does the hospital mandate certain shots for all newborns? What if I don't want my child to have them?
- What assistance is available for breastfeeding mothers? Is this hospital certified as "Baby-Friendly"?
- Are private or semiprivate rooms available? Is there an additional charge?

CHAPTER 18

Contested Conceptions and Misconceptions

Rayna Rapp

We were furious about the session they required us to attend before being allowed to do the amnio. These silly people made us pay $140 for a two-hour session, and it took us over forty-five minutes to get there and the same to get back. They explained, in the most elementary language, as if we were total idiots, a few basic things about amnio—information that we could easily have digested from a short pamphlet in ten minutes. . . . It was the clearest case of a for-profit bilking in the American medical system! . . . They could devise . . . a short test to be taken at home to prove that we understood. Then they'd have no excuse to spend so much of our time on so little information. (middle-class academic couple)

MOST COUNSELORS ARE QUITE AWARE that their clients come from diverse backgrounds: Some bring much knowledge of genetics and prenatal testing to the counseling session, others, almost none. Highly educated pregnant women and their supporters may find that the counseling session and prenatal testing offer only the most rudimentary of controls over hereditary health problems when compared to their fantasies of surveillance, while those with little access to education may be overwhelmed by both its content and assumptions. In this chapter, I describe the tension between the scientific meaning of heredity and a model for its control which counselors expound, and the range of popular conceptions of the same domain women and their supporters from diverse backgrounds express. That tension is multilayered, for it rests upon the difference between scientific language and worldview, and broader, more capacious culturally specific notions of causality. The tension also rests on the differences between genetic and socially gendered contributions to a pregnancy's health and well-being, and between medical and experiential understandings of what specific disabilities entail. Here, I will argue that the hegemony of the scientific model can never be absolute: Not only are the communicative resources on which it is based always expanding just below or beyond the reach of many clients; practical conceptions of heredity, maternal responsibility, and disability are also layered with many meanings other than those that genetic counselors can describe.

Many counselors attempt to address what they understand to be the problem of diversity in patients' knowledge of heredity by beginning the individual (intake) portions of their interactions conversationally. Often, they pose a variant of the question, "Do you know why you are here talking to me?" From the beginning, interactions are context-sensitive to the responses and resources that patients bring to the interaction. Middle-class, scientifically educated pregnant patients may respond, "We're planning to have amniocentesis," thus pushing the counseling script into high gear. Implicit in that answer is not only knowledge of appropriate medical indications for the test but also the existence of "the couple" as a decision-making unit. One white, highly educated husband (who turned out to be a biostatistician!) replied that he had come to get a decision-making tree in order to ascertain whether his pregnant wife needed amniocentesis, and what to do with the information, should the results be positive. His response effectively squelched any exploration of those counseling issues that could not be mathematically modeled.

A patient's answer may be much less formal than that of the biostatistician, but highly persuasive, convincing the counselor that the patient knows what she wants to do. As one white working-class clinic patient put it, "I know a little, my friend told it to me. It's quick, it doesn't hurt, no one said anything bad. There's no reason not to have this test." But a Dominican mother of three may answer, "Por culpa de mi edad" (literally, "For the fault of my age"), thus presenting the counselor with several options. She can assume that the woman "knows," since "age" is the factor that sends her here. Or she can confront the "culpa" head-on, explaining that older women having babies present no shame, just medical risks. Families from India may interpret such a direct and leading opening question as impolite; some African-Americans, especially if they come from rural Southern backgrounds, may remain silent, in deference to medical professionals. Wherever she begins her routine explanation, the counselor is likely to have to adjust her language to the language and assumptions of her pregnant patient (and sometimes the patient's mate).

NATIVE LANGUAGES

In adjusting (or not adjusting) to a patient's language, genetic counselors are bound by the limits of their own communicative resources. Although many languages are spoken by the pregnant women whom counselors see, most counseling sessions are conducted in English. Availability of fluent translation is a significant problem: Depending on their catchment areas, the hospitals in which I observed served patients who were close to 100 percent bilingual Spanish speaking, 50 percent French/Creole speaking, or about 25 percent monolingual Spanish speaking. Among the thirty-five counselors that I interviewed, there are at least five in New York hospitals who are native Spanish speakers, and another five who are comfortable counseling in Spanish.

Many others have learned a bit of medical Spanish and work through translators, ranging from trusted assistants who understand their agendas (a secretary in the office or a clinic nurse) to catch-as-catch-can interpreters. The problem of interpretation is not minor: An 8-year-old bilingual girl kept out of school to help her monolingual mother negotiate the prenatal clinic may have trouble translating the mysteries of LMP (last menstrual period) by which pregnancies are medically dated; male kin and neighbors may be too embarrassed to accurately call forth the information a genetic counselor needs when querying prior miscarriages and abortions. One white, middle-class counselor from a Jewish background described her baptism into the world of translation. Her first pediatric case was a Colombian mother whose newborn had just been diagnosed as having multiple congenital anomalies, an inherently serious and ambiguous situation. Unable to speak directly with the mother, the counselor worked through a Spanish-speaking visitor. Although the counselor chose her words very carefully, she could tell by the body language of the mother that her meanings were not getting through. The visitor wanted to spare the mother the pain of hearing the entire diagnosis and was dramatically editing the bad news. Distraught but determined, the new counselor spent her summer vacation in Spain at an intensive language school.

"Native language" only approximates the variety of communicative differences that genetic counselors confront. "Hispanic" glosses a range of Spanish-speaking cultures, especially in New York City. Many counselors, of course, know this. As one middle-class South American counselor told me, "I'm Spanish speaking, but I'm not Hispanic!" Another native Spanish speaker, also from a professional family, confessed that she found it tiresome to be asked to explain the hot-cold folk medicine beliefs of Central American patients. "I don't know anything about that, why should I?" she said. "Sometimes," she continued, "speaking Spanish gives you more problems, not less. People think you're from the same culture, but you really aren't." In both of these instances, the counselors were contesting a too-easy elision of language and culture. On the one hand, they were asserting that the class-based nature of their privileged education removed them from any automatic knowledge of, or identity with less educated, more "traditional" Spanish-speaking clients. On the other, they were pointing out that important national and regional differences separated clients from counselors.

The diversity of Spanish-speaking cultures at the present time in New York City (and most metropolitan areas in the United States) is quite profound. Some genetic counselors distinguished "Hispanic" (which often meant Puerto Rican and Dominican, the "old" migrants) from new migrants who might be "middle-class" Colombians and Argentineans or the "field mice" of Central America (by which the speaker meant "the poor, rural, and humble"). Although exact cultural differences among Spanish-speaking groups may be unknown, most counselors recognize something of the diversity in educational levels, familiarity with medical terminology, and religious observance that different nationalities may represent.

Nominal or deep fluency in another tongue does not ensure direct communication for science speakers. Language differences may signal communicative ambiguities far beyond the question of literal translation. Local metaphors of pregnancy, of birth, and of female and male contributions to parenthood do not necessarily translate easily into the realm of medical discourse. Two native Spanish-speaking counselors pointed out the far-reaching impact of their conversations with pregnant Spanish-speaking patients:

> This knowledge is more than genetic. They learn about things that were completely hidden—where the eggs are, what sperm does, how children get to look like their parents. They have ideas, but this is female physiology, it is knowledge, not just information. For this, they come back.
>
> When I see confusion, I go to work, I tell them in language they will understand, language of the streets. They are comfortable here, it is a good place to visit. They come back to see me whenever they come to the hospital.

Of course, not everyone is equally open to the complex relation between native tongue, knowledge, and communicative power. Two counselors, one of whom conducts group sessions for patients in Spanish, expressed irritation that so few of their clients "bothered to learn English": "They're here ten, maybe fifteen years. They learn enough English to pick up their welfare checks. Why don't they just learn the language? My grandparents did."

And if Spanish is a contested domain, French and Haitian Creole are virtually terrae incognitae. At the time of these interviews, only one genetic counselor felt comfortable counseling in French; none knew any Creole. The lack is significant: In at least one City Hospital, Haitians make up about 50 percent of the patients referred for counseling. In translating for counseling sessions, I discovered that there is no recognition of Down syndrome or "mongolism" among recent immigrants from the Haitian countryside. No word exists in Creole for the condition. In principle, the incidence of Down syndrome is invariant worldwide. But in a country with the worst infant mortality statistics in the Western Hemisphere, babies may die from many causes, and this one may go unrecognized as a "syndrome." Nonrecognition of the label may also reflect other cultural and political experiences. Haitians living in New York City have already confronted alternative definitions of their children's vulnerabilities. As one Haitian evangelical Christian father told me, while firmly rejecting amniocentesis on his wife's behalf, "What is this *retarded*? They always say that Haitian children are retarded in the public schools. But when we put them in the Haitian Academy [a community-based private school], they do just fine. I do not know what this *retarded* is." In his experience, "chromosomes" seemed a weak and abstract explanation for the problems a Haitian child may face. Thus a "language barrier" may eclipse a complex imbrication through which transnational migration, racial prejudice, religious beliefs, gender practices and assumptions, and scientific world-views may all be uneasily stitched together.

Indeed, commonsense, experiential explanations and scientific, abstract ones are often in tension, a point to which I return below. This is constantly reflected in a tug-of-war of words pitting the formal vocabulary of biomedicine against the informal lexicon of most women's lives. Both codes uneasily cohabit in a forty-five-minute intake interview. Code switching occurs rapidly as counselors feel out their clients: "Babies" vie with "fetuses" for space in "wombs," "tummies," or "uteruses"; "waters" or "liquid" or "fluids" may be "taken out with a needle" or "withdrawn through an insertion"; the "test" or "procedure" may involve "looking at the inherited material" or "examining chromosomes." And, in the worst-case scenario, women must decide to "terminate" or "abort" an "affected" or "sick" pregnancy in which "Down syndrome" or "mongolism" has been diagnosed. In the standoff between medical and popular language, the more distant idiom may provide reassurance by suggesting to some pregnant women that their experiences are part of medical routine (Brewster 1984). But for others, medical terminology may muffle anxiety-provoking choices until they are expressed through dramatic disruption:

So I was sitting and listening, listening and sitting and all the time getting more and more preoccupied. The counselor kept on talking but she never did say it, so finally I had to just say it, right while she was still talking, "You can't take the baby out *then* [i.e., so late in pregnancy], can you now?" I finally asked. (Veronica Landry, 36, Trinidadborn factory worker)

The tension between a distanced medical language and a more affective language of maternal-fetal connection may also be intertwined with often inaccurate pictures of prenatal testing. Most obviously and consistently, many Spanish speakers fear that the needle goes into the mother's navel or hits the fetal navel cord. The mother's navel, of course, is not the baby's lifeline, for it does not connect the pregnant woman to her baby, but is the severed cord of connection to her own mother, to her own babyhood. Yet both cords were intertwined as the object of concern when women told me they pictured the needle as damaging the *umbligo*. Puerto Rican and Dominican women were also the only ones who consistently brought their mothers as supporters to counseling or testing. And I often heard, of an unplanned pregnancy among women from these backgrounds, a statement like, "I'm 41. My daughter, she's 21 and pregnant. I didn't think I could get pregnant at my age if she's already started" (Feliciana Dominguez, Dominican factory worker).

Intergenerational closeness, or even fusion, appears to run deep through Puerto Rican and Dominican maternal social relations and cultural imagery. But I hazard this interpretation with some uncertainty; it is hard to know why fear of needles, or fear of striking the navel, or beliefs that the daughter's fertility affects the mother's are so pervasive among some Spanish speakers, especially Dominicans and Puerto Ricans. Only far greater familiarity with their cultural backgrounds and aspirations than I hold might reveal or repeal the validity of this explication.

And misinformation about the locus of the test and its relation to pregnancy is not confined to any one group. One 39-year-old African-American was sent to counseling, but came too late for amniocentesis. She had had the test in her prior pregnancy, and announced that she expected it to cover all her pregnancies. At first, there was barely concealed amusement on the part of counselors (and observers!). Later, we realized the logic of her position: She thought that the amniocentesis had probed her own health, rather than the health of the fetus, to ensure that she had no problem that might be passed on to any of her fetuses.

Some misconceptions are easily corrected: Many Philippinas, Dominicanas, and Puerto Ricans expressed their belief that Down syndrome occurs only in a first, late pregnancy. Some asked whether they needed the test, since their prior children had been born without chromosomal problems. "Is this the test for women having their first baby over 35 or is it for women who've had other children?" (Luisa Alvarez, 36, Puerto Rican social worker).

This idea is easily displaced by a counselor's scientific explanation about nondisjunction of chromosomes potentially occurring in any pregnancy, and becoming more likely with age. But some ideas are deeply embedded within other domains of knowledge and belief, and are less likely to be dislodged by a strictly scientific explanation. Juana Martes, a 37-year-old mother of three from the Dominican Republic, initially refused the test because members of her charismatic Catholic prayer group had already healed two cases of Down syndrome. When I asked for descriptions of the mothers and children involved, she said that praying over the pregnancy had entirely saved one baby from "a little mongolism," while the second child was cured by God, although she was still unable to speak at the age of 3. A Puerto Rican unemployed father told me

that his conversion to Pentecostalism had enabled him to dream the image of his as-yet-unborn daughter. In the dream, the child was at first blind and suffered from a hole in her heart, but both infirmities were healed through prayer. These two infirmities exist simultaneously as problems amenable to biomedical and religious intervention, since Jesus is believed to cure a hole in the heart, and to bestow clear vision. The power of religious imagery and beliefs to infiltrate and transform biomedical practices is profound, as I hope to illustrate below.

Some patients invoke a causality of their own to explain the existence of a disability. A U.S.-born Irish-American school administrator said of her Irish aunt with ten children, one autistic: "I think it was her life, that's what I think caused the autism. She was a farmer's wife, she had a very hard life; one of the twins was normal, and one just was not. It was the circumstances, just the hard lot of her life as a mother that caused it." An African-American secretary who came for genetic testing during her second pregnancy related a troubled family medical history. Her first child had tuberous sclerosis, a genetic disease transmitted from her father's side. One of the pregnant mother's sisters had severe asthma, and another was born with short, uneven limbs. The specific risks of recurrence of these family-related conditions were all explained to her, and she was asked about her anxieties and concerns. She replied:

> I don't think about it, if I do, I'm going to make myself crazy. My father's brother has a son that's very, very retarded. My mother always say she didn't like that boy and she saw a lot of him while she was carrying Laney [the sister with limb problems]. That's what marked the baby, that's what she believes.

The counselor said, "I told you what we know about how problems pass down in families, and it isn't by marking. Do you believe what your mother believes?" To which the woman replied, "Yes, I grew up in the country, and it's part of me."

Puerto Rican women (like some others from Latin backgrounds) also held theories about parental-fetal transmission in which rage is substantiated:

> On my husband's side, the mother suffered a lot. The father ran around, he had thirty-nine children, eleven with that mother. But those children, they suffered her rage: Two died as babies, two are retarded. It seems the suffering descended [motions to her womb] to her pregnancies. Do you understand me? (Merced Blanco, 37, homemaker)

A Puerto Rican postal worker was even more pointed in her discussion of life's stresses and their hereditary transmission:

> My husband, he's schizophrenic. It was the pressure of going from a tranquil country to a strong one. It was just too much pressure, he cracked from the pressure. No, I don't worry about it in the kids. We got five kids, they all come up normal. They don't have schizophrenia because they were born here, they're used to a strong country.

Here, a social psychological theory about the stress of migration displaces contemporary biomedical research on schizophrenia, in which genetic propensities are asserted and debated.

Some misconceptions about genetic transmission are also widespread. African-American clients, for example, held many beliefs about sickle-cell anemia, including the idea that the youngest child always gets the trait. "So me," one woman said, "I'm the youngest, and I got it." Many spoke of the trait as something one can have in degrees. For example, "I've got a trace of it, so does my uncle. My mother says it's on her side, there's a trace of it on my mother's side."

Such beliefs can cohabit comfortably with scientific explanations. That is, a socially inflected analysis of why any particular baby was born with a disability, can be engaged with the practical technologies biomedicine offers. One working-poor Dominicana, 37, described the rage that she said damaged family members this way:

> They don't say he had a sister. They don't tell you, the sister was full of rage at him, they fought about the inheritance, then her rage made a baby that's crazy. They don't say she's having another baby, but they did that test. They don't tell you why for the test, but I'm sure it's because of the crazy baby. Now he's in a special school, they don't want to believe it. The crazy baby, he can't learn anything. The Spanish people, they just say, "loco, loco," caused by her rage at that brother. Now she's having another baby. With the test. I think it's ok.

FEMALE ACCOUNTABILITY

Thus the familial theories some women express about hereditary disabilities are disconnected from the age-related chromosomal problems that are the focus of amniocentesis. They index social relations and responsibilities within families—migration or birth order, for example, or the inability to control rage and fear—rather than the genetic materials on which counselors dwell. Such social relations can, in principle, be affected by human agency, allowing participants a sense of their role in cause and prevention. And an obvious, widely shared common theory of agency affecting a pregnancy's outcome focuses on maternal responsibility. Across divides of class privilege, racial-ethnic or national background, and religious affiliation, many individuals hold mothers responsible for fetal quality and health, despite the insistence of genetic counselors that the production of chromosomal and genetic anomalies are not under human control.

This gendered standoff between biomedicine and popular ideas about heredity, the causes of hereditary problems, and what can be done about them, is built on two quite significant sets of foundational ideas that can run into conflict. Most obviously, scientific knowledge assigns each parent a 50 percent contribution to the hereditary materials of a fetus at the moment of conception. The "drama of the egg and sperm" (Martin 1991) is mirrored technically in the discourse of genetic counseling, where haploid and diploid germ cells, meiosis and mitosis, and mitotic reduction division are all narrated to explain how the life force enters each new conception already equally indebted to both its maternal and paternal sides. This discourse corresponds to a popular understanding in American culture that "blood" is passed on equally from both the father's and mother's sides (Schneider 1980 [1968]). But the egalitarian nature of genetic (or "blood") contributions is held in tension with a second popular, pervasive and nonegalitarian idea, the highly gendered notion of maternal responsibility. Here the discipline of biomedicine concerns female compliance with guidelines for health pregnancy behavior, but it does not include an assignment of responsibility for genetic or chromosomal normality. Yet women and their supporters from many backgrounds believe that the behavior they define as healthy or unhealthy is responsible for a pregnancy's outcome, and they do not distinguish genetic health from any other cause or manifestation.

The widespread, popular accountability of women for the "quality control" of fetuses and children contrasts with notions of male responsibility. While there are circumstances in which male nurturance is considered essential to the developing fetus (Battaglia 1985; Hewlett 1991), men in many cultures are pictured as providing the creative spark or seed which "causes" the pregnancy, without assuming any behavioral obligations that influence its outcome. Women carry the burden of nurturance in such popular models (Delaney 1986; Stolcke 1986).

Of course, the idea that women are responsible for the outcome of pregnancies, including the production of anomalous

or ambiguous births, has a long history in Western theology, natural philosophy, and medicine. Pregnancy, for example, figures in the tensions and agreements between medieval theology and natural philosophy. In that period, women's "fleshiness" was associated with the body in body/soul dualities, her fetus a cause for speculation about maternal and paternal contributions to God's purpose and perfection. Women's reproductive capacities invoked reflection on divine regulation and causes of oddity. Medieval texts and artifacts evinced enormous curiosity about pregnancy, monstrous births, and the relation of blood to milk, couched as problems of permeability and stability (Bynum 1992). This intellectual interest also flourished in the eighteenth century, when the representational arts, medical practice, and emergent scientific research all converged on grotesques, on anomalous embryos, and on "unnatural" births, using them to index debates on causality and regularity in nature. In both religious and secular discourse, women's role in purveying or perverting the life force generated by semen was a central concern (cf. Bynum 1989; Jordanova 1989; Stafford 1991). In its present incarnation, notions of women's embodied responsibility are played out inside an imaginary and bounded female-centered domain, drafting women as the nearly exclusive guardians of fetal and child health.

This engendered and entwined foundation—equal scientific material donations, unequal social practical burdens—corresponds to the scientific difference between genetic and gestational contributions. Not uncoincidentally, it also symbolically aligns women with all the labors of making a nurturant home for the pregnancy and for children while assigning men a proprietary interest, but not a practical responsibility, in a pregnancy's outcome. The consequences of such a widespread belief system have been the subject of much contemporary feminist scholarship.

This stance of holding a woman accountable for a pregnancy's outcome is undoubtedly helpful in linking some health problems like smoking or alcohol consumption to low birth weight or some congenital problems, for it suggests behavioral guides that many women can accommodate. But it doesn't aid in understanding chromosomes, whose patterns and pathologies are unaffected by maternal behavior. Yet many Puerto Rican, Dominican, and Haitian women rejected the test with a variant of this statement:

> I don't smoke, I don't drink, I don't take drugs. I eat good food, I take good care of myself. What do I need this test for? (Dominique Laurent, 39, Haitian garment worker)

> Me and my husband, we saw this program on Channel 13 [PBS]. This only happens if you take drugs, that's when it happens. Nothing to do with me. (Maria Dominguez, 38, Dominican day-care worker)

Often, an assessment of age-related risks is personalized and folded into an interpretation of family history:

> My family's all healthy, they're all professionals, they're active, they take good care. Me, I cut out smoking, I've been off birth control pills for ages, and two of my cousins had babies when they were in their forties. I'm not at risk. (Angela Storrman, 41, African-American public school teacher)

Female accountability also extends inappropriately to mysterious events over which individuals have no control. Mothers often blame themselves, or are blamed by family members, for problems with which their children are born:

> I fell down during my pregnancy with her two times, and then this happened. (Dominican mother describing the birth of her daughter with cleft lip and palate)

> My mother-in-law says the cleft [in the first son] was caused by me using scissors during the pregnancy. This time, I've come for your counseling, but I won't use scissors during the pregnancy. (Chinese garment worker, 32)

> My mom don't want me near his [boyfriend's] retarded brother now, when I come up pregnant. She's worrying in case my baby catch it. (African-American student, 17, sickle-cell trait carrier)

EMBEDDING DISABILITIES

But the problems about which counselors speak are independent of maternal agency, kinship problems, or other social interventions, for they depend on statistical models of risk, not gendered or familial preventative behavior. The complex nature of chromosome problems is condensed into counselors' discussions of the forty-seventh chromosome clinically expressed in Down syndrome, and its accompanying mental retardation. As I noted in chapter 3, the eugenics movement and contemporary genetic counseling practices both focused on mental retardation, indeed, on Down's, as an index of a range of individual and social problems. While this condition is almost universally recognized, the content of that recognition varies considerably, and may well stand orthogonally to the conventional scientific description of Down's. Many families share the counselor's concerns about the limitations on independence which mental retardation represents in our culture. Yet in families who have had direct experience with children with Down's, consciousness of disabilities is more finely honed: Children with Down syndrome may be mildly, moderately, or profoundly retarded, and most fall into the middle range; they run heightened risks of heart and esophageal problems, hearing loss, and increased risk for leukemia. "Mental retardation" provides an iconic description which blurs differences among children with Down syndrome, even as it categorizes them.

Counselors refer to the burdens of raising a child with Down's in a variety of ways:

> A heart defect, we can operate, pneumonia we can cure. But mental retardation, that we can't do anything about. Think about it: No babysitters, it's a twenty-four-hour-a-day job.

Sometimes, it causes problems between the parents, some men can't handle it, and sometimes the other children feel neglected.

We're only looking for fetuses whose inherited materials don't give them a chance of a good life, who will have *severe* handicaps, where life will become very hard for the family. I'm sure you know that in this society, the responsibility for a handicapped child rests on the mother's shoulders.

Embedded in such descriptions are images of mentally retarded children that are hardly value-neutral, where the differences between the medical diagnosis and management of a child with Down syndrome, and that child's location in its complex social map, are analyzed. But first it is important to point out that clients can and do contest these images:

I take in foster children, I had some that were mentally retarded. I saw a movie on Channel 13 about this. When the women saw the kids' pictures, they didn't want any abortions. Me neither. I don't want this, but I've thought about it in every pregnancy, and if it happens, I can handle it. I wouldn't want no abortion for this because it would be my child. If I make it, it's my responsibility, I wouldn't give it up or nothing. (Chloris Lewis, 38, Trinidadian foster mother)

Disabling conditions have specific local meanings that are not shared by all. Mental retardation may stand as an icon for some groups—especially, but not exclusively, middle-class professionals:

I'm sorry to say that I just couldn't accept that. I mean, I've worked hard to get where I am, I worked hard at Cornell. And I want the same for my child. I want to teach my child, and to have him learn. Maybe it's unfortunate, maybe I should be more accepting. But I don't want a child with retardation. (John Freeman, 32, African-American computer technologist)

There's a certain relationship I want to have with a child, a way of growing and being in the world. A retarded child, well, I imagine it would just be too dependent. (Cheryl Spencer, 35, white interior decorator)

The bottom line is what my neighbor said to me: "Having a 'tard,' that's a bummer for life." (Shelley Osteroff, 36, white real estate agent)

Having a retarded baby, well, we both feel life is difficult enough without putting this on a baby itself. We are practical people. . . . Having a retarded child, I suppose it becomes part of you. I know people with a retarded child, they learned a lot. But it is very hard. My husband and me, we haven't actually said this to one another, but we'll end it if it's like that. That's how we feel, I know it is. The biggest problem is, what would we tell our 5-year-old daughter? (Coralina Ramirez, 36, Colombian hairdresser)

But for some, different conditions evoke more fear. Among many of the Spanish speakers I interviewed, physical vulnerability, especially if it was highly visible, seemed a much more urgent problem for family life. Many Puerto Ricans and Dominicans expressed great anxiety about conditions that were visibly crippling. They seemed less concerned with functional disabilities, provided the child appeared "normal." At counseling sessions, questions were often raised about the appearance of children with the conditions the tests probed. A Dominican couple who were both sickle-cell anemia trait carriers, for example, queried whether a child born with that condition would ever walk; if not, they would seek abortion. When told by the counselor that the child would walk but suffer a painful blood disease, they were much reassured. Low-income Puerto Rican parents interviewed through an infant stimulation program generally expressed acceptance and confidence in their Down syndrome children being "normal," for example: "She's growing really well. We were only concerned that she wouldn't grow, that she'd be really small. But now that she can walk, and she's growing, she seems like a normal child to us." Thus, the "choice" any pregnant woman makes to take or reject the test, and to keep or end any specific pregnancy, flows from the way that both pregnancy and disability are embedded in personal and collective values and judgments within which her own life has developed.

One aspect of that totality is prior experience with specific disabilities. Migdalia Ramirez, for example, was sent for genetic counseling because her sister had spina bifida. Both she and her mother were devout Catholics, generally opposed to abortion, but determined to end Migdalia's pregnancy if the fetus had the sister's condition. Amniocentesis found no neural tube defects, but it picked up 47XXY, Klinefelter's syndrome. This sex chromosome anomaly is linked to hormonal and growth problems, sterility, and risks of learning disabilities and mild retardation. Migdalia kept the pregnancy. She explained:

> I was only concerned if my baby could walk and see. This other stuff, it didn't concern me. They said he'd be normal, he might be slow-minded, but that's ok, as long as he looks normal. I'll be there for him. If my first kid was having what my sister's got, I'd need a lot of help. But he's growing up normal: He looks ok, he acts ok, he's a really nice kid. I could never abort for *that*; he's developing each day, I can handle this, as long as the baby looks normal. (Migdalia Ramirez, 19, Puerto Rican waitress)

Lucia Morez's 5-year-old daughter has Goldenhar's syndrome, a condition involving heart defects and facial asymmetries. In talking about her daughter, she said, "Sometimes when we're out on the street, people look at her, they say, 'What happened?' She cries, she know she looks bad. That's the thing: She really looks bad." Although the child has serious heart problems that must be consistently monitored, they did not enter the mother's discussion spontaneously, but only after being prodded by many questions. She refused amniocentesis in her second pregnancy because it could not monitor and detect the problem from which her first child suffered, and she was not overly concerned

about chromosomal risks that could lead to mental retardation.

Family history also carves limits into the choices women make. Carol Seeger, a white Jewish museum curator, had prenatal diagnosis at 42, determined to abort if the fetus had neural tube defects, but not for Down syndrome. Having helped to raise a younger sister with Down's, she felt committed to living with that condition. Twig Hansen, a white Protestant homemaker, expressed reverse reasons when seeking amniocentesis: Her firstborn son had spina bifida, and her family was clear that they would meet that challenge again if the need arose, but they did not want to raise a child with Down syndrome.

Even the same diagnosis may evoke different interpretations and paths to decision-making. One genetic counselor encountered two patients, each of whom chose to abort a fetus, but for strikingly different reasons, after learning that its status included XXY sex chromosomes (Klinefelter's syndrome). One white professional couple told her, "If he can't grow up to have a shot at becoming the president, we don't want him." A low-income family said of the same condition, "A baby will have to face so many problems in this world, it isn't fair to add this one to his burdens."

And the interpretation of diagnoses may be deeply distorted, despite a counselor's best efforts. During my many years of participant observation, I was told similar stories three times about couples who chose to abort after a diagnosis of sex chromosome anomalies in their fetuses because they believed those anomalies would lead to homosexuality. In each case, counselors were unable to disabuse them of this wrongful interpretation; the fear of a homosexual orientation was so profound that sex chromosome problems and sexual "problems" were irrevocably conflated.

Such conflations are more likely to occur when diagnoses involve conditions about which a pregnant woman and her supporters have very little prior knowledge. When such shadowy diagnoses involve sex chromosomes, they often index anxieties about the limits of the natural bases of sexuality. A Colombian manicurist, for example, married to a Dominican factory worker, received a fetal diagnosis of Klinefelter's. They did not express much concern about the 10–20 percent risk of learning disabilities or mental retardation which accompanies this syndrome, and they listened to discussions of gynecomastia (male breast enlargement) and micro penises without intense distress. But the husband asked, "Is this going to make him homosexual? I don't want that." And the wife said, "He won't be able to have children; I wonder if he'll blame us." Both expressed concern about knowing something

hidden that the son won't know about himself until he was older.

The cultural logic of equating sex chromosome anomalies and homosexuality was enunciated in a group session at Middle Hospital in which a counselor was explaining these conditions. One father interrupted to say, "This question is not related, but does science know, if you believe homosexuality is from birth, how chromosomes are related? It's logical that if you have more Xs or more Ys, you should have more sex in that one direction" (Mort Lansberger, white accountant). Here, sex chromosomes, sexual drives, sexual orientation, and normative gender are streamlined into the mirage of a single, quantifiable trajectory.

CHAPTER 19

Motherhood Lost

Cultural Dimensions of Miscarriage and Stillbirth in America

Linda L. Layne

PREGNANCY AS A RITE OF PASSAGE

In many cultures including our own, pregnancy is treated as a rite of passage, especially if it is a first pregnancy. Furthermore, despite the feminist movement, some Americans still believe that a woman is not a 'real' or 'complete' woman until she has born a child (cf. Luker 1975). Hence the transition to the status of 'mother' may also entail the assumption of the status of 'real woman' and/or 'adult' as well. As a condition that marks these transitions, pregnancy has a liminal status and represents a temporary condition which places the woman between two structural states.[1] The pregnant woman, especially in the case of a first

child, is "betwixt and between fixed points of classification" temporarily set apart from the structural arrangements of the culture (Turner 1974:232, Davis-Floyd 1986, 1988).

Normally, the liminality of pregnancy ends following the birth of the child. For example, in the United States, at the end of a normal pregnancy a woman is gradually reintegrated into society in her new role through rites of reincorporation (e.g., flowers in the hospital, visits and gifts from relatives and friends, the lifting of taboos, being addressed as 'Mom,' etc.). However, when a pregnancy ends without a live birth, there are no rites to reincorporate the woman into her normal role. In a sense a pregnancy which ends in miscarriage or stillbirth might more accurately be described as what Crapanzano (1981) has called a 'rite of return' in that despite having gone through many of the rituals of pregnancy such as doctor's visits, maternity clothing, abstention from coffee, alcohol and cigarettes, the woman returns to her pre-pregnancy status rather than to the new (or renewed status) of 'mother.'

My research with members of pregnancy loss support groups indicates that many participants feel trapped in a liminal social position. One woman reports that after two stillbirths she was told by someone not to worry about 'Limbo' "because in God's house there are many mansions." Later she says she realized "that there is a Limbo, but it's not for the stillborn babies. It's for their parents," a state which she and her husband felt powerless to escape. "We gave birth – sort of. We had a child – sort of. Our child died – sort of. . . . Soon we learn to speak of things somewhere between birth and death, as we live in our someplace between heaven and hell" (Gana *Unite Notes* 1986 5(5):4). Another expressed similar feelings in a poem: ". . . a mother without a child. What am I? I had a baby, but she's gone. Am I a mother? What am I?" (Chaidez in Schwiebert and Kirk 1985).

These feelings may be particularly acute for members of the middle class because of the moral valuation placed on finishing what one starts. As one woman who had a miscarriage put it "no matter how you look at it, you've failed, because if you set out to do something, I believe you've got to finish it . . ." (Down 1986).

Ethnographic material on miscarriage and stillbirth is very difficult to locate, partially I would suggest, because of the tabooed status of the topic in the culture of Western investigators.[2] But my preliminary research on pregnancy loss in Jordan indicates that in some cultures miscarriage and stillbirth are marked by a ritual which both acknowledges the event and serves to reintegrate the woman into the flow of everyday life. In Jordan, in contrast to our tradition of waiting to announce a pregnancy until after the first trimester, a pregnancy is made public as soon as it is determined and if that pregnancy ends in miscarriage or stillbirth the loss is publicly acknowledged. For example, during the course of my dissertation research in the Jordan Valley a school teacher I knew had a miscarriage. At the end of a period of seclusion/recuperation her colleagues and I were invited to her home for a ritual meal which she prepared and served.[3] We offered our condolences and presented her with a gift of a blanket, an important form of women's wealth (Layne 1984). The following day she returned to work.

In many societies a pregnancy also represents a rite of passage for the father.[4] The ethnographic literature provides documentation of men's observance of food taboos and seclusion during their wives' pregnancies and of the birth process as a rite of passage for both parents in many societies (Paige and Paige 1981; Young 1965). Rothman (1982:99–100) has suggested that many of the new roles for American fathers such as actively preparing for the birth, helping the mother do pre-natal exercises, learning breathing techniques, etc., may represent new forms of couvade rituals in which the husband imitates to a certain extent the wife's pregnancy and her birth rituals.

Men have been remarkably ignored by most social and demographic studies of reproduction (Townsend 1988) and the area of pregnancy loss is no exception. None of the studies on reproduction loss have included fathers in their sample. Given the extent to which stillbirth or miscarriage is treated as an illness, it is understandable that the focus of friends and relatives, healthcare practitioners and social scientists alike tends to be on women and their bodies. But as the rite of passage framework makes clear, pregnancy loss is a social event as well as a biological one and one that involves both men and women although in different ways.

In many cultures gender influences the way that grief is expressed.[5] The folk knowledge of pregnancy loss support groups is that men and women react differently to a reproductive loss and grieve differently and that these differences often place a strain on marital relations. To fully understand the impact and meaning of a miscarriage or stillbirth for women, one must also understand what it means to their partners.

THE CULTURAL CONSTRUCTION OF 'CHILD' AND 'PARENT' IN A CONTEXT OF BLURRED BOUNDARIES AND CONTESTED MEANINGS

Pregnancies constitute a continuum that stretches from a single cell to a newborn human infant. The ambiguous status of embryos and fetuses has become a major public issue in the United States during the last twenty-five years. While the abortion debate is the most visible manifestation of this issue, as Luker has pointed out, that debate is part of a larger process in which ordinary Americans are grappling with the philosophical issue of personhood (1984:7). The legal, medical and social status of an embryo or fetus is clearly central to the meaning of miscarriage and stillbirth and yet, in each of these domains, there is currently a lack of consensus.

Medical definitions of miscarriage and stillbirth are also in flux. As advances in neonatal medicine push back the date at which a fetus has any possibility of surviving, currently at 24 weeks, the boundary separating miscarriage from stillbirth is being moved earlier and earlier. Because this is continually changing, at any given time different institutions and individuals may be utilizing different definitions.[6]

As a result of new technologies new lines are being drawn along the continuum of pregnancy. Sonograms are allowing women to "see life" long before they "feel life."[7] At the same time amniocentesis is delaying the time at which some feel they can safely start getting emotionally involved with the fetus (Rothman 1986). With in vitro technology, some women start marking the stages of their pregnancies even before implantation (Williams 1987). Genetic testing of the embryo or fetus following a miscarriage now makes it possible for bereaved parents to know what the sex of their child would have been, even if the demise took place before the sexual organs were physically differentiated.

Access to and use of these new technologies varies in different sectors of American society. In addition, the meaning of information gained through these technologies may vary from one group to another. For example, learning how knowledge of the sex of a miscarried embryo affects the experience of miscarriage should contribute to our understanding of the relationship between sex, gender and personhood in American culture. Yet, it may be that just as Rapp (1988a, b, in press) has shown for amniocentesis, ethnic background may significantly affect the meaning that such information holds for different individuals.

Given the culturally ill-defined status of an embryo, fetus or neonate, a miscarriage or stillbirth is open to a wide range of interpretations. The significance of a reproductive loss to the parents and the appropriate way of dealing with the bodily remains clearly depend on how it is defined. While the socially prevalent response is to deny or at least minimize its human status, for the most part pregnancy loss support group participants are struggling to define their loss as a child. This effort entails certain challenges because, unlike an adult who leaves behind a trail of existence, an unborn child lacks the material traces of social life. Groups such as UNITE and the Australian team featured in the film *Some Babies Die* seek to assist parents in this enterprise by encouraging parents to retain keepsakes such as pictures, locks of hair, hand prints, birth and death certificates, a scrap from the fetal monitor showing the baby's heart rate, and sonogram photos. All of these constitute evidence in the battle over whether or not a child actually existed.

It is important to note that not all men and women construct themselves as parents on the basis of a miscarriage or stillbirth. Indeed, as the title of this paper implies, a salient aspect of the experience, especially for those who do not have children, may be the *loss* of motherhood or fatherhood. As McCook (1987:1) has pointed out, during the course of a pregnancy, especially a first pregnancy, a woman develops two identities – a pregnancy identity and a motherhood identity. For many a miscarriage or stillbirth entails not only grief for the would-have-been child, but also for the loss (cutting short) of parenthood. Although most women who experience a pregnancy loss already have children or go on to bear children, for some multiple miscarriages or stillbirths are an unacknowledged form of infertility.[8] Both common sense and current research suggest that the experience of pregnancy loss in these cases differs from the experience of those who have children or still have the hope of having children.

Because the issue of pregnancy loss is so closely related to the issues which inform the abortion debate, the feminist movement and the pregnancy loss support movement have tenuously maintained strategic areas of silence. The appropriate position to adopt regarding pregnancy loss is a thorny one for feminists. A whole generation of feminists is now confronting a dismaying array of unexpected fertility problems (infertility, repeated pregnancy loss, positive amnio results, etc.), and as a result has reexamined the notion of reproductive rights. However, the perceived danger of adding fuel to the anti-abortionist fires has been reason enough for the feminist movement to maintain a studied silence on the issue. Similarly, the clearly divisive issue of abortion has remained submerged in the pregnancy loss support movement as leaders work to champion their shared goals with the added strength of unity. Thus, the meaning of pregnancy loss in American culture is being constructed in various ways by people situated at different positions along the political spectrum. Indeed, one of the reasons for the rapid development of the pregnancy loss support movement may be the multiple meanings (and political utility) 'pregnancy loss' has for various sectors of American society.

CONCLUSIONS

The topic of pregnancy loss has been relatively understudied. The topic of perinatal loss is a particularly illuminating area for studying the changing meaning of parenthood and provides a fascinating case study of culture-in-the-making, as members of a grassroots movement actively create new rituals – striving to transform personal symbols into cultural ones and to change the meaning of miscarriage and stillbirth in our society. In addition this area of inquiry promises to contribute to our understanding of the changing and complex relationship between birth, death, gender, and personhood in American culture.

NOTES

1. Death and rebirth symbolism is common to all rites of passage, the old self dies, the new one is born. It is not surprising then, that this imagery is common in contemporary accounts of childbirth (e.g., Chesler in Bergum 1989:37).
2. Flint's (1988) preliminary reporting of pregnancy loss practices she happened to observe in Indonesia during the course of field research in physical anthropology is the only cross-cultural study of pregnancy loss of which I am aware.
3. The serving of a ritual meal to guests is a critical element of all rites of passage in Jordan (e.g., marriage, high school graduation, death) save that of childbirth.
4. In the last few years a number of popular books have appeared with titles such as *The Birth of a Father* (Greenberg 1985; Bittman and Zalk 1978; Panuthos 1984, Chap. 7). These tend to focus on the man's role in delivery and changes in his life following the birth rather than his status and experience during the course of the pregnancy.
5. Rosenblatt, Walsh, and Jackson's (1976) cross-cultural study of grief and mourning in 78 world cultures found that in many but by no means all of the societies they studied there were sex-related

differences in the frequency of crying, attempted and actual self-mutilation, anger and aggression in the context of bereavement.

6. For example, Neugebauer (1987) continues to use 28 weeks gestation as the cut-off point between miscarriage and stillbirth.

7. Sonogram images appear in several of the poems written by bereaved parents, for example "10 Weeks Gestation" by Ingle, *Unite Notes* 1986–87:4.

See Petchesky (1987), Luker (1984:4), Rothman (1986:58), Swanson-Kauffman 1983, and Fletcher and Evans (1983) for more on the impact of these visual images.

8. Infertility is generally defined as "the inability of a couple to conceive after 12 months of intercourse without contraception" (OTA 1988:3) and thus women who conceive but cannot bear a child are still technically 'fertile.'

CHAPTER 20

The Risks to Reproductive Health and Fertility

Jackie Schwartz and Tracey Woodruff

CHEMICAL EXPOSURES AND FEMALE REPRODUCTIVE HEALTH

Exposure to chemicals can damage female reproductive function and health in a variety of ways. Some exposures cause structural malformations and disease; others more subtly damage tissues or cells of reproductive organs. Still others interfere with the endocrine system. Exposure to chemicals has been linked to impaired fertility and reproductive function as well as to a higher risk of cancers, diseases and disorders of the **female reproductive tract** and ovaries.

Fibroids

Fibroids are noncancerous tumors that grow in the middle muscle layer of the uterus. They are the leading cause of **hysterectomy** in the United States, can be extremely painful, and are also a risk factor for infertility, miscarriage, abnormal position of the fetus in the womb, premature labor, and complications with the placenta. Estimates are that between one half and three quarters of all women of reproductive age have fibroids (only some of these women are diagnosed because their tumors grow large enough to cause recognizable symptoms). Despite the common

occurrence of fibroids, little is known about what causes them. We do know that fibroids are partly genetic (hereditary) and that the hormones estrogen and progesterone, which are produced by the ovaries and can also be given as medication, cause existing fibroid tumors to grow.

Exposure to estrogenic chemicals in our environment may have a role in causing fibroids. Women exposed to DES [diethylstilbestrol] in the womb are two-and-a-half times more likely to develop fibroids. Rodents exposed to DES and other estrogenic chemicals also have an increased risk of fibroids. Recently, researchers have looked at how exposure to estrogenic chemicals in our environment might cause fibroids by studying the effects of chemical exposure on rodents. They have focused on exposure during the time that the uterus is developing, specifically, when muscle cells in the uterus are being genetically programmed for how and when they will respond to estrogen during the menstrual cycle, later in life. The researchers found that exposure to estrogenic chemicals during this period of development makes genes in the muscle cells permanently hypersensitive to estrogen. And, because estrogen triggers fibroids to grow, this hypersensitivity causes existing fibroids to grow faster and larger than they normally would in these animals. These experiments also showed that cells that will become fibroid tumors later in life may be created, in part, by exposure to chemicals in the womb.

So far, only a few chemicals have been screened for these effects in animals, including DES, genistein (a natural hormonal chemical found in soy food products) and bisphenol A (a chemical commonly used in clear, shatter-proof plastic water and baby bottles and in the material that lines the inside of canned foods and beverages). But it is likely that a host of other estrogenic chemicals may have similar effects on the development of the uterus and the risk of fibroids. It is also worrisome that these effects are not the result of unusually high exposures: In fact, exposure to the same level of bisphenol A that is currently found in our bodies causes these harmful effects in animals and in laboratory studies of cells.

Endometriosis

Endometriosis is a disease that causes the tissue lining the inside of the uterus (called the endometrium) to grow outside of the uterus and in other parts of the body, for example, the ovaries, abdomen and pelvis. Estimates are that about 10 percent to 20 percent of women of reproductive age in the United States suffer from endometriosis. Younger women are more frequently diagnosed with endometriosis now than in the past, and specialists believe that the disease has become more common since World War II. Endometriosis, like fibroids, can be extremely painful and is a leading cause of infertility and hysterectomy. Risk factors for this complex disease are largely unknown.

However, we do know that the immune system is involved, that the hormone estrogen causes endometriosis tissue to grow and that endometriosis tissue does not respond normally to the hormone progesterone.

The possibility that chemical exposures might be one of the factors that cause endometriosis was first recognized in 1993, when rhesus monkeys that had eaten food contaminated with dioxins (chemicals that are formed when items that contain chlorine are burned) developed endometriosis 10 years later. Researchers looked further at this possible link by using surgery to implant endometrial tissue outside the uterus of monkeys and rodents. Animals that were exposed to dioxins and certain dioxin-like polychlorinated biphenols (also called PCBs) developed endometriosis as a result. And, the more these animals were exposed, the more severe the disease became. Exposure to dioxins and dioxin-like PCBs also altered the way immune cells in the endometrium functioned and the way endometrial cells responded to the hormone progesterone. These effects in animals are very similar to what we see in the endometrial tissue of women with endometriosis.

Of particular concern is that humans are exposed to levels of dioxins that are two to twenty times higher than the levels that cause monkeys to develop endometriosis. And the question of whether exposure to other chemicals that affect the immune and endocrine systems also contributes to the development of endometriosis remains unanswered. Increased rates of endometriosis among DES daughters and higher levels of phthalates (an endocrine disrupting chemical used in fragrances and in soft plastics) in women with endometriosis suggest that the answer may be yes.

Reproductive Tract Development and Disease

Exposure to estrogenic chemicals during fetal development can also harm the development of organs in the female reproductive tract. Many women exposed to DES in the womb have a uterus that is abnormal in size and is shaped like a T instead of a triangle. These deformities make it harder to get pregnant and cause higher risks of miscarriage and premature labor and birth. Exposure to DES during fetal development also increases the risk of a rare form of cancer that can affect the cervix and the vagina. Recent inquiry has focused on how DES causes this harm. Researchers have found that exposure to DES causes permanent changes in the expression of a group of genes called Hox genes that are essential to the development of the reproductive tract and, later in life, to fertility. These permanent errors in how Hox genes function cause abnormalities in the tissues of reproductive tract organs (the fallopian tubes, uterus, cervix and vagina). As a result, the tissue in the uterus looks and behaves like tissue that is normally found in the fallopian tubes; the tissue in the cervix is more like uterine tissue; and tissues in the vagina look and act more like tissues normally found in the uterus and cervix. These errors in tissue development are believed to contribute to the increased risk of cervical and vaginal cancer and the high rates of infertility in women exposed to DES in the womb.

Researchers are beginning to look at whether the estrogenic chemicals we are commonly exposed to also alter Hox gene expression in reproductive tract tissues the way DES does. To date, they have found that exposure to bisphenol A and the pesticide methoxychlor during fetal development also modifies the programming of Hox gene expression in mice. As a result, fertilized eggs are less likely to implant in the uterus, offspring have abnormally developed bones and the uterus of female offspring appears to also have structural defects.

Effects on Ovarian Follicles

Healthy ovaries and **ovarian follicles** are essential to both a woman's fertility and her overall health. A woman's entire, lifelong supply of ovarian follicles is created during fetal development by about the 20th week of gestation. No new ovarian follicles are produced after this time. We know little about the conditions that support the growth of an ample and healthy supply of ovarian follicles prior to birth. However, there is growing evidence that exposure to estrogenic chemicals during development can affect both the quality and the quantity of ovarian follicles.

Alligators living in Lake Apopka, Florida, are exposed to pollution from nearby industry and agriculture and consequently suffer from reduced fertility and increased fetal death. Problems with ovarian development, caused by exposure to estrogenic chemicals in the water, contribute to this reduced survival. The female alligators have more ovarian follicles with two or more egg cells, instead of one. These deformed follicles, called multioocyte follicles, have lower rates of fertilization and embryo survival.

Laboratory mice and rats exposed to estrogenic chemicals, such as DES, bisphenol A, genistein or ethinyl estradiol (the synthetic estrogen in birth control pills), when their ovaries are forming also develop multioocyte follicles. Some women develop multioocyte follicles, but their association with exposure to estrogenic chemicals has not been explored. However, wildlife and animal data indicate that such research is needed.

Exposure to estrogenic chemicals during fetal development can also damage the genetic quality of ovarian follicles. For example, a recent study reports that when developing mice are exposed to levels of bisphenol A commonly measured in humans, nearly half of the eggs they ovulate later in life have **chromosomal abnormalities**. Embryos that develop from these eggs also have this genetic defect. Chromosomal abnormalities are the leading cause of miscarriage, birth defects and mental retardation in humans.

These findings are new and it is unknown whether these effects are also occurring in humans. However, an association between exposure to bisphenol A and recurrent miscarriages in humans has been reported.

Whether other similarly-acting chemicals that interfere with estrogen signaling can damage the genetic quality of ovarian follicles is a question that science has not yet answered, but the pattern and clues suggest the answer is likely yes.

Early or Delayed Puberty

Puberty begins a set of orchestrated biological events and hormonal changes that result in the ability to reproduce. A girl's age at puberty is a risk factor for diseases that are influenced by hormones that are produced in higher amounts after sexual maturity. For example, the duration of exposure to estrogen is a risk factor for breast cancer: The earlier puberty (and the production of estrogen) begins, the longer a woman is exposed to estrogen, and the higher is her risk of developing breast cancer. Accumulating evidence suggests that girls in the United States are reaching puberty at younger and younger ages, prompting attention to their exposure to chemicals that may adversely alter the timing of sexual development. Laboratory and wildlife studies point to numerous chemicals that can hasten puberty in animals, including the pesticides DDT, atrazine, vinclozolin and chlordecone; PCBs; dioxins; polybrominated biphenyls (a type of flame retardant); bisphenol A; alkylphenols (cleaning agents used in detergents and other consumer products); and DES. Recent studies in girls have found associations between younger age at puberty and exposure to many of these chemicals, including PCBs, polybrominated biphenyls, dioxins, phthalates and phytoestrogens (estrogenic chemicals found in plant foods such as beans, seeds and grains). We also know that exposure to lead delays puberty in girls. However, this harmful effect has been reduced by the removal of lead from gasoline and consumer products. It is likely that more connections between chemicals and altered timing of puberty in humans will be drawn as nascent research on this topic continues.

Menstrual Cycle Irregularities

Menstrual cycle irregularities (such as altered cycle length, abnormal bleeding, lack of ovulation, absence of menstruation and disrupted hormonal control of the menstrual cycle) can cause subfertility or infertility and can also be a sign of other underlying problems with reproductive health. Exposure to numerous chemicals has been linked to menstrual cycle irregularities in adult women. For example, women exposed to lead at work as well as those who drink water contaminated with chlorodibromomethane (a chemical that can be produced when water is disinfected using chlorine) have shorter menstrual cycles and, in the case of lead, more frequent, intense and prolonged bleeding. Women exposed to dioxins, endocrine disrupting pesticides, PCBs or chemicals used in the semiconductor industry have longer cycles and a higher chance of missed periods. Women exposed to a variety of endocrine disrupting chemicals have lower levels of hormones that regulate the menstrual cycle, including follicle stimulating hormone, progesterone and estrogen. No studies have examined the effect that exposure to endocrine disrupting chemicals during fetal development may have on menstrual cycle irregularities later in life.

Premature Menopause

Menopause begins to occur when the ovaries are no longer able to transform ovarian follicles into mature eggs that are ready for ovulation and fertilization. Normally, menopause occurs between the ages of 45 and 55. Premature menopause is when a woman experiences menopause before the age of 40. Premature menopause signals a problem with the supply of ovarian follicles or with the ovaries' ability to support the process of developing an ovarian follicle into a mature egg.

We have only begun to understand the role that chemical exposures play in altering the timing of menopause. We know that medical chemotherapy treatments can trigger menopause temporarily or permanently, and that women exposed to dioxins, DDT, DDE or other pesticides as well as women who smoke experience menopause at younger ages. The chemical benzopyrene, which is found in cigarette smoke, has been shown to destroy ovarian follicles in studies of both humans and animals. Animal studies provide hints about the ways that chemicals may cause premature menopause in humans. For example, exposing female mice to lead prevents their ovarian follicles from developing into mature eggs. And, exposing rodents and rabbits to a wide array of chemicals destroys ovarian follicles before they begin to mature into eggs. These chemicals include mancozeb (a pesticide), dibromoacetic acid (a chemical that can be produced when water is disinfected using chlorine), polycyclic aromatic hydrocarbons (a group of chemicals that are formed from the incomplete burning of coal, oil and gas, garbage, cigarettes or charbroiled meat), cyclophosphamide (a chemotherapy drug) and 4-vinylcyclohexene diepoxide (an industrial chemical). Whether these chemicals deplete the lifelong supply of ovarian follicles or interfere with the process of follicle maturation in women is an area of research that needs exploration.

CHEMICAL EXPOSURES AND MALE REPRODUCTIVE HEALTH

The development of the male reproductive system depends on sufficient production, by the male fetus, of androgen (male) hormones such as testosterone, dihydrotestosterone, Müllerian inhibiting hormone and insulin-like 3. Müllerian inhibiting hormone prevents the development of tissues that would otherwise transform into a female reproductive system. The other hormones cause the remaining tissues to develop into the male system. Testosterone is essential for the development of the duct system through which sperm travel. It is also the raw material for making the hormone dihydrotestosterone, which is essential for the development of the penis, the scrotum, the prostate and, along with the hormone insulin-like 3, the descent of the testes (testicles) into the scrotum.

The male fetus must produce quite large amounts of androgen hormones to support the development of the male reproductive system. For example, the levels of testosterone during fetal life can reach about two-thirds the levels in adult life. Anything that interferes with the production of androgen hormones can disrupt the development of the male reproductive system. In adult life, androgen and other endocrine hormones are needed to support the production of sperm.

Exposure to chemicals can produce a variety of effects on male reproductive health by interfering with hormone production or signaling, by altering the normal programming of gene expression or by damaging or destroying vital cells, to name but a few ways. These effects range from subtle problems with sperm production to obvious deformities or diseases in male reproductive organs.

Testicular Dysgenesis Syndrome

Research over the past ten years has drawn a connection between various malformations and diseases of the male reproductive system. These include a birth defect of the penis (**hypospadias**), a birth defect of the testes (**undescended testes**), low sperm counts and testicular cancer. These malformations and diseases tend to cluster in men (in other words, men with one condition are more likely to also have the other conditions). These four conditions are currently considered to be symptoms of an overarching **testicular dysgenesis syndrome** because they are thought to have a common cause: During the early stages of fetal development, something goes awry with the development and organization of two types of very important cells in the testes. One result of this problem is that the fetus does not produce enough hormones to support the normal development of the penis, which can lead to hypospadias, or to trigger the testes to migrate through the body to the scrotum, which leads to undescended testes. A second result is that the cells that support and nourish the development of sperm do not multiply enough, which limits the capacity for sperm production later in life. Sperm counts are also lowered because the cells in the testes are not organized properly, and this disarray destroys sperm cells throughout life. Although it is not known what causes testicular cancer, men with this disease have the same problems with the development and organization of cells in their testes. Also, men with hypospadias, undescended testes or low sperm counts have a higher risk of developing testicular cancer.

Some of the risk factors for testicular dysgenesis syndrome are known, including premature birth, **intrauterine growth restriction,** maternal stress during pregnancy and some rare genetic disorders. However, these conditions cause only a small percentage of testicular dysgenesis syndrome cases.

It is also known that interfering with the production of testosterone or its ability to trigger responses in cells that are necessary for development will cause testicular dysgenesis conditions. Therefore, increasing attention is being paid to the role of endocrine disrupting chemicals, which have been proven to disrupt the production or function of hormones, and to impair development of the testes and the male reproductive system in laboratory animals and wildlife populations. For example, rodents exposed to DDE, DDT, vinclozolin, PCBs, bisphenol A, phthalates, DES, flutamide (an anti-androgenic drug used to treat prostate cancer) or ethinyl estradiol during fetal development develop hypospadias, undescended testes, low sperm counts, testicular tumors and **hermaphroditism.** Alligators in the polluted Lake Apopka have abnormally small penises, and the high rate of undescended testes in the Florida panther is possibly due to exposure to DDE that has accumulated in the bodies of prey. Recently, the damage that phthalates cause in rodents has also been observed in exposed non-human primates. There is also evidence that, for at least one of these chemicals, the harm is passed on to subsequent generations of males.

Emerging studies are examining the relationship between endocrine disrupting chemicals and testicular dysgenesis syndrome in humans. Infant boys whose mothers have higher levels of phthalates in their urine during pregnancy were more likely to have a shorter **ano-genital distance**—a physiological measurement that indicates low testosterone production or function and a higher risk of testicular dysgenesis syndrome conditions. Boys in this study who had shorter ano-genital distances were also more likely to have undescended testes and a smaller penis volume. Also, a parent's exposure to pesticides at work or from living near agricultural fields has been associated with higher rates of undescended testes, and mothers of adult sons with testicular cancer have been found to have higher levels of PCBs.

Semen Quality

In 1977, an abnormal number of male workers at a dibromochloropropane (also called DBCP) pesticide plant in California were found to be sub- or infertile. They were producing either very little or no sperm, and the sperm they did produce had genetic defects. Wives of exposed workers had higher rates of pregnancy loss, and couples tended to have more female infants than normal. The discovery that DBCP was highly toxic to sperm raised awareness that chemicals could harm human reproduction.

Since then, a wide range of agricultural and industrial chemicals has been shown to negatively affect male reproduction in humans and animals. For example, exposure to the metals cadmium and lead has been linked to poor sperm quality. Men exposed to PCBs have reduced sperm counts and poor sperm quality and these effects appear to be passed on to male offspring when exposure levels are high. Men with higher levels of the pesticides atrazine, alachlor or diazinon in their urine have low sperm counts and poor semen quality. We know that exposure to the pesticide atrazine increases the conversion of testosterone into estrogen and decreases testosterone levels. Male amphibians and rodents exposed to levels of atrazine commonly found in our environment are both demasculinized (due to decreased testosterone) and feminized (due to increased estrogen) as a result. Effects range from low sperm counts, to the growth of eggs instead of sperm in testes, to overt hermaphroditism. Reduced semen quality, reduced fertility and fetal loss in animals and humans have been associated with bisphenol A, phthalates, ethylene oxide, glycol ethers, **solvents**, tobacco smoke, pesticides (DDT, vinclozolin), PCBs and dioxin exposure. Damage from some exposures, like lead and vinclozolin, can be passed on to subsequent generations.

DES: HARMING MULTIPLE GENERATIONS IN MULTIPLE WAYS

DES is a synthetic chemical that was first created in 1938. Although DES was known to be highly estrogenic and to cause cancer when it was first manufactured, DES was marketed as both a pharmaceutical drug and a growth stimulant for livestock.

Between the 1940s and the early 1970s, DES was prescribed to as many as 3 million pregnant women in the United States to prevent miscarriage and stillbirth. (Subsequent studies showed that DES is ineffective at preventing pregnancy loss.) In the early 1970s, some of the grown daughters of these women, who were teenagers or in their early 20s, developed clear-cell adenocarcinoma of the cervix and the vagina—a type of cancer

that was previously unheard of in young women. After the link to DES was made, the Food and Drug Administration banned doctors from prescribing DES to pregnant women. However, by then, 5–10 million people in the United States had been exposed to DES, either as adults or in the womb.

Since then, the health effects caused by DES have been studied extensively in both humans and animals. This chemical has become an example of how exposure to an endocrine disrupting chemical can harm multiple generations in multiple ways.

WHAT WE CAN DO

Expand Knowledge

We have learned a substantial amount about how chemical exposure can damage our fertility, reproduction and development. Yet we have many unanswered questions. Have we fully investigated whether chemicals affect development, including longterm consequences of exposure in the womb and early childhood? Do we know enough about the chemicals we have evaluated? What is the potential harm from chemicals that have not been studied? These are but a few of the questions facing scientists. We need to expand what we know about the health impacts of chemicals so we can do a better job of preventing and treating chemical-linked diseases and disorders.

Translate The Science

Researchers have been sending the message that chemical exposures can harm human and animal reproduction for decades, but the message has only partially reached the public and policymakers. Those of us who have heard the message can try to avoid potentially harmful exposures in our own lives. We can identify the largest industrial polluters in our neighborhoods. We can read product labels. As workers, we can follow the guidance of material safety data sheets. But these practices offer inadequate protection because our environmental laws and regulations protect commerce in several ways that have negative implications for public protection and disclosure. Small polluters fly under the regulatory radar. Chemicals in consumer products that are considered "trade secrets" do not have to be included on product labels. Material safety data sheets publicize only a narrow slice of information on the toxicity of a given chemical. Furthermore, as individuals, we can't protect ourselves from the contamination of our air, our water and our food supply by industrial pollution.

Effective protection from chemical exposures cannot be accomplished solely on an individual level. This is a matter for social action. Key partners in this endeavor include researchers, health care professionals, community groups, advocacy and environmental organizations, and policymakers, who must all voice a consistent and cohesive message that is rooted in science.

Strengthen Government Protections

Our current system of regulating chemicals is based on the assumption that chemicals are harmless until proven otherwise, and it places the burden of proof on the government. Labeling laws largely favor commerce over a user's right to know what ingredients are in the products they are purchasing or working with. Occupational exposure limits favor industry and do not protect workers' reproductive health or the health of their fetuses.

Evidence is accumulating that our regulatory system is failing to protect our bodies from exposure to chemicals and our fertility and reproductive health from harm. The increases in rates of chronic diseases such as testicular cancer, and declines in sperm quality show that we have reason to do better. Male reproductive development is being jeopardized by a mother's exposure to phthalates, while baby shampoos and lotions and soft plastic products continue to expose boys to phthalates after they are born. The average adult in the United States is exposed to as much as 20 times the level of dioxin that causes endometriosis in monkeys.

Furthermore, recent science teaches us that chemicals can scramble our hormonal messaging systems and permanently alter gene expression, that certain periods of development are particularly sensitive to chemical harm and that exposures in the womb can cause disease or disorders later in life. Yet the studies upon which our health standards are based do not adequately look for these effects.

A protective public health policy would turn our current paradigm on its head. It would take protective action when there is an indication of harm rather than waiting for absolute proof of harm. It would require information on the health effects of all chemicals used or registered for use. And, it would direct the most intensive action be taken on the most commonly used chemicals that we know the least about.

GLOSSARY

Female reproductive tract A term used to refer to the fallopian tubes, uterus, cervix and vagina.

Hysterectomy An operation to remove a woman's uterus, and in some cases, her ovaries and fallopian tubes as well. It is used to treat a variety of diseases or conditions, including fibroids, endometriosis and cancer of the uterus, cervix or ovaries. Hysterectomy is the second most common surgery among US women, with over 600,000 performed each year. One out of every three women in the United States has a hysterectomy by the age of 60.

Ovarian follicles A single egg, surrounded by layers of two types of cells which produce the hormones estrogen and progesterone and which nurture the egg as it matures during the menstrual cycle.

Chromosomal abnormalities A term used to describe problems with the number or the structure of chromosomes (the structures that contain genetic information) in a cell. These problems are inherited or can occur spontaneously in an individual. Chromosomal abnormalities produce problems with the genetic information in a cell: Genes can be missing or duplicated, or located in the wrong place or order. These problems prevent cells from functioning normally and can have a range of consequences on health.

Hypospadias A defect in the development of the urethra in the penis (the urethra is the tube through which urine and semen travel). The urethra normally runs the full length of the penis, with the opening at the tip of the penis. In hypospadias, the opening instead forms on the underside of the penis or below the penis. Hypospadias is the second most common birth defect in the United States and national studies report that the rate of hypospadias has more than doubled since the 1970s.

Undescended testes A birth defect in which one or both testes fail to move from near the kidneys into the scrotum during fetal development. This process of migration occurs in two stages and each stage is thought to be controlled by different hormones. The hormone called insulin-like 3 is thought to direct the first stage (when the testes move from near the kidneys to the pelvic area), which occurs between the 8th and 15th weeks of gestation. Testosterone controls the second stage (when the testes move from the pelvic area into the scrotum), which occurs in most cases by the 7th month of gestation. Undescended testes is a risk factor for testicular cancer and, if not corrected surgically, a risk factor for low sperm production later in life.

Testicular dysgenesis syndrome A collection of disorders and diseases of the male reproductive system that may be related to one another and have a common cause: abnormal development of the testes during fetal development. These include: hypospadias, undescended testes, low sperm counts, and testicular cancer.

Intrauterine growth restriction Also called IUGR. A condition in which the fetus does not grow at a normal rate and consequently is smaller than expected for its gestational age (the number of weeks of pregnancy). Babies who experience intrauterine growth restriction tend to be very light weight, and their tissues and organs may also be underdeveloped. These infants also have a higher risk of death shortly after birth, of problems with neurological and reproductive development and growth, and of cardiovascular disease later in life.

Hermaphroditism A condition in which either an animal's genetic sex is not consistent with the sex organs that develop, or the sex organs that develop are not entirely male or female. For example, a genetically female animal may develop testes, a male reproductive tract or male external genitalia. Or, both sperm cells and egg cells may develop in the testes of a genetically male animal.

Ano-genital distance A measurement of the length of the perineum (the *area* of the body between the anus and the genitals). During male development, the hormone testosterone triggers the perineum to lengthen as part of the normal development of male sex organs, such that the ano-genital distance of male humans and rodents is twice as long as that of females. Researchers study ano-genital distance because it is a sensitive measure of whether a chemical has interfered with testosterone production or action during fetal development.

Solvents Liquids that cause other liquids, solids or gases to dissolve. Solvents are most often used to clean things. For example, they are used in dry cleaning, spot removers, detergents, paint thinners, nail polish remover and perfume. They are commonly used in numerous industries to remove oil and grease from metals and electronics.

CHAPTER 21

The Liability Threat in Obstetrics

Theresa Morris

When I was a resident, I had a very old Chair who said something that stuck with me [and] helps me explain where we are now . . . He said that he's never done a cesarean that he regretted. He had done dozens and dozens of vaginal deliveries that he did, but never a cesarean. And I think that is where doctors are right now . . . You're unlikely to be the person who does the next section and gets surgical complications, but you could be the one regretting that vaginal delivery if the baby doesn't come out perfect.

—Physician Jacob Chism

Doctor Chism, an obstetrician of twelve years at the time of the interview, is quite frank about his concern with being blamed for a bad vaginal birth outcome. His is not alone in this concern. The American College of Obstetricians and Gynecologists (ACOG), the professional association representing most obstetricians and gynecologists in the United States, has named malpractice. liability a crisis for the profession and physicians' practice of defensive medicine a consequence. In a September 11, 2009 press release announcing findings from a survey of its members about professional liability, Albert L. Strunk, ACOG Deputy Executive Vice President, stated, "The latest survey shows that the medical liability situation for ob-gyns remains a *chronic crisis* and continues to deprive women of all ages—especially pregnant women—of experienced ob-gyns. Women's health care suffers as ob-gyns further decrease obstetric services, reduce gynecologic procedures, and are *forced to practice defensive medicine.*"[1] In other words, AGOG suggests that physicians practice defensively to avoid lawsuits-this is code for performing more c-sections.

THE LEGAL ENVIRONMENT OF OBSTETRICS

As discussed earlier, the legal environment of health care has gone through rapid changes. To understand these changes, it is important to understand the role of insurance cycles. All types of insurance are known to go through cycles. "Hard cycles" are characterized by a lack of insurance policies and high prices, while "soft cycles" are characterized by a good supply of policies, a lack of demand, and low prices. Thinking specifically about the market for malpractice insurance, physicians and hospitals feel the pinch in hard markets because malpractice insurance policies are expensive and sometimes hard to find.[2] Defined hard markets in the malpractice insurance industry have happened in the United States during 1975–78, 1984–87, and 2001–4.[3] Maternity providers and ACOG describe these as periods of "malpractice crisis." Notice that the hard cycles are relatively common and last for about three years. Although experts suggest that the most recent hard cycle in the malpractice insurance industry ended in 2004, it is not clear from talking with maternity providers or following statements from ACOG that they believe it has.

Obstetrics is notably one of the fields of medicine most affected by these cycles and has the added problem that malpractice claims are infrequent, large, and hard to predict, all of which contribute to uncertainty.[4] For obstetrical medical malpractice claims opened or closed during the period January 1, 2009, through December 31, 2011, the most common primary allegation of the claims was neurological impairment (28.8 percent) and stillbirth or neonatal death

(14.4 percent).[5] The most common neuro-logical impairment cases are for shoulder dystocia (where the baby's shoulders unpredictably get stuck behind the woman's pubic bone) and cerebral palsy (a disability involving the central nervous system that is largely believed to be due to something that occurs during a woman's pregnancy). Incidents of shoulder dystocia and cerebral palsy are notably difficult to predict or prevent, and thus maternity providers feel that most negative birth outcomes involving shoulder dystocia or cerebral palsy are due to obstetrical maloccurrence, defined as "a bad or undesirable outcome that is *unrelated to the quality of care provided*," rather than to obstetrical malpractice, which is defined as "a bad or undesirable outcome *caused by medical negligence*."[6] However, maternity providers believe that they will be held responsible for such birth outcomes regardless of whether they committed a medical error.

It can be argued that because most obstetrical lawsuits are tied to hard-to-predict events (shoulder dystocia and cerebral palsy) and may even occur before labor begins (cerebral palsy), the type of malpractice risk maternity providers face is markedly different from that in other medical specialties. Some births will have perfect outcomes, while others will involve birth defects and death regardless of the care a woman receives during labor and birth. Thus, one can see the precarious problem maternity providers face. This is not to say that malpractice in maternity care does not happen. Certainly there are documented cases of substandard care where women and babies are harmed because of the type or quality of care or lack of care they receive.[7] But the malpractice risk is quite different for maternity providers compared to other medical providers, and they feel this difference.

From the obstetrician's perspective, the risk of lawsuit is real. In a 2012 ACOG survey, 77.3 percent of responding obstetricians reported having had at least one lawsuit filed against them in their career, with an average of 2.69 lawsuits per obstetrician.[8] In fact, nearly every physician in high-risk specialties, including obstetrics, will be subject to a malpractice claim by the age of sixty-five.[9] While obstetricians have the third-highest rate of suit after neurologists and neurosurgeons, the average claim payment for obstetricians is almost 20 percent higher than the overall average claim payment for all specialties, and obstetricians have the highest total number of claims paid among all medical specialties.[10] The average claim payment for ob-gyns in 2012 was $510,473 and differs markedly by primary allegation: $982,051 for neurological impairment; $364,794 for "other infant injury—major"; and $271,149 for stillbirth or neonatal death.[11]

In terms of the disposition of malpractice claims, examining claims closed between January 1, 2009, and December 31, 2011, 43.9 percent were dropped by plaintiffs' attorneys or were settled with no payment to the plaintiff, 38.7 percent were settled by a payment to the plaintiff on behalf of the obstetrician, and 17.4 percent were closed through a jury or court verdict or through arbitration.[12] When the lawsuit went to trial, the court decided in favor of the obstetrician in 65.6 percent of those cases.[13] Doing some quick math, what this means is that payment on behalf of the obstetrician (either through settlement or court verdict) happens in less than half (44.7 percent) of malpractice cases.

These contradictory trends—a high risk of being sued but a smaller risk that the suit will result in a payment to the plaintiff—sometimes lead critics to question the existence of a malpractice crisis.[14] Other conflicting trends also lead to this doubt. For example, the *number* of obstetrical malpractice claims is *not* increasing and has actually decreased in the United States generally and in Connecticut specifically over the past twenty-five years.[15] But the average payment in malpractice suits are increasing nationally and in Connecticut. In the United States malpractice claim payouts increased from an average of $254,019 in 1991 to $330,435 in 2010 (in 2010 dollars), a 30 percent increase.[16] The average payment on a malpractice claim in Connecticut increased by slightly more, 38 percent, in the same period, from $314,206 in 1991 to $433,446 in 2010 (in constant 2010 dollars), although this average hides spikes in this measure, including an average of $817,092 in 2008.[17]

Malpractice insurance rates are also high and increasing at record rates nationally and in Connecticut. The average cost of policies offered to obstetricians by malpractice insurance companies in Connecticut increased by 92 percent from $73,451 in 1997 to $140,902 in 2012 (in constant 2012 dollars).[18] Although harder to document because of regional variation, obstetrical malpractice rates have also increased nationally. For example, by one measure malpractice rates increased by 70 percent between 2000 and 2004.[19]

Connecticut has other characteristics that make it an interesting state to study. A 2009 report from the State of Connecticut Insurance Department concluded that Connecticut has the highest annual cost per malpractice claim.[20] Further, Connecticut has had three record-breaking obstetrical malpractice awards in the past several years: in 2005 a $36.5 million cerebral palsy award; in 2008 a $38.5 million award for a neurologically impaired infant; and in 2011 a $58.6 million cerebral palsy award. The 2011 $58.6 million award replaced the 2008 $38.5 million award as the largest medical malpractice award in Connecticut history.[21] Connecticut also does not have a cap on noneconomic damages, commonly referred to as a tort-cap, which is something ACOG stresses as a cure for liability crisis.

At the same time that the liability threat has been emphasized for maternity providers, changes in malpractice insurance coverage have caused them increased uncertainty. To deal with the risk of malpractice suits, maternity providers carry malpractice insurance; in fact, they are usually mandated by hospitals to purchase malpractice insurance to protect themselves in malpractice claims. There are two types of malpractice insurance: occurrence policies and claims-made policies. Occurrence policies cover all incidents that occur in the year the insurance premium is paid, regardless of when the claim is filed.[22] For example, if a baby was born in 2008 and her parents file a malpractice claim in 2012, the physician's malpractice insurance premiums paid in 2008 will cover him or her for that claim. This is in contrast to claims-made policies, which covers claims *filed* during the year the insurance premium is paid.[23] In this same example, the physician's 2008 premiums would cover only claims *filed* by a patient in 2008, meaning that if a birth occurred in 2008 and a claim of malpractice is filed in 2012, the 2012 premium would cover the claim.

The malpractice insurance industry has increasingly shifted to offering physicians claims-made policies. For example, in 2012, 61.6 percent of obstetricians had claims-made policies, while only 30.3 percent had occurrence coverage (8.1 percent of obstetricians were self-insured or had another unidentified type of malpractice insurance).[24] Claims-made policies are advantageous to medical malpractice insurance companies because these policies decrease the length of time between policy payment and settlement.[25] Insurers prefer shorter lags between policy payment and claims payment because there is less of a chance that inflation will have an effect on the size of the settlement or that a precedent-setting case will be decided that will increase the likelihood of a family winning a malpractice case.[26]

However, this shift in insurance coverage has had deleterious effects on physicians, "trapping" them in the profession because if they retire or stop practicing obstetrics they must still pay malpractice insurance premiums to cover any future claims that maybe filed within the medical malpractice statute of limitations, which varies by state, but is on average twelve years for newborns.[27] To stop obstetrical practice, physicians must pay a hefty "tail insurance" premium—typically 1.5 to 2 times the annual premium—that covers claims filed after the year the last premium was paid through the last year a patient could file a medical malpractice claim under the current statute of limitations.[28] This disadvantage was noted by a number of obstetricians, one of whom, Rosemary Steel, a relatively young obstetrician in her mid-thirties, is already aware of this issue: "Most malpractice insurance carriers will give claims-made insurance coverage. . . . [I am] only covered for the time that [I am] around paying the bill, and then, if I want to move away, I need to pay a tail. . . . So, I'm kind of shackled to where I am."

MATERNITY PROVIDERS' UNDERSTANDING OF THE LIABILITY ENVIRONMENT

This feeling of being shackled because of changes in malpractice insurance policies is just the start of how aware maternity providers are of liability risk. Let me share a story to illustrate. I plan to drive across the state to interview physician Philip Burgin, but my schedule becomes too cluttered to manage the drive. I e-mail Doctor Burgin and offer to interview him by phone. I am surprised when he offers to make the three-hour round trip so that we can meet in person. Of course I agree, wondering why he is going to this trouble. We meet over coffee at a community college near my home, and it quickly becomes clear that Doctor Burgin is on a mission—to tell about the fear, anxiety, and worry he faces on a daily basis as an obstetrician. The meeting starts out as a lecture, but he softens once he figures out that I came not to indict him but rather to understand from his perspective why the c-section rate is increasing. What I learn from him is that every day he thinks about being sued and

worries about not being able to put his children through college because he might lose his ability to practice. "Do you face those fears as a college professor?" he asks me.

The fear and anxiety over liability expressed by Doctor Burgin are near-ubiquitous concerns expressed by the maternity providers I interviewed. Their anxiety and fear are tied to several potential professional and economic outcomes that might result from being named in a malpractice lawsuit, outcomes from which malpractice insurance does not protect them. I have grouped these anxieties into five themes.

The first anxiety is that if a maternity provider is involved in a malpractice suit, he or she may lose malpractice insurance coverage and subsequently face escalating malpractice insurance premiums. Physician Tony Oday says, "I know somebody recently who lost her insurance because she had three lawsuits. . . . She's a good physician. She just had some bad luck." Likewise, physician Leticia Stites worries that "if you have a case and you lose, you lose your ability to practice because your rates go so high you cart afford it." These two fears—being dropped from coverage and facing high premiums—go hand in hand. Malpractice insurance companies do not raise the premiums of high-risk physicians; these companies rarely "experience rate" medical providers.[29] What this means is that malpractice insurance companies charge the same premium to all obstetricians. Thus, rather than increasing the insurance rates of obstetricians who have malpractice claims filed against them, malpractice insurers may cancel their policies.[30] In such a case the provider will have to obtain malpractice insurance from a surplus line carrier, "insurers who specialize in hard-to-insure risks," and likely pay a much higher premium.[31]

A second anxiety is that a settlement or award will exceed a provider's malpractice insurance cap, usually $1 million, and that his or her personal assets will be vulnerable. Physician Lois Timberlake articulates this fear:

"I think we've all heard about these cases, where it's $15 million, $20 million [awards]. . . . You have limits on your policy, and if the award is beyond your limits, they can go after your house, your car, your whatever, which is a very scary thought." This concern is not without reason. A study of medical malpractice claims between 1991 and 2005 found that obstetricians were the most likely of physicians in all medical specialties to have claims closed in excess of $1 million.[32]

A third anxiety deals with the actual process of the lawsuit and the time and effort it takes to be involved in a malpractice proceeding. Nurse Jane Rios describes how this anxiety affects physicians:

> We've had . . . physicians [who] have gone through [a lawsuit], and they've actually won their cases. But the time, the effort, the gray hairs that lead up to that day that you actually win the case—you age yourself ten to fifteen years just with all the stuff that you have to go through to get to it. And, yes, you win [but] . . . you would never want to do [it] again.

Part of the frustration mentioned by Nurse Rios is no doubt due to the length of time it takes to resolve claims of medical malpractice. Between 1999 and 2002 the average length of time from the occurrence of an alleged malpractice to the closing of the malpractice claim in obstetrics was four years, but 13 percent of claims took seven or more years from occurrence to resolution.[33] Physician Philip Burgin pinpoints this anxiety when he tells me, "Being in a suit is a nightmare. It totally envelops your life for the five to seven years it takes to play out. You're constantly worried; you're constantly doubting yourself; you have nervous anxiety attacks; you have acid stomach . . . . Imagine the worst thing [that] can happen hanging over your head for seven years."

Beyond economic fears of paying high malpractice premiums or losing personal assets in a lawsuit, maternity providers worry about their reputations being impinged by being publicly exposed as having committed malpractice. Physician Joe Haley greets me in the lobby of the hospital. "Can I buy you coffee?" he asks. Fresh coffee in hand, we ride the elevator to the labor and delivery floor—he is on call today—and search for an empty seminar room. On our way he greets nurses by name with a smile and a wave. He is friendly and seems quite popular. We find a seminar room and sit down across the table from each other. He slides a few sheets of paper in front of me. He has printed out material from prosecuting malpractice attorneys' websites about obstetrical malpractice suits they have won and points out to me how they negatively portray the physician involved. He points me to one about a friend of his who was sued: "You're named on a public website [reading from the printout]: 'If the evidence had shown that [City] Hospital and Dr. [Jager] [his friend] were not at fault, we would have gone that way. We didn't see anything that showed us remotely that they weren't liable.'" Physician Haley was particularly disturbed by this case because, knowing the details, he felt that Dr. Jager had not committed a medical error.

Finally, maternity providers worry that a lawsuit will haunt them for the rest of their professional careers. Physician Geneva Spalding tells me, "Once you've been named in a suit, forever and ever . . . every time you apply for licensing . . . you have to write a whole paragraph about the [incident]. . . . It follows you . . . . If you move to another state, you need to get a certificate from the state." Midwife Rita Morey concurs with this frustration: "Once you have had a suit brought against you, regardless of the outcome, when you go to get privileged at any institution, you have to report it, and you have to explain what happened, why you were sued, what the outcome was, and why. And it becomes a really onerous process."

Being involved with a negative birth outcome exacerbates these anxieties. Physician Joe Haley tells me that after a negative birth outcome, "you look at the mailbox every day if you have an outcome like [shoulder dystocia], and you're going to see the return address from some sort of litigator's firm. And you watch the mailbox every day. It's really painful." It is clear from my conversation with him that Doctor Haley is consumed with anxiety, much of which is due to his being personally involved in a malpractice case.

Physician Andrew Robinette, another physician I interview in the hospital while he is on call, has a similar take on what it is like to be sued:

> The stress on family, on marriages, on sense of self-esteem . . . . There are better ways to make money than being an obstetrician—be an orthopedist, be a radiologist . . . . But people do this essentially because they really want to help people. And you get sued . . . . In cases that these often arise from, they are frantically trying to do their best. It's a situation of high stress where you've got to make on-the-spot decisions . . . . Their adrenaline is high; they're emotionally invested, and, yet, things don't go well. And then you get sued for it . . . . You're beating yourself up already. Can you imagine what that does to someone's self-esteem?

What was clear to me in talking with maternity providers and is so eloquently stated by Doctor Robinette is that maternity providers typically go into maternity care because they want to help women and babies. They fear bad outcomes not just because they'll be sued, but also because they want to promote the health of women and babies. The anxiety they face is that they will be held responsible for bad outcomes that they tried their absolute hardest to prevent. This is a common notion expressed by maternity providers. Physician Terri Diggs sums this up nicely:

> With obstetrics there is so much unpredictability, and bad things that can occur despite the most optimal care given. . . . It's likely that the doctor will be sued whether or not they did anything wrong . . . . You have a jury that feels

sympathetic to a damaged infant. They want to blame somebody, and they tend to blame the doctor, even if it has nothing to do with the care given by the doctor.

Doctor Diggs sees obstetrics as a special case, and most maternity providers feel this way. They feel that the unpredictability of bad birth outcomes means that these unfortunate occurrences are random events, though ones for which the doctors are held responsible. In fact, the academic literature on the malpractice supports this fear. For example, most malpractice payments are awarded for injuries that are not the result of medical error.[34] Further, research also finds that physicians who have had malpractice suits are not necessarily providing worse care than those who have not had suits.[35] This fear of the randomness of lawsuits is captured in the following interview excerpt from physician Leticia Stites:

> Most people have had lawsuits either discussed or papers served for a lawsuit, and I think it's random. It's like "ticktock" It's just going to happen to you one day because, again, it has nothing to do with how you practice, whether you're good or bad, whether malpractice has occurred or not, it just happens.

This feeling that obstetrical outcomes are not predictable and are not due to medical error is also apparent in way that physicians describe lawsuits. An example that came up repeatedly in my interviews is that of a severely disabled child. Physicians feel that monetary settlement happens in these cases regardless of whether medical error was committed. Research suggests that they have a point. The severity of a disability, rather than negligence, best predicts the payment of claims.[36] The following interview excerpt serves as an example of how physicians talk about being blamed for outcomes over which they feel they have no control. Notice in the following excerpt how physician Robert Hinson frames himself as a victim of the current malpractice legal environment, a common sentiment among obstetricians:

> I got sued for being a Good Samaritan once. . . . I got sued for a baby that had six feet of umbilical cord around the neck and a knot in that umbilical [cord]. And I delivered that baby by cesarean section. And that baby was not good neurologically thereafter. . . . And I settled that case because my [family member], who is an attorney, said to me, "If you take that baby and put it in front of the jury, they're not going to listen to anything that you have to say, and they're going to look at the baby and say, 'You're the deep pocket. We're going to give them more money than what you would have settled for,'" which was millions of dollars.

Another way physicians expressed this frustration of being held accountable for things beyond their control is how cases are sometimes settled on their behalf, because settling a case means admitting medical error. Physician Maggie Rust tells me, "We don't necessarily like that the hospital settles because then they're kind of admitting fault. And then . . . we get a little defensive: 'We didn't do anything wrong. Don't settle with them.' But we do understand that it's cheaper, sometimes for them to settle. But it is, it's frustrating either way." Notice again the articulation of a feeling of a loss of control.

It should also be understood that physicians are not the only ones who worry about being sued. Nurses and midwives share the fear that they will be held accountable for unpredictable outcomes. For example, nurses talk about the stress of dealing with patients who write down everything that happens during labor and birth and tell the nurses they will sue for any negative outcome. Nurse April Coleman describes this: "It's unbelievable how people come in looking for trouble. [They] tell you right off that they're keeping an eye on everything you do. . . . They're very forward about it . . . 'You better do everything right or I'm going to sue you.'"

I also heard of patients talking with providers at prenatal and well checkups about malpractice cases they know about from the news:

> People will come in and tell you these stories about how stupid this provider was and killed this baby, . . . and they dearly don't have . . . the clinical information to even know what really happened in the situation . . . . You have to be very careful because what they've said about other providers, goodness, they can be saying that about you if something bad happened.

Midwife Crystal Hereford is clear in her interview that liability is often on her mind. Similarly, nurse Anne Boudreaux shares this story with me: "When I worked at [City Hospital], I think that every nurse [who] worked there had been depositioned [in a malpractice case]. Every one. They were all talking about it all the time, [saying], 'Well, we have to do that because, what if we got sued?'"

I WISH I HADN'T GONE INTO THIS FIELD

Maternity providers' anxiety about liability has a number of consequences, one of which is a common regret about having gone into the obstetrics profession. For example, physician Joe Haley tells me that he discouraged his own children from entering a medical profession and was relieved when they went down different career paths. He did not want them to experience the anxiety he feels on a daily basis, an anxiety he believes is unavoidable in the medical world, especially obstetrics. Physicians expressed regret regularly about their own choice of occupation. Physician Janice O'Brien relays an interesting experience in which she and other obstetricians were attempting to recruit medical students into their specialty:

> The American College of Ob-Gyn [AGOG] put out a big effort to . . . recruit people to

our [specialty], and we had meetings with the students at Yale and [University of Connecticut]. . . . And it was hard because all the guys in practice are trying to say this is a great profession . . . and yet we're all going, "I [would not] to do it again."

She described their disingenuousness in their recruitment efforts because they recognized they would not choose this profession if they had it to do over again. They had regrets.

Beyond having negative feelings about the profession, some physicians drop out of obstetrical practice altogether. I interviewed two gynecologists who had recently stopped practicing obstetrics and heard tales of others who had done the same—one who is now "home baking cookies." Gynecologist Terri Diggs tells me of her decision: "The fear of litigation especially in regards to obstetrics is just profound in this state and the cost both financially and emotionally I just thought were in excess of what I, was willing [to pay] to continue doing OB." Doctor Diggs is not alone in her analysis. Survey research finds that physicians with high malpractice insurance rates are less satisfied with their careers, and physicians often cite liability risk as the reason they stop practicing obstetrics.[37]

Midwives and nurses also experience a desire to leave the profession to avoid liability threats. One nurse I interviewed is working on her credentials to become a nurse-practitioner, a job she thinks will be less stressful than being a labor and delivery nurse. Another nurse squelched her hopes of becoming a midwife because she did not want to increase her liability risk. Similarly, midwife Ada Medlin speaks about her dilemma with continuing obstetrical care: "There were some recent suits in the state [involving] . . . midwives [who] I knew very well, and who are great, wonderful providers, and it just makes you kind of think twice. . . . Do I want to take this risk? Is it worth it with a family, at this point in my life, to do this?"

PRACTICING DEFENSIVELY: A WAY TO SURVIVE

Another way maternity providers deal with liability anxiety is to practice defensively. It is common to hear that physicians practice "defensive medicine"—that is, they perform procedures and tests not to protect the health of the patient but rather to prevent malpractice liability. From my interviews, it is clear this is not just conjecture in the case of obstetrics. Defensive practices happen regularly. For example, physician Jack Bianco tells me:

> I will promise you a third of what I do is defensive medicine . . . if you really want to use honest criteria. Do I really believe I have to do everything that I do? No. But I do it because if something bad happens, someone can't blame me for not having done it . . . . Am I causing harm by doing a c-section in this situation? I potentially am. But I can't control that.

Renowned political theorist Carl J. Friedrich refers to such defensive practices as "the rule of anticipated reaction."[38] This concept refers to authoritative structures that guide individuals on how to act to avoid negative consequences or to secure positive consequences. In the context of c-sections, the rule of anticipated reaction operates when a physician decides to perform a c-section or other interventions because of a belief that he or she will be less likely to be sued for doing the surgery than for facilitating a vaginal birth. It is important to understand, however, that as much as the public responds negatively to the term "defensive medicine," individual maternity providers do not decide on the action that is defensive. Rather, defensive practices are defined by organizations as a way to prevent liability, in this case c-sections. Such a definition has authority over providers, even though it may not be obvious that organizations have this type of control. I argue here that organizations such as ACOG, malpractice insurers, courts, and hospitals have defined liability as a problem and c-sections as the solution to this problem. Practicing defensively takes a number of forms.

DOCUMENT EVERYTHING: THE BEST SOLUTION IN THE CASE OF A BAD OUTCOME

A common response to liability anxiety of maternity providers—nurses, midwives, and physicians—is a heightened focus on documentation. Documentation becomes a way for maternity providers to demonstrate that they are providing adequate care; they have learned that *lack of documentation* may be used in a malpractice claim to suggest that a bad outcome was due to medical error. Maternity providers must constantly document that they did the right thing. If something isn't documented, it's as good as not done. Especially because of the unpredictable nature of many adverse obstetrical outcomes, a focus on documentation of every labor and every birth becomes almost obsessive among providers. They don't know which labor will end badly. This means every case has to be well documented. Below are two telling examples of how maternity providers use increased vigilance in documentation to avert liability threats:

> I think about malpractice with every single patient I encounter, . . . and the doctor who doesn't is asking for trouble. . . Every phone call, every office visit, every hospital encounter-I think about malpractice. . . . Every time I write a note about a phone call, about an office visit, or about something else in the hospital, I think, "How will this look in court?" (Physician Philip Burgin)
>
> I'm always thinking, "Am I going to be able to stand up in court with what I'm writing? . . . Is this going to pass muster if I'm on the stand?" You always have to keep that in mind as you're doing your documentation. (Nurse April Colman)

Nurses face a particular burden of documentation because unlike most physicians—who are typically self-employed or employed by obstetrical practices—nurses are almost always employed by hospitals, and hospitals provide malpractice insurance for their employees. The hitch, however, is that hospitals will not cover a nurse in a malpractice claim if she did not document that protocols were followed. In fact, consistently breaking protocols is a cause for termination of employment. As nurse Michele Saxton tells me, "If you're not keeping up on your reading and you're not up on your standards of care and you don't know the protocols, you'll get yourself in trouble. They won't protect you if you didn't follow those procedural policies." Thus nurses become the "enforcers" of protocols; the burden of "compliance" is placed on the least-powerful professional actors, a common practice in organizations. This burden was a common concern of nurses. Some may be surprised to hear that most nurses with whom I spoke are very critical of the way maternity care is being delivered, with a particular scorn toward interventions, such as routine inductions, use of Pitocin for labor acceleration, and, especially, non-medically indicated c-sections. I think this would especially surprise many midwives, who often have a somewhat cynical view of nurses. Nurses are structurally placed in a situation where they must enforce protocols and document that those protocols have been followed.

Excessive documentation becomes a common practice, and this imperative is spread throughout the profession in conferences and workshops that focus on malpractice prevention. These conferences and workshops almost inevitably emphasize the importance of documentation. Doctor Burgin follows up our interview with an e-mail message about a conference that teaches the importance of documentation to prevent liability:

> I thought it might interest you to know that I am going to a full-day seminar entitled: "Advanced Fetal Monitoring 2007 and Legal

Implications." There's no mistaking what this course is about. One of the lectures is titled: "Monitoring for Asphyxia: What You Need to Know and *Document*," The reality of the event is the same, but how you document it (and therefore how it's presented to a jury) is what counts. I think about law all day long.

Conferences spread documentation as the answer to liability threat and also perpetuate a focus on law among maternity providers.

Nurses and midwives attend the same type of conference presentations on malpractice prevention, as this interview excerpt from labor and delivery nurse Margie Napolitano suggests: "Definitely in the past five years or so, it's become a lot more scary for nurses and doctors because of the lawsuits and the legal issues. And a lot of conferences are focused on legal issues and documentation and all that." Midwives also discuss these types of conferences and presentations; for example, midwife Rosalie Batten describes how "in [university] teaching hospitals we have a risk reduction program. . . . We have to do this continuing-ed piece specifically for the insurance company for the risk-reduction program. . . . So we are constantly being bombarded with, 'This is the best legal defense.'"

C-SECTIONS: THEY'RE JUST LESS RISKY FOR US

One can see how, put in such a position, maternity providers may focus too much on how attorneys will perceive their actions. For example, physician Philip Burgin tells me, "[I think], 'This wouldn't have been a shoulder dystocia if you hadn't delivered that head.' Because the question posed to a doctor [is], 'If you'd done a c-section, would this baby be paralyzed now?' I hear lawyers talking in my head all the time." It is clear that Doctor Burgin thinks about liability and how attorneys will interpret his actions constantly, likely obsessively.

I heard tales of maternity providers' observing deviations from a normal labor and dwelling on similarities to previous bad outcomes, another defensive practice. This tendency is described well by midwife Crystal Hereford: "I can just think of so many physicians, [when] I'd have somebody in labor, . . . [the] physician saying, 'She has twenty minutes more, and I'm doing the c-section, because all I can think about is that last bad outcome I had.'"

Imagining bad outcomes and lawyers talking in their heads is just a short step to intervening any time labor is not going according to plan. As Physician Leticia Stites tells me, "That's where the scariness comes in. That it can be no fault of your own, an act of God, or just a spontaneous event, and you still get sued, and you still lose. So, here you have no control over that situation and . . . it definitely leads to a higher c-section rate where the outcome is immediate, and it's controlled, and no one can blame you for it." Similarly, physician Philip Burgin said, "I think if we do more c-sections it is going to result in [fewer] lawsuits. Not because there will be less difficult babies. I think we're still going to have cerebral palsy because no one knows what causes it. But because if you do a c-section you've done all you can do. Now the only question is did you do it early enough."

This easing into c-sections as a solution to liability threats becomes more apparent after a maternity provider is sued for malpractice. The threshold to move to a surgical delivery slips lower and lower. Many physicians reported to me that after they had been sued they began to jump more quickly to performing a c-section, another example of Friedrich's rule of anticipated action.[39] They are performing c-sections because they have learned that doing so may prevent a malpractice lawsuit. The following two interview excerpts illustrate this:

It became more personal when I was sued. . . . There was particularly one case . . . I don't know if the child would have been OK or not. But that was the allegation—that a c-section would have helped. . . . After that my threshold became much lower. Although probably 95, 99 percent of the patients with that same situation would have been OK, I kept thinking to myself, "OK, for that one percent, it's such a catastrophic outcome for the child, for the parents, and then for me, not only because I care for the patient, but then going through the whole process of a suit." . . . Nobody really wants to take that chance. And so you don't. (Physician Lois Timberlake)

I have been [what] I'll call the victim of medical malpractice lawsuits, and with that experience and also . . . now paying over $120,000 a year for malpractice premiums, I've realized that there's a huge implication of our legal system on why the cesarean section rates are going up. And, I think, if I were to move tomorrow to Montreal [Canada] and practice medicine, my cesarean section rate would immediately go down because I would not be set up in the same manner of really intimidation by what's happening out there. (Physician Robert Hinson)[40]

Nurses also see physicians jumping quickly to c-sections, especially after a physician has been involved in a malpractice suit. Nurse Amanda Barnett tells me:

You watch how the physicians are practicing now, and because of malpractice and things that have happened in our own state. . . . Doctors [who] I have worked with for fourteen years, who we call the men and women with "all the feel," they would watch a strip [with] variables and decels, and they'd [say], "Let's try this, let's try that—change position, use amnioinfusion, give herb tea," whatever. . . . Let's just say there were five things that you could do when a strip looked bad. Now they are trying one or two things, and if it's not immediately better, we go down the hall for a c-section.

Perhaps the most shocking story I heard comes from physician Joe Haley, the mild-mannered, friendly obstetrician who bought me coffee. He lowers his eyes and speaks quietly when he says, "I call my wife when I'm hanging out in labor and delivery, and I say, 'Oh, the strip looks like this,' and she says, 'Just do a section.' [I feel threatened], and in a serious way, because . . . I mean, she's not a doctor. But you really are vulnerable, and there's really no protection." This is perhaps the most telling example of the fear maternity providers face in modern maternity care. Asking one's nonphysician spouse for advice on how to manage a woman's labor seems unbelievable, but it does happen, perhaps in this case as a way Doctor Haley manages his stress and anxiety over caring for women with complicated deliveries.

WHERE THE AUTHORITATIVE RULES ORIGINATE: THE ROLE OF ORGANIZATIONS

Maternity providers feel caught in a bind. The defined way to escape being held accountable for unpreventable negative birth outcomes is to perform a c-section. Then, if a bad outcome happens, they are less likely to be blamed—they did all they could. From the perspective of maternity providers, they are caught in the fundamental irrationality of organizational change. Organizations have defined c-sections as the answer to liability threat. This definition causes maternity providers to change their behavior and perform more c-sections because they fear if they do not they will be blamed for bad birth outcomes, even those outcomes that are not preventable or predictable. The current economic, political, and legal environment binds organizations, and organizations change to protect organizational interests. In this case, professional organizations, malpractice insurers, courts, and hospitals have coalesced in their suggestion that c-sections solve liability threats.

The most common way that providers learn about c-sections being a solution to liability is by being involved in a lawsuit or hearing about a malpractice lawsuit where the maternity provider is asked by the litigating attorney why a c-section was not performed, with the underlying accusation being that a c-section would have prevented the bad outcome. Physician Lawrence Rascon makes clear his feeling that courts have defined c-sections as the solution to bad birth outcomes and liability threats:

> Every time an obstetrician gets sued for a bad outcome of a pregnancy, the one thing in every trial is, "You should have done the cesarean section." . . . And I think you hear that every single time and every malpractice case you hear or read about: . . . "You should have done a section," or "You should have done a section earlier.". . . And after a while everybody says, "Well, if that's what we have to do, then that's what we have to do."

Courts also enforce this view by focusing on the timing of the c-section. For example, physician Robert Hinson tells me, "When you get deposed in a malpractice lawsuit . . . you will be asked if you could have done the cesarean five or ten minutes earlier or done it an hour earlier . . . and could that have made the difference." In short, what maternity providers tell me repeatedly is that the message they get from courts on how to prevent malpractice suits is to perform more c-sections and to perform them early. Surgical birth becomes the answer to preventing liability threats, even though there is little evidence that c-sections prevent most bad outcomes.

I also commonly heard about the role of professional workshops and conferences. As I mentioned just a few pages ago, these workshops and conferences teach maternity providers the importance of documentation in preventing liability threats. However, the messages from these workshops and conferences go beyond documentation that protocols were diligently followed. Physicians talk about how these types of conferences affect how they assess risk in labor. Physician Philip Burgin speaks about a workshop he attended in which a prominent malpractice insurance plaintiffs' attorney lectured: "One of the plaintiffs' lawyers said something I [will] never [forget]: 'OK, if you're thinking about a c-section, you should be doing a c-section.'" Similarly, physician Lois Timberlake tells me of a lecture she attended at a professional conference: "There was one lecture I heard at a New England ob-gyn society meeting. . . . He started out as an obstetrician, and then he got his law degree, and he was very much, 'When in doubt, section . . . don't even think twice about it.'" In other words, attorneys spread fear of bad outcomes *and* c-section as an answer to this fear.

Litigating attorneys also spread fear of liability by seeking potential clients through advertising on local radio and television stations. Physicians commonly spoke about litigation attorneys' television commercials that target them for malpractice lawsuits. Physician Rosemary Steel tells me, "I'm sure you've seen those commercials with the lawyers saying, 'Is your child not as smart as you think [she] should be? Maybe it was a birth injury. Why don't you give us a call?' I mean, those kinds of commercials, of course, drive me crazy because they're picking on things that don't even exist sometimes." These types of media presentations are perceived as threatening to maternity providers.

Once this definition of c-sections as relief to liability threats takes hold, the definition spreads among providers, even those who have not been sued. I heard this sentiment countless times in my interviews; it seems to be an unwavering belief among all types of maternity providers-nurses, midwives, and physicians-here expressed by physician Maggie Rust: "There is a whole perception that if you have a bad outcome but you've done a c-section that you're not as much at risk being the physician as you are if you had a bad outcome and you had a vaginal delivery."

ARE C-SECTIONS JUST MORE CONVENIENT FOR OBSTETRICIANS?

It is important here to digress for just a moment to examine the idea that physicians perform c-sections out of convenience, something that is heard in everyday conversation. I argue that convenience should be understood within the organizational constraints physicians face. For example, physicians would likely rather do c-sections outside of office hours rather than attend vaginal births during office hours because they need to see patients to earn money to pay skyrocketing malpractice premiums. Most health insurance companies pay a global fee for birth. That means that health insurance companies pay the physician a single rate, usually between $2,500 and $3,500, for all prenatal visits and the birth. Physicians are not compensated for attending a long labor, and if a physician interrupts office hours to attend a birth, he or she will potentially lose money by not seeing scheduled patients. Remember, as malpractice insurance premiums escalate, obstetricians must see more and more patients just to cover that increased rate. Protecting office hours becomes a necessity. Further, although providers performing c-sections in the evening may seem to smack of convenience, it is also the case that evening c-sections allow providers not to miss any office hours and to sleep at night. Getting a good night's sleep is in the interest of providers who, because of increasing malpractice insurance rates, feel a pressure to see patients as many days in the week as possible. Many maternity providers told me they often have a full slate of patients, even if they were on the call the night before. Obstetricians also expressed concern. about the safety of c-sections during the nighttime because everyone is likely to be more tired.

In other words, liability may underlie convenience, because of the pressure to earn money to pay malpractice insurance premiums. It may be that some physicians are performing c-sections to go play golf or to go to dinner, but with most physicians operating in group practices, this is not as much of a concern as it used to be with solo practices. In short, organizational constrains are a better explanation of practices that seem to be convenient for physicians.

CONCLUSION

"My goal is that everybody goes home healthy and happy, and I don't get sued. . . . That's my goal. And maybe I get paid. . . . Everybody's happy . . . For me that's a perfect case," physician Philip Burgin tells me toward the end of the interview. Maternity providers have learned from courts, conferences, professional organizations, hospitals, insurers, and the media that the way to prevent liability threats is to perform c-sections. Organizational structures define c-sections as an answer to the liability threats faced by maternity providers. The rule of anticipated reaction is in play. Maternity providers try to avoid negative consequences by jumping quickly to c-sections. This is a way that organizations control behavior, even though it may not be apparent that organizations are behind individuals' decisions. As physician Jack Bianco tells me:

> So why not? . . . We're not stupid. You kick us long enough, we respond. Do we believe in it? No. Do I believe we're doing far too many c-sections? Absolutely. But every once in a while, you'll try to let someone labor longer, even if it's unpredictable because nature's unpredictable, shoulder events, something will happen, and we'll get blamed for it. So until society decides it doesn't t want to put up with this anymore, we're going to continue to move in this direction because that's what society has asked us to do.

Organizations have responded to uncertain legal, political, and economic environments, and one response that has coalesced among organizations has been to define c-sections as the gold standard for a "safe" birth.

Still, women do not commonly perceive that their births are being held in the hands of providers who feel backed into a corner. They trust their doctors and believe that if they recommend a c-section, it must be necessary. The Listening to Mothers II Survey found that, while 62 percent of women believe that the current malpractice system causes providers to take better care of their patients, well less than half believe that providers would perform an unnecessary c-section to avoid being sued.[41] Trust in providers was a common sentiment, here expressed in the words of Dianne, a thirty-four-year-old woman who delivered her second child by c-section after two hours of pushing failed to result in a vaginal birth: "I mean I'm happy. The baby is safe, and I'm OK. I was avoiding a c-section. . . . I had to go through all possible ways of having a vaginal delivery, but I still couldn't get a vaginal delivery. Yeah, so it was a little disappointing, but at the end all that matters is a healthy baby and healthy me, of course. Right?" What would women like Dianne think if they knew how preoccupied their providers are with being blamed for a bad outcome? Would they so easily discount their desire for a vaginal birth?

NOTES

1. Klagholz and Strunk 2009 (emphasis added).
2. Sloan and Chepke 2008.
3. Ibid.
4. Ibid.
5. Klagholz and Strunk 2012.
6. Gherman et al. 2006; Clark and Hankins 2003; Sokol, Blackwell, and American College of Obstetricians and Gynecologists 2003; Blair and Stanley 1993.
7. See, for example, Baker 2005; and Centner 2008.
8. Klagholz and Strunk 2012.
9. Jena et al. 2011.
10. Greve 2009.
11. Klagholz and Strunk 2012.
12. Ibid.
13. Ibid.
14. See, for example, Baker 2005; and Centner 2008.
15. This is thought to be the result of both high costs of litigating malpractice suits and litigating attorneys' reluctance to assume any cases that do not have a good chance of a high settlement or judgment. See Sloan and Chepke 2008.
16. Ibid., 61.
17. Author's calculations from National Practitioner Data Blank public data set available from U.S. Department of Heal and Human Services 2010.
18. Author's calculations using data available for purchase from *Medical Liability Monitor*.
19. Sloan and Chepke 2008, 59.
20. State of Connecticut Insurance Department 2009.
21. Sturdevant 2011, 1.
22. Mello 2006.
23. Ibid.
24. Klagholz and Strunk 2012.
25. Mello 2006; Hay 1992.
26. Hay 1992.
27. Shea et al. 2008.
28. Shi and Singh 2012.
29. Sloan and Chepke 2008.
30. Ibid.
31. Ibid., 10.
32. Jena et al. 2011.
33. Mavroforou, Koumantakis, and Michalodimitrakis 2005.
34. Localio et al. 1991 also find that most victims of medical errors are not compensated.
35. Sloan and Chepke 2008.
36. Brennan, Sox, and Burstin 1996.
37. Xu et al. 2008.
38. Friedrich 1963, 16.
39. Ibid.
40. In 2001, the most recent comparison I could find, there were 350 percent more malpractice claims filed per 1,000 population in the United States than in Canada, although the actual claims paid in the United States were somewhat lower than claims paid in Canada. See Anderson et al. 2005.
41. Declercq et al. 2006.

SECTION V

Special Populations Targeted for Reproductive Control

When we talk about reproductive self-determination, we often imagine this is a situation in which individuals are—or should be—free to determine the families they want, under the conditions in which they want to live. This view accepts that individuals are experts on their own lives and know what they need. We easily assume each person is free to choose for herself what she wants and has the resources to implement her choices. Yet, if we focus solely on individual choice, it becomes easy to ignore how different groups face different kinds of state surveillance, stereotypes, or material obstacles to exercising that choice. Race, language, immigration, sexuality, disability, or criminal history might all make certain choices unavailable to some individuals, while making them easily attainable for others. Indeed, as we discuss in the introduction to the next section, scholars and activists associated with the reproductive justice movement have challenged the very use of the term "choice" with respect to reproductive issues for this reason.

In this section we consider how women who are in particularly vulnerable situations in a number of different ways face stereotypes about their adequacy as women and mothers, and experience additional barriers to reproductive self-determination. Although this is by no means an exhaustive discussion, we have selected a few exemplars among a wide array of groups that are targeted and whose reproduction is identified as a problem in need of control.

COERCED CONTROL

The willingness to control others' reproduction stems from a few sources. First, often one group's reproduction is identified as the *cause of social problems*. For example, poor women's reproduction has been blamed for welfare dependency, poverty, and poor child outcomes, and politicians have imposed social policies designed to discourage childbearing among this group, as discussed in the selection in this section from Rickie Solinger's book, *Beggars and Choosers*. Teenagers' childbearing is assumed to cause them to drop out of school, even as much research shows that most teen parents experienced failure in school before becoming pregnant (Geronimus and Korenman 1992; Luker 1985). Rather than addressing the underlying causes of poverty or the reasons why teens leave school, political and popular rhetoric focuses on the groups themselves.

Second, we note the persistence of eugenic ideology in the U.S. It is tempting to look at the flowering of eugenic thinking in the early 20th century that we mentioned in earlier sections—President Theodore Roosevelt's famous statement about "race suicide" because of his concern about higher birth rates among European immigrants than among white native-born Protestant women and the many states that permitted forced sterilization that lasted well into the 1960s—as unfortunate chapters in our national history, and no longer relevant. Yet, ideologies of eugenics—namely that some people's reproduction is more valuable than others and that some groups' reproduction leads to social problems or population inferiority—continue. In this section, we focus on a few different groups who have been targeted for reproductive control. As we discuss these groups, the reader should note that their experiences also intersect with other forms of inequality, most persistently race and class. So, for example, as we discuss the experiences of women who are sanctioned for drug or alcohol use, one should understand that these sanctions are disproportionately applied to poor women and women of color, even as much research shows that these groups do not use drugs or alcohol at higher rates (Chasnoff et al. 1990; Ellsworth et al. 2010). Similarly, the criminal justice system has significant racial and socioeconomic bias in conviction and sentencing (Mustard 2001; Petersilia and Reitz 2012). This means that while women who are incarcerated face significant barriers to reproductive health and self-determination, this is an issue disproportionately affecting women of color and poor women.

DRUG USE AND PREGNANCY

Public hysteria about the reproduction of women who use drugs became widespread in the mid-1980s. Building on the social panic known as the "crack epidemic," media reports often discussed the plight of newborns whose mothers had used cocaine during pregnancy. Although the reported crack epidemic has proven to have been mostly hype, the coverage focused largely on women who smoked this inexpensive form of cocaine, who reportedly lacked maternal instinct and who harmed their fetuses during pregnancy. These babies, quickly labeled "crack babies" by the media, were initially described as damaged, including small, "irritable, inconsolable, developmentally delayed, and incapable of love," reportedly suffered from "Alzheimer's-like symptoms," and were expected to be learning-disabled (Siegel 1997, 255). Long-term research shows that the effects of drug use during pregnancy were significantly overstated. In fact, when compared with other children in the same neighborhoods whose mothers did not use drugs, they were indistinguishable. More robust research shows that illicit drugs have virtually no effect on fetal development (Frank et al. 2001; Gomez 1997). Nonetheless, the legal responses to pregnant women who use drugs have been tough and unyielding. This is in notable contrast to alcohol use during pregnancy, which is more damaging but receives little attention.

One result has been continued efforts to drug test women and their newborns at delivery. One of the most dramatic early examples of this was a program in South Carolina where a county hospital reported any pregnant women who tested positive for illicit drugs to the district attorneys for prosecution. In the three years the program ran, 87 women were charged criminally with neglect or distribution of drugs to a minor, and at least 43 others were coerced into treatment with threat of prosecution. Most of the women who have been prosecuted for drug use—in South Carolina and other venues—have been women of color, a pattern consistent with research that shows that after controlling for poverty and other variables, women of color are still more likely to be reported for prenatal substance abuse than are other women, even though they are no more likely to use illicit drugs than white women (Chasnoff et al. 1990).

These criminal charges were later ruled to be unconstitutional. Challenging the South Carolina program specifically, the U.S. Supreme Court ruled in *Ferguson v. City of Charleston*

(2001) that drug testing pregnant women without consent and disclosing results to law enforcement represents an unconstitutional search. Nonetheless, the pattern of reporting drug using pregnant and perinatal women to law enforcement and child welfare agencies has continued.

One of the costs of these policies that target pregnant women is that they lose the ability to access care for fear of sanctions should they disclose their current or past drug use. In one recent case Alicia Beltran, a 28-year-old Wisconsin woman who was 14 weeks pregnant, told a physician assistant that she had become addicted to Percocet, a painkiller, the prior year but had stopped using the drug on her own. Despite evidence that she was indeed drug-free, she was involuntarily held in a drug treatment facility against her will for 78 days, in order to protect her fetus (Eckholm 2013). Wisconsin is one of four states with laws that allow authorities to confine pregnant women for substance use against their will. Other states allow family members to civilly commit a pregnant woman against her will. Others allow the state to take custody of newborn babies at birth if their mothers have used drugs before or during pregnancy. Some also permit women to be prosecuted. The Beltran case is one in which a woman was subjected to drug treatment she did not need, yet at the same time, as suggested above, pregnant women who *do* wish treatment for drug addiction are afraid to seek out such treatment because they fear that they will be arrested and their newborns will be taken away from them—again, an example of the "too much—too little" theme that characterizes the world of reproduction to which we have pointed throughout this book.

INCARCERATED WOMEN

Women who are incarcerated often face other challenges to their reproduction. Between 1990 and 2009, the number of women who are incarcerated increased by more than 150%, mostly for non-violent offenses like property crimes or drug-related offenses. Approximately 6–10% of women who are incarcerated are pregnant, with rates estimated to be higher in juvenile facilities (ACOG 2013b). Despite claims of concern for the well-being of fetal health, state agencies often fail to ensure that women who are incarcerated receive safe and appropriate healthcare. Women are assigned physically challenging work that jeopardizes their pregnancy and are denied access to good nutrition, supplements, or medical attention when needed (Flavin 2008). Although numerous professional organizations, including the American Public Health Association, the American Congress of Obstetricians and Gynecologists, the National Women's Law Center, the American Medical Association, the National Commission on Correctional Healthcare, the American Correctional Association, the Federal Bureau of Prisons, the Immigration and Customs Enforcement Agency, and the Association of Women's Health, Obstetric & Neonatal Nursing, have issued guidelines about appropriate care for incarcerated pregnant women, as of 2013, only 37 states and the District of Columbia have issued specific policies as to the care of pregnant women. But of these states, many provide very little specificity in their own policies or take few of the professional guidelines seriously. For example, according to a recent ACLU report, only 13 of these 38 states specify that medical examinations should be included in prenatal care and only seven states require that women's pregnancies be tracked and the outcomes recorded. Nationwide, only 20 states (plus DC) have policies in place which specify how incarcerated women who wish to terminate a pregnancy should be treated (ACLU 2013). The physician Naomi Stotland, in her selection in this section, gives a portrait of one dedicated obstetrician/gynecologist who is attempting to bring humane care to women in a California prison.

Women who are pregnant and incarcerated also face other challenges to their care. Until recently it was common for women, even those convicted of non-violent offenses, or simply detained for a traffic stop, to deliver their babies while shackled to the bed (Sichel 2007), as mentioned in the introduction and section six, or held in restraints. In 2009, the Eighth Circuit Court of Appeals ruled that woman have a right not to be shackled in labor, a decision that matched that of other courts. Even with these decisions, only sixteen states ban the use of restraints of pregnant women in labor in law, while another eight ban shackling as a matter of policy (ACLU 2013).

Women who are incarcerated also face assumptions that they should not reproduce. Echoing the eugenics rhetoric of the last century, many women find themselves facing pressure or deception to consent to sterilization. In a recent example, nearly 150 women in California prisons were sterilized between 2006–2010, despite state and federal laws that ban the procedure unless it is medically necessary. These women appear to have been targeted because prison staff perceived them likely to return to prison in the future or had previously been incarcerated. These inmates' history of poverty may have also been a motivating factor. James Heinrich, one of the physicians who performed many of the tubal ligations and received more than $147,000 for doing so, explained why his payments do not constitute much money. "Over a 10-year period, that isn't a huge amount of money," he explained, "compared to what you save in welfare paying for these unwanted children as they procreated more" (Johnson 2013, A1). This is a recent example that illustrates the ways the ideologies of eugenics still persist with real consequences.

In a landmark recent study (2013), lawyer Lynn Paltrow and sociologist Jeanne Flavin, both with the organization National Advocates for Pregnant Women, tabulated over 400 cases (between 1973 and 2005) of pregnant women who were subject to arrests, detentions and enforced medical procedures (such as forced Cesarean sections) for various reasons. Those targeted were disproportionately women of color. In the selection in this section by Paltrow, "*Roe v Wade* and the new Jane Crow," she summarizes this research and draws the connections between current attacks on abortion (particularly the efforts to established legal "personhood" rights for fertilized eggs and fetuses) and those on pregnant women.

DISABLED WOMEN

Reproductive rights are complex for women with physical or cognitive disabilities. In theory, women with disabilities are entitled to the same rights to determine their own reproduction as any other woman. Yet, their reproduction is frequently seen as a problem. First, many professionals assume that women with disabilities are uninterested or incapable of becoming pregnant, birthing children, or being a mother. While disabled women may face different challenges in caring for their children, they are able to do so with the necessary supports in place. For example, women with physical disabilities might need adapted changing tables, or other physical modifications to make their parenting work easier. Women with cognitive disabilities are more likely to succeed with family support or help from social services, but, again, in most cases they are capable of successfully parenting if these supports are in place.

Disabled women are often not assumed to be sexually active. This makes them less likely to receive comprehensive sexual education, information about contraception, or support in family planning. As women who are not imagined to be ideal reproducers, they often receive substandard care. A number of clinics, however, have long sought to tailor services specifically to women with physical and mental disabilities (Alvares et al. 2011), but this is not yet the norm. In general, disabled women face challenges of both continuing pregnancies they want or maintaining the ability to reproduce, even when others assume they should not. Several recent legal cases in which care providers, mentally retarded or mentally ill women, and family have competing preferences for pregnancy outcomes show how complicated these issues are. In one such case, a Massachusetts woman called "Mary Moe" was 31 years old, suffered delusions and schizophrenia, and was pregnant for the third time. Her parents, who had custody of her son, requested that she be declared incompetent so they could become her guardians and consent to an abortion on her behalf. While the initial judge granted her parents guardianship, an appeals court overruled that decision so that Moe could continue her pregnancy, even as she is not expected to be able to care for that baby after birth. Cases like these highlight the complex nature of reproductive decision-making and the challenges of supporting reproductive rights, of evaluating what informed decision-making might look like, including how pregnancy might exacerbate other health conditions, and considering what comprehensive care and support may be required.

A second bias limits disabled women's access to support for their reproductive lives. There is a fear that women with disabilities will pass down their condition to their children. Again underscoring the long history of eugenics, many attitudes about disabled women stem from a belief that they should not reproduce. While this is true of women with physical disabilities, it is more often seen with women with cognitive disabilities who face significant discrimination. Although some disabilities may be inheritable, which require more in-depth counseling and education for individuals to make informed decisions about their reproductive plans, in fact, the broader assumptions that disabled people should not reproduce are often more widespread and not closely linked to measurable health outcomes. The selection in this section by disability scholars Virginia Kallianes and Phyliss Rubenfeld further discusses the challenges of disabled women to achieve their reproductive rights.

IMMIGRANT WOMEN

Immigrant populations in the U.S. have greatly increased in the past 50 years. In 2011, there were 40.4 million foreign-born people residing in the United States, whereas the immigrant population in 1960 was 9.7 million. Today, women outnumber men among immigrants to the United States (Garcia 2013). Women who have emigrated from another country also face particular challenges to their efforts to determine their reproductive lives. First, women who are not citizens have limited options for health care. Most states and the federal government ban undocumented immigrants from participating in public health insurance programs, including the ACA. Although they can access emergency services, including labor and delivery, they do not have access to other services, including prenatal care, contraception, cancer screenings, or STI treatment which can prevent infertility. Immigrant women are most likely to work in hazardous conditions, including those that expose them to toxins that could be risky to their reproduction health, to be low paid, and to be vulnerable (ACOG 2013a). They are also more likely to be at risk because of their immigrant status. For women who are undocumented, access to care and navigating health systems can be difficult (Deeb-Sossa 2013; Hasstedt 2013), as can the risks of being pregnant while under investigation by immigration enforcement agencies. In fact, some of the high profile cases of women who have been shackled while in labor have involved women detained because of concerns about their immigration status. Other undocumented women have lost access to their young children when immigration raids have occurred in low paying factories where they were employed

(Capps et al. 2007). The selection in this chapter by Michelle Chen examines the particular difficulties that immigrant women have with respect to reproductive issues.

REFERENCES

ACLU. 2013. *State Standards for Pregnancy-Related Health Care and Abortion for Women in Prison*. American Civil Liberties Union.

ACOG. 2013a. *Environmental Chemicals Harm Reproductive Health: Ob-Gyns Advocate for Policy Changes to Protect Health*, September 23 2013a [cited January 3, 2014].

———. 2013b. *Health Care for Pregnant and Postpartum Incarcerated Women and Adolescent Females*. Edited by Committee on Health Care for Underserved Women: American Congress of Obstetricians and Gynecologists.

Alvares, Lisa, Heidi A. Case, Emily J. Kronenberger, Stephanie Ortoleva, and Joanne L. Tosti-Vasey. 2011. *Reproductive Health Justice for Women with Disabilities*. Center for Women Policy Studies.

Capps, Randy, Rosa Maria Castañeda, Ajay Chaudry, and Robert Santos. 2007. *Paying the Price: The Impact of Immigration Raids on America's Children*. Urban Institute.

Chasnoff, Ira J., Harvey J. Landress, and Mark E. Barrett. 1990. "The Prevalence of Illicit-Drug or Alcohol Use During Pregnancy and Discrepancies in Mandatory Reporting in Pinellas County, Florida." *New England Journal of Medicine* no. 322 (17):1202–1206.

Deeb-Sossa, N. 2013. *Doing Good: Racial Tensions and Workplace Inequalities at a Community Clinic in El Nuevo South*. Tucson: University of Arizona Press.

Eckholm, Erik. 2013. "Case Explores Rights of Fetus Versus Mother." *New York Times*, October 23, A1.

Ellsworth, Marc A., Timothy P. Stevens, and Carl T. D'Angio. 2010. "Infant Race Affects Application of Clinical Guidelines When Screening for Drugs of Abuse in Newborns." *Pediatrics* no. 125 (6):e1379–e1385. doi: 10.1542/peds.2008–3525.

Flavin, Jeanne. 2008. *Our Bodies, Our Crimes: The Policing of Women's Reproduction in America*. New York: NYU Press.

Frank, Deborah A., Marilyn Augustyn, Wanda Grant Knight, Tripler Pell, and Barry Zuckerman. 2001. "Growth, Development, and Behavior in Early Childhood Following Prenatal Cocaine Exposure: A Systematic Review." *JAMA* no. 285 (12):1613–1621.

Garcia, Ann. 2013. *The Facts on Immigration Today* (April 3). Center for American Progress, August 14, 2013.

Geronimus, Arline T., and Sanders Korenman. 1992. "The Socioeconomic Consequences of Teen Childbearing Reconsidered." *The Quarterly Journal of Economics* no. 107 (4):1187–1214.

Gomez, Laura E. 1997. *Misconceiving Mothers: Legislators, Prosecutors, and the Politics of Prenatal Drug Exposure*. Philadelphia: Temple University Press.

Hasstedt, K. 2013. "Toward Equity and Access: Removing Legal Barriers To Health Insurance Coverage for Immigrants." Guttmacher Policy Review, 16(1).

Johnson, Corey G. 2013. "Female Inmates Sterilized in California Prisons Without Approval." *Sacramento Bee*, July 7, 1A.

Kallianes, V., and Rubenfeld, P. 1997. "Disabled Women and Reproductive Rights." *Disability & Society*, 12(2), 203–222.

Luker, Kristin. 1985. *Abortion and the Politics of Motherhood*. Berkeley: University of California Press.

Mustard, David B. 2001. "Racial, Ethnic, and Gender Disparities in Sentencing: Evidence from the U.S. Federal Courts." *Journal of Law and Economics* no. 44 (1):285–314. doi: 10.1086/320276.

Paltrow, L. 2013. "*Roe v Wade* and the New Jane Crow: Reproductive Rights in the Age of Mass Incarceration." *American Journal of Public Health*, 103(1):17–21.

Paltrow, L. M., and Flavin, J. 2013. "Arrests of and Forced Interventions on Pregnant Women in the United States, 1973–2005: Implications for Women's Legal Status and Public Health." *Journal of Health Politics, Policy and Law*, 38(2):320–343.

Petersilia, Joan, and Kevin R. Reitz. 2012. *The Oxford Handbook of Sentencing and Corrections*, Oxford University Press.

Sichel, D. L. 2007. "Giving Birth in Shackles: A Constitutional and Human Rights Violation." *American University Journal of Gender, Social Policy and the Law*, 16(1):223–232, 239–243.

Siegel, Loren. 1997. "The Pregnancy Police Fight the War on Drugs." In *Crack in America: Demon Drugs and Social Justice*, edited by Craig Reinarman and Harry G. Levine, 249–259. Berkeley: California Press.

Solinger, Ricki. 2001. *Beggars and Choosers: How the Politics of Choice Shapes Abortion, Adoption, and Welfare in the United States*. New York: Hill and Wang.

Stotland, N. 2011. "Prescriptions: Dr. Carolyn Sufrin, Prison Ob/Gyn." *Mission Local Blog*, April 18.

CHAPTER 22

Invisible Immigrants

What Will Immigration Reform Mean for Migrant Women?

Michelle Chen

Patricia thought she had crossed the border to a land where she could finally earn a good living. She ended up in one of the worst places to be a woman. As a migrant farmworker, she was brutalized and raped by her supervisor, then left pregnant and alone. Her fear of her abuser was nearly matched by her fear of retaliation if she revealed her secret. She was almost too scared to file a police report, she later recalled in an interview with Human Rights Watch, because "I was afraid they would put me in jail; I was afraid [they'd] send me to Mexico because I was illegal."

Patricia eventually found her way to a social service agency, which encouraged her to report the rape after she sought assistance for her pregnancy. But countless other migrant women struggle with sexual trauma the same way they endure the everyday brutality of their work: silently.

One of the most ignored aspects of the debate on immigration reform—which has been largely focused on producing economic growth and legalizing undocumented workers—is what reform will mean for migrant women's rights. At a time when more American women are asking why they "can't have it all," immigrant women endure a much crueler work-life balance: mostly poor, often without papers, and largely Latina, they're exposed daily to chronic poverty, the threat of deportation, and sexual trauma. The struggle is inscribed on their bodies and reproductive destinies.

In contrast to the stereotype of migrants sponging off of welfare, in some border communities women are driven to look southward as a last resort for reproductive health care. "Immigrant women in Texas tell us that accessing birth control, cervical cancer screenings, and other reproductive care is so difficult here in the United States, they're forced to cross into Mexico in order to get the care they need," says Kimberly Inez McGuire, Associate Director of Government Relations and Public Affairs at the National Latina Institute for Reproductive Health. "One woman told us about how she literally swam across the Rio Grande to get access to reproductive care."

Under federal law, immigrants, including many green-card holders, face various bans and exclusions from federal health programs. For issues of sexual and reproductive health, immigrant women often find themselves doubly excluded from a health care infrastructure that degrades all poor women, unable to access or afford contraceptive and abortion services, prenatal care, or treatment for sexually transmitted diseases. Sexual violence or coercion by employers, inhumane conditions at detention centers, and a lack of legal recourse against abusers plague women with a precarious legal status. The dignity of reproductive sovereignty is a privilege that the low-wage economy forecloses for millions of immigrant women.

According to a policy analysis by the Latina Institute, "the majority of undocumented immigrant women do not have access to affordable health insurance," and "immigrant women are less likely to receive adequate reproductive health care, including cervical and breast cancer screening and treatment, family planning services, HIV/AIDS testing and treatment, accurate sex education and culturally and linguistically competent services." Even immigrants with green cards must generally wait five years to qualify for basic Medicaid programs. Some states have expanded coverage beyond federal law for select groups, including undocumented pregnant women and children. But overall, both federal and state health policies pose strict barriers for immigrant women and families.

The image of undocumented immigrants as welfare cheats and public charges all but guarantees that they will be the last group to benefit from any health care expansion. Two years ago during the health care debate, conservatives vehemently pressed for the exclusion of undocumented immigrants from benefits reforms, turning legal status into a threshold for rationing health care.

The Obama administration's health care reform legislation, the Affordable Care Act, could in theory extend Medicaid access and provide insurance subsidies for more immigrant households with legal status, but the undocumented generally remain excluded from essential federal benefits. And state lawmakers, facing fiscal constraints and conservative backlash against Obamacare, are unlikely to further extend benefits or dismantle existing restrictions imposed on immigrants. Meanwhile, without an overhaul of immigration policy that enables people to legalize and gain full citizenship, their communities' access to care will continue to be compromised by political and economic disenfranchisement.

Obama's reforms were "a largely missed opportunity to put right much of what has gone wrong with immigrants' access to affordable health insurance," because the expanded benefits for citizens end up being "disproportionately inaccessible to immigrants," says Kinsey Hasstedt, public policy associate with Guttmacher Institute, a reproductive health advocacy group. According to Guttmacher's analysis, immigrant women—who are more likely to be poor, young, and of color—are especially at risk of unwanted pregnancy and other reproductive health issues. They are less likely to use contraceptives, with cost barriers posing a major obstacle to preventive reproductive care. Federal Medicaid, moreover, explicitly bars subsidies for abortion services, a provision that disproportionately affects poor women of color.

By perpetuating those racial and economic divides among migrant women, these barriers, Hasstedt told me by email, "make it more difficult for them to realize the broader social and economic benefits linked to women's ability to determine whether and when to have children, namely educational and professional opportunities and economic and familial stability. These are all crucial considerations for immigrant women's full and productive integration into U.S. society."

GENDER AS OCCUPATIONAL HAZARD

Maria lost her motherhood in the fields. As she worked the California harvest last November, the young pregnant farmworker suddenly miscarried. She later recalled in an interview with an advocacy group, "I don't know what happened. I was working. The doctor told me that I just lost the baby. I don't know why." For a poor migrant worker, such tragedies are a regular occupational hazard—and to the agribusinesses that rely on immigrant labor, much of it done by undocumented workers, it's a rounding error in the cost of doing business.

Maria may never understand the reason for her miscarriage, but many potential causes surrounded her at work. Women's backbreaking toil in the fields, sometimes with their children in tow, exposes them to acute health hazards and threats of violence, aggravated by the underlying malaise of poverty and discrimination.

According to Levy Schroeder, Director of Health & Safety Programs with the Association of Farmworker Opportunity Programs (AFOP), the organization that recorded Maria's story, in addition to lack of insurance among most farmworkers, many migrants are constrained by "lack of transportation, language barriers, distrust of medical staff, immigration status, and cultural norms that discourage seeking medical care. . . . Even when a woman does seek medical attention, there are issues with continuity of care and mobility of medical records when the farmworker family moves on to their next workplace, which may be several states away." All those factors intensify migrant women's risk of HIV/AIDS, unintended pregnancy, and inadequate prenatal care.

Pregnant farmworkers are also extremely vulnerable to heat-related illnesses. A public outcry erupted in 2008 when a young pregnant migrant died after collapsing from heat exhaustion in a California vineyard. Pesticide exposure is extremely common, which in turn puts women at greater risk of birth defects and other reproductive health problems. But despite some recent state and federal efforts to revamp safety protections, regulations remain anemic, and brutal conditions in the fields persist.

And while all crop workers are subject to exhausting labor and poverty wages, women workers tend to be paid even less than male counterparts.

One woman interviewed by AFOP recalled that when she was working in the pumpkin fields during her pregnancy, "I had to bend over all day. I had a lot of [health] problems because the baby was slipping down too far. I [still] worked for two more months, until I was eight months pregnant."

According to a 2010 study on California farmworkers, about eight in ten female workers said they had experienced sexual harassment, such as degrading comments or groping. Domestic workers have reported similar abuses in private homes. In both sectors, women's vulnerability is deepened by fear of retaliation for reporting abuse, and a general lack of legal protections that apply to more conventional workplaces.

BODY POLITIC

When immigrant women and reproductive health are mentioned in the same breath in Washington, the discussion often reduces women to pawns in the culture wars.

Conservatives have long propagated the "anchor baby" canard to suggest, without evidence, that women are deliberately using U.S.-born children as a legal shield from immigration authorities. The myth has been used to justify proposals for harsher deportation policies and even repealing the constitutional guarantee of birthright citizenship for babies born on U.S. soil.

Parallel to the accusations of excessive breeding are warnings of excessive terminations of the immigrant "unborn." Last year, some conservative lawmakers pushed the Prenatal Nondiscrimination Act (PRENDA) as a supposed preemptive strike against sex-selective abortion, based on the presumption that gender-biased mothers were choosing to abort female fetuses (with a clear racial undertone linked to Asian American communities with a tradition of "son preference"). While the bill's purported goal was "ending discrimination against female babies," the legislation—which threatened to imprison doctors for performing a sex-selective abortion—was sharply criticized by reproductive rights advocates as another attack on abortion access, under the guise of supposedly "saving" women from their culturally regressive patriarchs.

Subtler gender bias surrounds the entire political discourse around immigration. The reform proposals currently before

Congress—focused on employment-based visas and establishing a tortuous "path to citizenship" that would stretch for over a decade—aim to expand labor migration in male-dominated sectors, namely the high-skilled "STEM" fields (science, technology, engineering, and mathematics). Yet visas for family reunification, which center on family and community rights, would be sharply restricted, taking a back seat to labor-market demands. This would in turn marginalize women and children who typically seek legal status as dependents of male workers.

Whether targeted by sexual violence at work, or cut off from prenatal care, migrant women are by turns exploited and invisible. Though they're working to raise the next generation of Americans, or to sustain families abroad with money wired home, the law degrades their social value as both workers and caregivers. Falling outside of traditional paradigms of feminism, migrant women confront racial and gender barriers that interlock with capitalist structures of citizenship. Their glass ceiling is the cold edifice undergirding the nation's economic hierarchy.

CHAPTER 23

Roe v. Wade and the New Jane Crow
Reproductive Rights in the Age of Mass Incarceration

Lynn M. Paltrow

All pregnant women, not just those who seek to end a pregnancy, have benefited from *Roe v Wade*. Today's system of mass incarceration makes it likely that if *Roe* is overturned women who have abortions will go to jail.

Efforts to establish separate legal "personhood" for fertilized eggs, embryos, and fetuses, however, are already being used as the basis for the arrests and detentions of and forced interventions on pregnant women, including those who seek to go to term.

Examination of these punitive actions makes clear that attacks on *Roe* threaten all pregnant women not only with the loss of their reproductive rights and physical liberty but also with the loss of their status as full constitutional persons.

In her book, *The New Jim Crow*, Michelle Alexander argues that the system of mass incarceration in the United States, fueled

by the war on drugs, operates in a seemingly color-blind, race-neutral way to create a new Jim Crow system that forces African Americans, especially African American men, into a permanent underclass.[1] I believe that attacks on *Roe v Wade*[2] and efforts to treat fertilized eggs, embryos, and fetuses as separate legal persons will establish a system of law in which women who have abortions will go to jail. Furthermore, all pregnant women are at risk of being assigned to a second-class status that will not only deprive them of their reproductive rights and physical liberty through arrests, but also effectively strip them of their status as full constitutional persons.[3,4]

Here I address major changes in US law enforcement since *Roe v Wade* was decided in 1973 that make it likely that if *Roe* is overturned women who have abortions will be arrested and sentenced to incarceration.

I discuss how efforts to undermine *Roe* and to establish separate legal personhood for fertilized eggs, embryos, and fetuses are already providing the basis for the arrests and detentions of and forced interventions on pregnant women. I conclude that these efforts, if unchecked, not only will result in massive deprivations of pregnant women's liberty, but also will create a basis for ensuring a permanent underclass for pregnant women or, for lack of a better term, a new Jane Crow.

In 1971, before *Roe v Wade* was decided, Shirley Wheeler was arrested and prosecuted for the crime of manslaughter after hospital staff in Florida discovered her illegal abortion and reported her to the police. After a two-day jury trial she was convicted of manslaughter, a crime that carried a possible penalty of 20 years' imprisonment. Although the conviction would later be overturned by the Florida Supreme Court,[5] the trial court sentenced Wheeler to two years' probation that required her to either marry the man she was living with or return to her home state to live with her parents.[6,7] Before *Roe*, other women were also arrested for having abortions.[8] It was far more common, however, for the abortion provider to be arrested and the woman suspected of having the illegal abortion to be subjected to grueling police interrogations designed to obtain evidence against that provider.[9]

Today's criminal justice system, however, is radically different from the one that existed when *Roe* was decided. In the 1970s, the United States had approximately 300,000 prisoners,[10] and relatively few women were prosecuted for any crime, including abortion.

Between 1970 and 2000, the US population rose by less than 40%, yet the number of people in prisons and jails rose by more than 500%.[10] The United States now has a prison–industrial complex that includes a for-profit prison industry that reaps enormous financial gain from building prisons, providing ongoing services to those prisons,

and ensuring that those prisons remain filled.[11–13]

Currently, US prisons and jails hold more than 1.5 million people, and 4.8 million more are under some form of criminal justice supervision in the community, such as probation and parole.[14] In 1977, the number of women in prison was 11,212[15] and in 2009, it was 105,197[16]—an increase of 938%. Today, more than 200,000 women are behind bars, and more than one million women are on probation or parole.[17,18] The fact that a woman is also a mother caring for one or more children is no deterrent to incarceration. Two thirds of the incarcerated women in the United States have at least one minor child,[21] and approximately five percent of women are pregnant when they begin their incarceration.[19,20]

This new era of mass incarceration—which is largely accepted by the public, defended by an army of lobbyists, and justified by a war on drugs deeply rooted in America's history of slavery and racism[1,22]—makes it far more likely today than in 1973 that if *Roe* is overturned women will themselves be arrested and jailed.[23] It is also likely that women having or considering having abortions will be subject to far more government surveillance than in the past.

Federal and state law enforcement agencies are twice as big as they were in 1973, and their investigative powers—including wiretapping—have been dramatically expanded.[24–26] Moreover, since 1973 drug testing has become a multibillion-dollar industry.[27] As a result of US Supreme Court decisions[28,29] and local policies, even middle school students who want to join the after-school scrapbooking club are being required in some schools to submit to urine drug testing.[30] Once a urine sample is in the possession of state authorities, it may just as easily be used to test for pregnancy.

In the post-*Roe* world, however, it is not only women who seek to end pregnancies who must fear the possibility of surveillance and arrest. Approximately one million women in the United States each year terminate their pregnancies, close to another million suffer miscarriages and stillbirths, and more than four million women continue their pregnancies to term.[31] Each and every one of these women benefits from the US Supreme Court's decision in *Roe v Wade*,[2] which not only protects a woman's right to terminate her pregnancy but also, as later US Supreme Court cases explained, has been "sensibly relied upon to counter" attempts to interfere with a woman's decision to become pregnant or to carry her pregnancy to term.[32] As a result, all pregnant women, not just those seeking to end a pregnancy, risk losing their reproductive rights and their liberty.

Indeed, pregnant women who have abortions, experience pregnancy losses, or fail to heed their doctor's recommendations, and even those who go to term and give birth to healthy children, are already being arrested and subjected to massive assaults on their physical liberty. A recent study that I coauthored with Jeanne Flavin found, between 1973 and 2005, 413 cases in the United States in which a woman's pregnancy was a necessary factor leading to attempted and actual deprivations of her liberty.[33] The evidence we obtained indicated that this was a substantial undercount, possibly by hundreds if not more, of the number of pregnant women subject to arrests or the equivalent during this period. In addition, we have documented more than 200 cases since 2005 in which pregnant women have been arrested. In almost all cases, the arrests and other actions taken would not have happened but for the fact that the woman was or had been pregnant at the time of the alleged violation of law.

Many states still have their pre-*Roe* abortion laws on the books, and virtually all have laws distinguishing between legal and illegal abortions.[34,35] Between 1973 and today, women in Idaho,[36] New York,[37-39] and South Carolina[40] who ended their pregnancies through abortion have been charged with violating state criminal abortion laws. Criminal abortion charges have also been filed against women in Florida,[41] Georgia,[42] and Tennessee,[43] who, in acts of desperation, shot themselves while pregnant. In an Illinois case, criminal abortion charges were filed against a woman who apparently attempted to remove a dead fetus from inside her after experiencing a pregnancy loss while at home.[44]

In light of the increasingly heated antichoice rhetoric routinely describing abortion as "murder," "killing,"[45] and "genocide,"[46] it should not be surprising to learn that prosecutors in Alaska,[47] Arizona,[48] California,[49-51] Florida,[41] Georgia,[52] Hawaii,[53] Indiana,[54] Illinois,[55] Kentucky,[56] Louisiana,[57,58] Massachusetts,[59,60] Mississippi,[61] New Jersey,[62] Nevada,[63] Oklahoma,[64] South Carolina,[65] Tennessee,[66] and Utah[67] have also used their existing murder, fetal murder, feticide, and manslaughter laws as a basis for arresting and prosecuting pregnant women who had abortions, who suffered miscarriages or stillbirths, or who were unable to guarantee that the children they gave birth to would survive.

Cases include a woman who used a knitting needle to end her own pregnancy,[56] a woman who delayed having cesarean surgery,[67] a woman who experienced an early miscarriage after receiving the medically prescribed contraceptive Depo Provera,[58] a woman who experienced a stillbirth while giving birth at home,[68] and women who suffered stillbirths and lost infants shortly after birth and were accused, without scientific evidence, of causing their pregnancy loss or newborn's death by taking an illegal drug.[47,65] In March of 2011, Bei Bei Shuai was charged in Indiana with murder and attempted feticide after becoming so depressed during her pregnancy that she attempted suicide and suffered the loss of her newborn.[69] Because murder is not treated as a bailable offense, Ms. Shuai was incarcerated in a county jail for more than a year before a court of appeals ordered her release. Thus far, Indiana courts have rejected attempts to have the charges dismissed; Ms. Shuai is now preparing for a murder trial.[54]

In a majority of the cases we documented, however, women went to term and gave birth to children who had no reported health problems.[33] These women, pregnant and alleged to have used an illegal drug or alcohol, were arrested for such crimes as child (fetal) endangerment and delivery of drugs to a minor through the umbilical cord. Women have been arrested while still pregnant, taken straight from the hospital in handcuffs, and sometimes shackled around the waist and at the ankles.[70] They have been arrested shortly after giving birth[71] and while still dressed only in hospital garb.[71–73] Pregnant women have been held in jails,[74] prisons,[75] and under house arrest.[76] At least one woman who was still pregnant at the time of arrest was shackled during much of her labor.[72]

State authorities have deprived pregnant women of their liberty not only through the criminal justice system, but also through civil commitment proceedings and actions taken pursuant to civil child welfare laws. Pregnant women have been held in locked psychiatric wards[77–80] and in treatment programs under 24-hour guard.[81] They have been forced to undergo intimate medical examinations[82] and blood transfusions over their religious objections.[83,84] Women have been forced to submit to cesarean surgery, and some have been physically restrained with leather wrist and ankle cuffs so that they could be subjected to medical procedures they opposed.[85]

Angela Carder was so debilitated at the time a court ordered her to undergo cesarean surgery that such restraints were unnecessary. Ms. Carder was 27 years old and 25 weeks pregnant when she became critically ill. She, her family, and her attending physicians all agreed on treatment designed to keep her alive for as long as possible. The hospital, however, called an emergency hearing to determine the rights of the fetus. Despite knowing that cesarean surgery could kill Ms. Carder, the court ordered it, claiming that the fetus had independent legal rights. The fetus was born alive but died 2 hours later. Angela Carder died 2 days later, with the surgery listed as a contributing factor.[86]

The highest court of the District of Columbia later vacated the order as one that violated Ms. Carder's right to "accept or refuse medical treatment"[86](p1252). Indeed, the vast majority of appellate court decisions in the United States have found that the arrests and interventions described here are contrary to law and public health policy.[53,87–105] Nevertheless, these arrests and interventions continue to occur, and virtually all of them rely on the claim that fertilized eggs, embryos, and fetuses should be treated as separate persons.[33] The decision in *Roe* explicitly rejected the argument that fetuses, at any stage of development, are to be treated as if they are separate constitutional persons under the law.[2] Despite this, passage of feticide laws[106] and anti-abortion measures (including those that have declarations of separate rights for fertilized eggs, embryos, and fetuses)[107,108] and efforts to pass so-called personhood measures[109] are providing the legal theory not only to justify the arrests of pregnant women, but also to deprive them of their constitutional personhood.

The dissenting judge's view in the Carder case makes this painfully clear. This judge argued that the viable unborn child is a person with rights separate from the pregnant woman[86](pp1254–1257) (Belson J, dissenting in part). He then articulated a clear rationale for the inevitable injury that the recognition of such rights would do to women's legal status: he claimed that "the expectant mother," by undertaking to bear another human being and carrying an unborn child to viability places "herself in a special class of persons"[86](p1254) (Belson J, dissenting in part). As exemplified in Carder's case and confirmed in the hundreds of others we documented in our study, when eggs, embryos, and fetuses are treated as separate persons, the state will have the authority to consign pregnant women to "a unique category of persons"[86](p1254) (Belson J, dissenting in part) in which they may be deprived of virtually every right associated with constitutional personhood, including, as in Carder's case, the right to life.[86,110,111]

In the name of separate rights for eggs, embryos, and fetuses, pregnant women have been locked up (deprived of the right to liberty) and forced to undergo major surgery (the right to liberty, bodily integrity, and medical decision-making),[112] sometimes over their religious objections (the right to religious liberty).[82,113–116] Women have been denied medical care[70] and have been forced to give birth while shackled and subjected to grossly disproportionate penalties (the right to be free of cruel and unusual punishment).[65] They have had bail deliberately set at levels so high that they were forced to remain in jail (right not to pay excessive bail).[70,117]

These deprivations have taken place after court proceedings where women were represented by inadequate counsel or no counsel at all (right to counsel)[118–120] and where they had no meaningful opportunity to challenge the claims being made against them (the right to due process).[118–122] Pregnant women have been prevented from leaving the state (the right to travel).[123] Pregnant women have been secretly searched (the right to be free of unwarranted searches)[124,125] and had their confidential medical information disclosed (right to informational privacy).[94] Pregnant women have been coerced into having unwanted abortions,[126] and they have been penalized for giving birth,[127] for experiencing pregnancy losses, and for terminating or seeking to terminate a pregnancy (the right to reproductive privacy).[128]

Pregnant women have also been denied the right to equal protection under the law. They have been required to prioritize their pregnancies over everything else in their lives, including their jobs[128] and their responsibilities for the children they already have.[129] And although our study confirmed that arrests and detentions of and forced interventions on pregnant women are happening in every region of the country and affect women of all races, we also found that African American pregnant women are significantly more likely than White women to be arrested, reported by hospital staff, and subjected to felony charges.[33,130,131]

These cases thus reveal that both pregnant women who have abortions and those who do not are already being arrested and incarcerated. They also demonstrate that there is no gender-neutral way to add fertilized eggs, embryos, and fetuses to the Constitution without subtracting all pregnant women from the community of constitutional persons and creating a Jane Crow system of law that disproportionately punishes African American women.

In light of the pressing need to dismantle the US system of mass incarceration, we must oppose the recriminalization of abortion and passage of so-called personhood measures that would expand it. In my experience, the majority of people, whether they identify as pro-life or pro-choice, do not want to see pregnant women who have abortions (61% of whom are already mothers),[132–134] who experience pregnancy losses, or who go to term sent to jail or consigned to a second-class status.[135,136] It is my hope then that we will be able to work together not only to oppose attacks on *Roe* and to defend reproductive rights, but more fundamentally to support a true culture of life: one that values and fully protects the personhood of the women who bring forth that life.

REFERENCES

1. Alexander, M. *The New Jim Crow:Mass Incarceration in the Age of Colorblindness.* New York, NY: New Press; 2010.
2. Roe v. Wade, 410 U.S. 113 (1973).
3. Daniels C. *At Women's Expense: State Power and the Politics of Fetal Rights.* Cambridge, MA: Harvard University Press; 1996.
4. Roth R. *Making Women Pay: The Hidden Costs of Fetal Rights.* Ithaca, NY: Cornell University Press; 2003.
5. Wheeler v. State, 263 So. 2d 232 (Fla. 1972).
6. Nordheimer J. She's fighting conviction for aborting her child. *New York Times.* December 4, 1971:37.
7. Deutsch D. Women's lib decries "crimes against women." *The Tech.* February 11, 1972:1.
8. Commonwealth v. Weible, 45 Pa. Super. 207 (Pa. Super. Ct. 1910).
9. Reagan LJ. *When Abortion Was a Crime: Women, Medicine, and Law in the United States, 1867–1973.* Berkeley: University of California Press; 1997.
10. King RS, Mauer M, Young MC. The Sentencing Project. Incarceration and crime: a complex relationship. 2005. Available at: http://www.sentencingproject.org/doc/publications/inc_iandc_complex.pdf. Published 2005. Accessed October 18, 2012.
11. Davis A. *The Prison Industrial Complex* [CD-ROM]. Oakland, CA: AK Press; 2000.
12. Mason C. The Sentencing Project. Dollars and detainees: the growth of for-profit detention. 2012. Available at: http://www.sentencingproject.org/doc/publications/inc_Dollars_and_Detainees.pdf. Accessed October 18, 2012.
13. Wides-Munoz L. Private prison companies make big money off detaining undocumented immigrants. Associated Press. August 2, 2012.
14. Glaze LE. US Department of Justice, Bureau of Justice Statistics. Correctional population in the United States, 2010. 2011. Available at: http://bjs.ojp.usdoj.gov/content/pub/pdf/cpus10.pdf. Accessed September 20, 2012.
15. Harrison P, James D. US Department of Justice, Bureau of Justice Statistics. Sentenced female prisoners under state or federal jurisdiction. Updated December 6, 2005. Available at: http://bjs.ojp.usdoj.gov/content/data/corpop37.csv. Accessed September 24, 2012.
16. US Census Bureau. Statistical abstract of the United States. 2011. Available at: http://www.census.gov/compendia/statab/2012/tables/12s0350.pdf. Accessed September 24, 2012.
17. Minton T. US Department of Justice, Bureau of Justice Statistics. Jail inmates at midyear 2010. Updated June 28, 2011. Available at: http://bjs.ojp.usdoj.gov/content/pub/pdf/jim10st.pdf. Accessed September 24, 2012.
18. Guerino P, Harrison PM, Sabol WJ. US Department of Justice, Bureau of Justice Statistics. Prisoners in 2010. Updated February 29, 2012. Available at: http://bjs.ojp.usdoj.gov/content/pub/pdf/p10.pdf. Accessed September 24, 2012.
19. Maruschak LM. US Department of Justice. Medical problems of jail inmates. 2006. Available at: http://bjs.ojp.usdoj.gov/content/pub/pdf/mpji.pdf. Accessed September 20, 2012.
20. Maruschak LM. US Department of Justice. Medical problems of prisoners. Revised April 22, 2008. Available at: http://bjs.ojp.usdoj.gov/content/pub/pdf/mpp.pdf. Accessed November 12, 2012.
21. Flavin J. *Our Bodies, Our Crimes: The Policing of Women's Reproduction in America.* New York, NY: New York University Press; 2009.
22. Blackmon DA. *Slavery by Another Name: The Re-Enslavement of Black Americans From the Civil War to World War II.* New York, NY: Anchor Books; 2008.
23. Diaz-Tello F. What's the answer to abortion in the age of the prison-industrial complex? Lock women up and throw away the key. *Reproductive Health Reality Check.* 2012. Available at: http://www.rhrealitycheck.org/article/2012/07/12/there-is-no-return-to-"pre-Roe"-in-ageprison-industrial-complex. Accessed July 12, 2012.
24. Duke SB. Mass imprisonment, crime rates, and the drug war: a penological and humanitarian disgrace. *Conn Pub Int Law J.* 2009(9):20–21.
25. Young MG. What big eyes and ears you have! A new regime for covert governmental surveillance. *Fordham Law Rev.* 2001; (70):1017–1026.
26. King RS. The Sentencing Project. Disparity by geography: the war on drugs in America's cities. 2008. Available at: http://www.sentencingproject.org/doc/publications/dp_drugarrestreport.pdf. Accessed October 18, 2012.
27. Riggs M. 4 industries getting rich off the drug war. Reason.com. Available at: http://reason.com/archives/2012/04/22/4-industries-getting-rich-off-the-drug-w. Published April 22, 2012. Accessed September 20, 2012.
28. Bd. of Educ. v. Earls, 536 U.S. 822 (2002).
29. Vernonia Sch. Dist. 47J v. Acton, 515 U.S. 646 (1995).
30. Pilon M. Middle schools add a team rule: get a drug test. *New York Times.* September 22, 2012:A1.
31. Ventura SH, Curtin SC, Abma JC, et al. Estimated pregnancy rates and rates of pregnancy outcomes for the United States, 1990–2008. Centers for Disease Control and Prevention. 2012. Available at: http://www.cdc.gov/nchs/data/nvsr/nvsr60/nvsr60_07.pdf. Accessed September 14, 2012.
32. Planned Parenthood v. Casey, 505 U.S. 833, 859 (1992).
33. Paltrow LM, Flavin J. Arrests of and forced interventions on pregnant women in the United States (1973–2005): the implications for women's legal status and public health. *J Health Polit Policy Law.* In press.

34. Center for Reproductive Rights. What if *Roe* fell? 2007. Available at: http://reproductiverights.org/sites/crr.civicactions.net/files/documents/Roe_PublicationPF4a.pdf. Accessed September 19, 2012.

35. Guttmacher Institute. *State Policies in Brief: Abortion Policy in the Absence of Roe.* New York, NY: Guttmacher Institute; 2012.

36. McCormack v. Hiedeman, 2012 U.S. App. LEXIS 19051 (9th Cir. Idaho Sept. 11, 2012).

37. People v. Jenkins, No. 900–84 (N.Y. Westchester County Ct. Nov. 5, 1984).

38. Carollo K. Woman charged with self-abortion after fetus found in trash. ABC News. December 2, 2011. Available at: http://abcnews.go.com/blogs/health/2011/12/02/woman-charged-with-selfabortion-after-fetus-found-in-trash. Accessed September 12, 2012.

39. Patten J. Woman charged with attempting to abort child with drug; infant girl survived four days. *Eagle Tribune.* January 24, 2007. Available at: http://www.eagletribune.com/local/x1876317741/Woman-charged-withattempting-to-abort-child-with-drug-Infant-girl-survived-four-days. Accessed September 12, 2012.

40. State v. Flores, No. 2006GS3203466 (S.C. Ct. Gen. Sess. Feb. 28, 2008).

41. State v. Ashley, 701 So. 2d 338 (Fla. 1997).

42. Hillman v. State, 503 S.E.2d 610 (Ga. Ct. App. 1998).

43. State v. Brown, No. 13952 (Tenn. Cir. Ct. Lawrence County Oct. 2, 1987).

44. People v. Lyerla, No. 96-CF-8 (Ill. Cir. Ct. Montgomery County May 1997).

45. Mason C. *Killing for Life: The Apocalyptic Narrative of Pro-Life Politics.* New York, NY: Cornell University Press; 2002.

46. Genocide Awareness Project (GAP). Center for Bio-Ethical Reform. Available at: http://abortionno.org/index.php/the_genocide_awareness_project_gap. Accessed September 24, 2012.

47. State v. Grubbs, No. 4FA-S89– 415CR (Alaska Super. Ct.-4th Oct. 2, 1989) (Hodges, J.).

48. State v. Robertson, No. CR2002–015076 (Ariz. Super. Ct. Maricopa County Oct. 21, 2003) (Reinstein, J.).

49. People v. Tucker, No. 147092 (Cal. Santa Barbara-GotetaMun. Ct. June 1973).

50. Jaurigue v. Justice Court, No. 18988 (Cal. Super. Ct. San Benito County Aug. 21, 1992) (Chapman, J.).

51. People v. Jones, No. 93–5 (Cal. Justice Ct. Siskiyou County July 28, 1993) (Kosel, J.).

52. State v. Moss, No. 99-FCR-276-J (Ga. Super. Ct. Franklin County Sept. 15, 1999).

53. State v. Aiwohi, 123 P.3d 1210 (Haw. 2005).

54. Shuai v. State, 966 N.E.2d 619 (Ind. Ct. App. 2012).

55. People v. Green, No. 88-CM-8256 (Ill. Cir. Ct. Winnebago County May 26, 1989).

56. Commonwealth v. Pitchford, No. 78CR392 (Ky. Cir. Ct. Warren County Aug. 30, 1978).

57. State v. Ingram (La. Jefferson Parish 1998).

58. State v. Greenup, No. 2003-300B (La. Dist. Ct. St. John the Baptist Parish Aug. 16, 2004).

59. Commonwealth v. Baker, No. 98– 912 (Mass. Super. Ct. Hampden County May 6, 1998).

60. DA: young mother botched abortion with ulcer medication. *Boston Globe.* January 24, 2007. Available at: http://www.boston.com/news/globe/city_region/breaking_news/2007/01/da_young_mother_1.html. Accessed September 20, 2012.

61. State v. Hart, No. 1702 (Miss. Cir. Ct. Madison County Oct. 18, 1991).

62. State v. Barker, No. 96-02-605 (N.J. Super. Ct. Essex County Jan. 3, 1997) (Goldman, J.).

63. State v. Flintroy, No. CR91–1818 (Nev. Dist. Ct. Washoe County Apr. 14, 1991).

64. State v. Hernandez, No. CF-2004- 4801 (Okla. Dist. Ct. Oklahoma County Dec. 21, 2007).

65. McKnight v. State, 661 S.E.2d 354 (S.C. 2008).

66. State v. Craig, No. S14068 (Tenn. Crim. Ct. Carter County July 13, 1999) (Cupp, J.).

67. State v. Rowland, No. 041901649 (Utah Dist. Ct.-3d Apr. 7, 2004) (Fuchs, J.).

68. Commonwealth v. Murphy, No. 82- CR-079 (Ky. Cir. Ct. Shelby County May 7, 1982).

69. Pilkington E. Outcry in America as pregnant women who lose babies face murder charges: women's rights campaigners see the creeping criminalization of pregnant women as a new front in the culture wars over abortion. Guardian. Updated June 27, 2011. Available at: http://www.guardian.co.uk/world/2011/jun/24/america-pregnant-women-murdercharges. Accessed September 20, 2012.

70. State v. Young (S.C. Ct. Gen. Sess. Oct. 5, 1989) (Guedalia, J.).

71. State v. Powell, No. C569305 (S.C. Ct. Gen. Sess. Charleston County Oct. 14, 1989).

72. State v. Griffin, No. C567255, C569256 (S.C. Ct. Gen. Sess. Charleston County Oct. 7, 1989).

73. State v. Brown (S.C. Ct. Gen. Sess. 1989).

74. State v. Hamilton, No. 1991001742FA (Fla. Cir. Ct. St. Lucie County July 31, 1992).

75. Whitner v. State, 492 S.E.2d 777 (S.C. 1997).

76. State v. Davis, No. 1990CF001924A (Fla. Cir. Ct. Escambia County Dec. 13, 1990).

77. In re Nicholson, No. T.D.D. 94-0185A (S.C. Prob. Ct. Charleston County Feb. 9, 1994).

78. State v. Ayala, 991 P.2d 1100 (Or. Ct. App. 1999).

79. State v. Lowe (Wisc. Cir. Ct. Racine County June 15, 2005) (Constantine, J.).

80. In re Steven S, 178 Cal. Rptr. 525 (1980).

81. People v. Moore (Ill. Cir. Ct. Winnebago County 1991) (Agnew, J.).

82. In re Unborn Child Corneau, No. CP-00-A-0022 (Mass. Juv. Ct. Attleboro Div. Aug. 29, 2000) (Nasif, J.).

83. In re Jamaica Hospital, 128 Misc. 2d 1006 (N.Y. Sup. Ct. Queens County 1985).

84. In re Fetus Brown, 689 N.E.2d 397 (Ill. App. 1997).

85. In re Triplets, (Ill. Cir. Ct. Cook County 1984).
86. In re A.C., 573 A.2d 1235 (D.C. 1990) (en banc).
87. Johnson v. State, 602 So. 2d 1288 (Fla. 1992).
88. Cochran v. Commonwealth, 315 S. W.3d 325 (Ky. 2010).
89. Kilmon v. State, 905 A.2d 306, 313–14 (Md. 2006).
90. State v. Wade, 232 S.W.3d 663 (Mo. 2007).
91. State v. Geiser, 763 N.W.2d 469, 471 (N.D. 2009).
92. State v. Gray, 584 N.E.2d 710 (Ohio 1992).
93. In re Unborn Child of Starks, 18 P.3d 342 (Okla. 2001).
94. State ex rel. Angela M.W. v. Kruzicki, 561 N.W.2d 729 (Wis. 1997).
95. Reinesto v. Superior Court, 894 P.2d 733 (Ariz. App. 1995).
96. Reyes v. Superior Court, 141 Cal. Rptr. 912 (Cal. App. 1997).
97. State v. Gethers, 585 So. 2d 1140 (Fla. App. 1991).
98. State v. Luster, 419 S.E.2d 32 (Ga. App. 1992).
99. In re Baby Boy Doe, 632 N.E.2d 326 (Ill. App. Ct. 1994).
100. Herron v. State, 729 N.E.2d 1008 (Ind. App. 2000).
101. People v. Hardy, 469 N.W.2d 50 (Mich. App. 1991).
102. State v. Martinez, 137 P.3d 1195 (N.M. App. 2006).
103. Collins v. State, 890 S.W.2d 893 (Tex. App. 1994).
104. State v. Dunn, 916 P.2d 952 (Wash. App. 1996).
105. State v. Deborah J.Z., 596 N.W.2d 490 (Wis. App. 1999).
106. National Conference of State Legislators. Fetal homicide laws. 2012. Available at: http://www.ncsl.org/issues-research/health/fetal-homicidestate-laws.aspx. Accessed June 9, 2012.
107. Mo. Ann. Stat. § 1.205 (West 2011).
108. Webster v. Reproductive Health Services, 492 U.S. 490 (1989).
109. Mississippi Secretary of State. Initiative #26—definition of a 'person.' 2011. Available at: http://www.sos.ms.gov/Elections/Initiatives/Initiatives/Definition%20of%20Person-PW%20Revised.pdf. Accessed June 9, 2012.
110. Kaplan M. "A special class of persons": pregnant women's right to refuse medical treatment after Gonzalez v. Carhart. J Const Law. 2010;13(1):145–206.
111. Minkoff H, Paltrow L. Melissa Rowland and the rights of pregnant women. *Obstet Gynecol.* 2004;104(6):1234–1236.
112. In re Madyun Fetus, 114 Daily Wash. L. Rptr. 2233 (D.C. Super. Ct. Oct. 29, 1986).
113. In re Bentley, 102 Daily Wash. L. Rptr. 1221 (D.C. Super. Ct. Apr. 25, 1974).
114. Broward Medical Center v. Okonewski, 46 Fla. Supp. 120 (Fl. Cir. C. 1977).
115. In re Jeffries, No. 14004 (Mich. Prob. Ct. Jackson County May 24, 1982).
116. In re Unborn Baby Wilson (Mich. Juv. Ct. Calhoun County Feb. 3, 1981).
117. Order, In re Unborn Child of Starks, No. 93, 606 (Okla. Sept. 23, 1999).
118. State v. Pemberton, No. 96–759 (Fla. Cir. Ct. Leon County Feb. 22, 1996).
119. Bennett v. Collier, 95 S.W.3d 782 (Ark. 2003).
120. Department of Human Services. v. Collier, 95 S.W.3d 772 (Ark. 2003).
121. In re A.C. 533 A.2d at 613.
122. WVHCS-Hospital, Inc. v. Doe, No. 3-E 2004 (Pa. Ct. Co. Pl. Luzerne County Jan. 14, 2004).
123. In re Twelve-Year-Old Pregnant Girl (Mich. Prob. Ct. Macomb County July 24, 1998) (O'Sullivan, J.)
124. Ferguson v. City of Charleston, 532 U.S. 67 (2001).
125. Ferguson v. City of Charleston, 308 F.3d 380 (4th Cir. 2002).
126. State v. Greywind, No. CR-92-447 (N.D. Cass County Ct. Apr. 10, 1992).
127. State v. Arnold, No. 94-GS-24-107 (S.C. Ct. Gen. Sess. Greenwood County Feb. 16, 1994) (Hughston, J.).
128. People v. Bremer, No. 90-32227- FH (Mich. Cir. Ct. Muskegon County Jan. 31, 1991) (Eveland, J.).
129. State v. Ferguson, No. 93OW102002142 (S.C. Ct. Gen. Sess. Charleston County May 3, 1993).
130. Roberts D. *Killing the Black Body: Race, Reproduction, and the Meaning of Liberty.* New York, NY: Pantheon Books; 1997.
131. Kolder VEB, Gallagher J, Parsons MT. Court-ordered obstetrical interventions. N Engl J Med. 1987;316(19): 1192–1196.
132. Jones RK, Finer LB, Singh S. Characteristics of U.S. Abortion Patients, 2008. Guttmacher Institute. 2010. Available at: http://www.guttmacher.org/pubs/US-Abortion-Patients.pdf. Accessed.
133. Jones RK, Darroch JE, Henshaw SK. Patterns in the socioeconomic characteristics of women obtaining abortions in 2000–2001. Perspect Sex Reprod Health. 2002;34(5):226–235.
134. Sandler L. The mother majority. Slate. October 17, 2011. Available at: http://www.slate.com/articles/double_x/doublex/2011/10/most_surprising_abortion_statistic_the_majority_of_women_who_ter.html. Accessed October 19, 2012.
135. World Public Opinion. World public rejects criminal penalties for abortion: public at odds with their country's laws in half of countries polled. 2008. Available at: http://www.worldpublicopinion.org/pipa/pdf/jun08/WPO_Abortion_Jun08_packet.pdf. Accessed October 17, 2012.
136. National Institute for Reproductive Health. Messaging project: how much time should she do? 2006. Available at: http://www.nirhealth.org/sections/ourprograms/HowMuchTime.asp. Accessed October 26, 2012.

CHAPTER 24

Prescriptions

Dr. Carolyn Sufrin, Prison Ob/Gyn

Naomi Stotland

Providing medical care for prisoners is not a popular (or well-reimbursed) endeavor. Only a handful of doctors and researchers work in this field; my colleague Dr. Carolyn Sufrin is one of them. Sufrin is an obstetrician/gynecologist at San Francisco General Hospital and is on the faculty at UCSF. I recently spoke with her about her work.

Mission Loc@l: How did you become interested in caring for incarcerated women?

Carolyn Sufrin: When I was a first-year ob/gyn resident in Pittsburgh, I delivered the baby of a woman from a nearby prison. She was shackled to the bed during delivery. I wondered what would happen to the baby when she went back to prison.

The next morning I was checking in on her and we had a discussion about contraception. She decided to use the vaginal contraceptive ring. So I wrote a prescription for it and placed it on her chart. I paused, questioning whether she actually needed birth control, and if the prescription I wrote would be honored at the prison.

ML: Can you briefly describe the clinical work you do in this area?

CS: I care for incarcerated women at the San Francisco County Jail. I work with a women's health nurse practitioner. Together we see women for a range of routine and complicated pregnancy-related and gynecologic concerns. This includes offering birth control options to women and, if they are interested, starting them on a method before they are released back into the community.

ML: What are some of the main health problems you see in incarcerated women?

CS: Many incarcerated women have had limited access to health care before they have come to jail. Sexually transmitted infections are very common. A very high proportion of these women have experienced physical or sexual abuse in the past, and this has long-standing effects on their health.

Many of these women have issues with substance abuse. When they are in custody and not using drugs, they often notice things about their body that they haven't before. So many of them come to us complaining of pelvic pain or abnormal periods.

ML: What about incarcerated men versus women?

CS: Compared to incarcerated men, women have a much higher rate of symptoms of a mental illness. Depression, anxiety, bipolar disorder, post-traumatic stress disorder—it's as high as 70% among some women. Pregnancy is an obvious health issue which differentiates incarcerated women from men.

ML: If women give birth while incarcerated, do they get to be with their infants at all?

CS: What is allowed varies from county to county, state to state. But in general, women get to be with their infants while they are both still in the hospital, which usually lasts two to three days. If the woman is being held in a local jail, then her baby goes either to a family member or into custody of the state. Usually she can see the baby once a week at visiting hours if a family member brings the baby.

Prisons are for people serving longer sentences, so some states have programs which allow the infant to stay with the mom in a special nursery wing of the prison. Depending on where the woman is, the baby can stay with her from four weeks up to 18 months.

ML: What about breastfeeding?

CS: This can be very challenging. If she is in a local jail and separated from her baby, then she has to pump breast milk. The clinic will store the milk until the family can pick it up, and then it is given by bottle to the baby.

ML: If incarcerated women want an abortion, is this available?

CS: Incarcerated women have the right to choose an abortion, just like every other woman in the U.S. In many facilities it is no problem for a woman to get an abortion in custody. The clinic at the correctional facility helps to make the appointment and facilitates transport. These are things that incarcerated women have limited ability to arrange themselves.

In reality, it is often restricted by rules and the political beliefs of the people who are in charge at a local level. I have heard stories from many women at other facilities about women not being allowed to leave the facility for an abortion. Or women may be required to get a court order for being transported, which is not required for all medical transports. This can take time and sometimes the approval comes through too late, when abortion is no longer possible.

And so some women are forced to carry undesired pregnancies to term. This is a kind of punishment which men don't have to experience.

ML: Do incarcerated women need birth control, and if so is it provided for them?

CS: The majority of incarcerated women are in their 20s and 30s—what we call "reproductive age." So family planning is an important piece of their comprehensive women's health care. The risks of a woman getting pregnant while she is incarcerated are low. Assault by male guards is known to happen, but it is highly underreported. At some prisons, women may be allowed to have conjugal visits from their male partners. And it's important that women have the option of starting birth control before they're released. If a woman wants to be on birth control, it should be available to her.

Despite research which shows the importance and feasibility of doing this, many facilities do not offer birth control. If they do, they might only have birth control pills available. I did a survey of correctional health care providers across the country and found that only 38 percent of providers were able to offer birth control to women before release. There are no standardized policies.

ML: What type of prenatal care do incarcerated women receive?

CS: Prisons and jails are required to provide routine prenatal care, either on site or at a local hospital. While clear standards exist from the National Commission on Correctional Health Care, there is definitely variation by state and county. A recent comprehensive report by the Rebecca Project found that 38 states had inadequate prenatal services.

ML: What changes would you like to see in the system?

CS: One of the most pressing issues is ending the practice of shackling of pregnant women in labor. Believe it or not, only 10 states—10!—have laws which prohibit this practice.

It is medically dangerous, as restraints can interfere with the need for unpredictable procedures during labor and delivery. In addition, the security risk of a woman in labor, with painful contractions, sometimes with an epidural, is low. More than 70 percent of these women have been arrested for nonviolent crimes, anyway. This is a barbaric practice that has been condemned by a number of medical professional societies and the United Nations.

I think we also need to work to standardize the services offered to women, including mental health care and access to contraception for women. Prison and jail administrators need to be made more aware about women's specific health needs, and how they differ from men's needs.

CHAPTER 25

Disabled Women and Reproductive Rights

Virginia Kallianes and Phyllis Rubenfeld

The women's movement has a long history of fighting for women's rights to self-determination and bodily integrity. An important part of the feminist agenda has been an argument against biological determinism and support for all women's rights to make decisions about their bodies, sexuality, and childbearing. The disability rights movement has also become more vocal in advocating for the rights of disabled people. Yet, according to disabled feminists, neither movement has adequately addressed reproductive freedom for disabled women. Disabled women have begun to articulate their criticism of the disability rights movement's failure to address gender issues and the feminist movement's failure to integrate into its agenda the perspectives of disabled women, particularly on issues of reproductive freedom, sexuality and mothering (Finger, 1984; Saxton, 1990; Boylan, 1991; Morris, 1991, 1993, 1995; Waxman, 1991a, 1993b; Begum, 1992; Hilyer, 1993; Hershey, 1994).

Although some may question whether the concerns of the disability rights and women's

movements are similar or different, disabled feminists say that they are, in fact, based on a similar foundation (Finger, 1984; Todd, 1984; Blackwell-Stratton *et al.*, 1988; Fine & Asch, 1988; Begum, 1992; Klein, 1992; Morris, 1993, 1995). Disabled and non-disabled feminists share many common goals, including: elimination of social attitudes that define women and disabled people solely on the basis of biological or physical characteristics; striving for self-determination; giving voice to women's experiences; elucidating the interaction of sexism, racism, homophobia and ageism in women's lives; and, exposing women's marginalized social status. Both movements maintain that the social context of 'difference'—the value imposed on biological characteristics—must be examined (Fine & Asch, 1988).

According to Finger, 'Because both the reproductive rights movement and the disability rights movement are rooted in our rights to control our bodies and our lives, there are strong links between the two' (1984, p. 294–295). Begum argues that the issues raised by disabled women 'strike at the core of both the disability rights and feminist movements' (1992, p. 70) because their experiences in a sexist and ableist[1] society highlight some major factors that play a critical role in understanding the social construction of women's lives, particularly gender roles and sexuality. Boylan, in fact, characterizes disabled women's rights as 'human rights' (1991, p. 52).

WHAT DO 'REPRODUCTIVE RIGHTS' MEAN FOR DISABLED WOMEN?

> Having sexual relationships (whether they are heterosexual or lesbian relationships), family relationships, bearing and rearing children, making a home—all these are important human and civil rights which, if denied to *non*disabled women, would be the subject of outrage.
>
> (Morris, 1995, p. 76.)

The question, then, is what does 'reproductive rights' mean for disabled women? Do they have the same or different interests as non-disabled women? The term has been used very basically to refer to women's right to be free of unwanted pregnancy—to obtain contraception and safe, legal abortion. The literature suggests that disabled women agree on these issues, but for them 'reproductive rights' is broader, and includes the right to bear and raise children.

In most contemporary societies women are still expected to marry and have children—they are sometimes seen as rebellious or 'deviant' if they choose not to and sometimes viewed with sympathy if they are unable to bear children. Despite some recent changes in women's status, women still experience subtle pressures to become mothers (Begum, 1992; Hershey, 1994). In fact, women are defined in terms of sexuality and reproduction, and, even more reductively, are sexually objectified.

However, a double standard exists for disabled women, who have been seen as asexual or 'defective' and undesirable as sexual partners or mothers. Both disabled and non-disabled women's sexuality and reproductive capacities have been regulated by patriarchal society, but here expectations of women's traditional reproductive role are reversed—what is expected, encouraged and, at times, compelled among non-disabled women is *not* expected, discouraged and proscribed among disabled women. Thus, disabled women have been denied sex education and contraception, discouraged from childbearing, forced to undergo abortions or sterilization, and lost custody of their children (Waxman, 1993a).

Disabled women, then, view reproductive rights as more than the right to choose *not* have a child; the concept also encompasses the right to be recognized as sexual, to bear children—even a disabled child—to be seen as 'fit' to mother and to refuse the use of genetic technologies (Finger, 1984; Saxton, 1984; Asch, 1988; Morris, 1991; Hershey, 1994).

It may seem a paradox that the issues for which feminists have struggled—for women not to be defined sexually, for the right to roles other than mothers—appear to be the opposite of what disabled women demand. Feminist arguments that women's lives must not be restricted by reproductive capacity have—by failing to address disabled women's experiences—inadvertently contributed to a binary construction that makes the reproductive concerns of disabled women seem opposed to those of non-disabled women. However, rather than differing perspectives, they are, in fact, two sides of the same coin (Hershey, 1994). Reproductive freedom for disabled women parallels abortion rights: if all women have the right to choose not to bear a child, then all women must also have the right to choose to bear children.

Of course, it is important to emphasize that 'disabled women' are not a monolithic entity, and reproductive freedom may not mean the same to all or impact all in similar ways. Not all disabled women are interested in marriage or mothering; some may be more interested in sexual freedom and access to contraception; some may be lesbians; some choose not to have children. Others have children prior to becoming disabled and wish to continue their mothering role. Also, there is much variability in women's experiences living with physical, sensory and developmental disabilities. Race and ethnicity, sexual preference and economic status also influence disabled women's reproductive interests and options.

FACTORS CONSTRAINING REPRODUCTIVE FREEDOM FOR DISABLED WOMEN

> Interference with reproductive choice for disabled women begins long before laws about access to reproductive services and technology. It starts in exclusion from sex education classes and in parental silence about sexuality and motherhood . . . inaccessibility of affordable gynecological services; lack of safe contraception . . . and the still-prevalent sterilizations.
> (Asch, 1988, p. 87.)

The literature by and about disabled women identifies a number of factors that interact to deny them reproductive choice, a primary factor being an assumption of asexuality.

Asexuality

At the root of the problem is the widespread belief that disabled women are asexual and could not possibly have concerns regarding sexuality (Finger, 1984; Saxton, 1984; Browne *et al.*, 1985; Fine & Asch, 1988; Morris, 1989, 1991; Lonsdale, 1990; Begum, 1992; *Disability Rag*, 1993; Hershey, 1994). Cole, for example, contends that the topic of sexuality and disability 'carries a double taboo' (1988, p. 278; also, Saxton, 1990). It has commonly been assumed that disabled people are either incapable of sexual function or 'just shouldn't want it' (Saxton, 1984,

p. 303; also Gardner, 1986). For example, a woman with spina bifida requesting contraception from her gynecologist was asked, 'What would you do with it?' (Saxton, 1991, p. 36). Finger also tells of disabled women being asked, 'How did *you* get pregnant?' (1984, p. 291). Leavesley and Porter note that 'developmentally-disabled people were rarely given any help with sexuality and physically disabled people were often told to think of other things (e.g. wheelchair basketball)' (1982, p. 418).

Patriarchal society has kept close control over women's sexuality, what sexual activity is socially acceptable and to whom. In a society obsessed with 'perfection' and health, and intolerant of difference, non-disabled people view sexual activity by disabled people with discomfort or alarm (Waxman, 1993a). Sex is depicted as a 'rare commodity . . . reserved for highly-valued people, able-bodied people' (Saxton, 1984, p. 303). These attitudes, along with narrow sexist definitions of female attractiveness, exclude disabled women from traditional standards of feminine beauty (Campling, 1981). While the 'sexual revolution' altered social attitudes about sexuality, disabled women have not enjoyed an expansion of sexual freedom (Romano, 1978). An early study probing college students' attitudes showed that among the aspects of sex viewed most negatively were sexual behaviour by disabled people and by older people (Haring & Meyerson, 1979).

Society has blocked disabled women from participation in the sexual sphere, where women are expected to locate a portion of their self-worth, 'by treating women in general as sexual playthings and yet women with disabilities as asexual' (Lonsdale, 1990, p. 7). Ironically, 'most able-bodied women experience problems in being treated as a *sexual* object, whereas many disabled women experience being treated as an *asexual* object . . . [and] may never have had the experience of flirting . . . being harassed, or objectified'

(Cole, 1988, p. 284; also Finger, 1984; Fine & Asch, 1988). As one disabled woman noted, 'It has been rare in my life that I have feared men getting sexual with me, because most men don't see me as a sex object in the same way as they see most women' (Campling, 1981, p. 32). The assumption of asexuality may exempt women from many sexist attitudes, but sexism also restricts their choices: 'Rehabilitation staff assume (if they do at all) that women will want to know only about heterosexual sex . . . and that women will only play a passive sexual role' (Lonsdale, 1990, pp. 70–71).

Parents of disabled girls are often overprotective and may 'withhold information about sexuality altogether' (Cole, 1988, p. 28; also Campling, 1981), or alternately, channel them into becoming 'super career women' believing they are not seen as 'marriage material' (Shaul et al., 1985). Something feminists may relate to is that disabled youth 'may not even acknowledge . . . ownership of his or her own body' because of experiencing excessive touching by physicians and attendants during health care tasks (Cole, 1988, p. 282). Not only do disabled girls face social isolation, and a lack of information about sexuality and their bodies, but their already vulnerable status leaves them susceptible to sexual abuse in medical settings, their families, or in intimate relationships. The history of sexual abuse of disabled women cannot be covered here, but a high incidence is estimated, particularly among children in institutions and among developmentally disabled women (Begum, 1992; Cross, 1994; McCarthy, 1996).

How does this belief that disabled people are asexual square with a history of coercive sterilization and abortion, and discouragement of childbearing? This is a clear contradiction, exposing the duplicity of representations of disabled women's sexuality. Some claim that sterilization protected disabled women from sexual abuse or, specifically, from pregnancies resulting from these rapes. Ironically, when disabled people have expressed their sexuality 'they were often treated as deviants or monsters' (Gardner, 1986, p. 61), who either were sexually promiscuous or desperate for attention. This stereotype plays into social fears of sexuality out of control, casting disabled people as a sexual threat (Finger, 1984; Saxton, 1984; Browne et al., 1985; Morris, 1989; McCarthy, 1996).

In reality, sexuality is a genuine concern for disabled people. An issue of *Disability Rag* devoted to sexuality and parenting offers telling articles: Gravitt, for example, says that after 'Will I walk again?' the most common questions asked by newly disabled people are 'Can I have sex?' and 'Will I be able to have children?' (*Disability Rag*, 1993, p. 30). Waxman contends that the disability movement has not adequately addressed disabled women's sexuality as a political issue, although 'many of us find sexuality to be the area of our greatest oppression . . . we are more concerned with being loved and finding sexual fulfillment than with getting on a bus' (1991a, p. 23).

Feminists and lesbians, in particular, may be interested in the implications of sexual activity among disabled women for expanding concepts of sexual expression. Narrow attitudes among non-disabled people tend to define 'real' sex as genital intercourse, to the exclusion of other sexual activity. As a result, non-disabled people assume that disabled people are not physically capable of 'real' sexual function. Thus, exploration by disabled people of what it means to be sexual can move the focus toward a broader view of sexual experience (Morris, 1989; Begum, 1992). Wendell points out that people who are 'Paraplegics and quadriplegics have revolutionary things to teach about the possibilities of sexuality which contradict patriarchal culture's obsession with the genitals' (1989, p. 120). Waxman also points out that laws restricting sexual practices depicted as 'unnatural' (oral or anal sex) can limit the sexuality of disabled people who may find these modes of sexual expression more attainable or pleasurable (1991a).

Despite stereotypes to the contrary, many disabled women report satisfying sexual experiences; some describe increased sensation in other parts of the body and say sexual experiences are enhanced because of 'having to take greater initiative in sexual relations, experimenting more' (Lonsdale, 1990, p. 73; also, Finger, 1984; Morris, 1989). Morris relates the experiences of one disabled woman who 'finally embarked on a sexual relationship [and] felt "delight, elation, triumph at the vindication of instinct over conditioning"' and another who claims 'sex is fun and there is no reason why a paralysed person should not get as much enjoyment from it' (Morris, 1989, pp. 81, 98). Potash writes 'While the rest of my life conspires to keep me isolated and alone . . . I feel powerful sexually' (Potash, 1993, p. 32).

Lack of Appropriate Reproductive Health Care, Contraception and Pregnancy Information

Feminists have noted that the medical establishment has been one of the loci of control over women's bodies and reproduction. This is exacerbated for disabled women when the denial of sexuality results in a lack of reproductive health information and services addressing their needs. Disabled women struggle to find providers sensitive to their health concerns and to overcome physical barriers to medical facilities (Gill, 1993). Medical professionals often respond with surprise when disabled women request contraception or pregnancy information and may be ill-prepared to provide appropriate care. Providers can be misinformed or biased, prescribe inappropriate treatments, and ignore disabled women's knowledge of their bodies and needs (Simpson, 1992). Physicians receive little training about or positive exposure to disabled people and virtually no education

on the social context of disability, much less the interrelated 'impact of sexism, racism, or homophobia on women with disabilities' (Saxton, 1991, p. 36). While all women may be subject to physicians' often condescending attitudes, providers more often treat disabled women as incapable of self-directed lives and choices, especially involving sexuality and pregnancy (Saxton, 1991; Ferreyra & Hughes, 1992; Simpson, 1992).

Due to inaccessibility, lack of information, insensitive treatment and the assumption they are not sexually active, disabled women may not receive necessary reproductive and obstetrical care, or appropriate instruction on protecting themselves from sexually transmitted diseases (STDs) and AIDS (see McCarthy, 1994).

The deficiency of a range of safe, effective contraceptives more seriously impacts disabled women, who may find hormonal methods—such as pills or injectables—contraindicated due to the nature of their disability and barrier methods such as diaphragms or condoms—problematic because of the physical dexterity needed for effective use (Morris, 1989; Boston Women's Health Book Collective, 1992; Simpson, 1992). In particular, provider-dependent contraceptives may leave disabled women vulnerable to coercion if method selection or use is not under the woman's control (Finger, 1984).

In reality, little research has been conducted on disability and reproduction (Fine & Asch, 1985; Beckmann et al., 1989). Thus, the attitudes of medical professionals towards disabled women as childbearers have often been based on myth rather than fact. Physicians often counsel disabled women not to have children merely 'because it has seemed "obvious" that people with disabilities would not make good parents' (Kaplan, 1988, p. 242).

Even within the disability community, there has been little information addressing the sexual and reproductive health needs of disabled women (Deegan & Brooks, 1985;

Begum, 1992). The Boston Women's Health Book Collective concurs that, until recently, 'literature and counseling about sex and physical disability focuses on men, penis-in-vagina intercourse and male concerns' (1992, p. 224).

This may be changing, as disabled women demand—and write their own—materials on the topic. Disabled women helped to update editions of the feminist health book *Our Bodies, Ourselves* (Boston Women's Health Book Collective, 1992). Improved reproductive health materials show that the concerns of disabled women can be addressed in a reassuring and sensitive manner (see Hare & Solomon, 1981; Congleton & Rotter, 1984; Morris, 1989; American Diabetes Association, 1990; Ferreyra & Hughes, 1992; Kroll & Klein, 1992; *Disability Rag*, 1993; Planned Parenthood, not dated; SIECUS, not dated).

Social Resistance to Reproduction and Mothering by Disabled Women

> i know i am not expected to have children.
> i don't know how i know, i just do.
> nobody ever said anything;
> it's probably what they didn't say
> that made the difference.
>
> (Duffy, 1994, p. 29.)

Since marriage and mothering signify sexuality and acceptance into the social mainstream, it is not surprising that disabled women face obstacles to sexual and reproductive freedom from the medical and legal communities, the public and their families. Many disabled women have experienced denial of their desire to become mothers through coerced sterilization, contraception or abortion, or have lost custody of their children (Finger, 1984; Cole, 1988; Callo-Brazil, 1993; Lonsdale, 1990). Disabled couples also face resistance to adoption of children (Campbell-Earl, 1993). Disabled women forgo childbearing plans due to social barriers, not physical incapacity. According to Waxman:

> No group in this country faces the sort of sexual and reproductive restrictions disabled people do . . . this is done tacitly to keep us from doing the thing that poses an overwhelming threat to our disability-phobic society: taking their sons and daughters as sexual and life partners, bearing their grandchildren.
>
> (1991a, p. 25.)

Many disability rights advocates suggest that a 'politics of eugenics' underlies this repression of sexuality and reproduction (Waxman, 1993a, p. 6; also Finger, 1984; Saxton, 1984). There are two misperceptions at play here: that a child will inherit a disability and that a disabled woman cannot possibly be a 'good' mother. Although a larger proportion of disabilities are not congenital, but develop later in life, the stigma of disability and the misconception that it is always hereditary result in attitudes that disabled women should not be permitted to bear children (Asch, 1988; Browne *et al.*, 1985). It is often assumed that the disabled mother will hurt her child or be unable to provide for its needs (Shaul *et al.*, 1985). People often assume that children seen with disabled women are likely adopted and even that they may be in danger (Saxton, 1984; Fine & Asch, 1988). The parent–child relationship itself is suspected of being defective: Hyler writes that her gynecologist and parents suggested she should not continue her pregnancy because the child would 'suffer psychological damage as a result of having a disabled parent' (1985, p. 282). Disabled women say that men seen with them are often presumed to be brothers or attendants rather than husbands or lovers.

The social proscription of parenting by disabled women was clearly highlighted by the controversy over the pregnancy of Bree Walker, a US television newscaster (*Disability Rag*, 1991a; Holmes, 1991a; *Newsweek*,

1991). A radio talk-show host, Jane Norris, criticized on air Walker's decision to become pregnant, since there was a 50% chance that the baby would inherit ectrodactyly. Norris invited listeners to comment on whether it was 'fair' that Walker was putting her baby at risk of being disabled. Callers to the show depicted Walker as irresponsible, saying she 'had no right to become pregnant and should have an abortion' (*The New York Times*, 1991a, p. 33). Walker was not invited to participate on the show or alerted that her pregnancy was to be discussed. She filed a complaint, claiming that Norris had invaded her privacy and incited negative, misinformed stereotypes about the rights of disabled women. A disability rights activist compared the situation to other civil rights issues: 'What's next, a discussion of whether black people should reproduce?' (Holmes, 1991a, p. 18).

Given this denial of disabled women's reproductive rights, it is not difficult to understand why Simpson claims that the disabled woman's choice to bear children is 'as daring as the choice to have an abortion was 50 or 60 years ago' (1992, p. 8). How does this repression of disabled women's desire to mother fit with feminist arguments for women's reproductive rights? Feminism has challenged the social conditioning that channels women to see their major, if not only, role as mothers and nurturers. At the same time, social prejudices virtually demonize disabled women, like women of other marginalized groups, who desire to be mothers. While many disabled women choose not to have children, some find it a rewarding experience, and resent the denial of their desire to form or continue intimate and familial relationships (Morris, 1995).

Is it an opposition to feminist ideology that disabled women demand the 'right' to be mothers? Are disabled women—although relegated to the margins of mainstream society—nonetheless influenced by the same patriarchal conditioning and notions that motherhood defines a 'real' woman? Morris says of disabled women, 'It is not surprising that many of us measure our "success" or "failure" in terms of whether we can return to the role of housewife and mother' (1989, p. 52), but cautions against viewing their desire to fulfill these roles as 'some kind of false consciousness', a result of 'sexist ideology' (1995, p. 76). Feminists have claimed that as an institution 'motherhood' has been used to force women into a subordinate status, 'glorifying self-negation', yet some disabled women have seen it as a 'positive opportunity for intimacy, regeneration, and human commitment' (Deegan & Brooks, 1985, p. 5). Disabled women claim that the denial of their mothering rights is itself an experience of oppression (Morris, 1993) and see the choice of childbearing as an opportunity to defy this social oppression (Morris, 1995).

Given society's insistence that disabled women are asexual and 'unfit' mothers, perhaps a disabled woman may wish to bear a child to disprove the stereotype of asexuality, to prove that she is indeed like other women, or to regain some semblance of an ordinary life (Rousso, 1988; Morris, 1989; Keith, 1994). Finger writes that she wanted to prove herself capable of childbirth and 'wanted something perfect to come out of my body' (1990, p. 172). A disabled woman described the experience of loving her baby, who also had osteogenesis imperfecta, as 'learning to completely love myself . . . rather than . . . trying to make up for the mistake of existing' (Lonsdale, 1990, p. 78).

Like non-disabled feminists and other marginalized women, disabled women also challenge traditional definitions of 'mothering' and 'family'. Disabled women make the connection between their oppression and broad concepts of 'rights':

Disabled women are systematically denied the most human of rights—the right to love . . . marriage . . . motherhood.

(Boylan, 1991, p. 52.)

I began to understand that my inability to be a full part of this society was not, in fact . . . because of my inability to walk . . . I was now living in a society which had permission to exclude me from things I had grown to consider my right.

(Keith, 1994, p. 2.)

The fact that disabled parents are frequently labelled 'unfit' and are vulnerable to losing custody of their children raises questions about not only women's 'reproductive rights', but also about the social definition of parenting (Browne *et al.*, 1985; Asch, 1988; *Disability Rag*, 1993). If child welfare laws define parenting in terms of physical capacity rather than love and nurturing, anyone who is temporarily able-bodied is vulnerable to losing their child(ren) due to future disability, injury or illness. Walstead, for example, asks if she would lose her child if something were to happen to her non-disabled husband, who helps her and cares for their child (1993). Callo-Brazil lost custody of her non-disabled children when she left an abusive marriage and was declared unfit as a single parent (Callo-Brazil, 1993).

This denial of disabled women's reproductive and parenting rights also relates to their social and economic marginalization (Waxman, 1993a). The reality of disabled women's lives has been compared to that of women of racial or ethnic minority groups, who are also disempowered and 'become scapegoats in a society that rations health care and other services' (Simpson, 1992, p. 8; also Waxman, 1993a). Because these women are themselves depicted as burdens to society and as irresponsible for having children, their sexual activity is open to public scrutiny and control. Waxman contends that the disabled woman who becomes pregnant is judged to be immoral and society seeks to punish her by removing her child(ren) from her: 'While a nondisabled woman's pregnancy is considered a miracle, a disabled woman's pregnancy is considered a crime against society' (1993a, p. 6). Discrimination against disabled women denies them reproductive 'choice' by controlling 'who may have sex . . . access to contraception . . . which babies should be born [or] allowed to live . . . who may raise these babies' (Saxton, 1993, p. 4). Such attitudes suggest that disabled people have fewer rights than other human beings, in fact, are seen as 'less than human' (Waxman, 1993a, p. 7).

ABORTION AND REPRODUCTIVE TECHNOLOGIES: IMPLICATIONS FOR DISABLED WOMEN

These topics comprise a vast literature that cannot be adequately covered here. Yet, they are an important part of this discussion, due to their impact on disabled women, as well as on the relationship between disabled feminists and pro-choice advocates.

Given the repression of sexuality and social proscription of mothering among disabled women, it is not surprising that they look suspiciously upon selective abortion or genetic technologies that are used to prevent reproduction by disabled women or the birth of disabled babies. Some of this concern arises from the legacy of sterilization abuse among disabled women, particularly the early 20th century US eugenics movement (Finger, 1984, 1990; Fine & Asch, 1988; Kaplan, 1988). For disabled women, this history underlies discussions of abortion and reproductive technologies. Many see in advancing reproductive technologies, such as genetic screening combined with abortion, the return of eugenic practices and claim society is reverting to attitudes such as those embodied in the 1927 United States Supreme Court case upholding compulsory sterilization in the state of Virginia, from which came Oliver Wendell Holmes' often-quoted statement: 'Society can prevent those who are manifestly unfit from continuing their kind' (Gould, 1985, p. 310).

Disabled women contend that sterilization abuse continues, either overtly—especially among developmentally disabled women—or when disabled women are denied appropriate contraception, sexuality and parenting information, and are left with no recourse but to resort to sterilization (Finger, 1984; Asch, 1988).

Abortion

Many disabled feminists voice support for women's right to abortion; in fact, some are among the most vocal supporters of reproductive freedom:

> We should know better than anyone why the government should not be allowed to restrict what one can and cannot do with one's body.
> (Reiskin, 1991, p. 2.)

> When the government can control such a personal decision as abortion, it can also control other aspects of sexuality, reproduction and childbirth . . . people with disabilities will once again find our choices limited.
> (Hershey, 1991, p. 2.)

There is a range of opinion about abortion among disabled women—just as among all women. However, when the discussion turns to abortions chosen because prenatal screening has detected fetal impairment, disabled feminists voice concerns that social prejudices and negative stereotypes about disabled people lead to automatic assumptions that disabled women should not bear children and babies who might be disabled should not be permitted to be born. These concerns are, in part, due to the history of disabled women being encouraged toward abortions. These experiences have given them another perspective on abortion: while supporting women's right to abortion, they assert that they have the right to refuse abortion for themselves.

Disabled women are most troubled that abortion is actively promoted to prevent the birth of disabled babies. They find it disturbing that 'birth defects' are the most socially acceptable reasons for women to have abortions, contending that fear and hatred of disabled people are exploited to advocate the right to abortion (Fine & Asch, 1988; Rothman, 1989; Finger, 1990; Morris, 1991; Hershey, 1994). They especially protest when fetal impairment is placed on par with rape as the 'worst-case scenarios' that are then highlighted to encourage support for legal abortion (Morris, 1991; Hershey, 1994). Surveys repeatedly show 75–80% of respondents agreeing that disability or fetal impairment are the most appropriate justifications for abortion (Asch, 1988; Rothman, 1989; Waxman, 1991b; Simpson, 1992; Hershey, 1994). One survey found that 83% thought abortion more acceptable in cases of 'birth defects'; in comparison, 44% thought it acceptable when a woman does not want more children (Uslaner & Weber, 1980). One might assume that mothers of disabled children oppose such abortions. Yet, a survey on attitudes toward abortion among mothers of congenitally disabled children and mothers of non-disabled children found very similar responses: while some of the mothers of disabled children opposed selective abortions, both groups of mothers also supported abortion at similar rates (Breslau, 1987).

While some disabled women strongly challenge selective abortion (Morris, 1991), others do not advocate prohibiting such abortions, but insist that pro-choice advocates should not prescribe *any* specific reasons—such as fetal disability—to justify women's right to abortion (Fine & Asch, 1988; Hershey, 1994). They assert that focusing on women's right to choose abortion in the case of a 'deformed' fetus exploits disability as a 'good reason' for abortion (Finger, 1990), thus disparaging the lives of disabled people. Emphasizing this rationale shifts the focus from a woman's right to make decisions about her body to the status of the fetus (Rothman, 1989). Women should not have to provide a socially acceptable reason for choosing abortion; the more compelling reason is the right to bodily integrity and self-determination. Finger believes we can 'defend women's right to have an abortion in such a situation without acting as if there were no other possible choice' (1990, p. 24). However, Johnson claims that abortion in cases of fetal impairment is not simply about women's right to choose, because women's decisions 'have been shaped by discriminatory attitudes—against disabled people' (1990, p. 34; also Morris, 1991).

Yet, some non-disabled feminists see in disabled women's challenge to abortions based on disability the potential erosion of tenuous reproductive freedoms that feminists struggle to maintain against ongoing attacks (Saxton, 1984; Fine & Asch, 1988). Feminists have also argued for women's autonomy, freedom from mothering as a confining role, and changes in women's sole responsibility for childrearing. They contend that the birth of disabled babies is regressive for women because, they claim, the added burdens of caring for disabled children will fall to mothers and threaten women's hard-won independence (Finger, 1984; Asch, 1988; Morris, 1991). While this is an important issue requiring further discussion among feminists, it does not seem that this must pose a contradiction. Feminists demand more partner and social involvement in childrearing—such as child care and other social programmes. Disabled women—in seeking supportive services to facilitate parenting or to care for disabled children—demand nothing less (Morris, 1995).

Reproductive and Genetic Technologies

How can I, a disabled person myself . . . regard this option to end the life of another one disabled? . . . I question the practice of systematically ending the life of a fetus because it is disabled. Real 'choice' . . . necessitates closely scrutinizing society's view of 'ablebodiedness'
(Saxton, 1984, pp. 301–302.)

Reproductive and genetic technologies—such as genetic screening and fetal therapies—have been proceeding dramatically, becoming more sophisticated and more routine, while scientists are developing ways to identify genetic predisposition to specific conditions. The literature on these technologies is huge and continually growing and cannot be thoroughly reviewed here. However, it cannot be overlooked that they have a disproportionate impact on disabled women.

While some view technologies such as assisted fertilization as potentially helpful, many disabled women see in these technologies not only increased medicalization and technological control over women's bodies, but also a potential return to eugenic practices (Finger, 1984; Tait, 1986; Asch, 1988). As such, some have been increasingly vocal in challenging the promotion and misuse of, for example, genetic screening (Saxton, 1984; Asch, 1988; Morris, 1991; Waldschmidt, 1992).

Most genetic technologies are developed to prevent or eliminate disability. Yet, it is not possible to avoid all disabilities, as many are not detectable prenatally and are not congenital, but develop at birth, through injury, degenerative conditions, or normal aging (Fine & Asch, 1988; Kaplan, 1988). Even when screening can detect impairment, it cannot predict the specifics or severity. Thus, disabled women claim that promotion and routine use of genetic testing inappropriately exaggerates and emphasizes negative aspects of disability—in reality, an occurrence in only a small percentage of pregnancies—while ignoring the worth of disabled people's lives (Finger, 1990; Simpson, 1992; Hershey, 1994).

As genetic technologies become more routine, based on avoidance of disability, what are the implications for people who are still born with or develop a disability? What of women who reject genetic screening and selective abortion? Some of the foreseeable results are less tolerance for and increased stigma of 'difference', blaming people for their disability, viewing pregnant disabled women as irresponsible and forcing them into abortions, and denial of social services to disabled people.

Promotion of genetic technologies can lead society to be unwilling to help people with any medical problem which could have been prevented 'had their parents had the decency to abort' and funding and services to help them live independently will seem less warranted (Johnson, 1990, p. 34). People who are born with or develop a disability, 'will be more the pariahs than ever', Johnson claims, as 'we're getting less tolerant of anything that deviates from the norm. And the norm's becoming more narrow' (1990, p. 34). Richter points to the implications for women considering genetic technologies: 'If society selects for totally healthy embryos, it is making a statement that there would be no circumstances under which a "normal" person would choose to bear a child who is not healthy'; women who make that choice may be viewed as not only irresponsible, but may ultimately be 'legally presumed to be incompetent' if they refuse abortion (in Corea, 1988, p. 91). Asch (1988) sees dangerous explicit and implicit pressures from the medical community and society on women to submit to genetic testing or abortion. The social forces may be more subtle than overt, claims Waldschmidt: 'The ban on childbearing . . . may not be expressly formulated in legal terms, but it is extremely effective on an informal, ideological, and moral plane' (1992, p. 160).

Reproductive technologies raise issues for feminists—non-disabled and disabled—to consider. Do reproductive technologies actually expand women's choices or result in increasing technological and medical control of women's bodies and reproduction? Are women permitted any decisions about use of reproductive technology? When technologies are presented as routine and women must opt out of them, are women really exercising 'free choice' or has the choice already been set up for women? Finger claims:

> This is a dangerous assault on women's bodily autonomy . . . social pressure can work to keep people in line . . . when a technology is available it becomes harder and harder not to utilize it . . . you have to explain your decision not to have amnio.
>
> (1990, p. 42)

If a woman refuses genetic testing or chooses not to abort an impaired fetus, will she then be refused social assistance if her child is disabled? Waldschmidt points out that 'disabled people themselves could be held accountable for their fate and left to cope with life on their own . . . they would have no essential right to existence any more' (1992, p. 166). We have already seen attitudes veering in this direction when mothers who seek public assistance are depicted as burdens on society, blamed for their condition and threatened with denial of services based on their childbearing; already, US courts have attempted to force women recipients of public funding to use provider-dependent contraception.

As important as the medical aspects, and rarely examined, is the social context in which technologies are developed and promoted. Who conceives of the need for genetic technologies, allocates the resources, and decides how they will be used—and for whom they are intended? Women, disabled people, and people of diverse races and economic status have not been making those decisions or even in the discussions. Ross points out that 'reproductive technology is not produced in a political vacuum . . . What technology is produced, for whom it's produced, who has access to it, whom it is forced upon, are all political questions' (1992, p. 9).

Feminists might question resources allocated for technologies which claim to eradicate disability and produce 'perfect' individuals when, concurrently, social programmes that provide necessary health and supportive services to poor women and children are being eliminated. In the United States, for example, disabled children and adults, and poor and elderly people face cuts in already-deficient services for medical care, nutrition, education, housing and more. Large numbers of women, in particular, lack health insurance for basic care, and have limited access to prenatal and infant care. More available, high-quality medical and prenatal services for all women will result in fewer disabilities at birth, while increasingly high-tech interventions are available only to a small number of more affluent women (Asch, 1988). Perhaps resources slated for genetic technologies would be better used to provide quality preventive health care and other services for persons already alive.

For disabled women, as for non-disabled women, 'choice' must be a broader concept: 'Perfect choice is the right to have the knowledge and means to make the choices that make sense to us [and] involves access not only to abortion, but to prenatal care, quality sex education, contraceptives, maternal, infant, and child health services, housing, and reform of the health care delivery system' (Ross, 1992, p. 8).

Disabled Women and the Pro-choice and Anti-choice Movements

I report to you as a disabled women, a potential target of the anti-choice movement, which capitalizes on my vulnerability and my tentative social status in trying to seduce me to join its ranks . . . Let us not accept the able-bodied guilt espoused by the anti-choice movement . . . We should fight for a pro-choice agenda and that goal must include all women. We, as disabled women, know better.

(Schneiderman, 1990)

No woman should be forced to bear a child, abled or disabled; and no progressive social movement should exploit an oppressed group to further its ends.

(Finger, 1984, p. 287.)

Disabled feminists contend that both pro- and anti-choice groups exploit disability in their arguments for and against abortion (Finger, 1990; *Disability Rag*, 1991b). This overemphasis on abortion of 'impaired' fetuses, is inflammatory, especially as fewer abortions are sought for this reason (Simpson, 1992; Hershey, 1994). Focusing on fetal disability deflects attention from women's rights to self-determination, while depicting disability as a 'tragedy' obscures the voices of disabled women who assert that their lives are worthwhile. Disabled feminists contend that pro- and anti-choice groups also fail to address the sexual, reproductive and parental rights of disabled women. These conflicts have enabled the anti-choice minority to make inroads into the disability community, focusing on abortion and euthanasia (*Disability Rag*, 1991b; Holmes, 1991b).

The abortion issue troubles many disabled women, who acknowledge that anti-abortion groups do not really support disability rights, especially publicly-funded services, much less women's rights (*Disability Rag*, 1991b; Reiskin, 1991; Hershey, 1994). Golden questions whether the disability and anti-abortion movements really share similar philosophies: 'Those who think we do, are ignoring a difference in approach . . . Self-determination is so integral to the disability rights philosophy that many disability advocates . . . are very skeptical of denying any choices' (1991, p. 4). Winter claims that 'the disability rights movement and the national right-to-life movement are at polar opposites' (*Disability Rag*, 1991b, p. 6). Waxman places the debate in a social context of 'the conservative Right wanting to get the state involved in women's reproductive decisions and the history of the state being involved in a disabled person's right to live as they choose' (*Disability Rag*, 1991b, p. 8).

Some disabled feminists disdain the anti-choice movement and support women's abortion rights, contending that the disability and pro-choice movements share similar political objectives, stressing self-determination. Reiskin states that the right to abortion, for any reason, is 'no less crucial to women than the right to access or attendant programs is for a person with a disability' (1991, p. 2). Hoell 'questions the right of any group to suggest that a person should have to exist for any reason or at any cost' (1991, p. 37).

Yet, their support is strongly informed by a disability-rights perspective that they say is missing from feminist discourse. Thus, there remains distance between disabled and non-disabled feminists. Finger contends that 'The feminist movement has by and large acted as if disabled women did not exist' (1984, p. 282). Disabled women criticize feminists' neglect of their concerns and, particularly, attitudes among pro-choice advocates toward disabled babies that they see as uncomfortably eugenic (Finger, 1990; Morris, 1991). Some disabled women contend that the pro-choice movement should be challenged on abortions for fetal impairment (Morris, 1991); overall, they agree that feminists must stop exploiting disability in their arguments for abortion rights and must integrate the perspectives of disabled women into their efforts (Finger, 1984; Reiskin, 1991; Begum, 1992; Hershey, 1994).

CONCLUSION

The literature shows a variety of issues affecting the reproductive rights of disabled women. Disability rights advocates have made inroads into changing social policies and attitudes, yet some feel that gains made may be threatened by reproductive technologies, misuse of abortion, and elimination of supportive social services—a combination that facilitates what some see as eugenic attitudes.

Disabled women are increasingly vocal and active in the disability and women's communities, aggressively raising a range of issues, including sexuality and mothering. It may be advantageous to ally with other progressive movements to influence their agendas and policies (Hershey, 1994). Saxton emphasizes the importance of disabled parents uniting with other marginalized people demanding parental rights, especially poor women, those of diverse racial backgrounds, and single or homosexual parents (1993). Some of the mainstream women's groups are slowly beginning to recognize the need to incorporate the perspectives of disabled women in their work. Waxman sees disabled women 'poised on a precipice' (1993b, p. 28) between obscurity and visibility, particularly with regard to sexuality, reproductive rights and mothering. Most importantly, disabled women themselves have written or compiled anthologies that give voice to their experiences, particularly with regard to mothering and sexuality (see Campling, 1981; Duffy, 1981; Browne et al., 1985; Saxton & Howe, 1987; Fine & Asch, 1988; Morris, 1989; Rousso, 1989; Finger, 1990; Mairs, 1990; Keith, 1994).

Yet, there is still a way to go to change the attitudes and practices that marginalize women, and to address what Fine & Asch decry as the 'social neglect of the sexual and reproductive roles of disabled women' (1985, p. 8). Morris suggests that non-disabled feminist researchers, for example, can be important allies for disabled women, providing 'space for absent voices' (1995, p. 68). Disabled women argue that feminism can itself be enriched by embracing the perspectives and experiences of disabled women (Finger, 1984; Fine & Asch, 1988; Saxton, 1990; Begum, 1992):

> Feminism is the poorer for its failure to integrate disability into the mainstream of its concerns and it has much to gain by redressing this omission.
>
> (Morris, 1993, p. 69.)

For example, mothers of disabled children are 'among the most politically active advocates of disability rights and . . . of disability experience' notes Hilyer (1993, p. 88; also Blackwell-Stratton *et al.*, 1988).

The disability rights, feminist and civil rights movements have created a foundation that could be used to further a collective agenda for an improved society. Disabled and non-disabled feminists may hold the key to bridging the distance between the movements.

NOTE

1. We are using 'ableism' defined as prejudice or discrimination against disabled people (*New Shorter Oxford English Dictionary*, 1993). Disabled women have also referred to these attitudes and practices as 'disablelism' (Morris, 1993), 'disabiliphobia' (Hershey, 1994), and 'handicapism' (Begum, 1992).

CHAPTER 26

Motherhood as Class Privilege in America

Rickie Solinger

Most middle-class Americans, including policy makers and politicians, seemed to agree that it was a "tragedy" when a middle-class woman could not have a baby. The president of a pharmaceutical company that manufactured fertility drugs spoke to a large constituency in the late 1980s when he defined "fundamental rights to life" as including "access to infertility therapy."[1] Yet many people seemed to draw the line at applying these principles to the family-building urges of poor women. Most Americans agreed that motherhood was "a source of self- and community esteem" for middle-class women, "of family life, of continuity, and of loving relationships."[2] Most agreed "that the desire to raise a family is a fundamental human longing for most adults, and to be denied that experience is a denial of the right to choose."[3] Yet when women with few resources had the desire to have a child or to build a family, many Americans freely and quickly applied a financial test for motherhood and found such women inappropriate candidates for motherhood. As we have seen, many argued that for the poor, motherhood was a source not of self- and community esteem or loving relationships but of dependency and even depravity.

During the same season that some members of Congress were promoting middle-class family-building activities, federal and state politicians were engaged in plans and fantasies to give governmental authorities greater power than ever before to control how resourceless women made fertility-related decisions, and to control the arsenal of punishments leveled against a poor woman who made the "wrong choice."[4] In the late 1980s, in Michigan and other states, politicians were working to cancel Medicaid funds that had given poor women the choice of abortion, at roughly the same time that Pat Schroeder introduced the bill mandating insurance coverage for middle-class infertility cures. On the federal level, President Bush approved big cutbacks in the WIC program—covering nutrition and health care for infants and their low-income mothers—while Pat Schroeder and some of her colleagues spoke piously to the middle class about the basic human right to create family and the joys of tending one's children.[5]

But the most dramatic and perhaps the most popular effort to restrict family building among the poor was the introduction of "family caps," a mechanism for uncoupling the size of poor families and the amount of the welfare check. For about forty years or more by this time, politicians had been claiming that poor women who collected welfare had sex—and so babies—for government money. The first success in passing a law to squelch this alleged form of prostitution was a Georgia bill passed in both houses of the state legislature and signed by the governor in February 1951. The legislation, which the federal Social Security Commission pressed Georgia state lawmakers to repeal before it went into effect, would have denied welfare grants to "more than one illegitimate child of a mother."[6]

For more than a decade following the Georgia effort, the federal government actively discouraged states from trying to constrain poor women from having babies using this kind of law. In 1960, a prominent government report on illegitimacy and its relation to the welfare program counseled state legislators and others: "An additional child may mean an increased [welfare] payment to meet part of the cost of the child's care. For the mother, no 'profit' is involved. Rather, an additional child adds to her responsibilities and in many instances, means spreading her income a little thinner."[7]

By 1970, however, signs of change in the government's attitude were apparent. When Maryland passed a law capping the maximum welfare grant at a figure fixed for a family of six, the state claimed it was providing incentives for family planning. In *Dandridge v. Williams*, the U.S. Supreme Court affirmed Maryland's welfare plan, and

the majority opinion spoke disapprovingly about poor women having babies.[8] According to legal scholar Thomas Ross, *Dandridge* constructed a poor mother's choice to have another child as "a choice to put her entire family in an even worse position." Ross points out that when the Supreme Court accepted Maryland's family planning argument, it accepted the charge that for a poor mother, becoming pregnant is an act of "moral weakness."[9] Ross suggests that to understand how this decision "draws on the theme of the moral weakness of the poor," we might "imagine the popular response to a similar, hypothetical state action directed against wage-earner families [that deduct dependents for tax liability-reducing purposes]."[10]

National attention was focused on the "family cap" as an effective way to get poor mothers to stop having children when Wayne Bryant, a "wealthy, patrician lawyer," the highest-ranking African-American legislator in New Jersey—he was the Democratic assembly leader—introduced family cap legislation in the spring of 1991. Bryant's plan denied increased benefits to mothers on welfare if they gave birth to additional children while they were on public relief. The proposal garnered so much attention in part because Bryant was African-American; many white politicians and others felt that a black insider was finally willing to stand up and speak the truth about his own people.[11] (Bryant apparently found it necessary to defend himself against the charge that he was prejudiced against his own people; when he appeared before the U.S. Senate, he said, "Let me state from the outset, sir, this is not a David Duke.")

The New Jersey family cap proposal also created sparks because of Bryant's timing: almost twelve years into the Reagan-Bush era, the majority of middle-class Americans had embraced the truth of the Welfare Queen and was eager for strategies to dethrone her, particularly during the economic recession of the early 1990s. Lawrence Mead accurately described just how hot the family cap plan was when he testified before the Senate in 1992: "There has been great interest in this. In fact, I spent much of the last two months on the phone talking to reporters about these proposals. I even got a call from *Glamour* magazine. When *Glamour* wants to write about welfare, then you know it's on the front burner."[12]

Throughout late 1991 and early 1992, states applied to the Bush administration for permission to bypass federal welfare guidelines and institute family cap regulations based on the New Jersey model.[13] Presidential candidate Bill Clinton, making a political calculation, spoke out in favor of the New Jersey plan in May 1992 after having opposed the plan previously.[14] Meanwhile, in New Jersey, the combination of the family cap and state funding of abortions for poor women apparently steered, and may have coerced, poor women to have abortions instead of children.[15] When the U.S. Supreme Court affirmed New Jersey's family cap regulations in *C.K. v. Shalala*, the majority claimed that this legislation could have "an ameliorative effect" on poor women by curtailing "family instability" and other social ills resulting from poor women having children.[16] Legal scholar Linda C. McClain argues that this court decision "seems to carry the further message that an important and legitimate way to end poverty is to end procreation by poor people."[17] Longtime New York senator and family poverty specialist Daniel Patrick Moynihan acknowledged how far Americans had come since the human rights era of the 1960s in accepting the proposition that public policy should constrain the reproductive choices of poor women when he said in 1992, "Twenty-five years ago [the New Jersey family cap regulation] would have caused howls."[18]

But by the early 1990s, the years of anti-poor, anti-welfare rhetoric beamed across the country had had what Cynthia Newbille of the National Black Women's Health Project called "a devastating effect on the public's perception of [poor] women."[19] In these years, conservative writers and policy makers frequently invoked frightening images of poor mothers and sometimes used these images to justify transferring their babies to middle-class couples or curtailing public support for these mothers altogether. Conservative analyst Heather MacDonald characterized a poor mother in 1994 as one "who has been beating her children, or failing to feed and bathe them." MacDonald discouraged funding for rehabilitative services because she doubted that such a woman could be rehabilitated. Instead, she championed child removal as the best solution for saving the children of poor mothers. Marge Roukema, U.S. representative from New Jersey, also championed removal because, she said, "ultimately . . . Americans and the Congress will not countenance children being raised in abusive drug-infested households or going hungry in the street."[20] Neither woman provided statistics or citations to bolster their characterizations.

Not surprisingly, Charles Murray and many Republican politicians who looked to Murray for policy guidance drew on these scary images of poor mothers—and on the uneasiness of many Americans responding to the news that their tax dollars were being thrown at these women—to trumpet a dramatic policy initiative based on the premise that poor women should not be mothers. Newt Gingrich and the conservative firebrands in Congress began to tout a plan to send children of poor mothers to orphanages.[21] This plan, they confidently claimed, would solve the illegitimacy problem and the welfare problem, and would finally convince poor women that the government was serious: no more help for their kind.[22] Tony Blankley, Gingrich's press secretary, explained why he thought this initiative captured so much attention. "Orphanage," he said, "is a term that communicates very well."[23] Numerous polls at the time showed that most Americans did not support the orphanage initiative, but Republicans continued promoting the idea.[24] One close observer commented, "Raising the specter of orphanages was viewed as a means to persuade unmarried mothers and welfare-dependent women into controlling their reproduction."[25] In an essay with a title that captured perhaps the most important domestic policy debate in the 1990s, "Do Poor Women Have a Right to Bear Children?," sociologists Christopher Jencks and Kathryn Edin characterized the Contract With America crowd as "welfare bashers [who] would like to prevent the poor from having children."[26]

Some critics pointed out that "welfare bashers" wanted to institutionalize the children of poor mothers simply because of "the absence of jobs for mothers willing to work" or the absence of jobs that paid a living wage.[27] Legal scholar Dorothy Roberts emphasized that policy makers were identifying a group of women—iconically Black—who were "less entitled to be parents." In various venues, Roberts asked Americans to consider the proposition that "denying someone the right to bear children deprives her of a basic part of her humanity."[28] Katha Pollitt, columnist for the *Nation,* argued that the "Murray-Gingrich orphanage proposal" did not simply threaten poor mothers. Rather, the proposal was an example of "symbolic politics" that aimed to teach Americans "to think of children who have living parents as 'orphans' just because those parents are young, female, unmarried and poor." Pollitt went on, "We are . . . being taught to see those mothers as having no rights and nothing to contribute—as being, in effect, dead."[29]

Someone sympathetic to the plight of poor mothers invited Clarissa Pinkola Estes, author of the enormously popular book *Women Who Run With the Wolves,* to speak at a congressional hearing on the Contract With America in 1995, when conservatives were promoting orphanages and other means of punishing poor mothers. Pinkola Estes, whose speech caused intense, partisan applause in the hearing chambers, echoed Marcella Mason's sentiments. She said, in part, "[T]he money that it takes to fund [orphanages and maternity homes] would more properly go directly to the recipients . . . As a woman myself who when I was eighteen years old had my first child—as a teenager—I think that most of us, even though we had made a mistake, does not mean that we are stupid." Fundamentally, Pinkola Estes argued that being young and being poor did not disqualify her or other women from motherhood.[30]

Politicians were largely uninterested in, or disagreed with, this argument as they pushed on toward "welfare reform" in the mid-1990s. In fact, the welfare reform bill that won bipartisan support in 1996, commonly called the Personal Responsibility Act (PRA), encoded a deeply negative assessment of poor mothers into law. Over and over in the introductory material appended to the PRA are "findings" that strongly suggest only women with proper and adequate resources can or should be mothers. The "findings" also indicate that poor mothers are illegitimate mothers, produce poor-quality children, and must be stopped from reproducing.

In the wake of the PRA, other government and community agencies have followed Congress's lead, adopting programs and slogans designed to convey (and enforce) this message: "Don't become a parent until you are truly ready to support a child."[31] In November 1999, the *Baltimore Sun* reported that some anti-teen pregnancy groups had adopted the slogan, "A baby costs $474 a month. How much is your allowance?"[32] These financial test/reality-testing messages mask a profoundly important set of issues about who can or can't "afford" to be a mother in the United States. The fact is, using the affordability test reveals that millions of girls and women cannot afford to become mothers because of circumstances beyond their own control. Jencks and Edin point out that "in 1989, a single working mother with two children needed about $15,000 worth of goods and services to make ends meet. Less than half the 25- to 34-year-old women [the demographic group with the fastest-growing number of single mothers] who worked in 1989 earned that much."[33] Using 1997 data, a study called "Equal Pay for Working Families" found that if women got equal pay, the annual family incomes of single working mothers would increase $4,459 on average—reducing poverty rates for this group by half, from 25.3 percent to 12.6 percent.[34] (Also important here is the fact that almost half of the children on welfare were born to women who were married at the time they gave birth.)

The most important point Jencks and Edin make is that economic policy in the United States creates and depends on sustaining a pool of low-wage workers, including women who make salaries too low to enable them to "afford" motherhood. The sociologists put it this way: "As long as America remains committed to competitive labor markets, open borders, and weak labor unions, most marginally employable adults will need some kind of public assistance if they have children."[35] In other words, using a financial test for motherhood would exclude millions of women in the United States from having children because their employers pay white women 73.2 percent and minority women 63.7 percent of what white men earn.[36]

These data seem never to make an impression on politicians. Nor have politicians and policy makers been moved by the data, available both before and after "welfare reform" was enacted, that many poor mothers have been stymied in their efforts to earn enough to "afford" their children because of the absence of day care opportunities. In 1994, Illinois had 34,000 families on a waiting list for day care, California families had a two-to-three-year wait, and thirty-three other

states reported substantial waiting periods as well.[37] In 1999, a study by the U.S. Department of Health and Human Services found that 82 percent of New York families eligible for government-subsidized child care were not receiving it, and that nationally the figure was even higher.[38]

In a brilliant study of poor mothers—their work and survival strategies—Kathryn Edin and Laura Lein emphasize the point that the financial test for motherhood would exclude millions of women through no fault of their own. Edin and Lein find that what poor mothers lack is "a living wage," not values or worthiness. They reject the personal attacks on poor mothers as dependents and bad choice makers and say, instead, that poor mothers' problem is a "labor-market problem." Poor mothers in their study "had made repeated efforts to attain self-sufficiency through work but the kinds of jobs they could get paid too little, offered little security in the short term and provided few opportunities over time. Meanwhile," they found, "mothers who chose to work were even worse off in material terms than their welfare counterparts."[39] Judging by the level of support for "welfare reform" rhetoric, most Americans would look at the bank balances of both the mothers on welfare and the ones at low-paying, dead end jobs and determine that neither group had the right to be mothers because they couldn't support children adequately on their own steam. By inference, it seems, most Americans embrace a proposition that is profoundly problematic in a democratic society, that motherhood should be a class privilege. Motherhood is appropriate, it seems, only for women with enough money to meet the financial test.

NOTES

1. Thomas G. Wiggan, president of Serono Laboratories, was the speaker. "Federal Employee Family-Building Act of 1987," Hearings, March 9, 1988, 67.
2. Carol Sanger, "M is for the Many Things," 63.

3. "Federal Employee Family-Building Act of 1987," Hearings, March 9, 1988, 24.

4. Reflecting and supporting the continued vulnerability of fertile women, U.S. Representative Dick Armey of Texas and five of his colleagues suggested in 1989 that the infertility problems of middle-class couples should be solved by canceling all women's abortion rights and transferring "1.5 million pre-born children each year . . . to infertile couples . . . This is a match which deserves much more attention . . . [It's] a genuine solution." "Infertility in America: Why Is the Federal Government Ignoring a Major Health Problem?" Eighth Report by the Committee on Government Operations together with Dissenting and Additional Views, 101st Congress, 1st sess., House Report 101–389, December 1, 1989 (Washington, D.C.: U.S. Government Printing Office, 1989), 34.

5. Seth Mydans, "U.S. Food Program Tightens Its Belt and Millions on Welfare Feel Pinch," *New York Times*, June 2, 1990, A10.

6. Bell, *Aid to Dependent Children*, 70.

7. "Illegitimacy and Its Impact on the Aid to Dependent Children Program: Implications for Federal and State Administrators," Bureau of Public Assistance, Social Security Administration, U.S. Department of Health, Education, and Welfare (Washington, D.C.: U.S. Government Printing Office, 1960), 47.

8. *Dandridge v. Williams* 397 US 471 (1970).

9. Thomas Ross, *Just Stories: How the Law Embodies Racism and Bias* (Boston: Beacon Press, 1996), 72.

10. Thomas Ross, "The Rhetoric of Poverty: Their Immorality, Our Helplessness," *Georgetown Law Journal* 79 (1991): 1520.

11. For *New York Times* coverage of these events, see, for example, Peter Kerr, "Trenton Legislator Proposes Overhaul of Welfare System," April 9, 1991, B4; Jason DeParle, "As Funds For Welfare Shrink, Ideas Flourish," May 12, 1991, IV, 5; Wayne King, "Maverick Democrat Confronts Trenton's Welfare Rules," September 4, 1991, B1; Wayne King, "Trenton Panel Supports Plan for Welfare," December 6, 1991, B1.

12. "Changes in State Welfare Reform Programs," Hearings, 7, 28.

13. For example, see Andrew Rosenthal, "Bush Backs Wisconsin Attempt at Welfare Reform," *New York Times*, April 9, 1992, D20, for a description of Wisconsin's family cap plans; and Jason DeParle, "California Plan to Cut Welfare May Prompt Others to Follow," December 18, 1991, Al, for a description of California's.

14. Gwen Ifill, "Clinton Backs New Jersey's Changes in Welfare System," *New York Times*, May 23, 1992, 8.

15. Linda C. McClain, "Irresponsible Reproduction," *Hastings Law Journal* 47 (January 1996): 398–99.

16. *C.K. v. Shalala*, 883 F. Supp. 991, 1014.

17. McClain, "Irresponsible Reproduction," 403. Welfare policy analyst Richard Nathan observed in 1992 that "New Jersey politicians have been kicked for a tax increase. They want something to kick back. In this case it is welfare babies. For a largely symbolic move, it is just not worth it. It sends the wrong message to people who have been down long enough—in some cases, all their lives." "Changes in State Welfare Reform Programs," Hearings, 94.

18. "Changes in State Welfare Reform Programs," Hearings, 28.

19. "Contract With America—Welfare Reform," Hearings before the Subcommittee on Human Resources of the Committee on Ways and Means, House of Representatives, 104th Congress, 1st sess., Part II, February 2, 1995 (Washington, D.C.: U.S. Government Printing Office, 1995), 1153.

20. Heather MacDonald, "The Ideology of 'Family Preservation,'" *Public Interest* 115 (September 1994): 45; "Contract With America—Welfare Reform," Hearings, Part I, 677.

21. Jason DeParle, "The 1994 Election: Momentum Builds for Cutting Back Welfare System," *New York Times*, November 13, 1994, Al. Eleanor Holmes Norton called the orphanage proposal "Murray's orphanage idea," and indicated that this type of child removal was "meant as a punishment and a deterrent for out-of-wedlock child-bearing." "Contract With America—Welfare Reform," Hearings, Part I, 584.

22. U.S. Representative Christopher Shay of Connecticut explained how the legislation ending AFDC would create block grants which "may be used to establish orphanages." Sheila Jackson Lee, a representative from Texas, pointed out how silly the orphanage plan was: "Under this [welfare reform plan], of the 541,000 children who are currently receiving AFDC in Texas, 288,000 would be denied benefits and only 310 federal orphanage slots would be funded." "Contract With America—Welfare Reform," Hearings, Part I, 735, 642.

23. Elizabeth Drew, *Showdown: The Battle between the Gingrich Congress and the Clinton White House* (New York: Simon and Schuster, 1996), 46.

24. See "Contract With America—Welfare Reform," Hearings, Part II, 841.

25. Ross D. London, "The 1994 Orphanage Debate: A Study in the Politics of Annihilation," in Richard B. McKenzie, ed., *Rethinking Orphanages for the 21st Century* (Thousand Oaks, Calif.: Sage, 1999), 98.

26. Christopher Jencks and Kathryn Edin, "Do Poor Women Have a Right to Bear Children?" *American Prospect* 20 (winter 1995): 47.

27. Eleanor Holmes Norton, "Contract With America—Welfare Reform," Hearings, Part II, 584.

28. Dorothy Roberts: "The Only Good Poor Woman: Unconstitutional Conditions and Welfare," *Denver University Law Review* 72 (1995): 931–48; "Irrationality and Sacrifice in the Welfare Reform Consensus," *Virginia Law Review* 81 (1995): 2607–22; "The Value of Black Mothers' Work," *Connecticut Law Review* 26 (1994): 871–78;

"Welfare's Ban on Poor Motherhood," in Gwendolyn Mink, ed., *Whose Welfare?* (Ithaca, N.Y.: Cornell University Press, 1999), 152–67; and *Killing the Black Body*, throughout.

29. Katha Pollitt, "Subject to Debate," *Nation*, December 12, 1994, 717.

30. "Contract With America—Welfare Reform," Hearings, Part II, 1344.

31. This motto comes from "A National Strategy to Prevent Teen Pregnancy," Annual Report, 1997–98, U.S. Department of Health and Human Services, June 1998, 1.

32. Kate Shatzkin, "A Better Message on Teen Pregnancy," *Baltimore Sun*, November 8, 1999, 1.

33. Jencks and Edin, "Do Poor Women Have a Right to Bear Children?" 45.

34. See, generally, "Equal Pay for Working Families" (Washington, D.C.: Institute for Women's Policy Research, 1999).

35. Jencks and Edin, "Do Poor Women Have a Right to Bear Children?" 47.

36. "Equal Pay for Working Families." Also see Abramovitz, *Under Attack, Fighting Back*.

37. Examples of presentations and reports targeting politicians and policy makers with this kind of information over time are: economist Nancy S. Barrett's testimony at "Economic Status of Women," Hearings before the Joint Economic Committee, Congress of the United States, 97th Congress, 2d sess., February 3, 1982 (Washington, D.C.: U.S. Government Printing Office, 1982), 85–86; "Mother-Only Families: Low Earnings Will Keep Many Children in Poverty" (GAO/HRD-91–62, April 2, 1991); "Testimony of the Child Welfare League of America," submitted to the Economic and Educational Opportunities Subcommittee on Early Childhood, Youth and Families on the Child Care and Development Block Grant and the Child and Adult Care Food Program, January 31, 1995, in "Contract With America: Child Welfare and Childcare," Hearings before the Subcommittee on Early Childhood, Youth and Families of the Committee on Economic and Educational Opportunities, House of Representatives, 104th Congress, 1st sess., January 31, 1995 (Washington, D.C.: U.S. Government Printing Office, 1995), 204–13.

38. "Millions in State Child Care Funds Going Unspent in New York," *New York Times*, October 25, 1999, A29. The article indicated that "the state has no detailed plan for getting the new money into the hands of low- and moderate-income parents."

39. Kathryn Edin and Laura Lein, *Making Ends Meet: How Single Mothers Survive Welfare and Low-Wage Work* (New York: Russell Sage Foundation, 1997), 220.

SECTION VI

The Way Forward

Moving Toward Reproductive Justice

The last twenty years or so have been particularly significant ones for reproductive issues, both globally and in the United States. These years have been marked by both a rethinking of "reproductive rights" and "reproductive health," and expanding our thinking of "reproductive justice," while also increasing interconnections between domestic reproductive politics and global ones.

Globally speaking, the most important events have been the two landmark United Nations (UN) conferences that took place in 1994 and 1995, the International Conference on Population and Development (ICPD) in Cairo and the Fourth World Conference on Women (FWCW) in Beijing (Petchesky 2003). Although held 20 years ago, these unprecedented conferences were significant in setting the stage for social change around reproduction in the subsequent decades. To offer some background, for some years these UN Conferences, particularly the ICPD, have been the sites of intense politicking over reproductive issues, sometimes setting the stage for the articulation of new policies by the United States and other developed nations, policies which have enormous implications for developing countries dependent on richer countries' aid. One of the best known of such policy announcements at an ICPD Conference was the so-called "Mexico City policy," unveiled at the 1985 gathering of this group in that city. The Mexico City policy, which originated during the presidency of Ronald Reagan, as anti-abortion sentiment was rising within the Republican Party, stipulated that the United States would give no funding to countries or NGOs (non-governmental organizations) which used their *own* funds to provide abortions or to refer women to abortion providing facilities. Since that time, the policy, now known as the "global gag rule," has become a proverbial ping pong ball of American domestic politics, being overturned by Democratic presidents, and re-instated by Republican ones. When in effect, this policy has been very costly to reproductive health organizations in the developing world, impeding the struggle to provide basic health services beyond abortion. In the selection in this section from her book *The Means of Reproduction*, journalist Michelle Goldberg describes the global impact on reproductive health when changes occur in the political parties of American presidents.

The main business of UN conferences is for the delegates to debate issues and eventually vote on a platform, which calls for member nations to adopt certain measures. To be sure, the agreed-upon platform does not have the binding force of law. Therefore it would be foolish to say that all the measures that were approved at these two conferences—or UN conferences more generally—are actually put into effect. Nevertheless, there is both a strong practical and symbolic value to agreements made at these UN conferences—countries do use these platforms as guidelines and often as justification for policies that might be controversial. This explains why the fights over the platforms at such conferences can be so bitter.

Both the Cairo and Beijing conferences were extremely contentious, with arguments about a range of issues and procedures, including who would compose official delegations, who would write up the official proceedings, what items would be voted on, and what language would be used in the final documents. The major fault lines that emerged in both instances was the "unholy alliance," as some have called it (Hartman 1995, p.151), between the Vatican and the delegations of several conservative Muslim and Latin American countries, on the one hand, and the delegations representing most of the rest of the 179 participating governments, including the United States, on the other. As Michelle Goldberg put it, in describing the highly contentious deliberations at these UN Conferences, it was "a fight over modernity itself" (2009, 104).

Because the Cairo and Beijing conferences took place during the presidency of Bill Clinton, a Democrat, the U.S. delegation was on the progressive side on issues of reproductive health, including abortion. At the Beijing conference, then First Lady Hillary Clinton gave a rousing speech in which she echoed a major conference theme, that of reproductive rights as human rights, and spoke of the important role reproductive health services play in the empowerment of women. A portion of that speech is reprinted in this section. In contrast, during the presidency of the George W. Bush (2000–2008), a Republican, the U.S. delegation at related UN conferences, such as one on the rights of youth, took on a very different, and far more conservative, character. For example, the U.S. delegation joined with the Vatican and a small group of very traditional countries to oppose a platform in support of comprehensive sex education and condom distribution (Associated Press 2002).

But if the major cleavage at Cairo and Beijing was between liberals and conservatives, or, to put it another way, between traditionalists and modernists, on reproductive issues, clear divisions also emerged *within* the reproductive rights community. These divisions can be described as between, on the one hand, the "population controllers" whose main focus historically has been on the widespread dissemination of contraception, typically through a medical model of intervention, and on the other hand, feminist activists who advocated the empowerment of women as the best way to help women in the Global South achieve their desired family size (Petchesky 2003). These divisions reflected a larger point of tension which runs throughout the field of reproductive services (and is mentioned periodically in this book): the fine, and sometimes confusing, line between viewing such services as emancipatory or coercive for women.

At both conferences, NGOs played a highly significant role, holding parallel meetings to the official proceeding, where positions on the often thorny issues of sexuality and reproduction were exhaustively discussed and negotiated. The NGOs in question are non-profit groups that are allowed by the UN to play a role in UN proceedings, including the advocacy and monitoring of agreed upon policies. Additionally, some influential leaders of these organizations, such as the head of the International Women's Health Coalition, also served on official delegations and played a key role in debating the final platform. At these conferences, reproductive rights activists made important conceptual and political gains. For example, the final platform passed by delegates in Cairo is the first international policy document to define reproductive health. That policy states (in paragraph 7.2):

> Reproductive health is a state of complete physical, mental and social well-being and not merely the absence of disease or infirmity, in all matters relating to the reproductive system and its functions and

processes. Reproductive health therefore implies that people are able to have a satisfying and safe sex life and that they have the capability to reproduce and the freedom to decide if, when and how often to do so. Implicit in this last condition are the right of men and women to be informed [about] and to have access to safe, effective, affordable and acceptable methods of family planning of their choice, as well as other methods for regulation of fertility which are not against the law, and the right of access to appropriate health-care services that will enable women to go safely through pregnancy and childbirth and provide couples with the best chance of having a healthy infant.

(UNFPA 2009)

Additionally, as revealed in the speech at the Beijing gathering by Hillary Clinton, mentioned above, the reformulation of *reproductive rights as human rights* gained currency and to this day continues to be used as a frame by activists globally and in the United States. Illustrating this, Human Rights Watch and Amnesty International, two of the leading human rights organizations, have explicitly endorsed this concept, in the aftermath of these meetings.

Abortion, predictably, was the most divisive issue at both of the UN conferences. The progressive-feminist coalition was not able to pass a resolution calling for abortion to be made available legally in all member countries. Note, for example, that the definition above from Cairo defining reproductive health does not mention the word "abortion" although it is alluded to. Indeed even the use of the terms "reproductive rights," "reproductive health" and "sexual rights" was opposed by some in the conservative faction at this and similar international gatherings. Nevertheless, some progress on the abortion front was made. The final document from the Cairo meeting acknowledged the problem of unsafe abortion and called on governments to make all abortions safe "where they are not against the law," and the Beijing platform calls on governments to review laws which contain punitive measures against women who have had illegal abortions (Petchesky 2003).

Delegates at these conferences also made progress on issues of sexual expression and sexual orientation, and, notably, the final Cairo platform called for the banning of female circumcision. In the selection in this section by Sonia Corrêa, Adrienne Germain and Rosalind Petchesky, the three longtime activist/scholars in the field of women's health, who were participants at both the Cairo and Beijing conferences, reflect on the aftermath of these historic meetings, and discuss the need for continued coalition efforts between those committed to reproductive rights, the gay rights movement, and HIV activists.

While the politics of these two landmark conferences still reverberate, and have unquestionably moved some policies in a positive direction, the daily lives of women in the developing world continue to be very challenging. In 1990, the Harvard economist Amartya Sen famously wrote about the "100 million missing women," the out of balance sex ratios between males and females in China, India and elsewhere in the developing world—an imbalance that has been attributed to sex selection abortions, the neglect of infant girls (such as withholding nutrition and healthcare), and even infanticide. Again illustrating the complex interplay of social structures, inequality, and individual choice, this problem of gender imbalance continues today, and the issue of sex selection abortions in places such as India is still highly relevant, as discussed in the selection by psychologists Ramaswami Mahalingam and Madeline Wachman in this section.

Moreover, the reproductive politics in the domestic United States and in the developing world are increasingly entwined. Beyond official policies of the United States—for example, the earlier mentioned "gag rule" which shifts with presidential administrations, and other restrictions placed on foreign aid, including whether condom distribution can be part of

HIV prevention campaigns—NGO activity in the developing world by those on both sides of the abortion (and gay rights) divide in the United States has had a dramatically increased presence in the years since the Cairo/Beijing meetings. For example, extreme anti-gay activists from the United States have been associated with the alarming rise in anti-gay policies in Uganda, including a discussion of a law that would permit the execution of gays (Gittelman 2010). At the same time, numerous medical and advocacy groups work to expand safe childbirth options and access to contraceptive services throughout Africa.

In the United States, an important rethinking has been occurring among those involved, as both activists and scholars, in reproductive issues. This shift is best described as a movement toward "reproductive justice." As described in the selection in this section by the sociologists Zakiya Luna and Kristin Luker, this reframing of the reproductive rights movement came about largely through the efforts of women of color who were dissatisfied with the narrow focus of that movement on abortion rights, to the exclusion of other issues. The concept of reproductive justice has been defined most clearly by Loretta Ross, one of the founders of the organization Sistersong, a coalition of groups of women of color focused on reproductive issues. As Ross has described the three core principles of this approach, every women has the right to: "Decide if and when she will have a baby and the conditions under which she will give birth; Decide if she will not have a baby and her options for preventing or ending a pregnancy; Parent the children she already has with the necessary social supports in safe environments and healthy communities, and without fear of violence from individuals or the government" (Ross n.d.).

The reproductive justice approach, it can be readily seen, while still firmly supporting legal and accessible abortion, also calls for renewed attention to other reproductive issues which have received less attention during the long struggle to defend abortion. Sterilization abuse (an issue which has not entirely disappeared, as the 2012 expose of California prisons mentioned in Section V revealed), the "family cap" provision of the 1996 landmark welfare reform legislation, cutbacks in social services such as food stamps and the WIC program (a nutrition program for women and infants) and quality childcare, the shackling of prisoners during childbirth, discrimination by service providers against disabled women's sexual and reproductive rights, coerced C-sections and other forced obstetrical interventions (typically on the most vulnerable women)—all represent examples of the expanded range of issues that occurs with a reproductive justice analysis (Luker and Luna 2013). Many of these issues have been substantively addressed elsewhere in this volume.

Beyond the attention to the specific areas mentioned above, a reproductive justice analysis has also focused on a critique of the concepts of "choice" and "privacy" as they have historically been used in the reproductive rights movement. "Choice," for example, which has been so central to the defense of abortion in the United States—as is obvious in the ubiquity of the term "pro-choice"—has been criticized by many (not only women of color) for its inevitable association with individualism and consumerism. The very use of the term "choice," as the argument goes, implies that women have the *means* to make a choice—whether it is to have an abortion, obtain birth control, or have the necessary income to adequately care for children. In a similar sense, "privacy," which is at the core of the U.S. Supreme Court decisions on both birth control and abortion, also has limitations. As Luker and Luna have argued in their discussion of reproductive justice, "Privacy assumes access to resources and a level of autonomy that many people do not have. A privacy approach cannot accommodate the fact that many people rely on government support for their daily activities. . .[including] family formation" (2013, 7). The fact that most insurance plans, even under the Affordable

Care Act, do not pay for assisted reproduction, and poorer women are more likely to suffer from infertility, is a prime example of the limitations of both "choice" and "privacy" when considering the reproductive situations of such women. Similarly, the enormous political pushback, discussed earlier in this book, against contraceptive coverage in the Affordable Care Act is another illustration of both how dependent some American women are on government provision of necessary reproductive health services and how difficult it is, for ideological reasons, to have these needs met.

As alluded to in the introduction and in the Solinger selection in Section V, "family caps" were a key feature of the Personal Responsibility and Work Opportunity Reconciliation Act of 1996 (PRWORA) as the welfare reform measure was formally named. These caps refer to the policy of not increasing the stipends of women receiving welfare if another child is born after she has already begun receiving public assistance. Aimed at discouraging childbearing among poor women, family caps have never been shown to affect how women and their partners make choices about family size (Donovan 1998). Though some states have opted to not adopt this feature, twenty-one states, according to the National Conference of State Legislatures, impose family caps on those receiving TANF grants, which in turn create new challenges for families already struggling.

A reproductive justice framework also reinforces the importance of attention to *coercion* in any discussion of reproductive services. Because so many contemporary reproductive struggles in the United States and globally are about gaining access—to birth control, safe abortion and obstetrical care, affordable assisted reproduction and so on—it can be easy to forget that some women face challenges of avoiding unwanted services. This coercion is shown most dramatically in the case of forced abortions, sterilization abuse, and forced obstetrical interventions, and less dramatically, in the economic pressures that lead women to become surrogates or egg donors—decisions that would not be made in many cases if the women in question were financially secure. Thus, the frame of reproductive justice creates a more comprehensive view of how best to support individuals in achieving their reproductive goals, irrespective of their resources and access to power.

CHAPTER 27

Reproductive Justice

Zakiya Luna and Kristin Luker

Reproductive justice (RJ) highlights the dynamic yet often tenuous relationship between the law, social movements, and academic scholarship.

The term reproductive justice itself is relatively new, conceived in 1994 by feminists of color to conceptualize reproductive rights struggles embedded in social justice organizing that simultaneously challenged racism and classism, among other oppressions (ACRJ 2005; Ross 2006). From its inception, the RJ movement called for recognition of the limitations of emphasizing choice, which had largely come to mean the choice to have an abortion (Luna 2009; Price 2010; Smith 2005). RJ encompassed the right to not have a child but also moved beyond that to include the right to have a child and the right to parent any children one has (Ross 2006).[1]

The legal framework of an individual's right to privacy, on which the right to abortion (and contraception) access was predicated, could not resolve the barriers to having children that many women of color and low-income women faced owing to their structural and political locations.[2] These roots notwithstanding, RJ's relevance goes beyond marginalized populations, because examining the reproductive disciplining some groups experience also highlights the reproductive privileging of others. RJ simultaneously demands a negative right of freedom from undue government interference and a positive right to government action in creating conditions of social justice and human flourishing for all.

An RJ analysis takes into consideration that the right to have a child and the right to parent are as important as the right to not have children. As such, issues of importance regarding the right to have children include population control, criminalization of reproduction, correlation of environmental degradation with infertility, cultural shunning of teen mothers, and access to assisted reproductive technology (ART). Issues of importance regarding the right to parent with dignity include incarcerated people's loss of reproductive rights, rapid termination of parental rights of people deemed unfit by the state, access to nonmedicalized birthing options, coerced obstetrics, and resistance to expanding definitions of family beyond a nuclear family unit.

RJ claims highlight more explicitly and proactively a foundational problem with which US abortion rights advocates have been unable or unwilling to grapple: Privacy assumes access to resources and a level of autonomy that many people do not have. A privacy approach cannot accommodate the fact that many people rely on government support for their daily activities, whether they be education (e.g. student loans), family formation (e.g., tax credits), or employment (Mettler 2011; cf. Reich 1964). The concurrent reproductive disciplining and reproductive privileging of different groups produce a linked set of experiences that point to devolution of the state in providing for the welfare of its members (Roberts 2005), the resolution of which requires more than protections of abortion rights.[3]

RIGHT TO NOT HAVE A CHILD

The legal battles around *Roe* have influenced jurisprudence beyond reproductive issues proper and public perception about the role of courts (Greenhouse & Siegel 2010), so the attention on the right to not have children, and on abortion in particular, is understandable. Yet, the lens of RJ is an enlarging one. Using the insights and expanded frameworks of the RJ movement and its scholarly companions, we see how a range of issues not traditionally considered under the rubric of reproductive rights become sites for activism and scholarship.

(WHO LACKS) THE RIGHT TO HAVE A CHILD

The breadth of this expansion is breathtaking, and we do not propose to examine it in its entirety. Rather, we present below some research that bears the imprint of the ideas of RJ. Emerging areas of scholarship deeply influenced by RJ as an analytic framework or movement have come to conceptualize the right to not have a child as intimately linked to the right to bear and raise that child with some measure of autonomy.

One particular area in this literature is the investigation of the differential targeting of what legal scholar Nancy Ehrenreich (1993) calls outsider women, whose reproductive decisions, once they are pregnant, are not considered worthy of respect. Thus, we turn to two overlapping areas of scholarship that elucidate how RJ is intimately linked to the right to have a child. The first is criminalization of reproduction, which highlights how some reproduction is not only discouraged but explicitly feared and penalized. The second is reproductive technology and the obstacles to having children that some groups face.

Criminalization of Reproduction

A small group of scholars have provided sustained analysis of the criminalization of reproduction, with particular emphasis on the impact of the drug war in constructing drug use and addiction as matters of crime rather than health, thereby moving the solutions from the health care system to legal system (Fentiman 2008; Janssen 1999; Paltrow 1990, 2009; Roberts 1991, 1996, 2009; Stone-Manista 2008). For example, in the wake of the moral panic over "crack babies," various states and administrative agencies have attempted to detain, confine, or incarcerate women whose behavior is thought to be damaging to their fetuses (Cherry 2007; Oberman 1991; Paltrow 2002), Although the American Medical Association (AMA) has noted that drug addiction is a disease, not a crime, legal and medical actors, using novel legal theories, have extended existing laws to punish women who use drugs. . . . Maternal drug use has thus been prosecuted as child abuse or as the delivery of drugs to a minor, resulting in lengthy sentences.

Analysis of the linkages between reproductive control and the criminal justice system also pointed to issues that go beyond traditional reproductive health or rights work. The term rights suggests placement within a legal system that recognizes a person's claim to protections or guarantees of freedom from certain interference of the state; in practice, however, many women cannot rely on these protections or guarantees.

Reproductive Technology

Debates about assisted reproductive technology (ART) reveal anxieties about who should reproduce and the relationship between law, science, and the private sector. Examining these practices also reminds us how gender and race stereotypes are perpetuated under the guise of neutral scientific progress (Almeling 2011; Roberts 2009; Thompson 2005). White, wealthy, heterosexual couples have used various forms of

ART without facing many questions about what burden such usage places on society; yet, being poor is perceived as a reason to not reproduce, and if a poor woman already has children, reproducing may even be seen as punishable. Infertility treatment is advertised to White and affluent couples (Hawkins 2013), whereas poorer women, nonnative English speakers, and women of color often find many barriers to receiving an official diagnosis of infertility—let alone treatment (Bell 2009; Guendelman & Stachel 2011; Harris 2014; Nachtigall et al. 2009; Ranji & Salganicoff 2009; Staniec & Webb 2007).

When women who use government insurance do access ART, they are questioned about their right to do so and represented as bad mothers whose actions require legal sanction (Forman 2011).

Limited regulation has . . . produced complex legal cases that push the boundaries of people's understanding of family. Populations that have had difficulty accessing ART include people with disabilities (Mutcherson 2009, Stafan 2008), prisoners (Roth 2004a), people with HIV (Keels 2010), single women (Lezin 2003), and same-sex couples (Anderson 2008, *Benitez v. North Coast Women's Care Medical Group* 2003). Reproductive technology is in practice still perceived as a luxury of which only a limited population should avail themselves (Jesudason 2009), which raises questions about whether and how social movements can meaningfully contribute to these debates.

RIGHT TO PARENT WITH DIGNITY

Concerns about the right to parent (healthfully and with dignity) range from the effects of the criminal justice system on families to the deleterious physical environments in which people raise children.

Birth Justice and Coerced Obstetrics

Within the concept of birth justice we find an emphasis on the actual conditions of birth, including access to culturally appropriate education about birthing options, freedom from undue medical intervention, and support for breastfeeding (Diaz-Tello & Paltrow 2010; see also http://blackwomenbirthingjustice. org). Scholars also argue that women of color experience a disproportionate amount of medical intervention in their births for non-medical reasons (Krauss 1991). Much like poor women and women of color who use drugs while pregnant, outsider women often find that their considered decisions during pregnancy and birth are deemed illegitimate and irrational (Ehrenreich 1993). For example, states have argued for the right to force a pregnant HIV-positive woman to take antiretrovirals against her will despite expert testimony suggesting that the risk of perinatal infection is small and largely unaffected by prenatal antiretroviral therapy (Halem 1997; *N.J. Division of Youth & Family Services v. L.V.* 2005).

However, higher-income women also find resonance with the desire to have one's birthing decisions respected. Forced cesareans for women whose labor is not progressing "properly" pit women's considered choices against their physicians' preferences (Chalidze 2009; Kukura 2010). More affluent women have organized to remove various laws that restrict their birth preferences for midwives or home birth, at times using disruptive tactics assumedly reserved for groups with limited access to the dominant political institutions (Craven 2010).

Incarcerated Women and Shackling

Racial disparities in sentencing, limited medical care, and overcrowding all become reproductive issues under the rubric of the right to parent with dignity as envisioned through this expansive lens of RJ. Some estimate that approximately one million women have a direct relationship with the criminal justice system; 20% of them are presently incarcerated (Sentencing Project 2012). Reproductive health services remain inadequate, whether in the context of pre-natal care or abortion, which, as a result of the Hyde Amendment, prisoners use their own funds to obtain (Roth 2004b, 2010). Approximately 70,000 incarcerated women are mothers, 2,000 entered prison pregnant, and more than 1,000 will give birth while incarcerated.

In various states, parental rights are termi-nated upon incarceration; in the remaining states, incarcerated parents face obstacles to maintaining relationships with their children during and after incarceration. These chil-dren, like others "at risk" or born of "bad" mothers, may become quickly incorporated into the convoluted child welfare system, which, some critics argue, meets the demand of wealthier people for adoptive children [Reich 2005; Roberts 2002; Solinger 2000 (1992)]. Thus, a larger concern of various RJ organizations is to understand how the criminal justice system facilitates the repro-ductive oppression of whole communities in terms of reproductive health and family structure.

One of the issues RJ organizations have made progress on is the shackling of preg-nant women. Shackling involves the use of restraints on the wrists, ankles, and/or abdo-mens of inmates, including pregnant women before and during birth (Ocen 2012; Suss-man 2008). Medical associations have stated that the practice is dangerous to both mother and fetus, as the restraints increase the risk of falling, impede the birth process, and result in injury (AMA 2011).

Predictably, federal and state policies and practice in this area vary widely. However, since 1999, 12 states, including Texas, New York, and Florida, have passed legislation to prohibit shackling during labor.

In 2012, California became the first state to ban shackling of pregnant inmates at any point during pregnancy. After multiple bipartisan attempts to pass the bill, it was signed into law after corrections eventually supported the change, which illustrates how expanding notions of a reproductive issue also requires expanding campaign sup-port. These victories are happening through organizing and coalition building aimed at drawing attention to laws that are already on the books (e.g., Supreme Court rul-ings on inhumane treatment of prisoners) but are not readily applied to vulnerable populations, such as incarcerated women, in the United States. The impetus for the campaign, however, was from community RJ organizations that worked in coalition with the American Civil Liberties Union of California and other organizations build-ing long-term support on a range of issues (Shain 2012).

DISCUSSION

Reproductive justice—as an analytic framework, movement, praxis, and vision—represents an advance in movement strategy and scholarship. RJ emphasizes how repro-duction must be considered among an array of social justice concerns. Consequently, reproductive justice is equally about the right to not have children, the right to have children, the right to parent with dignity, and the means to achieve these rights. As we first outlined, the movement emerged for many reasons, including the gap between the *Roe v. Wade* (1973) decision and the ability of laws to protect less-affluent popu-lations. Although rights are a part of justice, the nominal universalism of rights, espe-cially the right to privacy, masks structural disparities based on race, sexuality, gender, class, and disability, among other axes. RJ's expansiveness emerges from the need to account for the economic, social, and political disparities, and it is borne out in the array of issues taken up by activists and scholars.

Future Directions

RJ provides many fruitful avenues for future research in terms of theory, substance, and methodology. Theoretically, RJ speaks to, but does not resolve, some questions with which sociolegal scholars continually grapple: What are the limits of law for achieving justice? What nonlegal strategies do people use to overcome those limits? Can justice exist outside of law? How does legal mobilization by one movement have unintended consequences for linked or allied movements? What are the consequences of choices that cause lawyers make? What are the costs of legal strategies for groups supposedly represented by movements? How do countermovements affect movement strategy?

Substantively, there are many potential areas of research. One is the consequences of the Patient Protection and Affordable Care Act (ACA) of 2010. President Barack Obama's controversial inclusion of contraceptives implies a broader definition of health care. Many RJ activists would agree that by providing basic health care, the government is moving toward creating conditions that holistically support individual and community health, including having and parenting children. Yet, laws also must be enforced, and research on early implementation has already identified problems with vulnerable populations' access to the new resources offered through the ACA (Dennis et al. 2013; Sonfield & Pollack 2013). Applying a more radical RJ analysis could mean examining how the effects of the ACA are mediated by other phenomena such as environmental hazards or food insecurity. Further research could analyze what effect, if any, the ACA has on attitudes about who should and should not reproduce.

Other scholars may press forward examining the sociolegal implications of ART, including how globalization creates new dilemmas in the areas of ethics, commerce, and family formation (Lee 2009; Markens 2012; Twine 2011). With welfare reform and immigration reform on the horizon, the effects of family caps and health care waiting periods deserve renewed attention (Kelly 2010; Smith 2006). Sexuality

education has been a contentious issue for decades (Luker 2006), but there is still little understanding of how the ways in which youth themselves approach reproductive issues challenge adults' assumptions about the limits of reproductive autonomy. Yet other researchers may consider more deeply the intersection of reproduction and incarceration through persistent cases of coerced sterilization (Volz 2006; Johnson 2013) and criminalization of reproduction (Paltrow & Flavin 2013).

A Challenging Opportunity

In all modes of RJ, a key principle is to bring people made most vulnerable by issues to the center. These are often poor people, people of color, people with disabilities, and people with non-normative gender expression and sexualities. However, we want to caution against going too far in the direction of the "other" because the reproductive penalizing of some groups occurs within a context of the reproductive privileging of other groups whose experiences must also be critically interrogated. That said, the pressure for both scholars and movement actors to exclusively focus on abortion politics recurs as challenges to *Roe* are renewed in legislatures and courts. Ultimately, our review demonstrates how historically, there have been—and will likely continue to be—a variety of interrelated reproductive issues that deserve fuller attention despite the pressure. We look forward to seeing how scholars, practitioners, and activists take up the challenge of reproductive justice.

NOTES

1. A commonly referenced definition of RJ comes from Asian Communities for Reproductive Justice (now Forward Together), a founding organization of the movement: "the complete physical, mental, spiritual, political, economic, and social well-being of women and girls [that] will be achieved when women and girls have the economic, social and political power and resources to make healthy

decisions about our bodies, sexuality and reproduction for ourselves, our families and our communities in all areas of our lives" (ACRJ 2005, p. 1).

2. The idea of a coconstitutive relationship between (marginalized) social identities is often referred to as intersectionality, a term coined by legal scholar Kimberlé Crenshaw (1989). For more comprehensive discussion of this theory, its antecedents, and limitations, see Choo&Ferree (2010), Collins (1990), Guidroz & Berger (2009), Luft & Ward (2009), McCall (2005), and Yuval-Davis (2006).

3. Owing to space constraints, we focus on the domestic background of RJ, but international reproductive scholarship and activism are relevant. The RJ framework is often referred to as human rights based (Luna 2009; Price 2010; Ross 2006). The contestation over the meaning and goal of human rights occurs in movements worldwide with varying results (Merry 2006; Tsutsui et al. 2012). The RJ movement's engagement with international human rights discourse, particularly economic and social rights, however, makes it an outlier among US movements (Luna 2011) as a result of the US government's contentious history with the United Nations, containment of the meaning of human rights, and the early civil rights movement's unsuccessful attempts to engage with the United Nations (Anderson 2003; Somers & Roberts 2008; Soohoo et al. 2008).

CHAPTER 28

Thinking Beyond ICPD+10

Where Should Our Movement Be Going?[1]

Sonia Corrêa, Adrienne Germain, and Rosalind P. Petchesky

This conversation among three long time scholar/activists in the field of reproduction took place some ten years after the historic UN Conferences on women and population in Cairo and Beijing in 1994 and 1995. Yet, at the time of this writing, as we approach the 20th anniversary of these landmark Conferences, the issues raised by Sonia Corrêa, Rosalind Petchesky and Adrienne Germain are still very relevant. Their conversation points to some encouraging progress since the Conferences, yet also makes clear the huge amount of work that remains to be done by reproductive activists, and the new coalitions that should be pursued.

Ros: Let's begin by setting a frame for the history and legacy of the International Conference on Population and Development's Programme of Action.[2] When ICPD supporters refer to the Cairo agenda, they suggest a set of commitments not only going beyond but also very different from the family planning, population control and maternal and child health programmes of the 1950s to 80s. Less optimistically, many observers (including some feminists) have seen the Cairo and Beijing documents, like so many other human rights instruments, as at best noble words, with little practical follow-up affecting real women's lives. As leaders who work closely with women's groups in many countries and regions, what is your perception about actual implementation of the Cairo agenda?

Sonia: I'd like to make two points. First, we have to look at Cairo and our achievements and flaws in the longer term, *la longue durée*. People get very anxious and forget that ten years in this type of process is almost nothing, particularly when you're dealing with a debate that has been going on for 200 years. Second, the problems we see with Cairo are not just related to Cairo; they're related to the whole cycle of UN social conferences in the 1990s. The global climate of the 1990s was very different from today; it was a time of big promise because of the end of the Cold

War and the possibility of converting military expenditure into development, or better yet, human development. For the first time in 25 years, it was possible to discuss human rights as being universal. We forget that prior to the 1993 World Conference on Human Rights (in Vienna), the last UN conference on human rights was in 1968 (in Tehran). Another world conference on human rights was made possible in 1993 because of the climate, and now the climate has again become extremely chilly.

Ros: This wider context actually leads directly to my next question. From a more detached and slightly critical view of the Cairo and Beijing processes, the final documents were far from perfect. At the Global Roundtable in London a few months ago,[3] three major gaps that seemed very serious were identified. First was the failure to provide for access to safe, legal abortion as a basic human right. Second was the very limited way sexual rights were defined and not even named in those documents, even though we did make some progress. And third, the problem of resources and the failure of these documents to address the larger questions of privatisation, market forces, debt burden, militarisation, and all of the macro-economic and macro-political forces that have impeded making sexual and reproductive health and rights more than words. Do either of you want to add to or refine any of these points?

Sonia: First of all, those documents result from a political process; you don't just sit down and write them. Their ambivalences and gaps are a result of the political conditions and the balance of forces existing at the time. We didn't have the strength at that point to address abortion as a human right; we must now focus on building that strength. We are all aware of how contentious abortion rights and sexual rights are in international fora. The Programme of Action reflects what the political conditions allowed us to achieve at that point, and if you read

paragraph 8.25,[4] it's kind of a mixed picture. You can read the positions of the political forces at play in that paragraph very clearly. This is a clear example of the nature of the Cairo document.

Adrienne: I agree with Sonia's analysis. We must also look at the scope for practical action in today's world, having recognised that the context is not even as good as it was when the original documents were adopted. With regard to abortion, I'm not sure strategically that we can pursue it as a human right, in our global advocacy at least. The strategy adopted since Cairo – abortion as a public health issue – has been effective in forging WHO policy and technical guidance, and in various inter-governmental negotiations, where asserting a woman's right to abortion would not have worked. At the same time, all of us must take every opportunity, especially at country level, but even at global level, to bring the women's rights dimension into conversation and strategy, where possible. Of course, this is a strategic decision in each country.

Second, on sexual rights, in the political environments that we now face, both global and context-specific, we need to work on clarifying the concepts, and building the broadest possible support for language that could, with a lot of effort, be accepted in the global policy arena. Our biggest challenge is to get leading, sympathetic world governments to move forward on the recognition of sexual rights. In a way, the Brazilian government has set a marker with its 2003 resolution to the UN Human Rights Commission.[5] But the women's movement, together with the other constituencies (for example, lesbian, gay, bisexual and transgender (LGBT) groups and sex workers) that have the strongest vested interest, must think about how much we are able and willing to compromise, from our different perspectives, for the sake of progress in the global policy arena. We faced that challenge before Cairo with respect to reproductive rights, and I believe we can and should be doing the same with sexual rights.

Third, on resources, money is rarely the core problem. There's a lot of money out there under different labels which is badly used. So while the macro-economic picture is critically important, I also think that we should focus on reprogramming the resources that have already been allocated so that they benefit the people we are most concerned about.

Sonia: Brazil is a good example. In comparison with other developing countries, we have a huge health budget; yet it is still inadequate in the face of existing needs. Within that larger context, the resources for women's health and reproductive health are, and have historically been, much more limited than those devoted to HIV/AIDS. This budget imbalance between what is provided for reproductive health (elements of the Cairo agenda) and what is provided for HIV/AIDS can be explained by the sense of crisis. HIV/AIDS has much more capacity to mobilise the popular imagination, policymakers, providers, the media, civil society itself, than women's health does, which is viewed as "business as usual," not requiring significant technological or financial investment.

Ros: You've actually moved us toward my next question: What are the major obstacles holding us back, and what will be the most effective ways to surmount or transform these obstacles? Adrienne, you've pinpointed the misuse or distorted use of existing resources. Sonia, you're beginning to get at something much more elusive but critically important, and that is the question of popular perception and imagination, or what issues grab policymakers, media, opinion makers and the public.

Sonia: In Brazil, for example, we face a very mixed picture. As you know, Brazil was

ten years ahead of Cairo in the 1980s and a major leader in Cairo and afterwards on sexual rights. But since 2003, the Brazilian public has been discussing family planning in the most conventional neo-Malthusian way. What is grabbing society's imagination is the connection between poverty and the number of children poor women have. It's been very difficult for the feminists and even progressive demographers to shift that conversation in a different direction. It's not easy to convince the public and opinion makers that average fertility is already very low, and that the percentage of women who have more than three children is just 6% of women between 14 and 49. People see violence, they see beggars and homeless people living on the street and they connect that with women having too many children. The public do not yet fully understand the rights-based approach of Cairo. As an illustration, to address the "need for population control", some parliamentarians and policymakers are even urging a constitutional revision to authorise sterilisation (in the poorer sectors). It is very alarming.

On the bright side, we are starting to see a growing interest in the concepts of reproductive rights and sexual rights, terms which high-level policymakers are now using. More and more, journalists are asking feminists and LGBT activists about sexual and reproductive rights. The abortion debate has gained great visibility as a result of feminist activism on the subject; in 2004, the Minister of Women's Policies announced the creation of a working group to review punitive legislation. Conservative attacks on sexual rights with regard to LGBT communities have received great attention in the press, and two major legislative battles have just been won. State-level legislation restricting benefits for same-sex partners of public servants was defeated, as was a provision aimed at creating a government-funded programme to "rehabilitate" LGBT people. So this is all happening at the same time that we have this very tired debate about having fewer children as an antidote to poverty.

Adrienne: I would reinforce your point because we see the same phenomenon in the North: a resurgence of neo-Malthusian actors who were there pre-Cairo. And this phenomenon ten years after Cairo, this traditional demographic focus, goes hand in hand with the conviction among some actors that the Cairo reproductive health and rights agenda is too expensive and too complicated to implement, so why don't we go back to what we know and what we think worked earlier – in other words, vertical family planning. What they seem not to realise is that both the political and the demographic dynamics have changed since the 1990s. We now have the largest generation ever of people under 19 years of age who are, or are soon to become, sexually active.

For the first two to three decades of population policy, the focus was on women in their late 20s who had three or four children and were willing or could be persuaded to be sterilised. Most population growth will now come from much younger people. Where there are high prevalences of HIV and/or STIs, most modern contraceptive methods leave young people at risk of infection. In my view, we must offer young people the full range of contraceptive choices, while being very clear about STI and HIV risk, and ensure full access to condoms backed up by emergency contraception. The population field has never promoted condoms, however, is only recently taking up emergency contraception and has shied away from safe abortion. So, there is a dissonance that is worse than regrettable; it has led to enormous tragedy.

Of course, it's important to recognise, as Cairo did, that family planning is a crucial part of reproductive health services, and an essential right. Contraceptive prevalence has risen dramatically in the past 10–20 years, and that is to be celebrated, but there are millions of people around the world who still lack access to contraception. At the same time, some programmes are regressing to population control strategies. Such approaches foment resentment and fear among both women and men and in the end fail to achieve the fertility reduction they aim for.

Sonia: I agree with Adrienne. The fundamentalists' attack on Cairo, particularly backed up by pressure from the Bush administration, gives neo-Malthusians an opportunity to say: "Well, you see, it's so complicated. It raises controversy, so let's get back to family planning." Even the Bush administration, when it speaks out virulently in the global arena against abortions and reproductive rights, still gives some money, if not enough, to family planning and post-abortion care. What is being deleted from all sides is the feminist agenda, because of the big imbalance of power between the feminist movement and our allies on one side, and the other actors in this field.

Ros: So far, *gender* has not come across in all of what you've said. If the HIV/AIDS crisis grabs people, Sonia, why are the unnecessary deaths of 500,000 women a year from maternal causes not a crisis in the same way? Why do the murders of hundreds of women in Ciudad Juarez not grab people? Even with HIV/AIDS, the attention of media and politicians is not at all focused on black women aged 25–44 in the United States, whose risk of dying of AIDS is 13 times higher than that of their white counterparts. What is going on?

Sonia: One main problem, as I see it, is the way policymakers and epidemiologists view scale. They compare the number of women who die or have died because of HIV/AIDS in Brazil with the number of maternal deaths, and they say that maternal mortality is not a problem on the same level of magnitude. This is one of the reasons why it took six years, from 1997 to 2003, to institute a compulsory registration system for maternal deaths in Brazil in the national health surveillance system.

Ros: But is capturing the popular and political imagination really a matter of scale? Many more women in Brazil die of cervical cancer (or of breast cancer in the US) than die of AIDS, but where is the outcry?

Adrienne: It's true that epidemiologists weight numbers heavily. But issues like maternal death and lifelong maternal morbidity, or the death rates and lifelong consequences of violence against women, are still on the side burner because of the imbalance of power between men and women. Although women have mobilised in virtually every country, we are still very often marginalised when it comes to budgets, laws and policymaking.

Sonia: We feminists are very small in number. When even one of us moves from civil society to work in government, a big hole is left behind. So there's a problem of our human and institutional capacity that is also at play.

Ros: But vibrant, powerful, effective social movements have not been based primarily on numbers. One can think of many historical examples of movements that have prevailed without being enormous. Feminist leaders and organisations are only as effective and strong as the movements that stand behind them.

Sonia: I think that one problem is that we are kind of a guerilla movement. As feminists we are not many; we are very smart and can be very strategic, but we are small in comparison not just to institutions but also to other social movements. I can give you an example from Brazil, but it applies anywhere. If you compare the ability of the HIV/AIDS movement and the feminist movement in Brazil to make policy change, the big difference is that the feminists operate at the strategic level, trying to have experts in place, being very intelligent, with good policy formulation . . . but we don't have people screaming in the streets when things don't work. If the system is not working, HIV activists go to the streets; they have that capability of mobilising people.

Ros: Well, in the US more than a million people, mostly women and girls, marched in the streets of Washington DC last year for reproductive rights. An amazing moment, yet it seems to have disappeared from public memory. One important tool in spreading the word and mobilising people has been the internet, and it is being used more frequently to get groups of people to meet physically and work towards common goals. What else can we do to build a younger, more powerful movement for the coming decade that can sustain such actions? What do you think will be the most successful strategy for building that kind of movement?

Sonia: One challenge is that there's a new generation in the world. These girls (and boys) have grown up in conditions that differ widely from the conditions in which we became adult women. Our analyses and discourse on gender and reproductive and sexual rights don't always capture their imagination. My own daughter is often quite dissatisfied with the victimising tone of feminist analysis. Another challenge is the ability to make health systems work and to talk about them in a manner that responds to the needs and desires of people. What the intellectuals in the Brazilian HIV/AIDS movement demand is convergent with what people need on the ground. Sometimes, however, the feminist agenda is not exactly in line with what ordinary women want. One example is sterilisation. Many women want it as an option, but many intellectuals are critical of sterilisation. On the other hand, sometimes we do very well, as in the case of ensuring that women eligible under the law have access to safe abortion services, or as Uruguayan feminists did last spring when they pursued legal abortion through a broad reproductive health bill. Their public education efforts captured the imagination of many people, both younger and older. These success stories should be examined more closely for critical insights on how to move forward.

Adrienne: Regarding revitalisation, I don't actually think we've lost steam. Those of us who went into Cairo are ten years older now, we've been doing a lot of hard work in our own organisations and professions, and we're trying to carry the feminist movement agenda forward, often in our so-called "extra" time. What is revitalising me, and certainly should be part of the engine driving the politics of implementing the Cairo agenda, is the youth movement, in particular for their own sexual rights and health. Both young men and women, who at the same time as taking action and building networks that are coalescing into a movement, are changing how they themselves relate to each other and work together. While I want to recognise that it was largely women who initiated and brought the Cairo agreement to fruition – and until recently it was also primarily women who defended those agreements – what we've seen, even at the UN, is more and more of the youth, male and female, coming in to defend and take ownership of an agreement they realise is in their own interest.

In addition to the youth, to succeed and maintain our movement's legitimacy, credibility, and political power, we must do more to draw in the mainstream human rights community as our ally. They are still mainly preoccupied with civil and political liberties at the global level, with important exceptions such as Human Rights Watch and Amnesty International, and rarely engage with women, youth, sexual minorities and others at the country level. I also wonder why the wider women's movement is hardly working on sexual and reproductive health and rights in some countries and globally. Is it just a division of labour because we have so few resources to cover an enormous agenda?

Ros: If you raise the issue of HIV/AIDS, it really depends on which women's movement you're talking about. Women of colour organisations in the US are tremendously mobilised around HIV/AIDS because their communities are particularly at risk. They know HIV/AIDS is linked, for example, to prisons, because when men go into prison, they get infected and come back into the communities. Also, the rapidly growing number of incarcerated women get virtually no sexual or reproductive health care.

Adrienne: I agree, but my concern is that we must somehow mobilise greater interaction and solidarity across the many different elements of the women's movement, precisely to support each other. For example, activist women who are trying to work on behalf of women in HIV/AIDS movements are too often drowned out by other segments of those movements, even in sub-Saharan Africa where girls and young women are infected at much higher rates than men their age. So what can we do more broadly to support the struggle of HIV activists such as these? And how can they help us to work on changing global health policies and resource allocations?

Sonia: Certainly there are tensions. In Brazil, relations between many feminists, "ordinary" women, gay men, transvestites and sex workers, who are all major actors in the Brazilian HIV/AIDS scene, have not always been easy. This is true not just because of power differentials, but also because both feminists and the wider women's movement have difficulties dealing with sex workers and the issue of commercial sex. More recently, very productive dialogues on sexual rights have been evolving among feminists, LGBT groups and sex workers, but not everywhere, and often the greatest obstacle is the conversation between feminists and sex workers (of all genders). There's an ideological difference at play between and among women themselves. But the HIV/AIDS movement in Brazil has been able, with some disparities, to encompass a wide range of voices and positions, and HIV-positive women are gaining a voice and public space.

Adrienne: Exactly. Across the many elements of women's movements, as well as other social justice movements, we are not creating enough dialogue and engagement with each other such that we could build a much stronger political power base.

Ros: This really leads us to the issue of coalition building. Aren't you saying that if we could figure out good tactics for dialogue, the combination of the HIV/AIDS movement and the feminist sexual and reproductive health and rights movement, along with sex workers, LGBT groups and human rights groups, would be a very powerful political force?

Sonia: The creation of the concept of sexual rights is something we should value as a platform for conversation that may help drive coalition building. This is another conversation we have too rarely. While the definition of sexual rights in Cairo has limitations, we need to value it. It was the feminist community working at the UN level that crafted this incredible concept of sexual rights that goes beyond identity politics, allowing us to address issues of violence, race and disease prevention and at the same time issues of pleasure, autonomy and self-determination. Before this concept of sexual rights, we were talking basically identity politics, but that is not a lens through which we can effectively address or resolve political differences. We cannot continue to speak only among women.

Ros: The concept of sexual rights would never have been imagined without the LGBT movement, as well as the HIV/AIDS epidemic, which first made public discussion of sexuality unavoidable and then made it possible to speak about sexual rights. At the same time, it's also true that women's groups and feminist thinking were responsible for moving the sexual rights agenda towards a broader, more inclusive *human rights* frame.

Sonia: We did invent the sexual rights frame, but at the ground level, our rhetoric and activism are still mainly informed by identity politics. Sexual rights is the open platform to embrace everybody, but in daily political practice, we're still acting on the basis of our separate identities as (white) women, women of colour, sexual minorities, racial-ethnic minorities, which narrows our potential reach.

Adrienne: That's one reason I've been so energised by organised youth; those I know don't segment themselves by any identity except age. Rather, they take deliberate steps to be inclusive. In this way they may have the potential to reach more varied constituencies and to draw them in as they build their movements. I hope we can support and encourage their efforts to do this earlier and better than many of us have done.

Sonia: I agree with you, but it's not just a matter of gathering the different. You can gather people together, as in the World Social Forum (WSF),[6] without there being a genuine dialogue. We have to bridge differences. What is very interesting about the young people we met in London and elsewhere is that they have huge differences, yet they are able to weave their concerns and perspectives together to move beyond just "identities".

Ros: The crucial thing here is that "multiculturalism" as an approach to difference doesn't get us to transversal politics where people really listen to each other across differences and figure out together what those differences mean for building a coalition. That's something a lot of us who have been working on Cairo haven't been doing actively enough. We might look at the Rainbow Planet Coalition in South Asia[7] as a model of collaboration among women's groups, people living with AIDS, HIV/AIDS activists and sex workers.

Sonia: Yes, but we have to recognise that these conversations are just starting. Here we have a major problem when you get back to policy level; there's a huge tension and gap between the time-frame of policymaking, with many emergencies all the time, and the longer time required for building coalitions and bridges.

Ros: Another issue is that some of us have tended to operate in certain defined UN spaces. Should we attempt to have a stronger presence in alternative political spaces such as the WSF?

Sonia: The WSF is certainly a space where you are able to interact and to raise the agenda of sexual and reproductive health and rights, to make it visible and create awareness about how it links to other agendas. I would say the WSF works as a kind of marketplace for social advocates where we can publicise sexual and reproductive health and rights. This is important to ensure that WSF actors fully understand what the Bush war against women, young people and sexual rights advocates means, for example, and how it links to the neoconservative agenda more broadly. But whether the WSF can be a viable space for building cross-sectoral alliances remains to be seen.

Ros: In addition to alliances through the WSF, youth coalitions and other groups interested in sexual rights and HIV/AIDS, what about the more mainstream reproductive health and medical organisations, the kind of organisations that we were trying to interact with at the Global Roundtable?

Adrienne: First of all, I hate to label and to be labelled, but I would distinguish between the broader medical and public health community and the family planning community. One of the most tenacious commitments of family planning/population groups pre-Cairo was to avoid medicalising contraceptive services.

In Asia, for example, they favoured services that could be delivered by a specifically trained family planning worker who didn't have a medical background. In sub-Saharan Africa, family planning was often provided in maternal and child health services, but by mid-level workers not trained to address the many dimensions of reproductive health. By comparison, the Cairo agenda requires a functioning health sector. And it's precisely the health sector that the family planning and population movement didn't want to engage with except when absolutely necessary, in the case of complications and emergencies.

Partly as a result of this history of division between health and family planning, a substantial segment of health sector leaders I have met outside the US were narrowly trained in family planning, and are not at all persuaded that reproductive health should have priority. So we commonly see lack of investment in obstetric care, diagnosis and treatment of reproductive cancers, and diagnosis, testing and treatment for STIs in women. The longstanding family planning/population community – and here I'm talking about groups like the USAID population programme, or Washington DC lobbyists – appreciates and provides rhetorical support for the long-term vision of Cairo, specifically reproductive health, yet when you look at where their resources are going, it is family planning. They feel compelled to endorse the reproductive health agenda of Cairo but they also feel free to say that Cairo is too expensive and too complicated, so let's just do what we know how to do. The divide is now complicated with HIV/AIDS; we must promote and support universal use of condoms, but this is a technology the family planning field has said was not effective enough for contraception since the IUD and pill came on the scene.

Sonia: I agree with Adrienne's analysis in terms of the global level, particularly in the US, but there's a lot of variation across contexts. In the case of Brazil, our relationship with the medical community and public health professionals was a key element in the construction of the whole women's health agenda. The same applies to HIV/ AIDS policies. Because the women's health agenda was about reconstructing the health system, we have always had a kind of alliance with both health professionals and policymakers. But there remains an unresolved tension. Most public health advocates and managers tend to emphasise a universalist concept of collective health and resist any specific health agenda. They may rely on macroeconomics or scarcity of resources as their main argument (World Bank economists), or they may emphasise class dimensions and inequality (Brazilian public health advocates), but they often resist focusing on the needs and demands of specific social groups, such as women and sexual minorities.

Adrienne: The same resistance to a gender approach is true in some recent global initiatives and donor approaches to overall development strategies like the Poverty Reduction Strategy Papers of the World Bank, funding modalities like sector-wide approaches and even major reviews of health challenges such as the report of the Commission on Macroeconomics and Health.[8] Yet, where health systems are the weakest, and by weak I mean lacking money and also trained staff, the bulk of the most disadvantaged, or sickest, most incapacitated people are women and children. To change this, we must not only strengthen primary care, but also create an effective referral system to functioning secondary level care. If you undertake this strengthening, focusing initially on women's needs, you will at the same time build a health system capacity that ultimately serves everybody. A challenge that the movement faces is to convince people that reproductive health is not the demand of a special interest group but of the majority, especially if you include healthy babies and young children in reproductive health.

Sonia: Two things are missing in this discussion. One, looking to the Brazilian experience, which would also apply to other Latin American countries at least, is that most components of reproductive health or women's health are perceived and performed by the professionals in the health system as something secondary. This is because simple or routine and repetitive health measures are not as highly valued by many health professionals as high-tech ones. The director of one of the first clinics to provide abortions in Recife says that it's very difficult to introduce manual vacuum aspiration, for example, because the doctors tell her it is poor technology for poor countries.

The second missing element is that in the last 20 years, at least in Latin America, some obstetrician—gynaecologists have been our major allies on the very critical issue of abortion, committed and outspoken leaders such as Dr Anibal Faúndes and Dr José Barzelatto in Latin America, and Dr Mahmoud Fathalla in Egypt. Earlier, you had a handful of doctors, whereas now there are many in Brazil, Uruguay, Argentina, Mexico, who are really engaged in the conversation on safe, legal abortion. This is a major achievement we should not forget.

Ros: Good points. Before we close, I want to note that one part of the world we haven't talked about is Central and Eastern Europe. There weren't many women from that region at Cairo, and although there were more at Beijing, both documents are based on a North–South paradigm, which Central and Eastern Europe do not fit into very well. Often, their governments do not identify themselves with the developing world, which can be a huge barrier to implementation of Cairo and Beijing. Activists in that part of the world have had to work in unique ways when lobbying their governments.[9] So let's continue to broaden this conversation and make it more inclusive.

Now, to close, I want to take us back to questions of strategy. Given the state of health systems and the divisions among women's groups, family planning groups and health establishments, could you each try to map a few strategic priorities for the women's movement going forward?

Sonia: The many layers we've addressed suggest an array of challenges not easy to summarise. The international women's sexual and reproductive health and rights movement needs to understand and plan for the fact that our agenda is long term and that its translation into concrete policies and effective rights takes persistence beyond UN documents and demographic and epidemiological evidence. It is a matter of struggle, of political economy involving powerful forces that are often not in our control. With this in mind, there are at least three major tasks at hand. The first is to systematically connect microanalysis and processes with macro-trends in financial and trade policies as they affect governance at large and the structure of health systems in particular. An example would be developing a much more rigorous analysis of the impact on sexual and reproductive health and rights, in different contexts, of privatisation of health services and of trade agreements within the World Trade Organization (WTO), particularly GATS.[10]

The second area is partnerships and alliances. Potential partners and allies will differ according to context. For instance, in Brazil the demographic community has been a critical ally of feminists, but this is not true everywhere. At the global level, our conversation indicates that dialogue with the HIV/AIDS, LGBT and human rights communities is a priority, along with a range of actors involved in the World Social Forum. And while many tensions and misunderstandings persist among the feminist movement, family planners and the medical community, we must continue to work with these groups.

This leads me to the biggest challenge: we cannot move productively in all these areas with our current woman-power. For

that reason, a strategic and urgent effort is required to ensure an infusion of new energy from diverse groups of all ages, but especially the younger generation – women, men and other gender identities – in our debates and organisations. This renewal will take different forms in different settings, but it is not something that we can keep delaying as if the movement will renovate itself "naturally".

Adrienne: To achieve access to safe, legal abortion, realisation of sexual rights and provision of sexuality education and health services for the young people already born, we must hone our strategies even further. First of all, we must help HIV/AIDS policymakers see that prevention in girls and women requires full financing and implementation of the Cairo and Beijing agendas. We talked earlier of capturing the imagination and attention of the public and policymakers. We have a lot of work to do to convince HIV/AIDS leaders to invest their resources in expanding access to and strengthening condom provision, sexual and reproductive health services and sexuality education that promotes gender equality, women's empowerment and human rights.

Second, we need to heighten the movement's strategic investment in global processes and frameworks, and in today's world that means the Millennium Development Goals (MDGs) and Declaration. We have to take time to comment thoughtfully on documents, attend technical meetings, lobby governments and all the rest. We know that, perhaps more than any other UN conference in the 1990s, Cairo provides the foundation for the MDGs; just look at Cairo's chapter titles! These goals are now the world's shared destination, and Cairo is the most direct route to achieving them. People worry that Cairo's reproductive health goal is missing from the MDGs, but I say that if we get the global plan to achieve the MDGs right, sexual and reproductive health and rights will be the backbone.

Finally, and we've touched on this throughout, we need to deepen our commitment to each other and to those we represent, while at the same time, as Sonia says, building new allies and rejuvenating our own movement. Feminists, demographers, family planners, health service providers, AIDS activists, human rights advocates and youth leaders all want fewer women dying and suffering from complications of pregnancy, HIV/AIDS and violence. We all want kids to grow into healthy, happy adults. We all know that sexuality and power lie at the core of both pleasure and great pain. In October 2004, hundreds of heads of government and other global actors signed a World Leaders' Statement supporting ICPD on its tenth anniversary and calling for full funding and prioritisation of this historic action plan.[11] We need to help them make good on their commitment.

Ros: I want to go back to Sonia's point about the importance of realising sexual and reproductive health and rights beyond UN documents. It can move us, not to a conclusion, but to new points of departure. One of these, which we touched on earlier but bears further comment, is that of broader coalitions. If we think of the powerful, often pernicious forces driving today's world – neoliberal economic regimes, militarism and imperialist interventions, religious fundamentalisms – it's clear that all involve massive violations of sexual and reproductive rights. The positive side of these assaults (if there is one) is that they create new oppositional constituencies. I'm thinking of health care advocates, providers and consumers who oppose privatisation and shrinkage of public services; human rights and anti-war groups outraged by sexual torture in Iraq, Guantánamo and elsewhere, and the doctrine of imperial impunity that sanctioned it; and the sexual minorities, sex workers, youth, married women and others who suffer the greatest indignities from fundamentalist definitions of purity, manhood, womanhood and reproduction. All these constituencies are important allies in

the struggle for the right to bodily integrity. But what this means is we can no longer see women's bodies as the exclusive site of sexual and reproductive abuses, or women as the exclusive claimants of sexual and reproductive rights. We need to reaffirm Cairo and Beijing for sure, but we also need to move beyond them.

NOTES

1. "Our movement" refers to the feminists who helped generate the outcomes of many UN agreements during the 1990s, especially the 1994 International Conference on Population and Development (ICPD) in Cairo, and the 1995 Fourth World Conference on Women (FWCW) in Beijing, as well as many others who have defended those goals and are working in many and various ways to achieve them.
2. The ICPD was a landmark meeting at which 179 governments agreed to a comprehensive Programme of Action to ensure universal access to reproductive health, uphold fundamental human rights, alleviate poverty, secure gender equality and protect the environment. At the FWCW the following year, 179 governments agreed to a Platform for Action to secure women's human rights and to eliminate discrimination and violence from women's public and private lives. Hereafter, "Cairo" refers to the ICPD or the ICPD Programme of Action, and "Beijing" to the FWCW or the FWCW Platform for Action.
3. The Countdown 2015 Global Roundtable was an NGOled international meeting marking ICPD at 10, 30 August–3 September 2004, London.
4. "In no case should abortion be promoted as a method of family planning. All governments and relevant intergovernmental and non-governmental organizations are urged to strengthen their commitment to women's health, to deal with the health impact of unsafe abortion as a major public health concern and to reduce the recourse to abortion through expanded and improved family planning services. Prevention of unwanted pregnancies must always be given the highest priority and every attempt should be made to eliminate the need for abortion. Women who have unwanted pregnancies should have ready access to reliable information and compassionate counselling. Any measures or changes related to abortion within the health system can only be determined at the national or local level according to the national legislative process. In circumstances where abortion is not against the law, such abortion should be safe. In all cases women should have access to quality services for the management of complications arising from abortion. Post-abortion counselling, education and family planning services should be offered promptly which will also help to avoid repeat abortions."

5. This resolution is the first-ever UN resolution with a primary focus on human rights and sexual orientation, and would have condemned countries that discriminate based on sexual orientation.

6. According to its Charter of Principles: "The World Social Forum is not an organisation, not a united front platform, but '. . . an open meeting place for reflective thinking, democratic debate of ideas, formulation of proposals, free exchange of experiences and inter-linking for effective action, by groups and movements of civil society that are opposed to neo-liberalism and to domination of the world by capital and any form of imperialism, and are committed to building a society centred on the human person.'"

7. A coalition of groups working on the rights of sex workers and sexual minorities, under the rubrics of sexuality, HIV/ AIDS and minority status.

8. A WHO commission examining the interrelations among investments in health, economic growth and poverty reduction. At: <www.cmhealth.org>.

9. The authors would like to acknowledge the input of Wanda Nowicka.

10. The General Agreement on Trade in Services is an international trade agreement that was adopted as part of the Uruguay Round of trade negotiations and came into force on 1 January 1995, with the advent of the WTO. "The aim of the GATS is to gradually remove all barriers to trade in services. The agreement covers services as diverse as banking, education, health care, rubbish collection, tourism or transport." Its details continue to be under negotiation. See <www.gatswatch.org> and <http://tsdb.wto.org/wto/public.nsf>.

11. At: <www.icpdleadersstatement.net>>.

CHAPTER 29

The Globalization of the Culture Wars

Michelle Goldberg

One of the very first things that George W. Bush did upon taking office was to reinstate the global gag rule, resulting in clinic closures and contraceptive shortages worldwide. Still, early on it wasn't entirely clear just how much damage the new president would do to sexual health internationally. Colin Powell, the secretary of state, was a big supporter of the UNFPA, and, probably at his behest, Bush's first budget proposal asked for a $25 million appropriation to the agency, the same amount the United States had given the year before. In written testimony to the Senate Foreign Relations Committee, Powell said, "We recognize that UNFPA does invaluable work through its programs in maternal and child health care, voluntary family planning, screening for reproductive tract cancers, breast-feeding promotion and HIV/AIDS prevention. . . . We look forward to working with you and your colleagues to secure the funding necessary for UNFPA to continue these activities." Congress responded, exceeding the administration's request by appropriating $34 million for the fund.

Days later, though, Congressman Chris Smith joined with fifty-four other members of Congress to urge the president to freeze the money, citing the Population Research Institute's charges about UNFPA complicity in forced abortion in China. Smith is easily the Population Research Institute's closest ally in Congress, and he made sure the organization had a voice in government debates. In October 2001 he convened a House panel to look at the group's allegations, calling Mosher and his colleagues to testify, and on January 31, 2002, he wrote to Bush imploring him not to fund the organization. The UNFPA, he wrote, "clearly supports a program of coercive abortion and involuntary sterilization." He cited evidence from an "an undercover fact finding team" sent to Sihui, one of thirty-two counties where the UNFPA operates in China. "The investigators were told that family planning is not voluntary in Sihui, and coercive family planning policies in Sihui include: age requirements for pregnancy; birth permits; mandatory use of IUDs; mandatory sterilization; crippling fines for non-compliance; imprisonment for non-compliance; destruction of homes and property for non-compliance; forced abortion and forced sterilization," he wrote. The UNFPA, Smith charged, was complicit in these outrages.

That was the big lie. Early on, the UNFPA had failed to loudly and consistently condemn China's population-control abuses, but as a range of investigators would soon find, it was now working hard on the ground to combat them. The UNFPA had changed under Sadik's leadership and the mandate of the Cairo conference, and was now the only group able to work inside China to try to push the Chinese *away* from the compulsions of the one-child policy. When Bush took office, the UNFPA was working on a project in thirty-two Chinese counties that was meant to demonstrate how the state could move from coercive to voluntary programs. Suspending work in China would have meant giving up whatever influence the UNFPA had.

In his letter to Bush, Congressman Smith neglected to mention that the "investigators" who ostensibly uncovered UNFPA misdeeds were a Population Research Institute team. Based on their findings, Smith urged Bush to exercise a prerogative given presidents in the Kemp-Kasten Amendment, a Reagan-era law that orders money to be withheld from any organization or program that "as determined by the President of the United States, supports or participates in the management of a program of coercive abortion or sterilization."

Bush decided to freeze the money temporarily, pending a State Department investigation. Even before that team left for China, a three-person British delegation, chaired by Edward Leigh, an antiabortion Tory MP, embarked on its own fact-finding mission. Upon returning, Leigh told the *Washington Times* that "there was evidence UNFPA is trying to persuade China away from the program of strict targets and assessments. My personal line is British or U.S. funds should not be used for coercive family planning, and I found no evidence of such practices in China."

The State Department mission concluded exactly the same thing. "We find no evidence that UNFPA has knowingly supported or participated in the management of a program of coercive abortion or involuntary sterilization in the PRC," it said in a post-trip report. "We therefore recommend that [the] $34 million which has already been appropriated be released to UNFPA."

All the evidence, then, showed that PRI's allegations were unfounded. Indeed, by supporting the UNFPA the United States could have helped work against China's terrible abuses of reproductive rights. But instead of acting on the State Department's report, the White House kept it under wraps for almost two months, finally releasing it on the same day that it announced its decision to permanently cut off UNFPA funding. Powell was forced to defend a decision that contradicted his own office's findings, as well as his own evident beliefs. "Regardless of the modest size of UNFPA's budget in China or any benefits its programs provide, UNFPA's support of, and involvement in, China's population-planning activities allows the Chinese government to implement more effectively its program of coercive abortion," he wrote. "Therefore, it is not permissible to continue funding UNFPA at this time."

The American contribution represented more than 12 percent of the UNFPA's budget, and its loss was a harsh blow, one that would mean *more* unwanted pregnancies and abortions all over the world. By defunding the agency the administration established a pattern that would mark everything it did in the field of reproductive and sexual health. Henceforth, expert opinion and international consensus would be no match for right-wing shibboleths. Abstinence would be promoted as the only option for young people trying to avoid HIV. Groups getting American support to fight the AIDS epidemic had to pledge not to support prostitution, stymieing efforts to provide services to sex workers. (Brazil, which has been especially successful at curbing HIV, in part by working with prostitutes' rights groups, chose to turn down $40 million in American funding rather than cooperate with its restrictions. "We can't control [the disease] with principles that are Manichean, theological, fundamentalist and Shiite," said Pedro Chequer, director of Brazil's AIDS program.) American delegations to United Nations conferences on women and children began to look like panels at the World Congress of Families, staffed with people like Janice Crouse, head of Concerned Women for America; Christian radio host Janet Parshall, narrator of the hagiographic documentary *George W. Bush: Faith in the White House*; and John Klink, a member of the Vatican's team at Cairo.

"The Bush administration decided, for whatever reasons, that that was one area where they could throw social conservatives a bone," said Carlson, the World Congress of Families organizer. "I hope it was out of principle, but I'll settle for expediency." Either way, he noted, "they were very consistent."

Ellen Sauerbrey, a right-wing activist with scant experience in international affairs, became the American ambassador to the UN Commission on the Status of Women. "I always feel when I'm being introduced as a representative of the United Nations that I have to say I'm a conservative; I'm not a feminist," she told the Mormon group United Families International. She went on to cite that great expert in international human rights, Fox News demagogue Sean Hannity: "Sean Hannity, this morning, talked about visions and the differences in visions. My perception is that this prevailing vision at the UN is one that is based on rights, but rights without responsibility. Family, whatever you want it to be. Sexual freedom, anything goes. Practically every resolution that goes before the U.N. . . . somebody tries to figure out a way to put in 'reproductive services.'" In 2006 she was promoted, via recess appointment, to become assistant secretary of state for population, refugees, and migration.

It's important to note that throughout all this the United States remained the world's largest donor to global family planning. Funding for international reproductive health stayed stagnant during the Bush administration, in part because congressional family planning champions repeatedly thwarted administration attempts to make deep cuts. In the fiscal years 2006, 2007, and 2008, for example, the administration tried to slash more than $ 100 million a year from global reproductive health programs, representing almost a quarter of the total U.S. contribution. But Congress held the line, even increasing the budget slightly in 2008, from $435.6 million to $457.3 million.

Because of the global gag rule, though, none of this money could go to the two organizations, the International Planned Parenthood Federation and Marie Stopes International, that have the most extensive infrastructure in the developing world. America's antiabortion politics thus ended up undermining all kinds of women's health services worldwide. Both the IPPF and Marie Stopes provide abortions in countries where they are legal, but they also offer other kinds of care, including family planning, HIV counseling, STD treatment, prenatal care, management of delivery complications, and childhood immunizations. When they close, there are often no other facilities to replace them. Because of the global gag rule twelve countries—Cape Verde, Chad, Comoros, Gabon, the Gambia, Mauritius, Solomon Islands, Sri Lanka, Tonga, Vanuatu, West Samoa, and Yemen—lost access to USAID-supplied contraceptives altogether, because in each the local IPPF affiliate was the only outlet for them.

In other countries the gag rule forced clinic closings and led to contraceptive shortages. Kenya saw the closing of six of fifteen clinics run by the Family Planning Association of Kenya, the local IPPF affiliate—and the country's leading provider of Pap smear tests for cervical cancer. Marie Stopes, which provides half of all family planning services in Kenya, lost two clinics, while others laid off staff and raised their prices. Ethiopia's largest family planning organization, the Family Guidance

Association—also an IPPF affiliate—lost more than a third of its funding.

Meanwhile, agencies that accepted U.S. funds couldn't direct their clients to providers of safe abortion, even in cases where such abortion was legal. Ethiopia, for example, liberalized its abortion law in 2005 to allow women to end their pregnancies in the case of rape, incest, and on broad health grounds. In his guidelines for implementing the new law, the health minister emphasized the severity of the problem of unsafe abortion. "[U]nsafe abortion is one of the top 10 causes of hospital admissions among women," he wrote. "Unsafe abortion accounts for nearly 60% of all gynecologic admissions. . . . Due to the clandestine nature of unsafe abortion services, however, these figures represent only the tip of the iceberg and not the full magnitude of the problem." But because of the gag rule, employees of American-funded NGOs in Ethiopia couldn't tell women how or where to access abortion under the new law. The United States was undermining Ethiopia's life-saving reforms from within.

Diplomatically, the Bush administration moved to undo the progress that had been made under Clinton at Cairo and Beijing. In December 2002, at a UN conference held in Bangkok to discuss ways of implementing the Cairo program of action, the Bush administration shocked much of the world when it implied that it was withdrawing America's support for the historic agreement. The United States, declared Assistant Secretary of State Arthur E. Dewey, "supports the sanctity of life from conception to natural death. . . . [T]here has been a concerted effort to create a gulf by pushing the United States to violate its principles and accept language that promotes abortion. We have been asked to reaffirm the entirety of the ICPD [International Conference on Population and Development] principles and recommendations, even though we have repeatedly stated that to do so would constitute endorsement of abortion."

Arguing that terms like "reproductive rights and reproductive health" were code for abortion, the U.S. team tried to strong-arm other countries into jettisoning them, essentially amending Cairo. It also attempted to strike a reference to "consistent condom use" as an AIDS-fighting strategy.

"Our Philippine delegation received extreme pressure from back home, as well as inside the negotiation room, to come to the side of the U.S. delegation," said Filipino activist Gladys Malayang. But it didn't work. With discussions deadlocked, the United States forced a vote, a highly unusual move in the consensus-driven world of UN confabs. Except for two abstentions, every country present voted against America. It was a striking rebuke. "Given the way the U.S. participated during the negotiations, it was clear they were determined to influence us," said one South Asian delegate. "I don't think they expected to come up against this unified Asian position."

Unable to make common cause with Asian countries to fight reproductive rights, the United States, like the Vatican before it, found support in the more repressive quarters of the Middle East and North Africa. Even as the United States purported to fight a war against radical Islamism—a war it sometimes justified by the abuses Muslim fundamentalists inflict on women—American delegates joined hands with their colleagues from Iran and Sudan to undermine international agreements on women's rights. The country that once led the Western world in Cairo became the most powerful member of the fundamentalist alliance at the UN.

The right-wing Christian-Muslim coalition suffered a severe setback on 9/11, with hostility on both sides making it ever harder to work together. Before the attacks Carlson and Wilkins had been planning simultaneous World Congress of Families conferences in Mexico City and Dubai, with funding, Carlson said, from major evangelical organizations. After 9/11, that all fell apart. There were still contacts, "just at a much more careful level," he said. "We continued working with the Organization of the Islamic Conference up until 9/11. After that we had to be much more informal."

Eventually, however, Wilkins succeeded in partnering with the government of Qatar to organize a conference in that country's capital. Held in November 2004, the Doha International Conference for the Family brought together American groups like C-FAM and the Family Research Council with Muslim speakers, including Dr. Mahathir Mohamad, former prime minister of Malaysia, and Sheikh Yusuf al-Qaradawi, dean of the College of Shariah and Islamic Studies in Qatar. Qaradawi had earlier caused an uproar during a visit to Britain because of his support for wife beating and the execution of sodomites, though his apologists pointed out that he believes men should beat their wives lightly, and only as a last resort. Representing the Bush administration was Allan Carlson's close friend Wade Horn, then the assistant secretary for children and families in the Department of Health and Human Services.

The Doha gathering imitated the form and language of big UN meetings, replete with preparatory conferences, a declaration, and a call for action. There was an official conference report written in perfect UN bureaucratese: "The purpose of the Doha International Conference for the Family was to reaffirm international norms, and establish proposals for action, that can inform an agenda for cooperative research, discussion, and policy development related to family life for the next decade." Following the conference the government of Qatar put forward a resolution at the United Nations acknowledging the event and welcoming its findings, which was approved without a vote. Organizers then used this perfunctory UN approbation to claim, absurdly, that as a result "the Doha Declaration takes its place in the formal canon of legal documents comprising the growing body of international law."

Wilkins has since moved to Qatar to build a pan-fundamentalist think tank, the Doha International Institute for Family Studies and Development. According to its Web site, part of its writ is to combat mass media-engendered "moral globalization" that has "adversely altered long-standing societal norms and encouraged the disintegration of the family."

Carlson, meanwhile, remains convinced that conservative Christians have more in common with conservative Muslims than they do with Western liberals. "They share a common foe, which is a radical secular individualism that has turned against a common value system resting on the Abrahamic traditions, which involves a recognition of marriage and family as parts of the created order, as expectations," he said.

CHAPTER 30

Female Feticide and Infanticide
Implications for Reproductive Justice

Ramaswami Mahalingam and Madeline Wachman

Many demographers and journalists have noted the rising disparity in sex ratios in various Asian countries, such as China, India, and Korea (Croll, 2000; Das Gupta & Shuzhuo, 1999). Some scholars predict that, in the next few decades, this disparity will result in approximately 90 million men from India and China who will not be able to marry (Hudson & den Boer, 2004; Hutchings, 1997). These alarming sex-ratio disparities and the missing girls concern many demographers, planners, and economists. To develop meaningful interventions, we need to understand the cultural psychology of son preference and extreme neglect of girls. In this chapter, we argue that structural and cultural factors shape attitudes toward female infants, the most vulnerable members of society. We also explore the complex consequences of extreme neglect of girls in the form of sex-selective abortion and female infanticide and their impact on the lives of the men and women in these communities.

Our purpose here is threefold. First, we review the relevant literature on neglect of girls and infanticide in general, and then focus on India, which has a long history of neglect of girls that includes infanticide and sex-selective abortion. Second, we explore the complex consequences of systemic neglect of girls with respect to reproductive justice based on a cultural–ecological framework. Finally, we discuss the significance of these findings for combating extreme forms of neglect of girls (e.g., female infanticide, feticide) in places (e.g., Tamilnadu and Punjab, India) with a documented history of extreme sex discrimination and consider the implications for reproductive justice from a cultural-psychological perspective.

FEMALE INFANTICIDE AND SEX-SELECTIVE ABORTION

The female infanticide phenomenon is as old as many cultures. In many countries, governments have allowed, and sometimes encouraged, the killing of female, handicapped, or other unwanted children. Gender-specific infant mortality varies across cultures and regions of a country. Theories of why sex differentials in infant mortality occur also vary across and within countries. Although it is well known that sex ratios have historically been substantially higher in many Asian countries, the cultural and

psychological reasons behind these differences have not been sufficiently explored (Mahalingam, 2007). Most of the ethnographic and demographic research on sex determination has focused on the low status and oppression of women (see Hrdy, 1999, for a review). Female oppression is manifested in various forms. Female infanticide and sex-selective abortion are examples of an extreme form of neglect of girls, and gender inequality is one of its major contributing factors.

Sex determination is a dominant and persistent theme in countries with disproportionate sex ratios. Unequal power structures and gender relations are at the core of sex discrimination in cultural practices. Additional socioeconomic factors that contribute to female infanticide include irrational national population control policies and the unethical use of reproductive technology. In China, for example, the government implemented the one-child policy in 1979. This policy has achieved its objective of decreasing the country's fertility rate, but it also has provoked citizens to practice sex-selective abortion. The 2000 Chinese census indicated that, at birth, there are 100 girls for every 120 boys This number remained the same in the 2005 intercensus, and it left China with an estimated 32 million fewer female citizens under 20 years old (Zhu, Lu, & Hesketh, 2009). Moreover, the 2005 intercensus also reported more than 1.1 million more births of boys. Experts predict that the sex ratio in China will steadily worsen over the next two decades (Zhu et al., 2009).

According to Oster (2005), women who carry Hepatitis B are more likely to give birth to sons than to daughters. Based on census data from Tamilnadu, India, Srinivasan and Bedi (2008) argued that the Hepatitis B infection rate does not account for the disparity in the sex ratios in higher birth order (i.e., girls with more older siblings). They found that there were more late-born boys than girls, which could not be explained by the prevalence of Hepatitis B. Srinivasan and Bedi (2008) have also noted that the bulk of sex determination happens before birth and that cultural preference and access to sex-determination technologies are major proximal causes for the disparity in the sex ratio.

Improved ultrasound technology has allowed parents to determine the sex of the fetus. Increased access to this technology has led to increased rates of female infanticide, and thus the male-to-female ratio in many countries has become increasingly disproportionate (Das Gupta & Shuzhuo, 1999; Hesketh, Lu, & Xing, 2005). Sex-selective abortion was first documented in India in the 1970s. One of the first studies on sex-selective abortion in India showed that, in an urban clinic, 430 of the 450 women who were told that the sex of the baby was female went on to have an abortion, whereas 250 of the 700 who were told they had male fetuses went on to give birth, despite the risk of genetic disorders (Ramanamma & Bambawale, 1980). At the time of the study, sex-detection was done with amniocentesis at around 18–20 weeks of gestation. Now, modern technologies allow sex-selection to occur prior to conception, via in vitro fertilization and artificial insemination. However, most sex-elective abortion (i.e., female feticide) is a result of ultrasound imaging because the other techniques are more expensive. Though improvements in health care and conditions for pregnant women have resulted in reductions in infant mortality, advancements in technology to find the sex of the fetus have offset all of that progress.

Sharma (2008) noted that assisted reproductive technology has facilitated female feticide, which has contributed to 100 million girls missing from the world's population and led to a gendercide. Gender inequality and discrimination are problems of global importance, and extreme neglect of female infants underscores the various forms of sex determination over a woman's lifetime. In many cultures, women are blamed for not producing sons, despite the fact that women cannot control the sex of their children. Mothers whose children are only, or predominantly, female are blamed for the rest of their lives, and they are abused or mistreated for not producing sons. Such mistreatment affects the physical and mental health of mothers of daughters for the rest of the mothers' life. Thus, giving birth to daughters itself could lead to the maltreatment of mothers, and it is a potential risk factor that could seriously affect the health of mothers living in communities with extreme son preference (Shyama, 1996).

Few studies have been conducted to examine differences in infanticide rates across various cultural conditions; thus far, most hypotheses about neglect of girls and infanticide are relatively global (Keller, Nesse, & Hofferth, 2001). In order to mitigate sex determination and subsequent female infanticide and feticide, it is important first to understand the unique complexities of each community that has had a long history of infant gender disparities. We focus on India, but we also call for the need to identify culture-specific factors and psychological antecedents for female infanticide and feticide in other countries. Here we provide a cultural-ecological framework for the study of neglect of girls, and we also discuss how extreme neglect of girls could affect the psychological well-being of both men and women in communities with a long history of neglect of girls, as well as the social consequences of those "missing" girls.

THE PROBLEMS OF FEMALE INFANTICIDE AND NEGLECT OF GIRLS IN INDIA

During the 19th century, the colonial British government formed a committee to investigate the prevalence of female infanticide (Panigrahi, 1972). Fanny Parks (as cited in Panigrahi, 1972), a British traveler in the northern part of India, reported that she had never seen so few women as during her 4 years in India. The British government responded to reports about villages or tribes without even a single female child by enacting the Female

Infanticide Act in 1870, which was intended to abolish the practice of killing female infants (Miller, 1981). Although the colonial government claimed that they had abolished female infanticide in northwestern India, subsequent census records revealed enduring male-biased sex ratios over the next several decades (Miller, 1981). A century later, detailed ethnographic reports (e.g., Muthulakshmi, 1997; Shyama, 1996; Srinivasan, 1992; Venkatachalam & Srinivasan, 1993) left little doubt that female infanticide and feticide still exist today in Tamilnadu, India.

NEGLECT OF GIRLS: THEORETICAL PERSPECTIVES

To prevent female infanticide, one needs to understand the conditions under which it is likely to occur. Most of the research on neglect of girls and infanticide is primarily focused on explicating the structural and cultural reasons for differential treatment of girls. Two complementary perspectives dominate the current discussion of female infanticide: (1) the structural perspective and (2) the cultural-practices perspective. The structural perspective focuses on the contribution of structural factors (e.g., women's literacy, public policies) to the practice of neglect of girls. The cultural-practices perspective focuses on the role of cultural practices (e.g., the need to have son to perform funeral rituals) in fostering an unfavorable attitude toward girls. Below, we examine these perspectives in more detail.

Structural Perspective

Feminists have argued that women's low status and the structural differences between society's treatment of women and men are the main causes of neglect of girls and female infanticide (e.g., Dube, Dube, & Bhatnagar, 1999; Hegde, 1999; Muthulakshmi, 1997; Srinivasan, 1992). They advocate developmental programs geared toward improving women's educational and employment opportunities. Consequently, interventions by development agencies in India have been based on the assumption that improving women's literacy will lead to their empowerment and, subsequently, to declines in extreme forms of neglect of girls. However, recent demographic reports suggest that when women's status improves, preferential allocation of resources to sons also increases, which is the opposite of the desired outcome (Das Gupta & Visaria, 1996; Premi, 2001). It seems paradoxical that women's empowerment and status mobility result in increased investment in boys (Das Gupta & Visaria, 1996). In some parts of India, education of women correlates *positively* with neglect of girls (Das Gupta & Visaria, 1996). In Punjabi villages, for example, discrimination against girls and the "child mortality rate of higher-parity daughters" remains similar for educated and uneducated women (Das Gupta & Visaria, 1996, p. 124). Anderson and Romani (1997) found that, in Korea, although low infant mortality generally correlates with higher socioeconomic status (also see Anderson, Kim, & Romani, 1997), there is a greater differential between male and female infant mortality even in families of higher socioeconomic status. Therefore, when families have discretionary resources, they invest differentially in their sons and daughters. Therefore, it remains unclear that raising women's status *alone* will protect female infants; discrimination against daughters might actually *increase* with the upward mobility of women's status in India (Das Gupta & Visaria, 1996; also see Anderson & Romani, 1997; Anderson et al., 1997, for similar findings in China and Korea).

Ethnographers have pointed out that literacy is only one of several factors in women's decisions to keep a female child (Jeffery & Jeffery, 1997; Seymour, 1999). Other structural factors (e.g., federal policy that promoted smaller families, the easy availability of reproductive technologies) also contribute to the increase in male-biased sex ratios. During the early 1970s, the federal government of India promoted birth control programs and targeted women to implement various birth control methods (e.g., sterilizations; Ramasubban & Jejeebhoy, 2000). The Indian government also launched an advertisement campaign that emphasized the benefits of smaller families and depicted an ideal family with two children, a son and a daughter. Rarely did they present two daughters in any picture. Media theorists have argued that these implicit messages about gender shape and reinforce existing biases (Rosengren & Windahl, 1989). The Chinese government also used similar strategies to promote its one-child policy. Researchers have reported that, after China's introduction of the one-child policy, the abandonment of girls, female infanticide, and female feticide all increased dramatically (Hudson & den-Boer, 2004; Hutchings, 1997).

The easy availability of reproductive technologies to determine the sex of a fetus (e.g., ultrasound) has also contributed to the practice of female feticide. Noninvasive ultrasound tests cost as little as $10 (about 500 rupees) in India, and ultrasound clinics can be found even in small Indian towns. These technologies encourage people to achieve the ideal combination of one son and one daughter by aborting unwanted female fetuses; couples rarely abort male fetuses. In the government hospital of Amristar, in Punjab, for example, only one female child is born for every two male children (Natarajan, 1997). The technological control of achieving an ideal sex ratio for a family now affects even caste groups that did not originally practice female infanticide. Clinics offer their services to couples from all social strata, and, consequently, couples from any caste group can use technology to achieve an ideal gender composition (i.e., one boy and one girl) among their offspring. In sum, the structural perspective states that the increase in male-biased sex ratios is caused by a combination of structural factors (e.g., the low status of women, federal policies that promote small families, easy access to reproductive technologies).

Cultural-Practices Perspective

The cultural-practices perspective considers more context-specific reasons that might contribute to extreme forms of neglect of girls (i.e., female infanticide, female feticide). Some anthropologists (e.g., Gregor, 1988; Picone, 1998; Sargent, 1987; Scheper-Hughes, 1992) have suggested that female infanticide is tied to cultural practices and folk beliefs about what counts as a human being, such as questioning whether a baby should be considered a human being. Such folk beliefs exist cross-culturally (see Hrdy, 1999, for a review). Scheper-Hughes (1992) noted that, in poverty-stricken northeastern Brazil, people do not consider killing babies to be infanticide. Instead, they view babies as the *other*, and, because they are not truly human, babies might be left to die; therefore, mothers are discouraged from bonding with newborns. In other societies, children are not believed to be human beings until they reach school age (Hrdy, 1999). Picone (1998) found that, in parts of pre-World War II Japan, parents who had children with visible birth defects considered those children shameful and often killed them.

Scheper-Hughes (1992) examined the systemic nature of infanticide in Brazil. She argued that the social construction of mothers is always dichotomized between a *caring* mother and a *killer* mother. Based on her ethnographic work in poverty-stricken areas of northern Brazil, where there had been a high incidence of infanticide but no gender difference in infant mortality, Scheper-Hughes (1992) examined how material conditions shape maternal behavior. She reported that women often engaged in various discursive practices (e.g., not naming the child) to distance themselves from being mothers, and she argued that these impoverished mothers, who themselves needed nourishment, could not care for their newborns, who would often die from starvation. Examples of infanticide in Brazil and India call into question the universality of the notion of mothers as essentially "caring and benevolent" because of their dominant role in bearing children (Scheper-Hughes, 1992). Whereas abject poverty diminished Brazilian mothers' ability to nurture, there could be other factors and beliefs about gender that play a major role in the case of Tamil mothers. A key difference to note is that, in Brazil, infanticide remains gender blind, whereas, in Tamilnadu and elsewhere in India and Asia, it is almost exclusively female infants and fetuses that are killed (Harriss-White, 2001). In Tamilnadu, ethnographic reports provide graphic details about the various means used to kill a newborn female infant (e.g., Muthulakshmi, 1997; Venkatachalam & Srinivasan, 1993). In most of the cases, women (i.e., mothers, grandmothers, midwives) do the killing.

Ethnographic reports often suggest that, in India, the practice of giving a dowry to marry off a daughter remains a major stressor for parents, and it is a common form of transfer of marital goods (Murdock, 1967, 1981). Thus, each daughter represents a drain on family resources because the parents have to pay a dowry to arrange her marriage, and poorer families must pay proportionately more than wealthier families for a particularly desirable husband. As a result, spousal abuse is frequent when daughters of poorer families marry wealthier men (Rao, 1993a, 1993b, 1997). Most analyses attribute spousal abuse to the low status of women in a patriarchal culture (Dube et al., 1999; Muthulakshmi, 1997).

Neglect of girls is also related to religious and cultural practices that mandate the need for a son. Miller (1981) argued that Hindu beliefs and practices (e.g., only sons can perform funeral rites) contribute to neglect of girls. In the Hindu death ceremony, or *pind daan*, performed to ensure that the parent reaches heaven, only a son may set fire to the funeral pyre. According to the 1991 Indian census, the sex ratio of children under the age of six in the state of Tamilnadu is 945 girls to every 1,000 boys. Venkatachalam and Srinivasan (1993) described the various methods used to kill a newborn female infant. These range from starving the infant to feeding it paddy (i.e., rice with its outside husk) with milk or milk with a mixture of poisonous herbs (also see Vasanthi, 1995; Venkataramani, 1986). The cultural-practices perspective highlights the underlying social and cultural reasons for son preference that lead to extreme forms of son preference. The undervaluing of daughters due to various cultural practices, such as dowry and patrilocal system (where the woman has to relocate and live with her husband's family and become a member of her husband's clan), contribute to differential investment in daughters and sons.

Although several cultural psychologists have studied infanticide, very few of them examined the antecedents of female infanticide. Most of the psychological studies on infanticide were based on clinical cases conducted in the United States and Europe with mothers who had committed infanticide, and the researchers documented the women's underlying depression and other related psychopathology as major reasons for their infanticidal behavior (for a review see Spinelli, 2001; also see Chandra, Venkatasubramanian, & Thomas, 2002, for a similar study conducted in India). These researchers examined only the cases of infanticide that were clinically documented in relation to maternal depression or other severe mental illness. Although their studies help us to understand the psychopathology of infanticide, they may not help us to understand the cultural-psychological basis of the *systematic* and *gender-specific* nature of the female infanticide practiced in Asia. An understanding of the culture-specific moral underpinnings of female infanticide is of great importance as policy makers consider ways to combat female infanticide.

Despite the overwhelming evidence of the male-biased sex-ratio (see Harriss-White, 2001) in several communities in India, few cultural psychologists have examined the psychological consequences of neglect of girls. Mahalingam (2007) argued that cultural-ecological factors play a critical role in extreme neglect of girls. Based on field-based behavioral-ecological research on communities with extreme neglect of girls, he discovered that land-owning and warrior communities tend to practice extreme sex discrimination for very different ecological reasons. Agricultural communities tend to be patrilocal (i.e., women after marriage become part of their husband's family, and wealth is transferred from father to sons). Having more daughters depletes the land resources of a family because land would be given away as dowry, and fragmenting land depletes its value. In contrast, warrior communities need more sons to protect the community during inter-communal conflicts. Women are viewed as a liability in these communities because of the patriarchal notion that the purity of women holds the honor of the community.

Male-biased sex ratios need to be identified as a major risk factor for the psychological well-being and reproductive rights of women. Social and cultural interventions to combat female infanticide and feticide need to highlight the impact of male-biased sex ratios on the community's mental health. Social changes that encourage flexible arrangements for parental care (i.e., by daughters as well as by sons) and inter-caste marriages might change societal attitudes toward daughters. In addition to providing financial incentives to keep daughters and public policy that supports the empowerment of women, governments should invest in social programs that advocate practices that promote gender-egalitarian values (e.g., school curricula). Reproductive justice perspectives should be sensitive to the cultural-ecological factors that shape and constrain women's agency and pressure them to abort female fetuses. Culturally sensitive reproductive-justice perspectives will help us to understand the unique challenges of combating the practice of sex-selective abortions in various Asian countries. Successfully combating female infanticide and feticide is necessary to achieve reproductive justice for the women and girls who live in these communities and for those missing girls, who never had a chance to live.

CHAPTER 31

Excerpt from Remarks to the U.N. 4th World Conference on Women Plenary Session, delivered September 5, 1995, Beijing, China

Hillary Rodham Clinton

By gathering in Beijing, we are focusing world attention on issues that matter most in our lives – the lives of women and their families: access to education, health care, jobs and credit, the chance to enjoy basic legal and human rights and to participate fully in the political life of our countries.

There are some who question the reason for this conference. Let them listen to the voices of women in their homes, neighborhoods, and workplaces. There are some who wonder whether the lives of women and girls matter to economic and political progress around the globe. Let them look at the women gathered here and at Huairou – the homemakers and nurses, the teachers and lawyers, the policymakers and women who run their own businesses. It is conferences like this that compel governments and peoples everywhere to listen, look, and face the world's most pressing problems. Wasn't it after all – after the women's conference in Nairobi ten years ago that the world focused for the first time on the crisis of domestic violence?

Earlier today, I participated in a World Health Organization forum. In that forum, we talked about ways that government officials, NGOs, and individual citizens are working to address the health problems of women and girls. Tomorrow, I will attend a gathering of the United Nations Development Fund for Women. There, the discussion will focus on local – and highly successful – programs that give hard-working women access to credit so they can improve their own lives and the lives of their families.

What we are learning around the world is that if women are healthy and educated, their families will flourish. If women are free from violence, their families will flourish. If women have a chance to work and earn as full and equal partners in society, their families will flourish. And when families flourish, communities and nations do as well. That is why every woman, every man, every child, every family, and every nation on this planet does have a stake in the discussion that takes place here.

Over the past 25 years, I have worked persistently on issues relating to women, children, and families. Over the past two and a half years, I've had the opportunity to learn more about the challenges facing women in my own country and around the world.

I have met new mothers in Indonesia, who come together regularly in their village to discuss nutrition, family planning, and baby care. I have met working parents in Denmark who talk about the comfort they feel in knowing that their children can be cared for in safe, and nurturing after-school centers. I have met women in South Africa who helped lead the struggle to end apartheid and are now helping to build a new democracy. I have met with the leading women of my own hemisphere who are working every day to promote literacy and better health care for children in their countries. I have met women in India and Bangladesh who are taking out small loans to buy milk cows, or rickshaws, or thread in order to create a livelihood for themselves and their families. I have met the doctors and nurses in Belarus and Ukraine who are trying to keep children alive in the aftermath of Chernobyl.

The great challenge of this conference is to give voice to women everywhere whose experiences go unnoticed, whose words go unheard. Women comprise more than half the world's population, 70% of the world's poor, and two-thirds of those who are not taught to read and write. We are the primary caretakers for most of the world's children and elderly. Yet much of the work we do is not valued – not by economists, not by historians, not by popular culture, not by government leaders.

At this very moment, as we sit here, women around the world are giving birth, raising children, cooking meals, washing clothes, cleaning houses, planting crops, working on assembly lines, running companies, and running countries. Women also are dying from diseases that should have been prevented or treated. They are watching their children succumb to malnutrition caused by poverty and economic deprivation. They are being denied the right to go to school by their own fathers and brothers. They are being forced into prostitution, and they are being barred from the bank lending offices and banned from the ballot box.

Those of us who have the opportunity to be here have the responsibility to speak for those who could not. As an American, I want to speak for those women in my own country, women who are raising children on the minimum wage, women who can't afford health care or child care, women whose lives are threatened by violence, including violence in their own homes.

I want to speak up for mothers who are fighting for good schools, safe neighborhoods, clean air, and clean airwaves; for older women, some of them widows, who find that, after raising their families, their skills and life experiences are not valued in the marketplace; for women who are working all night as nurses, hotel clerks, or fast food chefs so that they can be at home during the day with their children; and for women everywhere who simply don't have time to do everything they are called upon to do each and every day.

Speaking to you today, I speak for them, just as each of us speaks for women around the world who are denied the chance to go to school, or see a doctor, or own property, or have a say about the direction of their lives, simply because they are women. The truth is that most women around the world work both inside and outside the home, usually by necessity.

We need to understand there is no one formula for how women should lead our lives. That is why we must respect the choices that each woman makes for herself and her family. Every woman deserves the chance to realize her own God-given potential. But we must recognize that women will never gain full dignity until their human rights are respected and protected.

Our goals for this conference, to strengthen families and societies by empowering women to take greater control over their own destinies, cannot be fully achieved unless all governments – here and around the world – accept their responsibility to protect and promote internationally recognized human rights. The – The international community has long acknowledged and recently

reaffirmed at Vienna that both women and men are entitled to a range of protections and personal freedoms, from the right of personal security to the right to determine freely the number and spacing of the children they bear. No one – No one should be forced to remain silent for fear of religious or political persecution, arrest, abuse, or torture.

Tragically, women are most often the ones whose human rights are violated. Even now, in the late 20th century, the rape of women continues to be used as an instrument of armed conflict. Women and children make up a large majority of the world's refugees. And when women are excluded from the political process, they become even more vulnerable to abuse. I believe that now, on the eve of a new millennium, it is time to break the silence. It is time for us to say here in Beijing, and for the world to hear, that it is no longer acceptable to discuss women's rights as separate from human rights.

These abuses have continued because, for too long, the history of women has been a history of silence. Even today, there are those who are trying to silence our words. But the voices of this conference and of the women at Huairou must be heard loudly and clearly:

It is a violation of human rights when babies are denied food, or drowned, or suffocated, or their spines broken, simply because they are born girls.

It is a violation of human rights when women and girls are sold into the slavery of prostitution for human greed – and the kinds of reasons that are used to justify this practice should no longer be tolerated.

It is a violation of human rights when women are doused with gasoline, set on fire, and burned to death because their marriage dowries are deemed too small.
It is a violation of human rights when individual women are raped in their own communities and when thousands of women are subjected to rape as a tactic or prize of war.

It is a violation of human rights when a leading cause of death worldwide among women ages 14 to 44 is the violence they are subjected to in their own homes by their own relatives.

It is a violation of human rights when young girls are brutalized by the painful and degrading practice of genital mutilation.

It is a violation of human rights when women are denied the right to plan their own families, and that includes being forced to have abortions or being sterilized against their will.

If there is one message that echoes forth from this conference, let it be that human rights are women's rights and women's rights are human rights once and for all. Let us not forget that among those rights are the right to speak freely – and the right to be heard.

Women must enjoy the rights to participate fully in the social and political lives of their countries, if we want freedom and democracy to thrive and endure. It is indefensible that many women in nongovernmental organizations who wished to participate in this conference have not been able to attend – or have been prohibited from fully taking part.

Let me be clear. Freedom means the right of people to assemble, organize, and debate openly. It means respecting the views of those who may disagree with the views of their governments. It means not taking citizens away from their loved ones and jailing them, mistreating them, or denying them their freedom or dignity because of the peaceful expression of their ideas and opinions.

In my country, we recently celebrated the 75th anniversary of Women's Suffrage. It took 150 years after the signing of our Declaration of Independence for women to win the right to vote. It took 72 years of organized struggle, before that happened, on the part of many courageous women and men. It was one of America's most divisive philosophical wars. But it was a bloodless war. Suffrage was achieved without a shot being fired.

But we have also been reminded, in V-J Day observances last weekend, of the good that comes when men and women join together to combat the forces of tyranny and to build a better world. We have seen peace prevail in most places for a half century. We have avoided another world war. But we have not solved older, deeply-rooted problems that continue to diminish the potential of half the world's population.

Now it is the time to act on behalf of women everywhere. If we take bold steps to better the lives of women, we will be taking bold steps to better the lives of children and families too. Families rely on mothers and wives for emotional support and care. Families rely on women for labor in the home. And increasingly, everywhere, families rely on women for income needed to raise healthy children and care for other relatives.

As long as discrimination and inequities remain so commonplace everywhere in the world, as long as girls and women are valued less, fed less, fed last, overworked, underpaid, not schooled, subjected to violence in and outside their homes – the potential of the human family to create a peaceful, prosperous world will not be realized.

Let this conference be our – and the world's – call to action. Let us heed that call so we can create a world in which every woman is treated with respect and dignity, every boy and girl is loved and cared for equally, and every family has the hope of a strong and stable future. That is the work before you. That is the work before all of us who have a vision of the world we want to see – for our children and our grandchildren.

REFERENCES

ACOG (American College of Obstetricians and Gynecologists). 2012. 2012 ACOG Workforce Factsheet. Acog.

ACRJ (Asian Communities Reprod. Justice). 2005. *A New Vision for Advancing Our Movement for Reproductive Health, Reproductive Rights and Reproductive Justice*. Oakland, CA: ACRJ. Online at http://reproductivejustice.org/assets/docs/ACRJ-A-New-Vision.pdf.

Adams, G.D. 1997. Abortion: evidence of an issue evolution. *American Journal of Political Science* 41: 718–737.

Agigian, A. 2004. *Baby Steps: How Lesbian Alternative Insemination is Changing the World*. Middletown, Conn.: Wesleyan University Press.

Alan Guttmacher Institute. 1999. *Sharing Responsibility: Women, Society and Abortion Worldwide*. New York: Alan Guttmacher Institute.

———. 2004. *Get "In the Know": 20 Questions About Pregnancy, Contraception and Abortion*. New York: Alan Guttmacher Institute.

Albert, G. 2011. Forced sterilization and Romani women's resistance in central Europe, *PopDev*, a publication of the Population and Development Program of Hampshire College, n.71.

Almeling, R. 2011. *Sex Cells: The Medical Market for Eggs and Sperm*. Berkeley/Los Angeles, CA: University of California Press.

Altiok, O. 2013. Reproducing the nation. *Contexts*, Spring.

AMA (American Medical Association). 2011. *Talking Points: Shackling of Pregnant Prisoners*. Chicago, IL: AMA.

American Diabetes Association. 1990. *Pregnancy and Diabetes*, Basic Information Series, No. 33. American Diabetes Association.

Amnesty International. 2010. *Deadly Delivery: The Maternal Health Care Crisis in the USA*. New York: Amnesty International USA. Online at www.amnestyusa.org/dignity/pdf/DeadlyDelivery.pdf (accessed January 3, 2011).

Anderson, B.A., & Romani, J.H. 1997. *Socioeconomic Characteristics and Excess Female Infant Mortality in Jilin Province, China* [Research Report No. 97–409]. Ann Arbor: Population Studies Center, University of Michigan.

Anderson, B.A., Kim, D., & Romani, J.H. 1997. *Health Personnel, Son Preference and Infant Mortality in China* [Research Report No. 97–401]. Ann Arbor: Population Studies Center, University of Michigan.Anderson, B.J. 2008. Lesbians, gays, and people living with HIV: facing and fighting barriers to assisted reproduction. *Cardozo Journal of Law and Gender* 15: 451–475.

Anderson, C. 2003. *Eyes Off the Prize: African Americans, the United Nations, and the Struggle for Human Rights, 1944–1955*. Cambridge, UK: Cambridge University Press.

Anderson, Gerard F., Hussey, Peter S., Frogner, Bianca K., & Waters, Hugh R. 2005. Health spending in the United States and the rest of the industrialized world. *Health Affairs* 24(4): 903–914.

Andrews, M. 2011. Health insurance rules may decide whether infertility treatment is essential. *Washington Post*. Online, January 24.

Andrews, R. 2006. The National Hospital Bill: the most expensive conditions by payer. In: *Healthcare Cost and Utilization Project, Statistical Brief*. Healthcare Cost Utilization Project Statistical Brief 2008: 7. Online at www.hcup-us.ahrq.gov/reports/statbriefs/sb59.pdf (accessed January 3, 2011).

APA (American Psychological Association). 2014. *Mental Health and Abortion*. American Psychological Association.

Arendell, Terry. 1992. The social self as gendered: a masculinist discourse of divorce. *Symbolic Interaction* 15: 151–181.

———. 1997. Reflections on the researcher–researched relationship: a woman interviewing men. *Qualitative Sociology* 20: 341–368.

Armato, Michael, & Marsiglio, William. 2002. Self-structure, identity, and commitment: promise keepers' godly man project. *Symbolic Interaction* 25: 41–65.

Asch, A. 1988. Reproductive technology and disability. In: N. Taub, & S. Cohen (eds.) *Reproductive Laws for the 1990s: A Briefing Handbook*. New Brunswick, N.J.: Rutgers University.

Associated Press. 2002. Conference rejects US stance on abortion, condom use. December 18.

Association of Women's Health, Obstetric and Neonatal Nurses. 2010. *Guidelines for Professional Registered Nurse Staffing for Perinatal Units*. Washington, DC: Association of Women's Health, Obstetric and Neonatal Nurses. Online at www.awhonn.org/awhonn/store/productDetail.do;jsessionid=D54A4918DF5BC334CD4681C94ECD3108?productCode=SG-910 (accessed January 5, 2011).

Baca Zinn, Maxine. 1990. Family, feminism, and race in America. *Gender and Society* 4: 68–82.

Bacak, S., Berg, C.J., Desmarais, J., Hutchins, E., & Locke, E. (eds.). 2006. *State Maternal Mortality Review: Accomplishments of Nine States*. Atlanta: Centers for Disease Control and Prevention. Online at www.cdph.ca.gov/data/statistics/Documents/MO-CDC-ReportAccomplishments 9States.pdf.

Bach, Amy. 1999. No choice for teens. *Nation*, October 11.

Baker, Tom. 2005. *Medical Malpractice Myth*. Chicago, IL: University of Chicago Press.

Balan, S., & Mahalingam, R. 2008. Culture, ecology, and lifegoals. Unpublished manuscript, University of Michigan.

Battaglia, Debbora. 1985. "We feed our father": paternal nurture among the Sabarl of Papua New Guinea. *American Ethnologist* 12(3): 427–441.

BBC News. 2013. "Test-tube baby" Brown hails pioneers on 35th birthday. Broadcast July 25. Retrieved November 24, 2013.

Becker, Gay. 2000. *The Elusive Embryo: How Women and Men Approach New Reproductive Technologies*. Berkeley, CA: University of California Press.

Becker, Gay, Butler, Anneliese, & Nachtigall, Robert. 2005. Resemblance talk: a challenge for parents whose children were conceived with donor gametes in the U.S. *Social Science and Medicine* 61: 1300–1309.

Beckmann, C., Gittler, M., Barzansky, B., & Anderson Beckmann, C. 1989. Gynecologic health care of women with disabilities, *Obstetrics & Gynecology*, 74(1): 75–79.

Beenhakker, B., Becker, S., Hires, S., Molano Di Targiana, N., Blumenthal, P., & Huggins, G. 2004. Are partners available for post-abortion contraceptive counseling? A pilot study in a Baltimore city clinic. *Contraception* 69: 419–423.

Begum, N. 1992. Disabled women and the feminist agenda. *Feminist Review*, 40, Spring: 70–84.

Behar, Ruth, & Gordon, Deborah (eds.) 1995. *Women Writing Culture*. Berkeley, CA: University of California Press.

Beisel, N. 1998. *Imperiled Innocents: Anthony Comstock and Family Reproduction in Victorian America*. Princeton, N.J.: Princeton University Press.

Beisel, N., & Kay, T. 2004. Abortion, race, and gender in nineteenth-century America. *American Sociological Review* 69: 498–515.

Bell, A.V. 2009. "It's way out of my league": low-income women's experiences of medicalized infertility. *Gender and Society* 23: 688–709.

Benbow, A., & Maresh, M. 1998. Reducing maternal mortality: reaudit of recommendations in reports of confidential inquiries into maternal deaths. *British Medical Journal* 317: 1431–1432.

Benker, Karen. 2001. Interviewed by Elena R. Gutiérrez, 26 June.

Berg, C.J., Callaghan, W.M., Syverson, C., & Henderson, Z. 2010. Pregnancy-related mortality in the United States, 1998 to 2005. *Obstetrics and Gynecology* 116: 1302–1309.

Berg, C.J., Hareper, M.A., Atkinson, S.M., Bell, E.A., Brown, H.L., Hage, M.L. et al. 2005. Preventability of pregnancy-related deaths: results of a state-wide review. *Obstetrics and Gynecology* 106: 1228–1234.

Berger, M.T., & Guidroz, K. (eds.) 2009. *The Intersectional Approach: Transforming the Academy Through Race, Class, and Gender*. Chapel Hill: University of North Carolina Press.

Bergum, Vangie. 1989. *Woman to Mother: A Transformation*. South Hadley, Mass: Bergin and Garvey.

Bernard, Jessie. 1981. The good provider role: its rise and fall. In: Mark Robert Rank, & Edward Kain (eds.) *Diversity and Change in Families: Patterns, Prospects, and Policies*, Englewood Cliffs, N.J.: Prentice Hall.

Bhagat, P. 2004. *India* (3rd edition). Oxford: England: Oxfam Books.

Bhowmick, N. 2013. Why people are angry about India's new surrogacy rules. *Time*, online. February 15.

Bittman, Sam, & Rosenberg Zalk, Sue. 1978. *Expectant Fathers*. New York: Ballantine Books.

Blackwell-Stratton, M., Breslin, M.L., Mayerson, A.B., & Bailey, S. 1988. Smashing icons. In: M. Fine, & A. Asch (eds.) *Women with Disabilities: Essays in Psychology, Culture and Politics*, Philadelphia, Temple University Press.

Blaney, C.L. 1997. Involving men after pregnancy. *Network* 17: 22–25.

Blankenhorn, David. 1996. *Fatherless America: Confronting our Most Urgent Social Problem*. New York: Harper Collins.

Bloch, Maurice, & Parry, Jonathan. (eds.) 1982. *Death and the Regeneration of Life*. Cambridge, UK: Cambridge University Press.

Boston Women's Health Book Collective. 2008. Choosing your health care provider and birth setting, *Our Bodies, Ourselves: Pregnancy and Birth*. New York: Simon and Schuster, pp. 13–28.

Boylan, E. 1991. *Women and Disability*. London: Zed Books.

Brennan, Troyen A., Sox, Colin, M., & Burstin, Helen R. 1996. Relation between negligent adverse events and the outcomes of medical-malpractice litigation. *New England Journal of Medicine* 335(26) (December 26): 1963–1967.

Breslau, N. 1987. Abortion of defective fetuses: attitudes of mothers of congenitally impaired children, *Journal of Marriage and the Family* 49: 839–845.

Brewster, Arlene. 1984. After hours: a patient's reaction to amniocentesis. *Obstetrics and Gynecology* 64 (3): 443–444.

Briggs, Laura. 2002. *Reproducing Empire: Race, Sex, Science, and U.S. Imperialism in Puerto Rico*. Berkeley, CA: University of California Press.

Brindis, Claire, Boggess, Jane, Katsuranis, Frances, Mantell, Maxine, McCarter, Virginia, & Wolfe, Amy. 1998. A profile of the adolescent male family planning client. *Family Planning Perspectives* 30(2): 63–66, 88.

Browne, S.E., Connors, D., & Stern, N. (eds.) 1985. *With the Power of Each Breath: A Disabled Women's Anthology*, San Francisco: Cleis Press.

Bryant, A., & Levi, E. 2012. Abortion misinformation from Crisis Pregnancy Centers in N. Carolina, *Contraception* 86(6): 752–756.

Bynum, Caroline Walker 1989. The female body and religious practice in the later middle ages. In: M. Feher, R. Naddaff, & N. Tazi (eds) *Fragments for a History of the Human Body*, Part 1. New York: Zone, pp. 161–219.

———. 1991. *Fragmentation and Redemption: Essays on Gender and the Human Body in Medieval Religion*. New York: Zone Books.

Cade, Toni. 2005. Black women and the pill. *The Black Woman: An Anthology*. Washington Square Press, pp. 203–212.

Callo-Brazil, T. 1993. Unfit because of my disability. *Disability Rag* 14(3), May/June: 9.

Campbell-Earl, L. 1993. A ramp to parenting. *Disability Rag* 14(3), May/June: 10–11.

Campling, J. (ed.) 1981. *Images of Ourselves*. London: Routledge & Kegan Paul.

Caplan, A. 1992. *When Medicine Went Mad: Bioethics and the Holocaust*. Totowa, New Jersey: Humana Press.

CDC (Centers for Disease Control and Prevention). 2010. *Use of Contraception in the United States: 1982–2008*. Atlanta: CDC.

———. 2013a. *Assisted Reproductive Technology*. September 10. Atlanta: CDC.

———. 2013b. *Reproductive Health: Infertility*. June 20. Atlanta: CDC.

———. 2013c. *Faststats*. Atlanta: CDC.

———. 2013d. *Pregnancy Mortality Surveillance System*. Atlanta: CDC.

———. 2013e. *Pregnancy-Related Deaths*. Atlanta: CDC.

Center for Reproductive Rights. 2013. *The State of the States: Targeted Regulation Of Abortion Providers in 2013*. New York: Centre for Reproductive Rights. Online at http://reproductiverights.org/en/the-state-of-the-states-2013/targeted-regulation-of-abortion-providers (accessed February 2, 2014).

Centner, Terence J. 2008. *America's Blame Culture: Pointing Fingers and Shunning Restitution*. Durham, NC: Carolina Academic Press.

Chalidze, L.L. 2009. Misinformed consent: non-medical bases for American birth recommendations as a human rights issue. *New York Law School Law Review* 54: 59–103.

Chandra, P., Venkatasubramanian, G., & Thomas, T. 2002. Infanticidal ideas and infanticidal behavior in Indian women with severe postpartum psychiatric disorders. *Journal of Nervous and Mental Diseases* 190: 457–461.

Chang, J., Elam-Evans, L.D., Berg, C.J., Herndon, J., Flowers, L., Seed, K.A., & Syverson, C.J. 2003. *Pregnancy-Related Mortality Surveillance: United States, 1991–1999*, MMWR surveillance summaries February 21: 1–8. Online at www.cdc.gov/mmwr/preview/mmwrhtml/ss5202a1. htm#tab3 (accessed January 3, 2011).

Chase, Allen. 1980. *The Legacy of Malthus: The Social Costs of the New Scientific Racism*. Urbana: University of Illinois Press.

Cherry, A. 2007. The detention, confinement, and incarceration of pregnant women for the benefit of fetal health. *Columbia Journal of Gender Law* 16: 147–197.

Chesler, E. 1993. *Woman of Valor: Margaret Sanger and Birth Control Movement in America*. New York: Simon and Schuster.

———. 2012. Was Planned Parenthood's founder racist? *Salon*, Nov 2. Online at www.salon.com/writer/ellen_chesler/ (accessed February 6, 2012).

Choo, H.Y., Ferree, M.M. 2010. Practicing intersectionality in sociological research: a critical analysis of inclusions, interactions, and institutions in the study of inequalities. *Sociological Theory* 28: 129–149.

Christian Medical and Dental Society. 2013. CMDA Ethics Statements. Christian Medical and Dental Society.

Clark, Martha Bittle. 1987. *Are You Weeping with Me, God?* Nashville: Broadman Press.

Clark, S.L., Belfort, M.A., Byrum, S.L., Meyers, J.A., & Perlin, J.B. 2008. Improved outcomes, fewer cesarean deliveries, and reduced litigation: results of a new paradigm inpatient safety. *American Journal of Obstetrics and Gynecology* 199(e1–105.e7).

Clarke, Adele. 1984. Subtle sterilization abuse: a reproductive rights perspective. In: Rita Arditti, Renata Duelli Klein, & Shelly Minded (eds.) *Test Tube Women: What Future for Motherhood?* Boston, MA: Pandora/Routledge and Kegan Paul, pp. 188–212.

Clinton, H. 1995. Remarks to the U.N. 4th World Conference on Women Plenary Session. September 5, 1995, Beijing, China. Online at American Rhetoric.com.

Coeytaux, F., Bingham, D., & Langer A. 2011. Reducing maternal mortality: a global imperative. *Contraception* 83: 95–98.

Coeytaux, F., Bingham, D., & Strauss, N. 2011. Maternal mortality in the United States: a human rights failure, *Contraception* 83(5): 189–193.

Cole, S.S. 1988. Women, sexuality and disabilities. *Women and Therapy* 7(2–3): 277–294.

Collins, Patricia Hill. 1990. *Black Feminist Thought: Knowledge, Consciousness, and the Politics of Empowerment.* Boston, MA: Unwin Hyman.

———. 1999. Will the "real" mother please stand up? the logics of eugenics and American national family planning. In: Adele E. Clarke, & Virginia L. Olesen (eds.) *Revisioning Women, Health and Healing: Feminist, Cultural, and Technoscience Perspectives.* New York: Routledge.

Collins, P. and Andersen, M. 2007. M. *Race, Class and Gender: An Anthology.* Independence, Ky: Cengage Learning.

Coltrane, Scott. 1998. Changing patterns of family work: Chicano men and housework. In: Susan Ferguson (ed.) *Shifting the Center.* Mountain View, CA: Mayfield, pp. 547–562.

Comanor, William S., & Llad Phillips. 1998. The impact of income and family structure on delinquency. Working paper, University of California at Santa Barbara.

Confidential Enquiries. 2007. *Savings Mothers' Lives: Reviewing Maternal Deaths to Make Motherhood Safer 2003–2005. Seventh Report of the Confidential Enquiries into Maternal Deaths in the United Kingdom.* G. Lewis (ed.). London: Wiley, pp. 1–260.

Congleton, J., & Rotter, J. 1984. Should we have a baby? *Diabetes Forecast.*

Connell, R.W. 1995. *Masculinities.* Berkeley, CA: University of California Press.

Conrad, Peter, & Leiter, Valerie. 2004. Medicalization, markets, and consumers. *Journal of Health and Social Behavior* 45: 158–176.

Corea, Gina. 1984. Egg snatchers. In: Rita Arditti, Renate Duelli Klein, & Shelley Minden (eds.) *Test-Tube Women: What Future for Motherhood?* London: Pandora, pp. 37–51.

———. 1985. *The Mother Machine: Reproductive Technologies from Artificial Insemination to Artificial Wombs.* New York: Harper and Row.

———. 1987. The reproductive brothel. In: Gina Corea (ed.) *Man-made Women: How New Reproductive Technologies Affect Women.* Bloomington: Indiana University Press, pp. 38–51.

Correa, S., Germain, A., & Petchesky, R. 2005. Thinking beyond ICPD+10: where should our movement be going? *Reproductive Health Matters* 13(25): 109–119.

Crapanzano, Vincent. 1981. Rite of return: circumcision in Morocco. In: Warner Muensterberger, & L. Bryce Boyer (eds.) *The Psychoanalytic Study of Society.* New York: Library of Psychological Anthropology, pp. 15–36.

Craven, C. 2010. *Pushing for Midwives: Homebirth Mothers and the Reproductive Rights Movement.* Philadelphia: Temple University Press.

Crenshaw, K. 1989. Demarginalizing the intersection of race and sex: a black feminist critique of antidiscrimination doctrine, feminist theory and antiracist politics. *University of Chicago Legal Forum* 139–167.

———. 1991. Mapping the margins: intersectionality, identity politics, and violence against women of color. *Stanford Law Review* 43(6): 1241–1299.

Crenshaw, K., Gotanda, N., Peller, G., & Thomas, K. (eds.) 1995. *Critical Race Theory: The Key Writings that Formed the Movement.* New York: New Press.

Croll, E. 2000. *Endangered Daughters: Discrimination and Development in Asia.* New York: Routledge.

Cross, M. 1994. Abuse. In: L. Keith (ed.) *Mustn't Grumble: Writing by Disabled Women.* London, The Women's Press.

Crummy, Karen E. 2000. My two mommies: court backs lesbian couple. *Boston Globe*, July 24: 2.

Cruz, Ricardo/Católicos por La Raza, Papers (CEMA 28). California Ethnic and Multicultural Archives, Department of Special Collections, Davidson Library, University of California, Santa Barbara.

Curran, Laura, & Laura Abrams. 2000. Making men into dads: fatherhood, the state, and welfare reform. *Gender & Society* 14(5): 662–678.

D'Angelo, D., Williams, L., Morrow, B., Cox, S., Harris, N., Harrison, L., Posner, S.F., Richardson Hood, J., Zapata, L. 2007. Preconception and interconception health status of women who recently gave birth to live-born infant–pregnancy risk assessment monitoring system (PRAMS), United States, 26 reporting areas, 2004. MMWR surveillance summaries, December 14: 4 and 17. Online at www. cdc.gov/mmwr/preview/mmwrhtml/ss5610a1.htm (accessed January 3, 2011).

Das Gupta, M., & Shuzhuo, L. 1999. Gender bias in China, South Korea, and India 1920–1990: effects of war, famine, fertility decline. *Development and Change* 30, 619–652.

Das Gupta, M., & Visaria, L. 1996. Son preference and excess female mortality in India's demographic transition. In: Korea Institute for Health and Social Affairs and United Nations Population Fund (eds.) *Sex Preference for Children and Gender Discrimination in Asia.* Seoul, Korea: KIHASA, pp. 96–102.

Davis, Susan E. 1988. *Women Under Attack: Victories, Backlash, and the Fight for Reproductive Freedom.* Boston, MA: South End Press.

Davis-Floyd, Robbie E. 1986. Birth as an American rite of passage. Ph.D. Dissertation, University of Texas, Austin.

———. 1988. Birth as an American rite of passage. In: Karen L. Michaelson (ed.) *Childbirth in America: Anthropological Perspectives.* South Hadley, Mass.: Bergin and Garvey, pp. 153–172.

De Beauvoir, Simone. 1952. *The Second Sex.* New York: Vintage Books. Quoted in L. Segal, *Slow Motion: Changing Masculinities, Changing Men.* London: Virago, 1990, p. 27.

Declercq, Eugene, Sakala, Carol, Corry, Maureen, & Applebaum, Sandra. 2006. *Listening to Mothers II: Report of the Second National U.S. Survey of Women's Childbearing Experiences.* Childbirth Connection. Online at www.childbirthconnection.org/article.asp?ck=10401 (accessed September 14, 2011).

Deegan, M.J., & Brooks, N.A. (eds.) 1985. *Women and Disability: The Double Handicap.* New Brunswick, N.J.: Transaction.

Delaney, Carol. 1986. The meaning of paternity and the virgin birth debate. *Man* 21(3): 494–513.

Dennis, A., Blanchard, K., Cordova, D., Wahlin, B., Clark, J., et al. 2013. What happens to the women who fall through the cracks of health care reform? Lessons from Massachusetts. *Journal of Health Politics, Policy and Law* 38: 393–419.

Denyer, S., & Wan, W. 2013. In reform package, China relaxes one-child policy, abolishes prison labor camps. *Washington Post.*

Deprez, E. 2013. Abortion clinics close at record pace after states tighten rules. Bloomberg.com, September 3. Online at http://www.bloomberg.com/news/2013-09-03/abortion-clinics-close-at-record-pace-after-states-tighten-rules.html (accessed April 20, 2014).

Derkas, E. 2012. The organization formerly known as CRACK: Project Prevention and the privatized assault on reproductive wellbeing. *Race Gender Class* 19: 179–195.

Devereux, G. 1954. A typological study of abortion in 350 primitive, ancient and pre-industrial societies. In H. Rosen (ed.) *Therapeutic Abortion.* New York: Julian Press, p. 98.

Dewans, S. 2010. Antiabortion ads split Atlanta. *New York Times* February 5. Online at www.nytimes.com/2010/02/06/us/06abortion.html?scp=1&sq=Shaila%20Dewan%20Margaret%20Sanger&st=cse (accessed February 6, 2012).

Dillingham, Brint. 1977. Indian women and IHS sterilization practices. *American Indian Journal* 3: 27–28.

———. 1977. Sterilization of Native Americans. *American Indian Journal* 3: 16–19.

———. 1977. Sterilization Update. *American Indian Journal* 3: 25.

Diallo, DD. 2004. Reflections of a human rights educator. *Meridians: Fem. Race Transnatl.* 4: 124–128.

Diaz-Tello, F., & Paltrow, L.M. 2010. Birth justice as reproductive justice. Working paper, National Advocates Pregnant Women, New York. Online at http://law.bepress.com/usclwps-lss/art68/.

Dickeman, M. 1979. Female infanticide, reproductive strategies, and social stratification: a preliminary model. In: N.A. Chagnon, & W. Irons (eds.), *Evolutionary Biology and Human Social Behavior: An Anthropological Perspective.* North Scituate, MA: Duxbury Press, pp. 321–368.

———. 1981. Paternal confidence and dowry competition: a biocultural analysis of purdah. In R.D. Alexander, & D.W. Tinkle (eds.) *Natural Selection and Social Behavior.* New York: Chiron Press, pp. 417–438.

Di Mauro, D. & Joffe, C. 2009. The religious right and the reshaping of sexual policy: reproductive rights and sexuality education. In: G. Herdt (ed.) *Moral Panics, Sex Panics: Fear and the Fight over Sexual Rights*. New York: New York University Press, pp. 60–68.

Disability Rag. 1991a. Bigotry in the air. *Disability Rag*, November/December: 4–13.

———. 1991b. Disabled activists outraged at idea of coalition with Right. *Disability Rag*, September/October: 6–11.

———. 1993. Parenting with a disability. *Disability Rag*, May/June, 14(3): 1–40.

Dixon-Mueller, R. 1993. *Population Policy and Women's Rights: Transforming Reproductive Choice*. Westport, CT: Praeger Publishers.

Donoval, Patricia. 1976. Sterilizing the poor and incompetent. *Hastings Center Reports* 6: 7–8.

Donovan, P. 1998. Does the family cap influence birthrates? Two new studies say "no." *The Guttmacher Report on Public Policy* 1(1).

Dowd, Nancy. 2000. *Redefining Fatherhood*. New York: New York University Press.

Down, Martyn Langdon, 1986. *Some Babies Die: An Exploration of Stillbirth and Neonatal Death* (film). Australia.

Dube, R., Dube, R., & Bhatnagar, R. 1999. Women without choice: female infanticide and the rhetoric of the over population in postcolonial India. *Women's Studies Quarterly* 27: 73–86.

Duffy, M. 1994. Making choices. In: L. Keith (ed.) *Mustn't Grumble: Writing by Disabled Women*. London, The Women's Press.

Duffy, Y. 1981. *All Things are Possible*. Ann Arbor: A.J. Garvin Associates.

Ebenstein, A.Y., & Sharygin, E.J. 2009. The consequences of the "missing girls" of China. *World Bank Economic Review* 23: 399–425.

Edwards, Sharon R. 1994. The role of men in contraceptive decision-making: current knowledge and future implications. *Family Planning Perspectives* 26(2): 77–82.

Ehrenreich, B., & English, D. 2005 (1978). *For Her Own Good: Two Centuries of Experts' Advice to Women*. New York: Anchor Books.

———. 2010 (1973). *Witches, Midwives and Nurses*. New York: Feminist Press at CUNY.

Ehrenreich, N. 1993. The colonization of the womb. *Duke Law Journal* 43: 492–587.

Ellberg, Amy (Rabbi). 1989. Halachic mourning practices for pregnancy loss. Paper submitted to the Committee of Jewish Law and Standards.

Embree, R.A. 1998. Attitudes toward elective abortion: preliminary evidence of validity for the personal beliefs scale. *Psychological Reports* 82: 1267–1281.

Evans, Ann. 2001. The influence of significant others on Australian teenagers' decisions about pregnancy resolution. *Family Planning Perspectives* 33: 224–230.

Fentiman, L.C. 2008. Pursuing the perfect mother: why America's criminalization of maternal substance abuse is not the answer—a comparative legal analysis. *Michigan Journal of Gender Law* 15: 389–465.

Ferreyra, S., & Hughes, K. 1992. *Table Manners: A Guide to the Pelvic Examination for Disabled Women and Health Care Providers*. San Francisco: Planned Parenthood.

Fine, M., & Asch, A. 1985. Disabled women: sexism without the pedestal. In: M.J. Deegan, & N.A. Brooks (eds.) *Women and Disability: The Double Handicap*. New Brunswick, N.J.:Transaction.

———. (eds.) 1988. *Women with Disabilities: Essays in Psychology, Culture, and Politics*. Philadelphia, Temple University Press.

Finer, L., & Henshaw, S. 2008. Disparities in rates of unintended pregnancy in the United States, 1994 and 2001. *Perspectives on Sexual and Reproductive Health* 38: 90–96.

Finer, L.B., Frohwirth, L.F., Dauphinee, L.A., Singh, S., & Moore, A.M. 2005. Reasons U.S. women have abortions: quantitative and qualitative perspectives. Guttmacher Institute. Online at www.guttmacher.org/pubs/journals/3711005.pdf (accessed April 20, 2014).

Finger, A. 1984. Claiming all of our bodies: reproductive rights and disability. In: R. Arditti, R.D. Klein, & S. Minden (eds.) *Test-Tube Women: What Future For Motherhood?* London: Pandora Press.

————. 1990. *Past Due: A Story of Disability, Pregnancy and Birth*. Seattle: Seal Press.

Firestone, Shulamith. 1970. *The Dialectic of Sex*. New York: Morrow.

Flavin, J. 2009. *Our Bodies, Our Crimes: The Policing of Women's Reproduction in America*. New York: NYU Press.

Fletcher, John, & Evans, Mark. 1983. Maternal bonding in early fetal ultrasound examinations. *New England Journal of Medicine* 308(7): 392–393.

Flint, Marcha. 1988. Before they are born. Paper delivered at the American Anthropological Association Meeting, Phoenix.

Forman, D.L. 2011. When "bad" mothers make worse law: a critique of legislative limits on embryo transfer. *University of Pennsylvania Journal of Law and Social Change* 14: 273–312.

Freedman, L. 2010. *Willing and Unable: Doctors' Constraints in Abortion Care*. Nashville: Vanderbilt Press.

Freedman, L., & Stulberg, D. 2013. Conflicts in care for obstetrical complications in Catholic hospitals. *American Journal of Bioethics Primary Research* 4(4): 1–10.

Freidson, Eliot. 1970. *Profession of Medicine: A Study of the Sociology of Applied Knowledge*. New York: Harper and Row.

Friedrich, Carl J. 1963. *Man and his Government: An Empirical Theory of Politics*. New York: McGraw-Hill.

Gal, S., & Kligman, G. 2000. *The Politics of Gender After Socialism*. Princeton, N.J.: Princeton University Press.

Gamson, J. 2013. The belly mommy and the fetus sitter: the reproductive marketplace and family intimacies. In: A. Frank, P. Clough, & S. Seidman (eds.) *Intimacies: A New World of Relational Life*. Abingdon: Routledge.

Gardner, N.E.S. 1986. Sexuality. In: J.A. Summers (ed.) *The Right to Grow Up: An Introduction to Adults With Developmental Disabilities*. Maryland: Paul H. Brookes.

Garg, B. 2005. Draupadis bloom in rural Punjab. *Times of India*, July 16. Retrieved from http://articles.timesofindia.indiatimes.com/2005–07–16/india/278617071agrarian-crisis-family-farm-punjab (page no longer available).

Gerson, Kathleen. 1997. Dilemmas of involved fatherhood. In: Estelle Disch (ed.) *Reconstructing Gender*. Mountain View, CA: Mayfield, pp. 272–281.

Gherman, Robert B., Chauhan, Suneet, Ouzounian, Joseph G., Lerner, Henry, Gonik, Bernard, & Murphy Goodwin, T. 2006. Shoulder dystocia: the unpreventable obstetric emergency with empiric management guidelines. *American Journal of Obstetrics and Gynecology* 195(3)(September): 657–672.

Gibbons, L., Belizán, J.M., Lauer, J.A., Betrán, A.P., Merialdi, M., Althabe, F. 2010. *The Global Numbers and Costs of Additionally Needed and Unnecessary Caesarean Sections Performed per Year: Overuse as a Barrier to Universal Coverage*. Geneva: World Health Organization.

Gill, C. 1993. When is a woman not a woman? *Disability Rag* 14(3), May/June: 26–27.

Ginsburg, F. 1989. *Contested Lives: The Abortion Debate in an American Community*. Berkeley, CA: University of California Press.

Ginsburg, F., & Rapp, R. 1995. *Conceiving the New World Order: The Global Politics of Reproduction*. Berkeley, CA: University of California Press.

Gittelman, J. 2010. Americans' Role Seen in Uganda Anti-Gay Push. *New York Times*, January 3.

Goffman, E. 1963. *Stigma: Notes on the Management of Spoiled Identity*. Englewood Cliffs, N.J.: Prentice-Hall.

Gold, R., & Nash, E. 2007. State abortion counseling policies and the fundamental principles of informed consent. *Guttmacher Policy Review* 10(4): 5–13.

Goldberg, M. 2009. *The Mean of Reproduction: Sex, Power, and the Future of the World*. New York: Penguin Press.

Golden, M. 1991. Do the disability rights and right-to-life movements have any common ground? *Disability Rag*, September/October: 1–5.

Gordon, Linda. 1990 (1976). *Women's Body, Women's Right: Birth Control in America*. New York: Penguin Books.

———. 2002 (1974). *The Moral Property of Women: A History of Birth Politics in America*. Champaign-Urbana, Ill: University of Illinois Press.

Gordon, Robert, & Kilpatrick, Cheryl. 1977. A program of group counseling for men who accompany women seeking legal abortions. *Community Mental Health Journal* 13(4): 291–295.

Gorrill, Marsha, Johnson, Lisa, Patton, Phillip, & Burry, Kenneth. 2001. Oocyte donor screening: the selection process and cost analysis. *Fertility and Sterility* 75: 400–404.

Gould, S.J. 1985. *The Flamingo's Smile*. New York: W.W. Norton & Company.

Grady, William, Tanfer, Koray, Billy, John O.G., & Lincoln-Hanson, Jennifer. 1996. Men's perceptions of their roles and responsibilities regarding sex, contraception and childbearing. *Family Planning Perspectives* 28(5): 221–226.

Greenberg, Martin. 1985. *The Birth of a Father*. New York: Avon Books.

Greenhalgh, S. 2005. *Governing China's Politics: From Leninist to Neoliberal Biopolitics*. Stanford: Stanford University Press.

Greenhouse, L. 2007. Justices back ban on method of abortion. *New York Times*, April 19.

Greenhouse, L., & Siegel, R.B. 2010. Before (and after) *Roe v. Wade*: new questions about backlash. *Yale Law Journal* 120: 2028–2087.

Gregor, T. 1988. Infants are not precious to us: the psychological impact of infanticide among Mehinaku Indians. Paper presented in the meeting of the American Anthropological Association, November 1988, Phoenix, AZ.

Greve, Paul. 2009. Labor pains: liability trends in obstetrics. *Medical Liability Monitor* 34(8): 4–5, 7.

Guendelman, S., & Stachel, L. 2011. Infertility status and infertility treatment: racial and ethnic disparities. In: A. Handler, J. Kennelly, & N. Peacock (eds.) *Reducing Racial/Ethnic Disparities in Reproductive and Perinatal Outcomes*. New York: Springer, pp. 93–117.

Guendelman, S., Thornton, D., Gould, J., & Hosang, N. 2005. Social disparities in maternal morbidity during labor and delivery between Mexican-born and US-born white Californians, 1996–1998. *American Journal of Public Health* 95: 2218–2224.

Gurr, B. 2012. The failures and possibilities of a human rights approach to secure Native American women's reproductive justice. *Society Without Borders* 7: 1–28.

Gutiérrez, Elena R. 2003. Policing "pregnant pilgrims": welfare, health care, and the control of Mexican-origin women's fertility. In: Molly Ladd-Taylor, Gina Feldberg, Kathryn McPherson, & Alison Li (eds.) *Women, Health, and Nation: The U.S. and Canada since 1945*. Toronto: McGill-Queens University Press, pp. 379–403.

———. 2008. *Fertile Matters: The Politics of Mexican-Origin Women's Reproduction*. Austin: University of Texas Press.

Guttmacher Institute. 2006. Contraceptive needs and services, Guttmacher Institute. Online at www.guttmacher.org/pubs/win/allstates2006.pdf (accessed January 3, 2011).

———. 2013a. Facts on Induced Abortion in the United States. Guttmacher Institute.

———. 2013b. Facts on Induced Abortions World-Wide. Guttmacher Institute.

Halem, S.C. 1997. At what cost? An argument against mandatory AZT treatment of HIV-positive pregnant women. *Harvard Civil Rights–Civil Liberties Law Review* 32: 491–528.

Haller, Mark. 1963. *Eugenics: Hereditarian Attitudes in American Thought*. New Brunswick, N.J.: Rutgers University Press.

Haraway, Donna J. 1997. *Modest_Witness@Second_Millennium.FemaleMan©_Meets_Onco Mouse™: Feminism and Technoscience*. New York: Routledge.

Hare, J., & Solomon, E.K. 1981. Giving birth. *Diabetes Forecast*.

Haring, M., & Meyerson, L. 1979. Attitudes of college students toward sexual behavior of disabled persons. *Archives of Physical Medicine and Rehabilitation* 60(6): 257–260.

Harris, A.P. 1990. Race and essentialism in feminist legal theory. *Stanford Law Review* 42: 581–616.

Harris, L.H. 2014. *Challenging Conception: A Clinical and Cultural History of In Vitro Fertilization in the United States*. Baltimore, MD: Johns Hopkins University Press.

Harriss-White, B. 2001. Gender-cleansing: the paradox of development and deteriorating female life chances in Tamilnadu. In: R. Sunderrajan (ed.) *Signposts: Gender Issues in Post-Independence India*. New Brunswick, N.J.: Rutgers University Press, pp. 125–154.

Hartman, B. 1995. *Reproductive Rights and Wrongs: The Global Politics of Population Control*. Boston, MA: South End Press.

Hartouni, Valerie. 1997. *Cultural Conceptions: On Reproductive Technologies and the Remaking of Life*. Minneapolis: University of Minnesota Press.

Hawkins, J. 2013. Selling ART: an empirical assessment of advertising on fertility clinics' websites. *Indiana Law Journal* 88: 1147–1179.

Hay, Iain. 1992. *Money, Medicine, and Malpractice in American Society*. New York: Praeger.

Health Research Group. 1973. *A Health Research Group Study on Surgical Sterilization: Present Abuses and Proposed Regulations*. Washington, D.C.: Public Citizens, Inc.

Health Resources and Services Administration. n.d. *Maternal Mortality: Child Health USA 2008–2009*. Online at mchb.hrsa.gov/chusa08/hstat/ hsi/pages/204mm.html (accessed January 3, 2011).

Healthy People. 2000. *2010: Midcourse Review*. US Department of Health and Human Services.

Hegde, R. 1999. Making bodies, reproducing violence. *Violence Against Women* 5: 507–524.

Hening, W.W. 1809–1823. *The Statutes at Large; Being a Collection of All the Laws of Virginia, from the First Session of the Legislature in the Year 1619*, 13 vols. Richmond/Philadelphia/New York: W.W. Hening.

Henshaw, Stanley K., & Kost, Kathryn. 1992. Parental involvement in minors' abortion decisions. *Family Planning Perspectives* 24: 196–207, 213.

Hern, Warren M. 1970. Family planning and the poor. *New Republic* 163, November 14: 17–19.

Hernández, Antonia. 1976. Chicanas and the issue of involuntary sterilization: reforms needed to protect informed consent. *Chicano Law Review* 3: 3–37.

———. 1996. Interviewed by Elena R. Gutiérrez, March 7.

Hershey, L. 1991. Letter, *Disability Rag*, November/December: 2.

———. 1994. Choosing disability, *Ms*, July/August: 26–32.

Hesketh, T., Lu, L., & Xing, Z.W. 2005. The effect of China's one-child family policy after 25 years. *New England Journal of Medicine* 353: 1171–1176.

Hertz, Rosanna. 2006. *Single By Chance, Mothers By Choice: How Women Are Choosing Parenthood Without Marriage and Creating the New American Family*. New York: Oxford University Press.

Hewlett, Barry. 1991. *Intimate Fathers: The Nature and Context of Aka Pygmy Paternal Infant Care*. Ann Arbor: University of Michigan Press.

Hill, K., Thomas, K., AbouZahr, C., Walker, N., Say, L., Inoue, M., Suzuki, E.; Maternal Mortality Working Group. 2007. Estimates of maternal mortality worldwide between 1990 and 2005: an assessment of available data. *Lancet* 370: 1311–1319.

Hilyer, B. 1993. *Feminism and Disability*. Norman: University of Oklahoma Press.

Hinson, D., & McBrien, M. 2011. Surrogacy across America. *Family Advocate* 34(2): 32–36.

Hirschenbaum, D. 2000. When CRACK is the only choice: the effect of a negative right of privacy on drug addicted women. *Berkeley Women's Law Journal* 15: 327–337.

Hochschild, Arlie. 2012. *The Outsourced Self: Intimate Life in Market Times*. New York: Metropolitan Books.

Hoell, K. 1991. Letter, *Disability Rag*, November/December: 2.

Holland, Sally, & Scourfield, Jonathan. 2000. Managing marginalised masculinities: men and probation. *Journal of Gender Studies* 9: 199–211.

Hollos, Marida, & Larsen, Ulla. 2004. Which African men promote smaller families and why? Marital relations and fertility in a Pare community in northern Tanzania. *Social Science & Medicine* 58: 1733–1749.

Holmberg, Lars I., & Wahlberg, Vivian. 2000. The process of decision-making on abortion: a grounded theory study of men in Sweden. *Journal of Adolescent Health* 26: 230–234.

Holmes, S. 1991a. Radio talk about TV anchor's disability stirs ire in Los Angeles. *The New York Times*, August 23, Sec. B: 18.

———. 1991b. Abortion issue divides advocates for disabled. *New York Times*, July 4.

Hoyert, D.L. (ed.) 2007. Maternal mortality and related concepts. NCFH Statistics: 1–13.

Hrdy, S.B. 1999. *Mother Nature: A History of Mothers, Infants, and Natural Selection.* Pantheon: New York.

Hudson, V.M., & den Boer, A.M. 2004. *Bare Branches: The Security Implications of Asia's Surplus Male Population.* Cambridge, MA: MIT Press.

Hull, G.T., Scott, P.B., & Smith, B. (eds.) 1982. *But Some of Us Are Brave: Black Women's Studies.* New York: Feminist Press.

Hull, K.E. 2001. The political limits of the rights frame: the case of same sex marriage in Hawaii. *Sociological Perspectives* 44: 207–232.

Hulse, Carl. 2005. Bipartisan group in senate averts judge showdown. *New York Times,* May 24.

Hutchings, G. 1997. Female infanticide will lead to an army of bachelors. *The Telegraph* (London), April 11. Online at www.telegraph.co.uk/htmlContent. jhtml?html=/archive/1997/04/011/wchill.html.

Hutchinson, Sally, Marsiglio, William, & Cohan, Mark. 2002. Interviewing young men about sex and procreation: methodological issues. *Qualitative Health Research* 12: 42–60.

Hyler, D. 1985. To choose a child. In: S.E. Browne, D. Connors, & N. Stern (eds.) *With the Power of Each Breath: A Disabled Women's Anthology.* San Francisco: Cleis Press.

Institute of Medicine. 2004. Keeping patients safe: transforming the work environment of nurses. In: *Institute of Medicine Committee on the Work Environment for Nurses and Patient Safety Board on Health Care Services.* Washington, D.C.: National Academies Press, pp. 229 and 386.

———. 2011. *Clinical Preventive Services for Women: Closing the Gaps.* Washington, D.C.: National Academies Press

Janssen, N.D. 1999. Fetal rights and the prosecution of women for using drugs during pregnancy. *Drake Law.*

Jeffery, R., & Jeffery, P. 1997. *Population, Gender, and Politics.* Cambridge, UK: Cambridge University Press.

Jena, Anupam B., Seabury, Seth, Lakdawalla, Darius, & Chandra, Amitabh. 2011. Malpractice risk according to physician specialty. *New England Journal of Medicine* 265 (7): 629–636.

Jesudason, S.A. 2009. In the hot tub: the praxis of building new alliances for reprogenetics. *Signs: Journal of Women in Culture and Society* 34: 901–924.

Joffe, C. 1995. *Doctors of Conscience: The Struggle to Provide Abortion before and after Roe v Wade.* Boston, MA: Beacon Press.

———. 2012. All common ground lost: the right's opposition to the Violence Against Women Act. Rhrealitycheck.org. Online at www.rhrealitycheck.org/article/2012/03/16/all-common-ground-lost-rightsopposition-to-violence-against-women-act (accessed March 20, 2012).

———. 2013. The politicization of abortion and the evolution of abortion counseling. *American Journal of Public Health* 103(1): 57–65.

Joffe, C., & Parker, W. 2012. Race, reproductive politics and reproductive health care in the contemporary United States. *Contraception* 86: 2.

Joffe, C.E., & Weitz, T.A. 2003. Normalizing the exceptional: incorporating the "abortion pill" into mainstream medicine. *Social Science and Medicine* 56: 2353–2366.

Joffe, C., Weitz, T., & Stacey, C.L. 2004. Uneasy allies: pro-choice physicians, feminist health activists and the struggle for abortion rights. *Sociology of Health and Illness* 26: 775–796.

Di Mauro, D., & Joffe, C. (eds.) 2009. The religious right and the reshaping of sexual policy. *Moral Panics, Sex Panics.* New York: NYU Press, pp. 47–103.

Johnson, C. 2013a. California lawmakers seek legislation to prevent prison abuse. Online at cironline.org/reports/calif-lawmakers-seek-legislation-prevent-prison-sterilization-abuse-5112 (accessed December 23, 2013).

———. 2013b. *Female Inmates Sterilized in California Prisons Without Approval.* Centre for Investigative Reporting, July 7. Online at: cironline.org/reports/female-inmates-sterilized-californiaprisons-without-approval-4917 (accessed April 20, 2014).

Johnson, D. 2008. "TRAP"ing *Roe* in Indiana and a common-ground alternative. *Yale Law Journal* 118: 1356–1359.

Johnson, M. 1990. Defective fetuses and us. *Disability Rag,* March/April: 34.

Joint Commission. 2010. *Preventing Maternal Death.* Issue 44, January 26. Online at www.jointcommission.org/sentinel_event_alert_issue_44_preventing_maternal_death/ (accessed January 3, 2011).

Jordanova, Ludmilla. 1989. *Sexual Visions: Images of Gender in Science and Medicine Between the Eighteenth and Twentieth Centuries.* Madison: University of Wisconsin Press.

Joyce, K. 2008. Missing: the "Right" Babies. *The Nation.*

Jump, Teresa L., & Haas, Linda. 1987. Fathers in transition. In: Michael Kimmel (ed.) *Changing Men: New Directions in Research on Men and Masculinity.* Newbury Park: Sage, pp. 98–114.

Kaiser Family Foundation. 1997. *A National Survey on Men's Role in Preventing Pregnancy: Women and Men Think Men Need to be More Involved in Contraceptive Choice and Use.* Menlo Park: Kaiser Family Foundation.

———. 2013. The impact of the coverage gap in states not expanding medicaid by race and ethnicity. December 17.

Kaplan, D. 1988. Disability rights perspectives on reproductive technologies and public policy. In: N. Taub, & S. Cohen (eds.) *Reproductive Laws for the 1990s.* New Brunswick, N.J.: Rutgers University.

Kaplan, L. 1997. *The Story of Jane: The Legendary Underground Feminist Abortion Service.* Chicago, I.L.: University of Chicago Press.

Keels, L.M. 2010. "Substantially limited": the reproductive rights of women living with HIV/AIDS. *University of Baltimore Law Review* 39: 389–422.

Keith, L. (ed.) 1994. *Mustn't Grumble: Writing by Disabled Women.* London, The Women's Press.

Keller, M.C., Nesse, R.M., & Hofferth, S. 2001. The Trivers-Willard hypothesis of parental investment: no effect in the contemporary United States. *Evolution and Human Behavior* 22: 343–360.

Kelly, M. 2010. Regulating the reproduction and mothering of poor women: the controlling image of the welfare mother in television news coverage of welfare reform. *Journal of Poverty* 14: 76–96F.

Kero, A., & Lalos, A. 2000. Ambivalence: a logical response to legal abortion. A prospective study among women and men. *Journal of Psychosomatic Obstetrics and Gynecology* 21: 81–91.

———. 2004. Reactions and reflections in men, 4 and 12 months post-abortion. *Journal of Psychosomatic Obstetrics and Gynecology* 25: 135–143.

Kero, A., Lalos, A., Hogberg, U., & Jacobsson, L. 1999. The male partner involved in legal abortion. *Human Reproduction* 14: 2669–2675.

Kimmel, Michael. 1996. *Manhood in America: A Cultural History.* New York: Free Press.

King, D.K. 1988. Multiple jeopardy, multiple consciousness: the context of a black feminist ideology. *Signs: Journal of Women in Culture and Society* 14: 42–72.

Klagholz, Jeffrey, & Strunk, Albert L. 2009. Overview of the 2009 ACOG survey on professional liability. Online at www.academia.edu/707493/Overview_of_the_2009_ACOG_survey_on_professional_liability (accessed October 26, 2012).

———. 2012. Overview of the 2012 ACOG survey on professional liability. Online at www.acog.org/About_ACOG/ACOG_Departments/Professional_Liability/2012_Survey_Results (accessed October 26, 2012).

Klein, B.S. 1992. We are who you are: feminism and disability, *Ms,* November/December: 70–74.

Kligman, G. 1998. *The Politics of Duplicity: Controlling Reproduction in Ceaucescu's Romania.* Berkeley, C.A.: University of California Press.

Knight, M., & UKOSS. 2007. Peripartum hysterectomy in the UK: management and outcomes of the associated haemorrhage. *BJOG* 114: 1380–1387.

Kolata, G. 1987. The sad legacy of the Dalkon Shield, *New York Times*, December 6.

Krauss, D.J. 1991. Regulating women's bodies: the adverse effect of fetal rights theory on childbirth decisions and women of color. *Harvard Civil Rights–Civil Liberties Law Review* 26: 523–548.

Krawiec, K.D. 2009. Why we should ignore the "Octomom." *Northwestern University Law Review Colloquy* 104: 120–131.

Krieger, Susan. 1991. *Social Science and the Self*. New Brunswick, N.J.: Rutgers University Press.

Kroll, K., & Levy Klein, E. 1992. *Enabling Romance: A Guide to Love, Sex, and Relationships for the Disabled (and the People who Love Them)*. New York: Harmony Books.

Kuklina, E.V., Meikle, S.F., Jamieson, D.J., Whiteman, M.K., Barfield, W.D., Hillis, S.D., & Posner, S.F. 2009. Severe obstetric morbidity in the US, 1998–2005. *Obstetrics and Gynecology* 113: 293—299.

Kukura, E. 2010. Choice in birth: preserving access to VBAC. *Pennsylvania State Law Review* 114: 959–100.

Lai-wan, C.C., Eric, B., & Hoi-yan, C.C. 2006. Attitudes and practices toward sex selection in China. *Prenatal Diagnosis* 26: 610–613.

Lamb, Michael E. 2000. The history of research on father involvement: an overview. *Marriage & Family Review* 29: 23–43.

LaRossa, Ralph. 1995. Fatherhood and social change. In: Michael Kimmel, & Michael Messner (eds.) *Men's Lives*. Boston, MA: Allyn & Bacon, pp. 448–460.

Larson, Kamet. 1977. And then there were none. *Christian Century*, January 26: 61.

Layne, Linda L. 1984. The use of space among settled Bedouin in the Jordan Valley. Paper delivered at Anthropology in Jordan: State of the Art Symposium, Amman.

———. 2003. *Motherhood Lost: A Feminist Account of Pregnancy Loss in America*. New York: Routledge, pp. 67–79.

Leavesley, G., & Porter, J. 1982. Sexuality, fertility and contraception in disability. *Contraception* 26: 417–441.

Leavitt, J. 1986. *Brought to Bed: Childbearing in America, 1750–1950*. New York: Oxford University Press.

Lee, R.L. 2009. New trends in global outsourcing of commercial surrogacy: a call for regulation. *Hastings Women's Law Journal* 20: 275–300.

Leth, R.A., Møller, J.K., Thomsen, R.W., Uldbjerg, N., & Nørgaard, M. 2009. Risk of selected postpartum infections after cesarean section compared with vaginal birth: a five-year cohort study of 32,468 women. *Acta Obstetricia et Gynecologica Scandinavica* 88: 976–983.

Lewin, Ellen. 2009. *Gay Fatherhood: Narratives of Family and Citizenship in America*. Chicago, IL: University of Chicago Press.

Lewis, Neil A. 2004. Bypassing senate for second time, Bush seats judge. *New York Times*, February 21.

Lezin, J. 2003. (Mis)conceptions: unjust limitations on legally unmarried women's access to reproductive technology and their use of known donors. *Hastings Women's Law Journal* 14: 185–214.

Li, L., & Wu, X. 2011. Gender of children, bargaining power, and intrahousehold resource allocation in China. *Journal of Human Resources* 46: 295–316.

Light, Donald. 2004. Ironies of successes: a new history of the American health care system. *Journal of Health and Social Behavior* 45: 1– 24.

Liss-Levinson, William. 1981. Men without playfulness. In: Robert Lewis (ed.) *Men in Difficult Times*. Englewood Cliffs, N.J.: Prentice-Hall, pp. 19–28.

Littlewood, Thomas. 1977. *The Politics of Population Control*. Notre Dame: University of Notre Dame Press.

Localio, A. Russell, Lawthers, Ann G., Brennan, Troyen A., Laird, Nan M., Hebert, Liesi E., Peterson, Lynn M., Newhouse, Joseph P., Weiler, Paul, C., & Hiatt, Howard H. 1991. Relation between malpractice claims and adverse events due to negligence: results of the Harvard Medical Practice Study III. *New England Journal of Medicine* 325 (July 25): 245–251.

Lombardo, P., & Hardin, P. 2013. Compensate eugenic sterilization victims. *USA Today*, August 21.

Lonsdale, S. 1990. *Women and Disability: The Experience of Physical Disability Among Women.* New York, St. Martin's Press.

Lopez, Iris. 1993. Agency and constraint: sterilization and reproductive freedom among Puerto Rican women in New York City. In: L. Lamphere, H. Ragone, & Patricia Zavella (eds.) *Situated Lives: Gender and Culture in Everyday Life.* New York: Routledge, pp. 155–171.

Lowery, A. 2012. The economic impact of the pill. *New York Times*, March 26: 1.

Luft, R.E., & Ward, J. 2009. Toward an intersectionality just out of reach: confronting challenges to intersectional practice. *Adv. Gender Res.* 13: 9–37.

Luker, Kristin. 1975. *Taking Chances: Abortion and the Decision not to Contracept.* Berkeley, CA: University of California Press.

———. 1984. *Abortion and the Politics of Motherhood.* Berkeley, CA: University of California Press.

———. 2006. *When Sex Goes to School: Warring Views on Sex—and Sex Education—Since the Sixties.* New York: W. W. Norton & Company.

Luker, K. and Luna, Z. 2013. Reproductive Justice. *Annual Review of Law and Social Science* 9: 327–352.

Luna, Z.T. 2009. From rights to justice: women of color changing the face of US reproductive rights organizing. *Society Without Borders* 4: 343–364.

———. 2011. "The phrase of the day": examining contexts and co-optation of reproductive justice activism in the women's movement. In: A.C. Snyder, & S.P. Stobbie (eds.) *Research in Social Movements, Conflicts and Change*, Vol. 32. Bingley, UK: Emerald Kingdom, pp. 219–246.

Lupton, Deborah, & Barclay, Lesley. 1997. *Constructing Fatherhood: Discourses and Experiences.* London: Sage.

Mahalingam, R. 2007. Culture, ecology, and beliefs about gender in son preference caste groups. *Evolution and Human Behavior* 28: 319–329.

Mahalingam, R., & Balan, S. 2008. Culture, son preference and beliefs about masculinity. *Journal of Research on Adolescence* 18: 541–554.

Mahalingam, R., & Haritatos, J. 2006. Culture, gender, and immigration. In R. Mahalingam (ed.) *Cultural Psychology of Immigrants.* Mahwah, N.J.: Erlbaum, pp. 259–278.

Mahalingam, R., & Jackson, B. 2007. Idealized cultural beliefs about gender: implications for mental health. *Social Epidemiology and Social Psychiatry* 42: 1012–1023.

Mahalingam, R., Haritatos, J., & Jackson, B. 2007. Essentialism and the cultural psychology of gender in extreme son preference communities in India. *American Journal of Orthopsychiatry* 77: 598–609.

Mairs, N. 1990. *Carnal Acts.* New York: Harper Collins.

Mamo, L. 2007. Debates of lesbian reproduction within lesbian/gay and feminist communities. *Queering Reproduction: Achieving Pregnancy in the Age of Technoscience.* Duke University Press: 47–57.

Marcell, Arik, Raine, Tina, & Eyre, Stephen. 2003. Where does reproductive health fit into the lives of adolescent males? *Perspectives on Sexual and Reproductive Health* 35: 180–186.

Mardorossian, Carine. 2003. Laboring women, coaching men: masculinity and childbirth education in the contemporary United States. *Hypatia* 18: 113–134.

Markens, S. 2012. The global reproductive health market: U.S. media framings and public discourses about transnational surrogacy. *Social Science and Medicine* 74: 1745–1753.

Marsiglio, William, & Shehan, Constance. 1993. Adolescent males' abortion attitudes: data from a national survey. *Family Planning Perspectives* 25: 162–169.

Marsiglio, William, Hutchinson, Sally, & Cohan, Mark. 2001. Young men's procreative identity: becoming aware, being aware, and being responsible. *Journal of Marriage and the Family* 63: 123–135.

Martin, Emily. 1991. The drama of the egg and the sperm: how science has constructed a romance based on stereotypical male-female roles. *Signs* 16(3): 485–501.

Martin, J.A., Hamilton, B.E., Sutton, P.D., Ventura, S.J., & Mathews Osterman, M.J.K. 2010. Births: final data for 2008. *National Vital Statistics Reports* vol. 59 no. 1. Hyattsville, MD: National Center for Health Statistics. Online at www.cdc.gov/nchs/data/nvsr/nvsr59/nvsr59_01.pdf (accessed January 3, 2011).

Matsuda, M.J. 1990. Beside my sister, facing the enemy: legal theory out of coalition. *Stanford Law Review* 43: 1183–1192.

Mavroforou, Anna, Koumantakis, Evgenios, and Michalodimitrakis, Emmanuel. 2005. Physicians' liability in obstetric and gynecology practice. *Medicine and Law* 24(1)(March): 1–9.

May, E. 2010. *America and the Pill: A History of Promise, Peril, and Liberation.* New York: Basic Books.

McCall, L. 2005. The complexity of intersectionality. *Signs: Journal of Women in Culture and Society* 30: 1771–1800.

McCarthy, M. 1994. Against all odds: HIV and safer sex education for women with learning difficulties. In: L. Doyal, J. Naidoo, & T. Wilton (Eds) *AIDS: Setting a Feminist Agenda.* London: Taylor & Francis.

———. 1996. Sexual experiences and sexual abuse of women with learning disabilities. In: M. Hester, L. Kelly, & J. Radford (eds.) *Women, Violence and Male Power: Feminist Activism, Research and Practice.* Buckingham: Open University Press.

McCarthy-Keith, D.M., Schisterman, E.F., Robinson, R.D., O'Leary, K., Lucidi, R.S., & Armstrong, A.Y. 2010. Will decreasing assisted reproductive technology costs improve utilization and outcomes among minority women? *Fertility and Sterility* 94(7): 2587–2589.

McCook, Leslie I. 1987. A study of the relationship between pregnancy identity and motherhood identity and the perception of loss in women who have a miscarriage. Doctoral dissertation proposal. Psychoeducational Processes, Temple University.

McKay, Jim, Messner, Michael, & Sabo, Don. (eds.) 2000. *Masculinities, Gender Relations and Sport.* Thousand Oaks: Sage.

McKinley, John, & Stoekle, John. 1988. Corporatization and the social transformation of doctoring. *International Journal of Health Services* 18: 191–205.

Mello, Michelle M. 2006. *Understanding Medical Malpractice Insurance: A Primer.* Robert Wood Johnson Foundation Research Synthesis Report no. 8.

Merry, S.E. 2006. *Human Rights and Gender Violence: Translating International Law into Local Justice.* Chicago: University of Chicago Press.

Messner, Michael. 1987. The life of a man's seasons: male identity in the life course of the jock. In: Michael Kimmel (ed.) *Changing Men: New Directions in Research on Men and Masculinity.* Thousand Oaks: Sage, pp. 53–67.

Mettler, S. 2011. *The Submerged State: How Invisible Government Policies Undermine American Democracy.* Chicago, IL: University of Chicago Press.

Mexican American Legal Defense and Education Fund (MALDEF). Papers. Stanford University Special Collections, Palo Alto, California.

Miller, B.D. 1981. *The Endangered Sex: Neglect of Female Children in Rural North India.* Ithaca, N.Y.: Cornell University Press.

Miller, Warren. 1994. The relationship between childbearing motivations and attitudes toward abortion among married men and women. *Family Planning Perspectives* 26: 165–168.

Minow, M. 1991. *Making All the Difference: Inclusion, Exclusion, and American Law.* Ithaca, N.Y.: Cornell University Press.

Morgan, L., & Michaels, M. (eds.) 1999. *Fetal Subjects, Feminist Positions.* Philadelphia: University of Pennsylvania Press.

Morgan, L., & Roberts, E. 2013. Reproductive governance in Latin America. *Anthropology and Medicine* 19(2): 241–254.

Morris, J. (ed.) 1989. *Able Lives: Women's Experiences of Paralysis.* London: The Women's Press.

———. 1991. *Pride Against Prejudice.* London: The Women's Press.

———. 1993. Feminism and disability. *Feminist Review* 43, Spring: 57–70.

———. 1995. Creating a space for absent voices: disabled women's experience of receiving assistance with daily living activities. *Feminist Review* 51, Autumn: 68–93.

Morris, T. 2013. *Cut it Out: The C-Section Epidemic in America.* New York: New York University Press.

Moynihan, Daniel P. 1965. *The Negro Family: The Case for National Action.* Washington, D.C.: Office of Policy Planning and Research, U.S. Department of Labor.

Muhajer, S. 2011. Octomom's doctor has license revoked for "mega-birth." *Huffington Post,* June 1.

Mukherjee, S., Velez Edwards, D.R., Baird, D.D., Savitz, D.A., and Hartmann, K.E. 2013. Risk of miscarriage among black women and white women in a U.S. Prospective Cohort Study. *American Journal of Epidemiology* 177(11): 1271–1278.

Mundy, Liza. 2007. *Everything Conceivable: How Assisted Reproduction Is Changing Men, Women, and the World.* New York: Knopf.

Murdock, G.P. 1967. *Ethnographic Atlas.* Pittsburgh, PA: University of Pittsburgh Press.

———. 1981. *Atlas of World Cultures.* Pittsburgh, PA: University of Pittsburgh Press.

Mutcherson, K. 2009. Disabling dreams of parenthood: the fertility industry, anti-discrimination and parents with disabilities. *Law and Inequality* 27: 311–364.

Muth, T. 2013. Death or imprisonment? El Salvador's strict antiabortion law. *Christian Science Monitor.*

Muthulakshmi, R. 1997. *Female Infanticide: Its Causes and Solutions.* New Delhi, India: Discovery.

Nabarette, Charles. 2001. Interviewed by Elena R. Gutiérrez and Virginia Espino, May.

Nachtigall, R.D., Castrillo, M., Shah, N., Turner, D., Harrington, J., & Jackson, R. 2009. The challenge of providing infertility services to a low-income immigrant Latino population. *Fertility and Sterility* 92: 116–123.

Nack, Adina. 2002. Bad girls and fallen women: chronic STD diagnoses as gateways to tribal stigma. *Symbolic Interaction* 25: 463–485.

Natarajan, S. 1997. *Watering the Neighbor's Plant: Media Perspectives on Female Infanticide in Tamilnadu,* monograph no. 6. Chennai, India: M. S. Swaminathan Research Foundation.

National Center for Health Statistics, U.S. Department of Health and Human Services. 1982. *Trends in Contraceptive Practice: United States.* Hyattsville, Maryland: Office of Health Research, Statistics and Technology.

National Conference of State Legislatures. 2009. Family Cap Policies. National Conference of State Legislatures.

National Council of La Raza (NCLR). 2001. *Beyond the Census: Hispanics and an American Agenda.* Washington, D.C.: NCLR.

National Fatherhood Initiative. 2004. www.fatherhood.org (accessed April 30, 2004). Gaithersburg, MD.

National Women's Law Center. 2013. *Health Care Refusals Harm Patients: The Threat to Reproductive Health Care.* Washington, D.C.: National Women's Law Center.

Neugebauer, Richard. 1987. The psychiatric effects of miscarriage: research design and preliminary findings. In: Brian Cooper (ed.) *Psychiatric Epidemiology: Progress and Prospects.* London: Croom Helm, pp. 136–149.

New York Times. 1988. Justice for all in the Baby M case. *New York Times,* February 4.

———. 1991. Official defends station's show on disabled. *New York Times,* December 15, Sec. 1, Part 1: 33.

Newsweek. 1991. Whose baby is it, anyway? *Newsweek,* October 28: 73.

Oberman, M. 1991. Sex, drugs, pregnancy, and the law: rethinking the problems of pregnant women who use drugs. *Hastings Law Journal* 43: 505–548.

Ocen, P. 2012. Punishing pregnancy: race, incarceration and the shackling of pregnant prisoners. *California Law Review* 100: 1–54.

Oomman, N., & Ganatra, B.R. 2002. Sex selection: the systemic elimination of girls. *Reproductive Health Matters* 10: 184–188.

Organisation for Economic Co-operation and Development. 2010. OECD health data 2010 — frequently requested data 2010. Online at www.oecd.org/document/16/0,3343, en_2649_33929_2085200_1_1_1_1,00.html (accessed January 3, 2011).

Osborn, R.W., & Silkey, B. 1980. Husbands' attitudes towards abortion and Canadian abortion law. *Journal of Biosocial Science* 12(1): 21–30.

Oshiro, B.T. 2009. Decreasing elective deliveries before 39 weeks of gestation in an integrated health care system. *Obstetrics and Gynecology* 113: 804–811.

Oster, E. 2005. Hepatitis B and the case of the missing women. *Journal of Political Economy* 113: 1163–1216.

Oudshoorn, Nelly. 2004. Astronauts in the sperm world. *Men and Masculinities* 6: 349–367.

Paige, Karen Ericksen, & Paige, Jeffery M. 1981. *The Politics of Reproductive Ritual.* Berkeley, CA: University of California Press.

Paltrow, L.M. 1990. When becoming pregnant is a crime. *Criminal Justice Ethics* 9: 41–47.

———. 2002. The war on drugs and the war on abortion: some initial thoughts on the connections, intersections and effects. *Reproductive Health Matters* 10: 162–170.

———. 2009. What to expect: legal developments and challenges in reproductive justice. *Cardozo Journal of Law and Gender* 15: 502–517.

Paltrow, L.M, & Flavin, J. 2013. Arrests of and forced interventions on pregnant women in the United States, 1973–2005: implications for women's legal status and public health. *Journal of Health Politics, Policy and Law* 38: 299–343.

Panigrahi, L. 1972. *British Social Policy and Female Infanticide in India.* New Delhi, India: Munshiram Manoharlal.

Panuthos, Claudia. 1984. *Transformation Through Birth: A Woman's Guide.* South Hadley, Mass: Bergin and Garvey.

Parsons, Talcott. 1951. *The Social System.* Glencoe, IL: Free Press.

Pepper, Rachel. 1999. *The Ultimate Guide to Pregnancy for Lesbians: Tips and Techniques from Conception to Birth. How to Stay Sane and Care for Yourself.* San Francisco: Cleis.

Petchesky, Rosalind. 1987. Fetal images: the power of visual culture in the politics of reproduction. *Feminist Studies* 13(2): 263–292.

———. 1990. *Abortion and Women's Choice: The State, Sexuality, and Reproductive Freedom.* Boston, MA: Northeastern University Press.

———. 2003. *Global Prescriptions: Gendering Health and Human Rights.* London: Zen Books.

Picone, M. 1998. Infanticide, the spirits of aborted fetuses, and the making of motherhood in Japan. In: N. Scheper-Hughes, & C. Sargent (eds.) *Small Wars: The Cultural Politics of Childhood.* Berkeley, CA: University of California Press, pp. 37–57.

Pillard, C.T. 2006. Our other reproductive choices: equality in sex education, contraceptive access, and work family policy. *Emory Law Journal* 56: 941–992.

Planned Parenthood/Shasta-Diablo Disability Program. (n.d.) *Reproduction, Contraception and Disability* (information flyer).

Popenoe, David. 1996. A world without fathers (consequences of children living without fathers). *Wilson Quarterly* 20: 12–30.

Potash, C. 1993. Sex: pure and not so simple. *Disability Rag,* 14(3), May/June: 30–32.

Premi, M.K. 2001. The missing girl child. *Economic and Political Weekly,* May 26: 1875–1880.

Price, K. 2010. What is reproductive justice? How women of color activists are redefining the pro-choice paradigm. *Meridians: Feminism, Race Transnationalism* 10: 42–65.

R., Kate. 2000. The crazy mixed-up world of donor insemination. *Volunteer Notes* (Fall): 2–4.

Rahman, A. 1994. A view towards women's reproductive rights perspective on selected laws and policies in Pakistan. *Whittier Law Review* 15: 981–1001.

Ramanamma, A., & Bambawale, U. 1980. The mania for sons: an analysis of social values in South Asia. *Social Science and Medicine* 14: 107–110.

Ramasubban, R., & Jejeebhoy, S. 2000. *Women's Reproductive Health in India.* Jaipur, India: Rawat.

Ramaswami, M., & Wachman, M. 2012. Female feticide and infanticide: implications for reproductive justice. In: J. Chrisler (ed.) *Reproductive Justice*. Santa Barbara: Praeger, pp. 251–258.

Ramirez de Arellano, Annette B., & Seipp, Conrad. 1983. *Colonialism, Catholicism, and Contraception*. Chapel Hill: University of North Carolina Press.

Ranji, U., and Salganicoff, A. 2009. State Medicaid coverage of family planning services: summary of State Survey findings. George Washington University School of Public Health Health Serv./Kaiser Found., Washington, D.C. Online at: kff.org/medicaid/report/state-medicaid-coverage-of-family-planning-services-summaryof-state-survey-findings/.

Rao, V. 1993a. Dowry "inflation" in rural India: a statistical investigation. *Population Studies* 47: 283–293.

———. 1993b. The rising price of husbands: a hedonic analysis of dowry increases in rural India. *Journal of Political Economy* 101: 666–677.

———. 1997. Wife-beating in rural south India: a qualitative and econometric analysis. *Social Science and Medicine* 44: 1169–1180.

Rapp, Rayna. 1988a. Accounting for amniocentesis. Paper for Wenner-Gren Conference "Analysis in Medical Anthropology," Lisbon.

———. 1988b. The power of "positive" diagnosis: medical and maternal discourses on amniocentesis. In: Karen L. Michaelson (ed.) *Childbirth in America: Anthropological Perspectives*. South Hadley, Mass: Bergin and Garvey, pp. 103–116.

———. 1999. *Testing the Woman, Testing the Fetus*. New York: Routledge.

———. (in press) Constructing amniocentesis: maternal and medical discourses. In: Faye Ginsburg, & Anna Tsing (eds.) *Anthropological Constructions of Gender in America*.

Raymond, E. and Grimes, D. 2012. The comparative safety of legal induced abortion and childbirth in the United States. *Obstetrics and Gynecology*, pp. 215–219.

Reeves, Jay. 1999. Bill would involve state attorneys in juvenile abortion cases. Associated Press State and Local Wire, February 23.

Regenstein, M., & Huang J. 2005. Stresses to the safety net: the public hospital perspective, Kaiser Commission on Medicaid and the Uninsured, report no.7329, June. Online at www.kff.org/medicaid/7329.cfm (accessed January 3, 2011).

Reich, C.A. 1964. The new property. *Yale Law Journal* 73: 733–787.

Reich, Jennifer A. 2005. *Fixing Families: Parents, Power, and the Child Welfare System*. New York: Routledge.

———. 2008. Not ready to fill his father's shoes. *Men and Masculinities* 11(1): 10–18.

Reich, Jennifer, & Brindis, Claire. Forthcoming. Conceiving risk and responsibility: a qualitative examination of men's experiences of unintended pregnancy and abortion. *International Journal of Men's Health*.

Reilly, Phillip R. 1991. *The Surgical Solution: A History of Involuntary Sterilization in the United States*. Baltimore: John Hopkins University Press.

Reiskin, J. 1991. Letter, *Disability Rag*, November/December: 2.

Riddle, J. 1992. *Contraception and Abortion from the Ancient World to the Renaissance*. Cambridge, MA: Harvard University Press.

Rindfuss, Ronald R., Morgan, S. Philip, & Offut, Kate. 1996. Education and the changing age pattern of American fertility: 1963–1989. *Demography* 33: 277–290.

Roberts, Dorothy. 1991. Punishing drug addicts who have babies: women of color, equality, and the right of privacy. *Harvard Law Review* 104(7): 1419–1482.

———. 1996. Unshackling Black motherhood. *Michigan Law Review* 95: 938–964.

———. 1997. *Killing the Black Body: Race, Reproduction, and the Meaning of Liberty*. New York: Vintage Books.

———. 2002. *Shattered Bonds: The Color of Child Welfare*. New York: Basic Books.

———. 2005. Privatization and punishment in the new age of reprogenetics. *Emory Law Journal* 54: 1343–1360.

———. 2009. Race, gender, and genetic technologies: a new reproductive dystopia? *Signs: Journal of Women in Culture and Society* 34: 783–804.

Romano, M.D. 1978. Sexuality and the disabled female. *Sexuality and Disability* 1(1), Spring: 27–33.

Roosevelt, T. n.d. On american motherhood. Online at www.nationalcenter.org/TRooseveltMotherhood.html (accessed February 6, 2012).

Rosenberg, D., Geller, S.E., Studee, L., & Cox, S.M. 2006. Disparities in mortality among high risk pregnant women in Illinois: a population based study. *Annals of Epidemiology* 16: 26–32.

Rosenblatt, Paul C., Walsh, R. Patricia, & Jackson, Douglas A. 1976, *Grief and Mourning in Cross-Cultural Perspective*. USA: Human Relations Area Files.

Rosenfeld, Bernard. Papers. In possession of author.

Rosengren, K.E., & Windahl, S. 1989. *Media Matter: Childhood and Adolescence*. Norwood, N.J.: Ablex.

Rosenwasser, Shirley Miller, Wright, Lloyd, & Barber, R. Bruce. 1987. The rights and responsibilities of men in abortion situations. *Journal of Sex Research* 23(1): 97–105.

Ross, L. n.d. Understanding reproductive justice. Online at www.trustblackwomen.org/our-work/what-is-reproductive-justice/9-what-is-reproductive-justice (accessed November 18, 2013).

———. 1992. In pursuit of perfect choice: feminism and reproductive technology. *Health/PAC Bulletin*, Summer: 8–11.

Ross, L.J. 2006. *Understanding Reproductive Justice*. Atlanta, GA: SisterSong.

Ross, L.J., Brownlee, S.L., Diallo, D.D., & Rodriquez, L. 2001. The SisterSong Collective: women of color, reproductive health and human rights. *American Journal of Health Studies* 17: 79–88.

Roth, R. 2004a. "No new babies?" Gender inequality and reproductive control in the criminal justice and prison systems. *Journal of Gender, Social Policy and the Law* 12: 391–425.

———. 2004b. Searching for the state: who governs prisoners' reproductive rights? *Soc. Polit.* 11: 411–438.

———. 2010. Obstructing justice: prisons as barriers to medical care for pregnant women. *UCLA Women's Law Journal* 18: 79–106.

Rothman, Barabara Katz. 1982 *In Labor: Women and Power in the Birthplace*. New York: W.W. Norton.

———. 1986. *The Tentative Pregnancy: Prenatal Diagnosis and the Future of Motherhood*. New York: Viking.

———. 1989. *Recreating Motherhood: Ideology and Technology in a Patriarchal Society*. New York: W.W. Norton & Company.

———. 2007. Laboring then: the political history of maternity care in the United States. In: W. Simonds, Barbara Katz Rothman, & Bari Meltzer Norman, *Laboring On: Birth in Transition in the United States*. New York: Routledge.

Rothman, S. 1978. *Woman's Proper Place: A History of Changing Ideals and Practices*. New York: Basic Books.

Rousso, H. 1988. Daughters with disabilities: defective women or minority women? In: M. Fine, & A. Asch (eds.) *Women with Disabilities: Essays in Psychology, Culture, and Politics*. Philadelphia: Temple University Press.

———. 1989. *Disabled, female, and proud!* Boston, MA: Exceptional Parent Press.

Rudrappa, S. 2012. India's reproductive assembly line. *Contexts. SAFE Publications* 11: 22–27.

Sabo, Don. 1998. Pigskin, patriarchy, and pain. In: Paula Rothenberg (ed.) *Race, Class, and Gender in the United States*. New York: St. Martin's, pp. 325–328.

Sargent, C. 1987. Born to die: The fate of extraordinary children in Bariba culture. *Ethnology* 23: 79–96.

Saul, S. 2009. Building a baby, with few ground rules. *New York Times*, December 12.

Sawicki, Jana. 1991. *Disciplining Foucault: Feminism, Power, and the Body*. New York: Routledge.

Saxton, M. 1984. Born and unborn: the implications of reproductive technologies for people with disabilities. In: R. Arditti, R.D. Klein, & S. Minden (eds.) *Test-Tube Women: What Future for Motherhood?* London: Pandora Press.

———. 1990. On being an outreach group: women with disabilities. *Sojourner: The Women's Forum*, November: 20.

————. 1991. Disability and the medical system. *Ms*, September/October: 36–37.

————. 1993. What's at stake. *Disability Rag* 14(3), May/June: 4–5.

Saxton, M., & Howe, F. (eds.) 1987. *With Wings: An Anthology of Literature By and About Women With Disabilities*. New York: The Feminist Press.

Scheper-Hughes, N. 1992. *Death Without Weeping: The Violence of Everyday Life in Brazil*. Berkeley, CA: University of California Press.

Schneider, David. 1980 (1968). *American Kinship: A Cultural Account*. Chicago, IL: University of Chicago Press.

Schneiderman, K. 1990. Disabled women need choice. *Sojourner: The Women's Forum* (December 1989), reprinted in *Utne Reader*, May/June.

Schoen, J. 2005. *Choice and Coercion: Birth Control, Sterilization, and Abortion in Public Health and Welfare*. Chapel Hill: University of North Carolina Press.

Schwalbe, Michael, & Wolkomir, Michelle. 2001. The masculine self as problem and resource in interview studies of men. *Men and Masculinities* 4: 90–103.

Schwartz, J., & Woodruff, T. n.d. *Shaping our Legacy: Reproductive Health and the Environment*. San Francisco: Program on Reproductive Health and the Environment, University of California, pp.14–26.

Schwiebert, Pat, & Kirk, Paul. 1985. *When Hello Means Goodbye: A Guide For Parents Whose Child Dies Before Birth, At Birth or Shortly After Birth*. Portland, Oregon: Perinatal Loss.

Seaman, B. 1994 (1969). *The Doctor's Case Against the Pill*. Alameda, CA: Hunter House Books.

Seaman, B., & Eldridge, L. 2012. *Voices of the Women's Health Movement*, vol.1. New York: Seven Stories Press.

Sen, A. 1990. More than 100 million women are missing. *New York Review of Books*, December 20: 37.

Sentencing Project. 2012. Incarcerated women. Factsheet, Washington, D.C.: Sentencing Project. Online at www.sentencingproject.org/doc/publications/cc_Incarcerated_Women_Factsheet_Sep24sp.pdf.

Seymour, S. 1999. *Women, Family, and Child Care in India: A World in Transition*. Cambridge, UK: Cambridge University Press.

Sex Information and Education Council of the United States (SIECUS) n.d. *Sexuality and Disability: A SIECUS Annotated Bibliography of Available Print Materials*. New York: SIECUS.

Shain, K. 2012. No more shackles: AB 2530 is signed! Strong Families Blog, September 28. Online at www.reproductivejusticeblog.org/2012/09/no-more-shackles-ab-2530-is-signed.html (accessed April 20, 2014).

Sharma, M. 2008. Twenty-first century pink or blue: how sex selection technology facilitates gendercide and what we can do about it. *Family Court Review* 46: 198–215.

Shaul, S., Dowling, P.J., & Laden, B.F. 1985. Like other women: perspectives of mothers with physical disabilities. In: M.J. Deegan, & N.A. Brooks (eds.) *Women and Disability: The Double Handicap*. New Brunswick, N.J.: Transaction, Inc.

Shea, Kevin G., Scanlan, Kevin J., Nilsson, Kurt J., Wilson, Brent, & Mehlman, Charles. 2008. 'Interstate variability of the statute of limitations for medical liability: a cause for concern?' *Journal of Pediatric Orthopaedics* 28(3), April/May: 370–374.

Shi, Leiyu, & Singh, Douglas A. 2012. *Delivering Health Care in America: A Systems Approach*, 5th edition. Burlington, MA: Jones and Bartlett Learning.

Short, Carroll Dale. 2000. *The People's Lawyer: The Colorful Life and Times of Julian L. McPhillips, Jr.* Montgomery, Ala.: New South Books.

Shostak, Arthur. 1987. Motivations of abortion clinic waiting room males: "bottled-up" roles and unmet needs. In: Michael Kimmel (ed.) *Changing Men: New Directions in Research on Men and Masculinity*. Thousand Oaks: Sage, pp. 185–197.

Shostak, Arthur, McLouth, Gary, & Seng, Lynn. 1990. *Men and Abortion: Lessons, Losses, and Love*. New York: Praeger Scientific.

Shyama. 1996. *Tamizaga gramangalil pen sisu kolai*. Chennai, India: Manimekalai.

Siegel, R.B. 2010. *Roe*'s roots: the women's rights claims that engendered *Roe*. *Boston University Law Review* 90: 1875–1907.

Silverstein, H. 2009. *Girls on the Stand: How Courts Fail Pregnant Minors*. New York: NYU Press.

Simpson, K. 1992. Disabled women and health care: the meaning of accessible, *The Women's Foundation Newsletter*, Summer: 7–8.

Sloan, Frank A., & Chepke, Lindsey. 2008. *Medical Malpractice*. Cambridge, MA: MIT Press.

Smith, A. 2005. Beyond pro-choice versus pro-life: women of color and reproductive justice. *NWSA Journal* 17: 119–140.

Smith, R.J. 2006. Family caps in welfare reform: their coercive effects and damaging consequences. *Harvard Journal of Law and Gender* 29: 151–200.

Snitow, Ann. (ed.) 1980. *Powers of Desire*. New York: Monthly Review.

Solinger, R. 2000 (1992). *Wake Up Little Susie: Single Pregnancy Before* Roe v. Wade. New York: Routledge.

———. 2001. *Beggars and Choosers: How the Politics of Choice Shapes Adoption, Abortion and Welfare in the United States*. New York: Hill and Wang.

———. 2013. *Reproductive Politics: What Everyone Needs to Know*. New York: Oxford University Press, p. 8.

Somers, M.R., & Roberts, C.N/J. 2008. Toward a new sociology of rights: a genealogy of "buried bodies" of citizenship and human rights. *Annual Review of Law and Social Science* 4: 385–425.

Sonfield, A., & Pollack, H.A. 2013. The Affordable Care Act and reproductive health: potential gains and serious challenges. *Journal of Health Politics, Policy and Law* 38: 373–391.

Soohoo, C., Albisa, C., & Davis, M.F. (eds.) 2008. *Bringing Human Rights Home*. Westport, CT: Praeger.

Spinelli, M.G. 2001. A systematic investigation of 16 cases of neonaticide. *American Journal of Psychiatry* 126: 325–334.

Srinivasan, S., & Bedi, A.S. 2008. Daughter elimination in Tamilnadu, India: a tale of two ratios. *Journal of Development Studies* 44: 961–990.

Srinivasan, V. 1992. Death for the female-foeticide and infanticide in Salem District. *Frontline*, October 9: 82–84.

Stafan S. 2008. Accommodating families: using the Americans with Disabilities Act to keep families together. *Saint Louis University Journal of Health Law and Policy* 2: 135–176.

Stafford, Barbara Maria. 1991. *Body Criticism: Imaging the Unseen in Enlightenment Art and Medicine*. Cambridge, MA: MIT Press.

Stacey, Judith. 2011. *Unhitched: Love, Marriage, and Family Values from West Hollywood to Western China*. New York: New York University Press.

Staniec, J.F.O., & Webb, N.J. 2007. Utilization of infertility services: how much does money matter? *Health Services Research* 42: 971–989.

State of Connecticut Insurance Department. 2009. Review of professional liability insurance rates. Online at www.ct.gov/cid/cwp/view.asp?Q=435460&A=3307 (accessed October 26, 2012).

Starr, Paul. 1982. *The Social Transformation of American Medicine*. New York: Basic Books.

Stolcke, Verena. 1986. New reproductive technologies-same old fatherhood. *Critique of Anthropology* 6(3): 5–31.

Stone-Manista, K. 2008. Protecting pregnant women: a guide to successfully challenging criminal child abuse prosecutions of pregnant drug addicts. *Journal of Criminal Law and Criminology* 99: 823–856.

Sturdevant, Matthew. 2011. Obstetrician held liable. *Hartford Courant*, May 26.

Sussman, D. 2008. Bound by injustice: challenging the use of shackles on incarcerated pregnant women. *Cardozo Journal of Law and Gender* 15: 477–502.

Swanson-Kauffman, Kristen M. 1983. The unborn one: a profile of the human experience of miscarriage. Unpublished doctoral dissertation, Health Sciences Center, University of Colorado.

Tait, J. 1986. Reproductive technology and the rights of disabled persons. *Canadian Journal of Women and the Law* 1(12): 446–455.

Tan, T. 2012. Looking to Mexico for alternatives to abortion clinics, *Texas Tribune*.

Tavernise, S. 2012. FDA makes it official: BPA can't be used in baby bottles and cups. *New York Times*, July 17.

Thompson, C. 2005. *Making Parents: The Ontological Choreography of Reproductive Technologies.* Cambridge, MA: MIT Press.

Throsby, Karen, & Gill, Rosalind. 2004. "It's different for men": masculinity and IVF. *Men and Masculinities* 6: 330–348.

Tita, A.T.N., Landon, M.B., Spong, C.Y., et al. 2009. Timing of elective repeat cesarean delivery at term and neonatal outcomes. *New England Journal of Medicine* 360: 111–120.

Todd, A.D. 1984. Women and the disabled in contemporary society. *Social Policy* 14(4): 44–46.

Tone, A. 2001. *Devices and Desire: A History of Contraceptives in America.* New York: Hill and Wang.

Townsend, Nicholas. 1988. "Spirit babies" and "blood children": the social meaning of paternity. Paper presented at the annual meeting of the American Anthropological Association, Phoenix.

Tsutsui, K., Whitlinger, C., & Lim, A. 2012. International human rights law and social movements: states' resistance and civil society's insistence. *Annual Review of Law and Social Science* 8: 367–396.

Tucker, M.J., Berg, C.J., Callaghan, W.M., & Hsia, J. 2007. The black–white disparity in pregnancy-related mortality from 5 conditions: differences in prevalence and case-fatality rates. *American Journal of Public Health* 97: 247–251.

Turner, Victor. 1974. *Dreams, Fields and Metaphors.* Ithaca, N.Y.: Cornell University Press.

Twine, F.W. 2011. *Outsourcing the Womb: Race, Class and Gestational Surrogacy in a Global Market.* New York: Routledge.

Umansky, Lauri. 1998. Breastfeeding in the 1990s: the Karen Carter case and politics of maternal sexuality. In: Molly Ladd-Taylor, & Lauri Umansky (eds.) *"Bad" Mothers: The Politics of Blame in Twentieth-Century America.* New York: New York University Press, pp. 299–309.

UNFPA. 2009. *Summary of the ICPD Programme of Action.* New York: United Nations Population Fund.

United Nations. 1948. *Universal Declaration of Human Rights*, G.A. res. 217A (III), in United Nations Doc. A/810. New York: United Nations.

———. 1994. *Report of the Commission of Experts Established Pursuant to United Nations Security Council Resolution 780 (1992).* New York: United Nations, p.33.

United Nations, Committee on Economic, Social and Cultural Rights 2000. *The Right to the Highest Attainable Standard of Health.* General comment no. 14 E/C.12/200/4. New York: United Nations.

U.S. Department of Health and Human Services. 2005. *Voluntary Relinquishment for Adoption.* Washington, D.C.: Health and Human Services.

———. 2010. *National practitioner data bank in U.S. Department of Health and Human Services.* Washington, D.C.: Health and Human Services. Online at www.npdb-hipdb.hrsa.gov/ (accessed October 26, 2012).

Uslaner, E., & Weber, R. 1980. Public support for pro-choice abortion policies in the Nation and States: changes and stability after the Roe and Doe decisions. In: C.E. Schneider, & M.A. Vinovkis (eds.) *The Law and Politics of Abortion.* Lexington: Lexington Books.

Van Dyke, N., & McCammon, H.J. 2010. *Strategic Alliances: Coalition Building and Social Movements.* Minneapolis: University of Minneapolis Press.

Vance, Carol (ed.) 1982. *Pleasure and Danger.* New York: Routledge.

Vasanthi. 1995. Salem, the killing goes on. *India Today*, September 30: 83.

Vélez-Ibáñez, Carlos. n.d. Papers. Personal collection (Vélez Papers).

———. n.d. Carlos Vélez-Ibáñez Sterilization Archives (Vélez Archives). Chicano Studies Research Library, University of California, Los Angeles.

Venkatachalam, R., & Srinivasan, V. 1993. *Female Infanticide.* New Delhi, India: Har-Anand.

Venkataramani, S.H. 1986. Born to die. *India Today*, June 15: 26–33.

Volz, V. 2006. A matter of choice: women with disabilities, sterilization, and reproductive autonomy in the twenty-first century. *Women's Rights Law Rep.* 27: 203–216.

Wade, Roger. 1978. *For Men About Abortion*. Boulder, CO: privately printed.

Waldschmidt, A. 1992. Against selection of human life: people with disabilities oppose genetic counselling. *Issues in Reproductive and Genetic Engineering* 5(2): 155–167.

Walstead, M. 1993. More love to give than anyone. *Disability Rag* 14(3): 9.

Watkins, E. 2001. *On the Pill: A Social History of Oral Contraceptives*. Baltimore: Johns Hopkins University Press.

Waxman, B.F. 1991a. It's time to politicize our sexual oppression. *Disability Rag*, March/April: 23–26.

———. 1991b. Protecting reproductive health and choice. *Western Journal of Medicine*, Rehabilitation Medicine—Adding Life to Years, Special Issue, 154: 629.

———. 1993a. The politics of eugenics. *Disability Rag*, 14(3), May/June: 6–7.

———. 1993b. The year of the disabled woman, or girls, it's time to flaunt your sexuality. *Disability Rag* 14(3), May/June: 28–29.

Wegner, Mary Nell, Landry, Evelyn, Wilkinson, David, & Tzanis, Joanne. 1998. Men as partners in reproductive health: from issues to action. *Family Planning Perspectives* 24(1): 38–42.

Weiss, K. 2012. Iran's birth control policy sent birthrate tumbling. *Los Angeles Times*.

Weitz, T. 2010. Rethinking the mantra that abortion should be "safe, legal and rare." *Journal of Women's History* 22(3): 161–168.

Wendell, S. 1989. Toward a feminist theory of disability, *Hypatia* 4(2), Summer: 104–123.

Wertz, R., & Wertz, D. 1989. *Lying-In: A History of Childbirth in America*. New Haven: Yale University Press.

West, Candace, & Zimmerman, Don. 1987. Doing gender. *Gender and Society* 1: 125–151.

Whitehead, Barbara Dafoe, & Popenoe, David. 1999. Defining daddy down. *American Enterprise* 10(5): 31–34.

Williams, Linda. 1987. "It's gonna work for me": women's experience of the failure of in vitro fertilization and its effect on their decision to try IVF again. Paper delivered at the Third International Women's Studies Congress, Dublin.

Worcester, Nancy, & Whatley, Marianne. 1988. The response of the health care system to the women's health movement: the selling of women's health centers. In: Sue V. Rosser (ed.) *Feminism within the Science and Health Care Professions: Overcoming Resistance*. New York: Pergamon, pp. 117–151.

World Health Organization. 2005. *Make Every Mother and Child Count*. Geneva: WHO.

———. 2010. *Maternal and Reproductive Health*. Geneva: WHO.

———. 2012. *Fact Sheet on Maternal Mortality*. Geneva: World Health Organization.

———. 2014. *Preventing Unsafe Abortion*. Geneva: World Health Organization.

Xu, Xiao, Siefert, Kristine A., Jacobson, Peter D., Lori, Jody R., & Ransom, Scott B. 2008. The impact of malpractice burden on Michigan obstetrician-gynecologists' career satisfaction. *Women's Health Issues: Official Publication of the Jacob Institute of Women's Health* 18(4), July/August: 229–237.

Xu, J., Kochanek, K.D., Murphy, S.L., & Tejada-Vera, B. 2010. Final data for 2007, *National Vital Statistics Reports*. Hyattsville, MD: National Center for Health Statistics.

Yim, J., & Mahalingam, R. 2006. Culture, masculinity, and psychological well-being in Punjab, India. *Sex Roles* 55: 715–724.

Young, Frank W. 1965. *Initiation Ceremonies: A Cross-Cultural Study of Status Dramatization*. New York: Bobbs-Merrill.

Yuval-Davis, N. 2006. Intersectionality and feminist politics. *European Journal of Women's Studies* 13: 193–209.

Zavodny, Madeline. 2001. The effect of partners' characteristics on teenage pregnancy and its resolution. *Family Planning Perspectives* 33: 192–199, 205.

Zelizer, Viviana A. 2000. The Purchase of Intimacy. *Law and Social Inquiry* 25: 817–848.

Zhu, W.X., Lu, L., & Hesketh, T. 2009. China's excess males, sex selective abortion, and one child policy: analysis of data from 2005 national intercensus survey. *British Journal of Medicine* 338: 920–923.

Ziegler, M. 2009. The framing of a right to choose: *Roe v. Wade* and the changing debate on abortion law. *Law and History Review* 27: 281–330.

CASES

Ankrom v. Alabama, [Ms. CR-09-1148, Aug. 26, 2011] So.3d (Ala. Crim. App. 2011)

Beal v. Doe, 432 U.S. 438 (1977)

Benitez v. North Coast Women's Care Medical Group, 31 Cal. Rptr. 2d 364, 106 Cal. App. 4th 978 (Ct. App. 2003)

Buck v. Bell, 274 U.S. 200 (1927)

Carey v. Population Services International, 431 U.S. 678 (1977)

Eisenstadt v. Baird, 405 U.S. 438 (1972)

Ex parte Anonymous, 531 So. 2d 901 (Ala. 1988).

Ex parte Anonymous, 720 So. 2d 497 (Ala. 1998).

Ex parte Anonymous, 810 So. 2d 785 (Ala. 2001).

Ex parte Anonymous, 889 So. 2d 525 (Ala. 2003).

Ex parte Martin, 565 So. 2d 1 (Ala. 1989).

Ferguson v. Charleston, 532 U.S. 67, 121 S. Ct. 1281, 149 L. Ed. 2d 205 (2001)

Griswold v. Connecticut, 381 U.S. 479 (1965)

Cleveland State Law Rev. 49:133–61

Harris v. McRae, 448 U.S. 297 (1980)

In re Anonymous, 720 So. 2d 497 (Ala. Civ. App. 1998).

In re Anonymous, 733 So. 2d 429 (Ala. Civ. App. 1999).

In re Anonymous, 810 So. 2d 784 (Ala. Civ. App. 2001).

In re T. W., 551 So. 2d 1186 (Fla. 1989).

Madrigal v. Quilligan, 639 F.2d 789 (9th Cir. 1981)

Maher v. Doe, 432 U.S. 526 (1977)

McCorvey v. Hill, 385 F.3d 846 (5th Cir. 2004)

N.J. Division of Youth & Family Services v. L.V., 889 A.2d 1153 (N.J. Super. Ct. Ch. Div. 2005)

Ohio v. Akron Center for Reproductive Health, 497 U.S. 502 (1990)

People v. Sanger, 118 N.E. 637 (N.Y. 1918)

Planned Parenthood v. Casey, 505 U.S. 833 (1992)

Relf v. Weinberger, 372 F.Supp. 1196 (D.C. Dist. Ct. 1974)

Relf v. Weinberger, 565 F.2d 722 (D.C. Cir. 1977)

Harvard Law Rev. 104:1419–82

Roe v. Wade, 410 U.S. 113 (1973)

Skinner v. Oklahoma, 316 U.S. 535 (1942)

STATUTES AND BILLS

Alabama Parental Consent Statute, Ala. Code S 26-21 (2004)

Patient Protection and Affordable Care Act, Pub L. No 111–148, 52702, 124 stat 119, (2010)

KRS S 311.732 (2004)

S.B. 389, 1999 Ala. Reg. Sess (1999)

CONTRIBUTOR BIOGRAPHIES

Rene Almeling is an Assistant Professor of Sociology at Yale University.

The late **Toni Cade Bambera** was an author, film maker and political activist.

Debra Bingham is Vice-President of Research, Education, and Publications at the Association of Women's Health, Obstetrics, and Neonatal Nurses (AWHONN.org) in Washington, D.C.

The **Boston Women's Health Collective**, publisher of *Our Bodies, Ourselves: Pregnancy and Birth* (OBOS), is a global nonprofit, public interest organization based in Cambridge, Mass.

Michelle Chen is a contributing editor at *In These Times*, and *Culture Strike*.

Hillary Rodham Clinton is a former Secretary of State, Senator for New York, and First Lady of the United States.

Francine Coeytaux is a project director at the Public Health Institute in Oakland, Ca.

Sonia Corrêa is a researcher at the Brazilian Interdisciplinary Association for AIDS (ABIA) and the co-chair of Sexuality Policy Watch (www.sxpolitics.org), a longtime transnational feminist and sexual rights activist from Rio de Janeiro.

Lori Freedman is an Assistant Professor of Obstetrics, Gynecology and Reproductive Sciences at the University of California, San Francisco.

Joshua Gamson is a Professor of Sociology at the University of San Francisco.

Adrienne Germain is President Emerita of the International Women's Health Coalition.

Michelle Goldberg is a senior contributing writer for *The Nation*.

Linda Gordon is the Florence Kelley Professor of History at New York University.

Elena Gutiérrez is an Associate Professor in Gender and Women's Studies and Latin American and Latino Studies at the University of Illinois, Chicago.

Virginia Kallianes is a project coordinator at the Population Council in New York.

Linda L. Layne is the Hale Professor of Humanities and Social Sciences, and Professor of Anthropology at Rensselaer Polytechnic Institute.

Annie Lowrey is an economic journalist at the *New York Times*.

Zakiya Luna is an Assistant Professor of Sociology at the University of California, Santa Barbara.

Kristin Luker is the Elizabeth Josselyn Boalt Professor of Law, Professor of Sociology, and Director, Center on Reproductive Rights and Justice at University of California, Berkeley.

Ramaswami Mahalingam is an Associate Professor at the University of Michigan in the Personality and Social Contexts program and in the Psychology and Women's Studies Joint PhD program.

Laura Mamo is an Associate Professor of Health Education and a core faculty member of the Health Equity Institute at San Francisco State University.

Theresa Morris is Professor of Sociology at Trinity College (Hartford, Conn.).

Lynn M. Paltrow, JD, is the Founder and Executive Director of the National Advocates for Pregnant Women in New York.

Willie Parker, MD, is an obstetrician gynecologist and a member of the Board of Directors of Physicians for Reproductive Health.

Rosalind P. Petchesky is a Distinguished Professor Emerita of Political Science and Women & Gender Studies, Hunter College and the Graduate Center, City University of New York.

Rayna Rapp is a Professor of Anthropology at New York University.

Dorothy Roberts is the George A. Weiss University Professor of Law and Sociology and the Raymond Pace and Sadie Tanner Mossell Alexander Professor of Civil Rights at the University of Pennsylvania.

The late **Phyllis Rubenfeld** was a Professor of Social Work and Special Education at Hunter College.

Sharmila Rudrappa is an Associate Professor of Sociology at the University of Texas, Austin.

Jackie Schwartz is a research scientist in the Program on Reproductive Health and the Environment at the University of California, San Francisco.

Helena Silverstein is a Professor of Law and Government at Lafeyette College.

Rickie Solinger is an independent historian and curator based in New York.

Naomi Stotland, MD, is an Associate Professor in the Department of Obstetrics, Gynecology, and Reproductive Sciences at the University of California, San Francisco.

Nan Strauss, JD, is a researcher with Amnesty International USA, where she has been working on maternal health and health care in the United States, in the context of the right to health.

Madeline Wachman is a student in the joint Masters in Social Work and Public Health program at Boston University.

Tracy A. Weitz, at the time of writing her article in this volume, was the Director of the Advancing New Standards in Reproductive Health (ANSIRH) program in the Bixby Center for Global Reproductive Health and an Associate Professor of Obstetrics, Gynecology and Reproductive Sciences at UCSF.

Tracey Woodruff is a Professor in the Department of Obstetrics, Gynecology, and Reproductive Sciences and Philip R. Lee Institute for Health Policy Studies, and the Director of the Program on Reproductive Health and the Environment at the at the University of California, San Francisco.

CREDITS

INDEX

*9 7 8 0 4 1 5 7 3 1 0 3 4 *

An environmentally friendly book printed and bound in England by www.printondemand-worldwide.com

PEFC Certified

This product is
from sustainably
managed forests
and controlled
sources

www.pefc.org

PEFC/16-33-415

This book is made of chain-of-custody materials; FSC materials for the cover and PEFC materials for the text pages.

#0313 - 260116 - C0 - 235/187/18 - PB - 9780415731034